MY BORING-ASS LIFE

MY BORING-ASS LIFE
THE UNCOMFORTABLY CANDID DIARY OF KEVIN SMITH
EXPANDED AND UPDATED EDITION
ISBN 9781848564978

Published by
Titan Books
A division of
Titan Publishing Group Ltd
144 Southwark St
London
SE1 0UP

First expanded edition September 2009
2 4 6 8 10 9 7 5 3 1

My Boring-Ass Life: The Uncomfortably Candid Diary of Kevin Smith copyright © 2007, 2009 Kevin Smith.
All rights reserved.

Front cover photo © Peter Sorel.

Visit our website:
www.titanbooks.com

Did you enjoy this book? We love to hear from our readers. Please e-mail us at:
readerfeedback@titanemail.com or write to Reader Feedback at the above address.

To receive advance information, news, competitions, and exclusive Titan offers online, please
register as a member by clicking the "sign up" button on **www.titanbooks.com**

A CIP catalogue record for this title is available from the British Library.

Printed and bound in the USA.

Snoogans.

MY BORING-ASS LIFE
THE UNCOMFORTABLY CANDID DIARY OF
KEVIN SMITH

TITAN BOOKS

INTRODUCTION

Why the Diary(ah)?

Since what follows is a shit-load of text detailing the minutiae of my daily doings, I'll forego the pages of pithy prose leading up to a retrospect and cut directly to the chase.

How the fuck did this happen?

Very simple: I've got a message board at one of our websites, www.viewaskew.com, that I've been actively back-and-forthing on since 1996. There, I've been engaged in a decade-long discussion with the folks who've paid for my house, my car, all my DVDs, and (quite probably) my wife: the audience for our pictures. For the last ten years, if you were adamant about tracking down the guy who cast the blight on contemporary American cinema known as "the Stink-Palm", a quick web-search would lead you to what's come to be known simply as "the board" — that magical system of ones and zeroes where you could ask the filmmaker in question what symbolism he intended with an ice hockey fight juxtaposed against a character's interrogation of his paramour's sexual history, and wind up with a half-answered query and a solicitation to purchase a t-shirt bearing said filmmaker's face or an action figure molded in his likeness.

Then, one day in March of 2005, a poster (meaning someone who posts on the board) posited a question so stymieing, I had to step away from the computer and truly ponder what my response should be:

"*What do you do all day?*" they inquired.

It was a staggering inquiry — because I honestly didn't know.

I mean, I had a *vague* idea of how my days were spent — and really, it was more of a vague idea of the *results* of my routines: still married, still a dad, still a filmmaker, still fat, still alive. But *how* did I reach these results, I wondered? What were all the exact steps that lead to the status quo, one more day above ground?

So rather than summon a sarcastic reply, I responded with a broad-stroked, moment-by-moment breakdown of that particular day. Question asked, question answered.

Sadly, the answer more than likely intrigued me more than it interested the inquisitor. I wasn't so much taken aback by what had transpired during the fourteen hours or so I was awake, but instead by how... well, *boring* it all seemed. It was rote. It was an every-life, chock-a-block full of inane elements that bore no significant impression of an existence well-embraced. If God was in the details, then surely God didn't exist; because no Supreme Being could suffer a creation of infinite promise who so often opted simply to lay on his bed and watch far too much television.

If all my days resembled the one I'd chronicled for that poster, then it was so dull that it demanded documentation. That way, upon my sure-to-be-premature death, when others would attempt to fill my daughter's head with tales of how much her father had done and how far he'd gone in his brief life, she could read for herself, in his own words, how little her old man had actually accomplished. Rather than buy into the legend of the convenience store clerk who risked money he didn't have via multiple credit cards he wasn't qualified for, culminating in an early 90s indie flick success story and career he didn't deserve, my daughter could read the cold truth about the shlub who begat her. My parting gift to my only child would be a full confession about how underwhelmingly human I ultimately was.

And so began the chronicles of My Boring-Ass Life — first as a series of entries on the board, and later at its own web locale — www.silentbobspeaks.com (and even later, at my MySpace page: www.myspace.com/therealkevinsmith). I was able to stick to the plan of an itinerary-style diary for a few good months before the experiment ultimately morphed into what it is now: a fucking blog like every other fucking blog, offering up unasked for opinions on any number of subjects. I'd hate myself for succumbing to a trend, were it not for the cool shit that came out of it in the process (namely the "Me and My Shadow" multi-parter that chronicled Jason Mewes's battle with addiction).

Still, for the most part, it'll serve its intended purpose: giving my kid a glimpse at a year (or so) in the life of her pater familias. And if it interests you at all, dear reader, then that's just gravy. That is, if you can get through it.

'Cause, y'know — it's kinda boring.

For those unfamiliar with my world, I'd like to offer up a quick reference glossary, so you'll know who I'm talking about when I drop names you're not savvy to.

Jen

This is my wife — she who holds my heart and dick.

Harley

This is my daughter. She just holds my heart.

Gail

This is Jen's mom who lives with us and also acts as my assistant. Having your mother-in-law as your assistant means you'll never chase your secretary around her desk.

Byron

Gail's husband, Jen's step-dad, who also lives with us. Without him and Gail, our lives (or lack thereof) as we know them wouldn't be possible.

Mos

Scott Mosier, longtime friend and producer. Essentially, my first wife.

Jay

Jason Mewes — the thinner half of Jay and Silent Bob and my unofficial first-born.

Bryan

Bryan Johnson, my oldest and dearest friend; also one of the funniest people I know. Born and raised in my hometown, Highlands, NJ.

Chay

Chay Carter, one of my wife's dearest friends (as well as mine). Also Ben Affleck's Gail.

Cookie

Alex Hilebronner Mosier, Scott's one-time girlfriend and present wife. I call her Cookie because she's a cook. I also once named a character Cock-Knocker because he punched people in the balls. I'm a simple man.

Malcolm
Malcolm Ingram, longtime (Canadian) friend, wing-man, and filmmaker. Director of the documentary *Small Town Gay Bar*.

Jackman
Jim Jackman, another Canuck compadre. Used to be a producer on *Degrassi: The Next Generation*.

Chappy
Bob Chapman, the guy who makes all the stuff that bears my graven image. Owns Graphitti Designs.

Gina
Gina Gozzi Chapman. Owns Bob. She and Chappy also used to run Jay and Silent Bob's Secret Stash West.

Phil
Sometimes Phil Raskind (my über-agent), and sometimes another Phil I don't have in my life anymore.

The other names that don't pop up quite as frequently but might still require explanation of sorts:
Andy (McElfresh), my *Tonight Show* friend.
Xtian, the fella who used to be the moderator at the board.
Endless, his wife.
Gabrielle and **Charlotte**, their kids.

The House is in the Hollywood Hills.

The Office is either the home office (right off my bedroom), or the View Askew West office, a few blocks away.

The Store is either of the two Jay and Silent Bob's Secret Stash retail emporiums: one in Red Bank, NJ, the other in Los Angeles, CA.

The Life is pretty boring-ass.

THE DIARY

Sunday 20 March 2005 @ 12:00 a.m.

21 March 1998: a much thinner, less bald Kevin Smith stands outside the Indie Spirit Awards tent on the Santa Monica beach, across from the Shutters Hotel. He's waiting for his 'date': Jennifer Schwalbach, a comely lass he'd met only a month earlier when, in her role as the youngest journalist at *USA Today*, she'd interviewed him for a piece about the début of his *Clerks* comic book. The pair had hit it off well — so much so that when the interview proper ended, they'd talked for another two hours, completely off the record. Since that day, they'd spent a suspicious amount of hours emailing and logging phone time with one another while Smith conducted Pittsburgh-based rehearsals of his fourth film, *Dogma*, and Jennifer continued to pen articles for the world's biggest newspaper.

This Spirits was the only awards ceremony that season which Schwalbach wasn't scheduled to attend or cover for the paper, so Smith had suggested they hit the awards together, strictly as friends. He sighted the dubious point that he didn't really know anybody out in LA when, in truth, he was supposed to attend those same Spirit Awards, extremely platonically, with awards presenter and *Dogma* co-star Salma Hayek. After pleading his case of cross-country puppy love to the Latina leading lady, Smith quickly dropped the on-screen muse like a hot rock the moment Schwalbach agreed to accompany him instead.

A miscommunication had the pair separated up 'til the start of the ceremony, with Smith waiting outside the tent, just off the red carpet, and Schwalbach — thanks to her press credentials — already inside. Figuring he'd been stood up by the prettiest girl he'd ever met, Smith was about to head inside to see if his previous flick, *Chasing Amy*, would fare as poorly as he seemingly had that afternoon. Then suddenly there at the entry to the tent, like an answer to a desperate man's prayers, stood the angelic Schwalbach, smiling, waving Smith inside, beckoning him to the rest of his life.

As if the gods were conspiring to keep them apart, Smith didn't get to spend much time with Schwalbach at the ceremony; he spent most of the day doing the press-room following his Best Screenplay win. At Spirits' end, Schwalbach drove Smith to her apartment in her Cherry Red Jeep Grand Cherokee, only after Smith assured her it was solely to change out of his suit jacket and jeans into a more comfortable hoodie and shorts. He wasn't, he promised her, making an attempt at any funny business; considering that he felt Schwalbach was altogether out of his league, why would he embarrass himself?

With half a day left before his flight back to Pittsburgh, Smith and Schwalbach spent hours chit-chatting over pizza bread sticks at Jerry's on Beverly. As his departure time drew near, the duo opted to head back to Schwalbach's Pointsettia apartment to run out the clock. There, the flirting shifted into heavy gear with Smith somehow convincing Schwalbach to lay her head, face-up, in his lap, so that he might play with her ears.

The rest, as they say, can be heard on *An Evening With Kevin Smith*.

Today's the seventh anniversary of the first time Jen and I ever kissed and fucked. And fucked. And fucked. And fucked. And fucked.

This day, more than any other, is proof positive that one excellent lay can change your whole life forever.

Happy Anniversary, Babe.

Now take those fucking pjs off and let's relive a fond memory.

But, y'know — without the heavy chafing.

Monday 21 March 2005 @ 12:06 p.m.

I get up and drop Harley off at school.

I pick up some McDonald's hash browns, two-dozen roses, and both hot and iced lattes for Jen to celebrate the seventh anniversary of the first time we'd ever fucked.

When I get home, I log a post on the board about said anniversary.

I go through the morning email, while watching a series of TiVo'ed *Simpsons*, while Jen continues to organize the poetry reading fundraiser we're hosting at the house for Harley's school.

FedEx delivers a box of *Silent Bob Speaks* books, courtesy of Kristin Powers at Talk/Miramax Books. I peep 'em out and re-read the introduction.

An awesome two-hour session of afternoon delight with the wife.

We go back to email/board stuff/general bid-ness while *The Pirates of Silicon Valley* plays in the background.

Shower at around 2 p.m.

Head to the food store with Jen to pick up some barbecue fodder for dinner.

Drop into Harley's school to watch the end of her karate class. Harley breaks a board. I start to fret that my kid can kick my ass.

Do a phoner with producer of NPR segment I'm to tape the next day, in which I interview Robert Rodriguez and Frank Miller about *Sin City*. We go over the points we want to make sure I hit during the chat.

I barbecue up burgers and chicken, while Byron handles the swordfish.

Family dinner. We're joined by Chay Carter.

I head downstairs to watch some TV and read the board. In the process of doing so, I fall asleep at around 8 p.m.

Jen wakes me to go pick up Malcolm at the airport. Mewes and I make the trek out to LAX and pick up the Good Load himself.

On the drive home, we crack one another up with the outlandish premise built off Mewes's meeting with Erin Gray (Wilma Deering from the *Buck Rogers* TV show) the previous day. Ms. Gray had generously invited Mewes to a ComiCon over in the UK in June. Mewes and I turn it into a what if scenario: what if Mewes gets there, only to discover that he's to dress up as Twiki from *Buck Rogers*, in complete Twiki costume, minus a face-plate. For the three days, he's expected to follow Ms. Gray around, doing his best Twiki impersonation, never mentioning that he's Jason Mewes. Mewes ups the stakes by insisting I go as well, only to discover the Con's insisting I hang off a chain around Mewes's neck and play the role of Dr. Theopolis. We riff on this for the entire ride home.

Back home, me, Mewes, Malcolm and Jen sit around the living room and chat for a bit, before me and Jen turn in.

Tuesday 22 March 2005 @ 12:07 p.m.

I get up around 6 a.m. with a wicked piss-boner. Jen's still sleeping, so there isn't much I can do with it. Jerking off isn't an option, as Harley's taken to sleeping on our couch. Two months ago, in an odd turn of events, she deemed her room too spooky, and refused to sleep in it. To accommodate her, Jen gave her the choice of sleeping anywhere else in the house that made her feel secure, so long as it wasn't Nan and Pop's bed, Mom and Dad's bed, or the couch in Mom and Dad's bedroom suite. First, Harley test-drove the living room couch. Then, it was the library floor. And just as she was settling into the guest room, Mewes moved back in, thus negating the guest room as an option. Mewes offers to pay Harley for the use of her room (which is much bigger than the guest room), but Harley insists on keeping her bedroom as her "playroom", while seeking a place to sleep elsewhere in the house. Somehow, that's become the couch in Mom and Dad's bedroom suite, which means Jen and I have lost a bit of the freedom we used to enjoy at night: Jen's freedom to smoke in bed or on her couch, and my freedom to watch movies with the volume turned way up — not to mention the freedom to wake up and tug one out if I feel the need, prior to the Schwalbach midday special.

I make the dreaded morning climb up the stairs to let the dogs out on the patio, take a leak, then head to my office to check email and read the board.

Harley wakes up, then wakes Jen. I kiss her goodbye and Jen gets Harley ready for school. I continue to putter online.

Malcolm gets up and we all chit-chat in the bedroom for a while before heading out for breakfast at the Griddle. We check to see if Mewes is awake yet, but he's still out cold (for the curious, Mewes tends to sleep in his clothes).

After breakfast, we speed home, and I jump in the shower. Following that, Malcolm and I head over to the NPR studio on Jefferson in Culver City.

On the drive, I talk with Matty, the producer from the Alice Morning Radio show, who's gonna help me with a four-hour test-drive broadcast I'm gonna do in LA the second week of April, if everything works out.

We get to NPR where I meet up with Robert and segment producer Jim Wallace. Robert and I cram into a small recording booth while the techs get Frank Miller on the line from NYC.

Interview goes great. It's about an hour long, and we cover the *Sin City* books, film, and ethos. Both Robert and Frank are articulate, eager speakers, so the hour flies by (Frank tells me I out-Catholiced him on my *Daredevil* run, which I find kind of funny). After we wrap, Jim tells me he's now gotta somehow cut the piece down to eight minutes for NPR broadcast (the entire interview will run on NPR's website shortly after the piece airs). I pick Robert's brain about using Troublemaker's Austin facilities for *Ranger Danger* (as always, he's very accommodating and encouraging) and Malcolm and I head back to the house.

Jen, Malcolm and I sit around bullshitting for a while and re-heat some of the leftovers from last night. Jen's off to the store to pick up some missing ingredients for a Bunny cake she's making for Harley's Fairy Tale Ball tomorrow in school, and Malcolm and I head to the Dome for a three o'clock tech scout with my Stash West partner in crime Bob Chapman, Q&A shooters Zack and Joey, and the Dome rep, Bob.

We tech scout the Dome with the very helpful Arclight folks, and figure out where folks are coming through, when the marquees are going up, what the schedule is gonna be, where the video projector will be stationed, the chairs for the various Q&As, etc., etc.

Malcolm and I head home in the pouring rain and find Mewes playing online poker. Based on the pouring rain, we opt out of the poker tourney at the Geisha House we were supposed to hit tonight at nine.

I find Jen upstairs slaving over the Bunny cake, then head down to the bathroom for a half hour shit/Nintendo DS session.

We order up some pizza and Jen and I settle into some TiVo.

Talk to Jeff on the phone for about a half hour, going over Vulgarthon and *Clerks 2* stuff.

Call Dwight, too.

We put Harley to bed and head upstairs to the living room. We watch an episode of *The Office* with Malcolm before digging into a little *Amongst Friends*. Mewes joins us after a bit. Twenty minutes in, I start taking shit from everyone else for making them watch the flick. I must be high or something, because I still think the flick's pretty watchable.

Jen and I head back downstairs and crash watching TiVo'ed *Law & Order*s.

Wednesday 23 March 2005 @ 12:07 p.m.

Fucking dogs wake me up again. This time I first take a leak in my bathroom (fuck them, I'm going first), then trudge up the stairs and let 'em out.

I hit the computer for a bit before Jen and Harley get up. When they wake, I'm rushed into the shower for a trip to Harley's school. Since Jen's got a facial at eleven, we take separate cars to the school. Malcolm and I are charged with safely delivering the Bunny cake.

It's Fairy Tale Breakfast day in Harley's class, which means that all the kids dress up like their favorite character and load up on eggs, sausages, donuts, cookies, juice, etc. Harley goes as Tinkerbelle. Me and Malcolm show up after Jen, and Byron and Gail follow us. Mewes wakes up late, yet still manages to get to the school in time to catch some costume action. Malcolm just about passes out when he sees Johnny Depp in the class. Depp's there to peep out his ol' lady and kid doing a reading of the classic Mulan fable (not the Disney version). Since he's currently shooting those *Pirates* sequels back-to-back, the Deppster's sporting silver-capped teeth beneath his facial scruff. He seems a little shy but very in love with his family. We exchange a very quiet "'Sup", as he heads off to his Valley-side set.

After an hour or so, we escape the Fairy Tale Breakfast, and Mewes, Malcolm, Jen and I grab some Griddle. Jen breaks away early to hit her appointment, and Malcolm and I head over to Laser Blazer on Pico to pick up this week's new DVDs.

On the way back, I stop at the Sprint Store to pick up a new phone. Unlike my last trip to a Sprint Store, this time everyone's pretty helpful, and we're out of there in half an hour, phone in hand, complete with old number switched over and address book intact. Oddly, a guy who waited on me and Mewes in a Sprint

Store back home in Eatontown now works at this Sprint Store out here. While I'm checking out, I'm chatted up by another Jersey relocator (this one from Wayne). Jersey represents big time, with three out of the ten people in the store hailing from the Motherland, which reminds me that I'm heading home next week. I take a pic with a non-Jersey guy who sped my order along, and we're off.

We hit the office. I have a long convo with Phil and Mos about Panasonic, Final Cut Pro, Apple, and whether or not we wanna shoot *Clerks 2* in digital.

I take a few minutes to talk to Devon at *Newsweek* about a possible *Revenge of the Sith* piece they might want me to pen, and then I hit the Avid and start digging back into *Jersey Girl* to pull together the longest cut of the movie I can for Vulgarthon. What I assume will take an hour winds up taking six. It's a real walk down Memory Lane, as I'm seeing footage I haven't seen in at least two years, so long ago was some of the stuff dropped from what would eventually become the movie.

Ten cases of the Silent Bob Speaks books show up at the office, and Mike lays them out for signing. Jen and Harley stop by on their way home from school to inform me that Harley took first place in her Karate class for an exercise in which she performs a series of moves (chaka, is it called?). Jen's had a hardcore facial (not like that, you fucks…) that leaves her skin very sensitive, so much so that we stretch our lips out cartoonishly to kiss, so as not to have my beard scratch her.

Over the course of my editing day, Mos, Malcolm and Phil head off to other stuff, leaving me and Biggie Smalls to hold down the fort. I finally wrap up the rebuild and head home around 7:45 p.m. to drive Jen over the hill to a girl's-night-out dinner with her friends.

Back home, I dig into some barbecue with Harley, Byron and Gail. Mewes shows up, and after I set Harley up in my bed with a new *Dora* DVD and the heat on, I head back upstairs where me and Mewes finally tackle a dining room table full of figures, comics, and posters that've been waiting for our signatures since before England. We listen to some King Diamond and talk about the flick he's starting the day after V'thon — an indie flick called *Bottoms Up*, co-starring Paul Walker and Paris Hilton. Jay's a little nervous, as he's the lead, but feels that by day two or three, he'll be settled into a groove. During a music change-up (from Black Metal to late eighties pop), I tell Jay the story of that summer of '89, when Bryan, Ed and I couldn't get into a party to save our lives, even though we were non-troublemaking non-drinkers.

I head to my office (the one in the master bedroom suite) and check some email for a bit when I get the call from Jen to come pick her up. Back over the hill I go.

On the short ride home, Jen's lamenting over how her face feels like it's been sun-burned, courtesy of the deep facial. We hold hands and listen to some Dave Matthews' 'Crash Into Me'.

We move the out-cold Harley from our bed to the couch and pop on some TiVo. We skip the nookie, as her face is still hyper-sensitive, and we can't kiss. Jen's out within five minutes of hitting the bed (after a nearly-fruitless quest to find some ice to rub on her face). Locked out, Malcolm rings the door at around midnight. I let him in then head back upstairs and fall asleep to a TiVo'ed *Law & Order*.

Thursday 24 March 2005 @ 12:07 p.m.

Fucking Mulder and Scully. Today, they wake me up at 6:45 a.m. I take a leak, let the dogs out, and then head to my desk-top computer to play catch up with the board diary-thing.

Harley wakes up and joins me at my desk. We watch the *Madagascar* trailer a record eleven times in a row before she heads off to find Pop and breakfast.

I jump onto iChat and IM who I assume is Walt regarding the *Silent Bob Speaks* book, and having a bunch in stock for next week in the east coast Stash when I'm back there for the Count Basie gig. Turns out it's not Walt but Mike Zapcik (Helpermonkey). We get 400 books ordered and I tell him that, post-Basie gig, I'll come back to the store for a signing, if they feel like staying open. They're down with it.

I'm still on iChat holding down convos with Ming, Helpermonkey and Joey (her appearance at Vulgarthon's up in the air, as she may have to leave for Arkansas earlier than expected to start the flick she's directing — which, as you might imagine, is quite the bummer), when I get an IM from Jon Gordon's assistant Leslye about having lunch with Harvey Weinstein that afternoon. Suddenly, the balance of the day changes.

Jen wakes up and summons me and Gail upstairs for a family meeting regarding Easter. Turns out we're having twenty people over for the early dinner, and Jen wants to go over the menu/figure out who's coming exactly and what we need. Malcolm's in attendance too, and he not only comes up with a helpful suggestion regarding feeding the masses Easter Sunday, but also volunteers to go pick up the near-pristine 35mm print of *Chasing Amy* I bought over the phone yesterday for the low, low price of less than five-hundred bucks. This will save me a trip to Palmdale.

Somebody posted on the board that, in his blog, Zach Braff reacted positively to my revelation in the press that I'd love to cast him as Fletch in *Fletch Won*. I forward Jon Gordon Zach's reaction, and he gets me Zach's number.

Gail moves up two phoners I'm supposed to do with McHenry area papers so that I can do the Harvey lunch. Both interviews are meant to pimp the Raue Theater screening. Both seemingly go well.

I jump in the shower, get dressed, and head to the office to pick up Mos for the lunch. As we jet across to Beverly Hills and meet with Jon Gordon (our friend and Miramax exec) and Harvey at Harvey's hotel, I call Zach Braff's cell. Surprisingly, he answers on the second ring. The convo goes something like this...

"Zach Braff?"

"Yes. Who's this?"

"Kevin Smith."

Beat.

"Kevin Smith?! No way!"

"Hello, sir."

"This isn't really Kevin Smith."

"It is. And I'm charmed by the fact that you answer your phone, sir. Are you working on *Scrubs* at the moment?"

"I am. We're between takes. Kevin Smith. This is awesome."

"So can we get together and chat about *Fletch Won*?"

"So the rumors are true?"

"They are, sir."

"Oh God, yes. I must have been really impressive in that PSA."

"I told you then I enjoyed working with you. What's your schedule look like?"

"I'm wrapping *Scrubs* on April 9th. After that, I'll have more time to meet up and stuff."

"So you wanna wait 'til sometime after the ninth?"

"I do. But I need your address. I want you to come to my birthday party."

"Right on. When is it?"

"Like April [DATE GIVEN]."

"I'll definitely be in town."

"Where can we send something?"

"Written invite or email."

"Written."

"Send it to [ADDRESS GIVEN]."

"Cool."

"So you wanna wait 'til sometime after April 9th to meet, right? Did my number come up on your cell."

"It did."

"Then just call that when you're ready to hook up."

"I will. They're calling me to set right now."

"Later, sir."

"Bye."

We get to the hotel and head upstairs with Jon to meet with the big man (or rather, not-so-big-man — Harvey's lost a shitload of weight) in his suite. He opts to head downstairs for a lunch meeting with us instead.

We go over *Clerks 2*-related business (turns out *The Passion of the Clerks* will hold the honor of being the first film put into production at New Co., the temporary moniker of Miramax v.2), as well as Harvey's feelings about Chapter Two of his epic career: the post-Disney Miramax v.2. He says he's nervous and excited. I ask why he's nervous and he says that it sucks to leave behind the 800-movie library and the name they spent two decades building. I say: "There's more than enough time to build another 800-movie library and a new name — however, this time, make only the good movies." To this, Harvey smiles and says, "Which means you'll never make another movie again." I love this man.

We talk about Zach Braff and *Fletch Won* (a combo Harvey loves) and then go over a list of possible Beckys (the female lead in *Clerks 2*). Harvey keeps pushing Amanda Peet who I agree is great but also know, in my heart, will never do this flick. I also think it's better to go with an actress who's less well known. We narrow the list down to a few names before Harvey gives me a peck on the top of the head and pimps off for another meeting. Scott, Jon and I sit around the restaurant for another forty-five minutes going over stuff and waxing rhapsodic about *The Talented Mister Ripley* before we have to head back to work.

At the office, Colleen Benn and Meredith Sachs from Universal Home Video are waiting to go over the *Mallrats* 10th DVD. I tell them I'll be ready to deliver the re-cut of the movie by mid-April. Phil Benson joins us, and we all go over what will be included on this two-DVD set. Thus far, we've got all the contents of the OG DVD, as well as the re-cut, the new documentary (in which we're gonna talk to everyone this time), the new commentary track, the 10th Anniversary Q&A we're gonna round the cast up for and shoot at the Arclight (in the coming months; not at Vulgarthon), storyboards, every draft of the script, tons of press, possibly the MTV Première Party special — just a bunch of stuff to make the double-dip worth the price. Smalls loads them up with a box of press, tapes, artwork. I even unearth my production binder, which has all the multi-colored schedules, one-liners, and drafts of the flick, complete with notes I wrote in the margins. I'm so glad I'm such a pack-rat; I save everything. Colleen says the street date for *Rats* will probably be in mid-September. Phil and I push hard for them to do a Region 2, but these ladies have no control over that; that's up to UPI — the overseas arm of Universal — and they're mainly into releasing the blockbusters. So if you're Region 2 and you want this new *Rats* DVD, best to start bugging UPI Home Video now.

During lunch, Jon Gordon reminded me of a shot from *Jersey Girl* that I'd forgotten to put back into the movie. I'd called Phil to ask him to slug it in. Now, Phil's showing it to me. I futz with it a little bit (move the sound, shave off the back half of the shot and lay a fade on that motherfucker) and with that, lock the version of *Jersey Girl* we'll be showing on Monday. It's about two hours and twenty-five minutes long, and based on the patchwork nature of it we'll be projecting a BetaCam copy onto the Dome screen that day. It won't be as lush to look at as a film print, but it'll get the job done.

From there, it's over to Phil's office for a brief tutorial on Final Cut Pro. I've never used FCP before (I've been an Avid guy since '96), so Phil hits me with the basics of removing chunks of media from a project, which is all I'll need to hack into *Oh, What a Lovely Tea Party*.

Tea Party is just too long to show at Vulgarthon in its present running time of three hours and forty-five minutes. For home viewing, sure — a VA enthusiast can watch it in a sitting or start and stop the flick according to their schedule. But at the tail-end of a loooooooooooooong day of watching movies, the far-from-'Snowball Effect'-tight/fly-on-the-wall-format of the nearly four-hour *Tea Party* might put motherfuckers to sleep. For that reason, and because we just don't have enough time to fit the monster version into our already-packed 'Thon schedule, Malcolm and I sit down and start the lugubrious task of finding an hour and forty-five minutes to hack out.

It turns out to be not as lugubrious as we thought. By midnight, we've tamed the beast into a hair over two hours without any really painful edits. Turns out there was a bunch of fat (mostly of behind-the-scenes angles of various scenes) that just slowly fell away like the pounds on Atkins. Midway through the cut, Malcolm and I are joined by Christian (Xtian to you folks) who is in town for Vulgarthon. Jen swings your beloved Mod, Endless and their two kids by the office before whisking the girls up to the house. The men are left to do the heavy lifting; the heavy lifting of sitting crammed behind a desk and pressing keys on a Mac keyboard.

We call it a night twenty minutes from the end of the doc, and head up to the house. Harley and Gabrielle are already out cold in Harley's barn bed (a bunkbed shaped/designed to look like, you guessed it, a barn), so Team Case opts to leave her here for the night and Malcolm and I take the remnants of their broken family back to the hotel. We gas up the truck on the way home.

Jen's out cold when I get home, so I jump online to check email. As I fall asleep in the process of doing so, I realize it's time to call it a night. I fall asleep watching TiVo'ed *Simpsons*.

Friday 25 March 2005 @ 12:08 p.m.

The dogs play it cool — it's the kids that wake my ass up at 7:30 a.m. Dressed in full princess regalia Harley and Gabrielle start banging on the door. Jen lets the dogs out, and I stumble to the bathroom with the computer to play catch-up with the diary-thing. I run out of battery juice in ten minutes, so I head back to the bedroom, sack out on the floor, and finish my entry.

Malcolm joins us (after being serenaded awake by Harley and Gabrielle doing their rendition of 'Good Morning, to You'), and we decide to take the girls to breakfast at Jerry's while Jen heads to the doctor's. I shower and we're off.

On the drive to Jerry's, we call Xtian and Endless to see if they're up for breakfast. They've already eaten, so me and Malcolm are on our own with the kids. I'd set my babysitting rate to be in line with my college-speaking rate, but Team Case's eldest is one of those rare good kids, who's low-maintenance and easy to be around (but, fuck does she love Sweet & Low).

After breakfast, we head over to the store so I can sign up the remaining 100 or so *Wizard*World Kevin Smith exclusive figures (we sent a few cases back east for the Red Bank Stash so there'll be some in stock post-Basie gig). Dave and I try to figure out what's creating this nauseating buzz in one of the lights at the back of the store and ultimately figure it's best left to an electrician. Malcolm keeps an eye on the kids while I re-stock the shelves and sign some bobble-heads and *Strike Back* figures. I buy two cases of Kevin figures for family and stuff, and we're off.

Jen calls and asks me to pick up a gift for Harley's friend whose birthday the girls are meant to attend that afternoon. We head across the street to Aaaah's and pick up some *SpongeBob* and Wonder Woman gear. I stumble across a few of those old school video games that consist of the games built into the joystick (the scrolling games that plug right into the back of your TV and run on batteries), including (to my utter joy) an EA Sports NHL '95 game. Malcolm finds an "I

Fucked Paris Hilton" t-shirt which we think (for twenty seconds) would be funny to give to Mewes (who starts shooting a movie with the fuckee in question on Tuesday), then move on.

On the ride home, [Jason] Lee calls to confirm he'll be rockin' the V'thon *Amy* Q&A mic (there was a question as to whether or not he was gonna be in town, but like a champ, he came through). We chit-chat the whole ride home (he's loving his TV show [*My Name is Earl*]) and he wraps it up by busting some Syndrome to Harley.

We get home and find Team Case chilling with Jen. I head into my office to do a phoner with the Bergen Record (to promote the Count Basie gig) and a phoner with *Entertainment Weekly* (to suck Criterion's cock; finally, Criterion's getting some mainstream ink). After that, we head to The Ivy for a late lunch.

Malcolm made the reservation at the wrong Ivy, so we stand there, displaced for a moment in the packed restaurant, at a loss. The Ivy kindly gets us in ASAP regardless. We're seven for lunch: me, Jen, Malcolm, Chay, Trish, Cookie (Mos's girlfriend), Xtian and Endless. I spend most of the lunch jawing with Trish about her new boyfriend.

We head home and after a moment of panic in which Gabrielle's 'Little Baby' (a small stuffed cow) has gone missing, shit's made right and I drop Team Case back at the hotel.

With Harley doing 'Movie Night' down in Gail and Byron's room, Jen and I settle into some of the first peace and quiet we've had since the anniversary. We rock a little *Without a Trace*, which, years later, still holds up. It's certainly as far-fetched as a child abduction movie can be (it makes *Ransom* look plausible), but totally watchable. I'm checking email through most of the flick, and then close up shop as we settle into that Robin Williams flick *The Final Cut*. It requires a degree more attention than we have to give at that point, as we're both kinda tired. We switch over to TiVo and fall asleep to some *Simpsons* eps.

Saturday 26 March 2005 @ 12:08 p.m.

Fucking dogs get me up at 5:45, but thankfully, Mewes is lingering about upstairs. I let the dogs out of my room (figuring Mewes'll let 'em out upstairs), take a leak, and go back to bed.

Rise from a bad dream at about 8:10, and throw on some clothes so I can get Xtian to the Stash. Once there, X, Bob and Gina put together the pickup bags (shirt, tip sheet, VA Almanac, comic), and I sign 500 copies of *Silent Bob Speaks*.

After some last minute rearrangement of the shelves, I'm out of there (joint opens at eleven, there's already a small crowd outside, and since I look like I slept in my clothes in the back of a car, I'm not in the mood to take pics and stuff).

I swing by the house, pick up Malcolm, and head to the office. Phil and I shift some of the *Jersey Girl* credits around on the Avid, render 'em, and Phil's off and running with the BetaCam output. I head over to Phil's office to finish off *Tea Party* and since Phil's taught me a few more tricks to Final Cut, I go back to the head of the flick to do a fine cut, whipping that motherfucker into a lean, tight (yet still oddly loose) one-hour forty-seven. I'm behind that desk from 12:30 p.m. to 11:00 p.m.

Along the way, my Canadian homey Jim Jackman (of *Degrassi* production fame) arrives, and after some initial histrionics from Malcolm (of the "There can be only one!" variety), all three of us mellow out with not one, not two, but three spliffs. Amazingly, I'm still able to edit (albeit more c-a-r-e-f-u-l-l-y, maaaaaaannn...). We order some food (natch) and it's about the best food I've tasted in what feels like eons (everything tastes better when you're baked — even when it's just a bun-less cheeseburger and some chicken skewers). We spend a long time laughing about shit which probably wasn't really all that funny, but fuck, I'm like crying at the time, unable to breathe. I don't spark up very regularly, but when I do a) it's usually with Malcolm, and b) it's usually an excellent time.

We drive home (s-l-o-w-l-y, maaaaaaaaannnnn...), making a pit stop at McDonald's for more chicken and beef. I get home and scarf two Atkins S'mores bars (because the first one tasted better than it usually does, somehow...) and climb into bed beside the slumbering Schwalbach. I'm out in less than a minute.

Sunday 27 March 2005 @ 12:09 p.m.

I wake up around 7:30 to find Harley waking up on our couch, ready to see if the Easter Bunny came. Surprise, surprise — he did (God bless Gail and Jen). Team Quinnster (Jen, Byron, Gail and I) head upstairs for the egg/basket hunt, with Byron firing away on his new Cannon 7MegaPixel SureShot.

Post holiday-lie-endorsement, we're joined by Malcom and Jackman and start the hour-long process of trying to figure out a table configuration for twenty-plus people. The dining room table is pretty long (it seats twelve), but not long enough. So the kitchen table is dragged into the living room, the dual leaves are put in, and we're off and running (with a tiny kids' table between the twain adult tables for the little ones).

I update the diary, shower, and head out to Bristol Farms with Malcolm, Mewes and Jackman to pick up a fruit and cheese platter, as well as some rolls and ice.

We eat at 3:00 p.m. The joint's packed. In attendance: me, Jen, Harley, Gail, Byron, Mos, Cookie, Jay, Chay, Phil, Malcolm, Jackman, Malcolm's friend Andre, Gina (Chappy's still stuck at the Stash), Bryan, Quinn, Andy, Xtian, Endless, Bry's brother Eric, Quinn's buddy Sal, Gabrielle and Charlotte (if I'm forgetting anybody, I'm sorry). I stick to the protein.

I talk to Phil for a long time, and later, while everyone's playing poker, Bob Schreck and Diana Schutz (both in town for the *Sin City* première) and Chappy join us for desserts.

I throw everyone out at 9:00 p.m., as we've got an early morning ahead of us.

Jen and I are asleep by 10:00 p.m.

Monday 28 March 2005 @ 12:03 p.m.

I get up before even the dogs, shower, send out last minute emails to Ben [Affleck], [Jason] Lee, Joey [Lauren Adams], and Jeff about the 'Thon. Then, me and Malcolm meet Jay and Jackman at the office so we can load some artwork for the glass cases at the Dome into the car.

I get to the Dome around 7:30 a.m. The line outside is huge (natch). Inside, we're all buzzing with pre-show activity, doing tech-checks, marking off reserved seats, etc. Smalls has done a great job of pulling the event together. Nothing is left undone.

I jump outside to do a quick interview with CNN.

I'm astounded by the video projection system. For weeks, we've been sweating what the projected BetaCams and DV tapes were gonna look like on the Dome's massive screen. But Vern and George's amazing machine somehow manages to not only keep all the resolution, but actually improve the picture too.

At 8:45, Mewes and I head outside to get the bracelets around the wrists of all 830 attendees.

Vulgarthon begins (and is fairly well documented over at News Askew).

I get home a little after two in the morning. Jen and I trade tales of Vulgarthon, and I fall asleep to a TiVo'ed *Simpsons* mid-conversation.

Tuesday 29 March 2005 @ 12:03 p.m.

Fucking bastard mutts. Goddamn 6:45 a.m.!

I cruise the board and the 'net to see what's what re: Vulgarthon, then call in to the Alice Morning Radio show at 8:00 for a promised on-air chat with Hooman (who was briefly in attendance yesterday). They're mid-commercials, so we opt to have them call me back.

I set about wrapping up last week's journal and store it in the new Boring-Ass Life forum, and get current with the new stuff.

Alice calls back, and I chit-chat with Sarah, No-Name, Hooman and Matty about the Vulgarthon.

Jen tells me I've gotta bring Harley to her spring break camp (she's on Easter break from school all week, but she's doing this day camp thing). I'm also to drop Xtian's Gabrielle off at the hotel, but her 'Little Baby' cow has gone missing. Ten minutes later, after said cow is unearthed, Malcolm, Harley, Gabrielle and I are off.

I drop both kids off at their separate destinations, and then call Joey, Dwight and Lee to touch-base about the night before. All enjoyed themselves (Lee I wind up getting via email later).

Malcolm and I swing by the Griddle, where I'm supposed to meet Brad and Chris for post-'Thon breakfast. Since I'm already a half hour late and we don't see them outside, we swing back home to grab Jen and Jackman for some Griddle instead.

The four of us Griddle it up, going over the previous night's activities. As we head off, we run into Bryan and Brian (Lynch) and get their thoughts on the 'Thon. As far as we can tell, everyone had a good time.

We pop into Rite Aid for some smokes (for Jen) and gum (for me), then head back home.

I talk to ********** who's come to town for this meeting with the folks at ********** about a ********** feature. We plan for her and *********** (her producing partner/husband) to come over to the house at nine tomorrow morning for a pre-meeting before we all head over to ***********.

(NOTE: As the above stuff is still in development stages, I've gotta leave the pertinent info out until deals are in place and signed. Sorry.)

I lay down to watch some TiVo and wind up falling asleep 'til four-ish. I talk to Mos for awhile, to get his thoughts about the *Amy* Q&A. Afterwards, Jay bombs by after his first day of working on *Bottoms Up*. He fills us in on the shooting, and then me, him, Malcolm and Jackman head to Baja Fresh to bring home some dinner. There, we run into Bryan and Brian (Quinn) and Brian's friend Sal at the adjacent Coffee Bean. We chit-chat for a bit, pick up the food, then head home.

Me, Jen, Jackman, Malcolm and Harley chow down. Following that, Jen and I put Harley to bed on our couch, and we close the curtains on the boudoir portion of the master bedroom suite and get into some TiVo. We're both asleep by eight or nine.

Wednesday 30 March 2005 @ 12:04 p.m.

Cursed dogs. 6:00 a.m. I let 'em out, take a leak, then head into my office for email and whatnot.

I shower at about 8:00 and then Jackman, Malcolm and I head to Coffee Bean to grab a box of coffee and pastries/bagels for the meeting. We get back around 9:00 to find Jen fixing up the house/living room for our meeting (fucking champ, that one). ************* and ********** arrive, and they sit down with me and Jackman to talk about what's going on with the ************ feature. All seems on track, as we're all on the same page. At about 10:30, ***********, ********** and I head over to the ************ lot.

The meeting goes insanely well, with the women in charge of both ********** and ********** as well the ************ and **********, the two folks in charge at ************* in attendance. Everyone seems to want this flick to happen. You couldn't ask for better feedback — even on the subject of me bringing ************* aboard.

********** and ************ head to the airport from the lot, and I head home. Jen's been planting, so she's a bit sweaty and dirty. While she showers, Gail comes up and we go over the schedule for my trip east, mid-west, and north. I fill Jackman in on my morning meeting, and then Jen and I head to Quizno's for some lunch. Following that, we head to the newspaper stand to grab the *Times* (*NY* and *LA*), *USA Today*, and sundry other papers that headline the Weinstein/Disney split.

We stop by the house so Jen can pick up some dry-cleaning and then head over to the Valley to drop said dry-cleaning off. Afterwards, I drop Jen back at the house and go to pick up Harley from camp. From there, Quinnster and I head to Laser Blazer for this week's new DVDs (it's a slim week for new releases). I chit-chat with store-owner Ron about the Vulgarthon (he was there for the first half of it), and then Harley and I are off for home.

I hear from Tony Angellotti (my publicist) that both CNN and KTLA ran pieces on the Vulgarthon, and that the *LA Daily News* is running something tomorrow, and that Marilyn Beck's column is supposed to be running an item about the Craig/UV engagement as well.

Once home, I climb back into my loungin' gear and hit the board/check email. Half an hour later, it's dinnertime. Gail cooked a chicken that me, Byron, Jen, Gail and Jackman dig into.

Post-meal, Jackman, Gail and Jen grab smokes on the deck, and I start signing a bunch of *Silent Bob Speaks* that Smalls laid out on the dining room table earlier that day. An hour later, Jackman's ride to the airport arrives. We say goodbye, and it's back to the Great White North for Jim.

I lay down and check email/the board while watching TiVo. At a certain point, I start falling asleep mid-post. Jen brings down some Jell-o which we dig into while peeping a *Law & Order* I've never seen. At the end of it, I'm already falling asleep. I'm out by nine.

Thursday 31 March 2005 @ 12:04 p.m.

Unholy floor-crawlers start the day at 6:48. Thankfully, I hear Byron at the top of the stairs, so all I've gotta do is let the mutts out the bedroom door. I take a leak and hit the board, figuring out when I'm gonna update the blog.

I take my laptop into the bathroom and check email during a good morning shit. I get through a lot of email, but there's somehow still another hundred left to address in the inbox.

Gail calls to let me know Josh Horowitz is calling to finish up his interview. Josh is writing a book about five young filmmakers, and we've already done about two hours on the phone a few weeks ago. This time, we do an hour and change. As he's great at posing queries and listening, the time flies by.

Jen wakes up as I finish the interview. She goes into the morning ritual of riding the couch while sipping coffee and having her morning smokes, while I update the diary.

We opt for a little Newsroom brunch. I take a shower and we're off.

Over turkey meatloaf (me) and artichokes (Jen), I ask the wife if she'd be interested in receiving her birthday/our anniversary gift today instead of waiting 'til next week. Naturally, she opts to get it today, so post-brunch, we head over to Beverly Hills.

I let her take over the wheel to circle Rodeo while I dash into Tiffany to pick up the gift I'd ordered oh, so long ago, yet couldn't wait another week to bestow. Before it's wrapped up, my Tiffany rep gives me a peek at the goods. As impressive as the box is, what's even more stunning is what's inside the box. What does a fella get the Queen of his world for her thirty-fourth birthday/six-year anniversary? A diamond tiara, of course.

I exit just as Jen's rounding the corner, and I hop into the driver's seat. She tears into the package and goes giddy. It's a nice fit and the design is subtle enough to wear everyday. As much as I was loved four minutes ago, my stock's somehow taken another jump.

We head home and fuck like stoned test bunnies.

I head over to the exo-house office to do an interview about Alanis and the tenth anniversary of 'Jagged Little Pill'. It goes really well. Before and post-interview, I rap with Smalls about the 'Thon.

Back home, I carry the new fireplace screen upstairs. Harley and her friend are in the pool, and Jen's outside planting and hosing down the deck. I sign up the rest of the *Silent Bob Speaks* books that're sitting on the dining room table, then head downstairs and get into the loungin' wear. Smalls comes over to box up the books and get 'em ready to send to Don in Florida.

While I'm laying down checking email and the board, Smalls comes in to schedule an appointment for when I get back from the east coast to talk about a raise. I say fuck the appointment, you got the raise (a roughly forty-five percent raise at that) and send him on his way.

I talk to Phil (my agent) for awhile and an hour later, I talk to Mos. We're all trying to come up with a formula for the *Clerks* 2 backend that we plan to share with Jeff, Brian and Mewes. During this, I eat some cheese from one of the pizzas Jen's ordered for the girls.

We watch some TiVo 'til it's time for Harley to go to bed (tonight, in Byron and Gail's room, thank God). We go downstairs and kiss Harley goodnight, then head up to watch a little *Law & Order*. As it ends, Chappy and Gina arrive. I put on my day clothes and head upstairs to the living room for a meeting.

Chappy, Gina and I go over all the post-'Thon data as well as other Stash details. The next two store-run events on the horizon are the *Silent Bob Speaks* book signing and the *Mallrats* tenth Anniversary screening/Q&A to be shot for the *Mallrats* tenth DVD. We opt to make a new shirt-as-ticket for this screening which we'll be holding in a smaller theater at the Arclight, if all goes well (looking at a 400-seater this time, so get your tix early). We decide to scrap the Kevin Smith InAction exclusive for the *Wizard*World Philly Con, as I'm not gonna make it (we'll be shooting *Clerks* 2 at that point), and move full steam ahead on the San Diego, Chicago and Boston variants.

Bob and Gina head off, and I head downstairs to find Jen and Chay kicking back on the couch. We all chit-chat for a bit, 'til Chay heads home and I put my loungin' wear back on. I settle into bed and check some final email/board stuff. Jen joins me and we cuddle up watching some *Simpsons* and eventually fall asleep.

Friday 1 April 2005 @ 12:05 p.m.

6:13. What the fuck possesses these varmints? Byron's upstairs, so I don't have to make the morning climb. It's freezing in the room, so I close the black-out curtains and crank the heat.

Take a leak and head directly to the desk-top to check email and start composing yesterday's diary. An hour or so later, Jen wakes up insisting I'm trying to roast her alive with the heat.

Harley calls up to the room (intercom system) to tell us there's a bird loose in the house. We head downstairs to investigate, only to discover we've been April Fooled by a five year old. We are filled with shame.

We drop Harley off at camp and head to the Griddle. Post-Griddle, we head home.

I have Gail switch my flight so that I'm not on the afternoon flight or the red-eye, but instead, a 7:15 flight the next a.m. which will get me to Red Bank three hours before showtime. This frees me up to lounge with Jenny.

Sacked out on the bed, in front of the TV, I watch the rest of *The Final Cut* while posting and checking email.

Gail serves up family dinner and following the meal, Harley heads to Nan and Pop's room for Movie Night (*SpongeBob* and *The Wind in the Willows*). Jen and I watch Sayles' latest, *Silver City*, during which Jen starts to get sick from some bad cheese she thinks she's eaten. She lays down, and I pack for the early morning airport run. We fall asleep watching TiVo'ed *Simpsons*.

Saturday 2 April 2005 @ 12:05 p.m.

I wake up before the dogs and jump in the shower. I check the board while I'm drying, get dressed, and kiss the sleeping Schwalbach goodbye.

Byron drops me at the airport and I jump on the plane for N.J. I'm ticked to discover the United flight I'm on doesn't have power-ports in the seats, so at a certain point, I'm gonna run out of juice for the laptop. The in-flight flick's *Ocean's Twelve* (which I'd never seen but wind up really liking), so that's two hours during which I'm not depleting the laptop battery. When the movie's over, I watch some *Degrassi* episodes from the current season that I'd missed. On the fourth ep, the battery dies, so I go back to reading the treatment for the ****** movie before I fall asleep.

We land at Newark. The weather's insanely shitty. I pick up a rental SUV and drive through the downpour to the MotherLand. Instead of taking the Red Bank exit, I get off at 117 and take Rt. 36 — the scenic route. It's always a roll down memory lane when I get back into town and drive past places like Bethany Rd. and Dante Tuxedos. I wouldn't be who I am or do what I do today without a lifetime of inspirado, courtesy of Monmouth County.

I get to the Molly Pitcher and check in. Thank Christ — they've finally upgraded and installed the ethernet. In fact, they've gone WiFi. I check the board and email and order some room service.

I head to the Basie, park at the loading dock, and head inside. After a few pics for and with Mark Voger (of the Asbury Park Press), I head outside, grab some fresh air before the long haul that's to come, then head out onstage for the Q&A.

Seven hours later, post-Q&A, I hit the store for a late-night signing. Walt, Mike Z (HelperMonkee to you folks) Ming and Xtian help out. By the time we wrap up, it's light outside. At 6:20 a.m., I head back to the Molly Pitcher for some sleep.

Sunday 3 April 2005 @ 12:05 p.m.

I get up at 11:00 a.m., take a shower, and head over to the store. Walt and Jeff lay out what's left of the *Silent Bob Speaks* books for me to sign, as well as a pile of *Evening With*s. The guy who runs the River's Edge Café next door sends over some breakfast which I down while chit-chatting with some board-ers who roll by.

I'm off to Newark where I turn the car in and jump on the plane to Chicago's O'Hare.

I sleep most of the flight, which winds up being extended because we're circling at O'Hare for a while, and when we land, we don't have a gate. I finally get off the plane and outside where I'm met by my brother Donald who's in town for the show. Mom was supposed to be there as well, but she's come down with a heavy-duty flu that's prevented her from attending.

Don and I drive out to Crystal Lake and we chit-chat about the gig, the online store (which he runs), Jen's impending birthday (7 April), and a bunch of other stuff. We stop at Quizno's so I can grab a Steakhouse Beef Dip on low carb flatbread before we hit the Raue.

We get to the Raue and a dude is waiting for me out back with some DVD covers and a Sharpie. My hands are full of my bags so I shrug and hustle inside, say hi to Judy Irwin and Co., and duck into my dressing room to change the shirt I've dripped some Quizno's onto earlier. Fifteen minutes after I get to the gig, I'm being introduced and rolling out onstage.

The gig goes swimmingly. Great house, great crowd, great questions. Before I know it, six hours have gone by. I say my g'nights, sign a few things for the Raue folks backstage, sign a few things for the guy who was waiting for me outside when I got to the Raue, then collapse into the car and go. On the ride back, I fight to stay awake by talking to Don.

We get to the Hilton at the airport (Don's staying elsewhere), and Don has me sign about twenty *Marvels, Mutants, and Monsters* DVDs before I hug him goodbye and stumble toward check-in.

I get to my room and open the computer. I check my email to see that Gail's changed my return flight to LA, which allows me to sleep in an extra two hours. I fall asleep watching a Spectravision-rented *Ocean's Twelve*.

Monday 4 April 2005 @ 11:56 a.m.

Because there are no dogs, I wake up at the Hilton Airport at O'Hare around ten o'clock. Ah, sweet no-dog sleep.

Rockin' the morning wood, and I've got a few minutes, so I tug one out to pics of Jen and head to the shower.

As I dry, I take a peek at the board to gauge reaction to this weekend's Q&As. I get dressed and walk to the airport.

At the gate, I'm told that I'm not on the 11:30, but on the 12:40 instead. I head to the other gate where I'm told I was, indeed, on the 11:30, but it's now locked out, and I'm currently on standby for the 12:40, but they can put me on the 3:00 p.m. I stare, dead-eyed, at the attendant and opt for the 3:00 p.m. to LAX.

Rather than bitch and moan, I head for the Admiral's Club lounge and, with over three hours to kill, order up a beer. Then another. Then another.

By two o'clock, I've got a good buzz going on. I'm checking the board, checking email, walking the LA-based Jenny through iTunes and iChat as I dirty talk her from my booth in the Admiral's Club. Even though I've snapped one off this a.m., I'm more than ready to be ravished by her when I get home. I contemplate getting flat-out sloppy drunk on the plane during the four-hour flight home, but decide instead to sleep the time away. In an effort to aid this, I order my fourth and final Michelob Ultra.

My brother Don rolls into the Admiral's Club and we talk about the gig the night before, as well as the friend of the poster in the Midwest Q&A thread who called me a jerk for not signing after the show. He drops me off at my gate before heading to his gate for his Orlando departure.

Prior to takeoff, I read some *Boondocks* until I fall asleep. I wake up during the food service to find that the two options for dinner are now one: all the chicken strips are gone, so all they have left is pizza. I pass on the pizza and crack open the laptop, plug in to the seat, and watch *My Own Private Idaho* for the first time in about a decade (it still holds up). Following that, I get through about half a doc called *The Secret Lives of Adult Stars* before it's time to land.

Jen's stuck in traffic, so I'm waiting at the arrivals level for a half hour. During that time, I talk to Mos on the cell, and he informs me that we've started getting some cashflow on *Clerks 2*. Jen shows up and we head back to the house.

I hit the bathroom, and then we hit the bedroom. After a quickie, we head upstairs for family dinner with Byron, Gail, and Harley. Quinnster's feverish — so much so that they sent her home from school today. She barely touches her food, so Jen sends me to the Ralph's for a thermometer, Pedialyte stuff (popsicles and fever reducer) and ice cream for the Sicko Chicko.

I get home, hand out the goods, and dig into some low carb ice cream in the kitchen. Jen appears and after we make out a little, she whips up a pair of strawberry milkshakes for Harley. I give the dogs some Milkbones and head down to the room.

I throw on the loungin' wear and catch up with Sunday night's *Simpsons* and *Arrested Development*. Jen brings Harley up to our couch where she'll be planted for the night. Harley shows me her third loose tooth and I kiss her g'night. As she falls asleep, I'm in the bed, updating my diary-thing, while Jen's upstairs smoking and watching TV.

Jen joins me in bed and I close up the laptop for the night, as we nestle ourselves in the sweet-yet-just embrace of Jack McCoy and *Law & Order*, during which we fall asleep.

Tuesday 5 April 2005 @ 11:58 a.m.

The dogs start getting restless at 7:20. Jen and I play the "You let 'em out"/"No, you are the one who should let the dogs out…" game for a minute or two before I lose and hoof it up the stairs to let the dogs out.

I head to the bathroom to shit, check email, and update the diary.

I switch from laptop to desk-top and continue with the email and board stuff. Over on iChat, Walt and I go over some light Stash East refurbishments I wanna do.

Jen gets up late and we hang out with Harley for a bit. She's still feeling under the weather, so she's gonna rest up today. I shower and Jen and I head to Quizno's for lunch.

Afterwards, I drop Jen off at the doctor's and I cruise over to Laser Blazer for the new DVDs. Following that, I stop by a newsstand and pick up the latest *Empire* magazine.

I pick up Jen and we head back to the house. She runs in and grabs a dress she wants to have tailored, and we head over to the Valley to the cleaners. While Jen's inside, I talk to Ernie O'Donnell on the cell about the Stash East refurbishments. Jen grabs some Coffee Bean and we head back home.

I sack out in front of the TiVo and do some iChat biz while watching Jack McCoy bust some ass on *Law & Order*. Jen has a meeting about our poetry event in the living room with Daniella and Russell Milton, as dinner begins in the kitchen for me, Harley, Byron and Gail.

I inhale a chicken breast and a cheeseburger while we all chit-chat about our respective days. At the tail end of the meal, Malcolm and Andre come over. They grab some barbecue as well, while I take Harley in to Jen to say goodnight. Quinnster heads downstairs with Nan and Pop while me, Malcolm and Andre head to my room to watch a new cut of their documentary, *Small Town/Gay Bar*. It's some excellent, excellent stuff and we talk about the possible involvement of Norman Lear and the Sundance Channel.

During the screening, Mewes comes home after a long day on the set of the new flick he's doing. We talk about maybe going to the Bicycle Casino in Long Beach, but opt instead to get him some In-N-Out so he can crash with a DVD full of *Murder, She Wrote*s. Malcolm and Andre head off, and me and Mewes take a ride down to Sunset for a Double-Double, Animal Style. He tells me about the shoot and how it's going on the flick, 'til we get home. He heads to his room and I head upstairs with some In-N-Out for Jen, whose meeting has ended. We fall asleep watching TiVo'ed *Simpsons*.

Wednesday 6 April 2005 @ 11:58 a.m.

6:30. Fucking 6:30. Why can't these dogs sleep 'til ten? I let 'em out of the room but, mercifully, Byron's upstairs to let 'em out-out. I head to the bathroom, take a leak, then retire to my office to update the diary.

Mewes wakes up, and I take him to get some smokes. We head down to the Ford dealer to pick up Byron (who dropped his truck off for some work), and I call Jen and ask her if she wants to get dressed and head to breakfast with me and Mewes, to celebrate his two years of sobriety.

I drop off Byron and pick up Jen, and her, Mewes and I hit the Griddle. We chit-chat about Mewes's new flick, and try to figure out whether or not we've got enough time to hit the Bicycle Casino near Long Beach before Mewes's call time. It would seem not, so we decide to scrap the Bike for today and do it this weekend instead.

When I get home, there's a situation heating up — a situation which could wind up pushing the *Clerks 2* shoot by a month and change. The producer Jenno Topping (who, aside from being a producer is also the main squeeze of Project Greenlight's Chris Moore) has sent me a script, not to direct (smart lady), but to act in. It's this movie Susanah Grant (writer of *Erin Brokovich*) wrote and is directing called *Catch & Release*, which stars Jennifer Garner and Timothy Olyphant. I'd be playing Sam, who's in the flick quite a bit. Somehow, off of *An Evening With Kevin Smith*, Susanah thinks I'm right for the role, and Jenno's not doing the smart thing and trying to convince her otherwise. So Jenno and I talk about it, and she says that Phil (Raskind, my agent) insists it can't happen, because we're due to shoot *C2* in June. However, that schedule's not set yet, and we're talking about pushing maybe a month and a half here (maybe two) to do something I've never been offered before: a big part in a big movie.

I call Phil about it, and we hash it out, and talk about whether it's even a possibility. By call's end, I decide I should talk to Harvey about it.

I call Harvey and tell him about the flick. Harvey says that I should probably read the script (I haven't, at this point; meant to take it with me to NJ and Ill last weekend, but my carry-on was overpacked already). He says: "If it's gonna make you Tom Cruise, then do it." I tell him it's not gonna make me Tom Cruise, but that nothing short of a deal with Lucifer is ever gonna do that anyway. He says: "My first instinct is to say you should keep your powder dry, because you've got *The Passion* coming up. But if they're gonna pay you a lot to do it…" I tell him I don't know what I'd be getting paid, and he says to call him back once I've read the script — as that's the key factor in deciding to make/be in any movie. He also tells me that Fox Searchlight might be coming in with New Co. on *Clerks 2* and handling the foreign side. Since Searchlight's had such a killer few years lately, and since both Harvey and Searchlight previously worked together on (and did so well with their respective releases of) *Garden State*, this is awesome news.

Jen comes home from a mani/pedi/brow, and I hit her with all of this. She's kinda floored. She says, "You never cease to amaze me." I say, "When I'm all kinds of terrible in this flick, you'll cease to be amazed." She says, "If I were you, I'd be really flattered that somebody thought of you to do this at all," to which I agree, but counter with: "But I'm not an actor. I don't wanna be an actor. I've never wanted to be an actor." She says, "Maybe that's why they thought of you." Regardless, she thinks I should at least give it a shot, inasmuch as I should read the script and meet with the director. I tell her I can't read the script 'til tonight, because I'm gonna be in the office all day working on the *Mallrats* re-cut, so she says she's gonna give the script a read in my absence.

I shower and take Byron back to the Ford dealer to pick up his truck. On my way back, I call Jen and suggest she meet me downstairs so I can take her to the cleaners to pick up her tailored dress. On the way over, she starts breaking the script down for me, talking about the first half, and whether or not I can pull this part off (she thinks I can; but then, she also thinks I'm attractive, so it's already been proven that this woman is delusional).

We grab her dress, and while Jen's getting some Coffee Bean, Jon Gordon calls. I debrief him, and he, too, is like "It might be worth pushing the *Clerks 2* shoot, because who knows what comes of you acting in this flick? Maybe you open yourself up to a completely different audience who'll try out *Clerks 2*?" I say "A completely different audience who'll then hate *Clerks 2*?" We talk about the Fox Searchlight development before he's gotta jump off the phone. I drop Jen off at the house and head to the office to talk to Mosier about all this.

At the office, I fill Mos in (not like that, you fucking children...), and we talk about the feasibility of moving the *Clerks 2* shoot by a month or two. It's do-able, but will anyone be happy about waiting? We talk about how Mos will fill in that two month gap, and come up with an option: if he gets bored, he can take over editing duties on Malcolm's doc (which is editor-less at the moment). Phil, meanwhile, has called to say this *Catch & Release* thing is getting serious, and that he's starting to feel like I should give it a shot, too. He's gonna read the script tonight, and I tell him I'll be doing the same.

Jen calls to tell me she's finished reading the script. She's not a chick-flick fan, but she loves this script. She says it's really warm, touching, and poignant. She says I can do Sam in my sleep (not like that, you fucking children...), and that she thinks I should give it a shot.

Mos and I head up to the house, where Jen's getting ready for her Birthday Dinner Girls Night Out with her friends. I tell her that Mos and I are gonna head to the Palm for dinner and then over to the Bike for some poker. She looks pretty-as-hell in her newly tailored dress and tiara, and I tell her so. I also tell her to have a good time, and with that, Mos and I are off to the Palm.

At the Palm, me and Mos both get Filet Mignon (his well-done, mine black and blue), and over some beers, we talk about this book he's reading in which a former travel writer breaks down science (from the Big Bang to evolution) into laymen's terms. After dinner, we opt to pop in on the Girl's Night Out at Koi, the sushi place on La Cienega. We valet the car, and head to the entry, getting snapped repeatedly by paparazzi standing outside. The paparazzi are an important aspect of the story solely because of what happens next: forty seconds later, the bouncer tells me I can't come in because I'm in shorts. I tell him I'm not staying, and that I just wanted to pop in and give my wife a kiss; it'll take four minutes, tops. He says it'll take no minutes, because I'm in shorts. Mos heads in to get Jen, while I stand at the entry, pretty okay with the whole affair, even if the paparazzi are snapping away at me. Seeing that I'm somebody the paparazzi seem to feel is worth wasting film on, the bouncer says, "You can step inside the door and wait right there." I tell him it's cool, I get it, and that I don't wanna get him in trouble. After a minute more, he says, "I'm gonna go to the bathroom, so I'm not gonna be standing here for a few minutes. If you were to walk in, I wouldn't know — ya' dig?" I tell him I've got no interest in flaunting house rules, but thanks anyway. Then, the Birthday Girl (well, tomorrow anyway) emerges and we make out a little in the doorway of Koi, until the Bouncer returns from his leak and says, "The boss says you can go in." So in I go with my wife, say hi to all the ladies at her table (Chay, Trish, Daniella, Lisa, Cookie, and Fanshen), kiss Jen again, and head off with Mos.

We stop at the house so I can grab more gum and Mos can grab the house keys he left behind, and we head toward the Pig 'n Whistle, where Mewes is shooting tonight. I call his cell, but no answer, so Mos and I take the 101 to the 5 to the Long Beach Freeway and the Bike. As we exit, Mewes calls, and I tell him we tried to swing by. He's bummed to not be going to the Bike too, and says if he gets off early, he'll call and join us.

At the Bike, Mos and I play 'til one or so. Our table's filled with the usual assortment of rounders and characters. Tonight, the highlight is the Mexican couple in their late twenties/early thirties, who're on a roll. The woman keeps saying to everyone at the table: "I'm not married, but my boyfriend is!" She digs this line, because she says it at least twenty times as the night goes on. A fan who'd been playing with us for half an hour quietly introduces himself and lets us know he's a fan, which causes a dude at the other end of the table to whisper to the couple "I knew it". By 1 a.m., Mos and I are ready to Donkey out, so we go all in on shit hands. We leave two hundred bucks lighter (we were only playing at the $2/$3/No Limit table) and head home.

I drop Mos off at his house, which is historic because, in the nearly-year he and Cookie have owned the house, I've never been over. It's in Echo Park, and it's pretty sweet, with excellent foliage up front, a nice backyard, and a killer fireplace. I peep it out, take a dump (couldn't hold it anymore), and head home.

At home, Jen's half in the bag after drinking martinis at Koi all night. But before I can take advantage of it, she falls asleep. Shortly thereafter, I do the same, watching TiVo'ed *Simpsons*.

Thursday 7 April 2005 @ 11:59 a.m.

The dogs get me up around 6:55. I let 'em out, take a leak, then climb back into bed.

I awake again at 9:30, to the sound of wife and child puttering about the room. Wife's trying to convince child that going to school today would be in her best interest, child's stalling. I sit up and wish the taller of the two a happy birthday. Wife takes child to get dressed for school, and I take morning shit.

With child off, wife and I sit around and play catch-up from last night. We then decide how we're gonna celebrate her thirty-fourth birthday. We cuddle for a while, and then talk about where to eat breakfast. Like every pampered Hollywood wife, Jen opts for Quizno's. Ever the love-slave, I head off to hunt and gather. Like a good caveman, I bring the dogs with me.

On the way to Quizno's, I go a few miles out of my way to Moe's on Melrose to get Schwalbach thirty-four multi-colored roses, as well as some gardenias to float in bowls of water around the room (she loves that) and some flowers for her mom (without whom there is no birthday girl). I then head to Quizno's, and stop at Wendy's for burgers for the Muttlies.

On the way home, I call Jenno and tell her I'm in, but that I think she's crazy for thinking I could pull this off, when this town's lousy with real actors. She tells me I'll be meeting with the director on Monday.

I get home, dump the booty on the respective booty-getters, and settle in in front of the TiVo to eat my low-carb Steakhouse Beef Dip wrap and dig into a little low-carb ice cream. We opt for *Dirty War*, an HBO movie on DVD about a dirty bomb going off in London that I picked up the other day.

Before we know it, it's three, and Harley's home. Jen and Harley bomb around for a while, and I try to get through the now-300 emails that're sitting in my inbox.

Suddenly, Harley decides it's present time. We head to the kitchen, where Byron, Gail, and Harley's gifts are all spread out. Jen unwraps and coos, and Quinnster and I fight about who gets to keep the boxes (I like to wind the kid up sometimes). Following that, dinner is served: lasagna for the Birthday Girl and family, bun-less cheeseburgers for me. Harley makes us go around the table, stating our name, age, and a memory of our favorite birthday. It's moments like this, I realize, that I'm really gonna miss in twenty years.

Post dinner, the candles are lit, and the Birthday Girl has at it. While the other four dig into what looks like just the flat-out best Duncan Hines cake ever made, I putter, trying not to think about all that sugar I'm missing out on. Quinnster and I adjourn to the living room to play some Tetris until it's time for her to go to bed.

I rendezvous with Schwalbach in our bedroom, and we go over the three scenes I'll be reading with Susanah on Monday. Immediately, I feel like a total fraud, but Jen seems into my horrible little performance. We go through the scenes for an hour, until I retire to the bed, where I fight with the room's WiFi for a decent connection. Around 10:20, mid-TiVo'ed *Law & Order*, I fall asleep. Jen wakes me up an hour later to say g'night and climb into bed beside me. It wasn't the best birthday in the world, but considering we did exactly what she wanted, it wasn't the worst either.

Friday 8 April 2005 @ 11:59 a.m.

6:45 with the dogs. It's like a fucking meat locker in our room. I let Captain Insecurity and the Brainless Wonder out, take a leak, and head to the computer to update the diary. I'm feeling kinda randy, but I don't wanna wake Jen up, so I click open my Jen nudes and tug one out in my office at the desk. From there, it's over to email.

Jen's got a doctor's appointment at eleven, so after she makes Harley's lunch and we see her off (Jen from downstairs, me from the upstairs balcony — she's wearing pony-tails to school for a class trip to see a stage version of *Aladdin* and looks adorable), Jen does the couch trip, the morning coffee, and is in the shower. I'm all over email and trying to sort out more *Clerks 2/Catch & Release* stuff.

Get an email from JJ Abrams, who's in for my guest-hosting episode of *Dinner for Five*. The final, locked five is JJ, Jason Lee, Stan Lee, Mark Hamill, and me. We shoot on Tuesday.

Jen and I make a post-doctor's lunch date (as well as a post-lunch fuck date), and she's off. Feeling a little randy again at the thought of the post-lunch fuck date, I head back to my office, break open the Jen pics again, and jerk off anew.

Off to the shower. I've got a noon meeting at the office with reps from the Director's Guild. I dry off, get dressed, grab some gum, and head downstairs.

Byron and Gail are off to Mammoth for the weekend for a ski trip we're send-ing Byron on for his birthday. We make arrangements to have Louis (the little Chocolate Lab Jen and I bought for Harley at Chay's insistence on New Year's Day that Byron has somehow inherited) shipped off to puppy camp (she's still in the stage where she needs constant supervision, lest she eat all Harley's crayons and shits all over the house). I kiss 'em both goodbye and then take the three-minute drive down to the Sycamore office.

There, Fern (from DGA East) and John (from DGA West) are already waiting with Smalls. I take them to my office and they chat me up about finally joining the DGA. I've been directing films for twelve years now, but I've never been a DGA member. It's kinda flattering that they're making the push to get me to join, because they feel that my inclusion sends a clear message to up-and-coming indie auteurs that the Guild is an essential part of any director's balanced break-fast. They tell me I'm one of the last holdouts (Quentin being another; Robert's been in and out of the Guild several times) and ask why I've never joined. I don't really have a good answer beyond the fact that I couldn't see the point in being part of another useless club. They maintain that, even though I'm deep enough in my career and have enough juice to not need Guild muscle behind me at the bargaining table, there are other benefits. They crack open a numbers sheet that makes it clear that if I'd been a Guild member since *Mallrats*, I'd have made close to a million dollars in residuals off of video sales. Also, by joining, the A.D.s and U.P.M.s I work with get protected and residuals too, as well as an insanely top-notch health plan. I suddenly remember why I didn't join years ago, and that's because I never want to throw that 'A Film By' credit in front of my name in the credit block. They say that, as a DGA member, it's not mandatory at all (in fact, they try to limit the 'Film By' credit so that it doesn't lose its meaning, and save it for folks like Scorsese, Lynch, Lucas, Spielberg, etc.). They cap it all off by telling me not every director is invited to join (or even accepted into) the Guild, and that I'd be a good score because I'm high profile, and if what it takes is an invitation letter from Guild President Michael Apted, then said letter will arrive next week. I say I'll give it all a serious think, and thanks for coming in. Nice folks.

Post-meeting, I pop into the editing room to see what Mosier's been doing with the *Mallrats* re-cut. We've decided that, instead of calling this The Director's Cut that we should call it The Cut That Should Never Have Been — as longer doesn't mean better (certainly in the case of *Rats*). Afterwards, while I'm chit-chatting with Smalls, Jen calls. She's home from the doctor's and ready to grab some lunch.

I swing up to the house, grab Schwalbach, and we head over to the Newsroom for lunch. The place is crowded, but we get a table and chow down: me on turkey meatloaf and chicken, Jen on some veggie soup and an artichoke. We talk about a bunch of stuff, including the Poetry Reading even we're holding up at the house next weekend to benefit Harley's school's Fine Arts program.

After lunch, we cross the street and go to Kitson's, this chick store on Robertson. Jen picks up an 'Award Winning Wife' t-shirt and an ashtray. Mos calls, and we talk about the *Rats* cut, and how we should perhaps deliver big chunks to Universal, as there's a lot of post-work to do to get it presentable (they've gotta go back to the negative, re-mix the sound, extend music cues, cre-ate new music cues, etc.). Done shopping, Jen and I head cross town to pick up Harley from school.

On the ride, Jen and I start talking sex, which evolves (or devolves) into dirty talk. I'm hard and she's wet, but the kid gets out of school in two minutes. All hot and bothered, we decide that, when we get home, we're gonna send Harley to watch some TV in her room for ten minutes while we go upstairs for a quickie.

Jen goes in to get Harley, and we head to Wendy's for some fries and chicken tenders for Jen and Harley respectively. We figure if the kid's chowing down when we get home, she won't notice the momentary absence of Mom and Dad. I get us home perhaps a little speedier than usual, and as we get out of the car, Jay greets us from the upstairs window. Beautiful: a built-in babysitter. I tell him to come downstairs and watch Harley for a few minutes so Jen and I can "talk".

With Harley safely in Jay's care, Jen heads upstairs, and I take Louis out for a brief walk (something Byron usually does, but he's on his way to Mammoth with Gail already). I put Louis outside with Scully and Mulder and head down to the bedroom, to discover the already naked Jennifer sprawled out on the bed. I lock the door, turn on the fuck-music (no, not 'Moonlighting', as Affleck's suggested), and we go at it. Ten minutes in, the door phone rings. We freeze, taking a beat to decide to answer it or not, as it may be the puppy camp people coming to pick up Louis, and the door phone doesn't ring in Harley's room, where Jay currently is. We give in, and Jen answers the phone (the phone's an intercom system, through which you can talk to people at the front door and buzz them in). Sure enough, it's the puppy camp folks. She buzzes the guy in, and we briefly debate who should go downstairs. I point out that, while she's wet, I'm hard, hence the more conspicuous of the two of us. Jen throws on a robe and races upstairs to get Louis. I call down to Mewes on the intercom and ask him to call for Louis downstairs and hand over the leash, the dog food, and the dog herself to the puppy camp pickup guy (so Jen doesn't have to go all the way downstairs). At this point, Mewes has figured out we're not "talking" and I hang up on his wink-wink, nudge-nudgey "Ohhhhh, shit!" Jen returns to the room, and we return to our regularly scheduled program, already in progress.

A half hour later, we head downstairs to retrieve the kid. Amazingly, she's asleep in her barn bed, and Jay's lying in the trundle beside her, watching *Scooby Doo*. We turn the TV down and leave Harley to nap for a bit, thank Mewes for the coverage, and head back upstairs. Jen rides her couch, smoking and checking email, and I head into the office to return a call to Jenno re: *Catch*. Jen asks me to send out some thank-you emails to folks who've agreed to do the Poetry Event, so I draft some missives to Anjelica Huston, Peter Coyote, Barbara Hershey and Ian McShane.

Harley wakes up and joins us upstairs, and with Jay off to play poker at Commerce, we try to figure out what the three of us should do for dinner. Harley opts for some leftover lasagna while watching *Fat Albert*. I join Jen up in the kitchen and make a low-carb pizza while we talk about the Poetry Event. She's stressing about it, trying to figure out if we've got enough booze and enough people coming to read, where the valet parkers are gonna put seventy to a hundred cars, etc. Tickets were $175.00, so she wants attendees to feel like they've gotten their money's worth. We've got two tickets left to sell, and we toy with the idea of putting them up for sale here on the board.

When *Fat Albert* ends, we start putting Harley to bed on our couch. She fucking loves that *Fat Albert* flick — particularly the song. I tell her that Jay and I sang that *Fat Albert* song in a movie once, and Jen suggests I let Harley see it (minus the guns in the scene). I grab *Dogma* from the library and pop it in the DVD player, jumping right to the cut scene. The kid's amazed (you've gotta impress them while you can, because kids grow up so fast these days, it won't be long before she's like, "You're a fucking jackass, Dad..."). When it's over, Jen reads Harley some books while I collect some DVD options to bring upstairs for Jen and I to choose from. We kiss Harley goodnight, turn on the house alarm, leave Scully and Mulder to keep an eye on her, and head upstairs.

Before we get into any DVD watching, Jen and I play a little Battle Tetris. While I'm whipping Schwalbach's ass, Harley joins us, claiming she's unable to sleep and tattling that Mulder's up on the couch with her. Jen deftly talks the Quinnster into going back to sleep, so back down she goes.

We decide on a movie: out of the pile of twenty, it all comes down to *Silverado*. We both rock our laptops while the movie plays on the big screen. About an hour in, Phil calls to talk about *Catch*. When we're done, Jen and I opt out of the movie (she's not into it, and I've seen it so many times already) and instead discuss the possibility of heading to Vancouver for three months, and what that means for the family (we travel in a pack) — particularly Harley's school.

Tired, we head downstairs and cuddle up while watching some TiVo'ed *Simpsons* until we both fall asleep.

Saturday 9 April 2005 @ 12:00 p.m.

With all the black out curtains closed and no school to get Harley to, I get to sleep in 'til around eight-ish before the dogs realize they've been outsmarted. I let 'em out and take a leak.

When I get back to the room, Harley's up too. She wants breakfast, but doesn't want to go sit at Jerry's or The Griddle to eat. We settle on some McDonald's, and I ask for five minutes to check my email before we go.

Two interesting emails: one from Richard Kelly, letting me know that all systems are go on *Southland Tales* and that I'll be needed for two days in August. The other email's from Edgar Wright, the director of *Shaun of the Dead*, who's in town for a week. I respond to both emails, throw on some clothes, pull a jacket over Harley, and we're off to grab some take-home chow.

As we drive, we decide that a Carl's Jr. breakfast might be more appealing. Far less than appealing, however, is the bird shit on my windshield. Harley suggests a carwash, so we're off to the Shell Drive-Thru wash on La Cienega and Pico. We play scream at the scrubbing brushes as they "attack" the car for five minutes, then head off.

We hit the Carl's Jr. drive-thru and load up on crap to take home. For Mom, we hit McDonald's on the way home (she's a McD's hash brown whore). Harley and I make a bet whether Mom's up yet or not (Harley says yes, I say no). It's ten to ten in the a.m.

We pull up outside the house and the bedroom curtains are still drawn, so I win the bet, and demand the kid give me a hundred bucks, lest I call in the goons to break her thumbs. She ignores me and carries the breakfast she apparently bought up to Jen. We snap on the lights and wake the dead, pushing greasy food and Diet Coke in her face to start her day.

Edgar Wright's called (I left the home number in his email). He's stranded at his hotel with nothing but winter clothing. I tell him I'll come get him and drop him off at the Gap.

As Jen heads out to look for plants, I swing over to Edgar's hotel, pick him up, and drop him off at the Hollywood and Highland Gap to grab some lighter gear. I head back to the house, take a shower, and retrieve Edgar a half hour later. We go back to the house, I give him the tour, and we retire to the living room bar for some beers and chit-chat about his new movie, *Hot Fuzz*.

I load the dogs into the car and drop Edgar off at his hotel 'round three/four. After that, it's over to Quizno's for me and Jen, and Wendy's for the accompanying mutts. I get back to the house and Jen and I dig into our Quizno's and beers. Mewes pops up and says that Paul Walker (through whose production company *Bottoms Up* is being made) can't break away from wherever he's currently shooting a movie to do his cameo on *Bottoms*. Mewes wants to know if I'll do it instead. The (brief) role is Mewes's home-town friend. I tell him that even though it's gonna be the biggest acting stretch of my life, I'll do it. Mewes takes off to play some online poker.

With Harley chilling with her friend Hans, Jen and I are free to grab some buzz-fucking time. We spend about an hour doing the nasty, and emerge from our room to take Harley to Astro Burger for some light dinner.

We take out, rather than eat in (a brief point of contention between me and Jen over that), and head home again. It's time for Harley to go to bed, on our couch once again. While Jen and Harley read some training books together, I download some classical music to play the kid to sleep with. We kiss Quinnster g'night and head upstairs. Oddly enough, the do-we-stay-or-do-we-go argument from Astro-Burger has followed us home, so we spat about it some more, and I opt to head downstairs to catalogue some mp3s. Jen sends me an email to get over it and come upstairs, so go upstairs I do to make up.

We opt for some *Scanners* while we go through our email. Jen's still putting together the pieces of the poetry event, and I'm still getting through posts on the board. About fourty-five minutes into *Scanners*, we decide to call it a night, and head back downstairs to some TiVo'ed *Simpsons* and sleep.

Sunday 10 April 2005 @ 12:01 p.m.

With the black out curtains drawn, the mutts are once again fooled into sleeping 'til 7:30. When they start stalking the bed, I get up and let 'em out, take a leak, and head back down to the bedroom office to plant myself in front of the computer.

Quinnster wakes up, and we opt to hit Jerry's (famous deli) for breakfast. On the way there, we play 'Sloop John B' over and over.

Post-Jerry's, we pick up an iced latte and a Quizno's veggie & cheese sub for Jen. The subject turns to tattoos and the 'Harley's' tattoo I've long promised I was gonna get for my right forearm to compliment the 'Jenny's' tattoo on my left forearm. I try to explain the process of getting a tattoo to Harley, and decide that showing her would probably be better. So we cruise Sunset, peeping out tattoo parlors — none of which are open before noon. Thwarted, we head back to the house, taking bets as to whether Jen's awake or not.

We get home at ten to noon and Jen is, indeed, awake. She's been shifting plants around the deck and library balcony for the last hour. I make with the sub and iced latte, and for a few minutes, I'm a true hero.

I take a shower, and decide that perhaps today is the day to get my daughter's name inked on my body. So I google Sunset Strip Tattoo, give 'em a shout to see if I need an appointment (I don't) and inform the ladies that I'm gonna get inked and read Catch & Release while I'm there. Jen says she'll bring Harley by in a half hour to check out the process.

At the tattoo parlor, I show the guy my 'Jenny's' tattoo and he looks for the exact font in his books. He preps 'Harley's', gets it to the right size, and we're in business. It's been four years since I last felt that needle, but it's a very singular sensation that's not too tough to take, yet not that comfortable to either.

Jen and Harley drop in about halfway through, and Harley's transfixed. The whole affair has a naughtiness factor (what with the naked ladies and devils on the walls, and the needle jamming in and out of Dad's arm) that appeals to the kid's wild side. I tell her she can come back in twelve years, and Jen takes her out to look for more plants.

Twenty minutes later, Mewes rolls in. He was next door picking up a modem for his cell phone and he saw my truck. He asks me to get 'Mewesy's' right beneath 'Harley's', but I tell him he'll have to settle for a Jay and Bob tattoo I'm thinking of getting on my calf.

The guy finishes up an excellent job, bandages my arm, and sends me on my way. As I'm leaving, I spy Mewes still in the Sprint Store. I pop in to see him (and his friend Molly), and then we sit outside the store, chit-chatting for a bit. Turns out I might have to head over to their set tonight to be in the closing shot of the flick. I tell him to let me know, and head home.

When I get there, Jen and Harley are chowing down on some Baja Fresh. I've gotta pick up some lotion for the tat, so I take Harley for a ride to Rite Aid and Wendy's (for some protein for me).

We get home and opt for a family game. So it's Disney Yahtzee in Quinnster's room. She wins (fuck…) and Jen gives her a bath while I go back to *Catch & Release* — a script I really wind up digging (it's about getting over grief, so it's appealing to the guy who made *Jersey Girl* on a couple different levels).

We put the Quinnster down for bed and rock the classical music. She wants to see my tattoo, but it's too early to take the bandage off, so she's gotta wait 'til morning. We kiss her g'night and head upstairs.

Jen's tearing apart the living room, trying to figure out where to stick the 100 people coming for the Poetry Event. The room fits more than that (party style), but this is a seated affair, so it's gonna take a well-organized layout. Mewes calls, and I am gonna be needed for the shot tonight. I call Phil to let him know I'm going, and he calls the producer to get some deal points straight before I head over.

I don't have to be there until 11:00 p.m., so I head back downstairs, draw the curtains on the boudoir portion of the master bedroom suite (so as not to wake Harley on our couch), and finish up *Catch & Release*, which turns out to be the kinda flick I'd see theatrically. The Sam part is pretty huge, though, so I'm a little nervous about jumping aboard, as I'm gonna be completely out of my depth.

I throw on some clothes (jeans, dress shirt, tie, and cold weather jacket) for the exterior night scene that's supposed to be set in Minnesota but is really being shot down near Westwood. I kiss Jen goodbye/goodnight and head off.

Thanks to a cell assist from Mewes, I find base camp and get shown to a trailer. The costume lady signs off on my outfit and I get put through 'the works' (makeup and hair). In the trailer, I meet David Keith, and remind him that this is our second movie together, though apart (we were both in *Daredevil* as well). Done with the vanities, I get shuttled off to set, where I meet the director. He walks me through what I'm doing (getting out of a limo at a première of sorts), meet my co-stars in the shot, and we're off and running. Two takes later, I'm done. Mewes's buddy Milo and his lady Christina drive me and Mewes back to base camp. We chit-chat for a bit, and then I head home.

It's 1:30 a.m., so Jen and Harley are out cold. I throw on the woobs (the lounge wear), and climb into bed beside Jenny, falling asleep to some TiVo'ed *Simpsons*.

Monday 11 April 2005 @ 11:50 a.m.

The kid tries to wake us up at 7:30, but it's just not gonna happen. Jen tells her to lie down again, and I don't know about Harley, but I take Jen's advice.

When I wake up again, it's a little past nine. I fly out of bed because I'm supposed to take Quinnster to school, but Jen puts the brakes on. She's sitting in the kitchen checking email and drinking coffee, informing me that she's already taken Harley to school. I shuffle off to take the morning leak/shit.

We opt for some Griddle breakfast, over which we discuss my *Catch & Release* meeting later today, as well as the Poetry Event later in the week. When we're done, we pop in to the pharmacy to drop off a prescription, then head home.

I hit the computer and update the diary while Jen continues planning the Poetry Event. Then, Jen runs lines with me. I don't know whether I'm expected to read at the meeting today, but I figure I'll be prepared. I try my three scenes a variety of ways, committing all the dialogue to memory, and soliciting Jen's take on each performance. After we run the scenes into the ground, I head off and take a shower.

Post-shower, I'm a little nervous about the meeting, so Schwalbach offers some tension relief in the way of a blowjob. But Jen never lasts too long in the oral department, as it gets her all wound up for sex, so a blowjob quickly turns into a champion fucking. We lounge a bit afterwards until I've gotta get dressed and leave for the meeting.

Gail (who's still up in Mammoth with the birthday-skiing Byron) has left directions to Fresh Paint, Jenno's production company. I fail to look at said directions, and wind up at what was formerly the Tall Trees offices — Jenno and the director Betty Thomas's old production company, located a few blocks from my house. Just as I'm about to head in, I look at the Mapquest Gail provided and realize Fresh Paint is all the way over in Santa Monica. I call Fresh Paint, let 'em know I'm a total jackass, and that I'll be twenty minutes late.

I rocket down La Brea to the 10 West and do the freeway dash to Santa Monica. I get off at the 4th/5th Street exit and find the 2nd Street address for Fresh Paint.

I head in and find Jenno, who gives me a big hug and introduces me to Susanah Grant and casting director Deb Aquila (who's cast, amongst zillions of other flicks, *The Shawshank Redemption*). We chit-chat for about forty-five seconds before the three ladies lead me upstairs for what I assume is a meet-and-greet in Jenno's office.

Low and behold, it's not a meet-and-greet: it's a flat-out audition. I get into

Jenno's office, and there's a video camera and a hot-seat chair that the camera's pointed at. A fourth chick is there to run camera, and I pretty quickly process that I'm gonna be immediately put on tape. So with little ado, I find myself on an end of a casting camera I am wholly unused to. Rather than sink, I dive in and swim.

There are three scenes I'm doing (and right about now, I'm really happy I'm off book on 'em). The first one is pure wise-assery, so I fly through it. When I finish, I move on to the next scene. At second scene's end, Susanah gives me a little direction, and I try the scene again, hoping to Christ I offer any difference in my performance. In my head, I'm thinking "It's cool — you've been in auditions before. Asking an actor to do another reading doesn't mean they're not doing well." I get the nod on scene two, and head into scene three — the weightiest of them all. At scene's end, Susanah offers more direction, so I try the scene again. When I finish, Susanah offers more direction. In the split second between her counsel and my third take, this is my inner monologue...

The little voice in my head wrote:

"You blew it. You have zero instinct for material you don't write yourself (and very little instinct for your own shit, at that). You're about to be rejected by not just one woman, but three women, as well as the chick running the camera you're fucking up royally on. What are you even doing here, Jerk-Stain? You're not an actor — you're just a guy who bugs his eyes out when another guy says 'snoogans' in some very small movies nobody's ever heard of. You soared too close to the sun on wings of wax, asshole, and now you're gonna plummet back to Earth. But don't panic. Don't let 'em see you sweat. Wait, who're you kidding? They can see your fat-ass sweat from space. Just hold it together long enough to get out of this office with a sliver of dignity intact. You've been rejected by plenty of chicks, so this should be easy for you."

I do the scene for the third time. When I'm done, the ladies and I chit-chat about *An Evening With Kevin Smith* (the flick which is largely responsible for my being in that room in the first place) and *An Evening With 2: Evening Harder*. I'm getting no read from the Women in Film beyond the *Arrested Development*-like "I've made a huge mistake..." expressions behind their smiles. All are kind enough to not mention the pooching of the part I just fumbled so massively, but I can feel it in the air. I've not only wasted their time and momentarily filled them with a false hope that I ultimately (and resoundingly) didn't fulfill, now I'm wasting even more of the time they're gonna need to go out and find their Sam by sitting here talking about my dopey Q&As. I do the only sensible thing I've done since I arrived by collecting my shades, sides, and scraps of pride, and bidding those standing in judgment of my feeble 'performance' adieu.

A block away from Fresh Paint, I call Jen to lament about my colossal failure. She's at home in a meeting with Cookie about the food for the Poetry Event, but takes the time to listen to my sad tale of woe and responds by telling me I'm over-reacting. "But you weren't in the room like I just was," I counter. "Trust me — I laid a big, fat egg." I get a call waiting signal and put Jen on hold to answer it. It's my agent, Phil, who wants to know how it went. I tell him "Badly…" and switch back to Jen to tell her I'm gonna debrief Phil. She tells me she loves me and that she'll see me when I get home, kiss it (whatever "it" is), and make it all better.

I switch back to Phil and fill in Phil with all the deets: I went to the wrong office, so I was half an hour late, and then I blew the audition I didn't know I was gonna have. Phil says: "Jenno just called." I ask what she said, and Phil says, "They're gonna talk about it and get back to us," which is code for "Don't call us, we'll call you". I'm like, "I knew it. When I was on the third take of the big scene, I…"

Suddenly, I'm reminded of an April Fool's joke from four or five years ago, when I called Phil and fired him, insisting he didn't "get" me, and that I was going back to CAA. It was a call that went on for fifteen minutes before I hit him with "April Fool". I'm reminded of this in the split second after Phil reveals, "Jenno says you nailed it. You got the part."

For the first time in, Christ, I don't know how long, I scream. "WHAT?! YOU'RE FUCKING SHITTING ME!" No, Phil tells me, there's no shitting involved: Susanah, Jenno and Deb were unanimous. They'd just called him right before he called me: essentially three minutes after I left their office. I'm the guy, they said. Inexplicably, the word "sexy" was used. Phil says they've still gotta make the deal (the money stuff), but the part's officially mine.

I can't tell you how unaccustomed to being "chosen" I am at this point in my career. I never have moments like this, because every script I've written to direct myself that I've turned in since Clerks has been greenlit, not selected. Granted, it's validation; but it's not the kind of validation you feel when someone says "I want you". This was up there with Schwalbach letting me into her body seven years back; not as physically gratifying of course, but up there nonetheless. For ten years, I've been the guy telling actors and actresses "I want you", and now, all the sudden, this person I have no connection to and have only met less than an hour before feels that a character she wrote without me in mind is me. It was one of the top ten best and most surprising moments of my life.

Jen can sense it too, when I immediately call her as I flip a bitch on Santa Monica Blvd to head back to Fresh Paint so I can bear hug those broads. She says,

"It's so nice to hear you excited about this. That's rare." And she doesn't mean that I don't get excited about my own flicks, because Lord knows I do. But the process of making a flick is so long and drawn out over time — starting with the writing and ending with the home video release — that there's rarely the rush I'm feeling right now, being tapped to act in someone else's flick. I've never thought of myself as an actor, but the director of a thirty-million-dollar flick disagrees with me to the point that she's done the unthinkable and cast me as a character who actually speaks. Jen's ecstatic, and I tell her I'm gonna be home right after I hit the Stash.

I get back to Fresh Paint, head inside, and find Jenno on the couch, smiling widely. "You realize you've just doomed your picture?" I tell her right before I practically squeeze the life out of her in a celebratory bear hug. Sadly, Susanah and Deb are gone, so Jenno becomes the focus of all my affection. We talk about what was said when I left, and how they were all psyched by my audition — so much so that moments after I left, they called the studio, then Phil. I'm flabber-gasted, and I keep waiting for Ashton Kutcher to pop out.

We talk about the schedule a bit and when she's heading up to Vancouver. Turns out Chris Moore (her man) is going as well, and he's gonna play Mr. Mom to their two kids during the shoot before he heads off to direct the *Race with the Devil* remake (a flick I've always loved). Jenno says I should call C-Moo, as he was the guy who suggested me in the first place, and I tell her I'm already on it.

I head over to the Stash to drop off two boxes of signed *Jersey Girl* DVDs. En route, I call Mos to let him know how it went and talk about the *Clerks* 2 push, which is now looking more and more likely — as long as the financials on *Catch & Release* work out.

I drop off the DVDs with Albert who tells me that John's in the back. I head back and talk to John about the email he sent to me and Chappy last night, let-ting us know he's gonna be stepping down as Stash manager to get back to pur-suing his acting career. I tell him it's probably the one reason for leaving I could never argue against, and let him know he'll be missed. I sign a bunch of *Clerks/Amy* books and some figures and head home. On the way, I drop C-Moo a call to thank him for starting the *Catch* ball rolling.

At home, I'm greeted by a round of applause from Jen, Harley, Cookie and Chay. Hugs all around, and I join the girls in what's gone from their meeting about the Poetry Event to a celebration of sorts. I call Mos down at the office and tell him to come up and join us as we suck back some beers and eat some barbecue.

Byron and Gail get home from Mammoth and take Harley to Bristol Farms to grab some filet mignon and burgers to grill up.

Mos arrives, and we get the party in full swing. All sitting around drinking and bullshitting while eighties tunes rock out from the iPod docked in the Bose speaker.

Byron, God bless him, does the grilling duties, and we all chow down. Mewes shows up later in the evening, and shortly after that, Mos and Cookie head home to let their dog Wolfie out. Mewes, too, heads off for another night's shooting on *Bottoms Up*, and while Byron puts Harley to bed, me, Jen, Chay and Gail sit around the bar, chit-chatting. It's about 10:30 when I'm ready to call it a night, buzzed not only from the brewskis, but also being cast. Jen and I head downstairs, get into our pjs, and curl up and fall asleep to some TiVo'ed *Simpsons*.

Tuesday 12 April 2005 @ 11:51 a.m.

I wake up at four, take a few Advil, down some water, and head to the computer to check email and read the board. About an hour later, Jen stirs and tells me to come back to bed. I do, and we cuddle up, falling asleep.

Somehow, I sleep 'til nine again. I intercom up to the kitchen to see if Jen's there and head upstairs to find her on her laptop, working on the Poetry Event and drinking coffee. We go over her concerns about the event, and then opt for some Griddle. We get dressed and head out.

Post-Griddle, Jen and I head over to the Valley to Linens and Things to grab some wine glasses. Next door, there's a Kaybee trumpeting the new *Star Wars* toys, so I head in to see what's what. I pick up a new Darth Vader figure (the first *Star Wars* figure I've bought since '97), a beanie Clone Trooper, and this Tiger plug-in-and-play Light Saber video game. On the way out of the store, I run into Jeff our computer guy and meet his wife.

Jen and I load the glasses and whatnot into the truck and head over to a nursery on Riverside. She buys a bunch of flowers to plant while I talk to Raskind on the cell about how the *Catch* deal's going. As we check out, I buy a carton of ladybugs (1500 per box!) to release in our yard. We head out and load the plants into the truck, and I meet a fella named Spencer who was at Vulgarthon and who posts on the board.

We get home and Smalls unloads the car. I head upstairs and check email and IM with some folks. Jen heads out again, this time to Target for napkins and shit.

Steve comes over to check on the back speakers upstairs. He swaps out the front channel speaker as well, which sounds great. Jon Gordon calls, and him and I talk about Miramax and stuff. Jen gets home and tells me to get off the phone so I can shower and head over to Le Meridien for the *Dinner for Five* taping, which I do.

I get to Le Meridien and meet up with Peter, Lisa, and Favs, and we go over the seating set-up. Favs and I tape some spots for IFC to hype the show, and guests start arriving. I head to the green room to say hi to Jason Lee, JJ Abrams, Stan Lee and Mark Hamill. We chit-chat for a bit, then head into the Fiesta restaurant to tape the show (which is the same location I shot the *Jersey Girl* cast episode of *Dinner for Five* at).

The show goes great (and long). After which, Pete and Favs do a post-mortem, I talk to Mark and his wife Marylou for a bit, say goodbye to Lee and JJ (the amazing Stan took off while I was taking a leak), and head home.

Jen calls me to ask if I could pick up a watermelon for Harley's class project (they're studying seeds), so I swing by Bristol to do so.

I get home around 11:00 p.m. just in time to watch some *Simpsons* and fall asleep next to Jen.

Wednesday 13 April 2005 @ 11:52 a.m.

Harley has a nightmare, and climbs into our bed, waking me up. I can't fall back asleep, so I get up and head to the computer. It's 4 a.m.

Around 4:30, I get up to take a leak and notice Harley's back on the couch, sleeping soundly. Nice move, kid: wake me up in my bed then flutter back to sleep in yours shortly thereafter. Thanks.

The dogs get up around seven and look at me like "What're you doing awake this early, asshole?" I let 'em out and get back behind the computer.

I run into John Sloss, my lawyer, on iChat. He wants to talk about the *Catch & Release* deal, so I head upstairs to call him (so as not to wake up the sleeping Jen and Harley). We wind up talking for an hour about a wide array of topics. When we're done, I shuffle by the kitchen to discover Mewes, sitting at the table, smoking and playing online poker. I play over his shoulder for a few minutes until I hear the front door signal, which alerts me that Harley's on her way out with Byron. I poke my head out the third floor window and yell goodbye to her down below.

Jen joins us and starts mixing up some coffee. Mewes, who's been shooting nights and has just gotten home, is debating whether or not to go over to a girl's apartment or crash in his own room. His libido gets the better of him, and he heads off. I follow Jenny downstairs and get back behind my computer.

I iChat with my Mom for a while and tell her about the *Catch* stuff while answering email and then head off to take a shower.

Mewes comes back from the girl's house, and Jen, Jay and I opt for some Griddle breakfast. Jen takes her own car, so she can then head on to the mall afterwards and I can head over to Burbank for a *Star Wars* interview for a British documentary.

At the Griddle, we run into Bryan Johnson, Brian Lynch, Bryan Strang, Matt Kawczynski (Charlie, from *Big Helium Dog*), and *Degrassi* head writer Aaron Martin (who's in town for some meetings). The Griddle folks give our party posse the back room, and we order, eat and joke around for the next hour, until Mewes wraps it all up because he's exhausted and still hasn't slept.

Jen heads out to the mall and I bring sleepy Mewes back the house. Since I'm already late for the *Star Wars* doc thing, I ask Gail to call them to see if I can head over later. It's about 12:30pm.

I lay down to watch some TiVo'ed *Daily Show*s and check email and promptly fall asleep for three hours.

Jen gets home from the mall and wakes me up, reminding me that I've got the CNN "Showbiz Tonight" thing to do. I take a leak, get dressed, and head over to CNN.

At CNN, I chit-chat with the makeup lady Necca and the camera guy Patrick as well as Jeremy, who I believe is the west coast segment producer. Then, I head into the tiny room with the backdrop, camera and chair, and Patrick shoots me out, live to New York, where *Showbiz Tonight* is shot. They ask me to stick around for the Ryan Reynolds segment, so Patrick and I watch the show, 'MST3K'-style, until Ryan comes on.

I head home, and tell the wife that I got off a "golden showers" reference on CNN. She's not impressed. I climb into lounge-wear and we head upstairs for some chicken breast Byron's grilled for dinner. Afterwards, Harley and I retire to the living room and set up the *Star Wars* lightsaber fighting game I picked up the other day. It takes about fifteen minutes longer than it should, because all these plug-in-and-play games have their battery compartments screwed shut nowadays. The game's pretty bad-assed, though, and we get up to stage three before it's time for Harley to go to bed. She's bunking down with Nan and Pop tonight, so Jenny and I are free to… watch TiVo'ed *Law & Order* eps.

But not before I hit the board again. I'm in my office, checking emails and posts when Bryan calls to see if I wanna swing by Mewes's set with him, as they're shooting pretty close to where I live. I opt out.

After about two hours of *Law & Orders*, the phone rings. It's Bryan, who tells me his harrowing (yet kinda funny) story about being car-jacked and kidnapped at gun-point right outside Mewes's set. The jackers ran up to his car, gun trained on Bry, and demanded his wheels. Bry, of course, told them to take it, but the jackers told him to get in the back seat, as he was coming with them. They got on the 101 (from Highland), and asked Bryan where an ATM machine was. Bryan had them get off at Alvarado, where one of the jackers took Big's ATM card and got money out of his account while the other stayed behind with him in the car, pointing a gun at my boy and telling him "This isn't personal. We don't wanna hurt you. Once we get the money, we're gonna drop you off and keep your car. But if you try anything, I'm gonna shoot the shit out of you." The other jacker got back in the car and wanted to hit another ATM, and at this point, Bryan gets out of the car, bewildering his captors, insisting they've gotten their money, so he's done. He said he ran across the street to a liquor store and called the cops (and Mos, who picked him up). I'm so flabbergasted, I have to have him repeat the story. I thank Christ he didn't get hurt and add that I'm suddenly really glad I didn't go with him.

Around eleven, with visions of moving to another, safer city dancing in my head, Jen and I fall asleep to TiVo'ed *L&Os*.

Thursday 14 April 2005 @ 11:52 a.m.

I wake up around 7:30 to let the dogs out, take a leak, and hit the computer.

While I'm wading through email and posts on the board, Byron calls up to the room to ask if I can pick him up at the Range Rover dealership where he'll be dropping off Jenny's car for a checkup. I confirm.

I hear the front door beep at 8:15, which means Harley's heading to school. I head out onto my porch to tell her goodbye, and Byron tells me he'll give me a shout from the Range Rover place with an exact address.

I check some more email when the call comes in twenty minutes later. I get dressed, take a coffee order from the couch-riding/Poetry-Event-fretting Jen, kiss her forehead, and make for the front door, closely followed by Scully.

Scully takes the ride as I go to pick up Byron at the Range Rover service place. On the way home, we stop at Carl's Jr. for some burgers for the dogs and a Low Carb Breakfast Bowl for me. Following that, we hit Starbucks for an iced latte for Jen, and Chi Lattes for Byron and Gail.

I deliver Jen's latte and she gets ready for a hair appointment and some other errands. She takes my car (as her car's being serviced) and heads off.

I hold down some iChats with my Mom, my brother, Chappy (my Stash West partner), Nicole (from *Degrassi*), and Ming. We take the tickets for the *Mallrats* public screening, and Scott IMs to remind me we've got a lunch date.

I shower and get a ride down to the office, where Scott and I watch some *Mallrats* re-edit he's been working on, and then head over to The Palm for some lunch steak.

After lunch, we stop over at Laser Blazer and pick up the new DVDs. Afterwards, we cruise back to the office and continue the *Rats* edit 'til six, when Mosier has to head out. He gives me a ride home, and I find Jenny in the bathroom, getting ready for her 6:30 Poetry Event meeting with Daniella and Russell Milton.

I head to the bathroom, then sack out on the bed and go over posts on the board while watching some TiVo'ed *Daily Shows*.

Around nine-ish, I head upstairs to pop in on the Poetry Event meeting. We talk about the possibility of making a few seats available to board members in the LA area, and go over the order of the readers for a bit before Jen heads downstairs to put Harley to sleep on our couch. I walk Daniella and Russell out, close up shop upstairs, and join Jen in bed. We watch TiVo'ed *Simpsons* 'til we fall asleep.

Friday 15 April 2005 @ 11:53 a.m.

I wake up at Jen's behest. She's telling me to let the dogs out. It's nearly seven.

I take a leak and hit the computer to update the online diary. Byron intercoms around 7:30 to wake Harley up. I wish him a happy birthday.

I open the curtains as Jen climbs out of bed to gently wake Quinnster. She takes her downstairs to get ready for school, and I go back to the computer.

I hear the front door, so I go out onto my office deck to say goodbye to Harley. When I go back inside, Jen and I start talking about the Poetry Event some more before she has Byron and I moving the blackjack table and sundry other pieces of furniture down to the library to clear up space in the living room.

I do something in the morning that I now can't remember (it'll come back to me), but I know I was doing something, because I remember getting home and the dogs being gone, picked up for doggie camp for the weekend.

Jen and I bicker a bit before she heads out to her mani-pedi-facial appointments at Burke Williams. We go back-and-forth about whether to take Byron out for lunch or just barbecue at the house before he heads for Big Bead midday. Jen finally decides we're gonna barbecue, and says she'll pick up some steaks from Bristol on her way home from her appointments, but before she picks up Harley, who's getting out of school early for a half-day. We bicker some more, and Jen's off.

The hundred or so folding chairs are delivered, and Gail calls up to ask me if Jen wanted white chairs or not. I tell her I'm not sure and call Jen at Burke Williams, because I don't wanna let chair one into the house if she didn't pick white chairs. After a few minutes, they track her down and I ask her about the chairs. She sounds frazzled, and says she thought it was some kind of emergency that they dragged her out of her pedi over. I counter with it'd be an emergency if she came home and found a hundred chairs she didn't order sitting in our living room. She signs off on the white chairs, so the white chairs start coming in.

When Jen gets home, we bicker some more (this time over the Burke Williams emergency phone call), and I head upstairs and fire up the grill. Gail's made Byron a birthday cake shaped like a pair of skis, so that's our steak followup. We sit down to the earliest family dinner on record and do the cake and candles thing afterwards.

We say goodbye as Byron loads Harley and Louis into his truck, headed up to Byron and Gail's Big Bear cabin for the weekend, skipping the Poetry Event altogether.

Jen and I hang around the house for the rest of the day, getting the living room in shape and moving stuff around. After much discussion about opening the event to some LA board folks, I throw a message up on the board about five tickets up for grabs, requesting some info from each applicant.

While I'm working on the board, Jen's holding a marg-tasting meeting upstairs with Chay, Bryan Johnson, Darrin Johnson and Brian Quinn, the Issacs for the Poetry Event (when they pour, they reign). Brian Lynch also comes by, and I head upstairs to join the boys in the kitchen while Chay and Jen chill in the living room. The men grill Bry about his carjacking, and we make copious jokes about all the head Bryan could've given to get out of it. A good time, as they say, is had by all.

The boys leave and, with Harley in Gail's room for the night, Jen and I bone hardcore and fall asleep to some *Simpsons*.

Saturday 16 April 2005 @ 11:53 a.m.

Poetry Event Day. The dogs wake me up around eight-ish. I let 'em out, then hear

Jen rustle and rise as well. With the whole house in pre-event mode, we skip breakfast.

I run into Mewes in the kitchen, where he's smoking and playing some online poker at UltimateBet.com — his new favorite pastime. I watch for a bit before heading back downstairs to my office to check email and deal with the board folks who're interested in attending the Poetry Event.

Cookie and Catherine McCord arrive early to start preparing the food. Jen asks Mewes and I to move a table from the foyer up to the deck, so we do so. Upstairs, I find Cookie and Catherine knee-deep in food prep and Jen setting up the outdoor martini bar. We all take a break and sit around on the deck, where I grill Catherine about her fiancé, Jon Gordon, our Miramax homeboy. Mewes is sitting with us, but he's rocking UB on his laptop, somehow managing to make out the screen despite the massive sunlight beating down that makes it almost unreadable.

Mewes joins me in my office with his laptop, still in the thrall of UltimateBet. After months of seeing him play and hearing all about the heady wins and bad beats, I ask if I can give it a shot. He lets me play on his laptop for a bit, and I'm instantly hooked. I give him back his laptop and jump online on my desk-top, hell-bent on buying a downloadable version of Virtual PC for Mac (UB isn't a Mac-friendly site) so that I, too, can become part of the poker action. Problem is, I can't find anyone selling it for instant download. My only option is to head over to the Mac Store, but I dare not attempt it, lest Jen rip my head off for trying to do something other than getting ready for the Poetry Event. I IM Matt Potter who's got Virtual PC on the G4 desk-top I bought him last year in exchange for editing the *Tea Party* doc, so he uploads a copy to our server site.

While it's downloading, I'm playing at the site on Mewes's laptop. Jen comes in to the office to tell me it's time to get showered and ready for the Poetry Event. After two warnings, I do so, and air-dry at the desk-top while I pull together some notes for each speaker's intro, as well as some opening remarks.

From about six o'clock on, as I hit and re-hit the IMDB for my intro material, the door phone's ringing like crazy and I'm buzzing people up left and right. I finally head upstairs to give Jen the cordless phone so she can be on door duty. While there, I see Bryan Johnson, his brother Darren, and Brian Quinn — all of whom Jen's recruited to work the bar at the event. Zak and Joey and their friend John are also in the house, handling the door and the crowd.

I go back downstairs and finish up my intro research. Chay delivers a beer which I slowly nurse while writing my Emcee material.

Around 6:30 p.m., I print up my intros and the reading order Russell and I went over the other night. I head down to Gail's office and cut the intros into little slips that I then staple together and organize into two piles of pre- and post-intermission.

I head upstairs to an already crowded deck, packed with guests and attendees. I say hi to folks like Will Wilkins (SilverLurker from the board), as well as the man and legend Stan Lee, before being introduced to Barbara Hershey, who I brow-beat into reading a poem later in the evening. Then, I go over the reading order with Russell, who informs me of a few changes. I alter my anal little list to reflect said changes, then go over the change of order with the recently arrived Mark Hamill. I greet Bernard Hill and Peter Coyote before heading back downstairs.

I hit my office, write an intro for Barbara Hershey, print up the new material, shoot down to Gail's office, rearrange my handy intro packet, then climb back upstairs.

Jason Lee is in the hizzy, so I chit-chat with him for awhile until we're joined by the very funny Jeff Garlin. It's almost showtime, so I head back to my room and practice my intro a bit in the bathroom mirror while sucking down another beer, trying to commit at least the opening remarks to memory. For some reason, I'm more nervous than I usually am to get up in front of this no-bigger-than-100-person crowd — probably because it's not a stacked-deck like it usually is when I get in front of an audience. These folks aren't a bunch of college kids who like my stuff; they're parents of kids in the school and various supporters of the fundraiser. But I'm safe; I mean, I'm in my own house. If everything goes wrong, it won't be a far walk to my bed, where I can cry myself to sleep at the end of the night. With that confidence inducing thought in mind, I head upstairs to start the show.

The show goes incredibly well. We've got a packed house, and all the readers do an excellent job. The order went like this:

1. JK SIMMONS
2. PETER COYOTE
3. STAN LEE
4. MARK HAMILL
5. BARBARA HERSHEY
6. PATRICIA VELASQUEZ
7. JEFF GARLIN

Break.

8. ANJELICA HUSTON
9. HARRYETTE MULLEN
10. BERNARD HILL
11. RAVI KAPOOR
12. IAN McSHANE
13. JENNIFER COOLIDGE

As the night progressed, beers progressed down my gullet. For the first time in my life (and probably the last), I'm rocking the mic drunk. And to be honest, I was still on point and pretty funny.

The night ends with just me, Jen, Chay, Russell, Daniella, Brian Lynch and his date Carrie, Joey, Zak and John sitting around outside, snacking out of Cookie's and Catherine's awesome leftovers. All in all, it was really an awesome night. An event that plagued the fuck out of our lives for the last month went off without a hitch, and better than either of us expected. Already, the school and the parents were calling for it to be an annual event, and I'm right there with 'em. Jen out-did herself.

The Mistress of Ceremonies and I stumble downstairs, too drunk to fuck, and pass out to no TV whatsoever.

Sunday 17 April 2005 @ 11:53 a.m.

Even without the dogs in full effect, I wake up at seven to a hangover forming. I head to the bathroom to down some Advil, drink some water, and climb back into bed. Jen's in and out of consciousness, chit-chatting with me about the previous night, wanting to cuddle up. Naturally, since it's morning and the morning wood's in full effect, any cuddling results with my cock pressing against her cocklessness. Since it's in the a.m., and she's still kinda sleeping, I don't push for any sex. But I do make the rogue's play of telling the wife I wanna jerk off onto her, regardless. Bless her heart, she says go ahead, and I slip her jammies and panties down and tug one out against her ass, showing amazing restraint in not attempting the slip-in.

I get up and head to the office, where I attempt to purchase some coin for my new UB account with a credit card. The attempt fails. I try again with another credit card. That also fails. I call my credit cards to find out what's up, and I'm told that it's MasterCard and Visa policy to not allow the use of the card for online gambling. What kinda crazy shit is that? Mewes gives me Annie Duke's

IM name, and I start hunting her down to purchase chips from her. We've sort of met before, via cell phone, when I bought a grand from her to dump into Mewes's UB account for Christmas. We spend some time chatting in IM, and she hooks me up. And with that, I begin my UB career.

Jen gets up, and we head out to breakfast at the Grand Luxe Café, at the Beverly Center. We stop at Bristol on the way home to pick up some turkey and potatoes for dinner, then spend most of the day doing nothing but laying around, eating, and watching some TiVo. Jen later comments on how surprised she was I didn't try for the slip-in this morning, as after a few minutes of jerking off with my cock pressed into her asshole, she was sleepily turned on (a foreplay pastime that was all the rage for us a few months back that we've since kind of moved on from). I tell her I like having sex with her when she's having sex back at me — that her presence (both physical and psychological) in the sex act is kinda vital for me. And naturally, this chit-chat leads to some awesome, late-day fucking.

We do family dinner, then I head downstairs and play more Ultimate Bet. Jen puts Harley down on our couch, and we head upstairs to the living room to watch some tube. I download Virtual PC to my laptop and Matt walks me through the installation process again. I follow that with a download of UltimateBet, and I'm soon playing some poker upstairs. Jen heads to bed, and I tell her I'll follow soon, but I wind up playing poker 'til two in the morning before finally heading to the room and crashing beside the sleeping Schwalbach.

Monday 18 April 2005 @ 11:28 p.m.

After the late-night UltimateBet.com bender, not a mutt in the world can wake me before ten. I shuffle to the bathroom to find Jen, watching old *Murder, She Wrote*s (box set!), smoking, and emailing with Chay. She's hungry, so I throw on a hat and we're off to the Griddle.

We sit outside on a blustery LÁ morning and bump into Carrie, the girl Brian Lynch brought to the Poetry Event. Later, Brian Lynch and Matt Kawczynski roll by for some breakfast and join us. We do an hour on the dancing Odie in the *Garfield* movie and anal (though, y'know — not in the same breath). Brian makes an awesome joke about lasagna at Garfield's expense, and it keeps me chuckling all day long.

On the way home, Jen stops for a Coffee Bean on Hollywood, across from Grauman's. I stay in the car, and I'm transfixed by the costumed Superman lurking in front of the theater.

For those who don't live here, in front of Grauman's Chinese Theatre you can find all manner of costumed characters: Elmo, Batman, Darth Vader, Chuckie, Michael Myers, Superman, Spider-Man, etc. Until Edgar Wright schooled me on the subject last week, I was under the mistaken impression that they were hired by the Hollywood Chamber of Commerce. Turns out, if you've got a costume that's remotely suggestive of a film or TV icon, you can chill out on Hollywood Blvd. and pose for pictures with tourists for a small fee. It's kind of fascinating because it's democratized the costumed impersonation/tribute artist biz. And utter proof of that is the Superman I'm obsessed with: he's blond (not brunette), short, his costume's saggy, he wears red bootlets over red Keds sneakers, and most heinously, he wears glasses. I'm not saying I'd make a better Superman than this guy, but based on the bar he's setting, I'd come pretty fucking close.

A blond Superman who wears glasses and has the gall to charge folks for pictures. How appropriately Hollywood.

We get home and Mos calls to remind me that we have to deliver the first big chunk of the *Rats* re-edit to Universal Home Video today, so I head down to the office to do a final pass on the stuff Mos and I have put together.

En route, I listen to a message from my brother about a few boxes of signed *Mallrats* books we sent to him that reached the Florida offices completely smudged. He points out that a simple layer of paper towels between the books would go a long way toward preventing this, just as I hit the office.

Phil Benson's in the editing room with Scott, as is Laura Greenlee (who I haven't seen in a dog's age). We chit-chat about the *Clerks* 2 move, and giggle over the mind-bendingly out there looooooooooong cut of the T.S./Mr. Svenning pre-pretzel scene, after which I learn that Tracy McGrath (a friend and colleague at Miramax) has been hospitalized with severe pneumonia and is only now being moved from ICU to the Critical list. This prompts a long discussion about how little any of us know about pneumonia before we dig into Laura's love-life a bit and let her head out. I watch some bloopers we've found and edit them a bit to just the really good stuff before I take off for home.

At home, Jen's waiting for me on the curb, and we load this massive blowup I got from Harvey's office of Jay and Silent Bob on the bike (that production still which was the most used to promote *Strike Back*). It was one of thirty massive Kodak-made blow-ups of stills from Miramax films that were hanging around the Pacific Design Center for the Miramax Pre-Oscar Party this year, and I'd asked Jessica Rovins if she could score it for me after the party. Harvey's office sent it out a month ago, but we're only getting around to having it framed now, so it can be hung in the guest room (aka Mewes's room).

We head to the valley, drop the six by four piece off at the framer's, along with that page from *Empire* magazine on which Mewes and I are making pussy-eating faces, with our tongues between our fingers — a piece we've decided to hang on family wall in the house.

After the framer's we pop into Koo-Koo-Roo for some chicken for Harley and head over to her school to pick her up from karate class. We get home, and Harley goes into max-and-relax mode with Jen, while I try to get through some email and posts on the board. An hour later, we play some Disney Yahtzee, after which Jen gives Harley a bath while I clean my office a bit.

We put Harley to sleep on our couch again, while I finish up some IM'ing, then meet Jen upstairs. She's jonesing to play some poker, so after we move all the furniture back into place (from the Poetry Event), I install Virtual PC into her laptop (thank you, Matt Potter) and download Ultimate Bet. After a brief tutorial snit (I can be impatient sometimes), she settles into some fake money play, and I bug Mewes for some chip transfer so I can play real stakes. Annie Duke pops up on my Buddy List, and I immediately accost her like a crackhead looking for a vial, asking her to dump some more cash into my account. We chit-chat for a bit, and then I'm all about the game. There we sit: husband and wife, side-by-side, playing online poker like a pair of junkies (or rather donkeys). Jen turns in around one, but I stay up 'til four, first building a heady little sum from my buy-in before losing it all as I fall asleep playing. I head downstairs, crawl into bed beside the out-cold Jen, and pass out rather quickly, with no help from the TV.

Tuesday 19 April 2005 @ 11:29 p.m.

I wake up at 9:30 a.m. and find Jen upstairs in the living room. As I tell her about my Ultimate Bet misdeeds of the night before, Gail joins us and we go over this week's schedule, as well as what the initial Vancouver *Catch* plans are. We do this for a half hour before Jen decides it's time to eat. We head downstairs and run into a sleep-eyed Mewes, who fills me in on his previous night's adventure (which includes him hiding behind a stove; don't ask) while I play a little UB. As Mewes retells his tale to Jen, I double-up on my chips, sign off, and get dressed.

We head to the Griddle for breakfast and run into Lynch, Matt, and Bryan Strang. After we order, Jen spots Joe Reitman entering with who I gather pretty quickly is Annie Duke. I head over to their table to say hi and thank her for the chip loan. I'm delighted with how utterly charming, personable and interesting she is, as this is the first time I'm talking to Annie in person (even though we did play together in that *Clerks X/Jersey Girl/Rounders* DVD-release promotional party at The Palms back in September). Joe and I do a post-mortem on his and Shannon Elizabeth's breakup before Mewes joins us with my food that's getting cold. Mewes jumps into their booth as well, and I slide back to mine, where Jen and the boys are chit-chatting. Since Mewes owes me some cash and has his checkbook on him, I have him write a check for Annie for the chips she loaned me before Mewes has to head off for his last day on *Bottoms Up*. Joe and Annie join us at our table, and we all sit around talking for an hour and change more (including the idea to make a View Askew skin for Ultimate Bet which we'd link up from our site) before heading our separate ways. It's the longest Griddle meal I've had since that five-hour breakfast I had with Dave Mandel at the Griddle a few months back.

I get home, play some Ultimate Bet for a bit, then say goodbye to Jen as she heads off to pick up Harley from school. Following that, I take a shower, shave, get dressed, and head over the hill to Burbank.

I get to the NBC lot, go through security, and get to the *Tonight Show*. I'm in my guest room about a minute before Leno drops by (he chit-chats with all the guests before the show). I ask him about what he'll do at the end of the four years — like if he'll just do more standup. He reminds me that 150 nights out of the year (three nights a week), he's doing standup somewhere other than the show. The dude's work ethic is insane. Kristin Powers from Talk/Miramax Books comes by as Jay's leaving, as does Dave Berg, the segment producer. We go over the stuff I'm gonna be talking about until Andy McElfresh (my *Roadside Attractions* partner-in-crime) shows up. Andy and I catch up as the show begins, and then he's off, back to an editing suite to finish his piece for tomorrow night's show.

I watch the show in my guest room and am floored by how fucking boring and what a terrible interview the *O.C.* chick is. I've now been a couch guest five or six times on *Tonight*, always as the second interview, and have figured out that there's this delicate balance you want in the guest who comes before you: you want them to be good, but not great. You want them to warm the audience up, so that when you get out there, you're not facing a sleepy crowd. At the same time, you don't want the first guest to kill — otherwise you're gonna have a tough time impressing the audience. The *O.C.* chick offers nothing. It's dead quiet out there — which makes my job harder, because I've gotta be even funnier than I planned on being and win the crowd within the first thirty seconds or risk tanking harder than the chick who just said she was lucky enough to be in Rome when the Pope died.

I'm sweating profusely (natch), so I get a little powder in the makeup room and trim my beard a touch. I get wired up and after the Human Ambien's segment is over, I head backstage to go on, post-commercials.

I do my segment.

Post-show, I talk to Rob Thomas for a few seconds, say goodbye to Jay. Debbie Vickers (the producer of the show and a chick I really dig) tells me I killed, and Dave Berg thanks me for a great segment. I head back to my dressing room where I talk with a guy who pops in to tell me he used to be an accountant on the *Clerks* cartoon, and how ABC fucked it up. Then Andy comes by to give me the thumbs up on the segment, as does Kristin and John Melendez (aka Stuttering John). John and I bullshit for a while about Howard and the Sirius move, as well as other non-Howard related stuff. Forty-five minutes later, it's just me and Kristin, and we go over stuff we wanna do for the book (I opt against taking out magazine ads, as it's a waste of money, and agree to do an interview on Air America if they can get me in), including a celebratory We Sold Out the First Printing signing party we're thinking of doing at the Stash before I head off to *Catch*. I drop Kristin off at the front door of the studio where her car's waiting, and head home.

I get into my woobs and sack out behind the computer for a little email checking and UB. Soon, it's dinnertime, and I head upstairs for a Byron-grilled cheeseburger while everyone else is doing tacos. We talk about the Vancouver move as well as Harley's day and what she wants to do in British Columbia. It's about then that I realize I still don't have directions to the *Bottom's Up* set tonight, where I'm supposed to be in an hour, so I head downstairs to call Mewes and play some more UB.

I collect a bunch of wardrobe possibilities (pjs and a robe), kiss Jen, and head off to the Valley for the *Bottoms Up* shoot.

Find the lot where they're shooting, pull in, and head to the trailer I share with Mewes for this, the last night of shooting. I whip out the wardrobe I brought for approval, go over last minute script changes with the writer, meet the producers, get hair and makeup done, and head to the set.

I share the scene with Mewes, an actor named Desmond Harrington, and two girls. The production's pressed for time, so the number of takes we do is limited. All goes well, and the night (and film) wraps around one in the morning.

I get home and play a little UB before crashing.

Wednesday 20 April 2005 @ 11:30 p.m.

We head to the Newsroom Café for some breakfast, and then swing out to Laser

Blazer to pick up new DVDs. Jen heads into some chick clothing store nearby and finds an awesome eighties-era DC Superheroines shirt titled 'Ladies Night'. As she buys three (one for her, one for Harley and one for Chay), I take a picture of the lineup with my phone so I can send it to Walter to discern who the one chick in the weird get-up is (turns out it's the circa eighties Zatanna, minus the top hat and fishnets). After the shirt store, Jen and I get into an argument because of the way I pull out into traffic while trying to send the picture to Walter. After a long period of silence, we argue some more, at which point she insists I "drive like an asshole". The fight gets worse, and we don't talk the rest of the way home.

We're home for about twenty minutes before we speak again, and it only makes things worse. I head off to the bathroom to shit and update my diary, during which the anger starts to subside, as I remember that a life with even a some-times-contentious Schwalbach is better than a life without one. I emerge from the toilet a kinder, gentler me, and set about putting the fight behind us by apologizing (though I didn't start the fight). We cuddle and opt to head out again, this time over to the Valley to finally get Jen's eyes examined and get her a prescription for glasses.

We're in Lenscrafters and the adjoining optometrist for two hours, during which Jen gets diagnosed and given a prescription. I have them swap out my scratched sunglasses lenses and have them re-do the lenses in my regular glasses while they're at it. Jen gets her pupils dilated, so for the next few hours, she's walking around with massive black dots for eyes.

We swing by Quizno's and down some subs, then stop at Koo-Koo-Roo for some Harley grub. After that, we stop by the cleaners to pick up stuff we dropped off the other day, and head back home.

Harley chows down while I go online beside her on the bed. We play some Disney Yahtzee, and then Jen takes her for her bath while I take care of some IM business. Mewes rolls in to say he's going to Commerce Casino to play some real poker (instead of UB, which we're trying to get in touch with Annie about so she'll dump some coin in our accounts). Jen reads to Harley and puts her to bed on the couch. I sit in my office while she tries to go to sleep, but she's chatting away for awhile before she succumbs.

Around nine, I take Byron and Gail to the airport. They're heading out to Florida on a red-eye to see some relatives. Mulder and Scully take the ride with us, and on the way home, I pick up some burgers for the three of us.

When I get home, Chay's there, chit-chatting with Jen and having some wine. I talk with them for a bit while I feed myself and the dogs the burgers I picked up. I head downstairs, jump online, IM with Annie, replenish my UB account, and gamble 'til Jen comes downstairs again. After that, I gamble some more, and go to sleep around 2 a.m.

Thursday 21 April 2005 @ 11:30 p.m.

I wake up around 9:30 a.m., and Jen's already taken Harley to school. She's upstairs checking email on her laptop when I find her. We sit around the living room and bicker for awhile, and then kiss and make-up.

We find Mewes in the kitchen, playing some UB. We chit-chat for a bit, then head downstairs and cuddle for a bit on the couch before I remember that my wardrobe fitting for *Catch & Release* is in a half hour. I look out the window and find Tish and Karin (the wardrobe chicks) already here, sitting in their car. I tell 'em to come up, and Jen heads into the shower.

This is the first time I've ever had a wardrobe fitting, really. On some of our stuff, I'd try on a shirt or two (*Dogma* particularly), but since my Silent Bob get-up never really changes, a long fashion show is never required of me. This time it's different: I'm in three-quarters of the movie, so there are lots of options required, hence the hour and change we spend going through clothes. I've been dreading this, because — I don't know if anyone's ever noticed this, but — I have, like, two outfits that I ever wear, really. The prospect of new clothes — clothes that may not fit me as well as the clothes I enjoy wearing do — doesn't really make me hard. But Tish and Karin make it a painless process, and pretty soon, I'm actually enjoying myself, digging out what a more 'granola' (the flick's set in Colorado) version of me might wear.

Tish and Karin leave, and I get into the shower. As I finish, Jen comes home from Bristol Farms (she left while I was doing the fitting) with some filet mignon and side dishes. As I dry off, I play some more UB until the door phone rings, heralding the arrival of Zach Braff. I tell him to head upstairs, buzz him in, and throw some clothes on.

I join Zach upstairs, then — at his request — give him the house tour. When we're done, we head back up to the kitchen where I prep the steaks and we talk about his being 'Punk'd', as well as a bunch of other topics.

While I grill, we chit-chat some more — mostly about his blog and this web-site. Once the steaks are done, we head to the dining room to eat and talk about *Garden State*, Natalie Portman, and all things *Fletch*.

As we finish, Mewes comes upstairs, balancing his laptop and cell phone. He says hi to Zach, then heads off deep into the living room to play UB while Zach and I finish up. I've met him before, of course (on the *Declare Yourself* PSAs), but this is the most time I've gotten to spend with him. He's an excellent guy.

The *Garden State*-er gives me his email address, and he's off. I call Mewes downstairs and we go into my office to play some UB: him on his laptop and me on my desk-top. While we're playing, Jen comes home from going shopping with Harley after school, before her gymnastics class. I'm told that I'm on Harley pickup, post-gymnastics, so twenty minutes later, I'm in the car, heading to grab the kid.

Thanks to the Hellish LA traffic patterns, I'm about seven minutes late. I'm handed a bawling Quinnster, who's the last kid to get picked up (what kind of anal-ass parents are there before class ends, making a brother look bad? Sheesh…). I apologize to the quivering, crying mass of tears and red cheeks that is my daughter, and we head for some ice cream (first at the food store, then at the ice cream parlor Mashti Malone's).

We get home, and Harley says hi to Jen, then heads off to play with Reyna. I sack out on the bed, watching TiVo'ed *Simpsons* and *Law & Order*s with Jenny while playing UB, until she moseys off to collect Harley and give her a bath. Phil Raskind calls, and we talk about the post-*Catch* and *Clerks* schedule 'til Jen and Harley return. They read books together, and then Jen puts Harley down on the couch. My gig is to stay with her in the room 'til she falls asleep, so I hang out on the bed, playing some UB. Twenty minutes later, I'm hearing the angelic snores of the slumbering heir to the Smith fortune, so I head upstairs to join Jen in the living room. We opt for some fine eighties cheese: *Dynasty*, season one. Jen's never seen an episode, but I was raised on it (Mom was an avid watcher back in the day). We cuddle up and watch the Carringtons for an hour before we get up from cuddle-zone — Jen to smoke and me to check email — still deep into a pilot episode that never seems to end.

Around eleven, we opt to head downstairs for some TiVo and sleep. We cuddle for a bit during *Simpsons*, until Jen's more or less asleep. Then, I play UB 'til I fall asleep mid-game.

Friday 22 April 2005 @ 11:30 p.m.

Harley wakes up at 6:30 a.m. and immediately sets about trying to wake us up as well. Jen sends her to let the dogs out and dig up some breakfast while we try to grab some more shut-eye. By seven-thirty, though, it's a losing battle, as the kid is just flat-out harassing us to wake up. Jen gets her ready for school while I take a leak and throw on some clothes.

I drop Harley off at school and swing by McDonald's for some hash browns and a large Diet Coke for Jen and some sausage patties for me.

Jen and I chit-chat up in the living room while we eat our breakfast. Following that, I head down to the bedroom, lay down again, and start playing some UB while watching TiVo'ed *Law & Orders*. Jen showers and heads off to her doctor's appointment while I wrap up my UB game and head to the bedroom office to start updating the diary. While doing so, I get a call to do an interview about my favorite birthday memory, and another call from CNN, asking me to come in and talk about comic book movies. Since they're less than five minutes from the house, I say "sure". Following that, I iChat a bit with Don about some missing signed stuff and Chappy about a new *Mallrats* script book we're thinking of making.

I shower and head to CNN. There, I meet up with Jeremy (the segment producer) again who tells me I had big fans in the NY and LA offices regarding the "golden showers" comment last week. While I'm waiting to tape my interview, I run into Brooke Anderson, who's apparently moved out to LA (the last time I saw her was when she interviewed me at the Atlanta CNN offices, circa *Jersey Girl*) and getting married. Following that, I do my interview and head home.

I'm home about ten minutes and answering some email when Jen comes home from the doctor's and lunch with her friend Lisa Roumaine. We opt to go pick up Harley together, hit the bank, and grab some grub. When Harley's loaded in the car, she chooses Koo-Koo-Roo for dinner, so we head over to the Valley. We hit the Roo and then the bank before going home.

At home, we all get into our woobs and lounge around. Harley watches a DVD of the puppet version of *Blue's Clues* called *Blue's Room* (in which, sadly, Blue speaks in a human voice) while I play UB beside her on the bed and Jen waters her plants upstairs. Jen joins us on the bed, and the three of us play a game called Traffic Jam that's really supposed to be only a one-player game. Jen orders some pizza, and Harley and I watch some more of *Blue's* before the pizza comes.

The pizza arrives, and I pick at the cheese, so as not to derail from Atkins. But the temptation proves too great, and I finally eat a whole slice. Then another. Since the twenty-or-less carb quota has been broken for the day, Jen and I opt to order a bunch of junk food from Yummy that we'll down while we watch more *Dynasty*.

We put Harley to bed, and I stay in the room with her, playing UB, 'til she's good and asleep. Then, I take my game into the shitter and drop a mean one. Following that, Jen tells me that her friend Trish is coming over for an hour before she heads out for the night. I give the girls their space while I order some Yummy.com in what the clerk must assume is a weed-induced selection of sugars and salts. As I wait for the delivery, I get the diary up to date.

Yummy arrives, and I dig in while I play some UB. After Trish leaves, I join Jen upstairs, and she makes cookies while we chit-chat. Following that, we hit the living room couch and watch some more *Dynasty* until I start dozing off — which now reminds me of being a kid and the many times my Mom would fall asleep on the couch watching *Dynasty* beneath this home-made afghan that laid across the back of our living room couch for years, *Roseanne*-style, before there ever was a *Roseanne*. Jen wakes me up and says we should go to bed (as I used to wake my Mom up and tell her to go to bed) and we head downstairs to fall asleep to some TiVo'ed *Simpsons*.

Saturday 23 April 2005 @ 11:31 p.m.

Harley gets me up at 6:45 a.m. I'm starting to group her in with the Alarm Mutts. I bring the dogs and Harley upstairs, my laptop under my arm. I let the dogs out, give Harley some milk and cookies for breakfast, and we head into the living room, opting for a first-time viewing (for her) of *The Karate Kid*. While Daniel-San learns the ways of the Force from Mr. Miyagi, I play UB. Harley loves the flick, and by the end, she's ready to go right into *Part II*. I suggest we skip to the fourth flick (in which Mr. Miyagi tutors Hillary Swank), but Harley — like all of us when we first peeped *KK* — has a thing for Ralph Macchio, so the much less engaging *KK2* it is.

Reyna and her boys Kevin and Hans show up, so Quinnster's off for the day. I take UB with me to the bathroom for what's not the eleven o'clock, late-morning shit. While in the upstairs can, I hear the half-awake Jen muttering about a broken sprinkler head that's gushing water all over the street outside. Through the bathroom door, I tell her that in my present condition — mid-shit — I can't do anything about it. Somehow, she handles it herself.

I join Jenny downstairs in the bedroom and lay on the bed playing UB, while she rides the couch checking email. Some TiVo'ed *Simpsons* act as white noise in the background. She's sweating getting a ride to Lisa Roumain's tonight for a little Coral Springs High-transplants get-together. Mewes IMs me, increasingly amused with how much time I'm spending on UB, and also offers to bring home some Coffee Bean for Jen.

I'm recruited to be the pick-up ride from Lisa's, post-party. I say it's gonna cost her in sex dollars, which Jen offers up. But I'm so full-tilt on UB that I forget to take her up on it. Then, Mewes and Chay arrive, thus killing any chances I've got at last-minute nookie as well. Jen signs Mewes up as the ride for her, Chay and Harley to Lisa's, and with that out of the way, the wife starts concentrating on the Festival of Books thing that's in two hours. Jen, Chay and Jay are all yammering on the couch in our room while I start dumping hands, chasing like a mother-fucker — which bugs me only because I was doing so well all morning. Finally, I somehow find the self-control to close the laptop and head to the shower. At this point, I've been playing UB for eight hours straight.

As I'm showering, Jen pops her head in to tell me she's heading over to the Festival of Books with Chay, Harley, Kevin and Hans. We're taking separate cars so nobody has to be at the mercy of my schedule). I get out of the shower, and as I air dry at my desk-top computer, I check the board and peep the link to Kirk Cameron's wacky Jesus website. Fuck, does that guy love the Lord — in that awe-some way that makes a motherfucker judgmental and sad. He's become one of those people who try to make the Bible say what they want it to say, and are way into telling people that they're sinners if they don't believe what he believes. I say the real sin is that flick he did, *Like Father, Like Son*. Still, the dude runs a camp for terminally ill kids, so he can't be all bad; just misled. At this point, I'm kinda dry, so I stop caring about Kirk's issues and get dressed and head out.

Jen and Chay call me while I'm en route to UCLA to tell me Sunset's jammed and at a stand-still, due to a faulty traffic light. I take some back roads and side-step the gridlock, and get to the school five minutes into my one-hour on stage. Jen, Chay, Harley, Kevin, Hans and I dash for Royce Hall, where I'm checked in and loaded onto an extra-long golf cart with the crew. They drop us at the foot of the stage, and I step up and do my Q&A thing for an hour to a nice, juicy crowd. Following that, I do a signing for a capped-line 100 people, offering more signing time at the Stash to anyone who didn't get served. The score of the day, though, is a ripe-for-the-framing sweet-ass blow-up of the *Speaks* book cover that I ask for and get. Jen and crew take it home with them as they head off. When I'm done signing, I head off as well, but to the Stash.

I sign at the Stash for about an hour and change, then chit-chat with Chappy about the new *Rats* book and other publishing stuff. Following that, I make for home, stopping at Quizno's for a Steakhouse Beef Dip and then next door at the pizza place for a calzone (in case I'm not feeling sandwich-y when I get home).

While en route, I call both Brian O'Halloran and Jeff Anderson to talk about the *Clerks* 2 move, and both fellas are awfully gracious about it. They're not only excellent actors, but excellent friends who're very supportive to boot. Jeff and I wind up talking about photography, and Jeff suggests he do a series of behind-the-scenes shots on *Clerks 2* with this Holga camera he's really into. I take it a step further and suggest he not only do that, but that we also publish a book of the pics when he's done. We talk about the next flick he's gonna direct, post *Passion* and, mid-convo, I decide I've gotta get some gifts for him and Brian for being so cool about what I promise is the last schedule change.

On the way home from Quizno's, I tear into my Beef Dip. Once home, I hit the shitter with my *Catch* script and start highlighting my lines for tomorrow's read-thru — an actorly pastime I've never really had to engage in before. When I get out of the bathroom, I hear Mewes bombing around upstairs, so I grab my calzone and laptop and join him in the living room. The plan is that we're gonna watch *Clone Wars* and play UB, but we wind up splitting the calzone and quietly playing UB without TV accompaniment, updating each other on our plays. Over the course of an hour or so, I turn $350 into $1000 before Chay calls to say they're all ready for pickup.

Mewes is in the middle of a tourney when we leave, but he's got a Sprint card that allows him to get online via his cell phone, so he brings his laptop with him in the car. We head deep into the Valley out by the Topanga exit and I swing into Lisa and Greg's place to say hi and grab my girls while Mewes throws down UB in the car. I carry Harley out, say g'night, and drive us all back to the house.

Jen puts Harley to sleep on our couch, as per usual. Chay sleeps over in Harley's room, and Mewes heads upstairs to play more UB and watch *Elektra*. I continue highlighting my script for a bit before cuddling up with Schwalbach and some TiVo'ed *Simpsons*, during which I fall asleep.

Sunday 24 April 2005 @ 11:31 p.m.

The heat wakes me up at three in the morning. I get up to shut it off and grab some water, but I can't fall back asleep. I opt to hit the desk-top and check the board to see what the reaction to the Festival of Books appearance was like. After doing that for a bit, I check email and update the diary.

I'm updating the diary from last weekend (the Poetry Event weekend), when I wind up going into rather blue detail about my sex life with Jen. Ironically, in writing about jerking off into her asshole (not inside, mind you; more against), I get turned on and decide to tug one out. Following that, I lay down again at about six-thirty in the morning, amused at how snake-eating-its-tail that spank was.

I wake up again at a little after nine, realizing I've now got less than an hour to shit, shower, shave and get over to Santa Monica for the *Catch & Release* read. I'm out of the house at five to ten, speeding down La Brea to the 10. Thankfully, there's very little Sunday morning traffic, and I make it to Casa Del Mar in fifteen minutes. As I'm about to pull up to the hotel, Jenno calls me to see where I am. I wave to her from my truck, hand it over to the valet guy, give her a hug and head into the read. Mercifully, I'm not the last person to arrive.

I give Susanah a hug, then meet Timothy Olyphant and the guy who plays Dennis to my Sam (whose name I don't wanna drop because I'm not sure if he's been announced yet, and I don't wanna ruin his chances of getting some *Variety* ink by spoiling it here). I re-meet Matt Tolmach (the president of production over at Columbia who I met years ago when he was working at Turner Pictures and I almost rewrote a script there) and Amy Pascal (Chair of the Sony Pictures Motion Pictures group) and say hi to a lot of other folks before we sit down at a long conference table to read, following the arrival of Jen Garner. We go around the room introducing ourselves, and dig into the script.

The read goes really well. I could listen to Olyphant read the phone book. The actress who's gonna play a character Sam gets involved with named Maureen isn't there for the read, so this actress stands in for her, and man is she good, great comedic timing. When it wraps up, Susanah thanks everybody and I say a bunch of goodbyes before heading outside with Jenno who delicately lets me know that there are those within the production that are made a bit nervous about the fact that I blog so, shall we say, intricately. I reassure her that I blog about my life, not other cats, and insist I'll use discretion when it comes to writing about my time on *Catch*.

With that in mind, I won't detail for you all the untoward comments made during the read by Garner about non-whites.

Kidding, of course.

While waiting for the car, I chat up Olyphant about his kids and thank Deb Aquila again for the kind words and vote of confidence. The paparazzi are in full stalk mode, waiting for Garner, but it's only three and they're apparently easy to ditch, as we watch them tear ass up the street to their cars, having missed Jen's secret exit. Some folks cluck their tongues in that "what a shame…" fashion, but it's hard to join in. Once you've seen paparazzi rent a helicopter to get pics of Ben in Central Park or watched fifty or more snappers come at JLo from out of nowhere like ninjas, three easily-ditched lens-crafters look less like an imposition and more like Moe, Larry and Curly.

I stop at the Vans store near the promenade, but alas, they've got no sizes in the style I want in stock. So I head back to the 10, grab some Quizno's, and speed home to find Jen, Harley, Chay and Jay chilling out by the pool. Soon after, Malcolm and his friend and producer Andre join us, and while margaritas are mixed, some poker ensues. Mewes turns the game into a tourney instead, and I donk out pretty quickly (pocket Kings vs. what turns out to be Malcolm's As and 8s), opting to head downstairs to grab some shut-eye. I play UB 'til I doze off, with Harley drawing in bed beside me, watching *SpongeBob*.

I wake up around six-thirty and head upstairs, over-tired and cranky that the party's still in full-swing. Renee Humphrey has joined the fun, but despite my fondness for her, I chase everybody out so I can grab some downtime with the wife. Chay stays to go swimming with Harley, and I go downstairs with Jen to do some 'night-swimming' of our own.

We emerge from the room an hour later and Jen sets about the task of getting Harley ready for bed while I clean up the living room. Scully's gotten at the ice cream and sour cream that folks left too close to the floor, so I throw out the remnants and give that bitch a dirty look as she stares up at me, guiltily (and blankly), from her Scully bed.

I head downstairs to Harley's room and walk in on Chay, getting into her pjs. We're both pretty embarrassed, but I assure her that I only saw one boob; it doesn't count unless the set are peeped. Chay's gonna sleep over with Harley, so they retire to Jay's room. Jay's gone out to some charity auction where you bid on girls, so it's not likely he's gonna be back any time soon. Jen and I kiss Harley g'night and head upstairs.

As I lay on the bed checking email and the board and IM'ing with Annie, Jen works on a writing project she's been putting together. We watch *Dynasty* until we can't take it anymore, then collapse into bed together to some TiVo'ed *Simpsons*, during which we fall asleep, minutes before our anniversary kicks in.

Monday 25 April 2005 @ 11:07 p.m.

I get up around five-ish, unable to sleep. The dogs aren't even up yet, and I toy with the notion of waking 'em up just to show 'em how it feels. But figuring that since they're dogs, the irony would be lost on 'em, I instead head to my office and put an anniversary post up for Jen, then check email.

The security system, in it's Hal-like tone, says: "Front Entry Door", so I look out my balcony to see Chay shuffling off. I call down to her to ask if Harley's awake yet and Chay whisper-shouts up that she's still sleeping. I tell her goodbye, and go back to checking email. Mom has sent me an iTunes Gift Certificate for the anniversary, which I redeem (she'd already sent Jen wine last week for the anniversary).

Harley shows up in our room around 7:30 a.m. I let her in and send her to Jen, who wakes up and shuffles to my office to wish me a Happy Anniversary, first verbally then with a smooch.

I get dressed and drop Harley off at school. Jen opted against Coffee Bean or McDonald's, so I head right back home afterwards. On my way past the library, I snag *Phantom Menace* and *Attack of the Clones* and bring them to our room. Jen gives them the nod and I throw my woobs back on, climb onto the bed with my computer while Jen rides the couch with hers, and we start our pre-*Sith* film festival.

With pauses to answer the door (Fed-Ex, the mail delivery, flowers from Byron and Gail, a muffin basket from my brother and Jerry), the phone (Scott, Raskind, Tony and sundry other well-wishers), and to chat with Mewes (who brought Jen some Coffee Bean and Baja Fresh), we get done with the flicks around 2:30 p.m. Jen's now completely refreshed on pre-*New Hope Star Wars* and ready for *Sith*. She jumps in the shower, and when she's done, I follow suit.

While I dry off, I check email, and find one from Tony that sort of disputes the second printing of *Silent Bob Speaks*. I call him to find out what he's heard, and then we get Kristin Powers on the phone and go over it until it's very clear that we have, indeed, moved to a second printing. During that call, Jen heads off to pick Harley up.

When Jen gets back with Harley, I get dressed. The idea is to leave around five-ish, and it's now four-ish. Chay's gonna babysit, but she's with Ben 'til five, so Mewes is gonna play Nanny in the interim. As we depart, he takes Harley upstairs to either swim or play the new *Star Wars* lightsaber game.

Jen and I head over to the Fox lot and talk about marital fidelity in regards to some friends of ours the whole ride. When we pull onto the lot, we can see a party getting underway on the same street where they had the *Daredevil* première party years back. As the security guard gives us our drive-on, I ask what the shindig is, and she replies that it's to celebrate the 350th episode of *The Simpsons*. I silently lament to myself that I won't be able to fall asleep to a TiVo'ed version of this party as we head to the parking structure.

Hand-in-hand, Jen and I search for the Zanuck Theater. We get there a half hour before the 6:30 p.m. start time, check in, then head back outside to chit-chat while Jen smokes. I love talking to Schwalbach. I can have endless conversations with her — which might have a lot to do with why I married her. After three cigarettes, we head inside to get seats.

There are about thirty-five people tops in the 400-seater. We're told the screening's being held for some marketing folks who are still in a meeting, so the flick begins a half-hour late. Jen and I spend the time talking about the upcoming schedule. Finally, the latecomers arrive, and the movie starts.

First off, never... never... see a movie as geeky-cool and momentous as *Revenge of the Sith* with a room full of marketing stiffs. While I "WOOOOOOOOOOOOOO-HOOOOOOOOOOOOOO!!!!"ed throughout the screening at stuff only the most moribund wouldn't be able to muster the enthusiasm to scream over, I stood alone. The only tepid interactive acknowledgment this sad little group could muster was a perfunctory smattering of near-golf claps for the Fox logo at the head of the film — and even that felt forced (pun intended). But fuck 'em — their disturbing lack of faith couldn't ruin this movie for me.

SITH SPOILERS

You've been warned...

Revenge of the Sith is, quite simply, fucking awesome. This is the *Star Wars* prequel the haters have been bitching for since *Menace* came out, and if they don't cop to that when they finally see it, they're lying. As dark as *Empire* was, this movie goes a thousand times darker — from the triggering of Order 66 (which has all the Shock Troopers turning on the Jedi Knights they've been fighting beside throughout the Clone Wars and gunning them down), to the jaw-dropping Anakin/Obi Wan fight on Mustafar (where — after cutting his legs and arm off, Ben leaves Skywalker burning alive on the shores of a lava river, with Anakin spitting venomous sentiments at his departing mentor), this flick is so satisfyingly tragic, you'll think you're watching *Othello* or *Hamlet*.

I saw a gorgeous digitally projected version of the flick, and lemme tell ya: this is a beautiful-looking film. The opening space battle sequence is the best in any of the six *Star Wars* movies. Grievous and Kenobi's lightsaber duel is bad-ass, with Grievous rocking four sabers. The Clone Wars end rather early in the flick (about the halfway point), leaving the rest of the film to concentrate on Anakin's turn to the Dark Side, and the resulting slaughter of the Jedi.

Perfect example of how dark shit gets: remember the Younglings — the kid Jedis in training from *Clones*? As a result of Order 66, when Anakin invades the Jedi Temple with an army of Clone Troopers, he enters the Council room to find a gaggle of said Younglings hiding behind the seats. They see Anakin and emerge, asking "What should we do, Master Anakin?" The query's met with a stone-cold

Anakin firing up his lightsaber. The next time you see the kids, Yoda's sifting through their corpses on the floor.

Yes, it's just that dark — and rightfully so. This is the birth of Darth Vader we're talking about. The only comic moments in the flick are given to R2D2, and while good, they're all pretty few and far between; the order of the day is dark, dark, dark.

Ian McDiarmid and Ewan McGregor steal the show, but Hayden Christensen silences any naysayers who wrote him off as too whiney in *Clones*. This is the flick that feels closest to Episodes 4, 5, and 6, because — for the first time since *Return of the Jedi* — there is a clear villain. And for all the shadow-play Palpatine has been up to in the last two flicks, his treachery is about as subtle as John Williams' score in *Sith*. Whether he's slowly drawing Anakin toward the Dark Side during an opera/performance art piece with his promise of the Sith's power of life over death, or he's engaged in a balls-to-the-wall lightsaber duel in the Senate with Yoda, his "Little, green friend" (his words, not mine — which I kinda dug, because, interestingly, I think it's the first time anyone's acknowledged that Yoda is green in any of the *Star Wars* flicks), this is the Emperor's movie.

The last fifteen minutes dovetail nicely into Episode 4 (or just plain *Star Wars* for you non-geeks), and the movie is full of link-up moments as well.

At flick's end, Threepio and Artoo are given to Captain Antilles (with the caveat that the Protocol's memory be wiped).

The twins, natch, are split up. Leia heads to Alderann with Bail Organa, and Obi Wan hands Luke over to Uncle Owen and Aunt Beru (indeed, the closing shot is Owen holding Luke while looking out over the setting suns of Tatooine — mimicking the shot of the adult Luke doing the same in *Star Wars*, complete with callback cue from Williams).

After he succumbs to the Dark Side, Anakin tries to convince Padmé that he can overthrow Palpatine, and together, he and Padmé can rule the galaxy as husband and wife.

Vader and the Emperor stand beside a younger Grand Moff Tarkin on the bridge of a Star Destroyer, overlooking the earliest construction stage of the Death Star.

Yoda telling Obi Wan that, as he heads to Tatooine to hand over Luke and go into exile, he should spend his time learning to commune with those who've crossed over to the next stage of life, as Yoda maintains he's been doing with Qui Gon (and Ben will later do with both Luke and Yoda, in *Empire* and *Jedi*).

And, hands-down, the best link-up to *Star Wars* moment that I enjoyed the most: Bail Organa and Yoda stepping into the hallway of the Rebel Blockade

Runner that opened *Star Wars*. Unlike all the high-tech CGI wizardry of the rest of the prequel Trilogy, this is a low-tech looking set, right out of circa '77, and for some reason, it really captured my imagination. I mean, this is the same exact hallway in which we got our first look at Vader, oh so many years ago, and I appreciated the hell out of Mr. Lucas including it — because it really felt like a nod to the hardcores.

Look, this is a movie I was genetically predisposed to love. I remember being eight years old and reading in *Starlog* that Darth Vader became the half-man/half-machine he was following a duel with Ben Kenobi that climaxed with Vader falling into molten lava. Now, twenty-six years later, I finally got to see that long-promised battle — and it lived up to any expectation I still held. I was sad to see the flick end, but happy to know it's not the end of the *Star Wars* universe entirely (I've read stuff about a TV show...).

Sith doesn't happen; *Sith* rules.

Following the flick, we head home to relieve Chay of her charge who, for the first time in months, has opted to sleep in her own bed... alone. Jen and I chit-chat with Chay up in the living room, and I hug her goodbye, as she's leaving in the morning to go to Toronto with Ben for the *Truth, Justice, and the American Way* [later retitled *Hollywoodland*] shoot. I'll miss her.

Jen and I lock up the house and head to bed, where we fall asleep watching TiVo'ed *Simpsons* — six years down, a lifetime to go.

Tuesday 26 April 2005 @ 11:15 p.m.

Harley wakes us up at 5:30 a.m., and wisely, Jen musters the enthusiasm to praise her for sleeping in her own bed throughout the night. I hear mention of a cele-bratory cake as I fade back to sleep.

Jen wakes me at about quarter to eight, informing me that I'll be driving Harley to school. I finally climb out of bed around eight, throw on some clothes, kiss the wife, and bring Harley to school, with Mulder in tow. We listen to 'Walking in Memphis' on the short drive.

I call Jen and let her know I'm gonna stop down at the office to go over the second half of the *Mallrats* re-cut. I tinker with the flick some more, swap out a few more shots, go over the eight-minute blooper/outtakes reel, and lock it up for the Universal folks.

I call Jen again, and tell her to get dressed so we can grab some grub. On the drive to the house, I chat with Jenno about *Catch* stuff, then pick up Jen and head to the Griddle. While we eat, Phil Benson calls to tell me Rick McCallum wants to know how I liked *Sith* (Phil worked Skywalker Sound for years, so he's tight with all those cats). I tell Phil to pass on the message that I loved it, and he says Rick might be calling me later.

While we eat, Jen and I are joined by Matt Kawczynski and his girlfriend, who're meeting Brian Lynch for breakfast. The cell rings, and it's Rick McCallum, so I step away from the table and enthuse about the movie to Rick for a while. I tell him I'll see him at the Lucasfilm/MTV screening up at the Ranch on the 6th, and he asks if we've booked our rooms yet. I tell him we'll probably stay in San Francisco and drive in, but he graciously offers me a room on property at the Ranch. Having stayed there many times during the *Dogma*, *Strike Back*, and *Jersey Girl* sound mixes, I gladly accept.

Lynch arrives, and I tell him about *Sith* before Malcolm and Andre appear. We chit-chat for a minute before Jen and I have to head to Bristol Farms for some cake mix and steaks.

Post-Bristol, I talk to our Miramax exec Jon Gordon on the cell while Jen runs in to Ralph's to get the strawberry cake mix Bristol didn't carry. Jon and I get done talking just as Jen emerges from the store, and we head home.

I jump in the shower and air dry in front of the computer until the door rings. I buzz up *Donnie Darko* director Richard Kelly, get dressed, and meet him upstairs on the patio deck. We're talking about the *Southland Tales* graphic novels he wants to do in advance of the flick, and I'm giving him all the comics publishing insight I have, pitching him to let me and Bob Chapman publish the books through a Graphitti/View Askew imprint. Mewes joins us for a few minutes to ask if I want to attend the *House of Wax* première (which I do). Following that, Bob Chapman shows up with a bunch of samples of the various hardcovers and trade paperbacks he's made over the years. I turn Richard over to Bob while I prep the filets for the grill.

Over lunch, we continue talking about the joint publishing venture, what it'll cost, and what Richard's looking for in the way of artists. Richard has a meeting to get to, so he heads off, and Chappy and I sit around and talk about the *Mallrats* ticket pickup, and check out the new 'Truth or Date' laniards we've introduced at Stash West in time for the *Rats* screening.

Chappy heads off, and I check my messages. Jen's left to pick up Harley between school and gymnastics, so I use the down time to check email and make some calls. I give Jeff Anderson a shout to see if he's around to grab this gift I picked up for him. He is, so I head out, passing Jen in the process, who's off to make the Harley Congrats for Sleeping in Your Own Bed cake.

I take Scully and Mulder with me and head over to the Valley. On the way, I return Susanah's call, and we talk about *Catch*. I call Jeff for more specific directions to his place, then see him waving me down outside his building. I give him his present, chit-chat for a bit, then head back home. On the ride, I talk to Matty from Alice about the re-scheduled radio gig I'm gonna be doing Saturday night.

As I pull up to the house, I notice it's time to grab Harley from school, so I call Jen to see if she wants to take a ride with me. She joins me, we pick up Harley, and try to get home through LA rush hour traffic. Mewes calls me to see if I'm going to *House of Wax*, but I decline, as I've got something else to do: which is drop wife, kid, and dogs off at the house, then head to the airport to pick up Byron and Gail, who're arriving from Florida.

On the way to the airport, I go through my iPod, looking for tunes we'll use as bumpers for the radio show. I find Gail waiting outside the American arrivals terminal, and we loop the airport a few times, as Byron waits for the bag. Once he's secured, we head back home.

Jen's ordered pizza for dinner, so the family sits down to a cake with two candles, celebrating Harley's conquest of her bedroom last night, and what we hope will be tonight as well. We chow down and chit-chat about Florida and the upcoming Vancouver trip. I kiss Harley g'night and head downstairs, nursing a sudden headache.

I check a little email, then curl up and watch some *Simpsons* while my head throbs. Jen arrives in the room from putting Harley to sleep, and checks email while riding the couch. I fall asleep only to be woken up by Jen around 10:30 p.m., moving me to a less-bed-hoggy position. I get up, take some aspirin, then go back to sleep, hand on my beautiful wife's back, head in agony.

Wednesday 27 April 2005 @ 11:15 p.m.

I wake up around 3:30 a.m., unable to sleep. I take a leak and head to my office to start updating the diary.

At some point in the night, Quinnster wound up in our room, sleeping on the couch. She's got a cough this morning when she wakes up, so I give her an ice pop and let her play with my Nintendo DS. She continues coughing until Jen gets up and barks at me about giving Harley something for her cough, to which I snap back that she should do it, as I've been up since 3:30 a.m. We both settle, and I go back to the board.

At around 6:30/7:00 a.m., viewaskew.com starts getting slammed hard. I track down Ming to see what's happening, and he tells me that it's the *Sith* review, getting hit like crazy, shutting down not just the board, but also the website. Ming labors like mad to get the site up and going and I discuss with Xtian his idea to take the Chatter section private, for registered members only. I hip Ming to the idea, and he agrees with Xtian and sets about initiating our own Order 66, while placing the *Sith* review on its own, accessible-to-non-members page.

Jen pulls me away from the computer, and we head to The Griddle for some eats. We're joined by Brian Lynch, who tells me about his secret girlfriend and tells me to keep it "off-the-blog" (a phrase that's getting more and more play in my life lately). Harley's friend Mina's dad David rolls by and joins us for breakfast too. I get a call from Casey, one of the producers on *Catch & Release*, who informs me I'm supposed to be in Vancouver on the 5th. I tell her this is impossible, as I'm gonna be up at Skywalker Ranch on the 6th for the MTV *Sith* première party. We try to figure out whether I'm gonna fly or drive, and then I head back to breakfast, just as we're joined by Malcolm and Andre. We can't stay long, though, as I've got a haircut at 10:30 a.m.

Jen and I bicker about my mullet on the way to the house (she can't stand it; I maintain it's a necessary evil) so I drop her off without saying goodbye and head over the hill to Nicole's to get my hair cut.

Nicole does as best she can with the little hair she's got to work with, mullet and all. I head back home to find Jen in her bathroom. We kiss and make up, and I head into the shower.

I head upstairs to do my *Degrassi* interview with Stefan 'Snake' Brogren for a CTV documentary that looks back on two decades plus of various incarnations of the show. During the interview, Mewes joins us to say hi and asks me what time we're heading over to the Arclight for the *Rats* screening. Stefan and Co. wrap up the interview, and I give them a tour of the house before heading back to my room.

I check email and the website, and IM Ming to see what's up with the traffic problem. He's put the *Sith* review on its own page with a hit-counter, and he tells me to look at the counter and click 'reload'. The number jumps substantially. Ming figures the review is getting 800 hits a minute, from all over the 'net. Shortly after that, I fall asleep for around two hours.

I'm woken up by Jen's return from shopping, and I groggily talk with her about her day. Gail calls down to let us know it's family dinnertime, and I drag my ass upstairs for steaks. During the meal, Mewes tells me that Run DMC are gonna be playing at Avalon on Friday. I tell him I'm all over it, and to sign me up. I top off the steak and baked potato with some leftover Harley Bed-Day cake and some milk.

Mewes asks if I wanna play some heads-up poker before we go to the Arclight, so I head upstairs and play for a while while Gail calls up periodically to give us time updates. Right before we leave, Mewes goes all in on a Jack/Ten, but I beat him with my Queen/Jack, winning his hundred bucks.

I kiss Jen and Harley goodbye and head down to the front door, where Mewes and I meet up with Byron and Gail, who're accompanying us to the Arclight. They opt to take a separate car and follow us over.

We get to the theater three minutes after the flick's supposed to begin. I ask the autograph seekers outside to wait 'til I get done with the intro, and head into the Arclight where I'm met by some Universal folks who lead me down the stairs to Theater 3. I say hi to JM Kenny and Meredith from Universal, grab a mic, and do some intro/Q&A for about twenty minutes. When I leave, I run into Jim Jacks in the back of the theater. We chit-chat for a bit, then I head outside, sign all the stuff I skipped on the way in, and chat briefly with Mewes and Malcolm before getting in the car and going back home.

On my way to my closet to change my shirt, I notice Quinnster's back on our couch. I quietly swap jerseys and join Jen upstairs in the living room to chill out for an hour before I have to shoot back to the Arclight. We watch *Everybody Loves Raymond* and I check email before and the board. An hour later, I kiss Jen g'bye again and head back to the theater.

I arrive with a few minutes to go before the credits. I talk with JM and Meredith about who's gonna be on stage, and decide to do Q&A until the chairs are set up and JM's ready to shoot. After about twenty minutes, we start the show, and I introduce Dave Klein, Jim Jacks, Scott Mosier, Renée Humphrey, Ethan Suplee, Jason Mewes, Jeremy London and Jason Lee. We do the Q&A thing for about two hours, then sign stuff for those in attendance. As I leave the theater, I find Mewes out in the hallway, ready to go home. Byron and Gail walk us to the car, and then we head to In-&-Out for some late-night snacks, and back home. Once there, Mewes heads off to "get up in dem guts", and I go inside to my office, where I chow down and check the board for Q&A reactions. I do this for a half hour, before joining the sleeping Schwalbach, beside whom I fall asleep, watching TiVo'ed *Simpsons*.

Thursday 28 April 2005 @ 11:16 p.m.

The dogs wake me up around 6:30 a.m. I let 'em out, take a leak, swish some mouthwash, then plant myself at my desk in my office, where I check email and read the reactions to the *Rats* Q&A.

I head out to my hallway bathroom to take a shit and further read the board. On my way out of the bathroom, I make the mistake of heading into the library, where the dusty gym equipment stares me down. I spy the doctor's office scale near the TV and decide to see what the damage is. It ain't pretty. Immediately, I head back to my room, throw on some sweats, pull on the sneakers, and head to the gym. I stick in some *Deadwood* and climb aboard the treadmill, where I do an hour. After I'm done, there's still some of the *Deadwood* episode left, so I chill out on the workout ball, taking it in.

I head to the room, where Jen's now awake, and wondering where the fuck I found the ambition to get up and work out. I tell her about my terrible meeting with the scale, and she gives me the "ahhhhhhh…", following it up with something about her being enemies with the scale as well. I point out that if she thinks she's on bad terms with the scale, then the scale and I are Jesus and Satan, so at odds are we.

I get in the shower, get dressed, and head down to the office, where Meredith and her post crew from Universal are there to do a spotting session on the new cut of *Mallrats*. We run through the flick, looking for places where new score will be added and old song cues will be extended. Mosier pops in just as the meeting's coming to a close, and as the Uni folks leave, he and I chit-chat a bit before I head back home. As I'm leaving, he gives me a piece he's done as part of his recent foray into painting. I love it.

I lay down to watch some *Simpsons* and fall asleep. Hours later, Jen wakes me up when she returns from shopping. She says the framers called, having finished with the big Jay and Bob piece from Harvey, as well as the me and Mewes page from *Empire* magazine. We decide to shoot over to the Valley to pick the pieces up and drop off Mos's painting for framing.

We get to the framers, do the drop off and pick up, grab some Koo-Koo-Roo for Quinnster, head to Quizno's for Jen and Ralph's for me (to get some canned chicken and Fat Free Mayo for my new diet). En route to Ralph's, I get a call from Casey (the *Catch* producer), and learn that I've gotta be in Vancouver by Saturday the 7th for rehearsal — which means the drive to the Van Jen and I were planning is facing a wrinkle. I tell Casey I'll figure it out and get back to her.

We get home and serve up the Koo-Koo-Roo turkey and mashed to Quinnster, who preps it (cut up turkey, mix into mash, cover with gravy). I climb upstairs to make some chicken salad (can chicken with fat free mayo), then adjourn to my room, where I slap on the woobs and sack out in front of some *Simpsons*. Jen and Harley join me for a moment to drop off Mulder. Jen stays too, and Harley heads back downstairs. I'm making goo-goo eyes at Schwalbach when the intercom buzz gives way to a screaming Harley, who informs us that Scully has eaten her beloved Koo-Koo-Roo. Jen and I race downstairs to find our apoplectic daughter screaming and crying her head off. I hunt down Scully, drag her into the room to remind her what she did, spank her turkey-stealing ass, and chase her upstairs, where I put her out on the deck by herself.

I get back to the room where Mulder (the extremely apprehensive, borderline neurotic Gallant to Scully's Goofus) is cowering behind the couch, terrified his shit's on the chopping block. I reassure the sensitive little man that he's in the clear and go back to watching TV and getting through email. Jen and Harley arrive, and it seems that Quinnster is so traumatized by the Scully Incident that she needs to sleep on our couch. Jen puts Harley to bed, just as Gail arrives to measure me for my neck and hat sizes for the *Catch* costume department. I talk to Quinnster for a bit, kiss her g'night, then join Jen upstairs.

Jen and I go over the upcoming schedule and how to handle being at Skywalker for Friday and Vancouver for Saturday at 1 p.m. We decide to drive to Skywalker Thursday night and do the preem/party on Friday. Then, I'll fly up to Vancouver for rehearsal on Saturday, turn around and fly back to the Bay Area, then spend Saturday night and Sunday driving to the Van. That settled we ride our respective laptops while rocking a little *Dynasty*. Around eleven, we decide to head downstairs to quickly fall asleep to some TiVo'ed *Simpsons*.

Friday 29 April 2005 @ 11:16 p.m.

My first words of the day are "…the fuck are you kicking me for?!" to a half-asleep Schwalbach who's kicking me to take the dogs out at 6:45 a.m. I do my Master's bidding, hit the head, swish some mouthwash, and check email. I plow through some responses and take a bit of time with Jeff Jensen's questions about *Sith* for the dreaded *Entertainment Weekly* (in an email the day before, I'd already asked him to relate the message to that book critic jerk-stain that he or she should go fuck him or herself).

During my email run, I say g'morning to both Quinnster and Jen, say g'bye to Harley as she heads to school, and mutter to Jen that I'm working when she hits my office 'fridge for her morning Diet Coke. When I emerge from my office, Jen's getting ready for her doctor's appointment. We're probably not gonna see one another most of the day, as I have a fly-fishing lesson (for *Catch*) at one, so I kiss her g'bye and head to the library gym — where I do another hour on the treadmill while watching *Deadwood*.

While I'm cooling down, watching the end of the second *Deadwood* of the morning, Mewes rolls in to tell me it's not Run DMC playing at Avalon, but instead Dougie Fresh and DMC. I ask him if he wants to go learn how to fly-fish today with me and Byron (who I've recruited to go with me), but he's not sure. We decide to have another two-man poker tourney after I take a shower.

I call down to Byron to see if he wants to join in on the poker action, and we've suddenly got a three-man tourney going. I whip up some chicken salad and the three of us play some cards. Jen returns while we're playing, just in time to see Mewes win his hundred bucks back with a pair of fucking sixes. I head downstairs to get dressed and Mewes pops in to tell us he's not gonna be home tonight (he's house-sitting elsewhere). When he leaves, the temptress that is my bride cuddles up to me on the bed, asking if I really have to go fishing today while grinding into me. I immediately cancel out on fishing as she heads off to get a manicure and her brow down, urging me to be home when she gets home and she'll make it worth my while.

With an hour and a half to kill, I opt to shoot cross town to Laser Blazer with Louis (Byron's Chocolate Lab puppy) in tow. I take Louis for a brief walk outside the store, grab some magazines at the nearby stand, then open the sunroof in the car, put Louis inside, and head into Laser Blazer. I talk to Ron for a few minutes about, amongst other things, his *Big Red One* signing next week. I chat with one of the clerks (who was at the *Rats* screening), then jump back in the car and round the block to McDonald's, where I grab a burger for Louis, an ice tea for me, and a pair of burgers for Mulder and Scully back home.

On the ride back to the house, Jason Lee calls. We do a post-mortem on the *Rats* screening and talk about his flick *Seymore Sycamore and Margaret Orange*. When I get to the house, we continue the chat. As I hang up, Jenny appears, flashing me. She throws on the music, we draw the curtains, and bone pretty hardcore, with a strong leaning toward "making love". This is incredibly rare, as we're not big into "making love". When it comes to sex, we're both pretty dirty — so we tend to fuck more than anything else.

We lounge for a bit, post-coitus, until Jen hits the couch to have a smoke. I doze for a few minutes, then do a few phoners with Mark Voger of the Asbury Park Press (about *Silent Bob Speaks*) and Scott Bowles of *USA Today* (about *Sith*). Following that, I start updating the online diary, while Jen heads downstairs to check on Harley.

As I finish getting the diary current, Jen hits the shower for her girl's-night-out with Harley's teacher and some other class moms. I've been slated to do the Morgan Freeman thing tonight, dropping her and Cricket off at Orso's. I hear the front door and wave to Harley, who's going out to eat with Nan and Pop at the Cheesecake Factory. Jen finishes getting ready and offers me a peek at her outfit (she looks stunning). She pops her tiara on; we pack Mulder and Scully into Byron and Gail's room with Louis, and head off to grab Cricket.

After I drop the girls off, I try to figure out what to do with the two or three hours I have to kill before pickup. I call Burke Williams about getting a massage, but they've got me on hold so long that I give up. I stop at Book Soup on Sunset to see if the new *Empire* is out (it's not), then opt to head home.

I let the dogs out on the patio, then grab a bite in the kitchen. I head downstairs to check out my TiVo options, and settle on a *Saturday Night Live* from 1980 (the barely-watchable Denny Dillon/Charles Rocket year before the rise of Eddie Murphy).

Jen calls, and I head over to the Valley to grab her from Orso's. I say hi to the mom-squad in attendance, then whisk Schwalbach away because I'm parked in front of a fire hydrant. Jen wants to stop at In-N-Out on the way home, so I grab an iced tea.

We get home, get into our jammies, then crash, watching some TiVo.

Saturday 30 April 2005 @ 11:17 p.m.

I get up around eight-ish, with Jen having let the dogs out already, apparently. I take a whiz then head to my office to check email and the board and start pulling stuff together for the radio show. Jen wakes up and says g'morning, but I'm knee-deep in pulling music for the show. Mewes calls to ask if Jen wants any Coffee Bean. He's babysitting his friend's Bulldog, Charles, and wants to know if he can bring the mutt by. Gail intercoms up to let us know she and Byron are heading up to Big Bear to check on their place.

I finally emerge from my office and head upstairs, where Harley and Reyna are watching Mulder adjusting to Charles out on the deck. We throw the pink bone for Mulder, and Charles chases it too. When we throw it in the pool, Mulder dives in after it, leaving the heavy-breathing Charles flummoxed. For the next half hour, we conspire different ways to get Charles to jump into the pool as well, including Mewes going in in his underwear, trying to lure Charles into following. Nothing works. Jen joins us, and we move some patio furniture around before I go downstairs to throw on my workout gear and hit the treadmill.

I do an hour on the treadmill, watching *Deadwood*. When I'm done, I take a shower and go upstairs to fix some chicken salad. I bring my grub downstairs and suck it down while laying on the bed, playing UB, and watching some TiVo with the couch-riding Jen.

While my IM's open, I see Lynch pop up and ask him if he wants to do the radio show tonight. He's into it, so I tell him to be at the house around 9:30 p.m. Edgar Wright calls soon after to let me know he's in town. I ask him if he wants to come by the radio show, and he's into it, too. Alice Morning Show producer Matty Staudt calls to tell me he's on the 405 and heading to the room we booked for him at the Renaissance. I tell him I'll pick him up there in a few.

I swing over to the Renaissance to pick up Matt. After I grab some gas, we go to my place. I give him the tour, then we hit the living room and start mapping out the show a bit, pulling news stories and listing the order of the music I've put together.

Around seven-ish a dressed-up Jen and Harley show up, signaling our departure. I leave Matty upstairs and head over to an engagement party for Harley Quinn creator Paul Dini and his fiancée Misty Lee, held at *Batman: The Animated Series* producer Allan Burnett's house. We chill for an hour, before heading back home, where we find Brian Lynch waiting outside.

Brian and Matt chat about the show, and I burn some cds with all the intro music I wanna use for coming back from commercials. Jen puts Harley to sleep on our couch and I kiss her g'night before going upstairs to collect the guys. After Jen wishes me good luck, I kiss her and head over to the Wilshire Blvd. KLSX studios. En route, we hit In-N-Out and Carl's Jr. for some pre-show grub.

We get to the studio and Mike meets us in the lobby. Mike's gonna be working the phones for us. He shows us into the studio, when Matty suddenly realizes he didn't bring any headphones. Oddly enough, headphones turn out to be a precious commodity at a radio station: there are none to be found. Mike and our board operator for the night, Dick, scrounge up enough cans for me, Bri, Mewes and Matt, as well as a pair for our eventual guest, Edgar. I'm going over all the stories we've pulled when Mewes shows up. Matt's giving Mewes the overview of the show when Dick tells us the CDs I burned won't play. I tell him they're MP3s, which is problematic, as the studio doesn't have a computer to play them on. Inexplicably, I'm thrown by this, because I'm not into any of the intro music Matty's pulled. But there's no time to fix the problem, as Dick is giving us the wave, indicating it's time to go on the air.

We have a haphazard start to the show, but by the second hour, we're in a good place with the whole affair.

I discover that I don't like being the front-man of a radio show. I liked my three days on Alice because it was Sarah's show, and she got to steer it, while I simply followed her lead and got to chime in with the funny. But I find myself in the Sarah role with Brian taking the role I was more comfortable inhabiting: that of sidekick. Riding shotgun, I discover, is way easier — because all you have to do is tag-up on the leader. If you go back and listen to the Alice stuff, that's all I did for three days. And that's a lot more fun for me.

Mind you, I don't want to take anything away from Brian or Mewes, who were great and did what they were supposed to do. But I learn that I'd rather be a guest or second banana. (It's really not that different than the Q&As: in that situation, the audience is in charge, and I'm just tagging up on what they say, in the form of story-telling.) If I were to do the radio thing again in the future, I'd wanna be paired up with someone like Sarah — who'd be in charge of running the show. In radio, I think I'd rather just be a sidekick.

Post-show, Mewes, Brian, Matt, Edgar and I do a post-mortem. Mewes heads off and I bring Edgar, Matt and Bry with me. We drop Edgar off at his hotel, then Matt off at his, then swing back up to my house where Bri's car is waiting. Lynch heads off and I go inside, chuck on the woobs, check the board reaction to the show and go to sleep.

Sunday 1 May 2005 @ 11:19 p.m.

I wake up around ten to find Jen getting ready. Harley and she are going to grab some Jerry's in the Valley and pick up her new glasses. I tell her I wanna go too, and jump in the shower. I get dressed, we collect Harley, and we're off.

We eat at the crowded Valley Jerry's, then head over to the Riverside Mall where Jen gets her glasses. She looks amazing, but I'm predisposed to dig her new look, as I'm soooooo into a cute chick in glasses (witness Brandi at the start of *Rats*, Serendipity in *Dogma*, Justice in *Strike Back*, and Maya in *Jersey Girl*). While mall-ratting, I grab some new running sneakers (to cut down on the blisters I'm nursing from the treadmill) and Harley plays at the indoor playground for a bit, before hitting a few of the fifty cents rides. While Jen picks up some Harley summer outfits at the Gap, Harley and I hit the Disney store, where we load up on *Stitch* barbecue stuff for me and *Violet Incredible* bathing gear for her. Jen finds us and we take off for the nursery down the road, where Jen picks up a gift for Cookie's birthday. While I wait in the car, Mewes calls me to let me know he's going to get a tattoo.

As we're heading home, I'm overwhelmed by the sudden shit I have to take. I drive like the Bandit to get to the house just in time to let 'er rip into the bowl.

I get back to my room and Harley's already taken up residence in our bed, watching *SpongeBob* and coloring. I join Jen upstairs in the kitchen where she's smoking, checking email, and watching a disc from the *Raymond* season three box set. I have a bit of low-carb ice cream and make a pitcher of decaffeinated iced tea. I down two glasses while getting caught up in *Raymond* (I don't understand why his wife doesn't just fuck him all the time; but I guess their lack of sex is what most of the show's best jokes are predicated on), then embark on a pantry-cleaning mission that's infectious enough to recruit Schwalbach as well. It becomes her gig, so I make some chicken salad and watch *Raymond*.

Jen decides she wants to go to Bristol to grab some sushi, but I decline, as I'm feeling like round two of my colon-blow is on its way. She brings Harley with her instead, and I sift through the DVDs in front of the bedroom TV, looking for something I can white-noise in the background while I update the online diary. Eventually, I settle on TiVo, and go back to watching that really bad *SNL* from 1980 (Christ, is it bad).

Jen and Harley return, and Quinnster takes the TV over again. We watch *SpongeBob* while I post. Jen calls down from upstairs to tell me to get the camera ready as Mewes is coming home with his new tat.

I've moved from the bed to the now-empty couch (as Jen's upstairs still) to continue blogging when Jay arrives. We head into the bathroom to remove the bandages and see what the new tat looks like.

I intercom up to Jen who comes downstairs for the unveiling to Harley. Harley is captivated. Both she and Jen coo over the spine-length tat of her moniker, and suddenly my forearm tag of 'Harley' seems a bit low-key. I take some pics, re-bandage Mewes, and he heads off, having completely stolen the hearts of a pair of chicks in their pjs.

I post the tat pics, then check some email before Jen reminds me it's 7:15 p.m. I get dressed and head out to Improv Olympic on Hollywood Blvd.

At the Poetry Event, Jeff Garlin (who most folks know from *Curb Your Enthusiasm* and *Daddy Day Care*) invited me to join him at this show he does every Sunday night at Improv Olympic, a small comedy club a few blocks from my house. It's a standup show that's generated by the audience: there are three comics who get up and talk a bit about themselves, then someone in the audience suggests a topic, and one by one, the three comics on stage take turns on the mic, making with the funny based on the suggestion.

Jeff maintained it was something I could do in my sleep (based on having peeped *Evening With*), so I took him up on his invite. When I show up at the joint, I'm not so sure. I'm not a comic; what am I doing at a comic's club NOT sitting in the audience?

I greet Jeff backstage and he goes over the program, then introduces me to the third in our party tonight: Andy Dick. As I'm a huge *News Radio* nerd, I'm delighted by this. I think about doing the fan-boy thing and doing Matthew's 'Little Billy' lines from the *Talent Show* episode back to the guy who played Matthew, but think better of it and let the man eat his Baja Fresh dinner in peace.

Jeff goes out on stage and does his intro and about fifteen minutes of standup. Then, he introduces me, and I get my first glimpse of the house: it's a smallish room with two levels that seats maybe 100 people max. I flash on the one and only time I ever attempted standup, back in '91, at an open-mic night at Rascal's Comedy Club, between the Monmouth and Seaview Square Malls in Eatontown. Though it did spawn the "you sucked your own dick" convo in *Clerks 2* from a routine I did that night, I was not good at it. At all.

It's always weird when folks who attend the Q&As tell me "you should do standup". Doing Q&A is simply answering questions posed, so there's a give-and-take with the audience; they're really the enablers, as without their queries, I cannot give replies. Standups have it much, much harder, as they're expected to get up and just generate, without any assist.

So I launch into a Q-less A, in which I talk about my day a bit, and dove-tail into some well-honed Q&A stuff, and shockingly, I go over well. I step off the stage and Andy goes on to do his intro, while backstage, I talk to Jeff about movies and heading up to Vancouver at week's end.

Jeff brings us both onstage. Andy and I sit while Jeff takes the mic and gets the suggestion from the audience. The suggestion is: "dentists". Jeff does a really funny ten minutes on everything but dentists, and then gives me the mic. I tag up on what Jeff was talking about (he ended with being Jewish), and do some Jewish stuff that dovetails nicely into my *Passion of the Christ* stuff, and hit on dentistry, which dovetails into my *Lord of the Rings* stuff. I kill with both, and give the mic to Andy. Andy does a fantastic fifteen minutes on being a tour guide in Chicago at the Water Tower and masturbating behind a screen that showcases a slide-show there (I can't do it justice), as well as a great bit about doing laughing gas at the dentist's office (even funnier). He kills, and gives the mic back to Garlin, who teaches us all a thing or two about stream-of-consciousness conversational comedy.

Before I know it, the night's over. We have to give the stage up to a comedy group called Cog, but it's my turn up at the mic. I've got five minutes, and I have to follow this Garlin/Dick tandem bit about Andy's drug problems vs. Jeff's food-aholism which fucking killed. I can decline and let Cog come on five minutes earlier or take the mic for five minutes and risk ending our show on a less funny note than these two pros. The bar's set pretty high, so the safe bet is to not be the closer. So, like a jackass, I get up and go for it.

And I'm so glad I did — not only because I would've always wondered what it would've been like had I chosen to not follow Jeff and Andy's genius bit, but also because it's the closest I'll ever get to doing something death-defying. I have no interest in hang-gliding, rock-climbing, or parachuting out of a plane now, because I've known the sheer terror and adrenaline rush of trying to be as funny as two standup pros who just finished rocking the mic so very thoroughly.

I finish with some stuff about Mewes's battle with drugs and dovetail into the bit about Jen and the *Playboy* spread. I go a little longer than five minutes, but I end on an insanely high note and leave 'em laughing.

I don't know why I feel so proud of it all, as it's the smallest room I've worked in years (mind you, the average college gig is about 800 to 1000 now). I guess it's because when I hit a stage for a Q&A, the deck is stacked in my favor, as (presumably) all in attendance are fans of the flicks I've done, hence are predisposed to root for me. This place, though? While some folks may have seen one or more of the flicks I've done, they didn't come to see me speak about what it's like to make movies; they just came to laugh. And I was able to make 'em laugh, even without the deck being stacked in my favor (although years of honing that Q&A material and style certainly didn't hurt). The whole night was fun and reinvigorating.

Post-show, I say g'bye to Andy and walk out with Garlin. We talk about the show, as well as *Curb*, and then I turn him over to a group of his friends, get in my car, and head home.

I find Jen up in the kitchen, emailing with the Toronto-imprisoned Chay, and we chit-chat for a bit while I make chicken salad. Angel the hamster's wheel is making a big racket, so I find a way to fix it with some tape, then head downstairs to throw on the woobs and grab *National Treasure* for Jen and I to watch up in the living room theater on the projection system. Halfway through, we're both feeling kinda tired, so we head downstairs and fall asleep to some TiVo'ed *Simpsons*.

Monday 2 May 2005 @ 10:54 p.m.

I'm about a week behind on this, so if it's a little threadbare, you're gonna have to excuse me, as I've forgotten stuff.

Wake up to a face-licking by Scully. I head upstairs, let the dogs out, take a leak, then head to my office to update the blog, check email, and work on the *Rolling Stone* Vader piece.

Jen gets Harley ready, and since Byron and Gail aren't back from Big Bear yet, I drop her off at school and grab some McDonald's for Jen and I. While I'm in the parking lot, I do a phone-in with Sarah and Matty on the Alice Morning Show for a post-mortem on our weekend radio gig. What was gonna be ten minutes turns into forty-five, and we talk about a bunch of stuff that doesn't have anything to do with the Saturday night show, including a poignant story about JLo and an unfortunate lack of toilet paper.

I head back home and get to work in my office. I IM back and forth with a few folks, including Ming — who relates the post-*Sith* review traffic info. He tells me to Google 'Kevin Smith Sith Review' and see all the links already out there. I do, and notice that there's one to RottenTomatoes.com. I click on it and find a message board — which is news to me, as I never knew Rotten Tomatoes to be anything more than a site that collects reviews. I read the thread and find, amidst a bunch of positive and negative comments about me and the review, a post from some jackass who's spouting off completely untrue bullshit about the box office of my flicks. So I put aside the *Rolling Stone* article to compose a response.

Here is said response (inclusive of the original post)…

Raziel wrote:

Originally Posted by Raziel

A couple of things….

1) Kevin Smith's review of *EPIII* can only be regarded as biased.

This is true. While it should probably go without saying, yes — my take on *Sith* is tainted by the fact that I like all the *Star Wars* films.

Raziel wrote:

He has gushed over *EPI* and *EPII* in the past and we know what happened with those films.

We do: those films were liked by some and not liked by others. This represented a development heretofore never recorded in over 100 years of cinema history.

Raziel wrote:

And aside from his zealot like devotion to the franchise, Kevin Smith has pretty poor taste in films.

I can't argue with this, as taste in film (and everything else in life) is pretty subjective. Yes, I've liked some pretty crappy flicks (*The Cutting Edge* is in my top 200). However, if this helps anyone get a better idea of the stuff I'm into, my top five favorite films of all time (in no particular order) are *Jaws*, *JFK*, *A Man for All Seasons*, *Do the Right Thing*, and *The Last Temptation of Christ*. The next three would be *The Talented Mr. Ripley*, *Citizen Kane*, *Jerry Maguire*. I'm still trying to figure out the last two to round off my top ten. Curiously, there are no *Star Wars* films in what is, thus far, the top eight.

Raziel wrote:

The man hasn't been able to create a decent film in years.

Also extremely subjective. That part about me being a man, I mean.

However, some (like me) could debate the poster's take on whether or not I've made a decent film "in years" or not. While the poster may not harbor any affection for my recent body of work, I can point him to a website full of people who'd disagree with him, or critics (both in print and on the web) who'd follow suit. In truth, it's probably more likely that the poster — a one Raziel, which I'm assuming is a 'net handle, because said poster feels the need to shield his secret identity from enemies who'd seek to do his loved ones harm — hasn't made a decent film (or any film, for that matter) in years, while I (like every filmmaker who's come before me and every filmmaker who'll come after me) have made films that have been considered to be shit by some and decent by others.

Raziel wrote:

His films combined have lost more money than they have grossed.

This is where the poster reveals him or herself (oh, fuck it — it's gotta be a guy; no woman could be this petty and sad) to be full of shit, because this statement is patently untrue.

Clerks

Cost: $27,575, Theatrical Gross: $3.1 million, VHS (DVD figures not available): $6.169 mill.

Mallrats

Cost: $6 million, Theatrical Gross: $2.1 million, DVD: Universal declines to issue figures, but Colleen Benn at Universal Home Video says, very coyly "Let's put it this way; we're doing a second version of the DVD. We only do that with titles that sell a lot. *Fast Times*, *Animal House*, *Jaws*, now *Mallrats*."

Chasing Amy:

Cost: $250,000, Theatrical Gross: $12 million, DVD: $12 million.

Dogma

Cost: $10 million, Theatrical Gross: $30 million, DVD: Col/Tri declines to give financial figures, but Michael Stradford informs me that they shipped

800,000 of the standard edition of the DVD, and over 300,000 of the Special Edition, one year later.

Jay and Silent Bob Strike Back

Cost: $20 million, Theatrical Gross: $30 million, DVD: $38.5 million

Jersey Girl

Cost: $35 million, Theatrical Gross: $25 million, DVD: Financials not available, but Miramax Home Video head Shannon McIntosh informs me that we shipped over half a million units in the first week.

Even when you factor in P&A and marketing costs, it doesn't require (good) Will Hunting to do the math and see that the poster's statement that my films have "lost more money than they have grossed" is an ignorant crock of shit.

Raziel wrote:

Smith is also rumored to be involved in the upcoming *SW* TV series project. Do you honestly think he would jeopardize his involvement with this by posting a bad or medoicre review of *EPIII*??? I don't think so.

Perhaps. Or before Fox Mulder here works himself into a frenzy with his conspiracy theory, might I suggest that if I, indeed, didn't like the flick, that I simply wouldn't have posted about seeing it in the first place.

See, in my world, if I don't like something, I try not to call attention to it. If I feel something sucks, I don't waste my time writing about it, unless I'm getting paid to state my opinion on the subject, or unless I'm asked about my take on it specifically (as with the *Magnolia* incident on my website, eons ago). The way-cool named Raziel holds forth on the subject of me and my flicks (even though, as he'd lead you to believe, he's not a fan) and as far as I know, nobody asked him his opinion, and he's not getting paid to offer it. This leads me to believe that Raziel — bad-ass name that, no-doubt, impresses chicks nothwithstanding — has a lot of free time on his hands; free time that would be better spent producing something rather than attempting to belittle those who do produce, or, say, chasing pussy. But no — here he sits, poo-pooing this film or that, as time marches on, bringing him ever closer to the grave and a legacy of invective-layered posts on a website.

Raziel wrote:

Smith is not a good candidate to use as a borometer for this film.

True enough — just as Raziel is not a good candidate for master speller (bator? Yes; speller? No).

Raziel wrote:

I'd wait until an unbiased review is posted...

Wait for what, exactly, I find myself wondering?

Raziel wrote:

Or even better, watch the movie yourself and create your own opinion.

Finally, a glimmer of intelligence from our hero.

Raziel wrote:

Also, as pointed out by someone else, what the hell is up with all the "darkness" crap?? "This is going to be the darkest *SW* yet!" "This one's darker than the last one!"....What is this??? Who cares if it's darker or not? Does "darkness" guarantee a quality film???

No. And yet, nobody maintained that "darkness" guaranteed a quality film. Raziel responds to an idea that nobody put forward, apparently falling into debate with himself.

Again, folks — I can't make anyone love me or the movies I've made (and will continue to make, long after the fire in the belly of the twelve year-old Raziel subsides). However, I can correct misinformation like Raziel's loopy and uninformed take on the box office of the films I've made. Even though some would consider it a waste of my time, I've always felt that if I can't spare a few minutes to show up the jackasses in life, I'm not living to my fullest potential.

Yours,

Kevin Smith

When I'm done with that, I write about 750 words for the *Rolling Stone* piece and then email it to Jim, the *Rolling Stone* editor, to see if it's what he's looking for.

Jen puts Harley down on our couch while I continue working in my office. I put on Harley's sleeping music, and Jen heads upstairs. Harley's not sleepy in the least, so we chit-chat a bit until the phone rings. It's Byron, telling me they're pulling up outside. Harley asks who it was, and I tell her Nana and Poppy are home. She asks if she can come downstairs to see them, and I say yeah. We get downstairs and Byron's immobile in the back of the truck. When he throws his back out like this, everything except laying down hurts him. Harley takes Louis's leash, and Byron rolls to the edge of the back of the SUV. He leans on me and we slowly make our way into their room and get him up on the bed. Gail intercoms Jen upstairs while I park and unload the truck.

I head to Rite Aid to grab a urinal and bed pan for the bed-ridden Byron, just in case he's in too much pain to get up 'til he gets in to see the doctor. I also grab some Carl's Jr. for him and Gail, and some chocolate (for the period-ravaged Jen).

I get back home, give Byron his gear and his cheeseburger and head upstairs, thinking about how comfort food really lives up to its name — as Byron rarely eats cheeseburgers (he's a health-nut), but was pretty happy to suck one down tonight, to take his mind off the pain. Upstairs, I give Gail her cheeseburger and Jen her chocolate and fries. The girls chit-chat while I suck back my chicken breast and the dogs look on, jealous. Gail heads downstairs, and Jen and I watch some tube while I respond to posts on the RottenTomatoes.com forum. I head to the bathroom downstairs and continue answering posts for a while.

When I get out of the bathroom, Jen's downstairs and in bed already. I climb in bed beside her and continue posting 'til three, outlasting everyone else in the forum and responding to every question before finally going to sleep.

Tuesday 3 May 2005 @ 11:02 p.m.

We all sleep in, and it's 9:30 a.m. before Jen rousts me out of bed to take Quinnster to school. Since she's late, I have to walk her in through the front office and the pre-K classes, which is always a bit harrowing, because you detour through their bathroom with the pint-size toilets to get to the outside campus, and every once in awhile, a little shaver's sitting there, taking a dump, asking if you'll wipe them. Thankfully, there are no shitters on the bowls today, so I get Harley to her class, kiss her g'bye, and head out. I call Jen to see if she wants to grab breakfast.

Jen meets me in front of the house, and we head to the Griddle, where we run into Brian and Matt. We spend the meal talking about the radio show and the latest bad bit of business to befall Bryan Johnson's ex, Suzanne. I get a call from Gail who tells me CNN has called to see if I'll jump on that *Showbiz* show again and talk about *Sith*.

Post-breakfast, Jen and I head over to Pico, and I hit Laser Blazer while Jen hits that girl store a few doors down. Since I've already grabbed a bunch of titles that streeted this week last week, my haul's kinda slim. I chat with Ron, and as I leave, I chat with Ron's mom outside. Then, I grab Jen who's bought this awesome Lois Lane t-shirt, and we head back home so I can work on the *Rolling Stone Sith* piece. I'm getting frantic calls from Tony Angelotti, my publicist, who's getting frantic calls from Jim, the *Rolling Stone* editor, who's now getting really panicky about not having the piece yet, because they go to press this week. On the way home, we stop in Westwood to peep out a hotel Xtian's gonna board his brood in for the first two weeks when he arrives in LA, while they search for an apartment. It's not a shit-hole, so I call X to let him know.

When I get home, Mewes is all over me about going with him to the Caddy dealership to co-sign a two-year lease for him (Mewes has shit credit at the moment). I tell him we can go right after I'm done at CNN, and he tells me he's heading to the bank to grab the deposit for the lease. I take a shower, get dressed, then head over to CNN.

I run into some of my old new friends at CNN; then, they put me in the chair, give me the earpiece, and get NY on the line. Apparently, they like me over at *Showbiz Tonight* (as this is the third time I've been on in four weeks) but they don't trust me to be on live anymore (because of the ol' "golden showers" comment). They're paying a bunch of dough in satellite time to have me comment on *Sith*, though you wouldn't know it based on the amount of yakking the hostess is doing in her lead-up to the question. Mid-answer, she cuts me off to comment on my commentary. It's a strange way to run a whorehouse (bring a guy all the way over to the office just to essentially listen to the host's thoughts on the topic at hand on-air), but eventually, we both get through it with little incident, and I'm off on my merry way.

On the ride back home from CNN, Mewes calls to see if I'm ready to hit the Caddy dealership. He's also out on the road, so I tell him to meet me at the View Askew office, where we'll leave his car and drive to the dealer in mine.

I get to the office and Susanah Grant calls my cell. I bitch about CNN for a beat, until she cuts to the chase and gives me some guff about not going to my fly-fishing lesson. I apologize and tell her I'll fly-fish my ass off the week before we start and all through the shoot, just hitting ten and two non-stop. She tells me that after rehearsal on Saturday, the hair department's gonna come look at my mop and see what's-what for the show. I ask if I'm gonna be allowed to rock my mullet, and — devastatingly — she tells me no: the mullet's not gonna be in the movie.

Now, am I insanely pro-mullet? No. But I've been growing this shit out for the last three months in prep for *Clerks 2* — fighting with my ol' lady about it, wearing it on national television — only to suddenly learn that I'm gonna have to hack it off. So when I hang up, I launch into a tirade for Scott and Phil about how powerless it is to be an actor and have someone telling you where to go and how to cut your hair. Mos and Phil are looking at each other like "karma, bitch…" Mewes arrives to hear me bitching about cutting my hair and immediately objects, as I haven't let him cut his hair in over a year in prep for *Clerks 2*. I tell him to shut the fuck up: actors are to do what they're told. Bryan Johnson pops in and opts to take a ride with Mewes and me to the Caddy dealer.

On the ride over, we talk about Bry's ex and the bad weirdness in her life. But the bad weirdness is yet to come, as we get to the Caddy dealer, pick out the car, and fill out all the lease agreements... only to then learn that California rolls a lot differently than Jersey when it comes to co-signing.

I was set to throw my name down as financial security for the dealership — so that if Mewes defaulted on his lease payments, they'd come looking for me. This is co-signing for a lease/loan as I've always understood it (and done it) back home. Out here, there is no co-signer; it's only co-buyers. What that means is that I'd be leasing the car with Mewes, right down to having my name on the registration too. This isn't good, because it means that if Mewes gets into an accident, I get sued as well. As much as I hate to, at this point I decline to co-sign/co-buy. Mewes understands, but is bummed — as he was a mere signature away from being a car-owner (he was leasing-to-buy). Thankfully, another option presents itself.

There's another Caddy, the same model that Mewes wants, only a few years older, with merely three thousand miles on it, available on the used lot. It's a thirty-thousand-dollar car, and the manager of the dealership says that if Mewes puts a third or more of the price down, he can probably get him financed for the rest. Mewes checks out the car, and likes it even more than the new Caddy he was gonna lease, so he's in. The manager says to give him a day to pull the paperwork together. Mewes — ever the very essence of patience and serenity — offers the guy five hundred bucks to make the paperwork happen now. The manager, bless him, says he doesn't need five hundred bucks that badly, and tells Mewes he'll call him tomorrow.

I drop Bry and Mewes off at the office and head home, just as Jen and Harley are coming back from Target and various errands. We put Harley to sleep and head upstairs, where we settle into an Anna Paquin flick called *Darkness*, while checking email and reading the board. When the movie wraps up, we head downstairs, cuddle up, and fall asleep to TiVo'ed *Simpsons*.

Wednesday 4 May 2005 @ 11:03 p.m.

It's not the dogs but Jen who wakes me up, as we're going into Harley's class to read books this morning. I quickly jump in the shower then go looking for a book to read. I dig out the DC hardcover from a few years back called *Bizzaro Comics*, leaf through it, find a pair of stories, and join Jen and Harley in the car.

At the school, we head to the front of the class to read to the group. I'm too leery to sit in one of the tiny chairs (lest I simply accept it up my ass, it's so small), so I take to the floor, while Jen sits in one of the kiddie chairs with Harley on her lap. Harley starts off the Smith Family Reading Extravaganza with one of her training books. Jen follows, reading a kids book about a young Mia Hamm and another book about a British kid with a weird fashion sense. Then it's my turn. When the kids hear the first stories about Hawkman, I immediately win over the boys in the class. When I move onto the story about Wonder Girl and Wonder Tot, I win the girls. And when I bust with the story about the little boy who finds the Bat Cave, I've got 'em all. It's weird, the power Batman has over little kids, even to this day. I guess it plays into what Stan Lee has always felt was appealing to kids about Spider-Man: beneath that mask, he can be anyone — so any kid can imagine he's Spider-Man. Batman has a little of that going for him, but he also has the credibility factor: he's not from another planet, he's not freakishly strong, and he's not invulnerable. It's his humanity that appeals to kids, I think, that and his suit and car.

Afterwards, Jen and I grab some Griddle and head home. I check email and get into updating the online diary when Mos IMs me about it being time to head to the store for the *Mallrats* documentary interviews.

I swing over to the office, pick up Mos, and head to the Stash. As we get there, Mewes is just finishing his interview. I jump in his grave, shut the store, and do an hour with JM Kenny about the history of the flick and how it found another life on home video. As per usual, sound asks that the air conditioner be shut off, so while we're getting good sound, I'm sweating my balls off. My face and hair look like I dipped them into a toilet.

When I'm done, I clear the way for Scott to do his interview and head outside to talk to Chappy. I suggest we go for a ride around the block so I can sit in front of the air conditioner in the car and cool off. We take a spin to In-N-Out, and Chappy and I talk about the Richard Kelly book project as well as a new trade paperback for the *Clerks* comics that'll include a story that happens between *Clerks* and *Clerks 2*.

We head back to the store and meet up with Gina and Scott, who has just finished his interview. Me, Chappy and Gina go over the proposed September street date for the *Rats* DVD and try to figure out if we can do a signing at the store in the midst of the *Clerks 2* shoot. Since we're only gonna be shooting five-day weeks on *C2*, a weekend signing sounds like it'd be in order. However, holding it the weekend after the title streets seems kinda pointless. We quiz Meredith from Universal about the feasibility of doing a weekend signing at the Stash the weekend before the disc streets (always an iffy proposition, as other retailers might feel you're getting an unfair advantage). Mosier delivers the coup de grace, pointing out that a weekend event would get on the Monday night news, *E.T.* and *Access Hollywood*, and presumably drive the sales of the next day release. Meredith agrees, and says she'll push it with the higher-ups.

Jason Lee is in the hizzy, so I say hi and give him a hug before he sits down to do his interview. While he's engaged, I hang out in the back alley with Bob, Gina and Scott. Mewes — who's not only there for his interview but is also working the store that day — joins us to reveal that the manager from the car place has given him the nod for the financing deal. Mewes wants to race over to the dealership immediately, but I tell him he's gotta wait, as we've got a new Stash commercial to shoot for the DVD.

Lee finishes up, and him, Mewes and I wing the commercial (a companion piece to the Stash commercial on the special edition *Dogma* DVD). Once he's done, Mewes is off Jesse Owens. We say g'bye to Lee, and then I head to the back of the store again to answer some EPK questions. Once that's out of the way, I also shoot a quick *Clerks 2* hype spot for Harvey to take to Cannes to amp up the overseas buyers. We wrap everything around seven, at which point Mos and I race back to the office so I can drop him off and he can get to Cookie's party before it starts.

I get home and Jen's putting Harley to bed. She doesn't want to tell her we're going out, as it's our last night at home before the Vancouver trek. So Jen, dressed up and in heels, fronts like she's just going upstairs to watch TV. My job is to sit downstairs until the kid's asleep. Once the coast is clear, I'm to collect Jen so we can head over to Cookie's party. Quinnster stalls and stalls, refusing to go to sleep. I put the dogs up on the bed with her, but she still won't close her eyes. Finally, I head upstairs and tell Jen we should just go, as we're already an hour late. We ask Gail to lay down with Harley and to tell her we went to In-N-Out if she asks where we are.

We get to Alex's party at this restaurant near Silver Lake. We're seated outside at a long table with like twenty-five people in attendance, most of whom I know, some of whom I don't. I sit next to some cats I know: Mos, Dave Klein, his wife Marty, and Sue McNamara, our production manager on *Dogma* and *Strike Back*. We chit-chat for awhile, catching up, and chow down while Jenny flits about, working the party, talking to Cookie, Catherine and Annaliese (who's back from a year in New Zealand, working on *King Kong*). The birthday girl, as one might imagine, is radiant.

At eleven, the outdoor portion of the restaurant stops serving booze, so the party starts breaking up to head inside. Jen and I excuse ourselves, as we've got to get up early to pick up donuts in the morning and then the drive ahead of us all day tomorrow.

We get home and Jen heads upstairs. I hear a car pull up to the house and take a peek out the library balcony to see a somewhat new, black Caddy pulling up. I head downstairs where Mewes is gingerly parking and re-parking his car as close to the garage doors as possible. He gives me the grand tour of the vehicle, then we say g'night and head inside.

I climb into bed beside Jenny and we fall asleep to a TiVo'ed *Simpsons*.

Thursday 5 May 2005 @ 11:03 p.m.

I'm with this girl who I don't know/can't place, who proposes a three-way with Jen, but then seduces me into some one-on-one. The chick kinda looks like Mewes's ex girlfriend Lauren, but it can't be her, as I haven't seen Lauren in a dog's age, and even when I did, she wasn't really my type. The weird thing about her is that this chick's got massive fucking nipples — monstrous even. They're so big and thick around that they're almost like a pair of cocks planted on her boobs (paging Dr. Freud…). I eat her out, she sucks my dick, we bone and cum, and then I excuse myself, as I have to get back to school. I rush back to my old alma mater, Henry Hudson Regional, where I'm somehow still a student, even though I'm also an established filmmaker. I hit the boy's locker room to wash my face off, so my high school wife, Jen, can't smell some other chick's pussy all over my muzzle. I'm hating myself for doing the unthinkable and cheating when I suddenly wake up and discover that, mercifully, it's all been a dream. I have the same sense of relief I have when I wake up from dreams about being murdered.

Since Byron's bed-ridden, letting the dogs out in the a.m. requires the climb up to the third floor. I make the climb, take a leak, swish some mouthwash, then head back to the room and open one of the black out curtains, so Harley and Jen can gradually wake up. I grab my laptop and head to the bathroom, where I open up a bunch of nude and sexy pics I keep of Jen, and tug one out in an almost conciliatory manner, to wipe any trace of the sex with a stranger out of my sub-conscious. After I finish, I check email for a few minutes before I hear the knock on the door of Jen, telling me to hurry up so we can get to school.

I get dressed and head downstairs. I grab the *Daily Variety* off the front stoop, load Jen and Harley into the car, and head over to Winchell's while reading the paper. When we get to Winchell's, I tell Jen I want to stay in the car, as a man on a diet shouldn't have to walk into a donut store. Jen points out that it's not a great neighborhood, and I grumble as I drag my ass out of the car and join the girls at the counter inside. I bury my face in the *Variety*, so as not to let a single one of those sweet temptations break my stride.

We bring the three boxes of donuts to Harley's class as a sort of going-away present. The kids are already in their reading circle, so we leave the donuts for them, say goodbye to Cricket, and kiss and hug Harley. I tell Harley that it's a safe bet we won't have taken to the road by three, so we'll probably see her after school anyway.

We stop at McDonald's on the way home and grab some hash browns and a Diet Coke for the Princess and some sausage patties for me. While in the drive-thru line, I throw out this suggestion: maybe we should skip the Skywalker Ranch première and drive straight up to Vancouver. As it stands, I have to be in Vancouver for three hours of rehearsal on Saturday afternoon, which was gonna require me to fly to Van and back to San Fran on Saturday so that we could continue our drive on Sunday. As much as I'd like to kick back in the Gershwin Room and see *Sith* projected and listen to it on the Stag Theater screen, the most responsible thing to do would be getting to Vancouver by Saturday morning and immersing myself in *Catch & Release*. Jen agrees.

When we get home, I head upstairs to grab a glass of iced tea for my sausages and sit down and finish reading *Variety*. Afterwards, Gail lets Scully and Mulder in and I feed the mutts before going back downstairs.

Jen's generously offered to help me pack (once she's done emailing Chay), so I pull all the clothes I wanna take with me out of my closet and dump them on the floor. I've opted against luggage, and instead, insist on using plastic storage tubs from Target. Since we're driving up, I can fit a shit-load of these buckets into the back of the Expedition, as well as the luggage Jen's bringing for her initial two-week stay.

I head to my office, plug in a 100-gig Firewire drive to back up my desk-top Mac. While it gobbles up all ninety gigs of my life's work, I forge ahead on the dreaded *Rolling Stone* piece 'til one-ish, at which point I give it a read and finally feel satisfied enough to turn it in. I email it to Jim, the *Rolling Stone* editor, and clean up some desk-top files before shutting down and emerging from the room, hands held triumphantly high to the couch-riding Jen, announcing the beast has been tamed. She's already packed all my clothes into the containers, so now all that's left for me to do is pack DVDs and sundry non-clothing items I'll be needing for my nearly three-month stay up north.

I pack a massive container full of movies, packed to the top largely with a slew of flicks I haven't even opened yet. I round up the comics I haven't gotten around to reading in the last few months as well, and put my office in order. With every-thing now sorted and packed, I head upstairs to sign the four hundred copies of *Silent Bob Speaks* that are waiting for me on the dining room table. Jen heads off to pick up Harley from school.

While signing the only amount of the second printing we could get from the book distrib (the second printing flew out of the warehouse, necessitating a third printing, which won't be available 'til mid-May), Gail comes upstairs to contin-ue making family dinner: spaghetti and meatballs. I tell her to call Smalls so he can load up the truck with the luggage and then pack up the signed books for shipping to Don in Florida. Harley and Jen return, and Harley joins me, helping me stack the signed books. Since we had such a smearing problem with the last batch, I'm now signing inside the book — and as she stacks each copy, Harley takes a moment to open the book and inhale the Sharpie smell. We get through the stacks and it's dinnertime. Byron appears for the first time, walking without wincing. Turns out the drugs the back doctor gave him are masking the pain enough for him to stand up and move around. He joins us for dinner.

It's an early family dinner — 'round 3:45 p.m. — because Harley has to go back to school for gymnastics. While the lucky sumbitches dig into pasta, I mix up some chicken salad and brew a glass of iced tea. We're all chatting up Harley about her day, but she's obsessed with this spider she spotted on the ceiling that seems to be making its way toward the stove.

I head downstairs closely followed by Jen and Harley. Jen's connection to Harley is, naturally, stronger than mine, so whenever we have to leave the Quinnster behind, it emotionally cripples Jen. They're going through their mother-daughter bond stuff, after which I hug and kiss the kid, tickle her and tell her I'll see her in a week, and send her off to gymnastics.

I take a shower, wrap myself in a robe, then head to my office to see if I've gotten a response from the *Rolling Stone* guy. Finding nothing, I shut the com-puter down, get dressed, and head upstairs to sign the last batch of *Dogma* UK posters we'll ever carry at the online Stash. When I'm done, I go back to our room, where Jen's drawing 'I Love You' signs for Harley to find when she gets home. I clean up the TiVo storage and cancel some programs off the Season Pass menu. We give the room a once-over, say g'bye to Scully and Mulder, and I carry the last few tubs of gear to the elevator. We pop in to Byron and Gail's room to say g'bye, then I head outside to spin the car around to the garage and load the last two containers from the elevator. Fully packed, we start our drive to Vancouver.

It's a straight shot up on the 5, but since we're leaving at about six, there's a bunch of traffic. We clear the city and it's smooth sailing. I call Don to tell him all the books are signed and we wind up talking for an hour. Turns out they're moving the Online Stash fulfillment center to a warehouse space, as it's gotten too big to keep in the offices they'd been in for the last year and a half. Don relates some amusingly horrifying tales of having to deal with the credit card companies until I lose connection to him in the mountains. Jen's been buried in *Newsweek* the whole time, so she relishes the opportunity to fill me in on some of the stuff she's read until we hit a gas and food stop. I call Don back and finish the convo while filling up the Expedition. Jen and I grab some McDonald's (Diet Coke and fries) for her, and some Carl's Jr. (bunless six dollar burger with cheese, chicken breast and iced tea) for me. We head back out to the road.

Harley calls in to say g'night. When that convo's done, the wife and I spend the next hour and a half chit-chatting. Aside from getting inside her body my favorite Jen/Kev pastime is getting inside her head. I find Jen insanely interesting, and I love hearing her talk and probing her verbally (orally and cock-ally, too). I tell her about my cheating dream, and we talk about my historical predilection for really pale girls, as well as which (if any) of her friends I'd fuck if we weren't together (turns out none). After awhile, we opt for some iPod. We listen to a lot of Springsteen before clicking over to Spalding Gray's 'It's a Slippery Slope', which takes us into Sacramento.

We get a room at the Sheraton and load all her bags out of the car. I grab a change of clothes from my tubs and we head upstairs. We both take long leaks before climbing into bed and purchasing some *Frasier* episodes from the in-room movie menu to fall asleep to.

Friday 6 May 2005 @ 11:04 p.m.

I wake up around eight-ish, take a leak, then head out into the living room part of our hotel suite to update my diary, letting Jen sleep in.

Jen gets up around 10:30 a.m., immediately searching for coffee. The room service folks won't do breakfast past ten, so we opt against eating here and decide to take showers and get a move on.

We drive about thirty miles down the road, then stop to gas up and grab some Quizno's. I pull the box of Trivial Pursuit cards out of the back, just in case the wife feels like playing Alex Trebek, then we get back on the 5 North and drive.

And drive, and drive, and drive. We drive and listen to the iPod while Jen reads. We barely talk for a couple of hours, just occasionally exchanging warm glances or holding hands. For a while, I'm the deejay. Then, Jen takes over. I chew gum, she smokes. It takes us hours to get out of California. We only ever stop for gas, Diet Coke, and Iced Tea; then, it's back on the road. We climb over the Shasta mountains and the hills of Oregon. We see America while listening to 'America'. We chit-chat, then fall into long silences. When we get a signal, we talk to Harley and Gail. Later in the day, Jen digs into the Trivial Pursuit questions and quizzes me for hours 'til it's too dark to see the cards. We succumb to the desire for comfort food and snack out on fries and Chips Ahoy. And before we know it, twelve hours have gone by.

We pull into Seattle at one a.m. The whole last hour of the trip, I've been saying how the car feels like it's out of alignment or something. As we pull into the garage of the hotel in the heart of the Emerald City, I discover why: we've got a pretty bad flat.

We get the bags into the lobby, check in, and head up to the room. I call AAA to see about getting the tire fixed in the a.m. It's about a two-hour drive from where we are to Vancouver, so I should make it to my noon *Catch* rehearsal with plenty of time, if AAA shows up early enough. Before I fall asleep, I check email and update the diary.

Saturday 7 May 2005 @ 11:04 p.m.

I get up at seven and take a shower. As I dry off, I call AAA. Jen wakes up, and we head downstairs to meet the Triple A guy in the parking garage. The guy swaps out our tire, I tip him, and we go back to the room to shit and pack (though not together). We head out on the road by twenty after eight.

We stop at McDonald's to fuel up, then race like hell to British Columbia. After clearing Customs, we cruise into Vancouver and check into the hotel. We're in the residence side of the hotel. Neither of us are really into it, but it's only until we secure an apartment.

Susanah's assistant Rhonda comes by with Forest from the hair department, who measures my bald spot for a possible piece. Susanah joins us, and she, Sam Jaeger and I rehearse for a few hours. I don't think I'm as strong as I was in the table read, but that might have something to do with the fact that I've only had four-and-a-half hours sleep. Sam's great, and fun to bounce off, so the time flies.

Afterwards, I head to the room and find a note from Jen telling me to meet her in the downstairs bar. We chit-chat for a bit, and then head out into the city to grab some pizza, over which we decide to change our room for something less on the residence side and more on the hotel side. We head back to the hotel, make the change at the front desk, have our luggage moved to our new suite, then head out to London Drugs to grab an Airport Express (to replace the one I forgot at the hotel in Sacramento). We grab some other stuff (snacks and water), then shoot back to our room, where we hunker down in front of some season six *X-Files* with our wireless laptops and snacks, exhausted. We're out cold by nine-thirty/ten.

Sunday 8 May 2005 @ 11:04 p.m.

Get up around seven-thirty, which bugs me because there are no dogs, and yet still I'm rising early. Jen's not in bed, so I sleepily call out her name and get a response from the bathroom. She emerges, and I wish her a Happy Mother's Day. I take a dumpski, do some Listerine, and we call home to talk to Harley. Jen gets blue because there's a full-blown Mother's Day celebration going on back at the house, with Chay, Gail, Byron and Harley, and she misses her daughter. As a distraction, we throw on some clothes and head downstairs to look for food.

We don't wander far. There's a Mother's Day brunch going on in the hotel restaurant. And since Mother's Day is the (allegedly) busiest day in the food service industry's calendar, the hotel's opened their upstairs ballroom and turned it into a makeshift dining room as well — where folks without reservations (like us) are shuffled. We chow down, trying to figure out why the Mother's Day motif (as represented on both floors, near the buffet table) is a little patch of faux garden with some flowers sprouting up and a small shovel and pitchfork nearby. Wouldn't a stroller have been more appropriate, as you can be a mother who's never been into gardening, but you can't be a mother without a kid being in the mix somewhere? "It's Canada-town, Jake."

When we're done eating, we saunter back to London Drugs to pick up an oscillating fan so Jen can smoke in the room without smoking me out. We grab some water and other stuff too, then stop by Starbucks to latte Jen up before lugging our booty back to the hotel.

Once in the room and in our woobs, Jen lays down and I call my Mom to wish her a Happy Mother's Day and fill her in on my life since my last call. I was having a Mother's Day gift made for her, but it's not done yet, so it may be either a Dad's Two-Year Anniversary gift or morph into an Anniversary gift.

When I get off the phone, I curl up in bed beside Jen, and we watch a bunch of season six *X-Files* while posting and checking email. Jen sends me a great piece she wrote about our drive that I urge her to post on the board, but she's feeling a little shy about it, so opts against. It's the second thing she's written in the last two weeks (other than all the email she writes to Chay), so I'm thrilled to read it and savor every word.

Hours slip by, during which time we snack out and eat lunch, all while watching Scully and Mulder run around the very town we're now in.

I use the one-line schedule provided by production to fill in my iCal with all the dates I'm shooting, so as to come up with some idea of when I can and can't fly home for long weekends and stuff. Jen and I go over it to map out how many times she'll be coming back to Vancouver before the big move, after Harley's done with school, when the entire family will come to town. Before we realize it, we've pissed away most of the day on *X-Files* and laying around — which was just what the doctor ordered, really. Jen wants a backrub, so she suggests we head downstairs, or take a walk to the water. I counter with suggesting a drive, instead, to take in our surroundings and get our bearings. We argue about this for a few minutes before switching positions on the subject (in arguments, we tend to try to out-think what one another is gonna say next or eventually), then settling on the drive. Harley calls as we're waiting for the elevator, so I talk to her a bit then pass the phone over to the parent she really wants to talk to. Jen opts against getting into the elevator, so as not to lose cell signal, and I tell her I'm gonna head downstairs and give the valet guy our ticket.

While waiting for the car downstairs, I run into Olyphant and we chit-chat about the next week's schedule. Jen joins us, says hi, and then Schwalbach and I are off, into the Vancouver non-night (it's past eight, yet still very light out).

I do the Kev/Van '92 Reality Tour with Jen, first showing her the old location of the Vancouver Film School (on Hamilton), then swinging over the Cambie Bridge to the other side of town, detailing the looooong walk to school I used to take, while searching for the house I lived in during my six-month stay (we look for a half hour, but I can't find it). All the while, I'm having flashbacks to the only time in my life when I was truly lonely. Aside from Mosier (who lived way out in Port Moody), I had no friends in this burg — nobody to hang with. Nobody from back home ever came out to visit me either, and since this was pre-internet, I had very little contact with Jersey. Of all people, Walter was my life-line to Highlands then — writing me handwritten letters detailing the misadventures of Mewes or chatting comics. He always included artwork in his packages, too; indeed, that's when he'd sent me the drawing of the clown in fishnets that would become our company logo for a decade. For the friend who probably understood what I was doing the least back then (nobody we knew had ever been to film school or thought about making a movie), Walt was my sounding board: I remember writing to him asking if he thought the name View Askew would be good for a production company. I still have all of his letters.

But when I wasn't trading correspondence with the Flan-Man or at the VFS, I was fucking lonely, kids. Weekends (with no school to break up the day) were the worst. I used to go to the movies a lot, paying to see one flick then staying all day to sneak into whatever else was playing at the multiplex. One weekend, I stayed at Mos's to watch the Oscars (when *Silence of the Lambs* won), and that was Heaven — just being around a family. But normally, I'd sit in my rented room in the house I stayed in with George and Ken (two dudes about ten years older than me) and watch laser discs or write, wondering if I wasn't wasting my time with this film stuff. But I remember feeling like, in some weird way, I was paying my dues; like after this period of my life, I'd never be lonely again. I remember feeling everything would work out for the best if I could just buck up and deal with this eight-month film school stretch (of which I only made it halfway).

And all of it seemed like a lifetime ago as I drove Jen around, showing her where a Jen-less Kevin would dwell, wondering if he'd ever get to make a film. Thirteen years later, I was about to co-star in someone else's flick, having already made six of my own. If only I could go back and visit that lonely motherfucker to let him know how well it all works out…

We get back to the city and stop at Chapters (which is like a Borders), where we pick up a shitload of new books for Harley and a few for ourselves. We stop at 7-11 to grab some snacks and look for baby oil (for the massage), but it's a bust. We get back to the hotel, shuffle to our room, get into our woobs, and pop in *Poltergeist* (which holds up). I spend the rest of the night snacking out (back on the diet tomorrow) while reading all about *Poltergeist* (including the sad story of Dominique Dunne) on the 'net.

Post-'*geist*, we pop some *X-Files* back in, and fall asleep.

Monday 9 May 2005 @ 10:56 p.m.

I get up, take a leak in the shower, check the board while I dry, write Jen a note in soap on the mirror in the bathroom ("Love you, Jenny") then head out the door. Just then, the phone rings, pulling me back in, so as to get it before it wakes Jen. It's Blake, the driver. He's come to pick me up downstairs. I tell him I'm on my way down, and as I hang up, the Princess stirs. She hauls her cookies out of bed long enough to tell me she loves me, then jumps back under the covers.

Downstairs, I meet Blake and tell him I'd like to follow him to the studio in my Expedition, so I can learn the way. He obliges, and we're off. Twenty minutes later, we're at the studios. I park my car near the trailers and I'm led over to the wardrobe department, where Karen and Tish have me trying on a bunch of different outfits. Jenno pops by to give me a welcome hug, then moves on, presumably to more producerial duties.

I head to the vanities — the hair/makeup trailer. Forest puts the hairpiece on me and...

shudder

...cuts my mullet. Before she does so, I ask her to memorialize the dreaded 'do with a photo. Next, I meet Margaret who'll be doing my makeup for the show. Like every makeup person before her, she tells me I have good skin. And, as with every makeup person before her, I explain that it's the only physical blessing the Lord gave me, as I was seriously shortchanged everywhere else. Margaret chuckles as she puts my face on for the camera test.

Lori, the 3rd A.D., takes me to my trailer. It's hands-down the biggest trailer I've ever had — which normally I wouldn't care about, since I'm usually always on set anyway. But since I'm not directing this picture, I know I'm gonna be spending a lot of time in my trailer, so I'm delighted with the roominess of it. I've got a bedroom to crash in, a living room with a big TV and DVD player for when I'm bored, and a kitchen and dinette, for when I wanna entertain. I check out the bathroom (which is wide enough) and note the shower (which I'll never use, as trailer showers — like trailer sinks — are woefully low on the water pressure).

On my bed, my first costume is laid out for me. I throw it on and Lori leads me over to the stage, where they're putting me on film to check out a few of my costumes and see what my glasses and hairpiece look like. Sam's already done his test, as has Tim, so it's my turn. I say hi to Susanah and meet Dave, our 1st AD. He in turn introduces me to John, the Cinematographer (who tells me he knows Bob Yeoman, my DP from *Dogma*).

For the test, I'm required only to stand on a mark and be filmed. Susanah calls out the angles she wants me to stand at (left, right, 360 degrees) while the camera pushes in to a closeup, or pulls out to a head-to-toe. We cut, and it's suddenly lunchtime. I skip lunch and head back to my trailer.

In my trailer, I meet the doctor for my cast physical. There's a form I've gotta fill out that leads with 'Artist's Name'. I insist I'm not an artist, cross out 'Artist's' and write, instead, 'Guy's'. The doctor finds no humor in this and crosses out my 'Guy's' and writes 'Artist's' again. In spite of this, I pass.

I change into my second camera-test outfit and Lori tells me they're ready for me. I run into Susanah and we chit-chat en route to the stage. After this test, I change into a third outfit in the stage bathroom. They shoot that one as well, and then I'm done. I head over to Jenno and Susanah and jokingly remind them that actors need lots of reassurance. They jokingly respond that I stood in front of the camera well, and satisfied, I head off.

I hit the vanities where Forest removes my hairpiece and Margaret does the same with my makeup, finishing it off with a quick skin moisturizing, pampering me just enough to almost commit my entire life to this woman.

I head back to my trailer and put on my Kev clothes. I'm done for the day, so I head to my car. On the way, I run into Tim. We bullshit for a little bit, and he gives me a tongue-in-cheek tutorial on the art of acting with props. Garner bombs by and we say hi. Tim heads off to rehearsal with Susanah and Jen, and I run into Jenno again. We chit-chat a bit more before I head for the hotel via a route that Lori gave me which turns out to be more direct than the route I came this morning. Ironically enough, it also brings me right through my old circa '92 hood.

I call Jen to tell her I'm stopping at the Safeway on the way home, and ask her if she wants anything. I'm in the market for fat free mayo and Jen's looking for Diet Coke.

On the way up the flat escalator into the store, I hear a guy on the descending side say "Kevin?" I say hi, and he spins around, heading up the down people mover, meeting me at the top. He tells me he's been reading and enjoying the online diary, and asks how rehearsals are going. We say g'bye, and I grab the groceries and head back to the hotel.

I get to the door of our room, but my hands are so full (my backpack, the bag of groceries and the twenty-four pack of Diet Coke), that I can't get the key in my pocket. I kick at the door so Schwalbach'll let me in. She opens the door slightly, revealing a dark, candle-lit room. As she lets me in, I see that she's dressed only in my 'Schwalbach/Jen's Bitch' shooter. She takes the groceries out of my hand and throws me on the bed and we fuck like crazy, letting the dirty talk fly.

Afterwards, as we lay around in afterglow, lavishing one another with compliments and affection, I insist she greet me at the end of every workday in such a fashion. She chuckles in that way that says "Don't kid yourself about who wears the pants in this family, actor-boy…" We then throw our clothes on and head out to eat.

We jump in a cab and find ourselves engaged in that rarest of commodities in the married world: a date. We try this steakhouse on Seymour that Chay had told us about called Gotham. Since it's not even five yet, we pretty much have the place to ourselves. Our waitress is attentive enough without being up in our grills all night, leaving the wife and me ample time to make goo-goo eyes at one another over our meals.

Post-Gotham, we cab back to the hotel and grab the car. We drive around for a bit, check out Stanley Park (for when Harley gets to town on Friday), then head over to the London Drugs on Robson. I buy a hot water brewer (for iced tea) and Baby Oil (for the massage Schwalbach says I owe her, post-nookie).

We get back to the hotel and lapse into some *X-Files*. I get an email from Gail, telling me I've gotta print up a watermarked copy of *Clerks 2* for Harvey to take to Cannes. I put together a watermarked PDF of the script and email it to Gail, walking her through the printing process via iChat. I finish checking email and remember that I've gotta start pulling together a draft of the *Rats* script for Chappy (for the book), so I spend an hour doing that while Jen emails with Chay. I shut down the computer and cuddle with Super-Vixen a bit before falling asleep to the *Files*.

Tuesday 10 May 2005 @ 9:40 p.m.

I go to the studio and Forest puts in my fake hair. Margaret's not on today, so Angela does my makeup. We're joined by Chris Henrickson, Susanah's husband, who plays Garner's character's dead ex in photos seen throughout the flick. Chris offers me a belated thank you for hosting his website for the last five years, then off my bewildered expression, explains that it was a site Ming built back when he worked at Live Planet, called DreamYardLA. Turns out Chris is a former AFI kid who's chucked the movie-making thing for the truly noble work of helping gang-banger kids find another way to express themselves without guns, violence or crime. After fifteen minutes of talking about the project, I feel like a sell-out piece of shit.

Outside the vanities trailer, Jenno introduces me to Juliette Lewis, who I take an immediate shine to. We bullshit for a few minutes before I have to head to my trailer to get into one of my costumes. Once I'm clad as Sam, I jump in my truck and follow Dave the driver (who's driving Chris, Sam and Karen, our 2nd A.D.) over to Stanley Park. We're gonna take some pictures of our characters hanging out in the great outdoors for use in scenes throughout the flick. Garner's there as well, as she's featured in some of the pics with Chris. I meet her dog.

Post pics, 2nd A.D. Karen, PA Shelly, Sam and I sit around bullshitting as we wait for Forest, who's doing me the kindness of driving all the way out to the location to remove my hairpiece so I don't have to drive all the way back to the studio. Forest joins us, does her magic with the glue solvent, and then I'm following Sam and Dave to North Vancouver for a fly-fishing lesson.

On the ride, I call home to talk to Gail. Byron tells me she's gone to Hawaii. Sadly, her brother — affectionately known to Jen, Harley and I as Uncle Ted — drowned while snorkeling in Fiji. Gail's flown to Hawaii to break the news to her mother, who was visiting Ted in Hawaii before Ted left for Fiji, and is still there, unaware of her son's death. I try to call Jen to let her know, but she's out on the road, looking at houses for us to rent for the Vancouver stay.

One of the first thoughts that goes through my head upon learning of Ted's untimely death is that we will no longer be receiving mysterious clippings in the mail. A few years back, we started getting letters with clippings from *USA Today*. Sometimes, the clippings were whole articles — some about current events, some about me. Then, we'd get these random clippings of one or two sentences from a paragraph in an article not included. The clipping would say something like "Global warming has the southwest weather patterns trending toward humidity." That was it. There would be no letter explaining why the clipping was being sent; just a few sentences from an article we'd never get to read in its entirety. There was never a return address, so for months, Jen and I were perplexed as to who was responsible for the odd mailings. Then, one Christmas a few years back, while Ted and Jen's grandmother, Peg, were in town, Ted asked me: "Have you gotten my clippings?" to which I busted out with "THAT WAS YOU?!" He never did explain why the sampling of stuff he sent was so all over the place, or what rhyme or reason they had, other than being factoids he must have found interesting. But that was Ted. He'll be missed.

Sam and I grab some eats at a bar and grill and chit-chat for awhile. Right before our food arrives, I spot a guy I recognize heading toward the bathroom: *Dogma* DP Bob Yeoman. He joins us for a few minutes, and we play a bit of catch-up. He's in town shooting a flick called *The Martian Child* with John Cusack, so we exchange numbers for a later hookup.

After our lunch, Sam and I meet up with props-guy Brian at a place called Ruddick's — a fly-fishing shop. The lady who owns the joint is gonna be our instructor, and she takes us to a park a few blocks away from her store to practice. There's something calming about the process of casting and re-casting: just dialing in and hitting ten and two, over and over again. It's not for me, but I can see why some folks get into it. The world just melts away.

I drive Sam back to the hotel with me then head upstairs to my room. Jen's there already, and based on the phone to her ear and the shocked expression she's wearing, I realize she's heard about Ted. When she gets off the phone, we set aside the grieving process to concentrate on damage control: in an effort not to disrupt our search for a permanent place up in Vancouver, Gail's gone to Hawaii by herself to tell Peg and wrap up Ted's life, while Byron's stuck at our house with Harley. All three were supposed to be joining us in Vancouver on Friday, but this is not gonna happen now. Now, our primary concern is getting Byron out to Hawaii to help Gail with the Herculean task of getting Ted's body back from Fiji (when an American dies abroad apparently an autopsy is mandatory), getting him cremated, cleaning out Ted's apartment, etc. Jen immediately books herself on a morning flight back to LA, and books Byron on a flight out to Hawaii.

Meantime, Jen reveals that the apartment/house hunt has been fruitless. Nothing she's seen will fill our needs. So instead of looking further, we opt to do the run of the show in a hotel in town. We're currently at the Sutton Place Hotel, but if we're gonna stay in a hotel for two months and change, it'd better have a kitchen. And since the residence side of the Sutton Place is out of the question (de-pressing), I ring Smalls back home to have him call around and look for alternative hotels: some kind of two-bedroom suite affair in the city. I also have him print me up a pair of Mapquests that'll get me to and from the airport in the a.m.

With tensions and emotions running high and the sudden flurry of activity, Jen and I get into a spat. It's quickly put to bed, though, so we can concentrate on the tasks at hand. I call 2nd A.D. Karen to see if tomorrow's photo shoot can be moved by an hour so I can drop Jen at the airport, and she accommodates my request. Then, Jen and I head over to a different hotel to see if their two-bedroom suite will work for us.

We get to the hotel, and get the friendly, "We know who you are"-type greeting from the valet guys. Led by one of the bellmen, we head upstairs to check out a pair of two-bedroom suites, one of which is the penthouse with a deck affair. The décor is a little mid-to-late eighties, but we're kind of into it. We leave my number so the guy who books this kind of apartment can call me in the morning with some figures.

Following this, we head over to Gotham for some steak for me and veggies and wine for Jen. The waiter comes to our table and reflexively moves the glasses and silverware. I jokingly ask "What'd you do that for? We'd just gotten them where we wanted 'em." This is met with a dead-eyed expression which screams "Fuck you, asshole…" and the waiter starts moving the cutlery back where it was. I tell the guy I'm kidding, but he apparently finds no humor in my borderline tepid attempt at jocularity. It's pretty clear this dude is not as warm as the waitress we had the night before, so when he leaves, Jen and I spend five minutes trying to decide whether we should move to another table. Since I always pathologically tip a minimum of fifty percent, I'd rather give it to the chick from last night. But we opt to tough it out at Guy Smiley's station and discuss, instead, our plans for the airport run.

We get back to the hotel and climb into our woobs and bed, where we work on our laptops while half-watching more *Files*. I iChat with Mos, who informs me that he got into a car accident on the freeway driving Cookie's car. While it obviously wasn't fatal, it was bad enough to set the airbag off which has left a burn mark on his arm. The car's totaled, but Mos is generally okay, thank God.

Before we know it, Jen and I are falling asleep.

Wednesday 11 May 2005 @ 9:41 p.m.

Jen wakes me up around 7:15 a.m., and I hit the bathroom. She tells me through the door that we've gotta be in the car by eight, so I climb into the shower.

While I'm drying off, Jen's putting together a bag to take home. She's already packed the rest of her luggage, which is staying with me, in anticipation of the move. We figure, best case scenario, Jen'll come back to Vancouver with Harley on Sunday — providing I've moved us into more permanent digs.

We get on the road and since it's pretty much a straight shot over the Granville Bridge, we get to the airport with very little trouble. We kiss and my love leaves me, heading back home to care for our kid.

On the ride back, I return uber-lawyer John Sloss's call from the previous day, regarding some loose ends on the *Clerks 2* deal that need to be tied up. With more than enough time to get to the studio, I head to the hotel to grab my backpack and chicken salad mix. I give my Mom a quick call to tell her about Ted, then make a glass of iced tea. In the quiet of the room, the place seems so empty without Jen. Suddenly, I start feeling randy. Something about an empty hotel room is a turn-on to me; I assume it's because it harkens back to my youth, when an empty house meant I could bring girls over. So I bust out my nudie pics of the wife and tug one out before heading off to *Catch*-land.

On the way, I pop into a McDonald's drive-thru to get an iced tea. There, I discover that Canadian McD's are now offering a low-carb menu: three 'dishes' with less than six carbs apiece. I grab the chicken dish (a chicken breast with a slice of cheese and a piece of bacon) and scoff it down before I get to the studio.

I drop my shit off in my trailer and head right into hair and makeup. While Forest puts my hair in, it dawns on me that the makeup trailer is missing tunes (indeed, every makeup trailer I've ever been in on any show always has the music blasting). I offer to pick up one of those Bose iPod speakers, so that when I'm getting my hair and makeup done, I can roll with some Wu Tang, and when I'm gone, Forest can rock her iPod (once she replaces the broken one she's currently sporting). Angela does my makeup, and then I head to my trailer to throw on my outfit.

I follow Driver Dave (who's got Sam and Chris), and we head out past North Van, near Deep Cove. On the ride, I return uber-agent Phil Raskind's call, and we talk about the post-C2 flick a bit.

We get to the location: a stream, where Dennis (Sam Jaeger), Grady (Chris Henrickson), and Sam (me) are fishing. Like the previous day, this is all about taking pics for use in the movie, so we do some make-pretend fly-fishing and male bonding while the photographer snaps away. We change into different wardrobe and take some more pics — this time in the middle of the stream. I lose my balance and, like an asshole, nearly fall in completely. At this point, my waders are full of water.

Following the shoot, I head back to the honey wagon with two soakers, which Sandra and Elaine, the on-set wardrobe chicks, help me get out of. I grab some directions back into the city and I'm off, while Sam and Chris stick around for one more Sam-less shot.

Back in town, I stop by the Future Shop to grab that Bose speaker for the makeup trailer. I pop into my hotel room to grab my highlighted script pages, then I shoot over to the studio for rehearsal.

Since it's still lunch, I head to my trailer to change back into my Kevin clothes, make my chicken salad and watch some *Krush Groove*. I get the call from the guy at the new hotel, who gives me the rundown on the prices of the two different rooms Jen and I peeped last night. Both, it turns out, are right in our target range, so I tell the room booker I'll give him a shout after I talk it over with the wife.

A half hour later, 3rd A.D. Lori knocks on the door to tell me Forest is ready to remove my hairpiece. I grab the Bose speaker and my car-based iPod and head to the vanities trailer. Once inside, I unwrap and plug in the Bose, slide my iPod onto the connector pin, and bust with some Method Man while Forest literally pulls my (fake) hair out. Susanah drops in to tell me she's heading to the stage for rehearsal, so I grab a warm towel to wipe my makeup off and follow suit.

I head to stage G, where Susanah, Garner and Sam are locked out of the rehearsal space. Garner and I talk about *Alias* for a few minutes until someone from the studio arrives to let us in. We're joined by the script supervisor this time, and we go over some scenes that Sam and I had done the other day, and some we haven't done at all yet.

Most of the scenes we're rehearsing are Gray (Garner) and Dennis (Sam) scenes, so I sit beside Susanah, watching the performances. We're joined by Tim and Juliette, but since Sam and Garner are in the middle of a pretty crucial scene, the three of us head outside, where we sit around chit-chatting until we're called back in to rehearse as a group.

Rehearsal ends, and Susanah tells us we're probably not gonna do the scheduled table reading of the script tomorrow, as she's got a ton of prep to do for our Friday start.

As we head back to the base camp, Sam and I are trailing the varsity team of Garner, Tim and Juliette, when Juliette hangs back and starts walking and talking with us. I gush about her for a bit, then point out that the inflection of her normal speaking voice never really imparts whether or not she's enthusiastic about a subject. She says she gets that a lot, then says g'bye and heads for her trailer. I offer Sam a ride back to the hotel, then jump into my trailer to grab my shit.

We get back to the hotel, and I invite Sam to some Gotham steaks. We head up to my room, drop off my backpack, and jump back in the car. A block from the hotel, I realize I've forgotten to bring some Splenda (my preferred iced tea sweetener), so Sam volunteers to run into Starbucks and grab some.

We get to Gotham and order up some filets, chit-chat about the show and acting in general, and people-watch the crank-addicts outside. Tonight, the waiter is top notch, as are the steaks.

Afterwards, we head over to the new place Sam has moved into (it turns out nobody digs on the residence side of the Sutton Place). He grabs his keys and fills out his paperwork downstairs, and then we head up to see his apartment (great view, though it'd be a little tight for me, Jen, Harley, Byron and Gail). I tell him to call me tomorrow if he gets bored, and I head downstairs.

On the way to the car, I notice there are messages from Jen on my phone. I give her a shout, and fill her in on my day. We talk about the suites at the new hotel and both agree that the penthouse with the deck is the way to go. I tell her the table-read has been called off and that I don't start shooting 'til Monday, so Jen suggests I move into the new hotel in the morning, then catch an afternoon flight home for the weekend. She's chilling with Chay, so we jump off the phone, with me telling her to jump onto iChat later on.

I was given a new one-line schedule (the overview of the entire show that breaks down what's being shot and on what day), so I spend most of the night fixing the dates in my iCal while the *X-Files* plays in the background. By the time I'm done switching stuff around, I'm feeling sleepy. I switch from iCal over to my nudie pics of Jen, tug one out, clean up, and fall asleep.

Thursday 12 May 2005 @ 9:42 p.m.

I get up around 7:30 a.m., take a leak and shit while I do a quick email check and respond to some Jen-mail she wrote me after I fell asleep last night.

Today marks the official one-year mark since I quit smoking. On the up side, my lungs must have cleared out (though not entirely, as Schwalbach still smokes like a chimney). On the down side, I've gained thirty pounds over the last year. I contemplate celebrating by smoking a cigarette when it hits me that I've fallen way behind on my online diary. So I start a Word document full of brief descriptions of everything that's been going on over the course of the last week, just to keep the days fresh in my memory.

My iChat's open, and I suddenly see Jen pop up. We chat back and forth about my potential homecoming and soon we're moving into the dirty-chattin'. We're gonna move it to phone sex, but Harley starts waking up, so Jen has to jump off. I crack open the Jen pics and start jerking off when the phone rings. I have a feeling it's Jen, whose stolen away from the kid to talk dirty and rub one out with me, and my feeling turns out to be only partially right: it's Jen… but she's putting Harley on the phone to say good morning — instant momentary mood killer. I put my dick away and tell the kid I'm coming home and that I love her. Jen gets back on the phone and tells me to go back to what I was doing, but save a drop or two for her. Since I always do what the lady tells me, I go back to jerking off.

Afterwards, I clean up and call the new hotel, to see if I can move my stuff over today instead of the Saturday move I'd originally asked about. While I'm waiting for them to get back to me with a response, I call the *Catch* office and see about grabbing a flight home for the weekend. I get yes on both, so I pack the rest of my stuff in the room and ring for the bellman. The guy has to make two trips, but we get it all downstairs and into the Expedition. I check out of the Sutton and head to the new digs.

I check in and head upstairs, joined shortly thereafter by the bellmen with the two carts full of my crap. The place is nice: roomy and lots of great views. The tech dude comes up and hooks up an air-port to our Ethernet, so we're all set, cyber-wise. I unpack a few things, throw my laundry in a bag to take back to LA with me, call Chay about picking me up at the airport ('cause Jen's taking Harley to a t-shirt party at school), and head out to the airport.

I park the car and head to my Air Canada gate. I'm flagged for inspection, so I go through two security pat-downs before winding up in front of a Customs agent who's a fan and wants to visit the set (he'd previously visited Garner's *Elektra* set). We exchange numbers, and I race to my gate to catch my flight.

I doze through most of the flight, listening to some Ol' Dirty Bastard. I wake only to have some airplane chicken, and then fall back asleep, thinking about how much I want to fuck Schwalbach when I get home.

I get off the plane and call Chay to let her know I've arrived. Chay says Jen's coming herself, so I call Jen and give her my whereabouts. She finds me, we kiss, and she launches into the harrowing tale of trying to get Harley's ears pierced earlier that day.

On the ride home, I call Shannon McIntosh at Miramax Home Video to see how my footage for the Cannes reel went over and to talk about the possible *Sin City* signing at the Stash with Robert Rodriguez and Frank Miller when the flick hits DVD in August. Shannon's two weeks from delivering her second kid, so Jen tells me to find out where she's registered before getting off the phone.

We stop at Baja Fresh for some grub for Harley. I hit the bathroom while Jen heads next door to Coffee Bean & Tea Leaf. When I get out of the bathroom, I'm waiting at the pickup end of the counter, when someone says "Kevin?" I look at the woman talking to me, and she kinda looks familiar. I immediately start trying to place the face, and I'm in the middle of the thought "I think she was crew on one of your flicks..." when she does me the kindness of putting the mystery to rest by introducing herself as Carol Leifer. This is a woman I've watched on TV for years: from the mid eighties, when standup became all the rage on cable, to the present, whenever she pops up in a *Seinfeld* (indeed, the Elaine character is based on her). She tells me she's been seeing me on the *Tonight Show* a lot, and we talk about *Roadside Attractions*. I ask her if she knows anybody over there, and she says "Well, Jay..." to which I'm like "Duh — yeah." She tells me she's heard from Garlin that our gig at the Improv Olympic last week went well, and I explain how the gig works and urge her to do it. Then, she's off... and I'm left with this warm feeling. This was a woman whose work I've quietly dug for years, as I was (and remain) a huge standup whore — and she started a conversation with little ol' nobody me. It was a really nice moment, actually.

Since I'd packed all my Splenda and brought it up to Vancouver, we stop at 7-11 on Sunset to see if they've got any. On the way out, the two panhandlers out front are like "Mr. Smith. You're making a movie with that girl, right? Is she pregnant or what?" I think this is pretty funny: I rarely ever stop at this 7-11 (I usually rock the La Brea and Sunset Sev), but two times out of the three times I have, these older, black Jay and Silent Bobs always seem to have their fingers on the pulse of what's going on in the movie biz. The first time they talked to me about my flicks, I was flabbergasted — as neither of them look like they've got enough scratch for an apartment, a TV, or a DVD player (plus, they're older black guys — historically not a big part of my demographic). Last time I saw them, they had a convo with me about *Jersey Girl* and Jennifer Lopez. This time, it's Garner. Either they're subscribers to The Affleck Journal, or they read a lot of *US Weekly*. I give 'em a buck and head off, as they wave at Jen in the passenger seat and call out, in flirty voices, "Bye, Mrs. Smith!" Ah, Los Angeles...

We get home and I get a huge greeting from the kid, who's in her room, playing with Reyna. I tell her to come upstairs when she's done, dump my laundry in the washing machine, and head upstairs to the bedroom. I get into woobs and climb the stairs to the kitchen to make some iced tea. On the deck, I see Chay checking her sidekick. She joins me in the kitchen and we talk about life in Vancouver before she heads out and I head to the room, where I get on the bed, slip back into my M.O. of watching TiVo'ed *Simpsons* while checking email and the board.

Harley joins me, and we lay on the bed talking about her day, the upcoming Vancouver trip, and our new home at the top of the hotel that's "like a little house in a hotel room" (her words, not mine). We haven't told her why Nan and Pop went to Hawaii yet, so she's wondering why the stability of her family unit (of which she's usually the center of attention) has been so disrupted, and is looking forward to getting to Vancouver and back to some sense of normalcy.

Harley's good at adapting, man. In her brief nearly-six years, we've lived in many different houses/hotels/apartments, and she's never really bitched. The kid takes well to each new place, which is a blessing, considering she could make life really miserable for us by objecting to any of the possible moves we make, forced on us by my job. Chay once uttered a phrase which quickly became the Smith Family Mantra: "Home is where the hotel is." It's kind of appropriate in this nomadic business of show.

I read Harley a *Junie B.* book while Jen deals with an issue at Harley's school involving a boy who pantsed her in gymnastics. When Jen's done, we kiss Harley g'night and head upstairs, allowing her to fall asleep in our bed.

In the living room, we crack open season seven of *The X-Files* and check email on our respective laptops. I start doing some more catch-up work on my diary with my iChat open. Then, from the other couch, Jenny IMs me, and we start a sweet convo that turns naughty, ultimately ending up with us fucking on the couch (something we rarely do, as most of our fucking is done in our bed).

We're laying around, engaged in some post-coitus chit-chat when we decide to get dressed. Good thing, as we hear the front entry alert telling us Jay's home. He joins us upstairs, and the three of us sit around the living room bullshitting about Vancouver and a Skywalker trip Mewes is taking tomorrow, as well as marital fidelity and whether or not girls can be trusted. Then, Mewes heads off to his friend's to play some video games, and Jen and I head downstairs. We bicker about what to do with Louis (the dreaded pup who eats everything, that Byron's left in our care), then cuddle up to some *Simpsons* and fall asleep.

Friday 13 May 2005 @ 4:08 p.m.

Harley tries to wake us up at 7:05 a.m., and succeeds in prying Jen out of bed. I sleep in a little while longer until Quinnster takes another run at me, insisting I take her to school.

I load the kid into the car and drive her to school, rocking out to the Ol' Dirty Bastard remix of Mariah Carey's 'Fantasy' (which the kid digs). I kiss Harley g'bye and drop her off, then head back toward the house. En route, I call Jen and ask her if she fancies a spot of breakfast at the Griddle. She meets me at the front door, jumps in the car, and we're off.

We stop for gas, then park in front of the Griddle, where we grab an outdoor table, order, and read our respective mags (*Newsweek* for Jen, *Daily Variety* for me). When the food comes, we chit-chat and flirt and try to figure out our day.

We head home, get back into our woobs, and I head downstairs to do some more laundry. I get back upstairs and Jen tells me to grab the *Files* DVDs from the living room, where we left them last night. I head downstairs to collect the laundry I did last night, then drop them off to Jen, offering that I'll go get the *Files* DVDs if she'll fold my clothes. The deal brokered, I head upstairs and find the dogs staring at me from the deck, forlorn. I join them outside and jump into the pool, throwing the ball for Mulder. Louis ventures close to the edge and I grab her and bring her in. She still doesn't have her sea legs, though, so she splashes about wildly, looking for an exit. I lead her to the stairs, where she dashes out and gets as far away from the pool as possible. Scully comes in and does a lap, and then I continue playing with Mulder for a bit until I decide to head inside. I grab the *Files* DVDs and go back to the room, where I take a shower and then climb onto the bed to update the diary.

Again, Schwalbach IMs me, and we start flirting. She joins me on the bed, dropping her gear and presenting me with massage oil. I give her a halfhearted rubdown, because with all her clothes off, I'm only thinking about being inside her now.

That's when the dirty talk kicks in.

She pulls me on top of her, and in an insanely rare show of initiative, I'm on top. Her cumming makes me cum, and since I'm still hard, she rolls me off of her so she can climb on top of me and cum again.

I have no illusions about myself as a master lover. I know I don't make Schwalbach cum; Schwalbach makes Schwalbach cum. She's easily the most orgasmic chick I've ever met, which makes my job a hundred times less tricky than it could be (or has been with some far less orgasmic girls I've been with). I love to fuck Jen, sure — but I'd be lying if I said I didn't dig the fact that it doesn't take much to get her off.

We cuddle up, spent, before heading back to our laptops. A half hour later, Jen announces that Trish and Chay are coming over after their lunch. It's decided that I'll pick Harley up and hang out with her while Jen chills with her friends.

Jen gets an email from the school, in which we learn Harley's been sort of naughty. When I pick Quinnster up from school, I confront her about the naughtiness in question. At first, she denies it, then blames it on another classmate. Finally, she admits to collusion. When we get to the house, Jen sits Harley down and gives her a stern talking-to. I add fuel to the fire when I share that Harley initially fibbed in the car, before ultimately copping to the indiscretion. Mom and Dad make with the angry disappointment and the stern punishment (no ear piercing today, and no TV), and the kid makes with the tears. We tell her that, even when she's naughty, we still love her — but won't tolerate a bad kid. Trish and Chay show up and Jen heads upstairs. I take Harley to her room so she can put on her pjs, and then we head back to my room, where we both lay on the bed — Harley coloring, and me updating the blog.

Two hours later, Quinnster's feeling hungry. We head upstairs to say hi to Trish and Chay and forage for some grub. Before I hit the deck, I can hear the blender going, which means it's gonna be a Margarita kinda night for the ladies — one that'll last well into the night, which is fine. What is not fine (or rather, what is fine, but in a way that I'm not supposed to acknowledge) is that, when I get out on the deck, I find Trish and Chay lounging poolside in their bikinis. Not good. Not bad, mind you (they're attractive ladies, to be sure, and both fill out bikinis well), but in the world I dwell, I don't really go to the beach or anything, so I rarely ever see any chicks that scantily clad, live and in person, outside of

Schwalbach. And what's worse is that these aren't random beach bunnies; these are chicks I know. Peeping little Chay-Chay Cartier and Trish the Dish frolicking in the nearly-altogether is enough to unnerve me and make me feel like a perve, so all sorts of embarrassed and shy, I excuse myself. Jen says Harley can stay with them and go swimming with the girls, and while Harley puts on her bathing suit, Schwalbach follows me into the house to poke fun at me for a few minutes for feeling weird around the bathing beauties.

I order some pizzas for the girls, wondering if I'm gonna succumb to the temptation of sucking down some slices myself, thus derailing my diet program. Instead, I heat up a low-carb pizza and brew a pot of decaffeinated iced tea.

Sometimes, the weight thing's a real struggle. I've found that I can be pretty good all week, but on the weekend, I usually derail and suck down garbage food or high-carb favorites (bread, mashed potatoes, various sugars). It looks like I'm heading that way today as well, until the pizza shows up and I hand it over to the girls. At this point, Chay's doing backward falls into the pool for Harley's amusement, and now the nearly-nude soaking wet Chay Carter is just a little much for my comfort level, so I excuse myself and head downstairs to continue updating my online diary, abandoning the pizzas to the girls. Somehow, my diet is saved by a pair of bikinis.

After a few hours, Harley re-joins me in the room. I ask her if she wants to go pick up new DVDs and grab some ice cream, and she's all into the idea. We get her dressed, then head upstairs to say g'bye to the ladies, who're now joined by Trish's friend Michelle (mercifully dressed more modestly). Chay snaps some pictures of Harley and I, I kiss Jen, and Harley and I head off into the Los Angeles night.

First stop is Laser Blazer, where I pick up this week's titles (and some of next week's too), and talk to Ivan about his script. After that, we skip over to Baskin Robbins on Westwood, where Quinnster indulges in some strawberry ice cream. We shoot up Westwood and stop at the Stash, which has just closed. I ring the store, and Albert's still in the back, closing. He let's me in and I sign some stuff, pick up some comics, chit-chat with Albert, and head off again. On the way home, Quinnster and I rock out to Mariah Carey's 'Fantasy' (really she rocks to Mariah, I rock to the ODB rhymes layered throughout the tune).

We get home and the girl party has dwindled down to just two chicks: Jen and Chay, who're sitting in the living room, toasted, oblivious to the fact that the dreaded Louis has eaten an entire pizza, shredded the box, and taken a shit in the dining room, despite the fact that the deck doors have been open all night. I bark a bit about the state of the room and insist I'm not cleaning it up. Even

Harley jumps on Jen and Chay's cases a bit. Chay invites Harley to sleep with her in Mewes's room (Mewes has jetted off to some *Sith* event in Modesto for the night), and Schwalbach invites me to sleep with her in our bed. I tell her I'll be down in a few minutes, as I just wanna sit up in the kitchen and finish updating the previous week's entries in the online diary.

But what I really wanna do is be alone so I can finally break my fast. It's been a year, which was all the time I'd planned for. I never said I was quitting for life; I just wanted to see if I could go twelve months without one, and I did it. The goal was achieved. The mission was accomplished.

But now it's time to smoke.

For the first time in over 365 days, I blaze up a Marlboro Menthol Ultra Light. I'd forgotten how good that first smoke can be. It immediately takes me back to Quick Stop, where I started my smoking career in earnest, back in '93. The ol' first smoke buzz returns — the one you spend the rest of your smoking days chasin' before you realize it'll never return, and all you have to show for all that smoking is lungs full of brown shit that you cough up every morning, shortness of breath, and a dipping of the libido (indeed, two weeks after I quit smoking, I was like a rabbit with Schwalbach; a rabbit that liked to fuck even more than the normal rabbit). As the heart specialist told me a year ago: smoking is about the worst thing you can do to the body. It taxes every major organ: brain, lungs, heart. It's a slow death sentence for the indignantly stupid.

But none of this fazes me at the moment, as I'm enjoying this cigarette. Following that first smoke, I enjoy the next three, while I update my week-old diary (the one that'd been long-stopped at Mewes's car-leasing fiasco). Suddenly, I'm smoking while writing again — one of my favorite pastimes. Not wanting to do too much of a good thing, I head downstairs, a bit lightheaded, climb into bed beside the sleeping Schwalbach, and fall asleep to some TiVo.

Saturday 14 May 2005 @ 2:56 p.m.

Harley gets me up. We let the dogs out, and decide to do some breakfast at Jerry's followed by an ear-piercing chaser. I get Quinnster dressed, then somehow manage to dress myself. We're about to leave when Genvieve Case calls. Apparently, Jen spoke to her at one point yesterday about a possible barbecue and she's wondering what time that might be. I tell her that, since it was such a late night for Jen and Co., it was doubtful we were gonna be having a barbecue today.

Harley and I head to Jerry's. En route, I decide that the recently-arrived Cases deserve some sort of welcome, so I call the Xtian Clan back and invite them to breakfast at Jerry's. I ask Christian if he knows where the joint is. He asks if I mean the one in Westwood, near where Team Case is temporarily housed. I say I'm more down with doing the Jerry's on Beverly, as the Claire's Harley wants to get her ears pierced at is right across the street, in the Beverly Center. I ask him if he'd like to meet us at that Jerry's or have me pick them up. Xtian opts for the latter. I tell him I'll be there in ten minutes, hanging up while thinking "Who am I, Morgan Freeman? Guy can't drive two miles to meet me instead of making me trek all the way to Westwood. Pampered fuck..."

I arrive in front of Team Case's temp housing with Harley all abuzz about see-ing Gabrielle. The family hauls their cookies into Jen's Range Rover (which I'm forced to drive, since my beloved Expedition — the Hate Tank — is up in Vancouver). While driving to Jerry's, I ask how the cross-country drive was. That's when it's made clear that the Cases didn't drive cross-country, they flew. So they're car-less at the moment: hence the request for pickup. Ah — not such pampered fucks after all.

We opt for the closer Jerry's, since going to the one on Beverly would mean a drive back to Westwood for me, and I'm all about the Daddy/Daughter Piercing Date immediately after brekkie.

The adults eat and chit-chat, while the kids throw stuffed animals around and order double helpings of their sides. When we're done, we drop the Cases off and head for the Beverly Center — Quinnster all atwitter with excitement about the impending ears piercing.

We park and head into the mall. Upstairs, the Claire's earrings emporium is situated right beside the Hello Kitty store — so that little girls can graduate to 'tweens in ten easy steps, from one door to the other.

Having grown up a dude, I've never spent much time in the 'tween stores. It's weird: they're peddling sex at such a young age. All the merchandise is cheap and kinda garish (like most sex), and it's branded by pseudo-celebs like Ashlee Simpson. The one thing I saw that I identified with was a small basket of pins on the counter. There were only three available, and they sported acceptable rebel-lion mantras like "I may be different, but you're ugly!" It took me right back to early high school, when I was a pin guy. Every weekend, I'd head to the mall to stock up on the latest pins at Spencer's, so that I could load up with a bunch of images and catch-phrases that I felt helped me express my individuality: every-thing from Bullwinkle pins, to pins that sported that most clever of witticisms, 'Who Farted?' It'd be a while before I realized that individuality can't be expressed by wearing something bought at a mall that thousands of other kids the world over were also brandishing to express their individuality, and that self-expression can't be purchased at a piercing pagoda. Still, even knowing what I now know, I had to resist the temptation to buy the snarky pin. Old habits die hard.

I let Harley go nuts, picking out a bunch of the cheap earrings, as the sales lady assured me they were all buy one/get one free. After about twenty minutes of pure, unadulterated consumerism, with Quinnster picking out dolphin earrings, guitar earrings, Royal Flush earrings (because Mom and Dad play cards), monkey face earrings, puppy earrings and the like, we finally approach the dreaded piercing chair.

This is when I detect a slight shift in Harley's once-joyous pre-piercing demeanor, and I get my first whiff that something might be amiss.

The sales chick comes to make with the piercing gun, and Harley's suddenly all a million questions: "Does it hurt? What's it feel like? What's that thing you're holding? Will I feel it?" Picking up on the apprehension, I decide that we should probably pay for the earrings we've picked out and the piercing charge in advance, before they actually make with the piercing, because I know my daughter's insanely low threshold for pain means that she's gonna be fit to be tied after they puncture her lobes on both sides. We pay, but I'm too fixated on Quinnster's mood to notice the total. We head back to the chair, where two piercing technicians are standing by, loading up the disposable piercing guns with Harley's chosen earrings: two purple-pinkish amethyst stones. They dot her ears with marker to make sure the whole affair's gonna be symmetrical. Harley's holding my hands tightly, getting more and more worried. Then, as the earrings are on approach, she starts in with the stalling. "Wait, wait — just a minute. Is it gonna hurt? What's it feel like? What're those things? Will I feel this?" This goes on for ten minutes, until I say, "You don't have to do this, kid," to which she replies "But I want to. I'm just scared." We talk about it for five more minutes, and then I'm like "If we're not gonna do it, that's okay. But we can't sit here all day. We're holding up these ladies and anyone else who wants to get pierced." Panicky, Harley elects to walk away.

Two steps out of Claire's, the Mighty Quinnster's all tears and agony. "I'm a failure…." she's wailing. "I can't do anything." I keep telling her it's cool, and that she almost did it, and that's brave enough for now. Next time, she'll totally do it.

We walk through the puzzle store, and she's still moaning about being afraid to go through with the piercing. We sit down outside the coffee joint and talk about it some more. I pull out one of the many earrings sets we bought and show her an admittedly tamer version of what she's in for by pressing the peg against the back of her hand, ever so lightly. "That's it. That's all it feels like," I lie. Based on that, she's ready to give it another try. As I put the earrings back in the bag, I notice the total on the receipt: $160.00! I nearly pass out. $160.00 for crappy, cheap-ass, I-could've-made-better earrings?!? Whoever Claire is, with all the loot she's pulling in from the legions of not-a-girl-not-yet-a-womans that people these joints, I wouldn't be surprised if she was snorting thousand dollar bumps of blow through hundred dollar bills, off the tight stomach of a high-priced male escort in Monte Carlo.

We head back to Claire's with a renewed vigor. Harley gets in the chair once again, the guns get loaded... and a familiar refrain fills the air: "Is it gonna hurt? What's it feel like? Am I gonna feel it? What if it hurts?"

Five minutes later, we're on our way back out of the store, the kid drenched in shameful tears. I keep telling her it's cool — that there's always tomorrow. The kid's coming at me like Apollo Creed with "There is no tomorrow!" She's apologizing to me, telling me she's sorry she wasted my time. I'm like "You don't have to be sorry. I don't care if you get pierced or not. In fact, I don't even want you to do it. Your Mom wanted to get your ears pierced when you were a baby, and I said we shouldn't do it, and that we should let you decide for yourself one day if you wanted holes in your head. And it's not a waste of my time, so long as we're hanging out together." But she's not buying it. She also lays into me for cock-blocking the infant piercing Jen was in support of, as that means we wouldn't be going through this shit now.

Looking for relief, I notice the *Sith* trailer playing on a flat screen in the Bose store, so I pull her toward it. We go inside and take seats in a pair of leather chairs they've set up in front of the flat screen display. As we watch it, again and again, Harley regains her composure. The sales guy keeps eyeballing us, and I feel bad that we're just sitting there. To assuage this guilt, I buy another Bose Sound Dock for my iPod (my third), since the one I usually have at home is up in Vancouver.

On the way to the parking lot, we pass a custard stand that sells low-carb custard. I get one for me, and Harley gets a regular ol' high-carb Strawberry custard. This seems to dull the kid's piercing-inspired self-loathing to non-existence, and soon, all is right with the world again. Fuck what the experts say: food cures all.

We head home and I swap the kid for the wife and the dogs: Harley goes to play with Kevin and Hans while Jen and I take our motley muttley crew over to the puppy camp in the Valley. On the way, I recount the entire sad tale of earring-less woe for Jen, who's like "been there, done that".

We drop the dogs off and while driving toward the freeway, I reveal that I smoked the night before. This delights Schwalbach no end, as she's a big fan of the taboo. She wants all the gossipy details, of which there are very few. Suddenly, there's a scent of sex in the air.

Jen and I stop for smokes, and I call Mos to tell him we're not gonna barbecue tonight, though I would still like to see him and Cookie before Jen and I head back to Vancouver. We decide to kill two birds with one stone by grabbing some early dinner at The Ivy.

The whole ride home, I'm smoking with Jen, and — mystifyingly, she's getting more and more turned on, insisting that the smoking version of me takes her back to when we first met. She recalls her initial fascination with my hands from that era, and how they looked when they held cigarettes. She announces that she's gotta fuck me when we get back to the house, so naturally, I lay on the gas pedal.

We get back to the house and let Chay in on the Ivy dinner plans, inviting her along. She heads home to get changed, telling us she'll meet us there. No sooner is the door closed than Schwalbach starts drawing the curtains. Two minutes later, we're engaged in some of the hottest, delicious afternoon sex we've had in a while (and, mind you, this is coming after a hot streak all week, too).

Post-coitus, I take a shower and get dressed. Mos and Cookie arrive just as we're heading downstairs, and the four of us head over to Robertson. Chay shows up as well, and our quintet digs into another exquisite Ivy meal.

After dinner, the five of us head back to the house. We send Harley to the Cheesecake Factory with Reyna, Kevin and Hans to celebrate Hans's sixteenth birthday, and then Jen ices some beers, pours some wine for the girls, and cranks the iPod in the Bose so we can settle into a nice game of poker.

While up most of the evening, by night's end, I've lost my initial twenty-buck buy-in. Mosier breaks even. Chay's in the hole, and Cookie and Jen are the big winners. Harley comes home in tears because the Cheesecake Factory was a bust (Saturday night, too crowded, no tables). We make with the goodbye hugs for Mos and Cookie, and by eleven thirty, everyone but Chay's gone. Chay's gonna stay downstairs in Jay's room, because Jay's driving her to the airport in the a.m. Harley sacks out on our couch, and Jen and I cuddle up to some *Simpsons*, to which we fall asleep.

Sunday 15 May 2005 @ 2:56 p.m.

We all sleep in 'til about nine. When I get up, Chay's already gone. Jay comes back from dropping her off, and the four of us (me, Jen, Jay and Quinnster) head over to the Griddle for some goodbye breakfast. Afterwards, Jen and Harley grab some Coffee Bean while Mewes and I chill in the car, chit-chatting.

We get back to the house and Mewes puts Jen's Range Rover into the garage while the three of us start packing. For me, this means loading up on a few more DVDs to bring back with my washed laundry. Fully packed, I take a shower, get dressed, and then sack out in front of the TV, while the anxious Schwalbach barks at me about leaving two hours before our flight. I pull Chay's Escalada around the front of the house and Mewes helps me throw the bags in the back. While I'm driving, the two kids (Mewes and Harley) fall asleep on the traffic-y trip to LAX.

We check in, head to our gate, and kick back while we wait for our delayed flight to board. Jen heads to the outside smoking area and Quinnster and I situ-ate the various Harley games and DVDs for the flight. We board and soon after, we're airborne, with Jen and Harley sitting in the two seats in front of me. I read a bunch of old issues of *Variety* and *USA Today* that had gathered at the house in my absence, and Harley either rocks the Nintendo DS or plays *SpongeBob* Uno with Jen during the two-and-a-half-hour flight.

We land in Vancouver and clear Customs. I have to get my working visa, which takes another twenty minutes. Then, I pick up the keys to my car at the valet desk, and we're off into the rainy Vancouver night.

We get to the hotel and up to the room. Harley rushes around, checking everything out. Jen immediately starts unpacking, so as to make the hotel a home, and I start adjusting my schedule, based on the new one-line and lat-est draft of the script. Each of us is buried deeply in our activities until we decide to do some room service. We sit down and eat as a family, and then it's time for Quinnster to go to bed. Jen lets Harley fall asleep to *Robots*, and we retire to our room to watch *Constantine*. Jen checks out of the flick early, leav-ing me to grumble to myself about the volume governor on the TV. I'm only half-engaged in the flick as I go through email on the laptop. I call down to the concierge about getting some DVD players brought up, but they tell me the tech department's closed, and the guy will have to take care of it in the a.m. Jen comes back to the room five minutes before the flick ends, looking to go to sleep. When the credits roll, we search for something... anything... to fall asleep to. Ultimately, we find a *Cheers* on one of the stations, to which we both konk out.

Monday 16 May 2005 @ 9:43 p.m.

I wake up around nine-ish, quietly vacate the room so Jen doesn't wake up, then take a dump while checking email.

The call sheet slipped under my door alerts me that I'm not due to set 'til 2 p.m. Harley gets up and I continué checking email while she watches some tube. In the kitchen, I answer a call from the tech guy who informs me that the price for DVD-player rental in the hotel is fifty bucks a day. Over the course of two months, this would be ridiculous. I ask him if I can bring my own TVs in, and he says sure.

Jen shuffles into the kitchen looking for non-existent coffee, and I tell her about the DVD sitch. We agree that we'll pick up some TV/DVD player combos and shit-can the hotel TVs (with their volume governors) altogether. I say let's get a move on, because before we know it, it'll be two o'clock and time for me to get to set.

I shower while Jen and Harley get dressed. We call down for the car and head over to Robson, on a mission to find some tumblers, plates, a shower caddy, and various other housewares. But before that, we stop at Starbucks for Jen.

It's drizzling, so I don't want to leave the car at Starbucks and walk the one block to London Drugs. We park in the underground parking lot and head upstairs, where we load up on sundry things, none of which are tumblers or plates (though Jen does score a shower caddy).

We swing back by the hotel and have the doormen unload our bags of booty while I get directions to the nearest Safeway. We drive the three minutes to Safeway, park, and head inside.

This is where we're confronted with the shopping cart conundrum. Any food store I've ever been in offers complimentary shopping carts to their customers. Here in Vancouver, shopping carts have to be rented. You stick a Loony (the popular dollar coin) into the cart handle, which unlocks it. When you're done, you return the cart to the rack, insert a key, and get your buck back. I guess it makes sense, but essentially what's being said is "for a buck, you can own this shopping cart".

Another thing that throws me for a loop is the paucity of product in Canadian food stores. In the States, we have copious choices for every item: you want to choose from thirty different kinds of peanut butter, you get your ass to America. You want to decide between, say, three? Oh, Canada. The former may be part of the reason our nation has such a problem with rampant obesity. The latter is enough to keep this anti-Bush-er from taking up residence in the Great White

North. I dig the socialized medicine and the crime statistics (550 murders in '04 — nationwide), but when I hit the food store, I need variety, bitch.

We're ten minutes into food shopping when I get the call from 2nd A.D. Karen, who informs me that they're pulling me in an hour earlier, as they're ahead of schedule with the first scene. Jen, Harley and I make a mad dash through the grocery store, check out, then head back to the hotel. We head upstairs, I grab my backpack, kiss the girls g'bye, and I'm off.

Even though I've got a directions map, Dave the Driver is downstairs, waiting for me. I tell him I'll follow him over, and we cross one of the city's many bridges to our location for the day, out past Kitsilano.

I get into my trailer and discover a big 'Welcome Aboard' basket filled with stuff reminiscent of the flick (lots of fishing gear, tea bags, kiddie tea sets, etc.) accompanied by a sweet note from Susanah. Beside that start gift is the studio start gift from Amy, Matt and Ange: a leather bag full of more *Catch* kinds of stuff and a Sony digital camera.

In the bedroom part of my trailer, Elaine (the trailer-based costumer) has laid out Sam's outfit for the day: a tie-dye Celestial Seasonings shirt over a long sleeve shirt, shorts, and sandals over socks. Adorably, Elaine has also labeled every piece of clothing with tags identifying each item ("these are your socks"), including a pair of non-costume slickers beside the bed that are marked "for comfort, if it rains".

I head to the vanities and Forest puts my hair on while I rock the iPod in the Bose. Lunch is called, so we opt to do the prosthetic and the makeup afterwards.

I chill in my trailer 'til after lunch, when Lori sends me back to Forest, who affixes my prosthetic. Because we're not sure if it's where Susanah wants it, Forest and I take a van to the set five blocks away to clear it with her. We're suddenly in a fictional Green Party candidate's campaign headquarters, where I spot Herr Director in the midst of making decisions between shots. I give Susanah a hug and let her gauge the prosthetic. She gives her notes, and Forest and I head back to the makeup trailer. Forest does touch-ups and turns me over to Margaret, who expertly does my makeup.

I head outside to grab a smoke, then head back into my trailer and rehearse my lines into the mirror a dozen times. I head back outside to discover a relative ghost town: everyone else is up at the set, shooting, so I'm kind of alone back at base camp.

It's a weird adjustment to make, not being in the thick of it all. There's no Mos, no Mewes, or no Affleck, and I'm not on set, surrounded by a full crew asking millions of questions. The more I think about it, I'm pretty lonely. I call Jen, who's assuaging my fears, when Lori the 3rd A.D. knocks on my trailer door, telling me it's time to head to set.

The set for my scene is across the street from the Green Party candidate's set. I arrive in time for the blocking rehearsal, with the vanities in tow. Shelly greets our van and leads me into the fake Celestial Seasonings office at which my fake character fake works.

The first set-up is pretty easy, with me having to enter my office, drop a bunch of folders on my desk, throw myself in my chair, look bored, and deliver only one line of dialogue. We rehearse it, getting the blocking down, and the crew takes over, lighting the set. I head outside and chit-chat with Forest (hair), Margaret (makeup) and Sandy (wardrobe). Then, it's time to shoot.

The weird thing about not directing myself (as I usually do) is that we don't stop when I think we've got it. Suzie Q's in charge, so that means we stop only when she feels she's got it. After six takes, she gets that feeling, and we block the next piece.

One of the most unsung entertaining aspects of being on any movie set is taking in the little details put in place by the props and set dec folks that are often ignored by the audience. This flick's no exception: on a corkboard in my fake office, there's a few concept drawings of animals for various Celestial Seasoning boxes. One of the drawings depicts a friendly looking owl holding a mug of tea. There's a Post-It stuck on the drawing that's meant to be put there by my character, with the words "Too scary for kids?" penciled on it. This cracks me up to no end.

Susanah chooses to shoot the next piece — in which I deliver a small monologue to an unseen boss — in a way that I never would have imagined. As I rehearsed the scene in my trailer, I assumed I'd be delivering lines to camera in a tits-up shot. Susanah has me in profile, standing in a doorway, delivering the lines to a person in the room. Outside the room, there's a large poster of a bear from one of the Celestial Seasonings boxes. As composed in the frame, the shot makes it look like I'm talking to the bear, kinda — the subtext of which is kinda funny. I internally note the fact that, even though it's her first film, Susanah already has more of a knack for telling a story visually than I do.

Outside, I bullshit with Jenno while the lighting crew tries to give John Lindley (our DP) and Susanah what they're looking for. Casey (the line producer) joins us and lets me know that, for insurance reasons, I'm not supposed to be driving my own car to set. I balk at this, as I can't stand being driven anywhere. I point out that I drove the hearse at my father's funeral, then quickly point out that there's no truth to that story, though wouldn't it have made my argument stronger if there was? Before long, I'm pulled back inside for the shot. I go over some word swaps with Susanah (she's very cool about ad-libbing), I tag Forest to play the off-camera boss who I'm addressing, and we shoot the one-er.

I'm a sweater. I sweat when I breathe. So under those hot lights and a crowded, body-filled set, I sweat an inordinate amount. Forest and Margaret are kept on their toes through both of my set-ups, dabbing away massive puddles and hair-dryer-ing a mop that looks like it's just come out of an old timey wash tub, where it was bobbing for apples.

And I'm sweating up a storm during shot after shot of this scene. Inside, I feel like I nail it on take two or three, but Susanah's looking for something, which I guess I finally give her on take eight, because that's when Dave Sardi (our first A.D.) tells the camera team to check the gate. With the gate declared clean, my first day on *Catch & Release* wraps.

Susanah and I thank each other and make sketchy plans to get our kids together the next day. Driven by Penny, I head back to base, trying to come up with a suitable Quote of the Day for 2nd A.D. Karen's call-sheet.

In the vanities trailer, Forest strips away my fake hair and prosthetic. Since there's glue in my hair, she offers to wash it. I practically dive into the sink, because getting my hair washed by someone else is one of my all time favorite pastimes.

Afterwards, it's over to Margaret's chair for the makeup removal with the warm, wet towel and the mini-facial. This, friends, is bliss.

I head to my trailer, get changed into my Kev Clothes, leave my costume heaped on the bed, and include a note to Elaine that reads "Elaine — Sorry I didn't hang up my costume. Kevin. P.S. — I realize in the time it took me to write this, I could've hung up my costume. P.P.S. — I heart you."

I load the welcome baskets into my truck and head for the city. Instead of going straight to the hotel, I head to the Future Shop instead, where I pick out a pair of TV/DVD player combos: one for Harley's room, and more importantly, one for me and Jen. The salesman helps me get them out to my already stuffed car (two welcome gifts, a wardrobe bag full of my clothes from home that costume designer Tish had borrowed to copy for the flick), and the still-flat tire from our drive up). I neglected to hit the parking meter in the garage when I pulled in, so my windshield is sporting a forty-dollar ticket.

I get back to the hotel and the doormen unload all my stuff and cart it up to the room. Marc (the bellman who'd showed us our room when we'd initially come to scout it out last week) helps with the swap-out of the TVs, while Jen orders me some room service. By the time the food arrives, Harley's TV is set up and programmed (putting her knee-deep in the new *Kim Possible* DVD), and Marc and the tech guy are hooking up the TV for my and Jen's room. Jen and I chit-chat over dinner while the tech guy drags TVs away.

I say g'night to Harley and Jen starts reading her books. The tech guy left the test DVD (*Fight Club*) playing in the room, so I let that spin for a bit while I check my email on the bed. Jen joins me in the room, and we kick back to some *White Noise*. Afterwards, we pop in some season four *Cheers* DVDs that we fall asleep to.

Tuesday 17 May 2005 @ 8:14 p.m.

I get up around seven-thirty, take a dump, and check email. I take a shower, kiss the girls g'bye, and follow Driver Dave over to the set in Kitsilano.

I get my hair put on and head over to the set with Sam for a blocking rehearsal. Today, it's me, Sam and Garner doing a kinda light scene. We block the scene for an hour; then head back to the trailers.

I call Schwalbach to see if she's gonna come over with Harley. Trailer world is adjacent to a nice park and it's not raining for a change, so I'm thinking Harley would enjoy coming over. I ask Lori if one of the Teamsters can pick up Jen and Harley from the hotel, then head back to set to shoot the master.

We shoot for a few hours, then I head back to base camp. When I get out of the van, I see Jen and Harley hanging out in the park. I introduce Sam to the wife and kid, then shuffle the family over to the catering truck for lunch. En route, we run into Susanah and Jenno, and I introduce Jen and Harley to both (though Jen's had something of an email introduction to Jenno the month before when she was inquiring about the Vancouver living arrangements). Susanah's assistant Rhonda tells us that, post-lunch, she'll take Harley to Susanah's to hang with Susanah's kids.

We grab some lunch, head back to the trailer and chow down. When we're done, Rhonda takes Harley to Susanah's, and Jen and I have a smoke. Then, Lori comes by to tell me we're back from lunch, and that the van's waiting to take me to set. I kiss Jen and head off.

Between set-ups, I hang out with Sam mostly. Sometimes, we chat up Garner, sometimes we just chill outside, smoking and talking to the crew. We're moving along at a nice clip, so I don't get back to my trailer for three hours. When I get there, Schwalbach's about ready to go home. We lay down together for fifteen minutes before I'm called back to set. I ask Lori to see if Susanah's assistant

Rhonda can bring Harley back from Susanah's place, kiss Jen g'bye, secure a ride home for her and Harley, and head back to set to shoot my closeup.

I shoot my coverage. Since I've been off camera most of the day, I've had the benefit of having plenty of time to get the lines and delivery down to a science. Susanah lets me ad-lib a few takes, but since I'm eating during the scene and trying to keep continuity as far as when I picked up what in the master, I don't stray too far from the script. When we're done, I head back to the vanities to get my hairpiece removed, and enjoy another hair washing and facial before jumping into the Hate Tank and heading home. En route, I ask Jen to order up some room service for me so that it's there when I get back.

After getting lost in Kitsilano for twenty minutes, I get back to the apartment just in time for family dinner. We chow down, telling each other about our days, and then Jen puts Harley to bed. Jen and I get into bed and start watching *The Life and Death of Peter Sellers*, but I fall asleep about an hour in.

Wednesday 18 May 2005 @ 8:15 p.m.

I wake up at seven, take a shit, and check email. Call time's eight thirty, so I shower, get dressed, and head out before the girls get up.

I get to the set and Forest puts on my hairpiece. A van takes us up to the set (the same house we shot in yesterday), and we block for forty-five minutes. It's a scene with a bit of physical comedy in it — physical comedy that requires a stunt double — so once Susanah and John have an idea of what they're looking for, the set gets turned over to the lighting department and the cast goes back to base camp.

I get dressed and bullshit with Jenno for a bit. Sam joins us and we talk about the show and speculate on the junket. Casey joins us and suggests a compromise, regarding me driving to set: so long as I do it in a car rented by the production, they're cool with it.

We head back to set and shoot 'til lunch. Sam, Garner and I all stay relatively close to set most of the day, 'til we're sent back to base camp for lunch. Instead of chowing down, I watch Sam's short film. It doesn't play in my trailer's DVD player, so I pop it in my laptop. About nineteen minutes into the thirty-four minute short, the disc kicks out — which blows as I was enjoying it. I use the remainder of lunch to grab some shut eye, before Lori wakes me up to tell me we're back, and that I've gotta head up to set.

When I get back to set, Chris Moore's there visiting Jenno. I give him a big hug (as he's the dude who suggested me for the role in the first place) and we bullshit for a while before I head into the house to finish the scene. When we're done, Garner's got another scene to shoot, so we say g'bye and Sam and I head out. We hang around outside talking to Jenno and Chris for a bit, before taking the van back to base camp. Sam and I jaw for a while before he wishes me luck on my scene tomorrow and heads off.

I bomb over to the vanities to get my hair and makeup removed and run into Sam again. Margaret had to leave early so Ange is removing my makeup today. I ask her if she's got a menthol blower (the minty apparatus that, when blown into an actor's eyes, produces tears), and I borrow it to take home for rehearsal for tomorrow. Hair and makeup removed, I jump in the car and head to the hotel.

I get upstairs and collect Jen and Harley for dinner at Gotham. We get to the restaurant, chow down, and head back into the (fairly early) Vancouver evening. Since it's only five thirty, we decide to hit the mall. However, once we park underground and get up into the mall, we learn it's only open for fifteen more minutes. This gives us enough time to hit the Sears, where I'm hoping to find an iced tea maker and a new showerhead. It's a bust for me on both fronts, but Jen finds some bowls, cups and pitchers, as well as a coffee maker.

We head downstairs to go back out into the mall, but some Sears broad tells us the store's now closed, and we have to exit the building. I tell her my car's beneath the other building, but she's not having it, so out we go. We get outside, and I opt to go get the car while Jen and Harley cross the street and hit the Chapters. I circle the building, looking for the entry to the parking garage, but for the life of me, I can't find it. The second time around, I pass a dude in a yellow and black *Jay and Silent Bob Strike Back* logo shirt. I'm sweating balls, lugging around two bags full of stuff, and trying to hike up my pants while looking for this parking lot entry. A girl stops me to say she's a fan, but I don't have the patience or the presence of mind to say much more than "Thanks — I appreciate that," before moving on. Finally, I hail a cab and ask him to drive around the buildings until I find the garage entry. This does the trick, as five minutes later, I'm getting into my car and leaving that cursed city mall.

I pull up to Chapters, where I've gotta jump out and pay for the books Jen and Harley have picked out (as Jen left her wallet back at the hotel). At this point, I'm in a pretty shitty mood, and I bark about having some silence in the car for the five-block ride home.

We get to the hotel and I head out onto the porch to have a smoke. I head inside and hit the bathroom with my lines for tomorrow. I shoot a scene I'm kinda stressing about: one that's less about making jokes and more about making with the dramatic. I copy the lines down onto another piece of paper, so it'll help me memorize my monologue. Jen finishes putting Harley to bed, and I ask her if she'll help me rehearse. I run lines with Jen for an hour and get to a place where I feel like I've committed the lines to memory and have made 'em my own. I make with the mentholator and try the speech in tears to see if it still works.

I call Susanah to ask if it's okay that I used the mentholator. We talk about it for a while, and she concludes we'll cover it both ways — with and without tears.

Jen and I chit-chat for awhile while she has some wine. We head to bed, where we engage in a little tension-relieving/confidence-boosting sex, after which I fall asleep.

Thursday 19 May 2005 @ 8:17 p.m.

I do my big scene.

Friday 20 May 2005 @ 8:18 p.m.

My first day off in a week, and I still get up at 7:30 a.m. I hit the bathroom, then lay on the floor in the living room, checking email. An hour later, Quinnster smokes out of her room, heading for ours. I stop her from waking up Jen, and talk her into grabbing some Denny's breakfast. I get her dressed, and when I head into my room to find some clothes, I discover Jen awake, brushing her teeth. I inform her majesty that me and the kid are bound for a Denny's breakfast, which she declines to attend. She kisses us both g'bye, and we're off.

Quinnster and I head over the Cambie Street Bridge to the Denny's on Broadway. En route, we pass a Toys 'R Us , which Quinnster's requesting we stop at after breakfast.

Harley's never been to Denny's, but at first glance of the menu, she's in love. I tell her she can join the Birthday Club which would entitle her to a free sundae on or near June 26th. She thinks we've passed into Shangri La.

Post-breakfast, we head to Toys 'R Us , where we buy a bunch of games (Bingo, Disney Yahtzee, *Madagascar*) and puzzles (*Scooby-Doo*, *Robots*, *SpongeBob*), as well as a travel version of 'Simon' and some room décor stickers.

Next, we drive around looking for smokes for Jen. We park and take a walk down Granville, stopping in smoke shops I'm hoping carry American cigarettes. I wind up getting three different kinds of Canadian smokes instead, then head across the street to Golden Age Collectibles — the comic store I used to shop at when I lived here back in '92.

It's exactly as I remember it. Everything looks the same, right down to the current release movie posters hanging on the wall. I thumb through two bins full of scripts and discover an entire section of Kevin Smith Scripts, which fills me with mixed emotions: elation, because I was successful enough in my career to warrant my own section in the Golden Age Collectibles script bin where, years earlier, I myself had bought scripts; and anger, as these folks were taking food off my table.

I chit-chat with the manager and sign some Askew merch (Jay and Silent Bobble heads, talking Jay and Bob and Bluntman & Chronic figures). Harley picks out a shirt, and when we go to pay, the manager offers to give it to me for free, as a thank you for signing the stuff. I tell him I'm happy to pay, as I'm loaded now, but if he really wants to thank me, he'll remove those Kevin Smith scripts from the bin. He agrees; I pay for my shirt, and Quinnster and I head back to the hotel.

We get to the room and show the rested and showered Jen our booty, and tell her about our day. I turn the kid over to Jen and chill for a bit, taking a shower and sacking out in front of the TV. An hour later, I decide to head down to the border to buy Jen her smokes. Jen's back is bugging her, so she elects to stay home. Harley agrees to go on the adventure with me, so she gets dressed, and we load into the car with the travel 'Simon' and the iPod.

Quinnster falls asleep on the ride. I try to wake her up when we get to the border, but she's out cold. However, we wind up waiting in line so long that she wakes up before we reach the booth. I ask the Customs guy where the nearest WalMart is, and he tells me it's Bellingham, about twenty miles away.

Back in the States, we stop at the first McDonald's without a maple leaf dotting it that we can find. Harley gets a Chicken Selects meal, and I get a chicken breast sandwich. Two guys come up to me separately to ask if I'm Silent Bob. I chat 'em up for a few, then head into the play area with Harley. She spends about fifteen minutes climbing up the ladders and slides of the screaming-kid-filled jungle gym room before I usher her out.

We stop to fill up on gas and I look for Jen's smokes, Marlboro Menthol Ultra Light. Not finding 'em, we head to Bellingham. On the ride there, I call Jim Jackman and we shoot the shit about *Degrassi* and other stuff. Mid-convo, a heavy downpour that makes it impossible to drive drops out of the sky. I don't know how people can live in the Pacific Northwest, what with all the constant rain.

We don't find a WalMart, but do find a Big K. Inside, we finally feel like we're in the good ol' USA, because there's so much of everything on display. Granted, it's all crap, but it's American crap (mostly made in Taiwan), which is just what the doctor ordered. We grab some supplies that can't be found in Canada (like an iced tea maker) and Harley asks for some DVDs. I grab *Son of the Mask* for her and *Back to the Batcave* and *Call Me: The Rise and Fall of Heidi Fleiss* for me. We pay and head out.

I stop at two gas stations and a Walgreens to find Jen's smokes. Loaded up with three cartons, we head back to Vancouver, with Harley watching *Son of the Mask* on the Expedition's DVD player.

I stop at the Customs gate at the border, and the agent asks to see the letter from Harley's Mom, granting me permission to transport her across international lines — y'know, the letter I don't have. Thankfully, the other Customs agent vouches for me as "the guy from *Jay and Silent Bob Strike Back*..." and I'm off.

We get home around nine. I talk to Jim Jackman again, and we decide to talk in the morning, once Linda's up. Jen puts Harley to bed, and we curl up with *Call Me: The Rise and Fall of Heidi Fleiss*, starring Meadow Soprano. I fall asleep toward the end.

Saturday 21 May 2005 @ 8:19 p.m.

Harley wakes me up at eight, and my throat's feeling like I've got some tonsillitis coming on. Ever since Harley was three, I've wound up getting tonsillitis at least twice a year. It's treatable with antibiotics, but it's still not pleasant.

I pop in a *SpongeBob* for Harley and play catch-up with the online diary until Jen wakes up. The girls want to go out for brunch, and Jen's pushing this bagel place a block away.

While they're getting dressed, Jim Jackman, Linda Schuyler, and Stephen Stohn call. During the call, I try to smoke a cigarette, but it's just not tasting good. Considering I'm nursing the sore throat already, I decide then and there to go back to being a non-smoker for another year.

When I'm done with my conference call, I meet Jen and Harley downstairs and we head over to the Great Canadian Bagel. I get a breakfast sandwich and a strawberry muffin, with some much-needed vitamin C, in the way of orange juice. Jen and Harley head over to the mall to return a pair of pants Jen bought for Harley yesterday, and I head back to the hotel.

I work on the online diary for a while, during which time I catch up on the parts of *Call Me* I missed when I fell asleep. I check email and write to the Funimation folks, regarding the forthcoming *Jay and Silent Bob Do Degrassi* DVD.

While I'm in the bathroom, Jen and Harley come home. Harley wants to play games, so her and I settle into a hundred piece *Robots* puzzle, while Jen grabs a much-needed smoke. Half an hour later, Jen joins us for the puzzle action, helping to bring it home. Following this, we settle into a few games of Bingo, then get cracking on some Disney Yahtzee, during which Jen heads out to grab some falafel. When she gets back, she joins in the Yahtzee action, kicking both my and Harley's asses.

I lay down on the bed and check email while Jen sits out in the living room and smokes. Harley comes in to tell me that Jen wants me to go to Starbucks for her. I send Harley to ask her what I'm gonna get in return. Harley comes back to tell me Jen said "Anything you want". I send Harley back to ask "Anything?" Jen sends Harley back with Jen's all-purpose notebook, so that I can write what I'm looking for in exchange for the Starbucks run, and we can spare the child the gruesome details of our private affairs. I take a moment to pen the following contract...

In exchange for a Starbucks run, I agree to give my husband, Kevin Smith, all sorts of dirty sex stuff, up to and including anal play.
Signed..........
Witnessed.......
Date.......

Harley brings Jen the notebook, and I hear chuckling from the other room. Harley brings back the document signed by Jen and witnessed by Harley. Quinnster launches into the questions: "What's it say? What'd I sign? Will you read it to me?" I read her a far tamer, fictional version of the contract, then get dressed and take Quinnster for a walk downstairs to Starbucks, passing the grinning, flirty Schwalbach.

Turns out this particular Starbucks closes at six, so Quinnster and I trek out further to find Jen a latte. We stop in two markets/delis and snag the coffee drink and sundry other items, as well as a bottle of wine for Jen.

We return to the apartment and vote unanimously to order room service rather than brave the pissy Vancouver weather this evening. I change into my woobs, and before long, our food arrives.

We sit down at the dinner table and eat as a family. Upon seeing Jen's crab cakes, I'm immediately taken back to the Trump Plaza in New York City, where one night years ago, Schwalbach ordered a shrimp cocktail from room service and came down with a case of food poisoning so bad, we had to call the hotel doctor, who wound up giving Jen a shot. Off the crab cakes, I remark that this evening will more than likely end with a hotel doctor injecting Jen's ass-cheek with some kinda anti-food-poisoning concoction as well.

Dinner leaves a little to be desired. All three of us pick through our unappetizing fare and agree that we should never order room service again.

Post-dinner, I'm revealed to be something of a prophet, as one of Jen's dishes — either the crab cakes or the cream of potato/leek soup — is disagreeing with her in a big bad way. She's dragging around a bucket, threatening to hurl. I put Quinnster to sleep, then lay down with the unwell Schwalbach — my Starbucks contract null and void for the night. Midway through a season four *Seinfeld* disc, we fall asleep.

Sunday 22 May 2005 @ 8:20 p.m.

I wake at up 3:30 a.m., unable to sleep. I'm really not feeling well. What I thought might be tonsillitis has turned out to be a head cold, and I'm congested as fuck, unable to breathe out of both of my nostrils. I clear my nasal passages as much as I can, take a leak, and read the news online for a while. On Google.ca, I peep an article about the impending release of Karla Homolka, which then leads me to a far larger article that provides all the lurid details of her sex-based killing spree with husband Paul Bernardo. I'm left feeling depressed and angry and, in my knee-jerk American fashion, wanna lobby for a Canadian death penalty. But considering the murders in Canada last year totaled 550 (as per the info provided on a cigarette pack, comparing smoking-related deaths to the relatively low count of suicides and unnatural deaths), I guess they're doing something right in this country. I watch a few trailers online as a kind of mental floss, then climb back into bed around six-ish.

I wake up around ten, and Harley and Jen are already hip-deep in activities. The weather is shitty as ever, but we elect to ignore it and go to Safeway.

I take a shower, get dressed, and then load the family into the Hate Tank. We get to Safeway and I load up on Nyquil and Robitussin, as well as a Vicks Inhaler, to help clear my breathing passages. We buy soups, oatmeal, fruit, and a bunch of other stuff to hold us over for the week, pay, and get out of dodge. Across the street from Safeway, I stop at London Drugs and pick up a frying pan, so Jen can whip up her quesadillas.

On the way home, Jen and Harley ask me to drop them off at the Children's Festival going on under the Burrard Bridge, near Kits Beach. We make plans to meet back at the drop-off point at three o'clock, I kiss the girls g'bye, and they're off.

I swing by the hotel and let the bellmen unload the groceries, then head back out, looking for a Mac-type store so I can grab Jen a new power plug and battery. London Drug only stocks the generic power plug, and the Mac store across the Cambie Street bridge on Broadway is closed, so I head back to the hotel.

I put the groceries away, heat up some soup, grab some iced tea, and settle in to watch Gaspar Noé's *Irréversible*, with Vincent Cassel and Monica Belluci. It's an amazingly good looking flick in which the story is told in reverse, but that's not even the most noteworthy aspect of the film — the centerpiece is a hardcore, merciless rape scene which leaves you nauseated and hating all men. While it's a well-made, well-acted, very French film ("Time destroys everything…"), the cumulative effect of sitting through *Irréversible* coupled with the still-fresh sense of unease caused by reading about the Homolka/Bernardo case makes me leave twenty minutes early to pick up Jen and Harley.

When I pick them up, I'm in full-blown agony mode with the head cold. I can't breathe through either nostril now, and anytime I blow out, yellow-brown shit bubbles up. Jen and Harley climb in, and we chit-chat about the shows they've seen on the way back to the hotel.

We get to the apartment, and Jen tells me to lay down. I sack out on the bed, composing a long-overdue intro to a *Degrassi* book that examines twenty-five years of show history. Jen insists I take some Nyquil and take a nap, so when I finish the piece I do so. I grab another bowl of soup as a chaser and put in *The Last Shot*, with Matthew Broderick and Alex Baldwin. A half an hour later, I'm out cold.

I wake up and drag myself out of bed. Jen and Harley are in the living room, working on projects. Harley's buzzing about a *Scooby Doo* puzzle they put together, which — according to Jen — really kicked their asses. I heat up another bowl of soup, which Harley uses a chair to reach the microwave to retrieve for me, sweet l'il Florence Nightingale that she is. I head back into the bedroom (when I'm sick, I just wanna be alone), and eat my soup while watching the parts of *The Last Shot* that I fell asleep on.

Jen joins me, and we opt to watch *Suspect Zero*. She's in and out of it as she puts Harley to bed. One of the moments she comes back for is a rape scene, and it's about all I can take for the day.

I don't know how chicks go to the movies, man. There's so much brutalization of women depicted, it makes you wonder who's greenlighting these flicks (though, in the case of *Suspect Zero* — a Paramount Film — the answer would have to be then-head of the studio Sherry Lansing). I realize I've only become more sensitive to this because I've got both a wife and daughter, which makes me sad to think that, as a single guy, this phenomenon was something I didn't notice at all, since I didn't have as much personally invested in the distaff. Does it make me want to campaign against those who tell women-in-peril tales? No — I'm for freedom of expression and all that. But it does make me want to turn off movies that show the first hint of brutality to women and opt to watch something else.

Which is what we do. Off goes *Suspect Zero* and in goes *Ocean's Twelve*, which we fall asleep watching.

Monday 23 May 2005 @ 3:34 p.m.

Once again, the weather is just plain shitty. After waking and doing the usual, the rest of Clan 'Couver gets up and decides, on this holiday, to hit the last day of the Kids' Festival. Seeing how sick I am, Jen suggests taking a cab to the fest with me doing a pickup at 4:00 p.m. I insist on dropping the Princesses off and picking them up.

Harley and I do a pair of puzzles, and I get lost in the wonderful simplicity of this forgotten pastime. Mercifully, they're only a hundred pieces, so it's not too easy and not too hard either — just vexing enough to shut down all the hyper brain activity for an hour or so and concentrate on basic problem-solving.

I throw on some clothes and a hat and load the fam into the Hate Tank. I drop the girls off, then head to WestWorld and Simply Computing on Broadway to look for a new battery and power cord for Jen's laptop. Alas, being that it's Victoria Day (a Brit-influenced Canadian holiday), both places are closed. However, down the street, I spy a Shopper's Drug Mart.

I pull into the underground parking structure and haul my congested ass upstairs into the Shopper's Drug Mart to pick up some Cold FX (suggested by Linda Schuyler as THE Canadian cold remedy) and tissues. While circling the aisles, Byron calls, and we discuss whether or not to leave the pooches in Puppy Camp for the week he and Gail are coming up here, as well as which account to use to pay for the Jeep repairs.

My old green Jeep Grand Cherokee — the one I bought while still dating Joey Adams, circa *Amy* — has managed to remain in the family even after I bought my Expedition. First, I gave it to my parents while my Dad was still alive. But the height of the vehicle proved too tall for my stroke-hindered Pop to navigate, so it came back to me. Next, we gave it to Jen's friend Bryony, who was car-less at the time. She used it for a little over a year, then called one day to say she'd bought a new car and figured we'd want the Jeep back. As Mewes was car-less at that point, he inherited it. Then, when Mewes bought his Caddy, we sent the Jeep into the shop for a complete overhaul to get it as close to mint as possible for its next (and probably last) owner: our housekeeper Reyna.

I pay for my over-the-counter crap and head outside, where I notice a Future Shop next door and flash on a brief convo Jen and I had about the living room TV in the apartment, and how it'd be much better with a DVD player. So I head into Future Shop and pick up a new TV and DVD player (separate units this time). While shopping, Sloss and Jackie call to go over some *Catch* and *Clerks 2* deal points so they can close both contracts. While on the phone, I sign a copy of *Clerks X* for a clerk. On the way out, I tag a copy of *Evening With* for the clerk who helps me downstairs with my electronics and loads them into the car. We chat a bit about *Degrassi*, and I'm off.

At the hotel, one of the bellmen brings the stuff upstairs and sends the tech guy to hook it up, during which I make some soup. While eating my soup, I kick back with one of my favorite flicks (definitely top twenty) *Grosse Pointe Blank*. I'm forty-five minutes into the flick when four o'clock rolls around, and I have to head off for the scheduled pick-up.

I pick up Jen and Harley and bring 'em home. Harley, Jen and I play some Bingo, and then I head back to the bedroom to finish watching *Grosse Pointe*. When it ends, I pop in the Director's Cut of *Ali* and check email while peeping the extended flick (same reaction: Will's great, and the movie's okay).

Toward the end of the flick, I get a call from Susanah, who's heard I'm sick and wanted to check in. I tell her I'll be fine to shoot by Wednesday and we chit-chat about the Friday shoot and how she feels about the flick thus far overall.

I finish watching *Ali* just as Jen joins me in the bedroom. We pop on some *X-Files*, and I take a big hit of Nyquil that puts me out by ten o'clock.

Tuesday 24 May 2005 @ 3:35 p.m.

I wake up feeling like the Cold FX has broken the back of this beast in my head and chest. I take a dump and check email.

Quinnster wakes and joins me in the living room for a while, where I'm on the computer. Then, she asks for some *SpongeBob* in her room, which I turn on for her. Jen wakes up, and we decide to grab some family brunch and hit Toys 'R Us for some more puzzles as well as the computer stores for Jen's battery/cord.

I take a shower, get dressed, and bring the brood across the Cambie Bridge to Broadway, where Quinnster somehow manages to convince us to eat at Denny's.

One incredibly unsatisfying meal later, the three of us vow never to eat at Denny's again, and stumble out into the parking lot. With Toys 'R Us in sight, Jen opts to take Harley for a walk to the store, while I head to WestWorld for the gear for her laptop.

At WestWorld, they have the battery I'm looking for, but not the Mac-made power cord. The clerk suggests Simply Computing down the street. I spot a backpack made especially for 12 inch Power Books and decide to upgrade from my *Jersey Girl* backpack. While the guy rings me up, I ask what his store — a Mac-only Mom and Pop shop — will do if Apple does a Toronto and opens an Apple Store in Vancouver. "Go out of business, I guess" he replies, and for a moment, the Apple-enthusiast side of my id is trumped by the Mom-and-Pop-Shop ideal-ist in me, and I find myself hoping the Mac-topus keeps its tentacles out of the Van, so these brand-committed guys can thrive.

I head over to Simply Computing and grab a power cord, then head down to Toys 'R Us where Jen and Harley are already waiting outside for me.

On the way back to the hotel, Jen asks if we could swing by Stanley Park to see if the Kids' Petting Zoo is open. We get to the Park and discover the Petting Zoo is a weekend-only affair, so we head to a playground in the park instead. Harley climbs around the activity center, and Jen shows off her hidden gymnast with some nifty monkey bar work that exhibits heretofore unrevealed upper body strength that impresses the hell out of me. Then, there's some drama involving Harley and her fear of sliding down a pole. Jen tries to work the Quinnster through her fear, but the five-foot drop is just too high for Harley to overcome her demons. She wails about this failure on the entire walk back to the car, calling to mind the ear piercing incident from last week.

The tears at an end, we head back to the hotel and relax for a while. I hook up Jen's new battery and plug and then the three of us play some Bingo and *SpongeBob* Uno. Jen goes outside to grab a smoke, and Harley and I start on two separate puzzles. Harley goes for the giant-sized big piece *SpongeBob*, and I go for a 100-piece Kodak photo puzzle of a bear cub in a pine tree. Naturally, Quinnster finishes first, and my puzzle kicks my ass for a bit before I conquer it.

Following that, I retire to the bedroom for a bit to lay down and watch the *Assault on Precinct 13* remake. When I emerge, Jen and Harley announce they're hungry again. We decide to head down the street to the Great Canadian Bagel joint and then walk over to Virgin to see if the *NewsRadio* box set is out.

Post-Bagel joint, we decide to add the place to our list of Never Agains, along-side Denny's. We take the short walk down to Virgin and pop inside.

Based on her fascination with 'Fantasy', I grab a Mariah Carey CD for Harley. As Harley and I hunt for the DVD, Jen weaves through the aisles then comes back, delighted to report that not only are some of my InAction figures on display, but HER InAction figure is on display. It's a nice moment for us both, that's quickly dashed one floor below.

We head down to the DVD department and peep out the selection. They do, indeed, have *NewsRadio*, and I flip-flop on whether or not to buy it, based on the fact that I've got Ron from Laser Blazer sending me out each week's new DVDs that I check off on a list he provides. The *NewsRadio* I bought from him will be arriving in two days, but I'm needing a fix now, so I throw it in the basket.

Jen asks about the hesitation, and I explain about the Laser Blazer set-up I've got going on. She deems this stupid and a waste, since I can just come down here to Virgin to grab the new titles every week. I argue that Virgin doesn't stock everything, and that I won't always have the time to get to the store while I'm shooting. The whole discussion leaves a bad taste in my mouth, and I pout for the rest of the time we're in the store.

Mewes calls to let me know he's coming up on Friday to record the *Degrassi* commentary track. We chit-chat for a bit, then I get off the phone to pay for our booty: *NewsRadio*, Mariah remix CD, Batman Uno, *Kim Possible* soundtrack, a yoga mat for Jen, and other stuff.

On the way out of the store, when prompted, I finally speak my mind on what I feel was a criticism of my decision to have new DVDs shipped to me, and charge the wife (awfully melodramatically and, in retrospect, wrongly) with shitting on something simple that makes me happy. This spoils the short walk to the Louis Vuitton store, and I slam the final nail in the coffin on the way into the store, when Jen suggests we just go back to the hotel, and I counter with "No — we're here now, let's stay. At least one of us should enjoy shopping today." With that, Schwalbach storms out of the store with Harley, and I stay behind, looking around, assuming she'll be back. Five minutes later, she is, so as not to confuse the kid as to why Dad's shopping in Mom's store and Mom isn't, without a birth-day, anniversary, or Christmas on the horizon.

We head back to the hotel in relative silence. Once up in the room, I rethink my petulance and apologize to Jen, giving her a hug.

The thing about the wife is, there seems to be very little point in getting into snits or fights. Granted, you spend as much time with anyone as I spend with

Jen, and you're bound to get on one another's nerves from time to time. But in pretty short time, I always arrive at the conclusion that my options are limited: I love this woman, am fascinated by, enthralled over, and obsessed with who she is, and have zero desire to ever be without her. Blowing off steam is one thing, but full-blown fights (particularly over opinions) are always a complete waste of time — especially when you never want to get divorced.

We pop in Harley's Mariah remix CD and dig into some family Batman Uno, Disney Yahtzee, and Bingo. After an hour or so of that, we pop in *NewsRadio*, I check email, and Jen and Harley work on birthday party invitations.

2nd A.D. Karen calls to let me know I've got a 7:30 a.m. call time to block, but will probably be sent home after that, as my portion of the large funeral scene that starts the flick won't be shot 'til later in the day. I call downstairs and get a wake-up call for 6:30 a.m.

Jen puts Harley to bed, and the two of us watch more *NewsRadio* eps, eventually moving it into the bedroom, where we fall asleep before eleven.

Wednesday 25 May 2005 @ 3:36 p.m.

Wake-up call gets me up at 6:30 a.m. and I immediately jump in the shower. As I'm drying, I check email, then take a shit. I call down for the car, then drive over to the set.

From base camp, I'm driven over to the set: a large mansion in Shaughnessy. On the ride, I meet Fiona Shaw, who's playing the dead fiancé's Mom, Mrs. Douglas.

I hang out with Sam and Tim for a bit before we head inside to block. Garner arrives, we say hi, and the blocking's off and running. Sam, Fiona and I chit-chat, as our portion of the scene involves just we three. We talk about Alan Rickman a bit, until Susanah gets to our section of the scene.

Blocking done, I head back to trailer world and hang out talking with Sam and Tim for a bit before heading to the vanities. Forest puts my hair on and Margaret does the makeup thing, after which I head back to my trailer and pop in *Kill Bill, Vol. 1* during which I sign hundreds of *Silent Bob Speaks* tip-in sheets while waiting for the official word that I can head back to the hotel for a few hours.

Chris Moore calls, and asks if I wanna interview Harvey Weinstein for this show he's producing for the Sundance Channel called 'Iconoclasts'. I tell him I'd be way down for it, and ask him when he gets back into town, and if he'll wanna check out *Madagascar* with me, Jen and Harley on Friday (which he does).

Vol. 1 ends, and I'm so digging on it again that I call Quentin and leave him a message about how genius I feel the flick is. Then, Lori comes by the trailer to tell me I can go home for a few hours if I'd like, and come back around three, when they think they'll get to my set-up.

I head back to the hotel and crash at the apartment, eating a sandwich and watching *NewsRadio* episodes. Karen calls to usher me back to set a bit earlier, and as I'm leaving, Jen and Harley return from shopping and lunch at a Thai restaurant down the street. I get kisses and hugs, and head back to set.

I get back to base camp and Lori tells me they're still three shots away from my scene. I get into my costume and watch *Kill Bill, Vol. 2* while signing more tip-in sheets. I get through the whole flick before Lori comes to let me know it's time.

I head back to the set, where I talk to John Lindley, our DP, about *The Last Shot* (which he shot), as well as some of the other flicks on his killer resumé, like *Field of Dreams* and *Sneakers*.

Fiona, Sam and I shoot our scene. Between set-ups, we chill outside, chit-chatting about UK real estate, American politics, *Dogma*, and other stuff. Susanah joins us and I ask if she wants to send her kids to *Madagascar* with me, Harley, Jen, Chris Moore and his daughter Maddy, but Susanah declines, as she's concerned the kids might not take to the flick well without her there.

We head inside for another take, before which I ask Fiona if she's a Dame yet. She admits that she's halfway there, having received the CBE — the Commander of the British Empire honor. Naturally, everyone in the near vicinity fixates on this, and Fiona seems a little embarrassed by the sudden attention.

Outside again, between set-ups, we continue our CBE discussion when Susanah joins us and states that she's instituting a new rule: we can bullshit all we want between takes, but we're not allowed to chit-chat on set right before a take. This is pretty much directed at me, because I'm the chatty one.

I'm a little stung by this, though, as I was chatting up Fiona a) because she's interesting, but chiefly b) to make her feel more at home on the set. Granted, she's almost a Dame, but she's also someone who didn't get a chance to bond with the rest of us during rehearsals. And every cast and crew tends to pussy-foot around British actors, for fear that their "process" will be interrupted somehow. But I remember Alan Rickman telling me that's irritating because it tends to isolate the Brits on a set, quite against their will. Based on this, I'm trying to make Fiona feel especially included.

I've always felt it's insanely important to make everyone on my sets feel completely at home and at ease, so I brought that sensibility to this picture. But I get the impression that Susanah was worried that my constant chatting and fooling around would throw Fiona off her game — hence this new "rule". Since it's Susanah's set, I abide by the rule, and keep my yap shut on set for the rest of the day.

I'm off camera keeping my mouth shut on the last shot of our coverage. Henry, the camera operator, lets me turn the camera on and off upon announcements of "Sound speed..." and "Cut". I suddenly realize that, in twelve years of making movies, this is the first 35mm camera I've ever turned on or off.

Our scene wrapped, I head back to base camp, get out of my clothes, leave the clothes in the living room to add some variety to Wardrobe Elaine's costume-retrieval routine, jot a quick note informing her of this, then head to the vanities trailer, where Forest removes my hairpiece and, God bless her, washes my hair. Margaret's up on set so Ange removes my makeup and gives me the mini-facial. I pop by my trailer, collect my signed tip-in sheets, and head home.

I call Jen, who tells me Byron and Gail have arrived, and they'd all like to grab something to eat. I pick up the brood and take them to Gotham for dinner, where we all catch-up. Afterwards, I swing us through Stanley Park to show off the town a bit.

We get back to the hotel and Harley elects to sleep with Nan and Pop, giving Jen and I our first night alone in over a week. Exhausted, we crash watching *NewsRadio* eps, which we fall asleep to.

Thursday 26 May 2005 @ 10:06 a.m.

I've got a 7:30 a.m. call time, which I'm twenty minutes late for — bad form in the movie world. When I get to base camp, I'm rushed to set for a blocking. It's a nice one-er which once again has me admiring Susanah's directorial instinct.

I head back to vanities and get hair and makeup done. Head to trailer and get dressed, then catch a van back to set before I'm called, so as to be in a state of cat-like readiness to make up for my lateness at call. I chit-chat with A.D. Dave for awhile about his time on the aborted *Mission: Impossible 3*, then shoot the shit with Susanah a bit before it's time to roll.

Sam and I shoot our scene. Four takes later, we're done for the day.

Forest removes my fake hair and washes my real hair. Margaret takes my makeup off and gives me a mini-facial. God, I love being in the movies.

On the drive back to the hotel, I call Byron to see if he, Jen, Harley, and Gail left already for their picnic in Stanley Park. He confirms that they're in the park, and tosses me over to Jen who gives me directions where to meet them.

We hang out in the park watching Harley play on the swingset. Quinnster wants to head down to the water park, so her entourage follows. I grab some grub from the concessions stand and chit-chat with Byron and Gail about the Ted cleanup while Jen and Harley pick up shells from the beach. Then, Jen and I leave Quinnster with B&G, and we head back to the hotel.

Back at the apartment, we get into woobs and kick back with some *NewsRadio*s. After a few hours, we head out to grab some dinner, opting for the Macaroni Grill. En route, we pop by the Thai place that Byron, Gail and Harley were supposed to be eating at, but they've already left. We meet them across the street at the food store, and invite Quinnster to a second dinner with Mom and Dad. She agrees to accompany us.

The three of us eat at Macaroni Grill, adding yet another restaurant to our Never Again list, then drive around looking for a magazine stand to pick up the *Rolling Stone* with my Vader piece. We don't find one, so we head back to the hotel.

I carry Harley's TV/DVD down to B&G's room, where Harley's gonna sleep again. We head back upstairs and chill in the living room, watching more *NewsRadio* episodes and a few *X-Files* too while checking email.

I move to the bedroom and fall asleep watching a *Simpsons*. Jen joins me and I cuddle up to her and fall asleep again.

Friday 27 May 2005 @ 10:15 a.m.

Get up at 10:00 a.m., after a good night of deep sleep. Jen wakes up not too long afterwards, and we watch some *NewsRadio* eps while checking email. Smalls made an appointment for me to check out the Vogue for the Vancouver Q&A I'm thinking of doing, but I call him to change the appointment from eleven thirty to one instead.

I take a shower, then head downstairs. While waiting for my car, I call Chris Moore to see if he's back in town, and if he's up for a little *Madagascar*. He's not answering, so I call Jenno to see if she knows where he is. We chit-chat about the show a bit, and when my car shows up, I head down to Granville.

At the Vogue theater, I meet with John Paul, the guy in charge of the place. He shows me around, lets me know about my TicketMaster options, and suggests I talk to the Georgia Straight about sponsoring the event. The place looks great, so I confirm for 16 July.

I call Smalls about the details, then head to Golden Age Collectibles on Granville to talk to the owner about possibly using their store as ticket pickup point.

On the way back to the garage, I talk to Jim Jackman about the commentary track we're gonna record for the *Degrassi* DVD tomorrow as well as other *Degrassi* stuff. Chris Moore calls to see what time we're seeing *Madagascar*. On my way back to the car, a dude named T-Roy who's shooting and performing in a music video for his resumé asks me to do an intro for him, which I do.

I get back to the hotel, take a shower, and get dressed. Sam shows up, and with Jen and Harley, we head down to the theater. C-Moo and his daughter Maddy get there just in time, and we head in to *Madagascar* (a cute and funny flick).

Post-flick, Jen heads off to run an errand, and me, Harley, Chris, Maddy and Sam go back to the apartment. The girls watch *Kim Possible* while me, Sam and Moore chit-chat out on the balcony.

Sam, C-Moo and Maddy leave, and me, Jen, Harley, Byron and Gail go out to eat at an Italian joint called Il Giardino's. We chow down then take a ride through Yaletown to scout for more restaurants we can hit in the coming months, before heading back to the hotel.

Jen and I say g'night to Quinnster, who heads downstairs to sleep at Byron and Gail's again. We get into our woobs and sack out in front of some *X-Files*.

Mewes finally gets to the hotel and calls up to our room. He comes by and we play catch up for a bit. We decide to check out the Holiday Inn Casino on Broadway, across the Cambie Bridge. Mewes wants to eat, so he orders some room service, then heads downstairs to switch his room so as to be closer to us.

While I'm on the living room floor checking email, Schwalbach emerges from the bedroom, standing in the doorway in her g-string, asking if I'm interested. As she's in her g-string, naturally I'm interested. As I get up to join her, Mewes returns. I figure he'll be too busy with his grub to realize I've popped off for a quickie, so Schwalbach and I bury ourselves in our room and bone a bit. Afterwards, we get dressed, then head off to the casino with the none-the-wiser Mewes.

The casino turns out to be a ballroom that the Holiday Inn has turned into a small casino. It suits me and Mewes just fine, but Jen finds the place sketchy. We put our names on the poker list and try to figure out whether we wanna stay or not. Jen and I kill some time playing blackjack while Mewes surfs a few other table games. An hour and change after we get there, they finally call our names for poker.

We join the $2/$4 Limit table, which is full of a regular bunch of rounders.

After twenty minutes, Schwalbach's way into casino (even this casino) poker: the camaraderie with strangers, the mystery of players you don't know, the thrill of multiple victories. She takes down some big pots — about six in a row. We wind up playing 'til one in the morning.

We head back to the hotel on a poker high, all of us coming home a little heavier in the pockets than when we left. We order room service and watch *Owning Mahowny*. Mewes plays some Ultimate Bet on Jen's laptop while I check email and update my diary. At the end of *Mahowny*, Jen and I crash, leaving Mewes to watch *Assault on Precinct 13* by himself in the living room.

Saturday 28 May 2005 @ 10:15 a.m.

I wake up and putter for a bit before Jim Jackman calls to say he's in the hotel. We make plans to meet up in my room before we head over to the commentary record.

Jen takes Harley to the Petting Zoo and I shower, get dressed and call Jim. He, Mewes, *Degrassi* head writer Aaron Martin and Stacie 'Caitlin Ryan' Mistysyn come up to my room for a bit.

We head over to the Warehouse Studio, a sound recording place outside of Gastown. All five of us sit around a monitor and record three different commentary tracks for the Kevin Smith/Jason Mewes episodes of *Degrassi: The Next Generation*. We're done around six, at which point we all head back to the hotel.

We retire to our respective rooms. In the apartment, I find Jen getting ready for dinner. At seven, we take Jay, Jackman, Aaron, Stacie and Sam Jaeger to Il Giardino's.

Afterwards, we all come back to the hotel and play poker 'til one in the morning. We say goodbye to Aaron and Stacie (who're leaving in the morning) and make plans to hook up with Jackman and Mewes in the a.m. Then, Jen and I go to sleep to some *NewsRadio*.

Sunday 29 May 2005 @ 10:16 a.m.

Jen and I wake up, putter, chit-chat, then, realizing we have the apartment to ourselves, we settle into some awesome pre-noon nookie.

Afterwards, we call Harley to see if she wants to grab breakfast. She tells us that she, Nan and Pop were about to head to breakfast downstairs, so we join them for some buffet.

Following brunch, the five of us head over to the food store to stock up for the week. We come back to the hotel, unpack the groceries, and get involved in some dollar-a-card family Bingo. Jay comes up to the room and joins us for a round as well. When Jimmy J. arrives, we set aside Bingo and play some poker instead, while Harley watches *The Incredibles*.

A few hours later, while we're still knee-deep in the game, Quentin returns my call from the other day, and we wind up talking for over an hour about his flicks, some of my flicks, a bunch of other flicks, Michael Parkes, how insanely famous a movie star Don Adams would be if *Get Smart* had been a ratings hit in the current TV climate, when directors should quit the game, *The Man from U.N.C.L.E.*, *Inglorious Bastards* and *Fletch Won*. When you can bullshit with one of your heroes, life is good.

I emerge from the phone call to find that Mewes and Byron have gone to the gym, Gail's resting in her room, and Jackman went down to his room to take a nap. Harley and I watch *First Daughter* while I swap the contents of my backpack into my new bag and sign the rest of the tip-in sheets for *Silent Bob Speaks*. Mewes joins us at one point to see if I'm up for some casino tonight. I tell him I will be up for it around eight, once I take a shower and such.

Harley goes to dinner with Byron and Gail, and Jen and I kick back with some *X-Files*. Then, I take a shower, kiss Jen and the returning Harley g'night, and head out with Jim and Mewes. We opt against the Holiday Inn casino and head out to the big, new River Rock casino near the airport.

We put our names on the poker list then bomb around the casino, playing blackjack for a bit. The beeper we were given goes off, and we head back to the poker room, where we manage to get on a $1/$2 No Limit table together. I kick some major ass, tripling up the hundred I sit down with (making up for my blackjack losses), and Mewes takes a bit of cash away as well.

We head home, chatting about *Degrassi* and tomorrow's schedule, with Jim and Mewes trying to figure out if they're gonna stick around another day to come with me to the set.

I climb into bed beside the half-awake Schwalbach, kiss her g'night, and fall asleep to some *NewsRadio*.

Monday 30 May 2005 @ 2:47 p.m.

I wake up, shower, and call down to Jim to tell him I'm heading downstairs. He says he'll collect Mewes and meet me down there.

Mewes, Jim and I follow Driver Dave over to Coquitlam for today's shoot. We get there a few minutes late, but I figure it's cool, as they're already shooting something else, and we can't even block yet. Lori leads Mewes and Jim to my trailer, and I grab my iPod and head to the vanities, where Forest slaps on my hair.

The transpo van brings me, Mewes and Jim to set, for the blocking rehearsal. Jenno, Dave and Susannah gather around me to let me know they've gotten me a gift and present me with a small, wrapped package. I open it to find an alarm clock. The message is clear: stop being late.

Susannah pulls me aside to tell me, with a smile, that there are two Ns in her name — a subtle reminder that even the director can read *My Boring-Ass Life*. I ask if she's bugged by anything I've written, and point out the glowing things I've penned about her, before we start chatting about the scenes she's cut together already.

I head back to base camp with Jim and Jay and they chill at the trailer while Margaret finishes my makeup. I get into my costume, then the three of us hang out outside the trailer, catching a smoke. Mewes reveals that he finds Susannah hot, "in a studious way". He also gives thumbs-up to Jenno, who I politely remind him is Chris Moore's ol' lady.

We head up to the set and Sam and I do the scene in three different set-ups. Take after take I bite into a smoker off a grill, delivering most of my lines through a full mouth. By the end of the scene, I'm feeling pretty far from hungry. The gate's checked, and I'm done for the day.

I get back to the trailer and get into my real clothes. I head back to the vanities and get my makeup taken off, my hair removed, and the day-closing mini-facial and a hair washing. As Jim, Jay and I are getting in the car to go, Tim pops by to say hi to Mewes.

On the ride home, we stop at McDonald's for Mewes. We get back to the hotel, and Mewes lays down in his room while Jim and I go over *Degrassi* stuff for a few hours in the apartment. We head down to Jim's room to conference call Linda and Stephen about said *Degrassi* stuff, then Jim gets ready to catch his red-eye back to Toronto. He comes up to say g'bye to Gail and Byron as well as Jen, then heads off.

Having put Quinnster to bed while I was downstairs with Jim, I crash with the increasingly ill Jen, who's suffering from the same shit I was fighting last week. I check email while watching *Law & Order* for a while, then cuddle up to Jen and fall asleep.

Tuesday 31 May 2005 @ 2:48 p.m.

Wake up, shit, check email. Wind up IM-ing with my sister Virginia, who lives in Kobe, Japan.

So as not to be late for work today, I decide to skip the shower and just throw on a hat, figuring Forest will wash my hair when I get to set. Mewes calls to tell me his car's waiting downstairs, and do I want to come get the fan he borrowed from us (Mewes always needs an oscillating fan to go to sleep with at night; he calls it his wooby). I tell him I'll meet him on his floor.

I wind up taking the elevator trip down to the lobby with Mewes. We stand outside, having a smoke, chit-chatting. Then, we say g'bye, and he's off.

I head upstairs, grab my bag, and go back downstairs where I follow the teamster driver to set in my rental.

At the set, Lori grabs me a breakfast burrito, while Forest, God bless her, washes my hair. She dries me up while I scarf the burrito then puts my fake hair in. We get the call for the blocking rehearsal, so Sam and I walk the forty feet from the circus (where all the trailers are parked) to the set (a stage, on which they've built a portion of a storage facility). We greet Garner and Susannah, then block and rehearse the scene. It's a quick one-er, with me having the only line of dialogue, but Susannah and John still find a way to shoot it more interestingly than I would have thought to shoot it.

When we're done, we head back to the vanities. Margaret does my makeup, and I chit-chat with Sam a bit before heading back to my trailer to get into my costume.

Lori knocks to tell me it's time to go, so I head to set and shoot the scene. By the fifth or sixth take, Susannah's got what she wants, so I'm wrapped for the day.

I talk to A.D. Dave about whether or not we're shooting the Juliette Lewis scene tomorrow, as scheduled. Since the weather's so pissy it might be called off, and the idea would be to shoot a cover set tomorrow (something indoors), and move the me and Juliette scene to Friday. This means the four-day weekend in LA I was gearing up for is shot. Dave tells me he'll let me know if that's the case by midday.

I talk to Tish about my wardrobe then run into Jenno. We hang by catering, bullshitting about stuff and the schedule for a bit, then I head to my trailer to get out of my costume, and to the vanities to get out of my hair and makeup. We go through an astrology book to see if any of us have the traits our signs are supposed to sport, and Jenno joins us to suggest I head home today and come back Thursday night for the Friday shoot. I tell her it's cool and that I'll probably just stay in Vancouver instead.

I drive home and find only the maid in the room. A quick call to Byron and Gail reveals Jen and Harley went shopping. Moments after I get off the phone, Jen and Quinnster return. We all hang for a bit, and I read a *Walter, the Farting Dog* book to Harley, after which Jen reads a *Junie B.* book.

An hour later, Harley heads out for tea with Nan and Pop, leaving Jen and I trying to figure out what our new schedule's gonna be, based on the elimination of the four-day weekend in LA. We finally settle on Jen staying with me in Vancouver 'til Sunday, then heading back to LA where I'll meet her on Friday. I'll head back to Van that Sunday, shoot all week, then head back to LA for Harley's kindergarten graduation and week-early birthday party. Then, we all come back to Vancouver to stay for the remaining month of the shoot. That settled, we turn on some *Law & Order* and I give Jen a baby oil massage. We indulge in a little room service, and then Harley returns with Nan and Pop and the five of us play Disney Yahtzee, *SpongeBob* Uno, and Bingo for about two hours.

I head to London Drugs to grab some water and other essentials, then come home and kiss the kid g'night. I check email and the board while watching more *Law & Order*, 'til we eventually go to sleep.

Wednesday 1 June 2005 @ 3:13 p.m.

I wake up around eight, shit, and check email in the living room. Harley bombs out of her room heading for ours when I stop her. She tells me Jen insisted she wake her as soon as she got up, so I let her go.

I call for the car, head downstairs, and load Byron and Gail's and Harley's luggage into the Hate Tank. While Gail and Byron check out, Jen and Harley go for Starbucks and I grab a toasted bagel with cream cheese from the nearby deli.

We drop Byron, Gail and Harley at the airport, loading 'em all up with hugs and kisses. Then, Jen and I head back to the city.

En route, we look for a McDonald's with a drive-thru, but find none. So we instead stop at the McDonald's on Broadway, where I grab Jen some hash browns and a Diet Coke, and an Egg McMuffin and an orange juice for myself. While waiting for the food, I sign a few autographs for folks in line. The clerk asks me what movie I'm in town doing, and I tell him *Catch & Release*. He then asks if there are props in the movie. I curb the instinct to stare at him dumbfounded for a long beat and instead affirm that there are, indeed, props in the movie. He then tells me his buddy works at a prop house. There seems to be no connector to his statement: it is a pronouncement set adrift on a sea of idle banter. Mercifully, the food comes, cutting our non-convo (or non-vo) short.

Jen and I get back to the hotel and get into our woobs. The hotel room empty, we indulge in some early-afternoon boning. Afterwards, we bomb out to the living room and watch some *Law & Order* while looking for somewhere to eat tonight. I comb through the restaurant guide provided by the production, but I've got calzone on the brain, so I jump online and Google 'calzones Vancouver'. Google hits me back with a few options, one of which is a pizza and live jazz joint called Capone's in Yaletown, located on Hamilton — the same street I used to go to classes every day before the Vancouver Film School moved to Hastings. I suggest it to Jen, who's down with it. We shower, get dressed and head over to Yaletown.

We somehow find a metered spot (finding parking in Yaletown is akin to finding American smokes in Canada), and as I park, I get a call from *Degrassi* producer Stephen Stohn. He's in town and staying at our hotel, so I tell him I'll call him after dinner.

Jen and I order, eat and chit-chat for an hour and a half, while a live jazz trio plays non-intrusive beats in the background. After some coaching, the calzone turns out spot-on, and Jen's way into her Portobello mushroom, so we both agree that Capone's is an excellent find.

When we're done, we drive around looking for an ice cream parlor. But they're harder to find than parking spots in Yaletown, so we head back to the hotel instead.

When I get into the room, I call my Mom. Today marks the two-year anniversary of my Dad's rather sudden death.

My father had always been in ill-health for as long as I'd known him. Like his parents and brothers and sisters, he was a life-long diabetic, which later in life had led to strokes, a heart attack, and the loss of a toe and most of his eyesight on one side. We'd almost lost him to a heart attack a few months prior, only to have him recover completely in what his doctors deemed an inexplicable turnaround. What none of us knew was that Dad was living on borrowed time, at that point. While he'd suddenly seemed more vital and in love with life than he had in years, his heart was slowing, counting down to a death I'd say was almost magical.

A month before, Mom had called to say she was thinking about coming to Philly for the *Wizard* World Comic Convention that I was scheduled to attend for another Q&A. Her idea was that since my sister (who was then living in Hong Kong) was also gonna be in Philly at the same time, she'd come up with Dad and Donald, and the whole family could be together for the first time in a year. My first instinct was to talk her out of coming up to Philly as I was planning a hit-and-run appearance at the Con: essentially, I'd Q&A and leave. Having her, Dad and Don come up from Florida meant I'd have to stick around longer than I'd intended, and I just wanted to get back home to LA to finish up the *Jersey Girl* cut. But Mom seemed committed to going and very into the idea of all of us being together, so I relented and said I'd stick around Philly for another day.

My parents got to town while I was doing a signing on the Con floor. Malcolm, who I'd been out of touch with for nearly a year after a drunken email fight (his, not mine), was in attendance at the Con to lend a hand at the booth, and I'd put him in charge of meeting my parents and brother and sister and getting them into the Q&A. They were running late, and the Con folks were eager to start my panel on time, but I kept holding out from going up on stage, as I wanted to greet the fam before starting the Q&A. Mom, Dad and Virginia finally pulled up in a cab a minute before I was to go on, and I helped Dad out of the car, while Malcolm secured a wheelchair. I gave 'em all hugs and kisses and told them Malcolm would get them in and seated, and I went backstage for my entrance.

I don't really remember that Q&A. I recall showing clips from *Jersey Girl*, but the caliber of questions or how long the panel lasted is all a haze at this point. What I do recall, however, was my Old Man sitting up front, in a wheelchair, next to my Mom and sister.

Rather than temper the show because they were there, I went for embarrassingly candid and frank, as per usual. After the panel, Virginia brought Mom and Dad backstage, where we talked to Joe and Nancy Quesada for a few minutes before I learned that Donald was stuck at the Philly airport with car trouble. Dad was wearing a *Simpsons* sweatshirt that Malcolm had bought for him on the Con floor after he'd mentioned he was feeling cold.

My panel was near the end of the Con day, so we waited ten minutes for the hall to clear out, and then I took the 'rents down to the floor to show them the Panasonic stock car that my man Ed Janda had emblazoned with a big blow-up of Jay and Silent Bob from *Strike Back*. I remember this impressed the hell out of Pop, for whatever reason, and then Ed Janda took a picture of me, Mom and Dad in front of the car.

I brought Mom and Dad back to the hotel, where Jen had already gone post-panel, as she wanted to get ready for the Morton's dinner we were planning. I gave Dad a pair of warm-up pants and drove him and Mom to where they were staying with my sister.

I'd reserved the private dining room at Morton's, and that night, the five members of the Smith family (Mom, Dad, Virginia, Donald and me) and two of our spouses (Virginia's husband Eric and my Jen; Don's husband Jerry was home in Florida, stuck working) gathered for a family dinner.

We sat around eating, drinking, talking, joking, bullshitting, and just generally having a great time. My father sat next to me, and in classic Don Smith fashion said very little, only occasionally chiming in with the well-timed joke. My sister has always maintained that I based Silent Bob on my Dad: the guy who never said much in social gatherings, whose lack of yammering set him up for perfect, well-timed *bon mots* when he did open his mouth. My Old Man was a pretty funny guy when he wanted to be.

That night, he seemed to wanna listen more than anything else. He laughed a lot, and put away a filet mignon, a trio of Manhattans, and a big chunk of cheesecake while the rest of us took the floor. The waiter was kind enough to snap a group shot of us.

It was, hands-down, one of the best evenings I'd spent with my father as an adult.

When dinner wrapped, I put Mom, Dad and Donald in a cab. I offered to drive them the few blocks to Virginia's rented apartment, but Mom said it would be just as easy to take a taxi. My father sat in the back seat on the passenger side, and I remember very clearly kissing his cheek and telling him I'd see him in the morning. He smiled and nodded and said g'night.

I got the call from Donald at around six in the morning. I tried not to answer the phone, assuming it was a Convention fan with no sense of time. When the hotel phone stopped ringing and my cell phone started, I figured it was important enough to wake up for. Donald told me that Dad had suffered another heart attack, and that they were at the hospital a few blocks away, and that I needed to get down there, ASAP.

I got up and got dressed, but didn't wake Jen, as I felt it couldn't have been all that serious if Don was calling. I got downstairs and cabbed it over to the hospital, entered the Emergency Room doors where Don had said to meet him, and instantly realized the situation was far worse than I'd imagined.

My mother was sobbing in such a way that I'd never seen her cry before. She was in a panic, unable to catch her breath, her eyes were wide and her skin pale. My brother, who's always been a rather quiet, dignified crier, was completely red and wet-faced. Between rounds of Hail Mary's, my mother told me Dad had had a heart attack, and the doctors were having a hard time bringing him around. She kept repeating "Not now, Lord. Jesus, please not now..." before diving back into a fresh Hail Mary. This was grief such as I'd never seen before, and I learned it was well-warranted when I made eye contact with Don over Mom's shoulder and he slowly shook his head "No".

I could only imagine it was like getting shot in the head. Life changed in an instant. My heart skipped a beat. At that moment, the Doctor came out and said we might want to come in and see Dad.

Upon entering the ER, the first thing I noticed was how quiet it was. There were no machines running, no activity swirling around my Dad. He was just lying on a gurney, awfully still. Mom was immediately at his side, holding his hand and stammering to him through thick, agonized tears. Virginia arrived, and the circle was complete: the man who'd taken me to the movies every week of my young life, the man who I loved most in the world, was very still and very quiet, surrounded by his wife and kids. All throughout my youth and through some of my adulthood, I'd seen my father asleep. This was nothing like that. The sheet wasn't rising and falling on his great barrel stomach. He wasn't snoring. He wasn't there.

Growing up, the Old Man and I used to watch TV together all the time. In those dark, pre-cable days, the selection was usually kinda weak, considering my father worked the night shift at the Post Office, and would only be able to watch the tube with me from three in the afternoon when I got home from school 'til six, when he'd go to sleep for a few hours before his five-day a week 11 p.m. departure. But I have very vivid memories of my Old Man lying on the floor with me, watching *Bowling for Dollars* every day, with me perpendicular to him, my chin on his belly, as if it were a great pillow. I hadn't done that since I was maybe seven. That morning, I recognized my last opportunity to rest my head on my father and seized it. As still as I thought he was before, my head on his chest confirmed for me that my father was truly gone. I kissed his head, told his empty vessel that I loved him, and headed outside to bawl.

I called Jen and told her the news, and she got off the phone to rush down to join us. Don filled me in on the particulars: how Dad had woken up around five, insisting he was overheated. How he was cold to the touch but sweating profusely. How he seized up in pain when they called for an ambulance. How it was all over by the time the ambulance arrived, and how the attendants knew this, but seeing how distressed and frantic my mother was, decided to go through the motions of getting Dad to the hospital anyway — a kindness that we all appreciated.

Almost immediately, I put up this post on the board...

June 1, 2003

Give your fathers a hug, if you can…

I'd hug mine if I could.

My father died very unexpectedly this morning around 5:30-6:00 a.m., suffering a massive heart attack. He'd just turned sixty-seven on 22 May.

Very emotional day, to say the least.

Pop meant the world to me. The man was an excellent father and directly responsible for my interest in movies, having taken me out of school early on Wednesdays to hit bargain matinees when I was a kid. A quiet man who only spoke when he had something funny or insightful to say, my sister often insisted he was the basis for Silent Bob. He'd survived congestive heart failure a few months back, and rallied quite nicely to better health and a more robust zeal for living than he'd had in years.

Fortunately, thanks to *Wizard* World this weekend, my entire immediate family was already gathered in the same place at the same time — a feat rarely achieved over the last ten years. My sister and her husband, who live in Hong Kong, were in town, and my Dad, Mom and brother had flown up from Florida to see the Convention and my sis and me. Last night, me, Jen, Mom, Dad, Don, Virginia and Eric had a great dinner at Morton's — talking, laughing, and shooting the shit. If he had to go, he chose the best time to do it, surrounded by the children he raised, their spouses, and the woman he loved and spent nearly every day of the past forty-one years beside. In this way, he died as he lived: generously and on everyone else's schedule.

I love you, Pop. I'll miss the hell out of you.

The wake followed two days later, and the funeral a day after that. I gave the following eulogy…

Looking at everybody in attendance this morning, I imagine my father would be really surprised if he were here. Not by how beloved he was — or still is, actually; but rather due to the fact that so many lapsed Catholics present in one church hasn't collapsed the roof… Yet.

What follows is a partial list, in no particular order of importance, of what my father taught me in the brief thirty-two years I spent as his son, his pupil, and an all-around fan:

My father taught me the importance of family, immediate or extended.

My father taught me how to be a man — and not by instilling in me a sense of machismo or an agenda of dominance. He taught me that a real man doesn't take, he gives; he doesn't use force, he uses logic; doesn't play the role of trouble-maker, but rather, trouble-shooter; and most importantly, a real man is defined by what's in his heart, not his pants.

My father taught me how to operate a Yo-Yo.

By example, my father taught me how to always strive to be the most loving husband I can possibly be. He taught me that, in marriage, the term "wife" doesn't preclude the terms "partner", "best friend", or "passion". He showed me that, even after nearly forty years of marriage, you can never be too romantic, and that there's no shame in being hopelessly in love with your wife; the only shame is in NOT being so.

He also taught me that — no matter what — your wife is always right. And if she's not, allow her the illusion that she is.

To clear his name, let me just say now that my father never taught me a single swear word. My Mom did, but not my father.

My father taught me that a father should serve as the best example of a man as possible for his daughter. That way, she'll never settle for anyone who's not at least as good as her Dad.

My father taught me to not be judgmental, and instead, simply accept the fact that most people are idiots.

By example, my father taught me how to be a good brother — and that being a sibling doesn't preclude you from being friends as well.

My father taught me that belief in God is only as meaningful as belief in one's family or one's self. To serve one and not the others is an empty gesture at best, and a betrayal of all three at worst.

My father taught me to weigh my words carefully, and speak up only when I had something insightful to add to the proceedings, or something really funny to say. He also taught me that if I couldn't be that kind of guy in real life, that I could earn a healthy living pretending to be that guy in the movies — particularly when paired up with a long haired stoner.

My father taught me the value of quality time with one's child — even if that quality time meant simply sacking out in front of the TV, resting your head on your Dad's stomach, and watching *Bowling For Dollars*. This weekend, my father taught me that there'd be no price to pay that'd be too high to be able to do that just one more time.

My father taught me how to pick the right girl.

My father taught me that it's okay to duck out of school early every once in awhile to see a movie. The benefit is two-fold: a) the bargain matinee will save you a couple bucks, and b) there's nothing they can teach you in school that the movies can't teach you in two hours or less, with a few car chases and good music thrown in to boot.

My father taught me that family comes first, and that family isn't necessarily limited to blood relatives only.

My father taught me how to feed twenty-eight cats at once.

My father taught me that, every now and then, you've gotta hold up in your room, turn on the stereo, and sing along at the top of your lungs.

Conversely, try as he might, my father was never able to instill in me an appreciation for Country Music.

My father taught me to respect men and women alike. But women more.

My father taught me that if you're ever gonna drive down to Busch Gardens in Virginia, you should first call to make sure the park is open.

My father taught me how to ride a bike.

My father taught me that it's possible to work in the United States Post Office for twenty-four years, and NOT show up to work one day to blow everyone away with a sawed-off shotgun.

My father taught me the value of hard work, and — by rooking me into mowing my grandmother's ridiculously huge lawn every weekend in my early teens — the importance of getting someone else to do the hard work for you.

My father taught me how to love and be loved.

My father taught me, much to the chagrin of my wife, that when it comes to gas, rather out than in.

My father taught me how to drive. No, wait — Ernie O'Donnell taught me how to drive. But my father taught me that it was okay that Ernie O'Donnell taught me how to drive. Obviously, my father never taught me how to gracefully recover from a mistake made when speaking in public.

My father taught me that all dreams are possible — even if your dream is nothing more elaborate than having a wife and children who love you.

Sadly though, the most useful lesson my father could've taught me was one he never got around to imparting: and that is... how to face the rest of my life without him.

Sometimes, it takes someone else's words to eloquently express what you can't compose yourself. Today, those words belong to the poet, W.H. Auden. The poem is called 'Stop All The Clocks' and it was featured in the movie *Four Weddings and a Funeral* — one of the only movies my father ever liked that didn't star Clint Eastwood.

[I read out the poem.]

I was lucky to have had Him for a Father.

I was lucky to have known Him at all.

So tonight, Mom and I made small-talk for awhile before getting into the heavy lifting of acknowledging that Dad's been gone for two years. I offered the simple platitudes that are easy to offer when you're not the one who lost your best friend: best not to think about his death when we can concentrate on his life instead, let's celebrate his birthday and not his death-day, etc. But, really — what do I know about loss of the scope my Mom's had to deal with for the past two years. To imagine it, I need only to imagine Jen dying, and how utterly bereft, lost and adrift I'd be — and even then, it's all speculation. My Mom has to live with my father's loss every day.

I live in a fast-moving world of many spinning plates. Days whip by and there's always something to preoccupy me: family, work, this board. I try not to afford myself too much time dwelling on my Dad, as it tends to bring everything to a screeching halt when I think about his absence. As it stands, most days, it almost feels like he's alive, well, and living in Florida: out of sight, out of mind. But all I need to do is talk to Mom for a painful reminder that things have fallen apart, and the center cannot hold in lieu of our missing lynchpin. And while, when I do give in to the melancholy of my own personal loss, I get very emotional, nothing... NOTHING about my father's death is more heartbreaking than listening to how crippling it has been and still continues to be for my mother. If I could trade in my own professional blessings in exchange for another few years of my Dad for my Mom, believe me when I say I'd be more than happy to go back to jockeying a register at Quick Stop. Sadly, there are just some things a son can't give his mother.

I get off the phone and head to the bedroom, a blubbering mess. Jen and I talk about our dead Dad's respective deaths for a while before I can cry no more. I dry my eyes, blow my nose, and go back to a life in which I busy myself regularly so as not to dwell on the fact that the most quietly impressive and admirable man I've ever known is but a memory.

I call Stephen and see if he wants to grab breakfast in the a.m., then Jen and I pop in some *NewsRadio* eps, to which I fall asleep.

Thursday 2 June 2005 @ 1:11 p.m.

I wake up around eight forty-five, take the standard morning leak and dump, call Stephen Stohn to see if we're still on for breakfast, then quietly dress in the room, so as not to wake the sleeping Schwalbach.

I head down to the hotel restaurant around nine and eat breakfast with Stephen, talking about all things *Degrassi*. He's got a ten o'clock meeting with some music guys who're waiting outside, so I say g'bye and head back up to the room.

Jen wakes up, and we chit-chat for a bit before digging in to some *Law & Order*. After an hour, she sends me to pick up Quizno's, and I tell her I'll do her one better and pick up the new *Moonlighting* seasons one and two box set as well. There's nothing that woman loves more than me, the kid, and a DVD box set, so she's on board with the idea.

I drive over to Quizno's and pick up her sandwich and a small sanny for me, which I eat in the car. I drop Jen's sub off with the valet guys at the hotel, asking them to send it up to our room. I high-tail it over to Virgin, park illegally, and race inside to grab *Moonlighting*. I can't find it on the New Release rack, so the insanely helpful guy at the counter tracks it down for me elsewhere in the store. I grab *Boogeyman*, *Tarnation*, and the season finale of *Everybody Loves Raymond*, as well, pay, and race back outside, so as to avoid getting ticketed. After that, I stop at IGA and grab some water, some bakery-fresh chocolate chip cookies, and a gallon of milk.

I get back to the hotel and we first watch the final episode of *Everybody Loves Raymond* while eating lunch. After that, it's all about *Moonlighting* — one of my all-time favorite shows, and one Jen's never seen (unlike me, Jen didn't watch much TV as a kid). It holds up like a motherfucker, and we watch the entire first two discs before deciding to go out and hit the Casino for a little poker. We shower, get dressed, and head out around eight.

We hit the River Rock Casino and immediately put our names on the list at the poker room. They give us the beeper, so we head down to the bar, grab some drinks, and hit the blackjack table while we wait. After about twenty minutes, the beeper goes off, and we head upstairs, where we both get on the same $1/$2 No Limit table.

We play poker for hours, watching our stacks go up and down, until 'round midnight, when I'm up, and Jen's down. When we cash in, collectively, we're about twenty bucks up. We say g'bye to our table-mates and head off. On the way out, a dude at the front desk gives us River Rock baseball caps.

On the drive home, the tipsy Schwalbach cranks the iPod. We spot a Tim Horton's twenty-four hour drive-thru and jump in line, but after a beat, we decide neither of us wants donuts, so we drive over the divider and get on the 99. Jen climbs out the window, sitting on the door, while I do eighty down the highway. For a moment, she says, she feels twenty-one again.

Back in the city, we stop at McDonald's on Granville. Jen opts to wait in the car, and I head inside and order some snacks. As I'm collecting our late-night booty, I hear an extended car horn. I emerge from the joint to see Schwalbach laying on the horn, and a car full of guys breaking a few feet away from the Hate Tank. When I get in the truck, Jen tells me the assholes pulled up to the truck moments before and were yelling "You're coming with us!" at her. They're still waiting in front of us, and the whole thing's looking one-in-the-morning sketchy, so we pull out, and Jen flips them the bird as we drive by, shouting "FUCK YOU, ASSHOLES!" Jen insists she saw that predatory look in their eyes and that they wanted to hurt her, and I assure her she's alright now, while checking my rearview mirror to make sure we're not being followed.

Back at the hotel, Jen's still pretty shaken up about the whole thing. We get into our woobs and climb into bed, where we eat our McDonald's and I rub her back. She says nothing for the rest of the night, as we fall asleep watching *Moonlighting*.

Friday 3 June 2005 @ 1:11 p.m.

I wake up and shit, checking email in the process. Afterwards, I get in the shower, get dressed, and head downstairs, following the driver over toward Kits Beach for Juliette Lewis's first day.

I get my hair and makeup done and meet Josh, the little kid who's playing Juliette's son in the movie. After Margaret and Forest are done with me, I head back to my trailer and find that Tish and Karin have a surprise for me: a baseball jersey, not unlike the shooters I wear all the time. Delighted by this addition to my costume wardrobe, I get ready and head over to the set: a set of train tracks where Juliette, Josh and I are doing a walk-and-talk.

To be fair, it's really Juliette's talk and my walk. She's got a big monologue to deliver, after which I have a single line, so Lewis is doing the heavy lifting. I enjoy the fuck out of watching her do the scene over and over, as Juliette's so damned natural. Her delivery is so casual and spontaneous that sometimes, she'll start talking and I answer her as me, forgetting we're in the middle of a scene.

On set, the hubbub is the weather next week. Monday, Tuesday and Wednesday, we're supposed to be shooting at a lake, but the forecast is bleak and rainy. It's looking like we're gonna go for weather cover at the stage instead, and the preliminary schedule has me working Monday, Tuesday and Wednesday. I let A.D. Dave know that Harley's got a school show on Tuesday morning ('E-I-E-I-

Oops') that I was planning to get to with the lake schedule, as I wasn't supposed to be working on Tuesday. This new schedule's putting the kibosh on that possible show attendance.

But I've made a few flicks myself, so I know how delicate a balancing act the schedule is, and if I've gotta work on Tuesday, then I've gotta work. But I ask Dave that if he can see any way possible to shifting my stuff around so I can get on a plane Monday night to be home in time for Quinnster's show on Tuesday morning, I'd love him forever. He says he'll see what he can do.

At this point, I feel like I'm now just flat-out IN *Jersey Girl* — except for the part where Ben Affleck is involved with the flick's leading lady.

Oh, wait…

Between takes, I tease Juliette relentlessly regarding her new beau she made the mistake of telling me about, and phantom-lightsaber duel with *Star Wars* fan Josh, who manages to nail me in the nuts, not once, but twice. Before long, we're done with the scene, which means I'm done for the day.

I come home around three to find the maid cleaning the room and Jen holding up in the office off the patio. I suggest we order from Capone's for pickup. Jen opts not to take the ride with me.

I head over to Yaletown and grab the grub. Afterwards, I stop at IGA to grab some cookies, as well as the *Rolling Stone* with my Vader piece and *Time* magazine, which has a blurb about the *Silent Bob Speaks* book. I shoot back to the hotel, and Jen and I dig into our Capone's while watching more *Moonlighting*. Between episodes, we talk to Harley, who's had a minor drama in school with some of her friends.

Jen and I spend the whole day watching *Moonlighting* episodes, barely leaving the bed. During one of the eps, I give Jen a prolonged massage, but outside of that, we're zombied-out in front of the tube from four 'til midnight — pausing only once around eight-ish, when Second A.D. Karen calls to deliver the good news that A.D. Dave juggled the schedule enough for me to get home on Monday night, in plenty of time for 'E-I-E-I-Oops'. I thank her profusely and ask her to pass on my undying loyalty to my new hero, Dave.

'Round midnight, we both fall asleep, cradled in the bosoms of David and Maddie.

Saturday 4 June 2005 @ 1:12 p.m.

I wake up and take a leak. Immediately, I start working on the conformed

Mallrats script for the 10th Anniversary DVD, laying on the floor in the living room.

Jen gets up, and we chit-chat for a bit before settling into some *Moonlighting*. I eat cookies for breakfast while Jen drinks her coffee.

Two hours later, Jen's hungry, so we order some room service lunch, and plow through *Moonlighting* episodes all day while I finish up the *Rats* script. After a full day of this, we decide to hit the Casino again, so we shower and head out around six-ish.

We do the River Rock 'til about nine. This time, I donk out and Jen's the big winner. Together, we leave the poker room a little over even (after all the tipping out and whatnot). We cash out and decide to head over to Yaletown for some Capone's, where we get seated on the patio.

After the first course, Jen runs out of cigarettes and asks me to go get her a pack. I tell her the nearest 7-11's a block and a half away, and I'd rather wait 'til we ate, and then grab her smokes on the way home. Jen starts talking about going to get smokes herself, which I point out makes no sense, since it's ten o'clock at night, and earlier at the Casino — with the events of Thursday night still fresh in her mind — she'd have me accompany her to the bathroom, just to make sure she was safe. This infuriates the tipsy Schwalbach, who feels like my observation was more of a dig than a simple caution. So, in typical Indignant-Jen fashion, she gets up and heads off the patio, in search of smokes.

I sit there for a minute, totally steamed, until thoughts of *Irreversible* come to mind. So I tell the waiter we're not ditching, and that the wife just went for smokes and I don't want her to go alone. He says he'll keep our food warm, and I head out to the 7-11 to get Jen.

Problem is, she's not at the 7-11. *Irreversible*-induced panic sets in, until I recall the many restaurants on Hamilton I passed on the way to the 7-11, and instead assume that Jen probably just stopped at one of them and bought smokes at the bar.

I get back to Capone's and, thankfully, Jen's sitting at our table again, a big smile on her face. She didn't find the 7-11, but she did wrap the block by herself in the dark, so she feels like she took back a bit of herself that was momentarily robbed the other night when the guys in the car harassed her. While this is all well and good for Jen and her self-esteem, I'm pissed that she just put me through this, and to top it all off, she gives me the tiniest bit of shit for being at a 7-11 and not getting her a pack of smokes. Steamed, I don't talk through the meal. We eat in silence, pay, and head home.

We pop in *Moonlighting* and don't really talk, finishing up the last episode in the set. At one point, I attempt a truce of sorts by rubbing Jen's back a bit. As we re-watch an episode of *Moonlighting* we'd fallen asleep during earlier in the week, Jen complains that I'm not being warm. I maintain the subtle back rub was my olive branch. She maintains spooning with my arms around her would be a better olive branch. At this point, I'm ready to jam an olive branch up her ass, I'm so ticked. We bicker some more, until finally, I just toss it all aside and take her in my arms. One thing leads to another, and we wind up fucking.

Post-sex, we lightly squabble some more, and then I fall asleep.

Sunday 5 June 2005 @ 1:13 p.m.

I wake up around ten thirty and Jen's already up. It's yet another rainy, shitty day in Vancouver. We talk about last night for a while, which leads to a long discussion about the assholes in the car who harassed Jen and how it affected her to the point where she had to prove to herself that she wouldn't let those fucktards take a piece of her away like that. I say that's totally fine — I get that. But it's fucking wrong of her to put herself at risk in that fashion when — if something bad happened — I'm left Jen-less over something so stupid as walking to get a pack of cigarettes at ten o'clock at night, in a crank-head littered town, when she could've simply waited 'til after dinner and gotten her smokes safely. We both have valid points, so we let the whole thing go and opt to get some food.

Jen feels like some falafel, so we get dressed and trudge out into the rain, only to discover that the falafel joint's closed on Sunday. We head over to IGA instead, but alas, there are no cookies. We grab some other groceries then head back to the hotel, where we pop in the Jeff Bridges flick *Door in the Floor* and check email.

Post-*Door*, we rock *The Notebook* and play some 500 Rummy. I find it tough to play by mid-flick, because I'm bawling (such a manipulative piece of mainstream movie-making). The flick ends in such a way that I'm completely taken out of the story, but at this point, I'm so deeply into thinking about love, marriage, and mortality that even the fumbled close of the flick leaves me really emotional and weeping into Jen's lap.

We cuddle for a while and try to figure out what to do for dinner. Neither of us feels like leaving, so we opt for the room service we'd previously sworn off. I hit the bathroom, and Jen checks her email.

We then order up some food, followed by a call to Harley to say g'night. She's expecting Jen home tomorrow, but I don't tell her I'm gonna make it for her show as well (cue The Cure's 'High').

Pre-food delivery, I watch some poker on the tube while Jen emails with Chay. The food comes, and we sack out on the floor, eating and watching an A&E Bigfoot documentary. We then pop in *Boogeyman* and rock some more 500 Rummy. Jen wins again, and I call 2nd A.D. Karen to find out what my call time is. Upon hearing it's 6:12 a.m., I hurl my ass into bed, falling asleep to *All the President's Men*.

Monday 6 June 2005 @ 8:57 p.m.

I work, then pick up Jen, and rush to the airport for the 7:40 p.m. flight home. Byron picks us up, and we head back to the house. Jen goes in first, as Harley was expecting her. Harley's immediately looking for the gift Jen promised she was bringing home. Harley covers her eyes, and I'm brought into the house. Harley goes nuts, genuinely excited to have me home, to the point of forgetting that there's no real present — just me.

Gail unveils Harley's awesome, homemade chick costume. An all yellow and feathered affair, it's a testimony to a grandmother's love for her granddaughter (and a testimony to how utterly craft-less the kid's actual parents are).

Quinnster hangs on me for the rest of the night, 'til she goes to sleep in our room on the couch. Jen and I crash to some TiVo'ed *Simpsons*.

Tuesday 7 June 2005 @ 8:58 p.m.

We wake up and get showered and ready for Harley's big show: 'E-I-E-I-Oops'. Byron and Gail take Harley over early, and Jen, Chay, Malcolm, his boyfriend Cubby and I follow shortly thereafter.

At the school, Byron gives me the Panasonic video disc recorder to work while he does the stills. We follow the kids into the theater and I find a place to plant myself where I can shoot the show and not be in anyone's way.

The show goes on. The first thing I notice is that my kid's about as stiff as an extra in an Ed Wood picture. But then, so is pretty much every kid up there. The teacher kneels down up front, directing the kids, and I see that my kid's eyes are glued on her director. I think "'atta girl…" After months of hearing Harley's rendition of these songs, I'm finally hearing the songs as they're meant to be sung (and I gotta say, I liked my kid's versions better). As adorable as the program is, mercifully, it's only a half hour long.

After the show, we all congratulate Harley and I use Byron's camera to snap some pics of Quinnster and her guests/fans. She's still got classes to attend, so Jen and I gather up the crew and head off campus.

Malcolm, Cub, Chay, Jen and I grab breakfast at the Griddle. Afterwards, I drop Jen home, and take Mitch and Cubby with me to the Stash. There, I sign a shit load of merch to hold them over while I'm gone, and chit-chat with Christian about his first week on the job. As I'm signing at the back of the store, I bullshit with some of the customers and personalize stuff for them before heading out.

The Malker, the Cub and I stop for ice cream at Baskin Robbins, then go to Laser Blazer and pick up new DVDs. I talk to Ron a bit, and then we're off.

On the ride home, Jon Gordon calls and we talk about *Fletch Won* stuff. I then call Gail and ask her to order some pizza for an early dinner.

I get home, say g'bye to Malcolm and Cubby, and chill out with Jen in the room before she has to head out for a hair appointment. We make out, get all emotional about separating for awhile, and then she's off.

I eat pizza and watch some *Simpsons*, before heading back to the airport with Byron. I get on the plane, and in two and a half hours, I'm back in Vancouver, picking up my car at the valet.

I get back to the hotel and pop in some *Chappelle's Show*, to which I fall asleep.

Wednesday 8 June 2005 @ 2:22 p.m.

Head to the studio, get the makeup and hair done, head to stage, where I shoot the scene in which Sam's asleep on the floor in the bathroom. As it requires merely that I lay there, I'm done in one take.

I head back to the trailer and watch some tube while they shoot something else, until I'm called back to the stage for a blocking rehearsal of the kitchen scene in which my character's dangerously drunk. We block it a few times, then I head off to get changed.

I'm kinda hoping we get this entire sequence done, as it would mean I can jump on another plane home for a nice four day weekend in LA. My hopes are dashed, as we reach the end of the day still owing a shot to finish out the sequence. Dave opts to move on to the stunt double portion of the sequence, so I'm wrapped.

At first I'm kinda miffed — as I don't work tomorrow, but will have to come back in on Friday to finish out the scene, thus ruining my dream of a four-day LA weekend. Then, I recall how these good folks got me home in time for the 'E-I-E-I-Oops!' and reign in the uncharacteristic diva-instincts. Since Dave's heading home this weekend for his kid's birthday, Karen's gonna be the A.D. on Friday. I ask her to move that remaining kitchen shot as early as she can, so I can at least catch a midday flight back to LA, and she says she'll see what she can do.

I head back to the trailer, and suddenly, Lori tells me to head back to the stage, as the stunt shot didn't take as long as they thought it would, and now I might be able to shoot out the rest of the scene before we wrap for the day. I run back to the stage and block the fall to the floor, complete with blood gag. The SFX guys rig up a hose beneath me, and we run the shot a few times, with Henry coaching me into the exact fall position in the frame. We finally nail it, and I'm calculating the flight I'll be able to get on in the morning, when Dave tells me there's one more set-up Susannah wants to get for the sequence, so it looks like I'm coming back Friday morning anyway. The only way I might not have to stick around is if they watch dailies tomorrow afternoon and Suzie decides she doesn't need the shot after all. Karen says she'll call me around production lunchtime tomorrow to let me know whether I'm on or not.

I get my hair and makeup removed and head back to the hotel, calling Jen to let her know the homecoming scoop. I grab some grub and watch some *Chappelle's Show*, before I tug one out and go to sleep.

Thursday 9 June 2005 @ 2:23 p.m.

I wake up, take a dump, and drop Jen an email about a dream I had in which she featured prominently. Then I finish up my diary from last week and get it up online.

I grab some cereal and pop in the bonus disc of *Chappelle's Show* season two box set.

Now, like every conscious motherfucker on the planet, I think *Chappelle's Show* is hilarious and brilliant. TV comedy hasn't been this consistently smart and good since the *SNL* '86 through '88 seasons. But the un-sung hero of the show has gotta be Charlie Murphy. The man is one of the most real human beings I've ever seen on TV and a dazzling storyteller. There are comedians, there are comic actors, there are monologuists, and there are storytellers, and Charlie Murphy is a phenomenal storyteller. After years of doing college Q&As and the *Evening With Kevin Smith* stuff, I've been told over and over that I'm a good storyteller. But Charlie Murphy is a master storyteller. He can make you laugh and make you feel, and he'll put you directly into the moment of the tale he's telling. The guy's amazing.

If you don't already have the *Chappelle's Show* season two box set, go out and get it now, and watch the shit out of it, 'cause Dave's brilliant. But then pop in the bonus features disc and go right to the Charlie Murphy story entitled 'That's My Brother'. Unlike the Rick James or Prince stories, there's no reenactment footage to fill out the tale. 'That's My Brother', therefore, is just Charlie, in front of a green screen, weaving a word tapestry that paints a picture so well, it makes me jealous. Watch this, and it'll be crystal clear how unbelievably good this man is at telling a story.

Lunchtime comes and goes, and I call Karen to get an update as to whether or not I'm working tomorrow. Turns out not only am I shooting the last bit of the kitchen scene, but they've added another scene to the schedule as well, pulling it up from later in the shoot. Best case scenario, I'm getting out on the last flight home tomorrow, at 7:40 p.m.

I get up and take a shower... which is about as ambitious as I get for the day. Sacked out in front of the TV, I wind up never leaving the apartment from morning 'til night. Aside from *Chappelle*, I watch the last four episodes of *Deadwood* season one, *The Best of Tom Hanks SNL* DVD, and all of the *Mallrats* extended cut and extras for the new DVD, jotting down notes and editing suggestions for the bonus stuff.

I talk to Jen, order some room service dinner, and fall asleep to some *Sopranos* season five.

Friday 10 June 2005 @ 2:23 p.m.

Wake up, shit, shower, roll to set.

Today, 2nd A.D. Karen's taking over 1st A.D. duties, because Dave has flown back to California a day early for his daughter's birthday. Immediately, I start badgering her about doing my shot in the scene they've added to the schedule right after we finish up the scene from Wednesday night, so I can get on the 7:40 p.m. flight home. The rumor is that pulling that scene up is a re-light issue — as the stage is currently lit for day, and the little piece I'm in later is a night scene, which would mean DP John would have to re-light the stage, then re-light it again just to accommodate me. I feel petty bugging a brother for my own selfish gain, but fuck it, I wanna go home. Lindley says he'll see what he can do, but adds that Susannah wants to shoot that new scene last, so she's the one to bug. I opt against this, because Suzie's got enough on her mind directing her show without me whining about going home early.

We shoot the leftover piece, and then I'm told I'm free for awhile. Rather than hang out around the set, I decide to kill a few hours at the casino, and recruit my boy Sam (who's done for the day) for some poker. Forest takes my hairpiece off and Margaret gives my face a washing, and we're off.

Sam and I roll out to the River Rock and play some poker. We both get fleeced pretty badly, and after a few hours, I throw in the towel. Sam had already donked out earlier, so he's bombing around downstairs. On the way to look for him, I hit a blackjack table. Over the course of forty-five minutes I rebuild my kitty, collecting back all the cash I lost at poker (excluding the buy-in I staked Sam with). Satisfied, Sam and I take off.

On the ride back, Karen calls to say my shot's been pulled up. This means there's a strong chance I can make the 7:40 p.m., although Karen tells me not to get my hopes up. I drop Sam off near his apartment, then hit my hotel to grab some clothes Jen wants me to bring back, which she talks me through collecting over the phone. Packed, I throw my bag in the car and rocket back to set.

I get back into hair and makeup, and get to set. My business in this scene is pretty straightforward: interrupt a potential tender moment between Garner and Olyphant's characters with a tray full of food, while singing a few lines of 'Suppertime', Snoopy's big number in *You're a Good Man, Charlie Brown*. We do it a few times, and it's looking like I'm in the clear to make my flight, when suddenly, I learn they've added another scene to the schedule: the continuation of this 'Suppertime' scene. It's about a half a page of dialogue between me and Garner, which means at least two shots of coverage. I'm about to throw a hissy fit, when I learn that if we don't shoot this scene today, we're not gonna get to shoot it ever, as it's a candidate for cutting to make room for another day they've added to the schedule. Garner and Susannah are both pretty in love with the idea of keeping the scene in the movie, so I give up all hope of getting on that 7:40 p.m. flight, bite the bullet, and do the scene. I live to serve.

Tim's in the background of the shot, so we chit-chat between takes, before wrapping around nine-ish. On the way off the set, a visiting Affleck buddies up to me a bit, but I blow him off, as I'm currently pissed at the guy. I get my hair and makeup removed, wish all a good weekend, and head back to town.

I grab some supplies at the convenience store, and head up to my room, where I order room service, eat, request an early wake up call, and kick back with *The Sopranos* season five box set, to which I fall asleep.

Saturday 11 June 2005 @ 2:24 p.m.

I get up early, shit and shower, then make the airport run, which at six-ish on Saturday morning takes me all of twelve minutes. I valet the car, check in, get my ticket, and head to the gate, tugging Jen's Louis Vuitton roller behind me, my backpack atop it.

I board the plane and get situated, only to learn that we're waiting a few minutes until some fuel issue gets cleared up. The few minutes turns into over an hour, during which I fall asleep. Before we take off, I call Jen to let her know we're gonna be late, so she's not sitting at the airport, waiting.

I eat a little breakfast on the plane, listen to Chris Rock's latest CD on my iPod, then watch some *Sopranos* until my computer's battery runs out of juice.

We land, and I find Jen and Harley waiting for me at baggage claim, carrying fresh-baked cookies with a thermos of cold milk. We family hug, and then Harley pimps her earrings, at which my eyes nearly bug out of my head. I look to Jen, who I'm assuming was there for the momentous occasion of the kid overcoming her piercing demons, but Jen reveals that they're just clip-ons. We head back to the car and out of the airport, bullshitting on the drive home.

We get back to the house, and Jen gets Harley ready for a classmate's birthday party. The theme is Little Divas or something, so Harley dresses up kinda fancy. Gail and Byron are up in Big Bear with their visiting Georgia friends Jimmy and Eileen, so we leave Harley with Reyna, who'll watch her until the party pick-up and head out to run some errands and grab lunch.

We head over to the Valley to rock a little Sparks, a restaurant we haven't eaten at in awhile. Alas, they're closed for lunch on Saturday. As we're both starving, we don't wanna head back over the hill for lunch, so we settle on the Daily Grill on Ventura, where neither of us has supped in a dog's age.

At the Daily Grill, we're all over each other like a couple of teenagers, sitting on the same side of the table at our booth, and making out, chit-chatting, and just enjoying the fuck out of one another, as if we'd been apart for months. We're both really crushing on each other, ceasing the light public petting only to eat when the food arrives. I toss back some turkey meatloaf and a couple of iced teas, while Jen rocks some salad and pasta, and then we stop downstairs for some Coffee Bean.

We drop off Jen's dry cleaning, then motor back to the Harley-less house to enjoy a quiet afternoon of hardcore fucking. It's one of those really awesome bone-a-thons, where we fuck for almost an hour, cum together, and lay around, enveloped in one another. I doze off for twenty minutes, then wake up and go for round two, managing to get off a second shot. It's pure fucking bliss being fucked by Schwalbach. Marrying that woman was the smartest move I ever made.

Post-coitus, I'm feeling like downing some ice cream. We throw on our clothes and head back out into the world, cruising over toward Beverly Hills. I don't spot a Ben & Jerry's or Baskin Robbins for miles, so we hit Coffee Bean and I try a Strawberry Cream Tea Iced Blended instead. It totally blows, so I chuck it and take Jen's suggestion to hit Jerry's Famous Deli for an honest-to-goodness strawberry milkshake instead. There, we order the shake, as well as some hummus for Harley, for when she gets home from the party.

We cruise over to Kitson's on Robertson, and Jen looks for a brown shirt to wear to Chay's hospital benefit on Tuesday. She doesn't find a shirt, but we score a Canada pillow (to match the LA and NJ pillows we've bought there previously), as well as some candles and an ashtray we think would be perfect for Malcolm. While I'm getting rung up, a guy who works at the store says "This is awesome: first George Lucas was just in here, and now you." Apparently, the Sith lord was shopping with his daughters in the store an hour before we rolled up.

We head over to Rodeo and bomb into the Louis Vuitton store, to pick up Chay's birthday present: a roller bag like Jen's. We pay, load the booty into the car, and head home.

Harley's back from her party and she wants to go swimming, so I strap on the bathing suit and take her in the pool. We spend an hour or two playing Shark, doing tricks, and throwing eight tennis balls for Mulder, including two sinker balls (tennis balls with holes cut in them that allow the ball to sink to the pool floor, driving Mulder ape-shit). Jen hangs out on the deck having a glass of wine while Harley and I frolic, until it's dinnertime.

In an insanely rare move, Schwalbach handles the dinner chores, whipping up some Quesadillas for the three of us. Following that, she bakes a cake. Harley loses her battle to stay awake 'til the cake's done, and I bring her to our room. We watch some of the new *Peabody and Sherman* DVD, before she finally falls asleep, and I rejoin Jen upstairs with some *Sopranos* discs I brought home.

Schwalbach suggests we cuddle up instead of rocking our computers, and we do just that on the couch, watching the show. She's hinting at going another round of nookie, but I'm wiped out, having woken up early that morning. Instead, she lets me lay in her lap and scratches my back and legs for an hour. As I love back-scratching more than massages, I'm in Heaven. We chow some cake and watch some more tube, until Jen heads downstairs, leaving me to finish watching the *Sopranos* episode I'm in the middle of by myself.

When I get downstairs, Jen's already moved Harley to the couch. We climb into bed, joined by Mulder. We pet the Mulder-Man while falling asleep to some TiVo'ed *Simpsons*.

It is, hands-down, one of the ten best days of my life. No shit.

Sunday 12 June 2005 @ 2:24 p.m.

I get up, take a leak, and go online. Harley wakes up, and we head to the library to find a DVD to watch upstairs on the big screen. We settle on *Gremlins*, which Harley's never seen. We dine on cake and make it through the flick with very little eyes-covering. Going for broke, we load up *Jurassic Park* and start watching when Jen finally wakes, joining us. Immediately, she gives me the "What the fuck are you doing letting a five year-old watch a killer dinosaurs movie?" look. We watch a little more, until Harley loses it when the T-Rex rips into a Galipo-something. Sometimes I forget the kid's not exactly familiar with the food chain yet. It makes me wonder if she knows what's in those McNuggets she likes so much.

Harley and I go swimming, while Jen joins us, poolside. We plot out the rest of the day while throwing the ball for Mulder and letting him drag us around the pool on his tail.

While watching some post-pool *Sopranos*, I check a message from 3rd A.D. Lori, in which she says I'm on a Will-Notify for tomorrow at noon. I'm flabbergasted, and I call back to double-check the time — as Will-Notify doesn't mean I'm going in at noon, but that they'll let me know what time I'm needed on set by noon. Lori calls back, but I miss the call. When I check the message, she confirms that, indeed, a noon Will-Notify it is. I immediately call Gail and ask her to book me on the early Monday morning flight back, instead of the 7:50 p.m. I'm currently scheduled to be on today. I tell Jen, and she's just as delighted that I'm getting to stay another night as I am.

Malcolm and Cubby join us, and we all head to The Ivy, where we meet Chay for late lunch. On our way out, Byron and Gail come home with their visiting friends Jimmy and Eileen, taking Harley off our hands.

On the ride to The Ivy, I call Bryan Johnson to see if he wants to join us at The Ivy, but he's not around. We get to the restaurant and dig into some sumptuous brunch, debating whether to call Mewes for his birthday now or wait 'til we're back home.

We head back to the house, where I lay down for an hour and watch the last episode of the *Sopranos* box set, digesting. Afterwards, I head upstairs and sit poolside with the crew, chatting with Jimmy for a while. Jen decides we should all play poker, so we head inside and get set up. Quinnster starts out watching a movie in our bedroom, but then joins us upstairs, where I set her up in front of the TV, within ear-and-eye shot of the adults. This perturbs Jen, as she wants to smoke and now can't. Things get momentarily chilly between us.

An hour and change later, Byron puts Harley to bed. The rest of us continue playing poker 'til midnight, chatting it up and having a good-ass time.

When we wrap up, Jen and I go to sleep to some TiVo'ed *Simpsons*.

Sunday 26 June 2005 @ 2:28 p.m.

Harley's Birthday. The kid wakes up at six to find the pink streamer-affair Jen's done the room up with. She wakes Jen and I up, and we collect Nan and Pop and head into the living room where Quinnster tears through her gifts. Having only gotten to sleep at three, when the last present's unwrapped, I go back to sleep at seven.

I re-wake at noon. Harley's at the pool, swimming with Byron, and Jen's heading out for a mani/pedi. I've missed the Denny's breakfast, which I'm not too heartbroken about.

While I wake up, I go online to look for birthday stuff we can do. I settle on Playland, a sort-of theme park with no theme that's down Hastings. When Harley gets back to the room, I hit her with the idea, and she's in. Jen returns from her spa trip, and we all gear up to go to Playland. Before I go, I look up a bowling alley as a fallback option, and discover that the Varsity Ridge bowling alley does that glow in the dark bowling thing. I file it away for later use.

We get to Playland and it's a mob scene: completely packed and sporting long lines at the ticket windows. Rather than brave it, we suggest to Harley that we come back during the week when the crowds might not be as big, and throw out glow-bowling as a viable alternative. She's in, so we head over to Arbutus to the Varsity Ridge.

We rent a lane, grab some shoes and socks, and are shown into a doorway at the mouth of what looks like a pitch-black closet. Once inside, our eyes acclimate to the lack of light, and we discover that not only are we gonna be doing some glow-bowling, but we're gonna be doing some Canadian glow-bowling: the balls are almost skee-ball sized, the lanes are thinner, and there are only five pins instead of ten. This suits Harley fine, and the afternoon turns into a smashing success, thanks largely to the beats they're pumping into the black-light-lit lanes. When she's not pitching rocks, she's dancing up a storm, or holding my hands while I spin her around, off the ground.

Jen blows us away the first game, and I win the second, but we tell Harley she won instead, then head out.

We return Uncle Don's missed birthday call before heading to Toys 'R Us , where we buy a bunch of puzzles, a Batman light-up keychain for me, and a bike that looks like a Harley for Harley.

We get back to the hotel and collect Nan and Pop for dinner at Capone's. While everyone gets ready, Harley returns her Grandma's birthday call. I ring up Capone's to make sure they can accommodate us, and brew up some iced tea for me.

Karen calls to say that I've got a noon call time up in Squamish tomorrow. This means I don't have to drive up tonight, so I tell her I'll shoot up in the morning and get there in time for the noon call time. I tell Jen, and she's elated that we don't have to rush out tonight, and can instead enjoy the kid's birthday.

We shoot over to Yaletown and dive into another Capone's dinner. I try to hook up the birthday cake/song thing with the waiter, but he does me one better and has the Bluesman who's up front doing the live music thing sing Happy Birthday to Harley from the stage, as they bring out a pizza with a candle in it.

We get home, and Harley crashes with Nan and Pop. Jen and I curl up on the couch and smooch for awhile, and even though we're both full from dinner, the smooching turns into some heavy petting, which leads us to the bedroom. We get into some really enthralling fucking for about forty-five minutes, then head out into the living room, where we hit the floor and watch *Race With the Devil* while playing Rummy. After the flick, we crash in bed, falling asleep to *The People Vs. Larry Flynt*.

Monday 27 June 2005 @ 2:29 p.m.

I wake up, shit, and check email. When Jen finally wakes, we both shower and get ready for the Squamish trip. We kiss the kid g'bye, and head out.

Squamish is this mountain town about an hour and change outside of downtown Vancouver, and about half an hour from Whistler, the big ski resort. *Catch* chose Squamish to double as a Colorado fishing river. We were supposed to be here three weeks ago, but the rainy weather moved us to the stage instead. Now, we're committed to doing the next three days here, and hoping to God it doesn't start pouring.

Jen and I listen to Spalding Gray's *Terrors of Pleasure* on the way up, and hit

Squamish in about an hour. I call Karen for directions to the hotel, and she talks me through it. We get to the hotel and Nick's there, waiting to drive me out to set, which is, apparently, another half hour away, deep in the woods.

At the check-in desk, there's a chick behind the counter who snaps at Jen and I about check-in time being 3 p.m. Granted, it's noon, but we were supposed to check in last night, so our room should be waiting for us anyway. The chick insists they were sold out last night, so there are no rooms 'til noon anyway. I remind her of what I just said: that we were supposed to be checking in last night, so one of those sold-out rooms is ours anyway. In a huff, she storms off to see if there's a room upstairs, and Jen and I look at one another and silently agree that this is the most hostile and agro Canadian we've ever met. She comes back and marches past us, goes behind the desk, and chit-chats with the other girl there who then tells us she's ready to check us in. I can tell Jen wants to bitch the chick out, but thinks better of it, and waits 'til we get into the elevator to say, almost in unison with me, "What a cunt…"

The room is a depressing, tiny affair, with no 'net access and no in-room movies. I urge Jen to come with me to my trailer instead, as I've at least got the DVD player and phat TV there, but she says she's fine and will stay at the hotel.

Nick takes me on the long drive out to the set, and we weave through the woods on a winding road, arriving at the circus almost exactly a half hour later. As I head to my trailer, I see Garner, who's just returned from a weekend trip to LA where she found out what sex the baby is. I ask her what baby Affleck's gonna be, she tells me, I congratulate her, and head to my trailer.

I check my cell — which is getting no signal whatsoever this deep in the woods — and notice that Jen called before I fell out of range. I head to the A.D. trailer to see if I can use Karen's cell, and Lori hands me a fax line to use. I call Jen repeatedly, but no answer. I call the hotel, but no answer. I'm getting a little worried, thinking maybe — between the altitude, the chick at the desk, and the tiny, box-like hotel room — Schwalbach has gone native on me and run screaming into the Squamish woods.

While I'm feverishly dialing Jen, I notice that both Karen and Lori are somehow online, out here in the middle of nowhere. Karen tells me they've got a WiFi hookup for the Squamish trip, and gives me the password to get online. I head back to my trailer, and sure enough — even though we're buried so deep in this forest primeval that I can't even get a bar on my cell phone — I've got full bars on my Air-port icon.

I jump online and IM Ming, and ask him to call Jen and act as a sort of go-between for us, as I can't call her myself. He reaches her, and I first make sure everything's okay, then urge her to let me send a driver down to get her, as I not only have the phat TV and DVD player, but now I've also got the Ethernet. Via Ming, Jen declines, saying she's fine. She's taken a ride into town and gotten some mags and other supplies, and she's biting the bullet and making it work.

I head to the makeup trailer, where Margaret asks me if I've loaded up her iPod yet as she does my makeup (I haven't). Little Josh shows up, and as his birthday is looming, I give him a couple of *Star Wars* figures I picked up for him at Toys 'R Us the other day. Then, Lori pops her head in to inform me that I may be wrapped soon. My eyes nearly bug out of my head, as I haven't shot anything yet. Suddenly, I'm filled with hope that I can get out of the woods and back to my on-the-edge wife. Sure enough, Lori tells me they're moving onto other scenes that don't involve me, so I can head back to the hotel. I gear up and grab a ride back to town.

I surprise Schwalbach, who's in her pjs, curled up with some gossip rags by the window, smoking and nursing her third Stella Artois beer. Since it's so early, we opt to head back to the hotel, and take the hour-plus ride home, listening to the rest of *Terrors of Pleasure* and giggling

We get back to the hotel and dive into our room, hoping to avoid Quinnster for a little while so we can play some cards and watch *The Jacket*. I'm kicking much ass in Rummy, when Jen orders a cheese platter. Fifteen minutes later, we hear the knock at the door. When I open the door to get the cheese platter, I come eye-to-eye with a shocked Quinnster, who's riding her bike in the hotel hallway, aided by Gail. The kid's like "Daddy?! What are you doing here?!" and I play it off like we just got home. Jen comes out and we both hug the kid and tell her we'll come get her in twenty minutes.

Busted, Jen and I finish our Rummy game, while she goes through her cheese platter. Then Jen goes to get Harley, and takes her to her bedroom to read a *Junie B.* book to her, while I finish watching *The Jacket* — a flick Jen's lost interest in.

A half hour later, I find myself under attack, as Jen and Harley are playing Tickle Monster, and I've become the focus. I give back as good as I get, and tickle the fuck out of that kid. Then, she's off to sleep at Nan and Pop's room, and Jen and I launch into another game of Rummy, while watching *Cursed*. I'm half in the game, as I'm loading Margaret's new iPod with tunes, so Jen beats the pants off me. When the flick ends, we head to the bedroom and continue watching *Larry Flynt*, to which we fall asleep.

Tuesday 28 June 2005 @ 11:29 p.m.

Jen wakes me up at eight. She's already showered and getting ready to head back to Squamish. I jump in the shower, take a leak, get dried and dressed, and we head out.

On the under-an-hour drive up (I'm a hardcore speeder), we listen to the first half of Spalding Gray's *Monster in a Box*. When we get up to the town of Squamish, we stop by McDonald's for a sausage egg McMuffin for me and some hash browns for Jen. While I'm looking at the board, I remember the many conversations with Jen Garner about the McGriddle, and how intrigued she is by the concept. My point to her has been "Now's the time to eat weird shit you'd never normally eat," but she seems too disciplined to go out and buy true junk food for herself, even in her current condition. So I grab a couple McGriddles to bring to set for her, and then Schwalbach and I begin the half hour journey from the center of town to the circus, getting lost a bit on the way.

We get to set, and I pass off the McGriddles to her security man, Walt, to give to Garner while she's in hair/makeup. I get Jen situated in the trailer, password her into the WiFi system, put on *Hysterical Blindness* for her, and head to the vanities.

As I head back to my trailer, Walt hands me the empty McDonald's bag, informing me Garner's left a note inside. I peep the note, which reads: "I heart K.S."

Get back to my trailer and get into the wardrobe. Chit-chat with Jen for a bit before I'm summoned to the set for a blocking rehearsal.

I climb into a little ATV and am whisked through the woods on tiny trails that lead to the shore of a river and mountain affair that can only be described as magnificent. I hate the great outdoors but even I was taken aback by the beauty of the living picture postcard we were standing within.

Ben's there as well, and we chit-chat for a minute or two before it's time to block a scene in which Garner, Tim, Sam, Juliette, Josh and I pull up and get out, readying for our day of fishing. It's the first time Garner, Tim, Sam and I are back in the car since the unpleasantness, so everyone's on their best behavior.

After we block the pull-up, Susannah and John decide to shoot a piece of me and Sam pulling stuff out of the back of the car first, so the crew sets up for that. I stand around smoking and jawing with Sam and Susannah 'til we shoot a few takes. I'm not needed in the next shot, so I catch a ride back to the circus.

I get to the trailer, and Jen's on her second flick of the day (*Wait Until Dark*). We crack open a game of Rummy and finish it before I'm called back to the set for another set-up: the background of Garner's coverage. After that, I head back to the trailer again and start another game with Jen.

Lunch is called and Schwalbach and I high-tail it into town for some Quizno's. Lunch is only a half hour, which usually means forty-five minutes. Regardless, I'm speeding through the woods like a madman so as to avoid getting in trouble for being late or holding up the shoot. We get back to the circus just in time, and I head to the vanities for a touch-up, telling Margaret that her iPod's all loaded and ready to go. As I head back to my trailer, she heads to the bathroom, before swinging back to my trailer to pick it up. There, she says hi to Jen, and seems taken aback a bit upon seeing her. I interpret this as the reaction some folks get when they meet Jen for the first time: it's this look that seems to say "Oh... THIS is your wife? Waitaminute: she's way too pretty for you. Are you sure this isn't a high-class call girl you've rented for the day?" Margaret goes, and I head back to the set for more shooting.

The rest of the day is spent getting into and out of the car. Susannah adds a little campfire bit, during which Josh and I improvise a lightsaber duel (the kid LOVES *Star Wars*). It's an unscripted, undialogued scene, so during the three takes, we're supposed to have a conversation amongst ourselves. I'm flabbergasted at how lost everyone gets without a script — me included. I throw out a convo starter to Tim-as-Fritz, and get nothing, and I mean N-O-T-H-I-N-G, back in return — so much so that I have to work his stoic silence into the scene, lest it be weird. When we cut, I harass him about leaving me in the acting equivalent of a hanging high-five, and he tells me he was thinking about a few different responses and wound up going with none. All three takes are funny in how quiet they are, but drop the sound out and cover 'em up with music in a montage piece, and they'd be totally usable.

Ben and Jen have some visitors on the set today: Joe Kindregan (a young man who is battling the genetic disease A-T) and family. I'd met the Kindregans on *Jersey Girl*, so I head over to say hi and chit-chat for a few, before heading to blocking for the last scene of the day.

Once we're done shooting, I head back to the vanities, get my shit off, then race back to the trailer to collect Jen and get the fuck out of Dodge.

We stop at the hotel to pack up the shit we'd left there last night and check out. The lady at the front desk tells me *Dogma* is her son's favorite movie, and I restrain myself from telling her the chick who was working the desk when we checked in was a total douche.

Jen and I hit the McDonald's drive-thru, then shoot back to the city, listening to the rest of *Monster in a Box*.

We get to the hotel and throw on the woobs, play Tickle Monster with Harley a bit, and have an ice fight, during which Schwalbach and Quinnster are trying to slip ice down my shirt. I hide in the closet for ten minutes to avoid this. The game wraps, and Jen reads Harley a book before putting her to bed.

Jen and I retire to the living room to engage in some Rummy and put on the ESPN poker show *Tilt*, which proves to be a guilty pleasure. We watch a few episodes before moving it into the bedroom, falling asleep to the show.

Wednesday 29 June 2005 @ 11:31 p.m.

Jen and I get up at seven, shit, shower, and shoot out the hotel, heading back to Squamish for the final day of shooting.

On the ride up, I call Marty at the Vancouver Film School to go over the Q&A deal we're throwing the school's way. We sold them a block of tickets at a discount, which officially sells out the floor of the Vogue, and forces us to open up the balcony for sales. The plan all along had been to just sell the seats down below and not open up the balcony, but now we're well into selling those seats too.

I get to set, drop Jen off at the trailer (where she pops in *Bonnie and Clyde*), and I head to set for a blocking rehearsal, immediately followed by a trip to hair and makeup. Forest is off for the day, so Cindy (the departing Janet's replacement as second on hair) winds up putting on my piece, even though I was supposed to be wearing a hat all day. It proves a wise choice, as I get a big, fat close-up at one point later in the day.

Today, it's just me and the little kid, Josh, doing a very sweet and funny scene in which my character teaches his character to fly-fish. The whole bit's poignant and chuckle-worthy, starting out with a shot of us from the back, as the two of us are standing on the shore of the river. I see a playback, and it's kind of adorable: there's big-ass me from behind, head-to-toe in the frame, with tiny Josh standing beside me. I suggest a button to a montage piece we shoot right after the scene, and Susannah uses it. Great stuff, all around.

We finish both sequences at midday, so I get my hair and makeup off, grab Jen (who's now climbed into the jimmies she brought with her), and high-tail it back to the city, stopping briefly at McDonald's for some protein. We don't listen to anything on the way home, opting instead to chat the whole ride down the mountain.

When we hit West Vancouver, the traffic's so bad we decide to detour into the town. We find a Whole Foods, and Jen opts to wear her pjs into the store, going nuts in the produce section, buying every veggie in sight. I stop by the meat counter and grab some Italian sausages, we check out, and brave the traffic once again.

We get back to the hotel and I hand off the sausages to Gail, who cooks 'em up for me. I get into my woobs and we chill with Harley, hearing all about Pony Camp. Jen and I are bushed, so we put Harley to bed early and sack out in front of the TV, getting deeper into *Tilt* while playing Rummy. We're both asleep by eleven.

Thursday 30 June 2005 @ 11:31 p.m.

I get up, take a shit while checking email, then shower and race over to Richmond for an appearance on Z 95.3 morning radio show with Nat and Drew. The format is more music than talk, but we manage to chat it up a bit, and I have a good time with the hosts. I offer to come back in a week from tomorrow, when I've got a day off, and do the entire morning shift with them. Nat, Drew and their producer Chad take me up on it.

Before I leave, Nat says "Man — we didn't get to this story," and flips her monitor around to show me the story of Ben and Jen's Caribbean Wedding on E! Online. The pair have copped to getting married, and finally copped to the impending KidFleck Jen's carrying. I mentally note that, as loose-lipped as I can be, I somehow managed to stay quiet about the baby for almost the entire show.

On the way back to the hotel, I call my agent Phil to talk about the future of *Fletch Won*. We're kind of at an impasse with the flick, inasmuch as I see the flick as more of a straight adaptation of the book, and Harvey and the producer David List seem to want to make something closer to the Chevy Chase version, with more sight gags and disguises. I told Harvey I was gonna do another draft of the script and turn it in by the end of *Catch*, but after re-reading the script, there's nothing I want to change. I see the flick along the lines of Soderbergh's *Out of Sight*, but, aside from me, Mos, Phil Benson, and Chris Moore (who at one point was in line to produce it with us), everybody else wants to do a version that's more commercial. Chris Tucker's name has been bandied about as Fletch on more than one occasion — which is all well and good, but I don't have much interest in making that version of *Fletch Won*. Being told I couldn't cast Jason Lee two years ago was hard enough, but now we're at a point at which Harvey and I aren't even on the same page in terms of tone or story-flow. So I tell Phil that I gotta go with the gut on this one and stick to my script, as-is. If they want to go another way without me I'll understand.

I get back to the apartment and pop in on Harley, Byron and Gail. I say g'morning to Quinnster, who's lounging in bed, chowing down on pancakes Byron made for her. Then Gail and I go over some business, before Jen shows up. I ask Jen if she wants to catch the matinee of *War of the Worlds*, and she's up for it. The show's at 12:10 p.m., so I call 2nd A.D. Karen to see if I can come to set a few minutes after my two o'clock call time, so I can peep out *War*. She gives me the okay, so I move the noon interview I'm doing with Sorelle Saidman at *The Province* earlier by calling her around eleven-ish. We chat for nearly an hour, mostly about the Vancouver Q&A gig, as well as the sudden nuptials of Ben and Garner. I continue my convo with Sorelle all the way to the theater, and wrap it up while Jen's buying popcorn. Then, we dive into *War*.

If you haven't seen it already, rush out and peep this flick. It's the best of the summer (*Sith* doesn't count, as that came out before when I feel the summer truly begins). As I sat down to watch it, I was thinking, "Why would Spielberg bother with this flick? We've seen the alien invasion movie before. How many ways can this cat be skinned?" But homeboy blew me the fuck away. Homeboy did more than skin the cat; homeboy reinvented the cat from the inside out, then skinned it, then put the skin back on, then skinned the motherfucker again with all the skill and grace of an amazing surgeon. It's the most tension-inducing flick I've seen since *JFK*. From the moment the lightning strikes my beloved New Jersey, you're sucked into the flick and feeling unsettled. It's so enveloping, I found myself feeling: "Christ, this is what it'd be like if aliens came. Never mind *E.T.* or *Close Encounters* — these fucks are all about destruction and extermination. I never want this to happen." I loved every second of this flick, man. It's just phenomenal.

At movie's end, sci-fi dork Schwalbach looked like she'd just had the most thorough and gratifying fucking of her young life. The whole flick, she was literally riding the edge of her seat, gripping the armrest. I was almost jealous, seeing her affected by another director so profoundly.

We kiss, and Schwalbach heads down to Robson to shop, while I head back to the hotel to grab my car. I get a call from Bob Weinstein, who asks what I'm doing after *Clerks 2*, and will I be ready to go into *Ranger Danger* for him and Dimension. I tell him that's what it's looking like, and he's all enthusiastic, insisting we're gonna knock it out of the park. Chuffed, I grab my car from the valet guys, and head to the stage.

En route, I call Walt to see if he's seen *War* yet. While I was watching the flick, I thought about Walt a lot, and how much he'd probably love the flick. He tells me he's going on Monday, and I tell him to brave the crowds and see it this week-end. I tell him the scene in which the TV news lady shows Cruise video footage of the Tripods traversing the landscape is worth the price of admission alone, it's so fucking creepy and awesome. He tells me he'll call me after he's seen it.

I get to the studio, jump into hair and makeup, and chill out in my trailer, watching *Metropolitan*, waiting for Tim and Juliet to finish the scene they've been shooting all morning. When that scene's wrapped, I do some off-camera for a Tim shot we owed from another day, and then block the two scenes I'm doing today: solo stuff of me unpacking a bunch of kitchen accessories, and then making a very messy smoothie with the new blender. We spend a couple hours getting it done, and end on a very high note with a nice bit of visual comedy. I get my hair and makeup removed, then hit the gas station on the way home, calling Gail to ask if she'll cook me up some more Italian sausages for when I get home.

On the way back I get a call from Phil going over the Harvey discussion he had. *Fletch* aside, we're also at an impasse with the female lead of *Clerks 2*. We've compiled a list of candidates for Harvey, but he wants us to aim higher. I'm all frustrated when I get back to the apartment, and ramble to Jen for an hour, before I realize the only thing that's gonna pull me out of my funk is the sugar I've been denying myself for the past two weeks. So Jen cracks open a bottle of wine, and I head for the Peanut Butter and Jelly, and the two of us indulge in our vices big time, watching more *Tilt*, to which we eventually fall asleep.

Friday 1 July 2005 @ 11:32 p.m.

I wake up to a very dreary, rainy Canada Day morning. I check email while taking a shit, and then lay on the floor in the living room, finally updating the online diary which I've fallen behind on. Harley wakes up and I take her next door to Byron and Gail's for breakfast. An hour later, I'm doing a phoner with a Seattle alternative station to pimp the Vancouver Q&A that's a week from tomorrow.

Jen gets up and we chit-chat, having some smokes. Today, we're going to Pony Camp with Harley, Byron and Gail, so we've gotta take showers and be on the road by eleven.

The five of us make the forty-five minute trek out to the boonies, almost near the US border. Since the entire *Catch* production has the day off due to Canada Day, Susannah and Jenno are out there with their kids as well. We all chit-chat, then wait while the kids decorate and dress up their ponies.

I do a few laps around the horse farm, picking up hay to hand-feed the horses. Every once in awhile, it's nice to do an up-close-and-personal with an animal you rarely ever see. I mean, I love my dog Mulder, but peeping the horses is a real treat.

The parents head to the corral to watch their kids ride. First up is Susannah and Jenno's kids. After half an hour of that, round two includes Tim Olyphant's kids and Harley. While it's a kick to see Quinnster trot her pony, Cricket, around the track, the shit gets pretty tired very quickly. Jen and I are in full agreement that Byron and Gail are fucking saints, as they've done five days of Pony Camp without bitching, and we couldn't even make it an hour before whining how boring it is.

As a close to their week, the kids all receive blue ribbons and get an ice cream party. No sooner does Harley swallow her last spoonful of sundae before we hurl her in the car and tear ass out of there.

We get back to the hotel around four, and try to figure out what to do with the remains of the day. Harley goes out to eat with Nan and Pop, and Jen and I sack out in front of the tube, watching more episodes of *Tilt* while playing Rummy. In a poker mood, we call up Byron and Gail to see if they're up for playing some poker in the room.

B&G come over with Harley, and Jen turns the dining room table into a poker table by tossing a sheet over it. Quinnster draws a birthday card for Jenno and Chris's daughter Maddy, who's having a party tomorrow at Jenno's Vancouver rental, while Byron, Gail, Jen and I play some forty-dollar buy in, $1/$1 No Limit Hold'em. We do this for hours, while Harley colors and dances to the iPod, listening to Gwen Stefani's 'Hollaback Girl' no less than fifteen times in a row. It's a relaxed, wonderful night full of cards, betting, laughs, chat and booze that ends around midnight (ending an hour or two earlier for Quinnster).

Afterwards, Jen and I hit the sack. She's making the moves on me, but I'm too tired to fuck or be fucked. We fall asleep to some *Tilt*.

Saturday 2 July 2005 @ 11:32 p.m.

I wake up, shit and check email, and go back to updating the diary. Jen rolls out of bed around ten, and we chit-chat in the living room. Jen asks me if I've written about Harley's birthday in the online diary yet, as well as that wonderful Saturday back in LA when we were really crushing on each other. The reminiscence of that day puts us both in a flirty mood. One thing leads to another, and we retire to the bedroom for a quickie before Jen has to rush off to a mani/pedi appointment. It's a delicious little fuck session that gets us off to a great start to the day.

Jen heads downstairs for her appointment, and I continue updating the diary. Her final instructions were for me to get in the shower, and get over to Toys 'R Us to pick up a birthday gift for Maddie Moore, but I get so wrapped up in the diary that, before I know it, Jen's back from her mani/pedi, and I haven't really moved. I jump in the shower, collect Quinnster, and head over to Toys 'R Us, with the mandate that I not buy anything too girly (Jen's against the Barbie stereotype that all girls want pink and frilly things). Any gift I get has to be non-gender-specific.

Harley and I chit-chat on the short ride to the store, and the moment we get inside Toys 'R Us, we find the perfect gift. The birthday party's a pool party type affair, so knowing the Topping-Moores have a pool (at least for their time in Vancouver), we pick up this amazing blow-up Wave Rider with battery-operated motor that actually allows kids to cruise around the pool. I call Jen to see if she'll give me shit for buying this, but she's down with the idea. I grab that, Disney Yahtzee (as a backup gift, in case Maddie already has the blow-up Wave Rider), some new puzzles for me and Quinnster, some gift bags to wrap the present, and we're off.

We get back to the hotel and Jen wraps the gifts. I chit-chat with Byron and Gail and talk them into going down to Blaine, Washington to grab some Marlboro Menthol UltraLights and Coke Zero (neither of which are available in Vancouver). Gail tells me the news story about the abducted girl they found in a Denny's, and we get into a long, depressing discussion about how alert and vigilant every parent has to be in this age of sexual predators, and how it never used to be like that, and how Harley will never know the simple joy of riding her bike to her friends' houses to play in their front yard, trick-or-treating alone, or selling shit for school fundraisers door-to-door.

Jen, Harley and I head off to the Moores, and it takes us about twenty-five minutes to get there. Chris and Jenno rented a great house with lots of room, and the party's just getting started as we get there. Since the kids are immediately headed for the pool, Jen suggests we break out Maddy's gift sooner, rather than later. When I describe it to C-Moo, he goes wide-eyed and insists we give it to Maddie now, so we can crack it open and see if it lives up to its promise.

After fifteen minutes of minimal assembly, we find that the kiddie Wave Rider does, indeed, live up to its promise. It works like a charm, and all the kids take turns riding it around the pool. C-Moo gets into the act himself and gives it a whirl, though it barely budges when there's more than eighty pounds on board, thus negating all urges to get one for myself once I get home.

We do the piñata and cake thing, and while the kids play, Jen, Chris and I chill out by the hot tub, talking about Ben and Jen getting married (who — if anybody — knew it was happening on Wednesday), and the fate of *Fletch Won*.

We chill on the porch talking to Chris and Jenno, and both Schwalbach and I are eyeing their toddler, Charlie (an insanely cute and laugh-y baby), thinking what we later discover is the same thought: wouldn't it be nice to have another kid, and maybe it wouldn't be so bad if it was a boy?

The party wraps up, and Schwalbach and I are the last to leave. We're not three feet up the driveway when Jen pronounces Chris, Jenno and Co. the coolest family we know. On the ride home, we talk about what it'd be like to have another kid, and Harley chimes in that she'd like a sister, if anything. We toss the notion of going out to eat back-and-forth, before settling on simply going back to the hotel and getting room service instead.

Back at the hotel, Quinnster and I engage in some puzzle-making while Jen relaxes in the bedroom. We finish a *Robots* puzzle in about a half hour and then embark on a 500 piece Mickey Mouse puzzle that proves to be soul-killing. Jen joins us, and the puzzle's defeating even her for awhile before we finally crack it to the point where we both feel like we'd done enough. I show Harley the 'Hollaback Girl' video online, and then we engage in some light Tickle Monster before Jen brings Harley to bed for some pre-sleep *Junie B.* reading, while I check email.

With Harley asleep, Jen and I settle into a game of Rummy while watching Alan Alda's *The Four Seasons*, an early-days-of-cable fave from my youth. We order some room service when Byron and Gail return from Blaine with our provisions. I crack open a Coke Zero, rock a smoke (we'd just run out that day), and I'm in Heaven. We load Byron and Gail up with some DVDs, make plans to hit the Edgewater Casino at BC Place in the morning, say g'night, and go back to our Rummy game, following up *The Four Seasons* with another Alda flick, *Sweet Liberty*. When that's over, we head to bed, falling asleep to *Goodfellas*.

Sunday 3 July 2005 @ 11:33 p.m.

I wake up, shit and check email, and bring Harley next door for breakfast with Nan and Pop. Byron's already dressed and ready to hit the casino, so I jump in the shower and get ready. Harley comes back and I let her wake Jen while I get dressed. The two of them are gonna hit the beach and go bike riding while Byron, Gail and I check out the casino. I kiss my girls g'bye and head out to gamble.

We cab it over, and I immediately head for the poker room and throw my name down on the list. They're just putting together a $4/$8 limit game at that point, so I get onto that table, rocking a little blackjack while I wait. Gail's a total slots junkie, but Byron's curious to try his hand at the poker room, so he puts his name down for the next table.

I'm doing well most of the morning, taking down some big pots and at one point, doubling up my buy-in. But as the game wears on, the ninety percent Asian table takes me down, 'til I wind up going all-in with six bucks and getting smoked on even that hand. I look over to the other table, where I see Byron sitting behind a huge stack of chips, then head to the blackjack table to see if I can win back the four hundred I lost at poker. I get close, and then wind up losing it all. By the time we leave, I'm five hundred and change down (Byron was up almost two hundred). The three of us get outside and discover it's five o'clock. We'd been playing for seven hours.

We get back to the hotel and Jen and Harley aren't back yet. Gail gives me the package that'd just been delivered to her: the first cuts of *Evening With Kevin Smith 2: Evening Harder*. I put them beside my backpack, figuring I'll watch them in my trailer between set-ups. I lay down in my room and snack out while watching the documentary on the *Goodfellas* DVD.

Jen and Harley get back from the beach, and Byron and Gail take Quinnster out to dinner, leaving Jen and I with some alone time. We're so into the *Goodfellas* doc that we put *Goodfellas* back on and watch it from start to finish. I order a chicken sandwich from room service while we immerse ourselves in Scorsese's brilliance. Goddammit, that flick is genius.

Harley returns and it's time for bed. I try to lay in bed with her and Jen, while Jen reads a *Junie B.* book to her, but apparently, I'm too distracting — as all Harley wants to do is play Tickle Monster. I get the boot, so I grab the Toronto version of *Evening Harder* and pop it in in the bedroom. Right off the bat, there's Harley introducing me, so before she falls asleep, I head back to her room and ask Jen if I can show Quinnster her intro. Reluctantly, Jen agrees, and Harley comes to our room to watch. Then, while swinging her Yay-Yay around, she pops one of her loose front teeth out. She's excited as hell about it, and we drag Nan and Pop next door to see it. It's her third baby tooth to go, so she knows the Tooth Fairy drill by this point, and insists Jen prep the tooth for the Fairy to pickup tonight, while she's asleep.

I show Harley, Jen, Byron and Gail the Harley intro from the tape, kiss the Quinnster g'night, then start watching the Toronto Q&A. I'm only intending to watch a few minutes, but I get sucked in, and wind up watching all two hours and eleven minutes of it. It's a totally fun watch, and I have little to no cut suggestions. It ends just as Jen comes back to the room. After Harley went to sleep, she'd opted to watch some TV out in the living room (she's seen me do Q&A so many times, the thrill for her is gone at this point), and now she's ready for bed. We pop in some *Cheers* episodes, chit-chat a bit, and fall asleep.

Monday 4 July 2005 @ 4:52 p.m.

On our nation's 229th birthday, I'm going to work.

Wake up, check email in the shitter, take a shower, and head to set.

The rain has moved us to weather cover, so we're at the stage again. The extent of my performance today involves me sleeping on a couch while two other actors do all the dialogue. God, I love my job.

I'm in the first set-up, and when we're done, I head back to my trailer and watch the end of *Metropolitan*, then get started on *The Daily Show* DVD box set, *Indecision '04*. I love Jon Stewart, Stephen Colbert, Rob Corddry, Ed Helms, and Samantha Bee. Even though the "fake news" is almost a year old, it's still hilarious.

The decision is made that I'm not gonna be in the background of anymore shots for the day, so I'm wrapped around four, and back to the hotel. We have family dinner at Byron and Gail's apartment (steak and sausage), and Harley talks about her Arts Umbrella Camp program, including day one of Tennis Camp. The idea of my uncoordinated kid playing tennis amuses me to no end.

After dinner, Harley and I play a couple games of Pick-Up Sticks, then launch into Tickle-Monster for awhile before Jen puts her to bed with a book-reading session.

After Harley's asleep, Jen and I retire to the living room. Jen has gotten into the box set of the new Kirstie Alley show *Fat Actress*, and she's insisting I'll dig it. After two eps, I'm in. It's weird, funny, and just out there.

We watch until eleven, playing Rummy, and then move it into the bedroom, falling asleep to disc two.

Tuesday 5 July 2005 @ 4:53 p.m.

Get up, shit and check email, shower, and race off to the stage again. The work today involves a continuation of yesterday's scene: I sleep on a couch. There's a question whether I'll even be on camera, though, so I don't get into makeup, hair or costume immediately.

Around 9 a.m., Lara and Sus from the Canadian *Entertainment Tonight*-like show *e-Talk Daily* come by the trailer. Lara, who I've done a piece with in the past, has been kind enough to come out west (she's based in Toronto) to shoot a couple of pieces pimping the Q&A gig. We shoot a piece in my trailer, and then make plans to shoot another at the Vogue if I'm wrapped early enough.

When the *e-Talk* crew goes, I continue watching *The Daily Show* box set, until I get the word around one that I won't be in any of the remaining shots.

Margaret comes to the trailer to say g'bye. She's cutting out of *Catch* early to start another show. I give her a hug and she tells me she'll see me at the Q&A on Saturday. After that, I pack up and head back to the hotel.

Harley's back from Pony Camp, so we chill with her for a while. I call Lara to tell her I'm available to shoot at the Vogue, if Jon-Paul can open the place up for us. She confirms a 5:15 p.m. shoot at the Vogue, to which Gail then adds a photo shoot with a photographer from *The Province*, to accompany Sorelle Saidman's piece that runs on Thursday.

I check email 'til I get a call from my agent Phil. Turns out I'm in trouble again for revealing too much in the diary. The passage in question is this...

The rest of the day is spent getting into and out of the car. Susannah adds a little campfire bit, during which Josh and I improvise a lightsaber duel (the kid LOVES *Star Wars*). It's an unscripted, undialogued scene, so during the three takes, we're supposed to have a conversation amongst ourselves. I'm flabbergasted at how lost everyone gets without a script — me included. I throw out a convo starter to Tim-as-Fritz, and get nothing, and I mean N-O-T-H-I-N-G, back in return — so much so that I have to work his stoic silence into the scene, lest it be weird. When we cut, I harass him about leaving me in the acting equivalent of a hanging high-five, and he tells me he was thinking about a few different responses and wound up going with none. All three takes are funny in how quiet they are, but drop the sound out and cover 'em up with music in a montage piece, and they'd be totally usable.

The fear is that the above can be construed as me saying "The actors in this movie suck". Only a moron would interpret that from the above paragraph. Anyone who reads this diary on a regular basis knows about my affinity for the entire cast of *Catch & Release*; shit, you can go back and READ the gushing shit I've previously written about all of them. I've gone on record as saying that I could watch Tim Olyphant read the phone book, I think he's such a great actor — and even THAT has gotten me spanked, because the studio feels it's sighting one actor above the others. I can't believe this shit sometimes, man. But for Jenno's sake, here goes...

The above story about the ad-libbing was in no way, shape, or form, meant as anything more than a humorous anecdote. Tim and I thought it was funny that day. Susannah thought it was funny, too. It is funny. It was one of those awesome human moments. It should not reflect poorly on what's already a wonderful flick (as I've pointed out many times in this diary); it should be taken as it was presented: as something funny that happened in the course of making a movie. Because making a movie IS fun — and I've always been about letting the audience in on that fun with stuff like the board at our website and now this diary. But because it makes folks on the studio side nervous when I write about the fun of making *Catch & Release*, or when I talk about how good I think the cast or director is, I'm just gonna knock it off. From here on in, all *Catch* entries in My Boring-Ass Life will be minimal.

At 5:15 p.m., it's time to go down to the Vogue. Byron drives and drops Gail, Jen, Harley and I off. We head inside, say hi to Jon-Paul and the *e-Talk* crew, and then I take the pic for *The Province*. After that, we shoot the *e-Talk* piece, then head out to family dinner at Gotham.

On the way to dinner, my pointer finger on the right hand starts aching, almost like it's sprained or something. This escalates through dinner, to the point where we stop at London Drugs on the way home to grab a finger splint. Don't know what I did to it, but I can't bend my pointer without feeling a surge of pain.

We get home and Harley spends the night with Byron and Gail, while Jen and I lay down. I'm whining up a storm about my finger, and Jen plays nursemaid. We put in *Glengarry Glenn Ross*, to which I fall asleep by 10:15 p.m.

Wednesday 6 July 2005 @ 11:26 a.m.

Wake up, shit and check email, shower, then head to the stage, running late. I get to the studio post-blocking but the first shot is something we owe from a scene we didn't get to finish a week or so ago, so I'm pretty much off camera.

I go through hair with Forest, and makeup with Deb, my new makeup person. After that, I get into costume and wait for the set call.

I head to set, and we shoot out the remaining coverage of the scene. Then, we block for the scene in the kitchen that we'll spend most of the day shooting.

I go back to my trailer and watch more of *The Daily Show* box set, 'til it's time to shoot the kitchen scene. I'm called back to set, and we get into the new scene.

Between takes, Forest and I stroll to the next stage, where they just started shooting *Dungeon Siege* with Burt Reynolds and Leelee Sobieski. The rumor is they've got Krispy Kremes on their craft service table, and we're in the market for some donuts.

We sneak onto the *Dungeon* set (a series of green screens and partial castle-looking sets), and spy Burt Reynolds dressed like a king or something. We mosey over to the snack table and Forest collects a quartet of donuts. Quickly, we race back to our stage, getting rid of the evidence by chowing down.

While we finish out the kitchen scene with little Josh, camera operator Henry explains podcasting to me in simple terms I can understand. We then block the last piece I'm in for the day with the female lead (studio Nervous Nellies... *sigh*). Afterwards, I chill in my trailer 'til I'm called to shoot, finishing up *The Daily Show* box set.

We roll on the first angle of coverage for the homecoming scene, and while the crew sets up for the reverse, Forest and I saunter back to the *Dungeon Siege* set. We roll up on the craft service table, and this time, we take a whole box of Krispy Kremes. Well, Forest takes the whole box, as I'm falling back on my splinted finger as an excuse to not do the pastry purloining myself.

We get back to the *Catch* set, and share our booty with whoever's into Krispy Kremes. All of the sudden, the craft service chick from *Dungeon Siege* is standing behind us, asking: "Did you just steal my donuts?" Midway through a jelly, I'm caught. As I start to sputter an excuse, Rob, the video assist guy, giggles, revealing that the craft service chick on *Dungeon* is his wife, and he'd ratted on us, texting her about the nipped KKs.

We shoot the reverse, and I'm wrapped for the day. I head back to my trailer and get out of my wardrobe, while watching *8 Mile*, following that up with a facial from Angela (the key makeup artist on the flick), in lieu of the now-departed (to another flick) Margaret, and a hairpiece removal and hair-washing from Forest.

I head back to the hotel, get into my woobs, and play with Harley for a bit. Jen and I both read her books in bed tonight, and then she goes to sleep. Schwalbach and I retire to our bedroom, where we watch the Bruce Willis movie, *Hostage*. When that's over, we try to watch *Be Cool*, but can't get through the first half hour. Instead, we rock some *Glengarry Glen Ross* to fall asleep to.

Thursday 7 July 2005 @ 2:04 p.m.

Wake up around ten, take a leak, and shit while checking email and updating the diary. I head into the living room and call down for the papers. Today, I hit the trifecta in Vancouver print media: I'm profiled in *The Province* (with a great entertainment section cover-story picture) and *The Vancouver Sun*, and get a small piece in *The Georgia Straight*.

Jen wakes up, and we chit-chat for awhile. With Harley in camp all week, we've got the mornings to ourselves. I sit at the desk that Jen moved into the living room yesterday, and Schwalbach sits on the couch across from me, checking her email. I jump onto iChat to go over last minute Q&A details with Ming, and I see Annie Duke online. We IM for a while, and she reveals that she's just bought a house down the street from mine. I give her the low-down on the neighborhood and the school she can send her kids to, and ask her to dump some cash into my Ultimate Bet account.

While still in iChat, I start flirting with Schwalbach, sending her instant messages, trying to seduce her into a little late-morning fucking before the kid gets back from Arts Camp. Tenacity pays off, and soon, we're in the bedroom, boning up a storm.

I shower, throw on the bathrobe, and head back out to the living room to continue updating the diary. Quinnster gets home from Arts Camp, and Jen takes her shopping at IGA, in preparation for Jay and Chay's arrival tonight.

Meanwhile, I get lost in the world of Ultimate Bet once again, watching my pot rise and fall over a two-hour period. Jen and Harley get home from the store, and I still haven't moved from my laptop. Both of them start bugging me to get dressed and head into work, as I've been called in to do some background work for a scene I've already shot with Sam. I throw on some clothes and head to the location.

Since we're matching a scene we shot over a week ago, Susannah shows Sam and I some playback on the video tap, so we can see what we did exactly, as well as how we did it. But what she shows us isn't just playback: she shows us the edited-together scene, fresh from Anne's Avid. I'm tickled by what I see: Sam and I are really funny together, and visually, the scene looks great. Watching it confirms my suspicions that this flick's gonna be really good.

When we're done shooting, I head to the backyard at the location to shoot a few pictures with Douglas, the stills photographer. They send me back to my trailer to change outfits, and then back up to the set to do some more stills. Then, A.D. Dave tells me I'm wrapped.

I hit the trailer and continue watching *8 Mile* while getting changed. I put it on pause and head to the vanities where Forest takes off the piece and washes my hair, and my new makeup person Deb gives me a killer facial. Following that, I go back to my trailer and watch the end of *8 Mile* before heading home (I'd never seen the flick, and I wound up liking it quite a bit).

I get back to the hotel to find Jay and Chay have already arrived. We hug and chit-chat on the deck, then head inside to play poker with Gail and Byron, while Harley dances around to 'Hollaback Girl'.

By midnight, Harley's in bed, and Chay's the big winner at the table. Since I've got to wake up at 5:00 a.m. to be in Richmond for the radio show at 5:30 a.m., I suggest to Mewes that we not go to sleep and instead head out to the River Rock Casino, which is near the radio station anyway. I kiss Jen g'night, and Mewes and I take off.

Friday 8 July 2005 @ 2:05 p.m.

Mewes and I get to the River Rock Casino at around one in the morning, and immediately head to the poker room. There's still a decent crowd there, so we jump onto the first table we can find with an open seat: a $3/$6 No Limit. As I hit the chair, I'm dealt pocket tens, but I don't bet aggressively: I just double the blind. We see the flop, and suddenly, a dude a few seats away from me bets up the pot. I'm prepping my chips to follow, when the dude beside him doubles the bet to fifty. I check the flop to see what's out there, but I don't see any flush draws or straights. The board hasn't paired up, so nobody can be holding a boat, and even if someone has a pocket pair, their set's not bigger than mine could be if I get another ten, as all three flop cards are single digits. The only thing either of these guys can be holding is pocket jacks or better, and I've still got a pretty great shot at another ten falling, so I stay in. Fourth street's still not a face card, but the board has now paired up with eights. If the river is a ten, I'm set like a mother-fucker. The two other guys bet the hand up again. I call, which takes us to the river: a king. The first guy bets fifty, and the next guy takes it to a hundred dol-lar bet. I'm thinking he's bluffing, as there's no way he was holding a king and betting as aggro as he was with those little cards on the flop and the turn. So I call, and all three of us open up. The first guy has pocket tens as well; we have the exact same hand, which would make it chop/chop, if the next guy didn't have a fucking king. Dude was holding king/three off suit, and calling big bets with just king high. But what do I know? It worked out for him. He rakes a fat pot, and I've suddenly got a little under a hundred bucks left from the three hundred I just sat down with.

Mewes, on the other hand, gets dealt two straights in a row, and takes down a pair of massive pots. The Pit Boss tells us that seats at the $1/$2 No Limit table have opened up, so we high-tail it over there, and play for a few hours.

Around five in the morning, I'm not doing so hot, so I head downstairs to play some blackjack, to see if I can win back some of my poker losses. For a while, I'm up. Then, as this is a casino, I'm down again. I hit the ATM twice, and keep giving it all back to the River Rock. I climb back upstairs to grab Mewes, as it's time to hit the radio show. I drag him, kicking and screaming, from the poker table. He's up about six hundred bucks, and I'm down more than that.

We head to Z 95.3 and jump on-air with Nat and Drew. For the next three and a half hours, I chat it up with the hosts of the morning show, while Mewes sleeps in the lobby, hand down his pants.

When the show's over, I collect Mewes, and we head back to the River Rock. I start donking at the poker table again, so I slip down to the blackjack table. I grab five hundred bucks from the ATM and head back to the twenty-five dollar table to play a couple hands. The dealer's about to give me all green chips, but I ask him for five black chips instead. Rather than feed it back to the casino slowly, I'm gonna play five simultaneous hands of a hundred each.

The first card out is a king. The second hand gets an eight, the third a four. The future's looking dark. Then, the Pit Boss comes over to remind the dealer that he didn't burn the top card. The Pit Boss is saying he's gotta take my king away and burn it, and move the eight and the four down to my first two hands. He's saying it's casino policy to burn the first card, and I'm saying "I know, but he already started dealing, and now you want to take away my one strong hand of the three he's started dealing. This is your error, not mine." In the end, the Pit Boss agrees to wipe the three partially dealt hands and burn the king. I start out fresh again, and I'm dealt face cards on all five hands, with a five up for the dealer. Then, he paints two of the hands with aces, giving me a pair of blackjacks, and couples the rest up with faces and nines. I stay on everything, but it doesn't matter, as the dealer goes bust, and I immediately double-up and then some, thanks to the blackjacks. I tip the dealer fifty bucks, head up to the poker room to collect Mewes, and head to the airport to pick up Malcolm, who's flying in today.

After a few laps 'round the terminals, we finally find the Malker, and head back to the hotel. Jen's already called to tell me she wants to go to lunch and then take Harley glow-bowling, so even though I haven't slept in thirty-six hours, I do my master's bidding. I call up to the room as I'm pulling up to the hotel, and Chay and Jen meet us downstairs. They get in the Hate Tank, and we're all off to Capone's for some lunch.

The food's great as usual, though I start falling asleep at the table. Then, I'm woken up by a bad blast of acid reflex, which sends bile as far up as the top of my throat, the lion's share of it landing in and around my epiglottis. The acid's burning my shit something fierce, and I'm downing water like a madman, to no avail (as we learned in *Fight Club*, water just spreads acid around; you've gotta neutralize the burn). Malcolm runs to get me Rolaids, but I remember I've got a bottle of Tums in the car, which Mewes runs to grab. I down five, and then we stop at a 7-11, where Mewes grabs me some milk. By the time we get to the Varsity Ridge Bowling Alley, the throat crisis is over.

We slip the attendant a hundred bucks to open up the glow-bowling earlier than usual for our little party, and grab two lanes, playing boys against girls: Jen, Chay and Harley vs. Jay, Malcolm and me. The boys win round one, and the girls take round two. Maybe it's the beats or the atmosphere, or the day-glo dark room, but Schwalbach and I get into some heavy high school flirting, that leads into some even heavier high school petting. I've got my hand down her skirt, she's grabbing my dick through my shorts; we just can't keep our hands off one another. We adjourn to a dark stairwell in the bowling alley that leads to an emergency exit. We're completely out of sight, so while Chay, Jay and Malcolm bowl with Harley, Jen lifts her skirt and I eat her out a little bit, before it's our turn to bowl. We make plans to meet at the stairwell again to fuck after the next frame. But lo and behold, Harley gets clingy, and won't let us steal away. So we all wrap up bowling and head back to the hotel.

Malcolm, bless his heart, takes Harley swimming, and Mewes and Chay putter around the living room, leaving Schwalbach and I alone in our bedroom, where we get into some heavy-duty fucking. Jen's still tipsy from lunch, and we're both still ravenously horny from the bowling alley. I'm face down in her ass for a few minutes before she climbs on top and fucks the shit out of me. Afterwards, we lay around cuddling for a few minutes, until we decide to wash up, get dressed, and rejoin our friends. I chit-chat with Jay, Chay and Jen for a few minutes, then lay down on the bed and play some Ultimate Bet, during which I fall asleep.

I wake up five hours later. It's about ten-ish, and Jen's going downstairs with Malcolm and Chay to meet this guy Chay's interested in. I'm barely awake, so I fall back asleep, waking up a half hour later to an empty room, except for Mewes, who's sleeping in his corner of the apartment. Feeling hungry, I grab some All

Bran cereal and kick back with some *Glengarry Glen Ross*, half cognizantly playing poker at the same time. Jen returns, more than half-in-the-bag, so I get her into her pjs and lay down with her 'til she falls asleep, then continue playing UB and watching *Glengarry* 'til I do the same.

Saturday 9 July 2005 @ 2:15 p.m.

I get up and play some Ultimate Bet while taking the customary morning shit. I hang out in the living room with Malcolm and Mewes, until Jen and Chay get up. I pick on Jen for being so blitzed last night, and then Malcolm and I decide to hit the Mongolian Barbecue joint on Broadway. Jen and Chay opt out, but Mewes opts in. I'm feeling a little stiff in the shoulders, so I make a massage appointment for three at Vida.

I take a shower, lounge with Jen for a bit, then get dressed and head to the Mongolian joint with the boys. I haven't had Mongolian in at least a year, so it's a real treat (though the chicken is cut a little too thick for my tastes). I load my bowl up with noodles, chicken, House Sauce, and a ton of garlic, opting for two servings.

When we're done, we head to Vida, where Jay and Malcolm opt for massages too. Malcolm's nervous, as he's never gotten a massage, and wants to know what the protocol is if he has to fart. I tell him it's never a problem.

But while I'm on the massage table, I'm proven wrong — as the Mongolian is doing weird things in my guts. My muscles are being relaxed by the massage, so it takes all the strength I can muster to clench that gas back, until the masseuse leaves the room, and I blow the first of what will be a mighty legion of farts throughout the rest of the day.

We head back to the hotel. Jen, Chay and Gail are heading down to the Vogue to start processing the ticket holders. They take Malcolm with them, and Mewes and I hang out on the bed, playing online poker: Mewes at FullTilt.com and me at UltimateBet.com. As we play, I continue farting up a storm, and as the fan is to my left, it blows the noxious fumes directly into Mewes's face to my right. We giggle up a storm, as farts — at any age — are still funny. Then, it's time to head to the Vogue.

Byron, Harley, Mewes and I jump in the hotel car and get dropped off at the back door to the Vogue around seven. Jen and the crew are still processing ticket holders up front, so Mewes and I chill in the back alley, grabbing a smoke. Harley's supposed to intro me, but she's feeling nervous and wants Jen. Brian, the theater guy, gets Jen, who joins us backstage, letting us know that they've sold a number of tickets to walk-ups, thus selling out the house.

Harley gets too nervous to do the intro, so Malcolm goes out instead, and then I bring Quinnster on stage with me to wave to the crowd before I get into the Q&A in earnest.

The show goes well, and I wrap it up around one. The crew heads back to the hotel, where we sit up, snacking out and doing Mad-Libs with Mewes. Around three thirty, I finally crash beside Jen, curling up to *Glengarry Glen Ross* again.

Sunday 10 July 2005 @ 2:19 p.m.

I get up at 5:45 a.m., after two hours of sleep, to take Chay to the airport. Mewes wants to take the ride, too, so that we can hit the River Rock on the way home. We load Chay and her gear into the Hate Tank and head out to the airport.

Jay brings Chay in to ticketing while I wait outside. They emerge five minutes later to say the airline's closed out Chay's flight. Apparently, the Passport Control line is so long, there's no way she'd make her flight. This is bad, as Chay's heading back to LA to run her sister's bridal shower this afternoon. I go inside with Chay to see if Air Canada has any availabilities, but after some back-and-forth with them, they can't help us. Finally, we located an eight o'clock WestJet flight, I throw down the credit card, and Chay jumps into the long-ass security line. I give her a hug, and Mewes and I are off to the Casino.

We both start off on the $4/$8 Limit table. After a few hands, Mewes moves over to the $1/$2 No Limit table, but I stay where I am. I dig my table today: it's a trio of fifty-something guys, a younger Asian dude who takes the game seriously, but is chatty and friendly, a fan, and me. When the fan goes bust, an Indian filmmaker joins us, and we talk shop for a bit. He goes bust, and an old timer who's trying casino poker out for the first time joins us, dumping his hundred pretty quickly. Jen calls to say she's awake, so I excuse myself (a hundred bucks up), collect Mewes (three hundred down), and head back to the hotel.

In the room, we all chill with Harley, playing Uno and doing puzzles. Malcolm makes a run to IGA for junk food, then takes Harley swimming while Jen and I watch the Mosier cut of Malcolm's documentary, *Small Town/Gay Bar* (which is just flat-out great). When Malcolm gets back from swimming with Harley, we chit-chat about showing the doc to Bob Hawk and submitting to Sundance.

Then, I lay on the bed and play UB while Harley watches TV in the living room, Mewes sleeps, Malcolm goes online, and Jen cleans up the apartment.

An hour or so later, we opt to take a run to Whole Foods over in West Vancouver. I pick up a bunch of Italian sausage for the week, and then we head back to the hotel, where Gail cooks some up. I get into my woobs, and Jen, Harley, Malcolm, the now-awake Mewes and I chow down. Afterwards, I lay down on the bed, updating my online diary as Jen lays beside me, reading *Specimen Days*. I fall asleep, mid-update, around 9 p.m.

Monday 11 July 2005 @ 2:17 a.m.

I call Karen to see if I have enough time to catch a flick before my two o'clock call time. She confirms that I can hit a movie, so long as I motor over to the stage the moment it lets out. Based on that info, I throw back a pair of Italian sausages, and Malcolm, Mewes and I hit the Paramount to see *Fantastic Four*.

Mewes and Malcolm come with me to the stage, where Mewes flirts relentlessly with Forest in the vanities trailer. Angela does my makeup, and I head back to the trailer, where Malcolm and Mewes are watching the *Evening With 2* tapes. I ask if we can swap *Evening 2* out with the latest cut of the new *Mallrats* doc, so I can let the good folks at Universal know that we're locked and loaded for the 20 September release date. The guys are down with it, so we watch the doc before I'm called to set to block.

Phil Raskind drops in and while I'm blocking Malcolm shows him a bunch of *Small Town/Gay Bar*. Later, Phil tells me he really dug it, but couldn't understand why Malcolm would say: "The film parallels my life." I'm like, "Well, because Malcolm's gay." Phil refuses to believe me, and I tell Malcolm to back me up (though not like that). Raskind makes me swear on my child's life that it's the truth, which I do. Phil spends the rest of the day in a fog, worried that his gaydar is worthless. We roll up on one of the *X3* stages, where we see the X-Jet being assembled, as well as the hallways of Xavier's mansion. Not content with a sneak peek into the mutant world, Mewes bums a Tim Horton off one of the X-ers. With that, we head back to the trailer, until I'm called to set.

The scene today went from being me walking through a shot, to me having lines. Susannah's added some dialogue that gives my character and Garner's character some closure. We roll through a few takes of the very sweet and funny bit, during which Ben and his mom, Chris, show up. Ben and Mewes chit-chat about the *Lord of the Rings* skirmish game, while I play catch-up with Mother Affleck.

A few takes in to the scene, Raskind has to bolt for the airport. I give him a hug and send him on his way. I shoot for about an hour more, 'til around seven, and then get my hair and makeup removed and head back to the hotel with Mewes and Malcolm.

We get back to the apartment to discover that Gail's made family dinner: spaghetti, meatballs, and sausage. Byron, Gail, Jenny, Harley, Mewes, Malcolm and I gather 'round the dinner table and throw back some good-ass Italian, while shooting the shit about our various days, and when we're all thinking about heading back to the States.

After dinner, we're all feeling lethargic from eating so much. There's a question about whether we're gonna play poker or not, but the idea is chucked, due to exhaustion. Mewes falls asleep on the couch, Malcolm watches *Murderball* in the living room, and Jen and I retire to the bedroom, where I play some Ultimate Bet and Jen reads. We throw on a flick and eventually fall asleep.

Tuesday 12 July 2005 @ 2:51 a.m.

I wake up, shit and check email for a while. Jen wakes, and we go over the schedule for the week. The idea is that we send Byron, Gail and Harley home for good in the morning. We'll be following the next day at the latest, going home for the weekend and heading down to San Diego for the big Comic-Con, so leaving B, G, and H up here only to return on Monday and send them home on Tuesday makes no sense. So it's decided: the 'rents and the kid will fly out on the morrow, and we'll follow the day after, if my work schedule is as it stands now (Thursday and Friday off).

Jen and I play some games and do some puzzles with Harley for a while. Then, somehow, Malcolm convinces us to give the Mongolian Barbecue another try. So Mitch, Jay, Jen and I head over to the Mongolie Grill on Broadway and chow down.

Afterwards, Jen wants to head back to the hotel to pack Harley's stuff, as well as some bags she wants Gail and Byron to take back ahead of us. We drop the wife at the hotel and the three boys head over to the Edgewater Casino, next to BC Place.

The poker list is pretty long, so we throw our names down and busy ourselves with other games. I turn $100 into $200 on blackjack, before joining Malcolm and Jay on a Caribbean Stud table. Then, our names are called, and we slowly filter onto the poker table.

I play for an hour and cash out with the same hundred I bought in with. I'm not feeling poker today, and would rather rock some blackjack. So while Mewes continues to play poker, I hit the blackjack table and turn $100 into $1200 before we all leave.

We get home, and Jen's dinner/karaoke plans with Julie Plec have fallen through. So I take her out to eat downstairs in the hotel restaurant, along with Harley, Malcolm and Mewes.

When we're done with dinner, we hand Harley over to Byron and Gail, and the four of us opt to hit Brandi's, the high-class strip club a few blocks away. I take a shower, get dressed, and cab it with the other three horn-dogs down the street.

At the door, we're greeted by the DJ — a guy named Jon. Apparently, Jon was at the Q&A last weekend, so he ushers us in without the requisite cover charge.

The manager seats us at a nice corner table in the VIP section, and we order some drinks and kick back just in time to see this dancer in a Spider-Man costume do an elaborate routine to a *Spider-Man* remix, spinning around the poles like the living incarnation of the WebSlinger and holding herself aloft upside down with feet wrapped around a pull-up bar suspended from the ceiling in inhuman positions that'd make Todd McFarlane proud.

When Spider-Girl's done, she joins us at our table, and Mewes is all over her. At this point, we opt to take the party to the back of the joint, into the private rooms. Malcolm, Jay, Jen and I recruit (or are recruited by) Spider-Girl and she brings another dancer along for what's presumably gonna be a girl-on-girl show.

The four of us last in the room only a matter of minutes before the lap dances start piling up around Jen, and she chases the boys off, leaving just her, I, and the dancers back there. Adult situations ensue.

We close the joint down at two in the morning, and catch a cab back to the hotel, where the randy Schwalbach and I head to the bedroom to fuck our brains out for fifteen minutes. Following that, Jen has a cheese platter while I have a bowl of cereal. We both fall asleep to *The Talented Mr. Ripley*.

Wednesday 13 July 2005 @ 2:20 a.m.

Up at 5 a.m. to head out to Maple Ridge, to finish the Disco Midge stuff that the weather's put off for weeks now. After the wake up call, I lay down for another five minutes, which suddenly turns into an hour. I spring out of bed, zero time for a shower, and drag Malcolm and Mewes out with me at 6 a.m.

I call Karen to talk us through the directions, as the driver I was supposed to follow has long-since left for the location with Sam.

I get to set an hour late, but it's cool, as they're nowhere near shooting me yet. I have zero dialogue today, and work solely as a member of a crowd gathered at a memorial.

I immediately head to Forest for a hair washing, and Mewes follows suit. Afterwards, Deb does my makeup, and I head back to the trailer to get into costume. Malcolm's already out cold on the couch, and Mewes has wandered up to the set to find coffee.

I work most of the morning, either on or off camera, up 'til right before lunch, when it starts raining. At that point I head back to the trailer to crash on the pull out couch, watching *Runaway Jury*. Mewes has taken up residence in the bedroom, out cold. Malcolm heads for some lunch and brings back steak and potatoes, which I pick at 'til I fall asleep.

I wake up three hours later, still not having been called back to set to shoot. Mewes continues sawing logs in the trailer bedroom, so Malcolm and I head outside to smoke and get an idea of what's what with the day's schedule, and ask Lori to see if Juliette is done with my *Chappelle's Show* season two box set yet.

It's a day of Garner proxies for me, as Malcolm and I run into Garner's stunt double Shauna, who was also Shannon Elizabeth's stunt double in *Jay and Silent Bob Strike Back* (she's the one who did the flips down the Diamond Exchange hallway). We chit-chat a bit, at the end of which Shauna offers "God, that was such a fun show to work on." Immediately, the wheels start turning, and I'm thinking "It'd be nice to make another Jay and Bob-only flick…"

I also have my first conversation with Nancy, Garner's stand-in, who, it turns out, is also from Jersey: the Morristown area, to be precise. We do the "What exit?" thing, as well as nail down which malls we frequented, until I head back to the trailer.

Bored, Malcolm and I grab the car and head down the road to McDonald's. Part of the deal in letting me go was that I pick up a Big Mac for A.D. Dave, so while in line, I figure maybe more of the crew are hungry. I order twenty large fries and twenty cheeseburgers, as well as six chicken McNuggets and a shake for me. While we wait for our bulky order, Malcolm and I rub off some *Star Wars* instant win tickets at the adjoining convenience store, winning two free tickets in the process.

We head back to the set and distribute the burgers and fries to a very thankful crew. Afterwards, we hit the trailer, where the *Chappelle's Show* has turned up. We wake Mewes so he can chow down on some Mickey D's, and the three of us watch highlights of *Chappelle*, including the Charlie Murphy stories on the bonus disc. Of everything Malcolm and I show Mewes, the one line that really captures his imagination (and has quickly become his new catch-phrase) is from the 'Three Daves' sketch, in which Chappelle yells at his Nick Cannon-loving son "I'm broke, nigga! I'm broke!"

Jen calls, and she's feeling super-depressed. Byron, Gail, and Harley have left for the airport to head back to LA, and Jen gets some big time separation anxiety when she's away from Quinnster. I talk her off the emotional ledge, and assure her she's an excellent mom, and take her mind off the Harley-lessness of it all by detailing how difficult it is for a fat guy to take a beer shit in a two-by-two trailer bathroom stall.

Soon after, I'm called back to set to shoot the last piece of the day: a high wide. The moment that's done, I rush back to hair and makeup, get my shit removed, hit the trailer, get out of costume, and jump in the car with the boys.

On the way home, we roll up on Tim Horton's for some donuts, which we throw back while bullshitting and rocking out to the iPod.

We get back to the hotel, and the mischief begins. Still randy from last night's strip club outing, Jen and I decide to hire-in a girl-on-girl show for the boys, the returning Chay, and us. Malcolm's always the event planner for stuff like this, and he locates an outcall service and hooks up our reservation.

Chay arrives, and Jen and her throw back some wine while I sit on the deck and talk to Malcolm, smoking. Mewes has taken up residence in Byron and Gail's now-abandoned apartment, and he's playing some FullTilt.com online poker, waiting for the chicks to arrive.

The chicks get there and Malcolm meets them in the lobby and brings them upstairs. They're really sweet and ready to get down to business, so they lay out what they refer to as their Stag Party itinerary: five songs worth of lap dances and sex show, followed by two mysterious sounding "door prizes".

Adult situations ensue.

An hour and change later, the girls are off, well paid and tipped galore. Jen, Chay, Jay, Malcolm and I sit around and do a post-game on the evening's events, until Schwalbach and I head back to the room for round two of some hardcore fucking, after which we snack out, and watch *Owning Mahowny*. Jen falls asleep, but inspired by the gambling flick, I jump onto UltimateBet.com and play poker.

At first, I'm on fire, starting out with $100 and working it up to $800. Then, I slowly start donking out, falling asleep mid-hands, playing bad cards, etc. Around five in the morning, I move from the $1/$2 No Limit table to the $5/$10 No Limit table instead. There, the pots are huge, and your stacks go up and down pretty quickly. I turn $100 into $500 in ten minutes, then jump to $700.

I'm dealt an ace and jack of spades, so I call the seventy-five bucks someone's already juiced the pot up to, pre-flop. The flop reveals a king of spades, a king of hearts, and a ten of spades. I'm one spade away from a flush, and one queen of spades away from that insanely rare royal flush, so I bet two hundred. Three others call, and then some chip-rich big dick throws down a two thousand dollar bet, essentially putting me all-in. There are two cards left to go, so I opt to go for it. Everyone else drops out, making it a heads-up game.

Then, a five of diamonds and a two of hearts falls.

Naturally, the dude's got trip kings.

I close my laptop, a super-donk, crawl into bed beside Jen, and go to sleep.

Thursday 14 July 2005 @ 2:21 a.m.

I wake up near noon, quickly grab a shower, then head to North Van with Malcolm in tow, over an hour late. After I get my hair and makeup done, Mewes and Chay show up at the set, having packed up all Ben's stuff to send back home. Malcolm goes with Chay to the stage, and Mewes comes with me to the house exterior location where Sam and I take some stills with a photographer friend of Susannah's that she brought in for some flick-specific shots.

Between shots, I offer Sam Gail and Bryon's apartment for the night, since they're not coming back again, and we've got the place 'til the 19th. He's down for it, so I tell him I'll leave the key in his name at the desk.

The stills finished, Mewes and I head back to the hotel, where Jen's packed ten bags to bring home with us. We shoot over to the airport and hit the check-in desk, where Malcolm secures a first class seat for an additional fifty bucks.

In the airport, I buy another Gameboy Advance and a Tetris cartridge, so I have something to do on the flight home. Once we're up in the air, I get tired and feel like laying down, so I head into the nearly-empty coach cabin of the plane and sack out on the floor in an empty row, listening to 'Freak Me' over and over, 'til we land in LA.

Byron and Jimmy pick us up in Byron's Expedition and Jen's Range Rover. They take all the luggage in the Expedition, and I take all the passengers in the Range, first dropping Chay off in Beverly Hills, then dropping Mewes off at his friend's house in Hollywood.

Malcolm, Jen and I head back to the house as Mitch's bag is missing, and we're hoping it got loaded into the Expedition (thankfully, it did). We get into the house to see Bob Hawk chillin' in the office checking his email. Bob's in town for Outfest, but whenever he's in LA, he stays at my place. He'd taken up residence in Harley's room 'til Harley came home the day before and booted him out. Now, he's on a floor mattress in the library.

Harley greets us, wide awake even though it's midnight. Jen insists we bring her along on the ride to drop off Malcolm in Silverlake. We get a few blocks from the house, and Jen's feeling hungry, so we stop at In-N-Out. While waiting in the drive thru line, Harley starts to fall asleep in the back seat, so Jen asks to be taken home, post In-N-Out. I'm feeling tired too, so the decision is made to have Malcolm sleep upstairs on the couch instead of being driven home.

Jen puts Harley to bed, and I climb into my woobs, pulling out some cereal I'd left behind on the last trip home. I down a few bowls, and while Jenny unpacks her bags, I fall asleep to TiVo'ed *Simpsons*.

Friday 15 July 2005 @ 2:22 a.m.

I wake up, take the morning dump, and check email until Jen joins the land of the living. I tell her I'm gonna take Quinnster to see *Charlie and the Chocolate Factory* and jump in the shower. Jen gets Harley dressed, and we're off on a Daddy/Daughter date.

We catch the flick at the Chinese, and it's pretty full for a 10:30 a.m. show. The flick starts out strong, but then doesn't live up to the original version — an opinion Harley doesn't agree with as, at the close of the flick, she states "I like this better than the other one." Fucking kids; no respect for history.

We decide to make a DVD run, so Harley and I head over to Century City. En route, Jen and I get into a tiff on the phone, regarding Bob, and we hang up angry. Harley's gotta take a leak, so we swing by the Secret Stash to use the shitter.

We head down Westwood and stop at Poquito Mas for some burrito action, during which, Jen and I reconcile, via the phone. Post-Poquito, Harley and I grab some Baskin Robbins, then shoot over to Laser Blazer, where I pick up two weeks worth of DVDs and chit-chat with Ron a bit.

We get home to discover a box from Toronto: my man Jimmy Jackman has sent me the first five episodes of the forthcoming season of *Degrassi: The Next Generation*. I throw on my woobs, and while Jen plays with Harley, I bury myself in the bedroom, closing the curtains to block out the blinding LA sun, glued to the TV and all that *Degrassi* goodness.

Jen was planning to have Trish over tonight, but she suddenly feels run down and wants to stay in and do nothing instead. Byron and Gail leave with Jimmy for Big Bear, taking the Quinnster with them, so we've got the house to ourselves.

It doesn't do us much good, as Jen's getting feverish, exhibiting flu-like symptoms.

Bryan Johnson comes by to drop Mulder off and we head upstairs to bullshit, so as not to disturb the suddenly sick Schwalbach. Bry and I chit-chat for an hour, firming up our Comic-Con plans for tomorrow, before I excuse myself to take care of Jen.

I get back to the room and Jen's feeling far worse. So I shoot over to Bristol to get her some soup, and then to Rite Aid, to get her some fever reducers and sundry sleeping aids.

I get home and nurse Jenny a bit 'til we crash, watching TiVo'ed *Simpsons*.

Saturday 16 July 2005 @ 2:23 a.m.

I wake up around 5 a.m., and for the first time in months, I let the dogs out. That's followed by the morning dumpski, after which I head into my office and check email for a while before getting in the shower. As I'm drying off, I call Bryan to tell him I'm on my way. I write the increasingly more flu-ridden Jen a love note and stick it on the bathroom door with a Band-Aid before grabbing my gear quietly, so as not to wake up Princess Sicky-Poo, and heading out.

I pick up Bry and shoot down the 101 to grab Malcolm in Silverlake. Our trio locked and loaded, we start the trek down to Diego.

What should only take me two hours winds up being a nearly four-hour trip, thanks to a few accidents on the freeway, as well as horrendous traffic. But I don't care, as I'm hanging with Big Bry — something I haven't gotten to do in awhile.

Bry is one of my oldest and dearest friends, and probably the funniest person I know. Even if I haven't seen him for months, ten seconds in, and we're back in the groove, bullshitting about movies, aging, relationships, Walt, our parents, Malcolm, Mewes, and especially life back in Highlands. Bry and I never take walks down Memory Lane; we patrol it, Neighborhood Watch style. We obsess over shit that happened fifteen years ago, dissect conversations we had with people in High School, reminisce about all the trouble we almost got into, and still wonder why the fuck three sober dudes (me, Bry, and Ed) got thrown out of four parties, back in the summer of '89. Jen hates being around us when we go on the Highlands rants; most other people except Mewes or Walt do too; I guess they always feel like "I don't know who Shubee, Neeny Balls, Johnny Ram, Stinkweed, or Big Lady are, so this crap doesn't interest me." But Bry and I can do hours on former classmates and people we haven't seen in nearly two decades — so much so that it'd probably scare some of those cats to know how often we talk about them, when they probably haven't given us a thought in years.

And it's not a Glory Days kinda misty look-back, where we pine for the girls we never got or something like that; it's far less sexy than that, really. It's conversation after conversation about Soukel's microscope (a yearbook photo of a girl we never really spoke to that captured our imaginations); about the way Ed would construct hockey nets for the Rec tennis court games every weekend, then destroy them in frustration over a missed shot; about that time we spied on Walt and Debbie when they were still just dating, and how we caught our friend in an uncharacteristic tender moment when he took his girlfriend in his arms and slow danced; about Tara and Jamie, the insanely young girls who Ed and Bry dated on the down-low for years; about Clearwater, the beach club landlocked on Memorial Parkway, a mile from the nearest beach, and its owner, Luke Penta, whose mantra was "Have fun, don't run..."; about eighties metal bands, and how white kids from the suburbs (like me) traded it in for another kind of bad-boy music called hip-hop, while Bry still rocks out to twenty year-old King Diamond jams.

Perfect example of what losers we are: last year, while Bry was living in Vegas for a few months, I was staying at the Hard Rock for a week, writing *Clerks 2* during the day and playing blackjack with Bry at night. One evening, we pushed away from the tables early and went back to the room, where we went online and looked up a slew of people we went to High School with, laughing our asses off about how there we were, in the middle of Sin City, where we could indulge ourselves in any form of debauchery known to man, and we were happiest Google-ing motherfuckers who probably hadn't uttered our names since we graduated. Bullshitting about the old days with Bry is one of my top five favorite pastimes, because we've never let them become the old days; with us, the past is the present.

Four hours whip by, and we're in San Diego, at the Marriott. The Con has gotten me a room cross town at the W Hotel, but even though we left LA at eight in the morning, we're arriving with about forty-five minutes to spare before my one o'clock panel, so I blow off the W and valet Jen's Range Rover at the Marriott. Bry, Mitch and I take leaks, then grab some quick lunch before calling Chappy to meet us at the back of the Convention Center with our badges.

Chappy walks us in, and I head straight to Hall H, where I'll be doing my panel. They're bringing people in, so the Con folks bring us up to the green room. I'm sweating my ass off after the trek around the Convention Center, so I'm grabbing napkins and scrubbing the copious amounts of perspiration off my brow. Then, they bring us down the elevator to the back of the stage, and I meet up with Richard Kelly, who'll be doing a brief *Southland Tales* thing at the end of my Q&A, when we announce the *Southland Tales* prequel graphic novels Richard's writing and Chappy and I are publishing through a joint View Askew/Graphitti Designs venture. Also backstage is Diane from Funimation, who's set me up with some *Degrassi* clips to show the crowd, from the Jay and Silent Bob episodes. I go over the clips with her, making sure they're whole scenes, and not just outtakes, and she assures me they are. With that, I head out.

I've never spoken in Hall H before, oddly enough. Not sure how new it is, but the biggest room I've ever done at Comic-Con has always been the biggest room I was under the impression they offered: the 3,000 seater. Hall H is more than double that; at 6,500, it's the biggest crowd I've ever spoken to before. And the house is packed.

Now I'm not stupid: I know all those people aren't there just for me. Some folks camp out in these lecture halls, watching a full day's worth of programming, waiting through shit they're not wild about to get to stuff they love. Even as I hit the stage, I know there are a bunch of folks in attendance holding seats for the *King Kong* panel later in the day. But I always dig having non-VA enthusiasts in the room, because if I do my job correctly, I can convert them by panel's end. I've read online many times the same sentiment, post-Q&A or panel: "I never liked his flicks, but he's pretty fucking funny." I'll take that. Not to say I want an audience of heathens, but mixing a few in with the hardcore keeps a brother honest, sometimes; makes him work harder to win the room.

I'm getting the big laughs, until I make the mistake of running the *Degrassi* clips, which isn't the whole Jay and Bob ninja fight scene I was assured it was, but is instead two whole takes of me talking to the Caitlin character, completely dry of sound mixing and score. Worse, those two takes aren't much different from one another, and they're played back-to-back; so the already tepid reaction the first take got seemed like a standing ovation compared to the relative silence watching it run again accompanied. I was so pissed; I mean, had I known what the clips were — and that they were identical, no less — I'd have kept answering queries instead. Indeed, I believe we probably put a few fence-sitters off from buying the *Jay and Silent Bob Do Degrassi* DVD, so boring were the clips.

The lights come back up and I recover pretty quickly, getting the Ha-Has back ASAP. When the Con folks tell me I've got to wrap it up (and I'm not used to an hour-only Q&A; the shortest I've done in recent memory has been four hours), I bring out Richard Kelly, who looks a little shell-shocked by the Sermon on the Mount atmosphere of Hall H. He drops a little science (and a clip) about *Southland Tales*, and then we're off.

I grab a smoke with the boys, then head to the booth to do some signing of the San Diego exclusive Kevin Smith InAction Figure. Five hundred people have just suddenly gathered at the Graphitti/Secret Stash West booth, and the Fire Marshal's threatening to shut the Con down, unless we can disburse the crowd and get the aisles clear. I agree to sign for the first seventy-five people at the booth, and then promise to tag for the remaining four hundred and change upstairs, in the autograph area.

All the signing takes me to about 5:45/6:00-ish, after which I wash the fuck out of my hands (shaking hands with that many people will make a brother germ-y, to say the least), then head back to the green room to chill and wait for the Big Show.

While I was signing, Malcolm and Bryan were badgering me about staying to watch the Tenacious D performance following the *King Kong* panel. But I was telling them "I've gotta get home to Jen. We've got a drive ahead of us." But Malcolm pleaded until I relented and offered, "If I can intro the D, I'll stick around." Malcolm's nothing if not a closer, so he went to work on securing me the Tenacious D intro honors. He came back in five minutes, offering, "It's done. They're psyched you wanna do it."

Smoking on the green room porch, I'm thrown by how star-studded the San Diego Comic-Con has become. Back in '95, the first time I ever attended, the biggest non-comics name in attendance was maybe Bruce Campbell. Now, it's like ShoWest Junior there. No less than three of the most recent Academy Award winners for Best Actor and Actress (Adrien Brody, Charlize Theron, and Jamie Foxx) were whoring their latest projects (*Kong*, *Aeon Flux*, and *Stealth*) to the Con crowds. It's nuts how much power the geek audience now wields, whereas we could never even so much as get a handjob back in the day.

I chat it up with Mark Steven Johnson, who's there with Eva Mendes, the female lead of Mark's *Ghost Rider*; I talk to Rob Cohen about *Stealth*; I talk to my man Jack Black (the guy I met with over a year ago to talk into playing *Ranger Danger*) about the flick he's gonna do with the *Napoleon Dynamite* director. And then, it's time to do the D.

I'm a huge Tenacious D fan. I remember the first time I saw the HBO shorts, back while we were shooting *Dogma* in Pittsburgh. Mos had gotten a bunch of tapes of the shows from Raskind I believe, and they were the buzz-watch of the show, passed from cast and crew member to cast and crew member. I'd seen them play in New York one night, years back with Jen, Malcolm and Alanis, of all people. We'd hit a PJ Harvey show at the Knitting Factory, and then shot over to what I'm thinking was the Hammerstein Ballroom to watch JB and KG own bitches. My fandom forced me to uncharacteristically ask if I could do something

I wasn't being asked to do in the first place — which has happened on only two other occasions I can think of: when I wanted to guest on *Law & Order* and *Degrassi*. But I didn't care. I am humbled by the D, and wanted to bring them out that night. Mercifully, the guys said yes, and suddenly, there I was: having another one of those "after this, I can die a happy man" moments.

So we're backstage, the house is packed, and the New Line trailer show is coming to an end, signaling the start of the Tenacious D set. I'm given the hand mic and told to go. I ascend the stairs, the happiest boy in the world.

And then trip on the top step and fall flat on my face in front of 6,500 people.

Yes, it was embarrassing as fuck — 'cause when a fat man goes down, he goes down hard. But I immediately leapt to my feet, dusted off, and got a thunderous greeting. I joke around for a bit, and then tell the crowd "There are only nine cocks in the world I would suck. There were ten, but I topped Affleck off and crossed his name off the list. These guys I'm gonna bring out are numbers six and five. Give it up for the men of Inspirado... TENACIOUS D."

As I leave the stage, I hug Jack and get stopped by Kyle, who turns his back to the crowd, drops his shorts, and thrusts his dick at me. I mime making the drop, and then rush off stage, through the backstage, and over to the small private seating area on stage right, where I watch the killer performance of two chubby guys who're flat-out geniuses drop on the crowd. Once the show's over, I collect Bry and Malcolm, and Margot and George, our escorts/security, bring us through the loading docks and back to the hotel, where we grab the car and hit the road.

Two hours and change and a McDonald's stop later, I drop Malcolm and Bry off, and head home to Jen, who's now so feverish, she's sweated through three pairs of pajamas — which is saying a lot because Schwalbach NEVER sweats. I lay down beside Jen, recounting the events of the day for her. Then, I load up her water pitcher with ice and fresh aqua and pop in a DVD of the eighties *Twilight Zone* from the new box set that just came out last week, to which we fall asleep.

Sunday 17 July 2005 @ 2:24 a.m.

I wake up around five, take a dump, let the dogs out, and check the boards and email. I bring my laptop upstairs and make some oatmeal, throwing it back while checking the weekend grosses. I'm feeling a little gross, so I jump in the pool for a while and play ball with Mulder.

Post-pool, I dry off and head downstairs, where I crawl back into bed and go back to sleep 'til noon.

I get up and putter with Jen before she sends me to Bristol for more soup and ice cream, to soothe her swollen glands and sore throat. On the way back, I hit 7-11 for some smokes and Emergen-C for Jen.

When I get back to the house, I indulge in some ice cream beside the wife, watching *Twilight Zone* eps. Later, I do laundry and make Italian Sausages on the grill, most of which I burn and give to the dogs. I convince Jen to come upstairs and relax in the sun for a while, then head downstairs to shit and shower. While drying off, I check the laundry again and bring up some new water for the office cooler.

We talk to Harley on the phone, who's still up in Big Bear with Nan, Pop and Jimmy, and opt not to bring her home, in case Jen's contagious. Gail jumps on and reminds me to get going, as I've got a 7:50 p.m. flight back to Vancouver to catch. Jen's saying she's gonna go, but I read her the riot act, as she's in no shape to travel upstairs, let alone to the Van.

I grab my laundry, fold and pack it, then get dressed and head upstairs to sign a bunch of *Jersey Girl* and *Dogma* grid posters for the online Stash. Mewes joins me, and we chit-chat a bit while I'm signing, then head downstairs, where he collects my bag to load into the car, and I say g'bye to my poor, sick One True, who's heartbroken she can't come with me in her condition, but will join me in a few days, when her fever breaks.

Mewes drives me to the airport, and I jump on the plane, taking some pics in the terminal with fans who'd been at the Con. On the plane, the dude who played Fat Albert (either Keenan or Kel) chats me up, saying he'd seen *Evening With* on cable, and was wondering if I'm a standup, and if not, what I do for a living. He's seated beside the chick from *ER* and *The Grid*, and as they seem pretty chummy, I'm assuming they're heading up to Vancouver to shoot a flick together.

I slap on my headphones and listen to 'Freak Me' about thirty times in a row, while playing Gameboy Advance Tetris. Before long, we land, and I shoot through Customs and wait for my bag to come down the carousel. I get to the valet desk, but nobody's there. I talk to Jen while waiting for half an hour, and then call the main office of the valet joint. Somebody comes down to give me my keys, and even though I've been waiting and I'm pissed, I still tip the guy. I'm dumb like that.

Fifteen minutes later, I'm back in City Center, at the hotel. I get into the apartment, throw on the woobs, and relax to some *Fight Club*, to which I crash.

Monday 18 July 2005 @ 4:38 a.m.

The will-notify I get at 10 a.m. notifies me that it's looking more like a 2 p.m. call time, so I opt to catch up on the diary.

At two, I get the call from Karen, telling me that they're knee-deep in another scene, hence not getting to any of my scheduled stuff today. I've got the day off.

I call Jen at home to let her know, and she's even worse than yesterday. She's gone to the doctor's office, where she was told that what she has started as strep has turned into something worse. She tells me she got a throat culture done, took a shot in the ass cheek (not like that, you fucks), and was prescribed a heavy duty antibiotic, before heading home to lay in bed. I tell her I'll call her later, and let her get some rest.

Meanwhile, over a thousand miles away, I make it an Anne Coates mini film fest in my room, watching first *Erin Brockovich* and following it with *Out of Sight* — the latter being one of the best edited films of all time.

I'd forgotten how good *Brockovich* was, too. The script is tight, and the performances wonderful. Susannah wrote it, so I suddenly feel a little chuffed peeping it out. The person responsible for a flick I've enjoyed/am currently enjoying likes me enough to put me in a flick she not only wrote, but is also directing. Maybe I'm not such a goon after all?

I spend the rest of the day/night playing far too much Ultimate Bet with UB points, as my account's out of cash. I do this until eleven or so, when I fall asleep watching *Fight Club*.

Tuesday 19 July 2005 @ 4:40 a.m.

Get up, shit, shower, and shoot the flick.

Between takes, I call Jen to see how she's doing. She insists that as she feels no better the antibiotics can't be working. Four hours later, Jen calls back to say the antibiotics finally kicked in, and she suddenly feels fifty percent better, and almost human again.

We wrap, and I head back to the hotel. I pop in *Crash* while playing some poker at UltimateBet.com, however twenty minutes in, I'm so sucked in by the flick, that I put the laptop to the side and devote all my attention to, what turns out to be, a great, great flick.

Post-flick, I put on some *NewsRadio* eps and jump back into some Ultimate

Bet. Annie Duke pops up on my iChat Buddy List, so I bullshit with her a bit. She's kind enough to reload my cash account at UB, so I play Hold 'Em 'til I fall asleep.

Wednesday 20 July 2005 @ 4:41 a.m.

Back to the stage, for the final few days of Vancouver production on *Catch*. Afterwards, at night, I head over to the River Rock for some blackjack. Jen calls me to let me know she's made a complete comeback, and that all the power's gone out in the Hills, so she'll be staying at the Standard for the night.

I get back to the hotel and play Ultimate Bet and watch *Fight Club*. I talk to Jen again, who's now back in the house as the power kicked back in. I tell her how much I miss her and love her, then hang up and go back to playing UB. I lose five hundred bucks and fall asleep.

Thursday 21 July 2005 @ 4:42 a.m.

X-Men 3 is taking up most of the lot at the Vancouver Film Studio, so this is the last day at the old lot. As of tomorrow, we move to First Light Stages, a few miles down the road. Between takes, I head up into the production office on the lot and IM Scott copies of the watermarked *Clerks 2* script for Ratface (our production designer), Tracy McGrath (our production supervisor), and Jim (the new locations guy). Once that's out of the way, I play some more Ultimate Bet until I'm called back to the set.

We wrap, and I head back to the hotel, stopping at the food store, where I grab some cereal and milk. I get back to the apartment, climb into my woobs, and play more Ultimate Bet while watching *Fight Club*.

I talk to Jen, who's booked herself on a flight out tomorrow, so she can pack up the room and drive home with me after wrap on Saturday.

When we hang up, I play some more Ubizzles. At first, I'm up a grand. Then, over the course of three hours, I donk out of not just my winnings, but my initial buy-in. On Tilt, I head to the $5/$10 table and throw up $400, of which I'm fleeced in a matter of fifteen minutes — a sure sign that I should go to bed; which I do, watching *Fight Club* again.

Friday 22 July 2005 @ 4:42 a.m.

Since my call time's not 'til noon-ish, I sleep in. When I get up and head to the kitchen, I notice an envelope stuffed under the door. It's the checkout bill. I call downstairs just to double-check that the hotel knows I'm not leaving 'til tomorrow, and I'm informed that they rented my apartment out already, as they were under the impression that I was leaving today. I tell 'em it's my fault that I never told them I was staying one more day beyond the contracted dates, but it's impossible for me to move out of the room today, as I haven't even started packing and I have to go to work. The front desk ultimately accommodates me, giving me twenty-four hours to check out. That fire put out, I shit and shower, then head over to First Light Studios, where the production's built a fake motel room that I'll be spending the next two days in.

This is the scene I've least looked forward to, as it's a scene in which Juliette Lewis's character gives my character a massage. And while it's not written into the script, I'm thinking that a massage means I've gotta take my shirt off.

Now, mind you, I almost never take my shirt off. I've always felt that, since I'm so fat and out of shape, it's kind of my civic duty to keep my white, flabby belly covered, and my man-boobs out of sight — just to keep the folks around me comfortable. Oh, sure — the wife asks me to take it off when we're fucking; she says she likes to feel my body against hers. But I rarely oblige, out of fear that she'll feel too much of my body against hers, realize she's been fucking a fat guy all these years, smarten up and leave me (or at least start fucking someone relatively toned-up on the side). I've got 'love handles' that go beyond the standard spare tire, and they're both lined with stretch marks. I mean, nobody should have to be subjected to laying eyes on this shit, which is why I leave my shirt on at all times — even when I'm being intimate. Fuck, I sometimes think about leaving it on when I take a shower, just so I don't have to deal with the view.

So based on all that, you'd imagine I'd especially never dream of taking my shirt off in public. Susannah, however — God bless her good heart — does dream of it... or at least assumes I'm okay with peeling. I discover this when I hit the set and chat up Susannah, feeling her out about what she's looking for in the scene.

"Suz," I say, "I don't have to take my shirt off for the massage scene, do I?"

"You don't want to?"

"Not really."

"Then no. But I thought you would."

"I'd rather not."

"Okay."

Alright. That was easy. No more worries.

I head to hair and makeup, then back to my trailer, to get into costume. Then, I get the word that Suz is gonna pop by the trailer. I already know what's coming.

"Suz," I say, before she can get her thought out, "I don't even take my shirt off in front of my wife."

"You're kidding."

"Nope. When we fuck, I leave my shirt on."

She measures this, then shrugs, heading toward the door.

"It'd be a kind of breakthrough for you if you did."

"I love you to death, but it's not gonna happen."

The whole moment — a director talking to an actor about being topless — takes me back to the set of *Mallrats*, when moments before we were to shoot the scene in which Silent Bob crashes through the wall of the changing room at Popular Girl just as Gwen is closing her shirt, Joey had a massive change of heart about doing the onscreen nudity.

Me? I didn't care. I like tits as much as the next guy, but having tits in the movie wasn't my idea; it was Jim Jacks's. He said his exhibitor friends always lamented that they missed the days of the teen titty comedy. Based on that, since we were already making something of a teen comedy, we might as well put some nudity in. Eager to please, I conceded.

So when Joey expressed hesitancy about flashing, I was like "It's cool. We don't need you to do it." However, Jim got super-pissed, insisting Joey had signed a contract saying she was going to flash in that shot, and if she didn't do it, why'd we bother casting her. On and on this went, with Jim getting more and more mad, and Joey getting more and more upset.

Finally, Joey pulled me to the side and said, "How long does it need to be?"

"You don't have to do it at all. Really. I mean…"

"How about this?"

And with that, Joey flashed me, on the second floor of the Eden Prairie Mall, during shopping hours. I was a bit flummoxed, going so far as to avert my eyes — which she pointed out was dopey, as she needed me to sign off on the duration of the flash. She was right, but I couldn't ogle her boobs — not even for work. It never felt right. It was just too weird a moment for me to be involved in — particularly because I'd have rather not include the shot in the flick in the first place.

And here I was, almost exactly ten years later, trying to keep from showing *my* tits in a movie.

Life takes you strange places, I swear.

Waiting to shoot, Juliette and I have a nice long bullshit session for the first time over the course of the shoot. With her character coming into the flick late, Lewis wasn't always around on set, so aside from the scenes we shared and some chit-chat in the vanities trailer, we never really hung out that much on set. Today was different as it was just us in the scene, and since it was something of an intimate scene, I think we were both kind of relating to one another in that "We're in this thing together" type of fashion. Regardless of why we're so suddenly bonded, I enjoy the hell out of talking to her.

We spend the rest of the day shooting two parts of the three-part scene, and Juliette does a brilliant bit of physical comedy on top of me, after the last take of which, we're given a round of applause. We watch the shot on the video playback, and it's really, really hysterical. Great stuff... and I got to keep my shirt on, bless Susannah's heart.

Right before we end for the day, the crew wrap gift is given out. Earlier, Jenno and Susannah had given everyone *Catch & Release* jackets, and Garner had given everyone LL Bean tote bags with *Catch & Release* stitched into them. Excellent swag indeed, but this wrap gift took the cake: a beautiful, printed and bound book of black & white behind the scenes photos taken by A.D. Dave Sardi over the course of production. Flipping through the pages, I see the last three months of my life splayed out across the pages, and it immediately fills me with warmth for all involved in the show. It's a brilliant wrap gift idea, and one I intend to steal and use myself.

I head home to find Jen waiting for me in the room already. We make out a bit, then chit-chat and get caught up, before I collapse onto the bed and order room service, while Jen starts packing up the apartment. After I gorge on my chicken sandwich dinner, I fall asleep watching *NewsRadio* while Jen continues packing.

Saturday 23 July 2005 @ 4:56 a.m.

This is the last Vancouver day of the show. Everything's all packed and ready to be loaded into the Hate Tank by noon. The big question is whether or not we bring home the three TVs we bought while up there. I decide to keep two of them and bring the third to the set to give to Lori, who — as the 3rd A.D. — had to put up with a lot of grief for my lateness.

I get to set, give Lori the wrap gift TV, get my hair and makeup done, get into costume, and get my ass over to the set, where Juliette and I do the more tender part of our characters' motel misadventure. Juliette, as always, is amazing, and so convincing that — for the first time ever on the show — I feel like I stop simply playing Sam for a moment and slip into *being* (not just *pretending* to be, but actually *being*) Sam.

The caterers do a massive lunch, and rather than eat in my trailer, I enjoy my steak sandwich in the lunch tent, with the rest of the crew.

Post-lunch, I realize I don't have my cell phone, so I borrow Shelly's and call Jen, who's already loaded up the truck, checked out of the hotel, and is at the Vida Spa, enjoying some treatments while she waits for me to wrap.

Post-lunch, as we set up for the last few shots, Susannah, Henry and I bond over Springsteen lyrics, and I drag the Bose iPod doc onto the set and hook it up at the playback monitor, where the three of us listen to the Boss. It's a wonderful, small moment I don't think I'll ever forget, as former Jersey girl Susannah reveals her lifelong crush on my one-time Rumson neighbor, Bruce.

Springsteen'll have that effect on a motherfucker. For years, I tried to deny the Boss — simply because I was a quietly rebellious Jersey lad who refused to dig on Bruce simply out of a sense of Central Jersey pride. But by the time I was twenty, I couldn't escape the fact that I, too, dug Bruce. I mean, the man wrote and sang 'Thunder Road', for Christ's sake. 'Thunder' fucking 'Road'!

I've never been a car-guy (indeed, I'm still not sure how an automobile works), but when Bruce romanticizes cars in his songs, it makes a brother wanna hang out around a garage or, at the very least, go to Pep Boys. The man's a fucking poet who, as Susannah pointed out, knows how to make the mundane epic. He takes small moments in the lives of the working class and reveals them for what they are: unsung miracles.

There was this one moment that Bruce Springsteen won me over for life. It was just after 9/11, during which Monmouth County was hit bad, losing about forty to fifty people from our neck of the woods — commuters who'd ferry or bus into the city everyday and work at the Trade Center. So a group called the Alliance of Neighbors of Monmouth County formed and put on two benefit shows at the Count Basie, featuring a lineup of Jersey music acts (and friends), all raising money for families who lost people in NYC. Bruce and Bon Jovi were the headliners, naturally. I was asked to emcee both nights.

So Thursday night, the night of the first show, I'm getting up and introducing each act to a packed-to-the-rafters Basie crowd. And between intros, while I'm backstage, I spot the man himself, hanging out with his wife Patti. From time to time, Bruce joins some of the acts onstage, doing the back-to-back rocker thing with Joan Jett on 'Light of Day', or joining former Elvis backers the Sun Records Rhythm Section for a few covers.

Ultimately, we said hi to each other, shaking hands, at which point, the Boss says to me "I like your flicks. *Chasing Amy*'s my favorite."

My head and heart almost exploded.

So the night goes on, with me introducing every act. Then, 'round midnight, it's almost time for Bruce and a scaled down version of the E Street Band to take the stage. However, Geraldo Rivera (a local) goes out to talk about the Bin Laden attacks and introduce some execs from Comcast, who were presenting the Monmouth County 9/11 widows with a big check. At the end of the presentation, the Comcast exec announces "And now, a man I'm sure needs no introduction..." essentially cueing Bruce. Bruce looks at me and shrugs and heads out onstage. And inside, I'm bumming a bit, because I would've loved to intro the guy myself. But this night isn't about me, and I'm getting ready to enjoy a stage right view of Springsteen live.

So Bruce walks out to thunderous, deafening applause, plugs in his guitar, and gets ready to play. Then, he looks around and says, "Where's the emcee?"

I just about faint.

Bruce looks at me, waiting in the wings, and says: "C'mon out. Let's do it right."

So I rush out onstage, giddy as fuck, and sputter, "I've lived here thirty-one years, and I never thought I'd have this moment. Ladies and gentlemen... BRUCE SPRINGSTEEN!"

From that moment on, I knew I'd take a bullet for Springsteen, if given the chance. I mean, the man went out of his way to have me come out and intro him, after he'd already *been* introduced, after he'd already *been* on stage for a minute and change. The guy knew how much it meant to me, and he wouldn't start his set until I got my geek-out moment. I'll take that with me to my grave.

After nailing a tricky little shot involving my gut, Juliette's hand, and my wide-eyed face, Sardi calls an official wrap on Vancouver. Hugs abound, as the champagne flows. I give Susannah a big kiss and thank her for the countless votes of confidence, not the least of which was casting me in the first place. The production now heads to Boulder to shoot a bunch of exteriors, including one in which I work. But as I don't have to be in Colorado 'til Thursday, *Catch* comes to something of a close for me. I say g'bye to all the Vancouver cats who aren't coming to Boulder (Elaine, Heida, Shelly, Lori), then head to the vanities trailer to get my hair and makeup removed, tell the rest of the crew I'll see 'em in Boulder, and get the fuck out of Dodge.

Since I'm pulling out of town, I leave the rental car at the set and get a ride back to the hotel from Blake. Jen's there waiting, and I ask her to dig around in the packed shit to find the remote for the TV I gave Lori. She finds it, and Blake's off, to deliver it to Lori.

Jen and I check out of the Sheraton Wall Centre, our home for nearly three months, get in the car, and start driving. In less than two hours, we're back in the States.

We're on the road for five hours, finally settling, ironically enough, in Vancouver, Washington, where we spend the night in their new Hilton, falling asleep watching an *X-Files*.

Sunday 24 July 2005 @ 4:57 a.m.

I wake up around six and check email. Jen wakes around nine and orders coffee, while I get in the shower. We check out and hit a Starbucks for coffee she can take on the ride.

We cross the bridge into Oregon and grab some Mickey D's breakfast to go, then drive like motherfuckers, listening to music and chatting the whole way. The goal is to get to Sacramento, stay the night, then finish the drive to LA Monday morning.

When we hit the Sacramento area, it's only 7 p.m. We make the decision to drive all the way home, which should put us in around midnight/one.

We stop at an insta-town just outside of Sacramento that seems to have just been inflated a minute before we got there. The tract housing and strip malls feel like they all went up at the same time to create a suburb around the Arco arena. Very weird place.

We stop at a joint called Pizza Pucks to grab some dinner, favoring the Mom & Pop shop over the Round Table Pizza in the other strip mall. The Pizza Puck, we're told, is a pizza done like a Cinnabun: thin dough, rolled up with the sauce and cheese. There's confusion with our order and what should take five minutes winds up taking forty. This may have something to do with the two twenty-some-thing cooks in the kitchen staring at me for fifteen minutes instead of getting our order right. In instances like that, I wish folks would just come over and ask: "Are you that fat director?" or something. The stare-down is a little creepy.

We hit the local Borders, where I take a dump, while Jen grabs a book to take home to Harley. We shake the 'burb dust from our sandals, and with that, we're back on the road.

After another five or six hours of driving, we finally pull up to our beloved home around 2:30 in the morning. We carry most of the bags in, then head to the bedroom to get into our woobs and sack out in front of the TV. I chug some cereal while watching TiVo'ed *Simpsons*, after which Jen and I fall asleep, elated to be home.

Monday 25 July 2005 @ 1:43 p.m.

Wake up, talk to Jimmy and Byron, then surprise Harley in Nan and Pop's room with being home.

I take Quinnster out to Jerry's Famous Deli in the Valley for breakfast, then head over to Castle Park, for a couple hours of skee-ball and other games of chance. We clean up, ticket-wise, and Harley trades them in for a bunch of crappy-but-cherished-for-a-half-an-hour prizes. We take photos in the photo booth and head over to Laser Blazer to grab DVDs. Ron lets us go through tomorrow's new DVDs as well, saving us a trip back this week.

We head home and Harley chills with Jen for a while, during which I lay on the bed and check email and update the diary on my laptop.

Gail makes family dinner, and me, Jen, Harley, Byron, Gail and Jimmy eat on the deck, joined by Bry and Mewes.

Jen puts Harley to bed, and I fall asleep around nine, watching TiVo'ed *Simpsons* while Jen unpacks.

Tuesday 26 July 2005 @ 1:45 p.m.

I wake up, take a dump while playing Tetris, then head to the office to check email. Axel Alonso at Marvel has forwarded me new pages Terry Dodson's drawn for *Spider-Man/Black Cat: The Evil That Men Do* — a mini-series for Marvel I started back in 2002. A few months back, I turned in the scripts for issues four and five while I was at the We Care Spa, doing a week-long fast and colonic program. At that point, I was in touch with both Axel and Joe Quesada (the artist on my *Daredevil* run from '98/'99, and now the Editor-in-Chief of Marvel) and let them know that I'd need to add one more issue to my run, as I'd written myself into a corner by the end of issue five. Joe was ecstatic, as I was finally finishing the book that had become the running joke of the comic book industry, sporting the rep of the latest comic in history (indeed, by the time issue four streets, it will have been three years between it and issue three). I was on such a roll, he invited me to write a *Moon Knight* revamp/ongoing series that he'd draw when I finished the script to issue six — at which point I reminded him that I was the guy with two and a half years between comic scripts for a mini-series that was supposed to be done in 2002. As tempting as it was to take him up on the offer — especially with him doing the art — I did the responsible thing and backed off.

It was the third Marvel series I begged off of doing in three years. I'd been offered *Trouble* — the Marvel girls-gone-wild series — as well as *Amazing Spider-Man* — a deal for which had actually been announced in *Wizard*, the comics magazine. I was already in arrears on not just the *Spidey/Black Cat* book, but another mini I started in late 2001, *Daredevil/Bullseye: Target* — for which I'd written only two scripts, about a year apart, resulting in only the first issue being published thus far. As much as I love comics, and as much fun as they are to write sometimes, I'm just plain lousy with hitting deadlines, and I over-commit like a motherfucker — usually resulting in chronic lateness or shit just never coming to fruition, due to the fact that writing comics is not my main gig.

Back in the day, it was *Jersey Girl* that pre-empted my work on the *Black Cat* mini. Then, almost anything else came first (*Tonight Show*, *Degrassi*, Vulgarthon, *Evening With 2*, the opening of the west coast Stash, *Clerks X*, *The Passion of the Clerks*, etc.). I'd gotten countless emails from Joe, insisting he needed me to finish the series; that he was holding the higher-ups at bay who were demanding another writer be hired to finish my arc, so that a solo *Black Cat* book could move forward. And countless times, I'd respond to Joe with "I'm on it..." only never to get on it at all.

Then, a few months ago, Joe had given me a drop-dead date, which I swore I'd turn in the final issue by. That date came and went, replaced by another drop-dead date — which also came and went with no script being turned in. Joe wrote me a very serious email giving a final date my script had to be turned in by, lest he have to give in to corporate and hire someone else to finish the series, so that the *Black Cat* monthly could proceed. But, knee-deep in *Catch & Release*, I missed that date, too.

I'd then received pretty depressing emails from Joe, chiding me for fucking him over, and informing me that someone else had been hired to finish my story. Few things suck as badly as letting someone you love down, and Lord knows this was an extreme case. Feeling like a putz, I dropped Axel Alonso (my editor on the *Black Cat* mini) a line, and we hatched a plan.

I asked Axel to let me write the last script, but keep it on the down-low, as a surprise for Joe. I insisted that if Terry started drawing issues four and five, that I'd get hyped seeing the art, and it'd power me forward through the script to issue six. Axel was down with the plan, but fairly, insisted that he still commission the alternative script from another writer, so that if I didn't deliver, he wouldn't be fucked, and the mini could finally end. I agreed, and we settled on the end of July as my deadline.

So for the last month, Terry's been powering forward on the art, and Axel's been feeding it to me, via email. And it, indeed, got me pumped, and made me want to finish the fucker in a big way. And as I sat at my desk-top Mac, I decided it was time to throw everything else aside, and concentrate on *Black Cat*.

The first order of business was doing a dialogue revamp of the first eight pages of issue four, as Axel's plan is to reprint the first three issues of *Spider-Man/Black Cat* as a Marvel Must-Have, that then concludes with an eight-page preview of the start of issue four. I polished up those pages and emailed them to Axel. Then, I continued rewriting some of the dialogue in the rest of the issue, before moving on to do the same for issue five, both of which I sent to Axel, getting the thumbs-up.

With that done, I finally… FINALLY start writing the end of *Spider-Man/Black Cat: The Evil That Men Do*.

I write for a few hours, before deciding to take a break, and heading out to run errands with Jen. We drop stuff off at the framers in Toluca Lake, hit Jen's bank to exchange all the Canadian cash we brought home, then pick up some lunch for Harley, Hans and Kevin, Reyna's boys.

When I get home, rather than go back to the script, I chill out and watch a documentary about John Wilkes Booth with Jen, while eating our late lunch. I'd picked up a bunch of Biography/History Channel DVDs, so they've become the watch of choice lately. After Booth, we pop in another doc about the Loch Ness Monster, which we chase with a doc about UFOs, during which I fall asleep. Jen wakes me, reminding me I'm supposed to go down to the store to sign a bunch of stuff that's being loaded onto the truck for Chicago. I hop in the shower and, joined by Mewes, truck down to the store.

At the Stash, I chill with Christian, Mewes and Bob, signing an ass-load of merch for not just Chi-town, but also the store. Bob and I go over the West Coast Stash schedule for the next few months, figuring out what dates the *Mallrats X* and *Jay and Silent Bob Do Degrassi* signings are gonna be, as well as a possible Alex Ross signing. I tag stuff 'til closing, then head back to the house, dropping Mewes off at his friend's so he can play the *Lord of the Rings* skirmish game all night.

I head home just in time to catch Quinnster before she goes to sleep, give her a kiss, head upstairs, throw on the woobs, and sack out in front of the TV with a box of cereal. Jen joins me, and we watch some TiVo'ed *Law & Orders* before falling asleep.

Wednesday 27 July 2005 @ 1:46 p.m.

In the early a.m., I head over to Scott's place to pick up Mos, Laura Greenlee, and Phil Benson.

We're tripping out to two locations to scout some space we're thinking of using for *Clerks 2*. I bring Mulder for a ride with us, as well. We stop at Jack in the Box for some road food, and spend the next three hours visiting and assessing the pair of locations. Out of the two, one is fantastic, so we decide to put all our efforts into securing it. I drop the trio off back at Mos's and head home with Mulder.

I get home and play Ultimate Bet for hours, while watching a few TiVo'ed *Law & Order* episodes.

At night, Malcolm, Cubby and Chay come over. Jen and I throw on some clothes and the five of us head over to a small theater on Melrose to see our friend Fanshen Cox perform in a show with her all-girl comedy troupe, Tomboys in Fishnets.

We get back home an hour and change later, and I throw on my woobs and get right back into Ultimate Bet, while Jen, Chay, Mitch and Cubby throw back drinks upstairs with Malcolm, Gail and Jimmy.

Jen comes back to the room an hour or so later, and I close up the laptop, cuddling up to her and falling asleep to *The Simpsons*.

Thursday 28 July 2005 @ 1:46 p.m.

I wake up early and bury myself behind my desk-top all day, knee-deep in issue six of *Spider-Man/Black Cat*. I'm digging the hell out of what I'm writing, and I'm suddenly glad I've waited this long to finish it, as it's far better an ending than it would've been had I completed it back in '02, or even six months ago. Jen comes in and out of the office all day, crushing on me for taking her out the night before. But I can't succumb to her charms; Spider-Man needs me. It's at this point that my journey into comics geekdom has taken a twisted turn, as I'm opting for

Peter Parker over pussy.

I finish writing and send the script off to Axel, then head out to bed to lay down and watch some *Law & Order* while eating the lunch that showed up an hour ago — the one I denied myself until I was done with *Black Cat*. A turkey/roast beef sandwich never tasted so good.

I look at the clock and realize I'm supposed to be leaving for the airport in an hour, so I call down to Gail to see if I can leave on a later flight out to Boulder instead. She books me on this, and I email back and forth with Scott about locations stuff, while watching TiVo'ed *Law & Order*s.

Jen joins me on the bed, and we cuddle up for twenty minutes before I have to get in the shower. Jen packs for me, and I get dressed and head upstairs for family dinner with Byron, Gail, Harley, Jimmy and Jen. I woof down Gail's awesome chicken and mashed potatoes, then collect my bags and drive to the airport with Byron and Jimmy.

I check-in, grab a smoke outside, then mosey to the gate, where I board and settle in for the two-hour flight to Denver.

We land in Colorado after a flight which consists of me watching half of what may very well be one of the most fascinating and delicious films I've ever seen: *Overnight*, the documentary which tells the story of the semi-rise and massive plummet of Troy Duffy, the *Boondock Saints* director who shot himself in the foot repeatedly. Good God, if you haven't seen this flick, track it down and watch it. It's a story of hubris and baseless arrogance so insanely pronounced, you spend most of the film talking at the screen, uttering phrases of disbelief like "oh my God..." and "holy shit!" If you're planning on being a filmmaker, this doc is like a primer of who you never want to become. See it, ASAP; you will NOT be disappointed.

I head out of the terminal and run into a fan who's trafficking the taxis and limos. He gets me into mine and I take the half-hour ride to Boulder, first playing Tetris, then sleeping a bit, before pulling up to the Saint Julien Hotel. I check in and head up to my room, where I immediately plug my laptop in (it'd died toward the end of the flight), and finish watching *Overnight*, going so far as to rock all the extras as well, something I rarely ever do. After that, I put on the TV and watch *State Property* on HBO while playing Ultimate Bet.

Friday 29 July 2005 @ 1:47 p.m.

I wind up playing Ultimate Bet clear until seven in the morning, absolutely on fire. I'm playing at the $5/$10 No Limit table called the Leominster, and it's like I can't lose. I pull down some massive pots and turn my initial five-hundred-buck buy-in into $2,700. However, roll or not, by seven a.m., I'm falling asleep at the keyboard, and I've got a noon call-time. So I finally close my eyes and catch some zs.

Wake up, shit and shower. I spend an hour writing out thank-you notes to all the key members of the crew I've worked with over the *Catch* shoot, and then start getting dressed. Liv Tyler calls and we chit-chat for half an hour, 'til I get the call from downstairs that it's time to head to set.

I'd had Chappy at Graphitti make five cases of exclusive *Catch & Release* Kevin Smith InAction Figures for a wrap gift, which he'd Fed-Exed to the hotel for delivery that morning, so I bring two cases with me to set, along with a few other more specific little wrap gifts for folks like Susannah and Henry.

Since I'm wearing a bandana in this scene, Forest doesn't really have to do my hair. Angela does my makeup, then I head back to my trailer to finish filling out thank-you cards for the crew. We're called to set for a pre-lunch blocking rehearsal of the shot, and then released for lunch.

During lunch, I start giving out the Kevin *Catch* figures, along with all the thank-you cards. I also collect a pair of gifts: a pretty funny t-shirt from Jenno and a framed trio of pics from Susannah that she signs: "I adore you, Kevin Smith. Chin down!" I know immediately that it's going up on the family wall back at the house.

Post-lunch, I get to set and see all the familiar faces from Vancouver nestled in the mountains of Boulder. The shot we're doing is a montage piece that features Garner, Sam and me moving furniture, with a gag as a button. We do about seven takes of it, at which point the gate is checked, and the three of us are picture-wrapped. It's hugs all around as I say goodbye to my extended family of the last three months. I give out the remaining *Catch* Kev figures, then head back to the trailer.

Forest washes my hair for the last time, and we bullshit for a bit before the car comes to pick me up to take me back to the hotel. I pack up my shit and play an hour's worth of UB, where I lose a grand of the chunk I'd won earlier that day, before heading downstairs to take the ride to the airport with the Boulder 2nd A.D.

En route, I call Jen to let her know I'm coming home and discover she's hammered. She's been sitting poolside with Chay, Trish, Michelle, Malcolm and Cubby, throwing back Margs. We get into a snit, and I get off the phone to try to track down Mewes by cell, to tell him he'll have to pick me up at LAX.

I fall asleep for the remainder of the ride to the airport and wake up to find out the flight home's been delayed by two hours. I check in and find a smoking lounge to hold up in, where I continue to donk out of my UB winnings until it's time to board.

I play Tetris for the whole flight home, listening to my iPod. At the airport, Mewes is waiting for me in my truck. We stop at McDonald's, then I drop Jay off at Milo's so he can play another marathon round *Lord of the Rings* skirmish game all night.

I head back to the house, kiss Jen, then proceed to get into a bigger snit over the afternoon party/no airport pickup, that puts us in separate rooms for an hour or so, until we think better of it and put the shit aside, cuddling up in bed, and falling asleep to *The Simpsons*.

Saturday 30 July 2005 @ 1:47 p.m.

Harley wakes me up around eight, and I take her swimming upstairs. Jen joins us after an hour or so, hanging out on the deck. Reyna and Hans arrive, so Harley heads off to hang out with them, and Jen and I head down to our room.

We engage in some pretty awesome late-morning fucking, after which I take a shower and check email, putting up the *Degrassi* trailer on the board.

Jen and I order sandwiches from Yummy and watch a documentary about the building of the Brooklyn Bridge, which turns out to be fascinating and informative as all hell (I finally understand how a suspension bridge works). We follow that with *An Empire of Their Own*, a doc about how five Jews from the shtetls of Russia created not only Hollywood, but fleshed out Horatio Alger's idea of the American Dream. It's another excellent doc that's worth checking out.

Catching Gregory Peck in the *Empire* doc makes me want to watch *The Omen* trilogy, so I suggest it to Jen. We tent off the curtains to the boudoir portion of our bedroom suite and dig in to the Dick Donner thriller.

Around six-ish, Jen, Harley and I head out to Coffee Bean and Rite Aid, then over to Baja Fresh, where we grab some take-home dinner.

Back at the house, the three of us chow down, then Jen reads Harley some books while I check the board and the weekend grosses, then watch a bunch of trailers. I kiss Quinnster g'night, and Jen puts her to bed, while I take a dumpski, playing Tetris.

Jen returns, and I pop in *Damien: Omen 2*. Dozing off, we turn stop *The Final Conflict* fifteen minutes in, opting for TiVo'ed *Simpsons* to fall asleep to instead.

Sunday 31 July 2005 @ 1:48 p.m.

I wake up and shower, while Jen gets ready to go to Burke Williams for a mani/pedi. I get dressed and load Quinnster into the car.

We head to breakfast at the Jerry's on Beverly, then shoot up to the Sunset Blvd. Aaahh's, the curio store, where we pick up some *SpongeBob* crap and a kid size 'College' t-shirt, made famous by Belushi in *Animal House*. We walk down the block to Tower, where Harley grabs a few kiddie DVDs, then head home.

I lay down for a half hour and take a nap before Jen wakes me up to let me know John Roshell's upstairs, waiting to go over the proofs of the *Mallrats* script book. I join John and we go over every page, making a few corrections and chit-chatting before he heads off.

An hour later, Chay and Jay show up, and I start prepping meat for the barbecue. Jen's iced down a bunch of drinks, and I call Jeff Anderson to see if he wants to come over as well. Annie Duke, two of her kids, and her boyfriend Joe (the A.D. who says "Or *House Party 3!*" to Chris Rock in *Jay and Silent Bob Strike Back*) arrive, and the kids immediately get in the pool with Mewes. Everyone else sits around and chit-chats while I'm grilling up some filet mignon and Italian sausage. It's a good-size barbecue crew, including me, Jen, Harley, Jay, Chay, Mos, Bryan Johnson, Brian Lynch, Malcolm, Cubby, Trish, her boyfriend Scott, Annie, Joe, and Annie's two kids.

Hours later, the crowd starts thinning out. I sit around with Lynch and talk about the last three issues of *Spidey/Black Cat*, as well as his awesome idea for a kids' movie. Annie and Joe have to get the kids back to Annie's husband, so we're left with just me, Jen, Chay, Jay, Malcolm and Cubby. We retire to the living room to play some poker, where we're joined by Jimmy. We play 'til midnight, then call it quits.

Jen and I head downstairs, get into our woobs, and fall asleep to TiVo'ed *Simpsons*.

Monday 1 August 2005 @ 10:27 p.m.

I'm up at five, unable to sleep. I take a shit and play Tetris, then head to my office to check email and update the diary a bit, before popping in a copy of *MurderBall* Phil Raskind sent me (he's repping the feature remake version). I watch half of the compelling doc before feeling tired enough to go back to sleep.

I wake again around noon, to the sounds of Jen and Harley rustling about.

Immediately, I check the showtimes of *Sky High*, as Harley's expressed interest in checking it out. I take a shower, get dressed, and load Quinnster into the car. We head to the Grove theaters, while Jen heads off to Burke Williams for the appointments she missed on Sunday.

At the theater, Harley and I load up on all sorts of what-seem-like-a-good-idea-at-the-time garbage snacks, then take in the flick. If you haven't peeped it yet, check out *Sky High*. It's really quite good, funny, and engaging as hell. A movie like this deserves to do well at the box office.

Afterwards, we head home. Harley and Jen go hang out in her room for a while, and feeling disgustingly full, I jump online to start tracking down the weight-loss program I want to enroll in.

It's been a hardcore four months of non-stop, unchecked, unabashed eating for me. Being away from home and stuck in Vancouver for nearly three months, I did no exercise and comfort-ate in a dangerous fashion. I come from a long line of diabetics, and for years, I've ignored that, packing sugar into my body like it was the key to eternal life. Not having been near a scale in months, I'm figuring that I'm at the top weight I've ever been at the moment, and it's time to change the nature of my relationship with food and get back into a regular exercise routine.

I'd already checked the Cedars Sinai site the other day, looking into their weight-management programs. I'd left a message but hadn't heard back, so today, I'm looking into any possible programs at the Century City Hospital. The Century City site links me to a site with a name I recognize: Novartis Optifast.

Back in late '97, while I was still living in the apartment on Broad Street in Red Bank, I'd heard about this doctor-regulated liquid-fast diet program that was run out of Riverview Hospital. The diet consists of five shake-meals a day, and nothing else. Each meal is a nutritionally balanced 160 calories, making it an 800-calorie a day diet. When I went through the program back in '97/98, I lost forty pounds, right before I lit off to Pittsburgh to shoot *Dogma*. It's just about the best diet plan I've ever been on, and it's pretty easy, so long as one doesn't mind not eating for months.

So I call the doctor's office and set up an appointment for the day after the birthday. With thirty-five looming, it's probably a good idea to start taking better care of myself.

I do some online work for a while, then fall asleep watching TiVo (or, "the 'Vo", as we affectionately call it in our house).

Tuesday 2 August 2005 @ 10:28 p.m.

The Birthday. Thirty-five. At least halfway to the grave. More than likely? More than halfway. Today is the last year that I can count myself part of the cherished key demographic of eighteen to thirty-five year-old males. From here on in, statistically, and as far as marketing goes, nobody will care about my opinion.

I'm woken up by the Quinnster who drags me out of bed, to be greeted by a massive birthday hug and kiss from Jenny. The pair of them plant a homemade paper crown on my head and pull me upstairs, where an awesome family breakfast awaits, courtesy of Jen, Harley, Gail, Byron, Mewes and Jimmy. We've got Italian sausages and biscuits, three birthday cakes that spell out "Dad", milk, OJ, eggs — the works. But before I'm allowed to feed, the group insists I open the gifts that are littered around the table.

Byron and Gail give me four new chairs for the poker table.

Jimmy writes me a poem about Harley.

Mewes and the absent Chay give me a new shooter (jersey).

Harley gives me a homemade card, as well as two massive, custom-framed gorgeous pieces of watercolor she did while in Arts Umbrella Camp back in Vancouver: one depicting the Vancouver skyline, the other depicting a guitar.

Jen gives me a shitload of History Channel/Biography DVDs, which I've found myself more interested in than watching movies, lately. She also gives me two new pillows and a bronze sculpture of a heart with wings that we immediately put on the mantle in our bedroom. She also tells me there's one more present, which we have to pick up tonight, around six, nearby.

We all chow down then dig into the cake, chit-chatting for a while before moving to the pool area to smoke out on the deck.

Downstairs, I find more gifts. From my brother: a *Mad* compilation (I was a massive *Mad* fan as a kid), an art of *Star Wars* book, and a gift certificate waiting for me at Laser Blazer. From my mom: a $200 gift certificate for the iTunes store. From Judy and my cousin Johnny (aka, Cohee Lundin): a big box of Kobe Beef steaks. From Ming (also born on 2 August): another iTunes gift certificate, as well as one to Whole Foods.

I push all the booty from the bed and lay down to check email while Schwalbach rocks her laptop on the couch. I've got an appointment for a pedicure (my feet are looking pretty ragged) and a facial at noon, and as it's 11:45 a.m., there's not much time for the sex Schwalbach has so generously offered on this fine birthday morning. Uncharacteristically, I say I'll settle for a blowjob instead, and the wife obliges, making me cum in under four minutes. I shower and head out to my spa appointments.

Afterwards, I come home and lay down on the bed, rocking some Ultimate Bet while digging into some of the History Channel/Biography DVDs. Around six, Jen tells me to get dressed so we can pick up the big birthday gift.

We get in the Hate Tank and head down the hill. Jen explains that the gift was made by a fan who was giving her a discount if I came in to take a picture with him when she picked it up. We pull into the Hollywood and Highland complex and park downstairs. I'm trying to figure out what in this place she could have possibly gotten me.

We cross the complex, passing store after store, and I'm no closer to figuring it out. As we reach the staircase that leads to the Highland side, I start thinking: "Are we going to Lucky Strike?" Lucky Strike is the high-end bowling alley I've never been too, nestled within the Hollywood and Highland mall. As if hearing my unspoken query, Jen offers, "I had a bowling ball made for you."

I register surprise, but inside, I'm thinking, "Good Christ — seven years together, and this woman still never knows what to get me. A bowling ball? Outside of Canadian six pin, when was the last time her and I ever went bowling?"

As my mind's racing to figure out what kind of bowling ball Jen would have had custom-made for me, we enter Lucky Strike, where I spy Malcolm, nursing a beer. Then, I see Mos. Then Mewes. Then Bryan and Harley. And suddenly, it's all clear…

That sweet-ass wife of mine — the one who'd already gone above and beyond with the Birthday Blowjob — is throwing me a Surprise Birthday Party.

In attendance: me, Jen, Harley, Byron, Gail, Jimmy, Mewes, Mos, Chay, Cookie, Malcolm, Cubby, Bry, Lynch, Andre, Trish, Catherine, John Gordon, Lisa and Greg and little baby Sky, Phil Benson, Donald, Joey, and McGuiness.

We bowl, drink, eat, and smoke for two hours, before it's time to go, as Lucky Strike doesn't allow little kids in after seven.

We take the party up to the house, where ten of us gather round the bar and start a Hold 'Em game, while Mos, Bry, Joey and the recently arrived Zack shoot pool. At first I'm on fire, tripling up my buy-in. But slowly, as the night progresses, I donk out of everything, including the twenty bucks in chips Jen gives me. My problem in poker (as in eating): I don't know when to simply walk away.

Everyone clears out by midnight, and Jen and I retire to the bedroom, where we fall asleep watching TiVo'ed *Simpsons*. It was an excellent way to cross into midlife.

Wednesday 3 August 2005 @ 10:29 p.m.

I wake up, shit and shower, then check email for a bit before heading over to Burbank.

I get to Next Wave and bury myself in the editing room with Mike and JM Kenny to cut some time out of *Evening With Kevin Smith 2: Evening Harder*, so we can make it an even four hours instead of the four and change it stands at now. The only real casualty is the long-ass *Degrassi* story, which will still be on the Toronto disc, as an Easter Egg, rather than in the body of the Q&A. Mike's done an excellent job in putting the cut together, so there's very little fat to trim. While we cut, I order some corned beef hash and egg whites from Jerry's, as well as pizza bread sticks. As this is the final day of eating for a while, I'm gonna enjoy this shit.

Col/TriStar Home Video's Mike Stradford comes by as I'm leaving, and we bullshit about the San Diego Con, the DVD, and other stuff.

Mike was the brainchild behind *Evening With Kevin Smith*. Back when I was in LA getting ready to shoot *Strike Back*, I did a Q&A gig at the Academy of Motion Picture Arts & Sciences — about the closest I'll ever get to the Oscar stage. Mike, who I'd met while doing the *Dogma* DVD, attended and after the show, asked me if I ever thought about taping one of these gigs to put out as a video release. The chat steamrolled from there into Col/TriStar putting up a modest budget (around $200,000) to shoot me speaking at five college gigs I'd had lined-up, post-*Strike Back*. The DVD was conceived as the first in a series of directors doing Q&As that Col/TriStar was gonna do, but apparently few directors are spotlight whores like me, so they never did another one. *Evening With* sold so well, though, that Mike got another one greenlit and, rather than do it on the college circuit again, we decided to make *Evening Harder* an international affair: shooting a pair of Q&As I did in Toronto and London.

I say g'bye to Mike, then head over to the doctor's office, for my Optifast appointment.

I fill out all the paperwork, then sit down with my counselor, Leslie, to discuss the program. Since I've been through it already, the consultation is pretty quick, bringing us to the part of the process where they go over all my medical particulars. First, there's a body-fat test, in which electrical pulses are sent through your body, gauging how much of you is lean and how much is fat. I'm expecting a ninety-eight percent fat reading, but it turns out to be thirty-eight percent, which the doctor feels is encouraging, as it means there's muscle under all that flab. The target body fat percentage we're now going for is seventeen percent.

The next test is for Metabolic Rate — how many calories I burn in a day, completely at rest (i.e. without exercise). You stick a tube in your mouth and breath into it normally for five minutes, and a machine calculates the estimates. My measured resting metabolic rate is 3,038 calories a day (almost 600 less than the caloric makeup of a pound — roughly 3,600, I'm told). The average resting metabolic rate for someone my age, sex, height and weight is 2,690, so the doctor's happy, as I'm burning calories (doing absolutely nothing, mind you) thirteen percent faster than the average.

That's all the positive stuff. I've been saving this next piece of data for the dramatic effect...

The weigh-in: when the scale comes to rest on a number, it's 319.

Yes, I know. Good fucking God is right. However, if there was any silver lining to that cloud it's that I was almost sure I was up to 350. Small consolation, I know, but it kept me from sticking a gun in my mouth at the time.

So, armed with enough shake mix for the next two weeks, my mission is clear: drop the pounds, lest they have to open a wall to get me out of my house in the near future.

I realize sharing this info positions me for nothing but ridicule from the portion of the online community that doesn't like me to begin with, but I figure if I'm gonna get serious about dropping the weight, it's best to just put all this on Front Street, as they say — haters be damned. I weigh 319 pounds. In six months from now, I intend to weigh far less than that (my goal is 230 to 250).

I head back to the house and pick up Jen, filling her in on the info (minus the actual weight number). I drop her off at the Mondrian Hotel, where her friend Dana is celebrating a birthday at the restaurant Asia de Cuba, then head down to Pico to hit Laser Blazer.

I pick up the new DVDs, then try to kill some time while I wait to pick up Jen. I figure since I'm already tipping the scales, and since my eating habits change drastically in the a.m., I might as well enjoy myself tonight. And enjoying myself means I hit Baskin Robbins for a scoop of peanut butter and chocolate on a sugar cone.

I shoot back up to Asia de Cuba, pick up Jen, and then we head out for the last restaurant meal we'll share in a while. We decide to make it good and roll up on The Ivy, where they always hook me up, with or without a reservation. It's pretty packed for 9:30 p.m., but the host jumps us in front of a bunch of people (tipping insanely well has its privileges), and we gorge — Jen on lobster pasta, and me on the Gumbo Ya-Ya and a bowl of spaghetti.

We head home, get into our woobs, and lounge in bed for awhile, before flirting ourselves into an uncharacteristic round of late-night fucking, during which I even further uncharacteristically take the top — an almost dangerous proposition, considering the weight info I now know.

Post-nookie, we watch a TiVo'ed *Law & Order* to which we fall asleep.

Thursday 4 August 2005 @ 10:31 p.m.

I wake up, shit while playing Tetris, then head to the office fridge for the first shake of the day. It goes down smooth; tastes good, even. Ask me if I feel the same way in two months.

I do online stuff most of the day then chill with Jen 'til it's time to hit the airport. Chay drops Mewes and I off, and we check in, bound for Chicago for the *Wizard* World comicon.

During the flight, I watch not only *Gray's Anatomy* and half of *X-Men 2*, but also the dude next to me eat his in-flight meal. I wanna dry-gulch him and take his bread, but practice civil restraint instead.

We land at O'Hare around 11 p.m., then take the five-minute drive to the Hyatt in Rosemont, where the convention takes place. We find Bry and Malcolm already checked into the two floor suite that'll be our home 'til Sunday and bullshit with them for a while. Then, Bryan and Malcolm go to bed, and Mewes and I launch Ultimate Bet and play Sit & Gos 'til five in the morning.

I head up to my bedroom and order a wake-up call for seven o'clock, then grab two hours of sleep.

Friday 5 August 2005 @ 10:31 p.m.

I wake up at 7 a.m., shower, and with two hours of sleep under my belt, I head over to Mancow radio show with Bry, to promote the *Wizard* Con.

I do the show from 8 a.m. 'til 10:30 a.m., alongside Sam 'Flash Gordon' Jones, Catherine 'Daisy Duke' Bach, Gareb 'Wizard Publisher' Shamus, and the voice of Space Ghost. I've been on Mancow probably five times (four in the studio) and always enjoy it. He's a funny guy, and what's more, he's a huge *Mallrats* fan.

We shoot back to the hotel, where Bryan heads over to work the Graphitti/Stash West booth on the Con floor, and I go back to sleep.

Wake up around three to Malcolm's call, telling me Gail needs to talk to me about changing my flights around. I call Gail, go over the flights to Jersey on

Sunday, and ask to talk to Jen, only to learn she's out shopping with Harley. With two hours to kill before I have to do anything at the Con, I jump onto Ultimate Bet and sign up for a Sit & Go tournament at a table for ten. I'm chip leader for a while, but ultimately come in second.

I head downstairs, where I find Mewes watching *Unleashed*. He passes on heading back to the Con, asking me to call him when it's time for the post-show poker tournament.

By the elevators, I run into my man Mike Oeming, the artist on the *Bluntman and Chronic* graphic novel. We chit-chat for a minute or two before I head over to the Con, where I meet up with Malcolm and head to the Marvel Knights panel. At Axel's behest, I pop in to announce the completion of *Spidey/Black Cat*, make some jokes, then head over to the Secret Stash West/Graphitti Designs booth, where I talk to Bry, Malcolm, Chappy and Gina. I tag a ton of merch at the booth until the Con folks shut the hall down for the night.

From there, I head to the big room at the Con for the *Wizard* Fan Awards, where I present Best Ongoing Series. Afterwards, I walk back to the hotel to chill with Bry, Malcolm, and Mewes for an hour, before we head over to Morton's Steak House to pop in on the Marvel dinner.

I talk to Joe Quesada for about twenty minutes and apologize for not just being late with the script, but for also not returning Joe's emails two months back. Rather than eat on Marvel's dime, Mewes, Bryan, Malcolm and I retire to the Morton's bar, where we can smoke and eat. Bry and Malcolm chow down while Mewes and I shoot back to the hotel for the Comic Book Legal Defense Fund's auction.

I arrive with the auction in full swing. Joe's ducked out of the Marvel dinner to auctioneer a few items, one of which is an appearance in a comic book called *Powers* (which Mike Oeming draws on a regular basis). Inspired by our earlier meeting, not to mention the good cause, I bid it up and close the auction out at two grand, the whole time trying to figure out who I'll give it to as a Christmas gift.

Mewes and I head outside to smoke, and fifteen minutes later, I'm pulled back in to play auctioneer on some stuff. I do about ten items, then, right before I go, I add an auction: a walk-on in *Clerks* 2. It also goes for two grand.

I head back to the hotel where I change my soaking wet, sweaty shirt. Then, Mewes and I head downstairs to the poker tourney.

Every year, Gareb Shamus, the creator and publisher of *Wizard*, the Comics Magazine, hosts a poker tournament, with a percentage of the gate going to charity, and the rest of it going to three or four winners. Feeling chuffed from my earlier, online tourney win, I'm ready to play all night. Mewes and I get separated and sat at different tables.

Mewes is the first knocked out, betting big on a pair of pocket aces, only to get rivered by Seymour (our Con Buddy and Security Man) with the flush. Ten minutes later, I bet heavily with a pair of pocket eights, only to have the comics writer Brian Michael Bendis knock me out of the game with a pair of nines.

Since it's so early, Mewes and I collect some other dudes who donked out too (like über-artist Jim Lee) and start a side game for real money. Our table swells to ten by midnight, and we play No Limit 'til 5:30 a.m. with Jim, Gareb, Dynamic Forces owner Nick Barrucci, and a bunch of other folks. I'm getting tremendous cards, and close out the night a big winner, with $730 from my hundred buck buy-in — essentially thirty bucks more than the second place winner in the tournament won (first place was two grand).

I head back to the hotel, check email and the board, write to Jen, then go to sleep around 7 a.m.

Saturday 6 August 2005 @ 10:31 p.m.

I sleep 'til two-ish, when I get up, do the morning shake drink, and sign some stuff Malcolm's brought over. Malcolm tells me business is brisk at the booth: we've sold out of the tons of stuff I signed the night before, as well as the 900 *Wizard* World Chicago exclusive Kevin Smith InAction Figures.

I watch some *Chappelle's Show*, take a shower, talk to Jen on the cell, then head over to the Con for my Q&A panel.

As it is every year for the past six I've been attending the Chicago con, the Q&A is packed, with nary an empty seat in the big room (which, Fred informs me, is four-hundred seats bigger than it was last year). I'm supposed to go from 3:30 p.m. to 5:30 p.m., but we're all having such a good time, I go 'til 6:30 p.m. instead, with the only negative aspect of the show provided by me.

In the course of telling a pretty funny story about working on *Catch & Release*, I use the phrase "nigga" to refer to Tim Olyphant, in the phrase: "Nigga, this ain't *Deadwood* and you ain't the sheriff." Too much Chappelle-watching for me, it would seem. While I obviously didn't intend it in any kind of racist context and no hush fell over the (largely white) room when I uttered it, I still feel badly. Dave Chappelle I ain't, nor do I — who's never been at the receiving end of a profiling, never been discriminated against, and never took any shit because of the color of my skin — have the right to employ the "N" term as even a colloquial term of endearment. Sure, I've been profiled, discriminated against, and took shit all my life because I'm overweight (which is still something of a minority in the aesthetic-obsessed culture of the US), but let's face it: fat ain't black. At the end of the day, I've prospered plenty in white America, and being white certainly didn't hurt.

The gay community co-opted "fag" as a means of taking the malicious power out of the term when used against them by homophobes, but I don't use "faggot" loosely either. Just because some of the black community has appropriated the "N" word for much the same reasons doesn't mean that I can use it too, even in a non-racist fashion (if there's even such a thing).

Sometimes I get carried away with my deep love for all things black and forget that I'm not black myself. Saying Jesus was black in *Dogma* doesn't make me black. Being called a "whigger" throughout high school because of my unfashionable early embracing of hip-hop (particularly Run DMC and Public Enemy) doesn't make me black. Wearing Fubu doesn't make me black. Identifying with black folks doesn't make me black. Wanting to be black most of my life doesn't make me black. Nothing will ever make me black (although, when I first learned that my mother had been adopted and learned, further, that she had no idea who her birth parents were, once the initial shock wore off, I immediately started fantasizing that somewhere in my bloodline I might have some black in me, as it would explain a lot).

So, to anyone in attendance at the Q&A that day, whether you were offended or not, I apologize. Rest assured, it'll never happen again.

I will, however, continue to use the term "motherfucker" as liberally as I can, even though it, too, is a term I got from the black community (from Chris Rock, particularly; Rock's use of "motherfucker" makes it sound like the most poetic adjective/noun ever invented).

By the time the panel ends, the Con's over. I'd mentioned not ever being able to walk the Con floor during the Q&A, so with the floor closed, Seymour escorts Malcolm and me around, and — for the first time in six years — I get to see every booth. I make a checklist of stuff I want to pick up tomorrow when the show opens, then head back to the hotel room, where Bry and Mewes are watching *The Longest Yard*.

Malcolm goes to sleep, Mewes and Bry head out to the *Wizard* wrap party, and I chill out in my room, playing Ultimate Bet for the rest of the night, watching *House of Wax*. I talk to Jen for a bit before she heads to a dinner with Chay back home, then fall asleep watching a PBS documentary about the history of pop music.

Sunday 7 August 2005 @ 10:33 p.m.

Wake up, drink a shake, then talk to Jen for a bit, before heading over to the Con for my noon to two signing at fountain in the Rosemont Convention Center. I do my time, then head to the green room for a general update interview with *Wizard*'s Richard Ho. Afterwards, I hit the booth and sign for another seventy-five folks and find out that the additional four cases of Kevin Smith Exclusive InAction Figures that were discovered buried at the booth have also sold out. We've sold out of so much merch at the booth that I wind up tagging InAction figures that aren't even me (discovering that, if I sign the Jen/Missy figure "had her" they go pretty quickly). I say g'bye to Bry, Malcolm, Chappy and Gina, and shoot back to the hotel with Seymour to collect Mewes and pack up for our trip to the airport.

We check in, head to the gate, and board. I play Tetris and listen to Luther Vandross's 'Don't Want to Be a Fool' on iPod repeat for the entire flight to Jersey.

Mewes and I touch down in the MotherLand around nine, collect my bag from baggage claim, and shuttle over to the car rental joint, where we grab an Explorer and head to Highlands, rocking out to the iPod the whole way.

I drop Mewes off at his family's place, then spin past the house I grew up in before heading toward Red Bank. I call my mom, who's in Jersey as well, down in Toms River with my sister. Virginia and her kids have been visiting from Japan for the last two months, so I'm gonna be able to catch her before she heads back to Kobe later in the week.

I check into the Marriott Courtyard (fuck you, they got free internet) and immediately take a load of laundry down to their coin-operated washer/dryers. I head back upstairs and call Jen, and we wind up getting into some steamy phone sex, after which I play some UB and go to sleep.

Monday 8 August 2005 @ 7:36 p.m.

Wake up around ten, take a shower, and head to Jay and Silent Bob's Secret Stash, Red Bank to see Walt and sign a bunch of merchandise.

Clete Shields comes by to deliver the bronze bust of Dad I had made for my mom, which turned out great. We chit-chat for awhile before Mewes pops in with some of his friends to say hi. He grabs me an iced tea from Starbucks, and then heads off. I pay Clete, finish signing all the books, figures, and posters, and head back to the hotel to get ready for the *Reel Paradise* première in NYC.

My sister Virginia calls to cancel Mom out of the première, as she's not feeling that well. I call Ming to see if he's already left for NYC, but he's well on his way. So I head up, solo.

Drive in to the city via Holland Tunnel and arrive an hour early, which is some kind of record for me. I park and head to the Tribeca Cinema, where I find Runshouse, Koala, Ralphy, Diff, Lithmick, and Magentalai waiting outside the theater. We all bullshit for a while, later joined by Ming.

Mark Tusk (the former Miramax acquisitions maven who brought *Clerks* in) shows up, followed by indie über-lawyer John Sloss. Shortly thereafter, John and Janet Pierson arrive, closely followed by Bob (he who discovered *Clerks*) Hawk, and it suddenly feels like a high school reunion.

These are the people who've been with me since the ground-up — the folks who I credit with keeping me honest for twelve years. Pierson, particularly, has been my sounding-board from the jump — a decade-spanning confidant whose approval I've always sought with every flick I've done since *Clerks*.

That's what makes tonight so special. It's the culmination of three years worth of me trying to give back to John what he gave to me. Without Pierson signing onto and selling *Clerks*, you would've never heard of the flick past Sundance. Without Pierson involving me in his seminal indie tome *Spike, Mike, Slackers and Dykes*, I might not have as much indie cred as I've sustained these many years. Without John jumping aboard *Chasing Amy* as an exec producer, Harvey might not have given us the $250,000, following the *Mallrats* debacle (or, at the very least, we might've been forced to make the Drew Barrymore, David Schwimmer, John Stewart version of the flick). He's been much more than just a mentor and guru to me, lo these many moons; he's also been one of my best friends in the world.

So when John had asked me, years ago, to invest in his dream of going to Fiji and purchasing what he calls "the world's most remote movie theater", I couldn't write him a check fast enough. And when he had the idea of turning that experience into a flick, I included the budget in my overall Miramax deal when I re-upped three years back. And it wasn't all just a way to say thank you to a guy I owe so much to; it was also because I believed in his vision. And that vision became the Steve (*Hoop Dreams*) James-directed *Reel Paradise*.

John, Janet, Georgia and Wyatt (their two kids and the scene-stealers of the flick), Steve James and I head inside to do some press pics while the crowd is loading in. We then intro the flick, and since there isn't an empty seat in the house, we head over to the bar side of the De Niro-owned Tribeca Cinema (formerly The Screening Room).

John, Janet and the folks from Wellspring (the distributor) head off to dinner, but since I'm not eating, I chill out at the theater bar. Sloss stays behind with me and we bullshit 'til the group gets back, then watch the Pierson Family/Steve James post-screening Q&A.

For the rest of the night, I pretty much chill outside the theater and do press, taking about a half hour off to talk to my other godfather, Bob Hawk, about Malcolm's doc, *Small Town/Gay Bar* which he loved and is highly recommending to Sundance (which is a great thing, as Bob also highly recommended *Clerks* to Sundance, back in '93).

By one in the morning, I'm tuckered out and ready to head back to Red Bank. Former Poop Shooter Jeff Wells shows up and takes a pic of John and I before I go, then I hug all the usual suspects goodbye, head back to the garage, get the car, and talk to Jen on the cell as I drive home.

I get back to the hotel and check email and do board stuff 'til I go to sleep around four.

Tuesday 9 August 2005 @ 8:18 p.m.

I wake up late, shit, shower, then head down to Toms River around two in the afternoon.

My sister's been back in the States for the last two months, but I haven't been east to see her because I was up in Vancouver all summer. A Kobe, Japan resident, she's come home to have her autistic daughter, Sabine, tested, to gauge the progress she's made in the two years since she was first diagnosed. Virginia and her husband Eric have been flying over therapists and specialists to help Sabine develop her language skills, as the five year old's at the end of the autism spectrum that allows for the greatest chance of developmental breakthroughs.

My mom, who's delved deeply into real estate in the wake of my father's death, bought a pair of houses down in Toms River a year or so back, so Virginia's staying with her kids in one of them (her husband after being here a month had to fly back to Japan for work).

Since I've never been to the Toms River house that my Mom shares with Judy (a woman Mom grew up with who was our 'Aunt Judy' growing up; the mother of my 'cousin' John — the guy who played Cohee Lundin) when she's not down in her Florida house. I call Mom when I get near the Toms River exit off the Garden State Parkway for more exact directions.

I pull up just as my brother Don (in from Florida, where he runs the Online Stash fulfillment center) pulls up with Andy (my mom's nephew-in-law).

I visit with Mom, Judy, Don and Andy, then meet up with Virginia outside, and get introduced to Sabine's younger sister, Delaney. Delaney stays at Mom's house with Don, and Virginia and I go to her place, where we walk around the neighborhood and catch up.

We head into her house, where Sabine's working with another therapist. In the two years since she was diagnosed, the kid's made great strides, and her language skills have developed to a point where she's actually speaking. Virginia and I bullshit for a while, then head back to Mom's with Sabine.

I spend the day chilling with my family. It's the first time Mom's had all three of us kids together since Dad's funeral, so she's glowing. I give her the bust, which goes over well. Judy serves dinner, but I opt to hang out on the porch, smoking and talking to Mom. Later, Don, Virginia and I hang out on the porch, and make jokes about how insanely awful our grandparents (on my Dad's side) were to us when we were kids.

Around ten, I say goodbye to Virginia, as she takes Sabine and Delaney home. I continue to hang with Mom, Judy and Don a bit, then head out around midnight, dropping Don off at Virginia's place before I drive back to Red Bank, talking to Jen on the way.

I get back to the hotel, climb into woobs, and jump online to check email and the board.

In the course of an IM conversation, I learn that someone pretty close to me isn't who I thought he was, and it's devastating. I call Scott back home and wake him up to talk about it. We go over it for an hour, and by conversation's end, *Clerks 2* loses a producer (not Scott, natch). I call Malcolm, too, after sending him the iChat conversation in question, and he's as flabbergasted as I am. We talk about it 'til six in the morning, before I finally go to sleep.

Wednesday 10 August 2005 @ 8:19 p.m.

I wake up two hours later, shower, and rush to Newark Airport, where American Airlines (now, officially, the worse airline on the planet) locks me out of my flight, even though it hasn't even started boarding yet. I call Gail and have her look for alternative flights back to LA, while I hit every other airline in the airport, doing the same.

Matty Staudt, the producer of the Alice Morning Radio show in San Francisco, calls regarding an Affleck story that's running in the NY *Daily News* that morning, in which I joke about fucking my wife as a wedding present to Ben and Jen

Garner. Since JLo's invoked, the story's now picked up on the wire service and running everywhere, reaching as far as San Fran. I call in to the show for a half hour and talk to Sarah and No-Name while waiting on a new flight. Afterwards, I email the iChat text from last night to Jen and we talk about it while I taxi over to JFK for a United flight Gail's found for me that'll get me into LAX around seven.

At JFK, I check in and hang out in the United lounge for two hours, IM'ing with folks and checking email, then talking to Scott and Jen before boarding.

On the plane, I make a big travel discovery. United runs a flight called United P.S., with routes to/from JFK and LAX that finally makes first class airfare worth the price of admission. They offer sleeper pods, not unlike the sleeper pods the Virgin Atlantic planes sport, handing out personal DVD players to boot. Exhausted from the lack of sleep from the night before, I'm out cold for most of the flight, waking with an hour and a half to go, during which time I write my *Degrassi* dialogue for the episodes Mewes and I are doing at the end of next week.

We land and Jen's there to pick me up. We grab my bag and head home, going over the iChat incident from the night before.

I get home in time to say g'night to Quinnster, then climb into my woobs, and Jen and I kick back and watch TiVo 'til we fall asleep.

Thursday 11 August 2005 @ 8:22 p.m.

Wake up, take a shit while playing Tetris, and update my online diary in my office 'til Jen gets up.

After an hour, we break into an uncharacteristic round of morning sex, during which I even more uncharacteristically get on top, going so far as to stand on the floor and pull Jen to the edge of the bed, fucking her like a 319-pound porn star.

I shower, get dressed, collect some clothing choices, then climb into the Hate Tank with Jen and drive down to San Diego.

On the way down, I talk to Scott for a long time about our *Clerks 2* woes. We're having difficulty locking up both a female lead and a location, and with a little over a month to go before the proposed start date, it's looking more and more likely that we'll have to move our start date yet again.

Jen and I arrive in San Diego two and a half hours later, and while she heads off to the W Hotel to chill, I head over to the set of the UPN series *Veronica Mars*.

Dan Etheridge (the priest in the opening scene of *Dogma*, as well as the voice of Mr. Plug) is the producer on *Veronica*, and he's asked me to do a cameo in the second episode of the new season. Because the dude's such an excellent friend (and because I'm a total whore who likes to see his fat self on TV), I jump at the chance to play, of all things, a convenience store employee.

I hang out with Dan a bit, meet the episode's writer Diane, then shoot the scene with Veronica Mars herself, Kristen Bell. The whole day lasts about five hours, and I have a blast doing it. Afterwards, I say g'bye to Dan and head over to the W to pick up Jen.

I meet Jen up in the room, and we immediately go at it again, fucking for twenty minutes before opting to get on the road and heading home to sleep in our own bed.

On the ride back to LA we rock out, singing power ballads at the top of our lungs and smoking up a storm. It's one of those really great moments that remind me how really wonderful it is to have a partner.

We get home, climb into our pjs, and go to sleep, watching TiVo'ed *Simpsons*.

Friday 12 August 2005 @ 8:25 p.m.

Wake up and take a leak. As I'm not eating solids, I find I don't shit nearly as much as I used to — maybe once a day, max, and rarely in the morning. It kinda throws off my whole day, now.

I shower and head over to the Weight Control Center for my EKG and weigh-in. When I step on the scale, it turns out I've lost a hefty seventeen pounds in a week. Most of it's likely water I'm told but still — seventeen fucking pounds. No wonder I'm fucking like a porn star.

I meet with the counselor and pick up a box of drinks for the week, this time in the pre-made, juice-box packaging.

As I head home, I call Jen with the good news. I ask her if I should wait 'til I pick up Quinnster to grab new DVDs, and she says to go now instead. I hit her up with the idea of having people over tonight, as a going away party for Bryan Johnson, who's leaving in the morning for a month-long motorcycle trip. She's into it, so we immediately start calling folks and inviting them over.

After stopping at Laser Blazer, I call Larry Krug, my trainer, and set up a work-out schedule for next week. Since I'm only taking in 800 calories a day, we opt for a Monday, Wednesday, Friday schedule to start with, instead of a daily thing.

I get home and check email, while Jen runs over to Bristol to pick up side dishes. When she gets back, I'm still working in the office as she sets up the deck and sides. Chay and her friend Chris arrive early to help out, and Jen summons me upstairs to prep the meat for the going away barbecue.

By eight, everyone's arrived, and we wind up with about twenty-five guests, all of whom are treated to filet mignon, swordfish, chicken breast, sirloin, and burgers. I manage to work the grill all night without eating a morsel.

A bunch of us adjourn to the living room and get into some poker. What begins with me, Jen, Chappy, Julie Plec, Malcolm, Andre, Trish, Scott/Cookie, and Joey (with the amusingly drunk Bryan passing in and out of the game), ends with me, Malcolm, Andre, Chappy and Chay's friend Chris playing 'til four in the morning, with everyone else either gone home or passed out. Chappy takes off, leaving me, Malcolm, Andre and Chris playing 'til six-thirty in the morning.

With everyone gone, I head downstairs to my room to find Jen and Harley sprawled out across the bed, leaving me no room. Since Mewes is still back in Jersey, I head to his room instead, closing the black out curtains and watching *Batman Begins* as I fall asleep.

·

Saturday 13 August 2005 @ 8:25 p.m.

I get up around 11:00 a.m. and head upstairs to the deck, where Jen is cleaning up. Harley joins us, and I go swimming with Quinnster 'til it's time for her play-date with Sam, a kid from her school.

I head downstairs and work on updating the online diary for a while, before it's time to head over to the Valley for a haircut.

Jen and I head over the hill and drop in on Nicole's for my standard, spiky haircut. It's the first time I'm getting my shit chopped since before *Catch & Release*, and when Nicole's done, I look about ten pounds lighter.

Jen and I then hit the frame store to have my *Reel Paradise* poster framed, as well as a vintage Disneyland Monorail poster (to match the vintage Tomorrowland Submarine Voyage poster in my office).

We come home and start watching the *Dallas* season three box set, while I sign a bunch of DVD covers for the online site and the Red Bank Jay and Silent Bob's Secret Stash.

After Jen puts Harley to bed, we watch more *Dallas*, while I empty out a big, catch-all box of stuff I found buried in my office that dates back to the *Jersey Girl* editing suite, while Jen rides the couch, shopping online.

Eventually, we get into two games of Rummy while watching *Dallas*, before falling asleep to a TiVo'ed *Simpsons.*

Sunday 14 August 2005 @ 8:31 p.m.

Quinnster wakes us up around seven. I tell her to let the dogs out while I go take a leak, and we head down to her room, so as not to wake Jen up. We watch *Monsters, Inc.* and some of the extras on the DVD, while playing the Guess Who Disney Edition game.

Around ten, we get dressed and head off to Castle Park over in Sherman Oaks, where we play a round of mini-golf. Afterwards, we duck into the castle to play some games, win a bunch of tickets, and redeem them for cheap-ass prizes.

On the way home, we hit Koo Koo Roo for Quinnster's take-home lunch. I call Jen to see if she wants anything, and then head next door to Coffee Bean for a Banana Carmel Ice Blended for Harley, an iced latte for Jen, and an iced tea for me. Following that, we stop at Quizno's to grab a veggie sub for Jen, then go back to the house.

I bury myself in my office for most of the day, updating the online diary and getting it onto the site, while Jen and Harley hang out.

After a few hours, Jen suckers me into taking her and Quinnster to the Paul Frank Store, where Harley gets a bunch of new school clothes.

Jen puts Harley to bed, and then her and I play Rummy for the rest of the night, watching more *Dallas*, until we're too exhausted to play anymore. We fall asleep to TiVo'ed *Simpsons.*

Monday 15 August 2005 @ 9:38 p.m.

Wake up at 8:45 a.m. and get ready for a workout with Larry, my trainer. I've been working out with Larry on and off for four years now. It's the perfect workout for me because he's not a drill sergeant about it, and we chit-chat all through it, about movies, relationships, biology, health, finance, South Africa (where he's from), the celebs he's trained, and all manner of other things. When your workout begins with a walk of the dogs up the massive hill beside your house, thus killing two birds with one stone, you know you've found the acceptable way to exercise.

Having not worked out in over three months, we start lightly. Even so, it still sucks ass, because any bit of exertion is a deviation from my current program of laying in front of the TV and eating. But the seventeen pounds I've lost thus far is an encouragement, so I muddle through the hour and change, before hitting the shower.

Jen and I head to the Beverly Center to look for standing oscillating fans at Restoration Hardware. When we get there, I call Scott, via cell, and talk about the Phil Incident at great lengths.

Mos is probably the most Zen person I know — maybe inching past Alanis by a nose. For thirteen years, he's been the sober ying to my (sometimes) raging yang. He keeps perspective on a very delicate situation, handling it fairly, even though, at the moment, I'm looking for blood. By the time my cell phone dies, I'm feeling better about the situation.

There are no fans at Restoration, so Jen and I try Bed, Bath and Beyond. No luck there either, but we pick up new standing paper towel racks on the way out. Afterwards, Jen pops into the Grand Lux Café to take home a salad, and we're off.

We grab smokes at 7-11 then head to Fred Siegel, where I buy shampoo and a frame for a picture I want to give to Scott. Following that, we shoot back across town to pick up Harley from gymnastics camp.

We stop at the Askew offices, where Jen drops Harley and I off and heads to yoga. Byron and Gail are inside, so me and the kid'll have a ride back. I just wanna pop in on the agent and manager of the actress we're going after, who're reading the script in advance of their client to see if she'd even be interested in *Clerks 2*. I chit-chat with them for a bit when they're done to learn they both really dug the hell out of it, with one of them offering: "I knew it'd be funny, but I wasn't expecting it to have as much heart as it does." Then, he offers what I feel is the pitch-perfect compliment: "It's like the best parts of *Clerks* combined with the best parts of *Chasing Amy*." They're going to recommend their client reads it this week, so things're looking good.

I head home with Byron, Gail and Harley, and chill in the home office, IM'ing with Scott about the actress update and answering email. Then, I'm IM'ing with Matt Potter, at which point we take the conversation to the phone.

Jen gets home while I'm on the phone. Then Mewes shows up as well. Jen heads up to dinner while Mewes and I bullshit in the room for a while.

I say g'night to Harley and Jen puts her to bed, while I watch more of *Batman Begins*.

When Jen gets back, we watch this Discovery Channel doc *Anatomy of a Shark Bite* while playing cards. If you haven't seen it, check it out. The lion's share of the eighty minutes is kinda dopey, as a crew of technicians and artisans try to build exact replicas of the sharks that attacked two victims. But the doc contains a pair of on-camera shark attacks that can only be described as "fucked-up". Totally worth sitting through for that footage alone, and further proof that I have no business being in any body of water outside of a swimming pool.

After our game of Rummy, I fall asleep watching *Simpsons* while Jen putters around the room, cleaning up.

Tuesday 16 August 2005 @ 9:38 p.m.

I wake up, shit while playing Tetris, then head to my office, where I work online all morning, going through email and iChatting with Mos and other folks.

Pre-noon, I drive Jen to Asia de Cuba at the Mondrian Hotel for her lunch with Cagney Jarvis, the mother of a kid in Harley's class and the woman Jen's launching a school paper with. Since Jen's early, she asks if I'll come in and sit with her 'til Cagney gets there. We get a table, order some drinks, and sit and talk for half an hour. It's times like this that I'm reminded how lucky I am not to have a nine-to-five job, as it affords me a bunch of opportunity to hang with my wife. And being that I married the woman because I find her so interesting, that kinda hang-time is pure bliss.

When Cagney arrives, I head to Laser Blazer. On the ride over, I call Chappy to hip him to my new clothing line idea. Then, I jump into Laser Blazer, pick up a bunch of DVDs, and shoot back to the Mondrian to pick up Jen from her lunch.

When we get home, I immediately take a shower, as I hadn't had a chance to do so before I ran my errands. When I get out of the shower, Jen's giving me the eyes, so we lock the door, turn on the fuck music, and bone for an hour.

Afterwards, we pop in one of the new *Simpsons* season six DVDs and check our email. Then, an hour later, we wind up fucking again. Once again, it's really nice not having a nine-to-five.

We get a call to attend an Easter Egg hunt in Harley's room that she's set up with Kevin and Reyna. Once all the eggs are unearthed, I kiss Quinnster g'night and head upstairs, where Jen and I watch *Simpsons* and play Rummy 'til we go to sleep.

Wednesday 17 August 2005 @ 9:39 p.m.

Wake up just in time to get dressed for a work out with Larry. When we wrap up, I check email and jump in the shower, then shoot over to the Valley to New Wave to meet with JM and Mike to finish the *Evening 2* edit.

I come home and play Ms. Pac Man with Harley upstairs, then we do a round or two of hide and seek in the living room. We head to my office and watch some trailers online, after which Harley goes to hang out with Gail.

I pop in *Hardcore*, a Greek flick about teenage prostitutes that turns out to be a pretty engrossing watch.

Before the movie ends, Harley intercoms up to invite me to a tea party in her room. While there, I get the call from the actress's agent, saying she just got done reading it in NYC, and he's happy to tell me that she's in. I ecstatically thank him, and call Scott to deliver the good news. Not only is she a score for us and someone we really wanted, but she's also on Harvey's pre-approved list, so he's gonna be delighted as well.

Jen comes home from yoga and the family heads upstairs to eat dinner while I relax in my room, watching the rest of *Hardcore*. I join the group, which now includes Chay, toward the end of their meal, to make my chicken soup shake replacement meal. Chay gifts me with a new jersey — the one she and Jay had made for my birthday, branding me "The King of Hearts", with a back that's labeled "All In". I totally dig it.

Suddenly, Harley launches a scavenger hunt on us, sending us all over the house to find odd bits of detritus to stuff into plastic bags she's provided. She winds up winning (surprise, surprise), and then it's time for Harley to go to bed. I kiss her g'night, then go back to my room, where I watch the Dave Chappelle standup special.

Jen returns from putting Harley to bed, and we watch more *Simpsons* DVDs while playing Rummy. Jen's pretty tired, so we wrap it up after one game, and she goes to sleep, while I watch more *Simpsons* and check email, 'til I fall asleep.

Thursday 18 August 2005 @ 9:39 p.m.

Wake up and head to the bedroom office (eating less means shitting less). While Jen goes off to yoga, I check email and board and do a bunch of IM'ing. I return calls to Tony Angellotti (the publicist) and John Sloss (the lawyer), then write the closing piece for the new *Mallrats* book.

Jen comes back from yoga and starts bugging me to get into shower for the CNN taping. I shower, get dressed, and head over to CNN to do piece on indie film.

Afterwards, I shoot over to Moe's on Melrose and pick up flowers for Jen, Gail and Harley. I come home, drop off the flowers to Gail, leave the flowers for Jen (who's out shopping), and bring Harley's flowers with me as I go to pick her up from gymnastics camp, bringing Scully along for the ride.

I grab Harley and present her with her flowers in the car, then drive home. Harley heads off to play with Hans, and I head upstairs to the flower-smitten Jen to play with her. We bone, and then she showers and gets semi-ready for her night out with Chay. We play a hand of Rummy before I head upstairs to meet with Chappy and Gina to go over the Boston Con schedule and the *Chasing Amy* inaction figures.

Jen heads out to a birthday dinner for Chay's roommate, while me, Malcolm, Andre, Mos, Byron, Gail and Mewes play poker all night. A buzzed Jen comes home and hangs out with us for a bit before heading to bed.

By night's end, it's just me, Malcolm and Dre playing poker. We quit around four, at which point they head home and I head to bed.

Friday 19 August 2005 @ 9:40 p.m.

I wake up around 8:45 a.m. and since Byron and Gail have left for Big Bear, I get Quinnster ready and drop her off at camp. On the way home, I pick Jen up some McDonald's hash browns — her favorite hangover medicine.

I get into my sweats and work out with Larry, starting with our routine dog walk and finishing with a serious set of squats.

Larry leaves, and I hit the shower, get dressed, and head over to the Weight Control Center. After the seventeen-pound loss from last week, I know not to expect to lose the same amount, but I'm not prepared for the precipitous drop the scale reveals: just four pounds. Granted, my two-week total is twenty-one, but after all that non-eating and working out, I was hoping for a little more. Leslie, the counselor, maintains that's a pretty normal figure, and when I go in to see the doctor, he explains how weight loss works (fat cells empty of lipid, but to maintain the enlarged cell structure, the body fills the cell with water; once the water is expelled from the cell, the cell shrinks; and since water weighs more than fat, that ongoing process does not provide an average weight-loss figure every week; one week you lose seventeen pounds, the next week you lose four, the week after you lose nine — all by following the exact same procedures).

I pick up Harley from gymnastics camp, then we swing up to the house and grab Jen, and the three of us head to the El Capitan to see *Valiant*.

After the flick, we pick up Baja Fresh for Quinnster, and head home. I watch TiVo'ed *Simpsons* and check email while Jen feeds Quinnster and puts her to bed.

Jen's feeling peckish, so she takes a run to In-N-Out, solo. When she comes back, she downs her grilled cheese, and we watch TiVo'ed *Law & Order* and *Simpsons* eps, and play Rummy 'til bedtime.

Saturday 20 August 2005 @ 9:40 p.m.

Quinnster wakes me up around seven and I let Jen sleep in, heading down to Harley's room to watch *Lilo and Stitch* and play Disney scrabble.

When Jen gets up, I turn Harley over to her and bury myself in the office, updating the online diary and posting it, as well as the original *Jersey Girl* trailer that I found on an old disc in the office.

Reyna arrives with Kevin and Hans, and Harley hangs out with them most of the day, heading to Chuck E. Cheese in the late afternoon. Jen runs errands and hikes Runyon, then comes home and goes swimming, while I continue to update the online diary. I join her upstairs in the kitchen and we chit-chat before heading back down to the room, where we start watching *The Mambo Kings*. The Cuban accent reminds us both of *Scarface*, and we decide we'd rather watch that movie, so we pop it in instead.

Harley gets home from Chuck E. Cheese and Jen and I read her a few books and put her to bed, then head back upstairs to continue watching *Scarface*, during which Jen falls asleep.

When *Scarface* ends, I pop in *School of Rock*, which the uneasy sleeper Schwalbach wakes to and barks at me about having the TV too loud (which it's not). I tell her to "Get off my ass," and it kicks off a fight that ends with Jen storming out of the bed, heading to the bathroom, presumably to smoke and fume. I go to sleep.

Sunday 21 August 2005 @ 9:40 p.m.

Feeling a little guilty about waking Jen up last night, I get up early with Harley so the wife can sleep in. We watch TV in her room and play games, then head upstairs to get Harley humus and watch some of the second *Looney Tunes* box set in the gym. I've seen all of these shorts so many times that I'm reciting lines to Harley and acting out the cartoons for her. She looks at me like I'm an asshole, but amusing nonetheless.

Jen finally gets up, and I crawl back into bed, falling asleep 'til 12:30 p.m. I wake up and check email, then realize I have less than an hour to shower, pack and get to the airport with Mewes for our Toronto flight. I call *Degrassi* producer Jim Jackman to see if I can get out on a later flight instead of rushing to LAX to possibly miss the flight. Jim books Mewes and me on a red-eye, so we've now got plenty of time before we have to head out to the airport.

We opt to have a barbecue and play poker. Malcolm, Andre, and Chay come over, and I cook up a bunch of meat my Mom sent me for my birthday. I try not to be too bitter as they scarf down burgers, hotdogs, and filet mignon, while I'm sucking at my 160 calorie drink box. Afterwards, the six of us play poker 'til it's time for me and Mewes to leave for the airport.

Andre drives us to LAX in the Hate Tank and drops us off. Mewes and I check in and head to the first class lounge for a bit to check email before we go, at which point I realize I've forgotten my cell phone.

We board and take the four hour and change flight to Toronto, sleeping most of the way.

Monday 22 August 2005 @ 2:57 p.m.

Mewes and I land in Toronto and head to customs, where we have to pick up our work permits. Forty-five minutes later, we're meeting *Degrassi* co-producer Jim Jackman out in passenger arrivals.

Jim whisks us out to the Epitome stages, where we're immediately put to work in the first shot.

We spend the day shooting the two-part follow-up to our three episode arc from last year, in which Kevin Smith and Jason Mewes are back in Toronto for the world première of *Jay and Silent Bob Go Canadian, Eh*. Today's all stage stuff, and tomorrow, we go on location for the fake première stuff.

I spend lunch talking to *Degrassi* creator/mastermind Linda Schuyler and her husband, exec producer Stephen Stohn about the *Degrassi* feature and the script revamp we're working on, coming up with 'It Goes There' storylines worthy of the *Degrassi* legacy. At lunch's end, Jim hands me his cell, saying Jen's on the line. Jen and I talk for a while, until I have to roll back to the set and shoot.

We shoot 'til eight or nine, during which we plan a post-wrap poker game with Stefan 'Snake' Brogren and I do an interview regarding the *Degrassi* twenty-fifth anniversary. But when we wrap, both Mewes and I are so bushed from our long day and lack of sleep from the night before, that we opt to crash at our hotel, The Grand.

Jim drops us off and gets us checked in, then gets us settled in our rooms. Mewes turns in to watch a movie and order room service, and Jim and I talk about the *Degrassi* feature for a while before he takes off.

I head upstairs in my suite and start to check email before crashing and falling asleep by ten-ish.

Tuesday 23 August 2005 @ 2:58 p.m.

I wake up around nine and check email while watching the new *Degrassi* season's freshly cut second five episodes (I'd seen the first five back home, a month before). I talk to Jen, then jump in the shower and get ready for our three o'clock call.

Jim picks up Mewes and I and takes us to the Eglinton, which is doubling for the movie theater at which the fake *Jay and Silent Bob* sequel is debuting.

We work 'til midnight, during which we knock out our three scenes, I visit with *Degrassi* folks I haven't seen in months, and I try to catch some Zs in anticipation of the late-night poker game we postponed from the night before.

At wrap, we head back to the hotel, where I talk to Jen, then head next door to Mewes's room, where the game gets going with eight of us playing.

Wednesday 24 August 2005 @ 2:59 p.m.

Mewes, Jim, Jim's friend Squally, Stefan, his girlfriend Yvonne, Mike 'Jay' Lobel, and me play all through the night. At one point, former show head-writer/current *Degrassi* feature writer Aaron Martin stops by with former Associate Producer Nicole Hamilton on their way home from catching a flick. By the time we wrap up at eight in the morning, the room's down to just me, Mewes, Jim, Stefan and Yvonne. While I donk out for most of the night, by the time we stop, I've won back everything I've lost, plus ten bucks.

I head back to my room to grab some sleep. I'm supposed to have a meeting about the *Degrassi* feature script in two hours, but I push the meeting 'til eleven so I can get some sleep.

I wake up close to eleven, shower, and head downstairs to meet with Linda, Aaron and his co-writer, Tassie. We jaw about the direction of the feature, breaking storylines, until it's time for me to head to the airport. But since we're not done tying up a third of the flick, I opt to take a flight that leaves two hours later, and continue with the meeting.

At meeting's end, I run upstairs, grab my gear, wake up Mewes, and head to the airport with Jim. Mewes opts to hang out in Toronto for another day and then shoot down to Jersey, so I'm heading back solo.

The guys drop me off at the airport, I check in, and head for the first class lounge, where I check email and IM Gail and Ming. I'm shooting on *Joey* in the morning, so I ask Gail to fax Ming the pages of the script, so he can scan 'em and email 'em my way for the flight home.

I board the plane and sleep for the first three-and-a-half hours of the five-hour flight home. When I wake up, I go over the *Joey* pages and rewrite all my dialogue, before I have to pack up for landing.

Byron and Jimmy pick me up at the airport, and we talk about being married the whole ride home. I get home around nine, where Jen's waiting for me. I jump into woobs, then email the rewrites to Scott, the *Joey* writer/producer, to make sure they're cool with my revisions. He calls back and jokingly offers me a job, before filling me in on the morning's shoot schedule.

Jen and I bone for an hour, then kick back with some TiVo 'til we fall asleep.

Thursday 25 August 2005 @ 3:00 p.m.

Wake up, shower, and head over to the Warner Bros. lot, for the *Joey* shoot.

Dave Mandel's friends with Scott Silveri, one of the creators of the show, who passed along an invitation to do a few scenes in one of this season's new episodes. Being a whore for seeing myself on TV, I said yes. To sweeten the pot, I'm playing myself — though not the unmarried, Quinnster-less version I play on *Degrassi*.

Before I left, I got a call from another producer on the show who asked me to bring some artwork from home for the show's version of my home office. I've brought along some of the framed, foreign editions of the *Clerks* posters. And when I get to the stage, the set dec folks load them out of my car while I'm led to my dressing room, and then makeup.

In makeup, I meet Matt LeBlanc, who seems like a really nice guy. He gives me a heads-up that the writers rewrote our scene last night. I tell him I rewrote the scene last night, to which he responds: "So that's why you have all the jokes now."

I smoke in my dressing room, going over my lines, until I'm brought down to the set for blocking. With a little time to kill, I head outside to smoke and run my lines. I'm joined by Matt and we chit-chat for a bit about the show and life on a sitcom in general, until Kevin Bright (the director, and co-creator of *Friends*) comes out to let us know we're gonna start blocking.

Stage-based sitcoms are great, because it's all about speed. There are usually four cameras shooting, so there's no wait between set-ups. Matt, Miguel (the other guy in the scene) and I blow through our two scenes in about two hours, and then I say g'bye to everyone and head out. On the way to my car, I run into Jennifer Coolidge, who I met during the poetry event we hosted at our house back in the spring, as she's a very cool person, we bullshit for a bit before I get going.

When I get home, I check out the sides for *Southland Tales* that Gail's left at the bedroom door. It's been about two years since I read the script, but even so, I don't recognize any of what's going on. Based on that, I start reading the new draft of the script.

Turns out Richard's given the script a complete overhaul. What was once a film that played like a cross between *Pulp Fiction* and *Short Cuts* is now a quasi-sci-fi epic that plays like a cross between *Dr. Strangelove* and *Donnie Darko*. Whereas the previous draft was set in a recognizable world, this version's set in the not-too-distant future, after a second terrorist attack on the US. Neither film is better than the other; both are pretty brilliant. This version, however, is more inscrutable — more *Darko*.

When I finish the script, I chit-chat with Jen in the bathroom as she gets ready for the *Reel Paradise* LA première. I get dressed as Scott arrives, and the three of us pick up Chay and head over to the Laemmle Music Hall, on Wilshire.

The line for the show is wrapped around the building, so I drop Jen and Chay off out front and go park. Scott and I hang out around the corner, talking about *Clerks 2* until Malcolm shows up — driving, no less (Malcolm never drives). With the crowd seated, I head inside, meet the Wellspring rep in attendance, and do the pre-flick intro.

We all hang out and watch the first ten minutes of the flick with the audience, then cross the street to Kate Mantellini's for appetizers and drinks. The Piersons meet us at the restaurant (they just flew in from San Francisco with Steve James, the director), and we all hang out, 'til it's time to head over to the theater for the Q&A.

Chay, Jen and I watch the Q&A, then head home with Scott, dropping off Chay on the way. We get back to the house, Mos heads home, and Jen and I go to sleep to TiVo.

Friday 26 August 2005 @ 3:01 p.m.

Wake up, get dressed, and work out with Larry.

Afterwards, I take a shower, get dressed, then toss Mulder into the Hate Tank and shoot over to Scott's in Echo Park. We then head over to the *Clerks* 2 location, where we meet Ratface and James, the locations guy. Rat, Scott and I go over the set design.

Two hours later, I fight the traffic back to our neck of the woods and drop Scott and Rat off. I'm running so late, I have to skip the weigh-in at the Weight Control Center. I head home, chill for a half hour with Jen and Harley, then head out to Beverly Hills for the *Southland Tales* shoot.

I throw my gear into the trailer and grab a smoke outside, before going into the makeup trailer, where makeup artist Louis Lazzara tells me they're going to change my look entirely. He asks if I can shave my beard off, but I tell him it's out of the question, as I'm gonna need it for *Clerks* 2 in a month and change. I start shaving it down a bit, then figure it'll grow back in time for the flick, and shave it to the skin, at which point I look like I'm sixteen.

That's when Louis starts with the prosthetics.

Three hours later, he has changed my look, entirely. Looking in the mirror, I see a sixty year-old version of myself, with a long, gray beard, and wrinkled, war-torn skin. Louis is pretty amazing at what he does.

I'm driven up to set, where I chit-chat with Richard a bit, who's happy with the makeup job. He helps me get a bead on my paramilitary, paraplegic character, Simon Thiery, before I climb into my motorized wheelchair to get a feel for the controls. Richard's cool with me ad-libbing, but my dialogue is so plot-specific, I don't alter it much — just flavor it up.

And, at 10 p.m., I start my day-long *Southland* shoot aboard the mega-zeppelin set.

Saturday 27 August 2005 @ 3:01 p.m.

We shoot *Southland Tales* 'til nine in the morning, during which I share dialogue with a non-present Janeane Garofalo (who's shooting her corresponding scenes weeks later), The Rock, Curtis Armstrong (Herbert Viola, from *Moonlighting*, and of course, Booger from *Revenge of the Nerds*), and Zelda Rubinstein ("This house is cleeeeaaannn…" from *Poltergeist*) — all three really sweet people. To write any more would spoil the flick.

After wrap, I spend forty-five minutes getting my makeup taken off, then head home to Jen and Harley at ten in the morning.

I get home and present the clean-shaven Daddy-Man to Harley, who Jen reported — via phone, last night — was in tears at the notion of a beardless father. Jen, too, isn't thrilled with the notion, offering: "You know you're not getting laid 'til the beard comes back, right?" Both agree that they'll learn to live with it for the time being.

Jen and Harley go out shopping, and I go to bed.

I wake up around five, and hang out with Jen before she has to go to her girls' night pot-luck at Scott and Cookie's. She's in the midst of her period, so we wind up getting into no less than two rather large arguments before it's time to go.

Harley and I drop Jen off at Scott and Alex's around seven, and go inside to hang out for a few minutes, at which time Scott gives me a belated birthday present: a framed blowup of a photo of the two of us that'd been taken for a *New York Magazine* story, circa *Clerks*.

I say g'bye to Jen and Alex, Harley and I head back to the house with Scott, where we're met by Malcolm, Andre and their roommate Jason. I put Harley to bed in my room with a bowl of popcorn and *SpongeBob* to fall asleep to, then head upstairs to play poker with the boys. We roll with cards and laugh all night, 'til we're joined around twelve by Jen, Chay, Fanshen and Julie Plec. Scott takes the Hate Tank home, and the rest of us play 'til four in the morning, with the only disruption being Malcolm throwing a hissy at Andre's betting strategy and storming off.

I head to bed around four thirty, cuddling up to Schwalbach, with Harley riding the couch.

Sunday 28 August 2005 @ 3:02 p.m.

Harley wakes me up around ten and I take her upstairs to get some grub, letting Jen sleep in. We try to decide what to do with our day, while we eat breakfast across from one another at the kitchen table: hummus and pitta bread for her, a drink box for me.

We make a game out of cleaning up all the empty beer cans and wine bottles in the living room. I burn a cork and draw a fake beard on, after which we put all the poker chips away, and play three hands of Go Fish. Finally, we opt to hit La Luz de Jesus — a notions store on Hollywood. We get dressed, careful not to wake Jen up, then head out.

We shop at Luz for two hours, buying a ton of books and rubber duckies of various shapes, sizes, and designs. While checking out, I get a card about a Shag gallery show next week, which reminds me how much I love my The Sun Also Rises print in the bathroom. I make a mental note to call about reserving a place at the show.

En route home, Jen calls, finally waking at two in the afternoon. Quinnster and I stop at In-N-Out and grab some hangover junk food for Jen and Chay, then go home, laying out all the swag for the girls to see and food for the girls to eat. I head to my office, and dig out this EA Sports plug&play combo game of Madden Football/NHL '95. I jam in some batteries, plug the game into the office TV, and start playing. I'm immediately taken back to '95, when Mos and I would play this same game (or NHL '93 — with the fights and blood — or NHL '94) constantly, during the *Rats* shoot.

EA Sports NHL series was not only the fav-rave game of me and Mos, but of our entire Jersey Mafia, from 1993 to 1998. Every Christmas, me, Walt, Bry, Ed, Mewes and later Mos would go out to the Marina Diner, exchange gifts, then come back to the condo and have a tournament, at the end of which the winner would take home a small Stanley Cup replica we passed around. The cup currently sits on my awards shelf, beside the Sundance Filmmaker's Trophy, the Prix de la Jeunesse, my DVD Visionary Award, my Independent Spirit Award, my Harvey Award, a Humanitas, and sundry others. I'm as proud of it as I am of the other tin I've collected over the years.

Hours later, I work on the online journal, as Jen puts Harley to bed. Afterwards, we kick back, bone, and watch TiVo 'til we go to sleep.

Monday 29 August 2005 @ 3:02 p.m.

I wake up, check email, then play NHL '95 all morning, stopping only to order a print off the ShagMart website.

With Larry out of town for the week, I spend most of the day playing NHL '95, stopping only to post the updated My Boring-Ass Life.

Around 4:30 p.m., I head out to the Weight Control Center for my weigh-in, where I discover I've lost another nine pounds, bringing my total weight loss to thirty pounds in three weeks. I pick up a new supply of drink boxes and head home, just in time for Malcolm's Going Away Party.

After spending all summer in LA, working on the edit of his doc *Small Town/Gay Bar* with Scott, Malcolm's heading back to Toronto. The film's been submitted to Sundance early with a strong recommendation from Bob Hawk, so there's not much left to do except wait to hear yes or no, so Mitch is making his way home to TO to see about getting a job. I chill on the deck with the crew of guests (including Sam Jaeger, who I haven't seen since we wrapped *Catch & Release* in Boulder) while they eat the Chay-prepared Mexican feast, then set up for poker.

We all play poker 'til two in the morning. When everybody leaves, I lock up the house and head downstairs to find Jen curled up on the couch in our bedroom. I try to wake her, but she's out cold, so I put a blanket on her and go to bed, watching TiVo'ed *Simpsons*.

Tuesday 30 August 2005 @ 3:03 p.m.

I wake up, hit the bathroom with my Tetris, and then head to the bedroom office, doing three hours of phoners for *Mallrats X*.

Afterwards, I pick up Harley from camp, with Hans in tow, and we head to the Coffee Bean on Beverly and Robson, followed by a trip to Laser Blazer, where I somehow spend $850 on two weeks' worth of DVDs.

I come home and chill with Jen for a while, then check email, watching the new *New Jack City* DVD.

After Jen puts Harley to bed, we watch *Witness* and play Rummy. After *Witness*, we pop in *The Truman Show*, and I fall asleep ten minutes before it ends.

Wednesday 31 August 2005 @ 3:03 p.m.

I wake up and head to the bedroom office to check email, during which I watch both the end of *New Jack City* and *The Truman Show*. I say g'bye to Jen, who heads off to yoga, then take a shower and answer more email.

I spend an hour inserting scene numbers into a script, then print up a few for the burgeoning crew, during which I let *Monster-in-Law* play in the background.

I do an interview with Kate O'Hare for a TV insert cover story on *Veronica Mars*, during which I don't have much to say about the show (as I've never seen it). We wind up talking about almost everything else going on in the TV biz instead.

Post-interview, I attempt to watch what I assume is a doc entitled *Confessions of an Adult Film Star* only to discover it's not a doc at all, but instead soft core porn. I turn it off after about ten minutes, because if I'm gonna watch people fuck, I'd rather see insertions and cum shots (gimme the "arching ropes of jism" as Bill Hicks would say) than simulated coitus.

I pick up Harley from camp, head over to Mr. Lee's to pick up a new jersey, go home, play Groovy Girls Bingo with Jen and Harley, and say hi to Mewes, who's returned from his Jersey jaunt.

I watch *Simpsons* on TiVo while Jen gets ready for Catherine McCord's bridal shower. Since Byron and Gail are heading up to Big Bear with Jimmy and Eileen, I watch *Lilo & Stitch 2: Stitch Has a Glitch* with Harley when Jen leaves. Post-flick, I put Harley to bed then watch a British flick called *Dog Soldiers* while signing three boxes of DVD covers for the online Stash.

Post-*Dog*, I prep the bedroom with candles and toys in anticipation of Jen getting home. When she arrives, I welcome her home in the hallway and escort her into the den of lust, at which point she hits the bed and we bust out with the sex.

Post-coitus, we sit around jawing for half an hour, then climb into bed, falling asleep to *Simpsons*.

Thursday 1 September 2005 @ 3:04 p.m.

I wake up and take Harley to camp, picking up McDonald's hash browns for the hung-over Jen on the way home. I take a shower, get dressed, toss Mulder in the car and shoot over to the *Clerks 2* production offices. There, I drop off scripts for Laura, pick up Scott, Dave, and Rat, and head out to the location where we meet James. Dave, Scott, Rat and I go through the entire script, running through all the exteriors, roughing out a shot-list of sorts for four hours.

We head back to the office where I drop off the guys, then I head home, talk to Steve (our electronics guy) for a bit, and chill out with Jen when she gets home from yoga. Jen heads out to grab Harley from camp and shoot over to the Grove for more school shopping, and I chill in my office, checking email and watching *St. Elmo's Fire*. I head up to the dining room and sign a bunch of posters for the site, then update the online diary 'til Jen comes home. We put Harley to bed, then chit-chat on the bedroom couch for awhile, after which we pop in the pilot for *Veronica Mars*.

Back before I did my stint on *Mars*, Dan Etheridge sent over the entire first season on discs, but I never got around to peeping 'em out. Big mistake. Because by midway through the pilot, Schwalbach and I are hooked, big time. We immediately watch the next two episodes before going to bed.

Friday 2 September 2005 @ 3:05 p.m.

I wake up after Jen's left to take Harley to camp. When she gets home, we continue watching *Veronica Mars*, and I'm so in love with the show that I call Kate O'Hare back to amend the interview, singing the praises of *Mars* now that I'm halfway through season one. I IM back and forth with Dan Etheridge telling him how genius this show is, and asking all sorts of fanboy questions about the mystery of Lilly Kane's murder (which, sadly, I already know the perpetrator of).

I get on the phone with Chap to talk about the new merch we're planning, and Jen goes to pick up Harley and hit the food store on the way home. When she gets back, Jen feeds Quinnster then goes to yoga, at which point I take Harley and the mutts for a ride to the Valley, where we drop my new Shag print off at the framers and pick up the framed Monorail and *Reel Paradise* posters.

We pick up Koo Koo Roo for Quinnster, grab some burgers for the dogs from Carl's Jr., and head home, where Jen puts Harley to bed, just as folks start arriving to play poker.

I play poker all night with Jen, Julie, Jay, Chay, Analiese, Miri, Judy, and Chappy. Post-midnight, Richard Kelly and some of his *Southland* mob join us, and I quiz Richard about the shoot thus far and my dailies in particular.

We play poker 'til three in the morning, when Harley joins us upstairs, awakened by the racket. She hangs out for a bit, then Jen puts her to bed in our room.

We wrap up the game and I join Jen and Harley in bed, going to sleep around four.

Saturday 3 September 2005 @ 3:05 p.m.

I wake up around eleven and head downstairs to find Jen in Harley's room, playing Groovy Girls bingo. I get dressed and head over to Quizno's to get Jen a veggie sub and Harley a turkey sub Kid's Meal. I bring the dogs with me and get them burgers at Wendy's.

I come home and the girls start eating in the room, 'til Reyna shows up, at which point Harley heads off to hang out with Reyna, and Jen and I spend the whole day in the bedroom, watching *Veronica Mars*.

Jay and Chay stop in, after grabbing Jen some In-N-Out. After our rave reviews, they take the first half of the *Mars* discs to watch downstairs.

Harley goes to Chuck E. Cheese with Reyna, then comes home around eight. We put her to bed, then finish watching out the rest of *Mars* season one.

This is, hands-down, the best show on television right now, and proof that TV can be far better than cinema. The cast is pretty uniformly excellent, and the dialogue crackles. Excellent characterization — even with the day-players — makes it the most engaging new show I've seen since *Degrassi: The Next Generation*, but the heart and soul of the show is the relationship between father and daughter, Keith and Veronica Mars.

The fact that Kristen Bell and Enrico Colantoni ("Those poor people..." from the severely underrated *Galaxy Quest*) weren't Emmy nominated proves how fucking out of touch and useless the Emmy Awards are to begin with. The tender and witty repartee between these two wonderful actors makes you want to be a better parent. And a big shout-out to Jason Dohring's Logan Echolls — a masterfully designed and performed nemesis whose twists and turns are always credible.

The show is basically an amalgam of some of the best TV ever produced, with each formula improved upon — chiefly, one clearly sees a *Twin Peaks* influence, with the year-long mystery surrounding the murder of party girl Lilly Kane. But whereas I always felt the brilliant *Twin Peaks* should've been a maxi-series, wrapping up the Laura Palmer murder in twelve episodes, *Mars* manages to thread the needle with the Lilly Kane murder so well, it never feels marginalized or played out over twenty-two episodes. And unlike *Peaks*, when the murderer is revealed and the storyline wrapped up in the final ep, it doesn't feel like the show's outlived its relevance; thanks to the crisp writing, the deft fleshing-out of the *Mars* universe and the endearing cast, you're left wanting Veronica's story to continue.

If you haven't seen this show, good God, get your hands on the season one box set. Sadly, it arrives in stores a few weeks after the start of season two, so if you haven't seen any of season one, make sure to TiVo season two's first few eps, but don't watch them, lest you spoil the amazingly plotted season one (however, I will say this: I was informed who the killer was before I even started watching *Mars*, and even so, it never took anything away from my enjoyment of the run).

In a lifetime of dedicated television watching, *Veronica Mars* is easily one of the five best shows I've ever dug.

After watching the seat-of-your-pants season finale, Schwalbach and I go to bed around one, as sated as if we'd been fucking for twenty-two hours, instead of simply watching a TV show.

Sunday 4 September 2005 @ 3:05 p.m.

I wake up around ten and head up to the pool deck, where I find Harley drawing, and Jen cleaning up the dog shit/watering her plants.

I take a shower and get dressed, and the ladies and I head over to the Valley to the Farmer's Market/Street Fair they hold every Sunday at Ventura and Laurel. Harley hits the petting zoo then goes to the bounce house. Jen buys Harley a pair of skirts, after which we hit Big Five Sporting Goods, where Jen picks up some workout stuff, and I buy a set of baseballs.

We go to the Daily Grill, where the ladies dine, and I toss back an iced tea, then shoot over to the Yellow Balloon, the kids' hair salon, where Harley gets a haircut.

The three of us head home, where I check email and the board. I call into Fan Boy Radio in Fort Worth and shoot the shit with Jim Mahfood for a bit, 'til Jen has to leave for yoga.

Jen leaves, and Harley and I chill out in her room playing Groovy Girls bingo and Pick-Up Sticks. Harley does some pre-school-year homework, and then we retire to my room to watch *Clueless* for a while, 'til it's bedtime.

Harley and I chill out on the front steps for two minutes until Jen pulls up. I kiss Quinnster g'night, and head upstairs to check email.

After Jen puts Harley to bed, we watch TiVo all night, and play a game of Rummy. When Jen goes to sleep, I pop in some *Twilight Zone*s to go to sleep to.

Monday 5 September 2005 @ 1:39 a.m.

While Jen chills with Harley, I wake up and check email and the board, before calling the Mondrian to make reservations at both Asia de Cuba and the hotel itself.

Reyna, Kevin and Hans show up, and Harley heads off to play with them while Jen works out in the gym and I get through all my email. When she's done working out, I tell Jen to get ready for our lunch date. We both shower, get dressed, and head over to the Mondrian.

I take Jen out to lunch at Asia de Cuba and we chit-chat. I down iced teas while Jen enjoys sushi and lobster rolls, and then I excuse myself to hit the bathroom, but instead check-in at the front desk and grab the keys to our single room. The guy at the front desk recognizes me and bumps me up to a suite instead.

The check comes and I pay with the house card they give you when you check-in, which surprises Jen. We head upstairs and lay around the bed for fifteen minutes, smoking and flirting. Then, the sex kicks in. The bed's situated beside a large mirror, so we spend most of the hour-long session watching our-selves fuck.

We wrap it up, and lay around, talking, enjoying the peace and quiet. Then, we get dressed, head down to the Hustler store, grab some toys, and come back to the room, where we rent a porno and go for round two, incorporating the toys. An hour later, we get dressed, check out of our afternoon-long den of iniquity, and head back to reality at the house.

I climb into woobs and watch the *Metallica: Some Kind of Monster* documen-tary (such a great watch) while checking email and the board. Jen puts Harley to bed, and we chill out on the couch, talking about the doc and the week ahead. I go back to my office to finish up some email, then close up shop and join Schwalbach in bed, falling asleep to TiVo'ed *Simpsons*.

Tuesday 6 September 2005 @ 1:56 p.m.

Wake up, shower, then check email and the board. Get dressed, grab the camera and head downstairs.

Today's the first day of first grade for Harley, so the whole family's heading over to the school to see her off. I take a bunch of pics of Quinnster, then we pile into two cars and head over to school.

We take Harley in and re-meet her new teacher. I take some more pics in the classroom and then we take off. Jen, Byron and Gail take B & G's car back to the house, and I head over to the Weight Control Center.

En route I call my Mom and talk to her for a while. Then, since I'm early, I pop into Office Depot and buy some odds and ends.

Afterwards, I head into the doctor's. At the weigh-in, I've lost another seven pounds. I meet with the counselor, then pick up new shakes and take off. I shoot over to Laser Blazer for new DVDs, then head home.

I head upstairs and Byron snaps a quick pic of me by the grill, which I for-ward to Ming. Then, we launch the Auctions Askew benefit for the Hurricane Katrina victims.

Head back to the school with Jen to pick up Harley, who tells us all about her day. When we get into the house, a very excited Louis almost pushes Harley down the stairs, and tears ensue.

The family eats dinner upstairs, and since I'm not eating, I chill in my office, checking the auction, the board, and email. Post-dinner, Jen and I get into a spat. I head upstairs and talk to Gail and Byron for a while, then come back to the room and continue to spar with Schwalbach. After an hour, we kiss and make up, then pop in the *Buffalo Bill* season one and two DVD, to which we fall asleep

Wednesday 7 September 2005 @ 2:14 p.m.

Wake up, shower, and head to Harley's school, where we drop off a bunch of her old toys and books and head to a meeting of first and second grade parents with the new Principal.

An hour and a half later, we head home, and I check email 'til it's time to work out with Larry. We do the dog walk, during which he tells me all about his week at Burning Man. We shoot back to the home gym and do legs (weights, squats, and lunges) for an hour. When we're done, I climb into my woobs and bury myself in the home office most of the day, iChatting with Scott about *Clerks 2* stuff, including the A.D. choices. By day's end, we hire the dude who's gonna be the 1st A.D. for our seventh film.

I iChat with Chappy about new posters we're doing in time for Christmas. In the midst of that, Mewes drops by and tells me he's going to play some UB. I ask him to transfer some chips into my account, so I can play alongside him, but my Virtual PC is acting buggy, so by the time I get on, Mewes has donked out of his cash.

Head down to Harley's room and help her do homework, then spend a couple hours playing Hide and Seek and Go Fish.

At night, I talk to Annie on iChat about our kids and school, and then get infusion of cash into my UB account.

Jen comes back from Yoga and puts Harley to bed. I'm knee deep in UB, so she busies herself with other stuff. I watch *The Sting* in my office while playing, before moving to the bed, where I kiss Jen g'night, then crack open the laptop. I play UB while watching the *Roseanne* season one DVD box set, then close up shop around two and fall asleep to a TiVo'ed *Law & Order*.

Thursday 8 September 2005 @ 2:15 p.m.

I wake up and do some phoners for the *Rats X* DVD, then secure the details for the *Rats* signing with Lee, via email. Go over the signing with Chap and lock in Mahfood for live art show, then post the info on board.

I shower and head to VA office for an interview with a British network that's named *Clerks* as one of the fifty funniest movies of all time and chit-chat with Smalls between takes. After we wrap it up, I head to the *Clerks 2* office for a meeting with Roseanne Fiedler, our costume designer (who was a wardrobe assistant on *Mallrats*), going over what Dante, Randal, Jay and Bob will be wearing. Meet with Scott and Laura about the schedule, then meet with Rat about production design.

Arrive home just in time to bring Jen to Asia de Cuba, where I sit with her 'til Daniella Milton arrives. I head home and watch the Kinison tribute DVD while playing UB. Jen calls for her pick up, so I head back to Asia de Cuba, grab Jen, and head home. We bone for a little bit, then head upstairs to the kitchen where Jen makes Harley's lunch for the morning, and we retire downstairs, falling asleep watching the *Roseanne* season one DVD box set.

Friday 9 September 2005 @ 2:16 p.m.

Dogs wake me up at seven, so I trudge upstairs, let 'em out, and go check email in my office, then play some more UB. I say g'bye to Harley as she leaves, as she's heading to Big Bear with Gail and Byron after school.

Around ten thirty, I realize Larry's running really late, so I leave a message on his cell phone that we can just skip the workout 'til Monday. Instead, Jen and I take the dogs for my workout warm-up walk up the hill. Schwalbach being all sorts of in-yoga-shape smokes me, with the always energetic Mulder in tow, while Scully and I, the Fat-Ass Twins, do our slow ascent and descent.

Come back and chill in my office, checking the board and email, until it's time to do an interview with the *Toronto Globe and Mail* about the *Degrassi* 25th Anniversary.

Around one thirty, I take a shower and get dressed, and drive Jen, Mewes, and myself down to the doctor's for cast physicals. Jen's is done pretty quickly, but Mewes and I — who are run of show — have to give blood, urine, and get an EKG, so we take a bit longer.

We race back to the house to drop Jen off so she can head over to yoga, and she sends down her cell phone, which Mewes and I are going to replace today with a phone that actually rings. We head over to the new Schwab's shopping complex on Hollywood and Vine, park, and head toward the Verizon store, getting sidetracked by the EB Games next door. I buy the *Spider-Man 2* and World Poker Tour games for my Nintendo DS, and well as *Batman Begins* for my Gameboy Advance.

We head to the phone store, pick out a new phone for Jen, and check out, which winds up taking almost an hour. While we wait, Mewes IMs with Annie and gets chips dumped into his account, so the plan is to go back to the house and play UB 'til I have to meet Jen for our massages.

We pick up In-N-Out for Mewes, then head back to the house and play UB for awhile, 'til I head over to Burke Williams, where Jen's booked massages for us (sadly, in different rooms). I follow up my massage with a facial (not like that, you fucks), then head into Virgin, where I pick up Metallica's *St. Anger*, Eric B. and Rakim's *Gold*, Mitch Hedberg's *Mitch All Together* and a Public Enemy *Greatest Hits* cd I'd never seen before. I drive home where I find Mewes asleep in his room. I start burning my new cds for my iPod while playing UB when Jen comes home. We both putter for an hour, before settling in for some Rummy and *Million Dollar Baby*, which I've been bugging her to watch with me ever since I checked it out back in December.

Post-flick, Jen goes to sleep to some TiVo'ed *Simpsons* while I play some more UB. When I donk out of all my cash, I start a TiVo'ed *Law & Order* and fall asleep.

Saturday 10 September 2005 @ 2:18 p.m.

I wake up and check email and the auction. I talk to Mewes upstairs for a bit, then head back to the office and post the artwork for the Ultimate View Askew DVD box. Afterwards, I hit the shitter and play *Batman Begins* on Gameboy, then go to work updating the online diary.

Jen goes to yoga and I chill out online, answering email and checking the board. I clean up my Mac desktop, putting pictures away in iChat, then jerk off to some pics of Jen, before showering and loading the Disneyland Submarine Voyage poster into the car to get re-framed.

I head over to the Valley, drop the poster off at the framer, pick up the new framed *Shag* print, then shoot over to the cleaner's to pick up Jen's dress, at which point I'm informed they didn't start the alteration yet, and that I'll have to come back at seven to pick it up before they close.

Call Jen on the way home to deliver the bad news, and she's devastated, as she was counting on wearing that dress for the party. She goes into damage control mode and jumps off the phone.

Get home and find Jen tearing apart her closet, looking for a dress to wear. I lay on the bed and play more *Batman*, 'til I hit the final level and can't beat the Scarecrow. Jen comes out wearing a gorgeous dress I've never seen before, which she reveals she bought when we went to Japan, back in '03 and hasn't worn yet. She looks truly dazzling, and I give the outfit the thumbs-up.

We head over to Jon Gordon and Catherine McCord's wedding bash at Mexico City. Since Jon starts his new gig as President of Production at Universal October 1, Jon and Catherine have opted to do the whole wedding thing in reverse, honeymooning over the summer, having the reception today, and finally tying the knot in a small ceremony in Manhattan later next week.

They've set up an old photo booth so guests can take pics and paste them into a book of well-wishes, and Jen and I take a set for the book and a set for ourselves. Mewes and I smoke and chat outside, later joined by Jen, Chay, Julie, Judy and Miri. I see and talk to Ben and Jen for the first time since we wrapped *Catch & Release*, as well as Jenno Topping and Chris Moore. I hang with Mos and talk shop for a while, until the food comes, at which point I go outside with Jen to smoke and chit-chat. We head back in and do the rounds for another hour, saying hi to Phil Raskind, and of course, Jon and Catherine.

Around 10:30, I drive Jen and Chay home. Jen almost immediately passes out, and I head upstairs to play poker with Chay, Fanshen and Diego, during which we talk about Italy and Mewes 'til two in the morning. Afterwards, I head downstairs and play *Batman* on Gameboy 'til I go to sleep.

Sunday 11 September 2005 @ 2:18 p.m.

Wake up around nine and let the dogs out, then take what — now that I've been on the shake diet for a month — passes for a dump while playing the *Batman* game on Gameboy.

I check email and the board 'til Jen gets up, then sit around chatting with her 'til she asks me to make an In-N-Out run. I throw on some clothes and head downstairs, stopping at Mewes's room to see if Chay wants anything as well. Mewes is there, so I recruit him for the ride, and we load the dogs into the car and head out.

Mewes and I bullshit about what he did last night post-party, grab In-N-Out for him, Jen and Chay, grab Burger King for the dogs, then shoot back to the house.

While they eat, we all sit around in the bedroom living room chit-chatting and checking out the birthday video Chay made for her father. I head to the bathroom and play *Spider-Man 2* on the Nintendo DS for a while, then lay down on the bed, doing more of the same. Chay and Jay head off, and Jen and I watch a review copy of *My Name is Earl* a journalist passed off to me, as well as the first two episodes of the new season of *Curb Your Enthusiasm*.

Earl is a great, original show, and both Lee and Ethan are fantastic in it. There's a *Raising Arizona* flavor to it, and Lee is pitch-perfect in the single-camera show. Mercifully, there's no laugh-track, so it plays like a feature, and the premise — Earl has over two hundred mistakes he has to make up for in order to balance his karma — is such that if the critical gods keep smiling down (or up) at the show, it'll run for years. This is one time you can believe the hype; even without my boys on the marquee, I'd still think this is the best sitcom I've seen since *Seinfeld*.

After watching the new *Curb* eps, we pop in the box set of last year's *Curb* and get through two episodes before Harley gets home from Big Bear. Jen chills with Harley for a bit before she leaves for yoga, and then Harley and I head over to Westwood.

We stop at the Stash where I drop off the new Matt Potter in-store reel, and pick up a few hardcovers. Then, we roll over to Aahhh's, where their Halloween section's up and running already. Harley picks out a pirate girl costume, and we grab Snow White and Superman costumes for Scully and Mulder. We pay and head home, listening to *Some Kind of Monster* on the way home and wrapping up with Harley's current fave, 'Hollaback Girl', before getting back to the house.

Jen's back from yoga, so Harley wants to boutique her Halloween threads. I get Harley into her outfit and ta-da it for Jen, before heading upstairs to show Byron, Gail, Jimmy and Ween. I pop the dogs into their outfits and try to take some pics, but Mulder — who's deathly afraid of cameras — slinks away to hide, a cowardly Krypto.

Chay makes Jen a salad for dinner, then spends the night, watching *Veronica Mars* eps. Jen puts Harley to bed, and we watch more *Curb*, during which Jen falls asleep and I play more of the *Spider-Man* game on the DS, 'til I close up shop and hit the hay.

Monday 12 September 2005 @ 1:21 p.m.

Wake up, work out with Larry, shower, and then head over to the *Clerks 2* office, where I pick up Mos, Dave and Tony, and we head out to the location to start shot-listing.

We spend half a day shot-listing all the exterior scenes at the location, and when we're done, we discover there are more planned shots in the first five scenes of *Clerks* 2 than in all of the original *Clerks*.

We head back to the office where I drop the guys off and I shoot back down the 101 to home.

I get into the house and play a game with Harley before she goes to bed, then crash with Jen, watching TiVo.

Tuesday 13 September 2005 @ 11:13 a.m.

I get up, throw some clothes on, and drop Harley off at school. Then, I come home and do some *Rats X* DVD phoners, including a great one with Bob Grimm of *Las Vegas Life* and the *Reno News and Review*, during which we talk about how puzzling it is that the new generation of film school kids haven't seen *Jaws*, much less *Do the Right Thing*.

I get in the shower, get dressed, and head over to Burbank to do some ADR [additional dialogue recording] on my *Veronica Mars* episode. The drive there is far longer than the ADR itself, which I hit in two takes, and I'm out the door and on the way home five minutes later, talking to my Mom on the cell en route.

I get back to the house and chill with Jen and Harley a bit before Larry comes by at 6:30 with his friend Jerrod, a guy who runs a pretty big t-shirt company. We spend the next three hours talking about doing a new Askewniverse line of t's for Hot Topics.

They leave and I climb into my woobs, crashing with Jen, watching TiVo'ed *Simpsons* and playing *Batman Begins* on Gameboy before falling asleep.

Wednesday 14 September 2005 @ 11:13 a.m.

Wake up and work out with Larry, then do another interview for the *Rats X* DVD.

I shower and head over to the *Clerks* 2 office, where I meet with Scott Purcell, the brilliant graphics guy we've used since *Chasing Amy*. I go over the shirt designs for Randal and Jay for a bit, then chit-chat with Roseanne about Becky's costume before collecting Mos, Dave, and Tony and heading over to the location to start shot-listing the interiors.

Dave and I are shooting the shit out of this flick. We're doing very little of the static two shots we did on the first *Clerks*, with a ton of hand-held coverage planned instead. What would've been one set-up on the first flick will now be five set-ups, minimum. This time around, the look of the flick will be as important as the performances and what's being said.

We shot-list 'til seven thirty, at which point Tony, Dave and Scott head back to the office and Chappy meets me at the location to lead me back to Graphitti Designs.

Back at Graphitti, Chappy meets with Jerrod and his art team to talk about the shirts we're gonna do. When they go, Chappy and his son Kevin start laying out the 750 Boston variants of the Kevin Smith InAction figure that we're selling at the WizardCon in Boston, and I sign 'em all. Even if I can't be there myself (due to the heavy pre-production build-up), we figured it'd be good to offer the Boston variant signed for any VA fans showing up to the Con. While I'm signing, Chappy shows me the *Mallrats Companion* script book, which blows the original *Rats* script book out of the water (John Roshell — the guy who designed the View Askew Almanac Calendar we did two years back, as well as some of our posters — is a genius).

I head home around midnight, get into my woobs, crawl into bed beside Jen, and go to sleep to TiVo'ed *Simpsons*.

Thursday 15 September 2005 @ 11:14 a.m.

Wake up, shower, and head to the office to do an early a.m. interview for an IFC doc on censorship. After we're done, I ask them if they can shoot a five-minute intro for me, for my induction into the Henry Hudson Hall of Fame. Apparently, my high school alma mater is officially recognizing that I've done something with my life, which is rather bittersweet. Sadly, with *Clerks 2* looming, I won't be able to attend the presentation, so I'm sending this PG-13 rated video intro instead.

After that, I head back up to the house to shot-list the opening scenes of the flick with Dave, Scott and Tony. We're done by three, at which point I chill out downstairs, answering email before the 7 p.m. meeting with Laura, Scott and a guy we want for a key crew position.

Post meeting, I climb into the woobs and hit the board for a bit before climbing into bed and watching TiVo with Jen 'til we fall asleep.

Friday 16 September 2005 @ 11:15 a.m.

Wake up early to let the dogs out, then drop Harley off at school, come home, check email and post a bunch of pictures up on My Boring-Ass Life.

I get showered and dressed and head over to the *Clerks* production office to say hi to Derek Raser, our transpo guy from *Strike Back* who's doing the new flick too. After that, I meet with Gary Jenson, who's on board as our stunt coordinator again, then head out to scout another location with Laura, Scott, Dave, Rat, Tony and James.

From there, Scott, Dave, Tony and I head back to the main location to finish shot-listing. We're done by 5:30, but with traffic, it takes us about an hour to get home.

Back in the house, I check email as well as the finals on the View Askew Katrina Auction, posting the results on the board.

With Harley gone for the weekend, up in Big Bear with Byron and Gail, Jen and I are alone in the house. We seize the opportunity and make with the hour-long fuck session, and then kick back to watch the new *Cheers* box set.

Mewes comes home from his three days in Utah where he was shooting at a prison on an indie flick. He's severely under the weather, sporting a mouthful of cold sores. Chay comes over to take care of him, and Jen and I fall asleep around ten.

Saturday 17 September 2005 @ 11:16 a.m.

I wake up around six, let the dogs out, then head to the office to check email and the board. Jen gets up and starts rushing me and Mewes out of the house, so she can prepare for her big girl's night sleepover party (no boys allowed). I wake up Mewes and tell him to get showered, while I shower, get dressed, and pack for the night, throwing 250 *Rats X* covers into my bag to sign if I wind up donking out early at the Casino that night.

I kiss Jen g'bye, then Mewes and I jump on the 10, bound for the Casino Morongo, in Cabazon, out near Palm Springs.

We bullshit the whole way down, listening to Metallica, with Mewes dozing off sometimes, as he's not feeling that great — a condition that immediately changes once we hit the casino.

We check in, at which point the guy at the front desk upgrades us to suites, as he's a fan. We dump our shit in the rooms, then head straight down to the poker room, where we get onto separate (then the same) $5/$10 tables. We play poker from three 'til midnight, stopping only to eat (in Mewes's case) or grab some air and play blackjack (in my case). When we're done, I hit the $100 black-jack table to win back some poker losses, then head up to the rooms, roughly even from where I started.

Mewes suggests we watch a flick, so we rent *Kingdom of Heaven* while Mewes eats room service and I sign the 250 *Rats* DVD covers I brought with me. I talk to Jen and say g'night around two in the morning. Post-*Kingdom*, around three in the morning, Mewes and I head back downstairs to the casino where I donk out at the poker table after a few hours. I head back to blackjack to win my losses back, only to lose even more cash at blackjack this time around. I go back to the poker room, but the only seat open is at a $1/$3 table. I lose about a hundred bucks as I start falling asleep at the table, and opt to hit the hay instead, at nine in the morning, Sunday.

Sunday 18 September 2005 @ 11:20 a.m.

The wake-up call at eleven makes me drag my ass out of bed. I pack up, bang on Mewes's door and tell him we're leaving, check out, and get on the road around 11:45. Malcolm calls in from Toronto while we're driving and we talk to him for a bit, getting an update on his dad's health.

Since there's no traffic, Mewes and I get home an hour and five minutes later, at which point Mewes heads out to play the *Lord of the Rings* game, and I head upstairs to kiss Jen and say hi to Lisa Roumaine and Lisa Weitz, the only two chicks left from the sleepover rager. I'm sent to Baja Fresh and Coffee Bean to pick up snacks for the girls, and then I retire to my room, where I watch *25th Hour* and sign another 250 *Rats* DVD covers, to send out to Don in the morning so he can start filling online Stash pre-orders.

The girls leave, and Jen joins me on the bed. We cuddle and chit-chat for a bit before we hear Harley coming home from Big Bear with Byron and Gail. She joins us in the room, and the three of us sit around, catching up, before Jen heads downstairs with Harley, and I finish signing the covers and watching *25th Hour*.

The two of us put Harley to bed, then head upstairs and kick back with some *Cheers* episodes from the new box set. I play more of the *Spider-Man* DS game, until I get too frustrated, unable to beat the Doc Ock final boss and shut the game down for the night, going to sleep to *Cheers*.

Monday 19 September 2005 @ 11:21 a.m.

Wake up at 5:45 to do phoner with Mancow radio show out in Chicago, then check email and the board taking Harley to school. I come home and print up a bunch of scripts the office needs, then wire the intro for Bry and Walt's *Karney* trade paperback. Afterwards, I play the *Spider-Man* DS game for a bit before showering and heading to office to rehearse with Jeff and Trevor.

Jeff's electric. He's got the whole script memorized, and every piece of his delivery is gold. After working at it for an hour, we finally find Trevor's voice for Elias, the character he plays, and the scenes begin to really sing, cracking me up (a good sign, as I believed I was already too familiar with the material to find it laugh-out-loud funny anymore). After four hours of rehearsal, going over all their shared scenes, we call it a day, and I head back to the house.

I check email while the family's upstairs eating, then play a few games with Harley and Jen (Disney Yahtzee and Uno), before kissing Quinnster g'night and heading back to my room.

Jen and I watch a few episodes from the new *Cheers* box set while I continue answering email, then call it a night, falling asleep around 9:30.

Tuesday 20 September 2005 @ 11:22 a.m.

Wake up at 5:45 for *Mallrats* DVD radio tour, which wraps up around 8:30. Afterwards, I go through email and hit a few posts on the board before rehearsing with Jen in our room for an hour and getting showered and dressed.

On the ride to the production office, I get a call from a comedienne I went after for a *Clerks* cameo who confirms that she's in, which makes me pretty happy.

I pick up Scott, Dave, and Tony and we follow Derek, Laura, and James and meet Ratface for a location scout. The place checks out really nicely, so we lock it up for the flick.

From there, I head over to the Weight Control Center to weigh in and pick up new shakes. I've lost another five pounds and change, bringing my total weight loss up to forty-five pounds in a month and a half.

I rocket over to Laser Blazer and pick up $400 worth of new DVDs, including Criterion's *Naked* and *Over the Edge* — one of my favorite flicks from the early days of cable. After that, I hit the Stash where I sign a bunch of *Rats X* DVDs and chat up Xtian and Dave for a bit before heading home.

On the drive back, I get the call that my new shooters are done, so I grab a check from the house, load the dogs into the car, and cruise back across town to pick 'em up. I stop at McDonald's for the dogs (you can't beat $1.00 double cheeseburgers), then get back to the house, where I chit-chat with Jen and fill her in on the day's activities before shooting back out to Harley's school for a back-to-school night function.

We come home and I set-up TiVo for an *Earl* season pass, then check email and chill with Jen, watching *Thirteen Days*. When it ends, we pop on some TiVo'ed *Simpsons* and go to sleep.

Wednesday 21 September 2005 @ 11:24 a.m.

Wake up and check email and the board while watching a pretty low-rent shark attack flick called *Blue Demon*. Order up some smokes from Yummy and watch the Sandler *Longest Yard* flick, then do an interview with *Maclean's* (the Canadian mag) and print up some more scripts.

I shower and head down to the office, where Mos, Dave and I watch a chunk of *25th Hour*, a film whose look I like quite a bit for *Clerks 2*. The *C2* brain-trust then goes over the options for a digital intermediate — a process in which you shoot on film, then transfer the footage into a digital format, where you have unprecedented color correction control, and spit the results back out onto a digital master from which all the film prints are made. The process is probably most easily recognizable in the Coen Brothers' flick *O Brother, Where Art Thou* — where colors were deeply saturated to give whole sections of the flick a golden hue.

We're going the opposite way. Amongst other things, our plans are to de-saturate the colors of all the scenes that take place at work, to give Dante and Randal's jobs a bland, hell-ish feel. The idea is the culmination of months of back-and-forth about whether or not to hone close to the low-rent look of the first *Clerks*. At the end of the day, we figured shooting on 16mm or shooting the flick as flatly and *mise-en-scène* as *Clerks* would be disingenuous and feel like we were trying too hard to catch lightning in a bottle twice. The look of *Clerks* — long held to be a big part of the flick's charm — was born out of a lack of budget and a trio of amateurs' eyes. This time around, we've got a budget and a decade of experience on our side; making the flick look bad on purpose would make us feel like we were posers. However, it doesn't mean we can't fuck around and try something creative with the look to invoke the first *Clerks*, while still applying everything we've learned since '93.

We wrap up at the office and I head back up to the house, take a dump, and then meet Jeff downstairs. We make the drive out to the location, where Trevor joins us. Tony, the 1st A.D. arrives, and based on the shot-list notes he took all last week, we do a blocking rehearsal of all the Randal and Elias scenes.

Trevor is slipping into a deeper comfort level with his Elias delivery, and in the process, finding funnier and funnier bits of business. Jeff is just on fire, having honed Randal to a finely tuned instrument of pitch-perfect delivery. It's a thing of joy listening to them together.

We wrap the rehearsal around seven and Jeff and I head back to Hollywood, chatting the whole drive home about how the rehearsals are going, as well as folks we went to high school with.

We get back to the house, and Jeff heads home. I join Schwalbach upstairs and we chit-chat a bit, before she hits the hay, tuckered out from a day of yoga and abs classes. I finally pick the Gameboy *Batman Begins* game back up and figure out how to beat the Ducard/Ra's Al Ghul final boss. Not wanting to wake up Jen, I retire to my office, where I watch the late-seventies classic *Over the Edge*, while checking email. When the flick's done, I crack open my Jen nudie pics, tug one out, and go to sleep around two in the morning.

Thursday 22 September 2005 @ 11:25 a.m.

I wake up, check email and the board, and some Canadian interviews for the *Rats X* DVD release while Jen hits yoga. Afterwards, I bury myself in the *Spider-Man* Nintendo DS game, finally bringing down the final Doc Ock boss and completing the game. I take a shower then head upstairs.

Zack and Joey show up around two, and we record the intros to the online video journal we're gonna be doing throughout the production of *Clerks 2*. At the tail end of that shoot, Jeff arrives, and the two of us then load into the car, pick up Brian at his hotel, and head down to the location for rehearsal.

The drive is spent, naturally, catching up with Brian, who's not only been through a cancer scare with his girlfriend Diana over the last few months, but also had gall bladder surgery himself. We get to the location just as I'm finishing up my story about the Phil Incident, and I tour Bri around the set a bit. Tony arrives, and since Brian's still on book, we settle into a read-thru with some minor blocking.

It's awesome hearing Brian and Jeff's voices together again, at last. For the past week, I've been filling in the Dante stuff for Jeff's and Trevor's rehearsal, but I'm not fit to fill O'Halloran's shoes. By the time we get to the car scene, the two are on fire, tearing it up in classic Dante and Randal style. The car scene, for me, is the highlight of the day, as it's hysterically funny, envelope-pushing outrageous, and then suddenly resolves itself into something really touching. Listening to Bri and Jeff reminds me I made two brilliant choices way back in '93.

Trevor arrives and joins the read-through, slipping more and more comfortably into Elias' particular patois. We wrap up the rehearsal close to eight and head back to Hollywood, dropping Brian off at the hotel on the way. Back at the house, Jeff heads off, and I head inside, finding Jen upstairs in the kitchen, making Harley's lunch for the morning.

I climb into woobs, and Jen climbs into bed, falling asleep by nine thirty. I check email, watching TiVo'ed *Law & Order* eps, until I opt to head to my office, where I watch the new *Justice League* DVD. Afterwards, I finally crack open *Rats X* and give it a test drive, peeping the whole disc, end-to-end, 'til two in the morning. I'm amazed at how good the extended cut looks, in terms of the extra footage. I've never seen that cut stuff taken through to the digital master stage, and I wasn't really prepared for how clean it all finally looks.

It's weird: for years, all that extra footage existed solely on a VHS in my office. Then, it finally saw the light of day on the first *Rats* DVD. Now, it's been reintegrated into the flick, and actually color-corrected and finished.

And yet, that opening still stinks.

It reminds me of the more humble beginning of *Rats*, back before the "Julie Dwyer died in the YMCA pool" start, or the "I got a musket tangled in my girlfriend's hair!" stuff. In the first draft, before the studio encouraged me to "open up" the start of the flick, to "make it bigger", we launched the film on a much more subtle note.

From the original file, dated August 13th, 1994 (written before *Clerks* even opened in theaters), this was the OG opening of *Mallrats*...

INT GAME SHOW SET — COLLEGIATE SHOWDOWN

A simple set: a three-seater of contestants on either side of a podium, at which stands a HOST. The one side is labeled SETON HALL; the other side is labeled MONMOUTH. Seton Hall has 275 points; Monmouth has 260. A BELL rings.

HOST
That's the one-minute bell which means this will
be the final question. Monmouth has an impressive
two hundred and sixty points, and Seton Hall is in
the lead with two hundred and seventy five — but

that can all change with this next question, a twenty
pointer, which goes to the first team that buzzes in:
Name the body of water of the Atlantic Ocean that is
formed by the north coast of Spain and the west
coast of France.

T.S. slams his buzzer; a light goes off.

HOST
For Seton Hall — T.S. Quint!

T.S.
(urgently)
The Bay of Bisquick!

QUICK CUTS -
The Host's face drops.
The team's faces drops.
The opposing team's faces drop.
The camera man's face drops.
SVENNING'S face drops.
The small audience's faces drop.
BRANDI'S face drops.
At home watching, BRODIE starts laughing.

BRODIE
Quint, you numbskull…

IN THE STUDIO

T.S.' face begins to drop as he notices everyone else's reaction.

T.S.
What? We win, right? What's with the faces?

The Host shakes his head somberly.

HOST

Oh! I'm sorry, Seton Hall — that answer is… bizarrely
incorrect.

(to other team)

Monmouth, do you have the correct answer?

The Monmouth CAPTAIN is all smiles as he leans into his microphone.

CAPTAIN

Bay of Biscay.

HOST

Bay of Biscay is right, giving Monmouth twenty
points, and making them the winners! Monmouth
College wins the Collegiate Showdown!

The winners rejoice. The losers are stunned. Half of the crowd joins
Monmouth on stage. And T.S. snaps out of his daze.

T.S.

That's what I said.

(to team-mate)

I said Biscay.

TEAM-MATE

(shakes head at him)

No you didn't.

T.S. looks at the other team-mate, who also shakes his head. He spots the Host
and raises his hand.

T.S.

Excuse me… I said Biscay.

HOST

(all smiles)

No, you didn't.

T.S.

(insisting)

No, I did. You asked for the name of the body of
water that is formed by the north coast of Spain
and the west coast of France, and I said "Bay of Biscay."

HOST

No, you said "Bay of Bisquick." I'm sorry. But we
have some great parting gifts for your school.

T.S.

(moving from behind desk)

No, we get the grand prize. I said Biscay.

MONMOUTH PLAYER

(from other side)

You did not, you retard. You said Bisquick. Now
sit back down and lose like a man.

T.S. glares at the Player and launches over his podium. His team-mates react.
The Host moves to play interference. T.S. throws a round-house at the Player. He
ducks and T.S.' punch lands squarely across the jaw of the Host who falls down
flat. The Player grabs T.S. from across his podium. T.S. pulls back hard to free
himself and falls against a CAMERA. He catches himself on it and hangs there
for a second — then falls forward with it. The camera slams against the ground
with a resounding crash and lets out a great spark, followed by a puff of smoke.
T.S. surveys his handiwork.

T.S.

Shit.

OPENING CREDIT SEQUENCE

with music, of course. But a few cards in we CUT TO...

INT T.V. STUDIO

C.U. on SVENNING as he screams at OC T.S.

SVENNING
…not to mention the goddamn camera! What are
you?! Some kind of idiot?! No! Don't answer
that! You'll probably get the answer wrong and
knock over another piece of equipment!

T.S. finally gets a word in.

T.S.
Mister Svenning, I can pay the camera off over a
couple years. It was an accident, I swear.

SVENNING
You're the accident, you moron! You have no idea
what you've cost me! But you're right! You'll pay
for what you've done! Nobody fucks with Jared
Svenning's career and walks away clean! I
promise you that!

Svenning storms away. The OPPONENT from Monmouth that T.S. lunged at
walks by, holding the trophy with two beautiful girls on his arm. He stops and
gives T.S. a sarcastic salute, then walks away. T.S. stares after him.

T.S.
Shit.

MORE CREDITS AND MUSIC

for a few cards, and then CUT TO…

INT T.V. STUDIO

C.U. on BRANDI, T.S.' girlfriend. Or rather…

BRANDI
…We have to break up.

T.S. is in shock.

T.S.
WHAT?!?!

BRANDI
It's just not working, T.S. And don't think it was
the bad answer and the camera. I just can't date
you anymore.

T.S.
But... but what about Florida? We've got an eight
thirty flight!

BRANDI
We had an eight thirty flight.
(touches his face)
Goodbye, T.S.

She walks away. T.S. is flabbergasted.

T.S.
Shit.

MORE CREDITS AND MUSIC

for a few cards, and then CUT TO...

INT BUS — NIGHT

T.S. stares out the window. The MAN next to him talks incessantly.

MAN
So you're heading home from college. Isn't that
something? I remember being in college. Best
years of my life. Which one do you go to?

T.S.
(hardly paying attention)
Seton Hall.

MAN

Seton Hall. I saw something on the news about that
place before I got on the bus. Now what was it?
(thinks)
Oh yeah. Some kid went crazy and took a machete
to some game show host. He went to Seton Hall.

The Man looks at T.S. and suddenly recognizes him. He jumps up.

MAN

STOP THE BUS!! THIS GUY'S A WANTED MAN!!

T.S.

(nervous as hell)
No, no I just knocked over a camera.

MAN

HE KILLED A GAME SHOW HOST!!!

EXT HIGHWAY — NIGHT

The Bus skids to a halt at the side of the road. People pile out in droves.

INT BUS

T.S. throws his head back and stares at the ceiling.

T.S.
Shit.

FINAL CREDITS

INT BRODIE'S ROOM — DAY

BRODIE is sitting up in bed, but his eyes are closed. A girl's form passes in
and out of the frame, pulling on clothes. Brodie opens his eyes and tries to focus.
He looks at the OC girl and yawns.

BRODIE
What time is it?

RENE (OC)
Nine thirty.

So that was the version of *Rats* we wanted to make on a three million budget — an odd hybrid of indie and studio flick. There was some nice symmetry to the film in that draft, inasmuch as it opened and closed with game shows. But alas, the studio felt the opening was too "small", and they asked me to create a "bigger" opening sequence. I came up with the Governor's Ball thing, which they liked much more, and we wound up shooting... only to cut it after the initial, disastrous, unofficial test screening and re-shoot a different opening that was even smaller than the proposed College Bowl intro.

But after reading that aborted opening scene, one thing's pretty clear to me: I tend not to let ideas die. The bus skid moment later showed up in *Dogma*.

Friday 23 September 2005 @ 11:29 a.m.

Wake up around 8:30, just as Jen's getting back from dropping Harley off at school. We sit and chit-chat for a bit, then get into some rehearsal, which goes really well. Jen heads out to yoga and I answer email and check the board, while watching *Chasing Freedom*, a CourtTV made-for with Juliette Lewis as a lawyer trying to get an Afghani woman out of jail. After that, I start watching *Inside Deep Throat*, until it's time to jump in the shower and head down to the office for rehearsal.

I get to the office to find Mewes playing Scrabble with one of his girl friends. As I head into the main room, Rosario Dawson's coming through the front door, tissue to her nose. She's got a cold, so Mewes runs out to Greenblatt's to grab her some matzah ball soup.

We chit-chat in that getting-to-know-you fashion for a bit, until Brian shows up, rounding out the convo even more. Mewes returns with the soup, tries to flirt with the very taken Rosario a touch, then heads out, leaving us to finally rehearse.

Within two lines to one another, Bri and Dawson have me smiling ear-to-ear. There's instant chemistry, and the two are bouncing off one another incredibly well: sweet, funny, touching — it's all there. I'm in heaven.

Then, Trevor and Jeff show up, and after some chit-chat, the four leads launch into a near-read-through of the entire script (we skip the first few scenes and concentrate on Becky's entrance forward).

As good as the boys have been in our previous rehearsal this past week, the introduction of a girl (a girl actress, to boot) suddenly enhances all three of their performances; ie — it seems like all three guys have ratcheted it up a bit. Brian's taken a massive leap since yesterday, Jeff — who's been camera-ready since Monday — informs today's rendition of Randal with not just the big laughs, but also sincere pathos, and Trevor is now locked into Elias' tone and mannerisms so completely, it's a night-and-day difference between the actor and the role. And Dawson — gift from the acting gods Dawson — redefines the read-thru, by actually becoming Becky, raising a bar that's well-met by Brian, Jeff, and Trevor.

Each of the guys are on point and flawless — so much so that I don't even interject with direction/correction, speaking up only to cover the lines of cast that isn't there. We could've shot that rehearsal and it would've been release-worthy, so excellent were the performances across the boards. Invariably, on every production, there comes a moment when the reality of what you're doing — creating a fake world populated with people who don't really exist — kicks in, and you know it's time to start committing it to celluloid. For me, that moment was triggered in that room. It's time to actually take *Clerks 2* from theoretical to film.

By five, I'm so happy with the read-thru that I break the rehearsal and let everyone go home early. Rosario hangs out, waiting for Roseanne to drop by to discuss wardrobe, and Brian and I sit around talking to her on the front porch of the office. She's a totally cool chick — well-rounded and versed in a great many subjects, and incredibly friendly and real (any girl who can talk about her favorite moments in *Johnny, the Homicidal Maniac* gets a cool sticker in my book). Roseanne shows up and talks to Rosario for a few minutes, and then we say g'bye to Dawson, who's off to *Killshot* next week.

Roseanne and I go over the pictures from Brian's, Jeff's, Trevor's, and Zack's wardrobe fittings, and I pick out what the boys will wear the entire flick. Mos shows up, and we chit-chat for a bit before I drop Brian off at his hotel and head home.

I get to the room, and Harley's on our couch, drawing, while Jen wraps a gift for the birthday party Quinnster's attending in the a.m. The pair relate the sick tale of Scully eating shit out of the toilet, so I start drawing cartoons about it, to the delight of Harley. An hour later, I put Quinnster to bed, head to the kitchen to make some program-approved cup-o-soup, and watch some TiVo'ed *Simpsons* while Jen talks to Brian O's girlfriend Diana on the phone. When she's done, we pop in *Swimming to Cambodia*, to which Jen falls asleep, and I sign another 250 *Rats* DVD covers. At flick's end, I pop on another TiVo'ed *Simpsons* to which I go to sleep.

Saturday 24 September 2005 @ 12:04 p.m.

Wake up to let the dogs out at 6 a.m., then take a leak, head to my office to check email and board, then get to work updating the online journal.

Jen gets up and gives me shit about not also feeding the dogs. She's in a snippy mood, so I hang low in my office for a while, staying out of the crosshairs, 'til Nicole Venables shows up. I take a shower, then head upstairs, where Nicole cuts my hair, and we chat about the flick (on which she's splitting the hair department with Janine Thompson — who was on *Strike Back* and *Jersey Girl* doing Ben's hair). Nicole leaves, and I head back to my office to hide out from the snippy Schwalbach, until she appears in my office door as the sexy Schwalbach, inquiring as to whether or not I'd like to massage her in the boudoir.

I give Jen a thirty-minute massage that leads into some sweet (rather uncharacteristic) love-making, and the two of us feel worlds better. Having been inundated with working out (for her) and rehearsing (for me) all week, it's been eight days since we last fucked, and man, was it just what the doctor ordered — especially in advance of the long day ahead.

I get dressed and head over to Westwood, where the line for the *Mallrats* 10th Anniversary DVD signing is already wrapped around the block. I tell Chappy to cap it, and hang out in the back alley, smoking and talking to Scott, Renee, Jay, and the Universal and PR guys, as we wait for Ethan Suplee. Ethan arrives, we all chit-chat a bit, then head in to take pics, do some press, and start the signing, a half-hour or so late.

Unlike the signing event we had for the grand opening of the west coast Jay and Silent Bob's Secret Stash last year (the *Clerks X* and *Jersey Girl* DVD signing event), the signing goes smoothly this time around, and doesn't nearly kill us all. Last year, when we opened the west coast Stash on September 7th, the signing started at 6 p.m. and went 'til 6 a.m. the next morning. It was not intentional — we just had thousands show up, and never capped the line 'til midnight. Thankfully, by staying 'til 6 a.m., everybody who made it into the line before it got capped was taken care of.

However, this time around, while capping the line early indeed, helped, the big credit goes to Gail, who played line cop, dealing with each customer as they approached the signing tables, having them get their three items ready, and feeding them to us in an orderly fashion — all while doing it with a smile. Thanks to Gail, the signing didn't turn into another all-night affair.

Big ups to Christian, as well. More than a few people who came through the line effusively praised him, unsolicited, as a great manager. A rapier wit and ever-helpful attitude will flood many a set of drawers (that the drawers in question belong to a bunch of guys is beside the point).

At 6 p.m., Mos and Renee had to bolt, so we used the opportunity to take a break and let Jim Mahfood and Dave Crossland set up for the live art jam. To celebrate the store's one-year anniversary, Chappy and I decided to commission Jim and Dave to do a mural on the back wall, that featured a slew of Askewniverse characters. They brought in the Root Down Sound System DJs, who spun records, mixed and scratched, and turned the place into SoHo, while Jay, Ethan, Brian O'Halloran and I continued with the signing, off to the side.

Around seven, the man of the hour, Jason Lee, showed up, looking bushwhacked after a week of non-stop travel for *My Name is Earl* press, and a full Saturday of shooting the pilot for his MTV variety show. As exhausted as he was, like a champ, he still showed up. We fed him pizza, bullshitted for a bit, then sat him in front of nearly two hundred people who had made it in to the Lee-only line.

By nine, Lee had gotten to everybody who wanted a signature, and headed off for home to sleep. Ethan and Mewes cut out as well, and the signing proper was pretty much done. Jen, Chay, Harley, Trish and I hung out with Ain't It Cool Mike (aka Mysterio Mike) and Silverlurker Will, chatting and watching some of the mural going up. The mural was so fantastic, it had me smiling ear-to-ear... until I realized that if we shuttered the store one day, it couldn't go with us.

By ten o'clock, I pick up two Jim Mahfood pieces he'd brought along to sell, and then Jen, Bri and I cut out of the store, after a very successful signing event. We sold a shitload of the *Mallrats* X DVD, naturally, as well as a slew of the *Mallrats Companion* screenplay book. Chappy and I both agreed it was the model against which all future Stash events would be measured.

We drop Brian off at his hotel and head home, where we climb into bed. Jen immediately falls asleep, and I do the same after posting a signing post-mortem on the board.

Sunday 25 September 2005 @ 12:05 p.m.

I wake up around nine to see Jen already up, riding her couch, checking the board, re: last night's signing. I head to the office to check email and see if any pics of the finished Stash mural have been posted, then look up what time *Corpse Bride* is playing.

I shower, get dressed, and Harley and I are off to the Chinese Theater to check out Tim Burton's latest (which I really love, despite the songs). We head home, and when I get to my room, I discover Schwalbach's already set the place up for our afternoon rehearsal. I collect my iPod and slug in the microphone adapter, so that I can record the sessions and cut together a file of her best readings, so she can listen to it while she hikes Runyon or runs on the treadmill.

Rehearsal goes great. Jen takes another huge jump — so much so that I decide to wrap it up an hour and change later, so I can cut together her rehearsal MP3. A half hour into the cutting, Gail reminds me that I've got an interview with FanBoy Radio (out of Dallas/Ft. Worth), so I take an hour off to chit-chat comics and stuff with the hosts and callers, before getting back to the MP3 edit. Then, Jen heads off to yoga, and Harley and I kick back and watch *Shark Boy and Lava Girl* (a pretty sweet flick) before I put her to bed.

I spend the rest of the night cutting the MP3 together, then crash beside the already-sleeping Schwalbach around 11:30, falling asleep to a TiVo'ed *Simpsons*.

Wednesday 28 September 2005 @ 9:58 a.m.

Hit TriStar Medical to discover I've only lost three pounds. Kinda bummed. Still, losing three is better than gaining three, so I stop at the Fox Hills Mall and pick up a bunch of new jeans shorts, in sizes I haven't seen in quite some time.

Afterwards, I head over to Sony to do some looping for *Catch & Release*. Susannah's having a screening for some friends, so she wants to fill in some dialogue holes or make a few muddled lines more clear.

While there, I finally get to see a bunch of *Catch* footage. I enjoy the hell out of it. Sam Jaeger (who also shows up to do some ADR) and I are pretty funny together, and the flick looks great. Can't wait to see it all put together.

I chit-chat with Suz, Sam, sound man Mike, and later, Anne Coates, who drops by while we're looping. Anne, who's used to seeing me everyday in the footage she's cutting, is taken aback at the slimmer-looking me in real life. I hip her to Optifast, then Sam and I head out. I drop Sam off at his car in another lot and boogie home for some rehearsal action on my own flick, up at the house.

Thursday 29 September 2005 @ 12:05 p.m.

We take the Train Wreck: The Making of The Passion of the Clerks site live, jump-starting what we hope will be a year-long interactive experience between filmmakers and audience.

Unlike the first *Clerks*, during the production of which nobody really knew we were making an honest-to-goodness film behind Quick Stop's closed steel shutters at night, word's out what we're up to this time around. There are expectations — shit that I've spent my career trying to avoid, because expectations are hard to live up to. So rather than ostrich-it and pretend like we're eight kids making a movie after hours at work, we've opted to go another way, and pull the curtain way-the-fuck back for anyone remotely interested to take a look at our goings-on. Good idea or not, we're committed at this point.

Zak Knutson and Joey Figueroa, long-time co-conspirators of ours (Zak we met on *Strike Back* and Joey, his friend, joined us in post on *Jersey Girl*), got a budget approved by the Weinstein Company for a behind-the-scenes project that's made up of two parts: weekly production pieces for the www.clerks2.com site, and a massive making-of documentary for the eventual DVD. Having worked closely with Phil Benson on the Snowball Effect doc on the *Clerks X* DVD, these guys know what they're doing. Together with Webmaster Ming Chen and trailer maven Matt Potter, they'll be providing the curious with a relatively spoiler-free, inside look at what goes into making *Clerks 2*.

Initial response to the shorts seems to be good, so we're off and running.

Saturday 1 October 2005 @ 12:05 p.m.

The day is spent laying around the room with Jen and watching a lot of the *Desperate Housewives* DVD box set, a show I kinda dig on. While checking email, someone directs me to the Ain't It Cool News forums, where some jag-off is spreading misinformation about my Vancouver Q&A from a few months back.

Now, normally, I avoid the AICN talk-backs like they're KKK rallies. I get a lot of trashing thrown my way from the talk-backers, but I figure there's little point in getting into a flame war with someone over their opinion. Movie-loving is a subjective thing: either someone does or doesn't like what I make, and telling 'em how wrong I feel they are for not digging on what I do is never gonna change their minds. About as far as I used to go at the AICN talk-backs (as I'd never joined, hence couldn't post) would be to email posters directly if they put up factually inaccurate info about me.

The day I stopped reading the talk-backs altogether was when I'd emailed a guy who was maintaining I'd done something I hadn't, re: *Dogma*. I started off with "Look, I can't help it if you don't like what I do or the movies I make, but I feel the need to correct you on this issue of" whatever it was "because it's factually inaccurate". And the response I got back was pretty much this: "I don't particularly like or dislike you or your movies. But you're one of those people that talk-backers will attack and defend with equal vehemence, so I just jumped into your thread to stir up some shit and get into fights with other posters. It's cheap, good fun to read how worked up these people get."

Paraphrased, natch, but that was pretty much the sentiment. And once I'd read that, I realized that even looking at the titles of the AICN talk-backs was probably a dumb move on my part.

However, with the *Clerks 2* site going live earlier that week, there was a story and link up at AICN, and the requisite love-fest/bash-fest had begun. And based on this tipster email, I found myself doing something I hadn't in almost six years: actually reading an AICN talk-back thread about me.

Now, I've got a pretty thick skin: saying my movies suck, I'm a hack, or I'm fat doesn't really rile me. However, when fuckers are low enough to go after my wife… well, that's when shit's on. So I decide to finally join AICN so I can respond in the talk-backs thread… only to discover registration is temporarily down. Rather than let it go, I copy and paste all the questions to a Word document and spend a half hour answering them all, then posting the entire thread up at viewaskew.com. I drop Harry Knowles a line about putting up a link to it, and we're off to the races.

So, for the curious, my fireside chat with the AICN talk-backers is at:

http://viewaskew.com/theboard/viewtopic.php?p=1192656#1192656

Sunday 2 October 2005 @ 12:06 p.m.

Wake up, shit and check email. I cruise the board and discover an enormous views count on my AICN topic, which means that Harry's already put the link to my viewaskew.com thread up at Ain't It Cool News. In addition, he opened up registration and gave me an account name and password, so I can head back to his site and respond to the talk-backers responses to my responses to their responses to the opening of the *Clerks 2* site.

An incredible waste of time for a guy who's about to start shooting a flick in a week? Maybe. But I still indulge in it for two hours, before logging off, taking a shower, playing some more of the Nintendo DS new *Spider-Man* game, while Jen and Harley eat lunch at The Grove. Then, I join them at The Grove, pick up Harley, and head out to Speed Zone, the go-kart fun park in City of Industry. Quinnster and I ride the go-karts, then play games of chance for two hours, winning a bunch of useless crap. Then, we head to Toys "R" Us to pick up some board games.

On the drive home, I'm feeling unwell, so I have to cancel out on Lee's variety show shoot. Jen goes food shopping, and I play more *Spider-Man* 'til I fall asleep rather early.

Monday 3 October 2005 @ 12:07 p.m.

Get up, shower, and head out to the location for a meeting with the crew and Michael Rooney. Later in the day, we have the production meeting — this conference in which all the department keys go through the entire schedule, scene-by-scene and trouble-shoot or raise questions about what's needed or left open for that shoot day. However, I've got about three hours before that kicks off back at the production office, so I hit the Bicycle Casino for a couple hours of poker.

I head to the studio, two hundred bucks poorer, and do my bit at the production meeting, seeing a lot of familiar faces of folks who've worked on a bunch of our other flicks, as well as some new cats.

When the meeting's finished, I talk to Carla Gardini (our Weinstein Company exec) for a while, and then check out some new production artwork with Rat and Scott Purcell before shooting home for an evening rehearsal at the house.

Bri, Jeff, and Trevor come over to rehearse, and our co-key hair person Janine Thompson stops by to take a look at Trevor's hair. Janine, Trish, and Jen hang out in the room, downing wine and bullshitting, while the boys and I run through all the scenes upstairs in the living room. Afterwards, when Janine and Trish have left, Jen comes upstairs, and the five of us (Jen, Jeff, Brian, Trevor, and me) sit around the bar, drinking, smoking and bullshitting 'til two in the morning, having a great time.

Tuesday 4 October 2005 @ 12:07 p.m.

Hit Laser Blazer for new DVDs, then go to TriStar Medical where I learn I've lost four more pounds, putting me at the fifty pounds total loss mark in less than two months. I started at 319, and I now weigh 269. I'm staying on the all-liquid phase of the diet 'til Thanksgiving, which gives me two more months, during which I will hopefully shed another twenty pounds, at least.

I opt against another night of rehearsals, and instead concentrate on locking in Randal's shirt, which I've decided to change at the last minute. Once I saw what a great job the ever-genius Scott Purcell did with Randal's hat, I decided to switch up his shirt design, and give him something different than what I'd originally intended (a design which will be used elsewhere in the flick). After much thought, it hits me like a cum-shot in the eye: *Ranger Danger*.

I'd pulled together some visual references for what I generally want the lead character of the flick we're getting to within the next two years to look like, and put Purcell on a path. The man hit me back with utter genius. Just looking at the shirt makes me happy, and I suddenly feel ready to roll on the flick.

Wednesday 5 October 2005 @ 12:08 p.m.

Jen and I pick up Brian O'Halloran and head down to the location for rehearsal. Rosario returns, so we get to go through almost the entire script with almost the entire cast of Jeff, Brian, Rosario, Trevor, and Jen. It all sounds so ready to be shot. We head home around nine.

Thursday 6 October 2005 @ 12:08 p.m.

Do an eleven o'clock phone interview with *New York Magazine* about the AICN talk-back fiasco, then shower and get ready to head down to the location.

We do a full-cast run-through of the entire script for some of the department keys. Afterwards, we take a few pics of the cast for scenes in the movie.

We're done and home by 6:30.

Friday 7 October 2005 @ 12:12 p.m.

Harley's sick, so we can't hit *Curse of the Were-Rabbit* as we'd intended. I spend most of the day printing up scripts and finishing off the *Desperate Housewives* box set with Jen.

At five o'clock, I've got an interview upstairs on the deck with Craig

Modierno, who's doing a *New York Times* piece regarding the website collective I've created (The ViewAskewniverse, Movie Poop Shoot, My Boring-Ass Life, The Online Secret Stash, Train Wreck) as well as the two I didn't create but host (NewsAskew and Newsarama at ViewAskew.com). During the interview, Vince Rocca arrives with the new Hold 'Em McNeil poker table Ming and I came up with for Vince to build. It's a thing of fucking beauty.

Afterwards, I make my diet soup and kick back for some *Veronica Mars* action with Jen. When it's done, we pop in *The Big Lebowski*. Ten minutes in, I start rubbing Jen's back. Twenty minutes in, I start rubbing her front. We turn the flick off, and get into some mutually much-needed loooooove-making. When we're done, we have the first good convo we've been able to have in a week. Then, we turn the flick on again and fall asleep.

Sunday 9 October 2005 @ 12:15 p.m.

Wake up to discover Jen's really pretty sick. She must've caught the bug Harley had the other day, as she can't keep anything down or in. This pooches our plans of heading down to the location and spending the night together in advance of the first day of shooting, and Jen's pretty bummed about it.

I spend most of the day packing a month's worth of clothes, a bunch of DVDs, my drink boxes, and sundry other things I figure I'll need during production. Even though the location's only thirty miles away, you've gotta take the 5 to get there — and the 5 is one of the most congested freeways in America. So rather than drive home every day after wrap, I've opted to stay down at the nearby motel, where we also host the cast dressing rooms (in lieu of trailers), the on-location production offices, and the editing suite for the run of the show.

At 5:30, Mos comes over, and we make our traditional pre-shoot trip to church, hitting Blessed Sacrament on Sunset. There's additional significance to this particular church, as it was in Blessed Sacrament's parking lot that I finally hipped Mos to my idea of doing *Clerks 2*, back when we were coming out of our traditional pre-release trip to church the weekend before *Jersey Girl* came out.

I get home, drop Mos at his car, head inside and kiss the kid g'night, then head over to Bristol Farms to grab Jen some soup. Once home again, I set Schwalbach up with her soup, have Mewes load all my shit into the Hate Tank, kiss the sickly and depressed Schwalbach g'bye, and truck down to the location, followed by Jay.

For a guy who's not in the flick that much, Mewes is excited as hell. He sees the whole thing as a camp-like endeavor, with all of us living out of the motel and walking one minute to set every day. Even though he doesn't shoot until Tuesday, Mewes insists on coming down tonight and being on set for the first shot.

This is a different Jason Mewes than I've ever made a movie with before — something him and I figure out once we've dropped our shit at the motel and head over to the drug store together for some essentials. On *Clerks* and *Rats*, he was a drinker/stoner. On *Amy*, he was just getting into heroin. On *Dogma*, he was knee-deep in heroin and Oxycontins (something we didn't learn 'til years later). On *Strike Back* he drank the whole show, and then got back into Oxys during the last week. And on *Jersey Girl* — well, he was on the run. This will be the first time I make a flick with a completely clean and sober Mewes. And based on his enthusiasm for something as simple as checking into the motel and getting set-up, I'm loving it already.

Settled-in, I say g'night to Jay and retire to my room. There, I do something I rarely find myself doing: I pop in a DVD and actually watch it. Normally, while watching DVDs or TV, I'll check the board or play video games at the same time. But tonight, I sit on the bed and smoke while simply watching a flick.

Naturally, I watch *Clerks*.

It's an odd experience. Here I am, thirteen years older than the kid who made that movie, and still, the enthusiasm, the trepidation, the confidence is all the same. I don't know what drove me back then. Why the fuck did I think I could make a film? What the fuck makes me think I can make a film now? And why the fuck am I doing a follow-up to the first film I ever made, possibly tainting the good will and fondness people hold for that spit-and-glue production? Is this re-visitation to Quick Stop and Company as bad a move as some folks have theorized? Will this latest foray into the lives of the pilgrims of the Askewniverse ever hold up to the OG journey? Am I out of my fucking mind?

And then, halfway through the flick, I get all the answers I need to step onto that set tomorrow morning. I love these characters. I love their story. And just as their original story reflected my life over a decade ago, this new chapter in their fictional lives closely follows my arc as well.

This is a story about me and Scott. This is a story about me and Jen. This is a story about me and Bry and Walt; about me and Mewes. And, yes — this is even a story, to some degree, about me and Harley.

And while the external trappings of my life are certainly different than they were twelve years ago, the song remains the same: I want to make a film about me and my friends, for me and my friends. I want to take a snapshot of a particular time in my life, when I was at (and still am at) a crossroad. This isn't a return to the roots; the roots — even in *Jersey Girl* — have always been maintained. Like that first flick — like every flick I've ever done — this is just a way for me to hurl a message into the void to see if anyone else is out there; to see if my human experience is echoed by others. The only difference this time around is that it'll all look a lot better.

Which is not to say that *Clerks* looked bad. In watching it again tonight, haters-be-damned, I find a new appreciation for the simplicity of the shot composition. I joke around a lot about the standard two-shot I did (and still do), but it's not there because I don't know how to or am unwilling to do any other kind of shot: I do it because it tells a story. So much of my life is spent standing beside someone in conversation; that two-shot reflects this. It may not be Scorsese-cool, but it not only serves my purpose; it's how I see life. And I got into film in the first place because I wanted to show people how I see life.

That being said, I now also see life in other dimensions as well (singles, overs, etc), so expect a better looking flick overall.

And funnier, too. In re-watching *Clerks*, I put to sleep any remaining demons that sat on my shoulder and whispered doubts of "You'll never be able to catch them by surprise again." This time around, I'd wager the laugh count is higher, scene-per-scene, and that the places we go in conversation are even edgier than "How many dicks have you sucked?!" And it's all wrapped up in this bittersweet undercurrent of two guys, well, one really, who's desperately trying to hold onto the only world he's ever known and felt at home in.

Kinda like me.

Please, God — don't let me fuck this up.

Monday 10 October 2005 @ 3:44 p.m.

Production begins. This'll be the first film since *Clerks* in which I don't begin the day with a breakfast burrito (as I'm still full throttle on the liquid diet). In fact, this will be the first film ever in which (if I'm able to maintain my diet throughout the show) I don't gain weight during the run of the show.

The set looks amazing. Ratface and his crew worked up 'til the last minute to make a living, breathing fast food joint that doesn't really exist. All the details are in place: the worn down, scratched counter, the grease stains caking the walls, the logo-stamped bags, cups, and wrapping — it's all there.

However, we're not on the main floor of the restaurant today. This day's shooting is gonna be spent in Becky's back office, doing three scenes that total up to roughly seven pages of the script — ironically the same amount of pages we shot on the first day of the OG *Clerks*. And while, also similarly, it's pretty much all Dante and a girl, this time around, it won't be a seven minute single take. For the lion's share of the pages, we've got about ten set-ups planned; ten set-ups for one conversation.

The day goes swimmingly. Brian delivers, and Rosario can do no wrong. The chick oozes chemistry, and even when she's not delivering lines, she's still giving me tons to cut with. Dawson can hold a frame like a fat man holds his lunch tray.

We wrap without quite finishing all the work we'd set out to do (we owe an eighth of a page from the third scene we'd planned to shoot), but everybody's ecstatic — because what we did shoot was gold.

All day, Mewes and I plan a trip to Target to grab sheets and other essentials (never sleep on hotel sheets if you can avoid it, unless you dig rolling around in dried jizz). Rosario's staying down at the location tonight as well, so she opts to take the ride with us. On the way home, we stop by a Thai food place so she can get something to eat, and plan to head over to the Bicycle Casino to celebrate a successful first day with poker.

I get back to the hotel and call the sickly Schwalbach to check in and see if she's doing any better, only to hear in her voice that she's not on the mend. In addition to her physical condition, she's also nursing a case of the blues, having missed the first day and feeling like the train has kinda left without her. At this point, I decide to scrap poker for the night and drive home to see Jen, and try to lift her spirits. I leave Mewes and Rosario to watch some DVDs and chill, while I speed back home.

Jen's caught by total surprise at my return, and immediately, her spirits are lifted. Still, she's weak and achy, so I hang with her for about two hours, then head back to the location, getting into the room around midnight. I pop in *Empire Falls* to which I fall asleep around two.

Tuesday 11 October 2005 @ 3:45 p.m.

Up at six to block and shoot the ATM scene, in which Mewes and I debut as Jay and Silent Bob in the background of the shot. We're working in the third shot of the day, so I get hauled off to the hair and makeup trailer, where Tricia Sawyer does my face and Nicole Venables does my hair and beard. I peep out Mewes in his full, new "Jay" ensemble, and the only remaining issue is what hat to put him in. We have the ol' *Rats* skull cap on standby, but the rest of his outfit's so dark, another piece of black clothing (like the skull cap) would make him more Johnny Cash than Jay, so we start coming up with alternate head gear. Having just watched *Clerks* again the other night, I opt to throw a baseball cap on him again. But both of us in caps looks weird. Then, I ask Roseanne to rip the brim off the baseball cap Mewes is sporting at the moment. She does, and suddenly, with the addition of a pin, we've got the full Jay look locked and loaded.

We spend the whole day shooting the very funny, funny scene (which is predominantly Dante and Randal, before they're joined by Becky), and wrap around six thirty, after grabbing a few shots from the Becky office scene we didn't get to the day before.

After wrap, I talk to Jen (who's feeling much better), and head off to the Bicycle Casino with Mewes. We play 'til midnight, then head back to the hotel, where I get about four hours of sleep.

Wednesday 12 October 2005 @ 3:46 p.m.

We spend most of the day shooting a tent-pole scene that features Dante, Randal, Becky, Elias. Wanda Sykes and the comedian Earthquake join us for the day, and they take two small roles and knock 'em out of the park, proving to be fantastic casting choices. Everyone's in top form, and we get through the planned first chunk of the three-chunk scene that's spread over two days. When we wrap, I head to the editing suite, where three days worth of footage awaits me.

I love editing, as it's almost like getting to do another draft of the script. I slip behind the Avid for the first time since *Jersey Girl*, and in a matter of minutes, it all comes back to me. I'm off-and-running, cutting the ATM scene, while next door, Mewes, Mos, Rosario, Brian, Trevor, Location-James, and Mewes's friend/Jeff's stand-in D.K. play poker and down beers (Red Bull for Mewes, natch).

When I get the ATM scene done, I bring 'em all next door to peep it out. Everyone's psyched with the results, so I send them back to their poker game and chit-chat with Mos a bit while cutting. He heads to bed at one in the morning, and I opt to do the same… until I decide to cut just a little bit more of the third scene: the monster office scene between Brian and Rosario. The plan is to cut just the Randal opening of the sequence, but I keep going until I get through a fine-cut of the entire scene.

Thursday 13 October 2005 @ 3:46 p.m.

Upon completion of the editing of the monster office scene, I open the door to the editing suite to see not only daylight, but also the crew eating breakfast at the location below. Lalida the P.A. tells me they're requesting I come down to set to block the first shot. I haven't slept at all in twenty-four hours, so I stumble to set, un-showered, and sleepily set up the first shot.

After blocking, I bring Jeff, Brian, and Rosario back to the editing suite, and show them their three scenes, fully fine cut. They're all a little surprised at how finished the scenes are, but are more delighted than anything else at how insanely well they come off, and how funny and sweet the scenes are. It puts a spring in their steps that results in them going even more hog-wild in the scenes we shoot for the rest of the day.

All day, between set-ups, I'm rushing back to my room to try to grab some sleep. Each time, though, I get about ten minutes before it's time to go back to the set and shoot. Byron and Gail bring Harley down around lunchtime, and I escort her around the set, showing her the face restaurant. Being my kid, she's far more interested in the craft service table, and the "free" Milano cookies contained therein.

Lunch ends, and I kiss Harley g'bye and go back to work. At the next break between set-ups, I've got a half hour while Dave and his crew re-light, so I bury myself in my room and sleep. I get the knock on the door and stumble out to see Jen's arrived with Chay. I give Jen a kiss and hug and drag my tired ass down to the set, where we finish out the day.

At wrap, I head upstairs to see Jen and crew. She's getting her hair done by Nicole, and has already turned her room into party central, with everyone hanging out and drinking/bullshitting. I hit the editing suite to check on the previous day's footage, and discover there's a shot we've gotta re-do — which is convenient, as we're at this location for quite a while. I let Mos and Tony know, then kiss Jen g'night, give her my room key, and head to bed around 9:30.

At 11:30 p.m., an inebriated Schwalbach wakes me up. Cranky and exhausted, we get into it a bit (instead of simply fucking, which would've made a lot more sense), and she goes to sleep in her dressing room, while I crash in mine.

SPOILERS BELOW!!!
Friday 14 October 2005 @ 3:55 p.m.

Back when we were making *Clerks*, there was so little to worry/care about beyond making the flick itself. Now, in the age of the internet, the playing field has changed considerably. As quiet as we've been able to keep the details of the flick, all it takes is one joker with a camera to spoil the virgin viewing of the flick for anyone with access to a computer.

So I'm gonna be that joker.

We've had a few snipers with cameras lurking around the set, so rather than let them get images of our flick out there, I'd rather do it myself. I'm gonna burn down this village to save it. Sucks that I've gotta do it, but then again, maybe it doesn't.

So here's a pic of our movie that kinda lets the cat out of the bag (somewhat)...

[The website ran a picture of Trevor Fehrman, Brian O'Halloran, Rosario Dawson and Jeff Anderson, standing in front of the counter in Mooby's.]

Based on this image, I'll pre-answer some of the queries I can already hear buzzing through your heads:

Does this tell the whole story? No.

Is our movie *Waiting 2*? No.

What about Quick Stop?

What about it?

Is it still in there?

Of course.

Is there a God?

Yes. It's either a Supreme Being who crafted the universe and plots all our moves outside of the free will choices we make, or Clapton. I lean toward the former — especially after shooting *Clerks 2* for the last week. Because God's been good to us — inasmuch as, thus far, it's a funny, wonderful-looking film. The performances of the main cast have been tight and spot-on, and the day players have been great as well. I don't know if the flick'll live up to anyone else's expectations, but it's sure as fuck met and exceeded mine (I should point out, however, that as a fat man, I maintain very low expectations when it comes to anything in life but lard-based food). Can't wait to share it with ya'll.

Back to work for me.

I wake up, shower, and head downstairs to the set, setting up the first shot of the day. When I emerge, I see Schwalbach, already awake, and standing on her balcony. She joins me downstairs and we do a post-fight wrap up, while Dave and company shoot some inserts that don't involve the actors. I get Schwalbach fed and pumped with coffee, and head in to the set to shoot some Dante and Randal stuff.

After setting up the next shot, I head upstairs to find Jen, Chay, Jay and Trevor hanging out in Mewes' room. I tell Jen I've got about twenty minutes, and we immediately retire to her dressing room, where we fuck for fifteen of those twenty minutes. Then, we chit-chat a bit, and I head back down to the set, a few ounces lighter.

Most of the day is spent shooting the back exterior scene with Jeff, Brian, Rosario, Jay and I. It's a steadi-cam shot, and Brian and Jeff tear it up — resulting in a funny, tight, good-looking scene. At day's end, we grab a pair of insert shots we owed from Monday, and at wrap, I take the cast and crew out to Medieval Times for a wrap-of-first-week-of-shooting celebration.

Afterwards, we head back to the motel, where I show Rosario's boyfriend Jason all the cut scenes, and then Jen and I head back to Los Angeles, getting to sleep in our own bed.

Saturday 15 October 2005 @ 3:47 p.m.

I wake up and chit-chat with Jen about the day's schedule. Byron and Gail are heading up to Big Bear, and Jen wants to hit a yoga class, so I elect to be on Harley duty all day. I shower, get dressed, load Quinnster into the car, and head to the Weight Control Center, where I learn that I've lost another six pounds, bringing me to 263 and my current weight loss to fifty-six pounds.

Afterwards, Harley and I hit Laser Blazer, then shoot over to Sony to do some more *Catch* looping with Susannah. Thankfully, Susannah's brought her daughter as well, so the girls occupy one another while I do about twenty on-camera and off-camera ADR lines. I get to see even more of *Catch* which looks great.

Harley and I head home, and fifteen minutes after we get there, Jen calls from Crunch to say she needs a ride home. I load Quinnster back into the car, and we pick up Jen, grabbing smokes on the way home.

While Jen putters, Harley and I lay in my bed watching *Kicking and Screaming* during which I fall asleep.

Three hours later, I wake up, and Jen and I watch *Land of the Dead*, while I check email. After that, we watch the *Amityville Horror* remake, then do *Simpsons* eps 'til we fall asleep.

Sunday 30 October 2005 @ 6:57 p.m.

My apologies for the lack of updates, but we've been pretty fucking busy. Week

3 is wrapped, and tomorrow, we start our second to last week on the show. Both cast and crew continue to dazzle. I continue to dream about getting more sleep, as I spend all day on set, then lock myself in the editing room 'til usually two or three in the morning. I may be sleepy, but I've cut every frame of film we've shot already, resulting in one hour of the movie completely assembled. The simultaneous-to-shooting editorial has been tremendously helpful in allowing us to go back to scenes and shoot any missing pieces I didn't know we'd need, or allow me to revisit scenes I feel need a bit more (or less) detail. If you're ever gonna make a flick, cut it (yourself) while you're shooting, kids; you won't regret it.

We went an extra day last week, shooting on Saturday to get Lee on his *Earl*-free day. The Randal/Lance showdown is a real highlight of the flick, but the award for scene-of-the-week goes to Mewes. When you see the film, you'll know what I mean.

Saturday 12 November 2005 @ 9:07 a.m.

We celebrate the LA wrap of *Clerks II* with a party up at the house. I play poker most of the night, and Trevor's band plays out on the deck, joined for three songs by Sarah. Everyone seems to have a great time.

While most of the keys are coming with us to NJ for the three-day shoot there, a bunch of the crew isn't being flown out (due to budget constraints). I'll miss 'em all. Fifty percent comprised of folks who'd worked on *Clerks*, *Mallrats*, *Chasing Amy*, *Dogma*, *Jay and Silent Bob Strike Back* and *Jersey Girl*, plus another fifty percent of new, excellent cats, this was easily the best crew I've ever worked beside. It's my intention to bring everyone back on the next flick we shoot, whatever that may be. But for now, the least I can do is throw them a thank you shindig, which wraps at about four in the morning.

Tuesday 15 November 2005 @ 9:33 a.m.

After wrap tonight, I took Jen up to NYC to peep out the latest staging of Sondheim's *Sweeney Todd* at the Eugene O'Neil Theater on 49th. Anyone who's seen *Jersey Girl* (all six of you) know what a *Todd*-fag I am, as the flick closes with a grade school rendition of 'God, That's Good!' — the show-stopping Act 2 starter from the grisly play about a vengeance-bent barber who cuts throats and sends the freshly dead below to the meat pie shop run by his partner in crime,

Mrs Lovett, who promptly serves them up as the best pies in London. Grim, fun stuff, this musical — as it has been since 1979.

But this current version of *Sweeney* is not my favorite incarnation of the production. I wasn't a fan of the Beckett-like approach to the normally grand guignol material. I didn't dig on the actors doubling as the orchestra. I missed the upstairs/downstairs set and the fabled barber chair. I didn't cotton to the actors not delivering their dialogue to one another, and instead casting their performances out at the audience. Maybe I'm revealing myself as a traditionalist, so mired in memory that he's closed-minded to new ideas, but Doyle's vision of *Todd* wasn't my cup of tea. I guess I'm just an old fuddy-duddy, but it would seem the gushing *NY Times* reviewer and I saw two different shows (though this wouldn't be the first time the *Times* and I didn't see eye-to-eye; anyone remember their *Jersey Girl* review; makes my *Todd* review seem like a Joel Siegel-like rave).

That all being said, the cast was great (Patti LuPone's Mrs Lovett, while very different from Angela Lansbury's, was still really enjoyable), and kudos to them all for pulling off the score while acting as well.

To me, more interesting than what was going on on stage that night was the fact that Angela Lansbury was sitting in the row ahead of me, five seats over. My heart went out to Patti LuPone: how nervewracking that must've been for the former *Evita* to be assayed by everyone's favorite Cabot Cove-ian — the OG Nellie Lovett — as she brought to life her version of the beloved character in an already controversial mounting of the Sondheim classic! I'd be lying if I said I didn't glance over in Mrs Potts' direction more than once during the show to see if she was as crestfallen as I was that the hallmarks of *Todd*s past weren't in evidence (for the record, she seemed to dig on the show).

My God, all this theater talk! I'm such a gay man in denial, aren't I?

Quickly! Must... fuck... beard...

WIFE! I meant WIFE!

Tuesday 22 November 2005 @ 4:33 p.m.

Spent an hour responding to a Talk-Back thread at Ain't It Cool News. Peep it here...

http://viewaskew.com/theboard/viewtopic.php?p=1273146#1273146

Why do they make it so easy?

Friday 16 December 2005 @ 9:01 a.m.

Tonight, we had a small, private test screening of sorts over in Burbank. We put up a 1:38 cut of the flick in front of about thirty-five View Askew message board folks, thirty-five friends and folks whose opinions we trust, and twenty west coast Weinstein Company colleagues.

The screening went amazingly well — fucking gangbusters, really. I was delighted to finally show the flick to people outside of the inner circle. We held a focus group afterwards that yielded some great input, but what was most helpful was just sitting in the back, listening to audience reaction during the screening. As a result, I found some more places to make trims in the flick.

The plan is to take the flick to Cannes in May (if they'll have us) and come out in either August or September.

Fuck, did the flick turn out well...

Fletch F. Fletch
Wednesday 21 December 2005 @ 2:45 p.m.

From time to time, I'm asked "Why doesn't Chevy Chase like you?" It's a question usually prompted by someone seeing an interview with Chase, like the one with James Kanowitz (aka Laker Jim) found at www.fletchwon.net.

Laker Jim: After Kevin Smith's *Jersey Girl* (NOTE: and now *Green Hornet*) he is going to do *Fletch Won* (the first Fletch novel) which will be the story of a young Fletch and his first big case. He's recently said *"He [Chevy] was excellent. I mean Chevy is a comedy god. I want to work in Chevy Chase. Which would require a framing device where he's telling the story. So we'd start with him and segue to Jason Lee. But that's if he's willing to do it."* Without agreeing to anything, would you at least consider it? Fletch fans everywhere want you to be a part of this.

Chevy Chase: For the record, Smith invited me to lunch about five or six years ago to talk to me about doing another Fletch movie: with me obviously, playing Fletch. He was ebullient about it; about working with me; and said he was writing it as we spoke. After that lunch, he never took or returned a call from me. After two years, I was called by Alan Greisman, producer of the Fletch films, saying, "Kevin doesn't want to do it." PERIOD! So I waited for three friggin' years to hear from someone else that Mr Kevin Smith was, for all practical purposes, lying to me to begin with — having written nothing — rudely deceiving me, and all with no apparent concern for how easily (facile) one can hurt another human being and his family... he can shove it up his hole. If this is the type of director he aspires to being (the type of person I've seen a million times in Hollywood), I hope he gets the karma he's owed. As for me, he owes me one hell of an explanation. (But, with some, when you're "hot" the rest of the world owes you).

If I played any part in the Fletch remake, think about it: as soon as I appeared on the screen people would say, "Hey... There's Fletch, man!" Silly idea. Keep me out of it. Fletch is me.

In the interest of fairness, here's my side of that story...

Chevy Chase: For the record, Smith invited me to lunch about five or six years ago to talk to me about doing another Fletch movie: with me, obviously, playing Fletch.

True. Here's how it happened...

Mid-'97, after the success of *Amy*, Universal asked me to come in and discuss working there again. I met with Stacy Snider and told her the only thing Universal would have that I might be interested in would be *Fletch*. She said she didn't realize they even had the rights still. I told her I'd like to do an original script called *Son of Fletch*, which was to star Chevy as Fletch, Joey Adams as his daughter (the titular *Son of*), and Jason Lee as her boyfriend, with a cameo by Goldie Hawn as Joey's mom/Fletch's one-time love (I was a big fan of the Chevy/Goldie starrers *Foul Play* and *Seems Like Old Times*). Stacy said yes, and sent me over to meet Brian Grazer, who she wanted as a producer on the flick.

So I head over to Imagine, meet Grazer, and tell him about my idea for the Chevy-starring flick. He says "Chevy Chase? Why him?" I remind him that Chevy has played Fletch twice already. Brian points out that Chevy hasn't had an audience in years, and he's legendarily hard to work with. Still, I back Chevy. Brian relents, and suggests I meet with Chevy. So a few days later, I go to Jerry's Famous Deli on Beverly with one of my all-time heroes, Chevy Chase.

Chevy: He was ebullient about it; about working with me;

True.

Chevy: and said he was writing it as we spoke.

Not true. I told him the ideas I had for *Son of Fletch*, but not that I'd started writing it.

Chevy: After that lunch, he never took or returned a call from me.

I haven't spoken to him since that lunch, yes. Here's why...

At the lunch, Chevy went on to claim he invented every funny thing that ever happened in the history of not just comedy, but also the known world. I made the mistake of telling him my favorite moment in *Fletch Lives* — when Fletch enters the faith healer's service.

"What's your name?"

"Fletch."

"Full name?"

"Fletch F. Fletch."

"What's your address?"

"Seven."

The "Seven" line was what I focused on, and he then offered, rather enthusiastically, that he wrote that — that he says that kind of thing all the time. The waitress was bringing us the charge receipt at that point, and he said to her "Ask me what my credit card number is." She obliged, and he said "Seven." Then turned to me, smiling widely, with a Krusty-like "Funny? Right? Funny?" expression.

You ever sat down with somebody who claimed responsibility for stuff he did AND didn't do? It's really off-putting.

But, whatever. When the lunch (mercifully) ended, we exchanged numbers, and I was off. I told him I'd call him when I had some pages to read.

Over the course of the next few months, Joey and I broke up, my grandmother died, and I learned Jason Mewes was a heroin addict. Naturally, Jason became my priority. So he moved in with me and we started the methadone/twelve inch Greedo dolls program (that's a whole different story), which pretty much took up the entire day — leaving little writing time.

Six months later, we were off to Pittsburgh to make *Dogma*. During two months of rehearsal and pre-production, I didn't write any scripts, and just concentrated on making *Dogma*.

By the end of production (two more months), I still hadn't written anything. Phil, my agent, called me while I was on set doing the third act church-front finale and says "Universal and Grazer wanna know where the *Fletch* script is and when it's coming?" I told him I hadn't written anything yet. He asked if I was gonna start after we wrapped *Dogma* and I told him I was immediately going into edit mode after *Dogma* wrapped. Phil suggested, rather than let this go on any further and anger Universal to the point of never being able to work there in the future, I let *Fletch* go for the time being, because I wasn't gonna get to it for at least a year. I thought it over, and then agreed. Phil then told Universal and Grazer that *Son of Fletch* was a no-go for now.

It'd been almost a year since my initial meeting with Universal. During that time, I hadn't spoken to Chevy again — certainly not because I was

"Hollywood"; more because I was in the midst of making a very un-"Hollywood" movie.

Chevy: After two years, I was called by Alan Greisman, producer of the Fletch films, saying, "Kevin doesn't want to do it." PERIOD!

Alan Greisman was a producer on the first two *Fletch* flicks. He was gonna be taking third chair on *Son of Fletch* behind Grazer and Mosier. I guess Alan was called about the no-go after Grazer.

However, it wasn't two years since my Chevy meeting. It hadn't yet been a year, really.

Chevy: So I waited for three friggin' years to hear from someone else that Mr Kevin Smith was, for all practical purposes, lying to me to begin with — having written nothing — rudely deceiving me, and all with no apparent concern for how easily (facile) one can hurt another human being and his family…

Look, I'm sorry the flick didn't happen. However, I wasn't lying to the guy. I *did* want to make that flick. But I was dedicated to *Dogma*, and I had to make a choice. I chose *Dogma*. I didn't "rudely deceive" the *inventor of all things comedic since the start of time*; I wanted to make a movie and it didn't pan out. That meeting certainly didn't prevent him from taking other jobs if they were available. It's not like I said to the man "Do absolutely nothing until this flick happens! NOTHING!"

I mean, shit — at least my heart was in the right place. I was pulling for the guy when both Universal and Imagine were like *"That* guy? Are you *sure?"*

Chevy: he can shove it up his hole.

Because of all the many hours of entertainment Chevy Chase has given me over the years, I'll give it a shot and "shove it up" my "hole." Hold on.

****

Nope. Didn't fit.

Chevy: If this is the type of director he aspires to being (the type of person I've seen a million times in Hollywood), I hope he gets the karma he's owed.

Here was the karma in question: back in 2000, I got a fax on my desk from a David List — the book agent for Gregory McDonald. He was letting me know that the entire Fletch library (with the exception of the two that feature Flynn) was up for grabs, as Universal let the option lapse. I called him and we spoke about it for ten minutes, after which I called Harvey and filled him in on the details. He asked me if I wanted to make a Fletch film from one of the books in the library. I told him I'd love to make *Fletch Won* — the origin story, and the best book in the bunch. Harvey was like "So Chevy wouldn't have to play Fletch?" I said no, the role would require a younger Fletch — like Jason Lee. He said "We'll get into it with List now." Less than five hours later, the deal was struck. While I was sitting in on a test screening of *Bounce*, Harvey leaned forward and whispered "Congrats. We're in the Fletch business." It was the fastest deal made in Miramax history, according to Harvey and the Miramax legal team.

Six years later, *that* Fletch film has never come to pass, either. I spent all that time trying to convince Harvey and David List that Jason Lee *was* the young Irwin Fletcher. I adapted the book into first a 170-page draft (which Fletch author Gregory McDonald had called the best adaptation of his work he'd ever seen), and subsequently, a more manageable 125 page draft, pulling for Lee all the way, and constantly being shot down. During that time, I've worked on the *Clerks* cartoon and wrote and shot *Jay and Silent Bob Strike Back*, *Jersey Girl* and *Clerks II*... and still, I was told "Lee's not big enough to play the lead."

Then, when *My Name is Earl* made Jason Lee a household name, I went back for one last shot at getting a Lee-led *Fletch Won* made... at which point, I was told "He's too old now."

sigh

So, Chevy? If I there was any karmic debt to be paid, I guess I've paid it — because I never got to make a Fletch flick at all, with or without you.

Chevy: As for me, he owes me one hell of an explanation. (But, with some, when you're "hot" the rest of the world owes you).

Like I've ever been "hot"...

But I owe that guy nothing. A few years after things went south on *Son of Fletch*, I read a story about the fifteen-year anniversary of *Fletch* in the NY Post. Chevy's all over the story, naturally, and he took the same "Hollywood" pot-shots at me. At that point, I kinda lost all interest in Chevy Chase.

Chevy: If I played any part in the Fletch remake, think about it: as soon as I appeared on the screen people would say, "Hey... There's Fletch, man!" Silly idea. Keep me out of it. Fletch is me.

Well, apparently, not anymore. If Harvey has his way, Fletch is Zach Braff.

But I'll never have as much enmity in my heart for Chevy Chase as he seemingly has for me. Aside from *Foul Play*, *Seems Like Old Times*, *Caddyshack*, the first *National Lampoon's Vacation*, and *Fletch*, Chevy was in one of the most influential four minutes of media of my teenage years: the music video for Paul Simon's 'You Can Call Me Al'.

I was still in high school when that video was in heavy rotation, and man, did I take a verbal beating by folks for liking that song (or *any* Paul Simon, for that matter). Then, I'd show folks the video for 'You Can Call Me Al'...

And I'd *still* take a verbal beating. Didn't matter, though — I thought that clip was pure genius (so much so that I cribbed the idea for the Soul Asylum 'Can't Even Tell' video I directed for *Clerks* years later).

Here's how nuts I was for that video: I tried desperately to buy an off-white suit jacket for months. And I recall, one specific shopping trip with my parents to a Mervyn's in Shrewsbury, when my Mom was looking for dress pants for me. I always hated clothes shopping with a passion — when you're a fat kid, it's never as simple as going to the Gap and grabbing a pair of cords or something. So while wandering the aisles, dreading having to try on multiple pairs of slacks, I stumbled across an off-white suit jacket. Excitedly, I tried it on, and while it was a little snug, I didn't care — I was gonna convince my Mom to buy it.

So I track her and my Dad down, and insist this jacket must be bought. My mom's like "A white suit jacket? That goes with nothing. And you can't wear it after labor day." To which I countered "I'd wear this all the time, I promise." Then, she looked at the price tag.

I think the jacket in question was between $50 and $75 — a pretty sizeable amount of loot to our one-income, $30,000 a year family. My mother's eyes bugged and she said "Did you see how much this cost?! You can get a whole suit for that!" Certainly, one could, indeed, get a polyester suit at K-Mart for $75 in those days (maybe still; I don't know — I don't buy suits), but I didn't want a whole suit; I just wanted this jacket. And sensing I was losing ground in the fight for the off-white jacket, I pleaded "If you buy it, I'll pay you back for it, with my bussing tips this month! Please?!?" My Mom was starting to get suspicious, and hit me with "Why do you want this so badly anyway?"

That's when my old man stepped in.

My father was a man of few words. He never really spoke unless he had some sort of *coup de grace* to deliver — either comedically or as a conversation closer. My sister, in recent years, has suggested that, in many ways, Dad was my model for Silent Bob — a theory I disagree with, but can still see the relevancy of the correlation between. Regardless, point being, when pop spoke, folks tended to listen.

"He just wants it because it's like the one Chevy Chase wears in that music video."

My Mom shot me that look which instantly communicated that any chance I had of convincing her to purchase the off-white jacket for me had just flown out the window.

"Oh, no way," she said, hanging the jacket on a nearby rack. "You're not Chevy Chase."

At the time, I was devastated. As I drove home with a new pair of navy blue poly-weave slacks in my near future, I was pretty resentful of Dad for tipping my hand, and Mom for the utter insult of saying I wasn't Chevy Chase. I mean, who didn't want to be Chevy Chase?

Years later, after having met and dealt with the man, my mother's sentiment was about as unintentionally complimentary a thing as anyone's ever said to me.

Saturday 31 December 2005 @ 8:58 a.m.

With Jen three days into quitting smoking, we opt for a low-key, non-celebratory New Year's Eve. Harley's in Big Bear with Byron and Gail, so Jen's free to thrash about on the bed for the last two days, her body going through serious nicotine withdrawal as her system gets adjusted to a lack of carcinogens. Going from three packs a day to zero can wreak havoc on a person's health, ironically.

We lay around all day, watching the latest *Battlestar Galactica* box set, wrapping up the run with the final episode of the partial season two. Not wanting to let 2005 end without getting a last fuck in, we bone for a bit, then pop in season two of *The Office* (UK version). Around five to midnight, we click over to *Dick Clark's New Year's Rocking Eve* and watch the ball drop while Jen sips champagne and I toss back junk food.

Then, about fifteen minutes later, a quarter hour into the year 2006, the old married couple that we are is fast asleep.

Sunday 1 January 2006 @ 5:15 p.m.

Sorry I've been gone for a while. Been working on the flick. Let's just take up like old lovers, as if nary a day's gone by since our last frolic, and continue sans update for now, shall we?

So I normally get hemorrhoids three or four times a year. It's never pleasant, natch, but it's also never crippling. However, close to a month ago now, I had a hem flare-up that felt like I was sporting two or three — which makes shitting, as you can imagine, something of a project and a painful inconvenience. But over the course of the last two weeks, I've learned to look back fondly on shitting through hemorrhoids — for I've had to learn to shit through...

An anal fissure.

Those of you who are long-time Stern listeners have probably heard the term before, but according to my proctologist, almost sixty percent of any given collection of one hundred people are familiar with the condition itself, if not the clinical term. An anal fissure is a tear or rip in the sphincter that travels up the colon in varying lengths. I'm guessing mine happened when a hemorrhoid broke during a particularly tough bowel movement (though, after watching *Brokeback Mountain* last night, I can't imagine how Jake Gyllenhaal's character couldn't *not* be sporting an anal fissure of his own after his first, spontaneous mountain-top tryst with Heath Ledger's Ennis Del Mar, when only a palm full of saliva acted as lubricant; fucking ouch), and it's made my life a living hell ever since.

Those of you who're regular readers of this site know how much I enjoy shitting. It's one of my favorite pastimes, really. I normally grab my laptop (or a comic, or a video game) and sit on the bowl for nearly an hour, shitting in the first thirty seconds, and just enjoying the stinky solitude for the rest of that time, with that exhaust fan white noising-out the real world beyond the door. Now, I have to learn to shit and go; get in, drop brown, wipe, and get up and out. According to the doc, it's a big preventative measure in the battle against hemorrhoids, which in turn will help me win the war against anal fissures. A lifestyle change of this magnitude is akin to stopping smoking; or even breathing. But it's all coming from a guy who's a bigger man-ass authority than (insert your best friend's name here), so I'm inclined to change me ways.

But how'd I get to the proctologist in the first place? Me — the guy who doesn't even have a regular GP of his own?

By way of the courts, naturally.

After a year of dodging jury duty notices thanks to valid "I'm in the middle of being in/making a movie" excuses, I finally had to face the music and pay the heavy cost of registering in LA to fucking vote in a losing battle against George Bush's America by showing up for a jury pool at the courthouse downtown. I packed a bag with busy work (a PSP, the VA Christmas card list), and trudged off to do my civic duty, hoping against hope that I wouldn't be selected to sit beside eleven of my peers and preside over an actual case.

Within minutes of signing up, I was pulled into a department (ie court room) for voir dire. The judge first asked what each prospective juror did for a living. As prospective juror number three, I had a few minutes to figure out what I'd say, and went with simply "Film", to which the judge queried "Well that's a pretty big field. What do you do in film?" Now, as a guy who doesn't like to talk about what he does for a living in forums outside of the ones where people gather to hear *specifically* about what I do for a living, I'm never comfortable saying I'm a writer/director. It just feels so showy or braggy, not to mention very unrealistic:

where most people have proper jobs, I have a gig in which I'm paid to make pretend for a living. But since the court was asking, and I was already under oath, I ultimately confessed "I write and direct." The judge said "Writing and directing. You must be talented," to which I responded "That depends on who you ask, really." And then, the voices of what I'd hoped would be my saviors piped up like a choir of angels, as one young woman said "He's talented", and was seconded, thirded and fourthed by some other potential jurors. I smiled and nodded thanks, but not for the props; I was thanking them for what I was certain was a sure ticket off the jury: recognition. Could either counsel possibly want someone sitting on their jury who was, even in some small way, in the public eye? Wouldn't I be bounced for being Bob?

Apparently not. As voir dire continued, other jurors would be excused by opposing counsels, and still, I remained juror number three — largely because I made the mistake of responding to the question "Have you ever hired a lawyer?" with "I've got a lawyer on retainer at all times, to handle contracts and deal paperwork." And then further, to the question "Do you have any biases against lawyers?" like a jackass who takes that dopey oath about telling the truth to heart, I replied "I love my lawyer."

That, apparently, sealed my fate — as the case I was to hear was a civil suit between a lawyer and client. But, like Heath Ledger's cow-poke (pun intended) character in *Brokeback Mountain*, I wasn't going down without a fight; I wasn't gonna spit into my palm without one last defensive swing at juror nullification.

The judge asked "Is there anything you should disclose to either counsel that you feel they should know before they make their final jury selections?" Here was my moment, I thought, and I raised my hand and offered "I'm suffering from some crippling hemorrhoids right now, so I hate everyone." Surely, I thought, *that* disclosure would get me bounced; because, really — who wants someone already in a volatile state (both physically and psychologically) deciding the fate of their case?

Apparently both sides, as neither booted me for my hems-confession. And one secondary swearing in later, I was suddenly on a jury.

As a longtime fan of *Law & Order* and courtroom drama in general, let me tell you: legal proceedings are nothing like they're portrayed on TV or in the movies. Witness examinations aren't nearly as dramatic as when Jack McCoy is tearing into a killer on the stand, and nobody ever bellows "You can't handle the truth!" After two days of watching the plaintiff be questioned by her lawyer and then cross-examined by the defense, I was ready to find in favor of neither party, as both were too fucking boring to deserve any monetary judgment. Add to that the fact that I was constantly squirming in my very uncomfortable seat due to what lied beneath, and fuck, was I ready to hang not just the jury, but myself as well.

Then, on day three, something wonderful/horrible happened.

I hadn't shit that morning, and I'd learned over the course of the past two days that it was only after shitting that sitting in the jury box was so physically hellish. All that morning, I was able to sit in peace and not squirm out of rectal agony, listening to the droning testimony in relative physical peace. However, at the lunch break, I finally had to give in and shit, which re-opened what I'd later learn was an anal fissure, and put me into an intense state of shit-hole torture. Remember that famous scene in *Un Chien Andalou* in which a razor is drawn across an eye? I felt like that, except my eye was brown.

So, in deep pain, I dragged myself back into the courtroom and asked the bailiff if I could stand, instead of sitting in my seat. I was granted permission, and stood beside the jury box, attempting to listen to more cross-examination, but almost unable to hear anything over the din of my screaming anus (which, by the way, would be the name of any garage band I put together: My Screaming Anus). When there's something wrong with your asshole, you figure out pretty quickly that the sphincter is like the fulcrum of your whole body, as any move you make is felt there — something you become keenly aware of when any move you make ripples down to your blow-hole and results in spasms of anguish.

Unable to even *lean* on the jury box without wincing, I ultimately laid down on the floor, hoping that taking the weight off my feet by being prone might lessen the pain. At this point, the judge puts a stop to the cross-examination and says "Did we lose someone? Juror number three?" I weakly respond "I'm down here, your honor." Nice guy that he was, the judge said "I understand you're having some problems, but I really think it's important you see the witness' face as she testifies." I replied "I'm in such rectal agony right now, I couldn't care less about seeing the witnesses face, your honor." When he asked what the court could do for me, I asked for a ten-minute break, which he quickly granted.

I dove into the jury deliberation room and climbed onto the plastic couch department stores usually provide in the entrance of the ladies room (presumably for the distaff dealing with menstrual issues), where I laid on my stomach, praying for death. The bailiff checked in on me ten minutes later, at which point I confessed "I can't go back out there, unless you guys wanna bring this couchthing into the courtroom for me to lay on. I can't stand, I can't sit. The only way I can not be in pain is to lay like this — and even this still hurts."

So the bailiff asks me to join her in front of the judge and counsels (the rest of the jury was still on break). As I leaned against the jury box, clutching the railing, cold sweat running down my face, the judge (who was a really sweet guy) said "It would seem you're having some problems, juror number three." I nodded and said, on the record "I think one of my hemorrhoids broke. I'm bleeding rectally and I feel like someone slid a knife up my ass, your honor. I've never had that done to me before, but it's what I imagine that'd feel like."

At that point, I was excused from the case.

To Be Continued.

Monday 2 January 2006 @ 5:46 p.m.

The sad tale of My Boring-Ass Anal Fissure continues...

I was really sweating the visit to the proctologist, as I'd never been to one before, and the only touchstone I had for an ass-doc was that scene in *Fletch* where Chevy Chase sings "Moooooooon Riverrrrrr!" while M. Emmett Walsh probes him with "the whole fist". I confessed this to my good friend, über-producer Dan Etheridge (Mr Plug) before a private *Clerks 2* editing room screening. Dan must've sensed I was trying to use the screening as an excuse to not keep my proctology appointment for that morning, as he hit me with a little supportive chat that calmed my nerves somewhat. As a man who'd had some experience with proctologists, Dan summed it up thusly: "Going in, you want to cancel, because you can't imagine a more humiliating position to be in than bent over an examination table, with your ass in the air. But once it's done, you're really glad you went, because you'll probably find it's not as bad as you're imagining it is back there, and they'll try to get you fixed up quicker than you'll heal on your own." And based on that sage-like advice, I shot over to Beverly Hills for my first visit to a proctologist.

My initial impression was "I'm the youngest person here by thirty years." Predominantly, it would seem, sphincter-trauma is an old man's game, not a worry of the young. Indeed, as I filled out my paperwork, I glanced over to see the great Sidney Poitier leafing through a magazine. This relaxed me somewhat, as I thought to myself "Any ass-doc that's good enough for Mr Tibbs..."

Once in the examination room, I was joined by the doc, who was much younger than I'd imagined he would be. I told him about my symptoms, and he told me to drop trou and get up on the table, laying on my side, in that colonic position I'd come to know over the last few years. Prepared for a probing finger or camera tool of some sort to intrude upon the solace (or sole-ass) of my rear end, I was shocked when he merely opened my ass cheeks a bit, let 'em close again, then stood up and said "Alright, we're done." As he washed his hands, the doc explained there was little point in looking beyond the surface, as he could easily see I was suffering from an anal fissure, and that any probe deeper would cause me to leap off the table. He gave me prescriptions for two creams — one to be applied three times daily around the "peri-anal" area, and the other to be applied when needed, for pain. I'm not sure what the first cream does, but the second is essentially a topical numbing agent. I rub it in, and my asshole goes to sleep. If I ever found myself up on Brokeback Mountain, this is the cream I'd want to have in my rucksack... and in my asshole. Sadly, however, the fissure travels up the colon a bit, so while numbing the surface provides some relief, it's the cut deeper up the mine shaft that I feel after shitting, which the doctor described as an "involuntary constriction of the sphincter and colon". He explained that the pain didn't come from the cut itself so much as the colon's reaction to the fissure once feces traveled over it. His metaphor was this: "If I cut your arm with a razor, you'd draw your arm as close to your body as possible and apply pressure to the wound, right? That's what's going on down in your anus now, only that clenching is involuntary, and no matter what you do, you can't relax it. Your body's just protecting itself from more pain, but it's creating more pain in the process."

But hearing my asshole was rebelling against me wasn't nearly as disquieting as the info the doc imparted regarding the creams he'd prescribed: "In a few weeks," he said. "You'll feel fifty percent better."

I was quietly outraged. Was this the best modern medicine could offer? Fifty percent better *in a few weeks*?! I don't wanna hear about anything less than one hundred percent better in a few hours, if not "After I tap you with this magic wand, your asshole will not only be instantly healed, but from now on, it'll periodically release a pleasant scent that's a natural aphrodisiac." And failing magical cures, where are all the *Star Trek* healing lasers and shit? We're in the 21st fucking century, people! I wanna walk into a doctor's office, lay on the table, and say "Bones, run that light-thingee over my bung-hole and high-tech my fissure shut, post-haste!" And then I want to shoot a fucking Klingon.

In the midst of this, I did, however, learn some fascinating trivia about anal hygiene. My biggest concern about my condition (outside of when it would heal) was the idea of toxic waste traveling along a path that sported an open wound. How could this *NOT* lead to infection, I asked the ass-doc, to which he replied "Your anus isn't nearly as virile as your mouth. The bacteria that lives in your mouth thrives on oxygen, so it's much worse than any of the bacteria in your stool. If you had an open wound on each arm, and you rubbed shit into one and your saliva into the other, the saliva-treated wound has a much higher chance of becoming infected." This doc, it seemed, really relied heavily on the cut-arm metaphors to get his points across, but it was effective, as he was able to make me understand a concept my conservative critics have been trying to unsuccessfully impart to me for over a decade now…

I've got a dirty mouth.

And apparently, it's dirtier than my asshole.

But this all begs the question that if a dog's mouth is supposedly cleaner than a human's mouth, would that put a dog's mouth on the same hygienic level as your asshole? And is that because dogs eat shit, and shit's apparently cleaner than saliva? The mind reels.

Regardless, that's where I've been for the last month: in varying states of little brown starfish distress. The moral of the story: drink lots of water (it's a natural stool softener, apparently), spend as little time sitting on the bowl as possible (stop, drop, and go), never "bear down" (if the shit ain't ready to come out by itself, don't force it out by straining; just wait), and don't lick cuts on your body — you'd be better off rubbing shit into them instead (though don't do that either).

Without good rectal health, you have nothing.

The *Clerks II* Teaser
Monday 9 January 2006 @ 7:31 a.m.

Over the last week or so, I've been cutting together a teaser for the new flick, and this morning, we post it over at the *Clerks II* website. Cruise on over there and peep it when you get a chance.

For those who're trying to avoid spoilers, don't worry: it's not a very *revealing* two minutes, as it gives away precious little about the movie's plot. It's merely a sneak peek at what *Clerks II* looks and feels like, set to one of my favorite tunes of all time: 'Among the Living', by Anthrax (for the curious, this isn't the original recording of 'Among'; this is a re-recording of the song from the excellent album *The Greater of Two Evils*).

Some folks have asked why I'm even bothering to put any footage of the flick out there, eight months before it'll hit theaters. The only reason I can cite is that I'm proud of the flick; I fucking love it, and I can't wait to share it with the world. Just as *Clerks* was a film about what I felt it was like to be in my twenties, *Clerks II* is a film about how I feel it's like to be in my thirties, and for the audience which has made that trans-generational journey along with us over the last decade, I think it's gonna really connect in a big way. But chuck that aside: after the great test run of the flick last month, as well as the enthusiastic response from Quentin and Robert, this just felt like the right time to put up some footage for the fan-base.

But to do a full trailer this far in advance of our theatrical release would be akin to us getting into a sixty nine with the viewer, blowing (or licking) them while hovering our sopping wet pussy/throbbing hard cock within an inch of their face, and then quickly dismounting before any spasms of release and euphoria could occur, getting dressed, and telling them we'll see 'em in August, while heading out the door. Rather than subject folks to that, we present, instead, the cinematic equivalent of a genital flash: just a quick enough glimpse of what we have in store for you to give you something to think about while you're tugging/rubbing one out over the next few months, with the added promise of three-hole input down the road (sorry ladies: I couldn't think of the male equivalent of three-hole input... except maybe the utter and complete lack of *request* for three-hole input).

So without further adieu, I give you a little whiff of *Clerks II*...

http://www.clerks2.com/teaser/

Wednesday 18 January 2006 @ 1:26 p.m.

In an effort to fill out my Academy Awards ballot (due tomorrow), I went over the handy booklet AMPAS included with their mailer that catalogs all the 2005 releases and came up with a list of what flicks I'd seen from the last calendar year. To wit...

White Noise
Assault on Precinct 13
Boogey Man
Inside Deep Throat
Constantine
Cursed
Be Cool
The Jacket
Hostage
Sin City

The Amityville Horror
The Hitchhiker's Guide to the Galaxy
Crash
House of Wax
Kingdom of Heaven
Monster-in-Law
Revenge of the Sith
Dominion: Prequel to Exorcist
The Longest Yard
Madagascar
The Adventures of Shark Boy and Lava Girl
Mr. & Mrs. Smith
Batman Begins
Herbie: Fully Loaded
Bewitched
Land of the Dead
War of the Worlds
Dark Water
Fantastic Four
Murderball
Charlie and the Chocolate Factory
The Island
Sky High
Pretty Persuasion
Skeleton Key
Valiant
The Exorcism of Emily Rose
Corpse Bride
A History of Violence
Capote
Good Night and Good Luck
In Her Shoes
The Squid and the Whale
Wallace and Gromit: Curse of the Were-Rabbit
Dreamer
Jarhead
Harry Potter and the Goblet of Fire
Walk the Line

Rent
Mrs. Henderson Presents
Syriana
King Kong
Munich
Match Point
Brokeback Mountain
Cinderella Man
Wedding Crashers
The Constant Gardener
The Cave
Upside of Anger
The 40 Year Old Virgin
Transporter 2
November
Cry Wolf
Junebug

Of that entire list, I'm kind of ashamed to admit only sixteen were viewed theatrically (and most of those were the kid flicks I saw with Harley). Granted, I was working on *Catch & Release* and *Clerks II* for most of the year, but still — why didn't I make the time to see stuff at the movies instead of in my bedroom?

I blame the shrinking theatrical-to-DVD window, myself. Once upon a time, at the dawn of the VCR, you'd have to wait upwards of a year for a flick to wind up on home video after its initial theatrical release. Now? Sometimes, the window is as small as three months. Folks looking for a reason for the Great Box Office Slump of '05 need look no further than this factor. When given a choice, most folks will opt to watch movies in the comfort of their own home, on their DVD players. By rushing these flicks from their theatrical run to their home video run (in an effort to capitalize on the marketing dollars spent opening a flick theatrically), the studios are muffling the siren's call that tempts most of us from our flat-screen cocoons and into the multiplexes. Why leave the house when you can peep the same flick in less than six months while laying on your couch? Nude, if you want, to boot.

I can recall a specific example of this kinda "Let's wait" attitude: the wife and I were thinking about going out to see *The Exorcism of Emily Rose* when it was in theaters. We started to throw the face-the-world clothes on, when both of us started backpedaling with "Do we *really* wanna get dressed, get in the car, head down to the Arclight, park, buy snacks, watch the flick, get back in the car, and drive home when this flick'll be on DVD a few months from now?" The answer was no, and we wound up watching some other flick at home instead, catching up with *Emily* less than a year later. Fuck the alleged rampant piracy that's supposedly crippling the movie industry; *this* is what's hurting the box office.

But fuck my politics. Since I got the list of what I bought, how about a list of what I thought? At least in regards to my favorite flicks of the year.

My Faves of 2005

The One I'll Take Shit For, Part 1: *War of the Worlds*

Fuck you, I dug it. It was my favorite movie of last year, hands-down. *War* is a well-made, edge-of-your-seat thriller, and Dakota Fanning is awesome in it. Even though we all knew the ending, Mr Spielberg somehow made this a gripping watch.

The One Everybody Likes: *Brokeback Mountain*

This ain't just the gay cowboy movie: it's the saddest flick I've seen all year. And I love sad flicks — particularly well-made/well-acted ones about people not living their lives the way they really want to. Heath Ledger didn't give a performance in this flick: his Ennis *exists* — that's how genius his non-performance was. Not since Billy Bob Thornton in Raimi's underrated *A Simple Plan* has an actor been buried so deep in a character that you forget there's acting going on. Ang Lee, whose film directorial choices are always all over the place in a great way (*Wedding Banquet* to *Sense and Sensibility* to *Hulk* to *Brokeback*) made a great, great film.

The One I'll Take Shit For, Part 2: *Revenge of the Sith*

Fuck you, I dug it. I thought it was a great way to end the *Star Wars* saga. Dismiss me all you want, but c'mon: that was a fantastic opening half hour. And at the end of it all, we got Vader back in black.

The One That Made Me Happy: *Crash*

Such a good flick. And no unhappy endings (well, mostly).

The One That Made Me Feel Dumb: *Syriana*

I loved *Traffic*, so it was no stretch to love this flick, too. Great script, great performances. And it confirmed my worst fears about pool lights.

The One I'll Take Shit For, Part 3: *Dreamer*

Fuck you, I dug it. The trailer made me cry more than the movie, but I felt it was still a great watch. Once again, that Dakota kid's awesome. And why didn't anyone else ever think to pair up Kris Kristofferson and Kurt Russell as father and son before? "I love the stupid King" too.

The One That Surprised Me: *Cinderella Man*

Alright, there were one too many instances of "People were so poor during the Depression…" ("How poor were they?"), but the second half of the flick more than made up for it. Great performances all around (especially Russell Crowe and Paul Giamatti), and an unusually good job by Ron Howard. And not being well-versed in sports lore, I was so glad to not know how it was gonna end.

The One That Made Me Feel Guilty for Not Doing More: *The Constant Gardener*

Strong, well-made flick, with great performances, but fuck, did it leave me feeling like I'm not doing enough for the world outside my own.

The One That Did the Impossible: *Sin City*

Robert and Frank Miller somehow managed to take the *Sin City* graphic novels and put 'em up on screen as… the *Sin City* graphic novels. This flick was, visually, an amazing achievement, and fun as fuck to watch.

The One That Reminded Me of Why I Got Into Film in the First Place: *Junebug*

It's out on DVD now. Pick it up and give it a watch — not just for Amy Adams' performance, but because it's a really wonderfully drawn, quiet portrait of small town life and manners. This flick really stuck with me.

Honorable Mentions

A History of Violence: Yay, Cronenberg and his great cast.

Capote: For Phillip Seymour Hoffman's performance alone.

Wedding Crashers: Vince Vaughn made this flick for me.

The 40 Year Old Virgin: Two words: Seth motherfuckin' Rogen.

Inside Deep Throat: My second favorite documentary of the year.

Sky High: It was a Kurt Russell kinda year for me, and this clever flick was another reason why.

Good Night and Good Luck: David Strathairn, an actor I've always dug, in another impressive, Clooney-helmed flick.

Mrs. Henderson Presents: What can I say? I'm a Judy Dench-whore.

Batman Begins: For Morgan Freeman and Michael Caine alone (not to mention Christian Bale, Liam Neeson, and Cillian Murphy).

And last, but certainly not least, my favorite documentary of the year, *Reel Paradise*. Yes, I was an exec-producer on this flick, and some may say it's kinda gauche to champion your own shit, but fuck you, I dug it. It's a doc about some of my favorite subjects on the planet: movies and John Pierson. It's coming to DVD in a few months, so keep an eye out for it.

Friday 20 January 2006 @ 11:14 a.m.

Professionally speaking, 2004 was a pretty bad year for me. It was the year of *Jersey Girl* — a film that I loved dearly, but will forever be remembered as "that other Bennifer movie" to most. After wrapping the flick in November of 2002, we embarked on what turned out to be a far longer post-production journey than we ever imagined traveling. Delivering that flick to theaters was akin to the loooooong-ass, three-flick walk of the Hobbit movies to Mount Doom. However, whereas Frodo got to complete his quest by pitching the One Ring into molten lava, thus saving Middle Earth, and Peter Jackson ended his chautauqua with a fist full of Oscar and box office gold, the end result of our *Jersey Girl* march of death saw me and Mos watching our flick engulfed in a swirling maelstrom of lava like the Ring itself. And then, a big bird carried us off, where our story continued for another twenty minutes.

Never mind that, in a post-*Gigli* climate, the flick managed the nearly-Herculean feat of crawling to a $25 million box office gross; the flick was still considered a failure. I mean, think about it: we were following the universally derided first Ben/Jen flick that grossed merely $6 million in its entire theatrical run. It would stand to reason, then, that *Jersey Girl* (a flick that essentially had the pre-hype of "Remember those two actors you hated so much in that massive bomb from eight months ago? Here's another helping! Choke on it, motherfuckers!") would fare even poorer at the box office; an *under* $6 million gross was prognosticated by some. It'd be like Warren Beatty and Dustin Hoffman releasing a new flick eight months after *Ishtar* and hoping for the best, or Mariah Carey offering the world *Glitter 2* less than a year after *Glitter*. And yet, miraculously, we got to $25 million, out-grossing *Gigli* in our opening weekend of $8 million on 1500 screens. Still, there are no silver linings to clouds in the movie biz, and a loser is a loser, great Roger Ebert review notwithstanding.

But to add to the professional misery of '04, I was taking far more well-deserved lumps in the comic book community for my utter unprofessionalism in not finishing not one, but *two* comic book series I'd started years prior: *Daredevil/Bullseye: Target* and, far more infamously, *Spider-Man and the Black Cat: The Evil That Men Do*. That I seemed to get something of a pass with *Target* was solely because only one issue had ever come out, compared to the three issues (ending with a cliffhanger) of *Black Cat*. That *Black Cat* fiasco haunted me for years, finally coming to a close of sorts in July '05, when I wrapped up the mini (or now, maxi, in terms of years it took to finish) series. The long-delayed, bare-ly-awaited-anymore issues four, five, and six are now available. Sales were not great, but not bad either (considering the lag time of three years between issues three and four) with issues four and five charting at 31 and 33 in top 100 sales figures for the month of December. With the release of the final issue this month (and the inevitable hardcover and trade paperback down the road), I can finally put to rest this self-imposed unfortunate chapter in my short-lived comics career.

However, the tarnish will forever mark me in the comics community. All over the web, folks have called me to task for being professionally irresponsible for starting a series I took so long to finish. And while my laze was cited often and much, my *ethics* in regards to the situation were really roasted. "He got paid to write something, and he didn't deliver" I'd read. "For that reason alone, Marvel should fire his fat ass and let another writer finish the series, and then sue fat Smith for taking the money and not delivering what fatty was contracted to do." It was an interesting position to take on the subject, and one not entirely with-out merit (all the "fat" jabs notwithstanding). I *had* been paid to write scripts; wasn't I somehow reneging on my *Black Cat* contract with Marvel Comics? Couldn't The House of Ideas take me to task in a court of law for not living up to my agreement?

And then, yesterday, my longtime friend and Marvel Comics Editor-in-Chief Joe Quesada and I made a startling (and pretty funny) discovery.

It all started with an email exchange between me and Carol, my major domo — the woman in charge of all my finances. In putting all 2005 business to bed, I was listing all my sources of revenue for the last calendar year, so we could cross the T's and dot the I's on the financial books. On my list, I included scripts three, four, and five of *Black Cat*, as I'd finished those scripts, and naturally, assumed I'd been paid for them. Then, in an email from Carol, I read this...

"Regarding Marvel. I haven't seen a comic book check for writing (versus roy-alties) since 11/12/02 for $4400.00 and I labeled that one *Daredevil — Target #1*."

I wrote back that I'd check with Joe on the subject, as the checks had proba-bly come in under some other heading or something (in the film biz, you often receive checks for your work from organizations you've never heard of, that are essentially loan-out companies; very rarely did I receive checks from "Miramax" — instead, the checks came from a Miramax loan-out company with a complete-ly different title). What follows is the Instant Message exchange between Joe Quesada and I.

AIM IM with JOE QUESADA.

12:55 PM

Kevin: You there?

Joe: Yup whatup?

K: Just got an email from Carol (the biz-ness manager).

J: Uh huh.

K: Seems she never got any checks for the last three *Black Cat* scripts.

J: That's possible, I'll check for you.

K: From Carol "Okay, regarding Marvel. I haven't seen a comic book check for writing (versus royalties) since 11/12/02 for $4400.00 and I labeled that one *Daredevil — Target #1*.?

J: I'll look into it. We went all electronic so it could be that you're not in the system.

Also, unless something different occurred while I wasn't paying attention, I don't think you signed any of the paperwork we sent you. Still, if there's unpaid balances all will be taken care of.

K: What paperwork?

J: Contract we sent a long time ago.

Did you sign that?

K: Which one?

K: For *Black Cat*?

J: Yeah.

K: Because I'd imagine I had to have (signed a contract) — unless she never got any *Black Cat* checks ever.

Hmmm...

Lemme ask her.

J: LOL!

You're lost.

Okay, here's who Carol can contact.

Tell her to drop an e-mail to —————— and CC the following people:

——@marvel.com

1:00 PM

——@marvel.com

——@marvel.com

I'm working from home today so I'll make a call as well.

K: Cool, cool.

As per Carol: "Black who?"

J: LOL!

K: Apparently, I never got paid for any of the six scripts.

That's pretty fucking funny, sir.

J: That's because without the signed paperwork you never went into the system.

K: Wow. I'm an idiot.

J: We went all computerized shortly after so the minute a script is logged in some machine spits out your check.

K: Still — at least with that three-year gap, you guys never had to pay a brother.

So there it is. While I can never be excused for the insane lateness and unprofessionalism with which I handled *Spider-Man/Black Cat*, comics fans can take some small comfort in knowing that I never got paid for any of the books 'til after the entire series was done anyway. That means no royalties (yet) on those first three issues either. Nada. Not a penny for my *Black Cat* work, heretofore. Until this moment in time, I essentially did *Spider-Man/Black Cat* for free.

Justice, in some weird manner, has been served, I guess.

Monday 27 February 2006 @ 4:22 p.m.

Wake up early and head over to Opie and Anthony show (now on XM), where I hang out the whole morning, chatting and taking calls. The gig starts off with a bang, as a couple who're fans of the show set up a web-cam in their Long Island apartment and do some pretty nifty sucking and fucking. After they wrap, they chat with us, via the web-cam and phone. The whole thing is pretty surreal, as it's like interactive-after-the-fact porn. Chatting up a couple you've just watched be physically intimate (and an attractive couple to boot) is one of those very adult situations that your teenage self's mind would've been blown to hear you'd wind up doing one day, but not nearly as mind-bending as the first year of conversations you have with folks you've been engaged with in a three-way.

Post-ménage relationships are awfully difficult to maintain. I've been involved in four different threesomes and one foursome, and of all the parties involved, I still remain friendly with only two of the players (one, naturally, being Jen). There's this fall-out involved in crossing that line that makes for awkward conversations in the light of day, once everybody's clothes are back on, and nobody's inside anybody else, that's not unlike chatting up your ex, but even more delicate. Try as you might, regardless of the topics of conversation, your mind inevitably arrives at "I've been involved in an out-of-the-ordinary sexual situation with this person."

The first three-way I'd ever had was with two high school friends, long after we'd graduated, on a Halloween night right around the release of *Clerks* in '94. It was boy/girl/boy, and while the guy and I stayed safely at either end of our friend, the whole thing was made salacious regardless, due to the fact that the woman safely separating us from any same-gender antics was engaged to a guy who wasn't involved in our debauchery. From my vantage point behind her, I remember seeing her hand and being struck by the sight of her engagement ring-finger wrapped firmly, along with the other four ringless digits, around the cock of a guy she wasn't set to marry within the year. I've had very few walks of shame in my sexual history; of the thirty plus different women I've been fucked by, the lion's share of my post-coital demeanor has always been "My God, I can't believe I get laid at all…" But that night, heading back to my Red Bank condo, all I could think was "You were just enrolled in a three-way with an engaged friend whose fiancé is on a weekend trip. In their pre-marital bed, no less. You're going straight to hell, buddy."

The whole night-long affair really strained the friendship after that. Whenever I'd see either of them, we didn't really talk much (especially when, in an odd turn of events, I was forced to drop by the woman's wedding reception months later). That's why, with the exception of two other times, any other threesomes I've allowed myself to be involved in have involved total strangers or people I'd never see again.

Post-Opie and Anthony, I head back to the hotel, and Jen and I head down to the Village to do some shopping. She hits Marc Jacob's store, and then we grab some cupcakes at the Magnolia Bakery (where I taste my first red velvet cupcake). As part of my month-old ongoing love affair with Pinto/refried beans, we hit the Caliente Cab Co. Mexican restaurant before heading back to the hotel to relax before the screening.

Around five, we head back downtown, where Jen and I hook up with Janet Maslin for a pre-show meal/drink. When Kate shows up, Jen and she retire to the bar, while Janet and I further discuss the possibility of her writing a column for the revised Movie Poop Shoot site.

An hour and change later, it's time to head to the IFC Center for the *Clerks II* screening.

After the screening, I spend a lot of time talking to the folks from the board at www.viewaskew.com before Scott and I head into the adjacent bar to talk to Harvey, Michael Cole, Carla Gardini and Kelly Carmichael about a release strategy. When Harvey leaves, I chill with Mos, Mike and Carla for a bit before collecting Jen and heading back to the hotel. We stop at an all-night bakery next to the Westin Times Square, grab some late-night chow, and retire to the room. The wife and I snack out to TV, then fall asleep around two in the morning.

Tuesday 28 February 2006 @ 4:25 p.m.

Jen and I are up at the crack of dawn, packing and showering before catching our ride to JFK for the 8 a.m. flight home.

If you've gotta fly from one coast to the other, and you've got the scratch, I can't recommend the United P.S. flight enough. It's the closest domestic equivalent to the Virgin Atlantic flights, and their awesome First Class pod seats that turn into flat-out beds, complete with sheets and a comforter. The United P.S. first class cabin (which you can only take between JFK and LAX, and JFK and San Francisco) offers not only these easy-sleepers, but they have power outlets that allow you to plug your computer's AC cord into the chair, without the bother of an airline adapter. This is the standard all US first class flights should be held to, if the airlines are gonna have the balls to charge as much as they do.

We land, collect our bags, and head out to the curb where Byron picks us up.

At home, we chill with Harley for a bit and relax, checking email and watching TV. John Pierson and I confirm plans to host a midnight screening of *House Party* at the world-famous Alamo Drafthouse in Austin, following John's master class on Monday. I throw the invite up on the board to let any Texas-area folks in on the fun.

At night, Gail, Byron and I head over to the Sony lot for a friends and family screening of *Catch & Release*. I see Juliette Lewis again, for the first time since we wrapped in Vancouver, as well as Sam Jaeger, Susannah Grant, and Jenno Topping. The flick turned out great, but Susannah says she wants to tinker with it more, now that she's got 'til January's theatrical release.

I get home and Jen's already asleep, so I watch some tube, check my email and the board, and fall asleep to a *Law & Order*.

The *Clerks II* screening
Wednesday 1 March 2006 @ 12:48 p.m.

Monday night, we showed *Clerks II* to an audience for the second time. It really couldn't have gone better than it did: laughter in all the right places, gut-punched silence in others. So delighted to know that the flick works for more people than just me.

The two highlights of the night…

1) Bob Weinstein (who hadn't seen the flick before) gushing after the screening, insisting it was the best flick we've made thus far. Bob is not normally an effusive guy, but he was so wonderfully dialed-into the flick and he expressed what I've thought for a while now: *Clerks II* takes the best elements and stand-out stuff from our six previous flicks and puts them to work in a cohesive, ultimately satisfying fashion, under one roof. Bob said, "It's like watching a movie where the filmmaker puts everything they've learned over a decade into one movie, and it works on every level." That made me feel terrific, considering the source.

2) Janet Maslin, the former lead critic of the *NY Times* (the woman who wrote a great review of *Clerks* twelve years ago) shot me this email when I got home…

So where/how/when can I talk to you? Either phone or I.M.? I don't want to type out a whole long screed this way. But I will give the highlights:

1) It's beyond funny. A great job, and a fantastically good time. This is fact, not opinion.

2) You barely have to sell it. It'll sell itself.

3) The zigging and zagging you mentioned: that's what makes it work. The audience goes up and down and all over the map, but they never get a chance to figure out where it's going. And you never have to stop to explain anything. Whatever longer version you had, you haven't lost anything: short works great.

4) And it is so good-hearted. So cheery, in its crazy way. It's such a moving experience in spite of all the funny stuff. I think for that reason it can cross over to people who know about the first one but never saw it. Especially if you tone down a little of the mildly freaky stuff (this thought brought to you courtesy of the person who bitched about the Poop Monster). By freaky I don't mean the **SPOILER DELETED**. The **SPOILER DELETED** is a delight.

5) You have defanged any possible criticism. Nobody can say these guys are too old for this: you've made that part of the joke. Nobody can say it's sophomoric because it's so clever. Nobody can say it's trivial because you've elevated all this to the level of homage to your own earlier work and who knows what else. The French will see this as a witty critique of American popular culture. Which in fact it is.

6) You can't wait until August. You just can't. Your audience is as web-savvy as an audience can be. And it is simply human nature to go home and say hey — I just saw a movie with a **SPOILER DELETED** and a **SPOILER DELETED** and a

SPOILER DELETED and a **SPOILER DELETED** and a **SPOILER DELETED** and a 30-second **SPOILER DELETED**. Nobody will keep quiet about this. Every story out of Cannes will be a spoiler.

So: can't you get it out there ASAP? Is it being shown in competition? If not, can't it open here just before it gets there? I know there's the worry of too many big summer things but this doesn't have to open on a huge scale. It can be in fewer theaters and just stay and stay and stay. You will get repeat business and a terrific grapevine thing. People will find it for themselves. It's barely going to have to be marketed.

Congratulations in a big, big way. I hope this is helpful. And thanks for a gut-busting good time.

I mean, Janet's *Times* review practically made my career twelve years ago, as it gave a lot of folks the impression I was legit. To have her dig on *Clerks II* as well brought my career full circle.

Amy Taubin, the first person to ever write about *Clerks* (waaaaaay back in '93, in her IFFM wrap-up piece in the *Village Voice*) was also in the house (I didn't get to speak to her after the screening, but Mos did, and reported that she loved the flick). Mark Tusk, the man responsible for bringing *Clerks* to Miramax, was on hand, too, and dug it. Harvey Weinstein, naturally, was there and still digs it (might even dig it a little more, after watching it with an audience and hearing the response). And many folks who post on the message board over at ViewAskew.com (some of who've been around since we first opened the site back in '95/'96) filled out the screening room and also seemed to be into the flick. All in all, it was one of the ten best screenings of one of our flicks I've ever attended.

Post-screening, me, Mos, Harvey, and Weinstein Co.'s Michael Cole, Carla Gardini, and Kelly Carmichael huddled in a corner of the bar attached to the IFC Center theater (where we screened the flick) and talked about what's left to do (lock up the music rights, screen for the Cannes programmers). I saw a couple poster concepts, and one really leapt out at me; hopefully, it'll be what eventually hits the theaters.

We're now pretty much locked-and-loaded for 18 August — a date that can't come soon enough...

Thursday 2 March 2006 @ 4:26 p.m.

I wake up early and take Harley to school, then grab coffee for Jen on the way home.

Get up, check email, shower, and head over to Sony lot to do one line of ADR for *Catch & Release*. I talk to Susannah for a bit, then head back to the house.

I get a little writing done and iChat with a bunch of folks about business stuff before picking Harley up from school and hitting Marix for an impromptu daddy/daughter date.

Back home, I crash on the bed for a while, checking email and watching TiVo while Jen hangs with Harley. The rest of the day is spent lounging with Jen, during which we manage to squeeze in some fucking and watch copious amounts of TiVo. That evening, Schwalbach and I engage in yet another late-night eating extravaganza, downing Pinto bean-covered nachos and other gastric delights, all the while swearing I'm gonna get back on my diet. I've now gained back twenty of the seventy pounds I took off while on Optifast, so it's time to get back into a program of sorts and take another vacation from food.

B-Star G

Friday 3 March 2006 @ 4:36 p.m.

Tonight, I do something I haven't done in a while, if ever: I get my geek on by attending a panel I'm not a part of, as an audience member.

At this point in my life, there's only one show in the world that'd make me leave the Elysium comforts of my bedroom and venture out into the world.

That show is the ever-genius new version of *Battlestar Galactica*.

The Museum of Television and Radio holds the William S. Paley TV Festival every year, in which well-regarded shows have screenings of unaired episodes, then assemble the cast and crew for moderated chats before opening up the floor to questions. Since the MTR is in Beverly Hills, Jen and I head over earlier than the scheduled start of the panel so we can kill two birds with one stone and pop into Tiffany to grab some gifts for Gail and a few other folks while we're in the neighborhood. With time to spare, we shoot over to the MTR only to discover that this year, the Paley fest is being held at the cushy DGA Theater, in their building on Sunset (next door to the Griddle), very close to our home.

We race back to Hollywood and get into the theater with two minutes to spare. The crowd in attendance looks like the same folks who show up for my Q&As at colleges and ComiCons, which results in much "Hey, Kevin Smith" and "Can't wait for *Clerks II*"-type shout-outs. My cell phone vibrates and I see Dave Mandel's name show up. I answer it, looking around the room, immediately asking, "Don't tell me you're here too." Dave tells me to look to my left, and I spot him across the theater, smiling and waving. I tell him we have no life, then settle in for the start of the program.

This v.2 of *Battlestar Galactica* is so insanely amazing, I'm sometimes flummoxed watching it. When I started seeing billboards around town advertising the show when it débuted, I remember thinking "Wow. Why?" The OG *B-Star G* (as we've taken to calling it around the house) was a fun piece of disposable youth cheese that, even as a seventies pre-teen, was easy to recognize for what it was: a *Star Wars* rip-off. Granted, I had a Colonial Viper and a Cylon Raider as a kid; but my mother bought them for me from the sale rack at the now-defunct Two Guys store, where each set her back less than a buck. Compared to the hundreds (maybe thousands) she and my father spent on Kenner's *Star Wars* line of action figures and accessories for me over the years, the two bits she dropped on *Galactica* crap probably made her wish I was a bigger fan of Starbuck than Han Solo.

The notion of an updated *Galactica* was about as far off my radar as an Amanda Bynes picture (which, in name-checking, I realize reveals an actual near-proximity of said flick to my radar; damn you, Harley). And the fact that none of the advertising I'd seen depicted any Cylons (always the most interesting part of the show, if for no other reasons than their pong-like red "eyes" and their "Funky Town" voice patterns) didn't help matters much.

It wasn't until we were in pre-production on *Clerks II*, and Tony, our A.D., started waxing rhapsodically about the show during a location scout that I even remembered it existed. Based on his fervent recommendation, I picked up the season one box set when it came out, during a later visit to Laser Blazer. But even when season two made its DVD appearance, neither box set had emerged from their wrappers until two days after Christmas, when the cold-turkeying Schwalbach, detoxing from a suddenly abandoned three-pack-a-day cigarette habit, was sacked-out in bed, barely able to move, asking what we were gonna watch next.

We'd gone through all our Academy screeners, and — surrounded by a banquet of nicotine-replacing junk food — my miserable-from-missing-smokes wife was looking for something to take her mind off lighting up.

"I just read in *Time* magazine's year-end issue that the new *Battlestar Galactica* was their favorite show," I offered.

Weakly, she countered "There was an old *Battle*-thing whatever?"

After a brief explanation of *Battlestar* classic, Jen's already withering glares — those glares that come from someone who's forsaking the only true indulgence they feel makes them whole — morphed into that old favorite blank expression of mine; the one that I've been at the receiving end of many times throughout our marriage, when my wife, with a look, communicates utter disbelief and near disgust as I reveal a familiarity with something far more geeky than I should know/enjoy. I call it the "I Can't Believe I Let Someone Like You Stick His Cock In Me" look.

Still, in her weakened, non-nicotine fueled state, she was in no condition to offer alternative suggestions on what to view. She moaned "Let's try it."

The V.2 *Battlestar Galactica* kicks off with a killer mini-series event that sees the civilizations of the Colonies all-but completely annihilated by a new breed of Cylons — Cylons that, instead of clunky, faux-metal fourth-rate Stormtrooper proxies, are now human in appearance (and some even super-human, if you count Six — the Cylon babe who wouldn't look out of place at the Playboy grotto).

Adama, keeper of the about-to-be-mothballed Galactica looks less like the dude from *Bonanza* and more like the dude from *American Me*. Starbuck has joined the distaff and is now a chick (depicted as a dickless dude). Boomer went from being a black dude to an Asian woman. The evil Baltar is now a somewhat hapless agent in humanity's destruction who carries on a constant conversation with the Cylon babe in his head. And the leader of the 50,000 remaining humans in the not-so-free world is the only surviving member of the Presidential cabinet — the Secretary of Education who was something like twentieth in the line of succession.

Without changing much of the original *Galactica* premise, the creators and folks involved with the show have done the equivalent of taking a covered wagon and creating a BMW from the design: it still takes you from place to place, but now it does so while keeping you safe from the elements, getting you there quicker, warming your ass with heated, leather seats, and bathing your ears in audio delights from an iPod-friendly sound-system. With the mini-series alone, these people managed to not simply just teach an old dog new tricks; they taught that bitch to speak, travel to alternate dimensions, fold space, and cure cancer.

How was this accomplished? How did the new *B-Star G* peeps spin straw into gold? How did they make the human beings as interesting (if not more so) than the fucking Cylons? Like all great art, they simply held a mirror up to our culture. *Galactica* V.2 is an allegory for 9/11 and the War on Terror viewed from both sides. It offers a far more complex view of two opposite ideologies in juxtaposition to one another, presenting neither side as particularly evil — just terrifying. Extremely well done science fiction has always been most powerfully effective when it lays out humanity naked and shows us ourselves, warts and all. Whether it's *Planet of the Apes*, *Star Trek*, or almost anything by Philip K. Dick, the best sci-fi isn't simply laser-beam driven shoot-'em-ups between good guys and bad guys; it's the abyss we look into and see someone awfully, sometimes painfully familiar looking back from. There will always be a place in science fiction for the Joseph Campbell-described archetypical hero's journey of the *Star Wars* saga, but what sci-fi does best is allow the author to comment on what it's like to be a human being — the shame, the miracle, the sacrifice, the desire, the grand heights, and the abject lows. And if an author can accomplish this in stealth mode — be entertaining while not calling attention to his or her loftier goals — so much the better.

And fuck, does *B-Star G* entertain. Jen and I were so gripped, we went through two box sets in two days. Would-be sci-fi (or just excellent television) creators take note: if you want to seduce a female audience (so that bi-mon sci-fi cons aren't just massive sausage parties), include strong, interesting, and indispensable female characters. I can't say *B-Star G* made my wife kick the habit, but nestled in the bosom of this wonderful show, my wife forgot about her self-imposed smoking moratorium for a long enough period of time that the initial detoxing transition wasn't as bad as it could've been (ie, she stopped yelling at and cursing me for introducing her to smoking). While the wife may be a massive Starbuck fan, I dare say that President Laura Roslin is the most interesting character in a show that has no weak links. Neither a figure of Clinton-ian valor or GDub-ian misguidance, Laura Roslin is a President we'd all be lucky to elect, and a sad reminder that the best-and-yet-heretofore-dismissed candidate to lead this nation would probably be a person born with the biology to create, carry and nurture life.

If you haven't seen this show yet, throw together a few shekels, set aside a few hours, and get your hands on the DVD box sets. A better use of your time-wasting I can't imagine. I mean, my affection for this program actually inspired me to go to a fucking panel and sit in the audience like every other fanboy and fangirl, gawking dopily at the cast and crew behind its creation.

The highlight of said panel was a screening of the episode that was running that night — the penultimate chapter in the second part of season two. This was an unexpected delight, as I'd never watched the show with anyone but Jen. Sitting amidst three hundred or so other *B-Star G* enthusiasts and hearing what they responded to was pretty cool.

After the screening, the cast and crew were brought up and interviewed, and I was reminded why I don't go to panels in the first place: there are no gods behind the stuff (movies, TV, comics) you're drawn to or love; there are actual people. Some folks came off as arrogant; some folks came off as boring; thankfully, a few realized that, if you're gonna stand up in front of a crowd, you should try to be funny, or at least entertaining (the Brit contingency especially — the guy who plays Apollo and the guy who plays Baltar — made the sit much easier).

When all was said and done, I'm glad I attended, but in the future, I will limit my enthusiasm for a show to the show itself (and to hours of web-investigation on the subject).

Following the audience-driven portion of the Q&A, Jen and I head for home, pop on our jammies and woobs, and curl up in bed. We briefly contemplate re-watching the TiVo'ed episode of the *B-Star G* we just watched in the theater, but then decide we've been geeky enough for one day, and instead fall asleep to a TiVo'ed *Law & Order* episode.

Two Big Anniversaries
Saturday 4 March 2006 @ 8:32 a.m.

Today, I'll be presenting at the Independent Spirit Awards (broadcast live on IFC at 2 p.m. PST). The last time I was at the Spirit Awards, I not only won Best Screenplay for *Chasing Amy*, but also, the heart (and vag) of one Jennifer Schwalbach. Yes, that Spirit Awards ceremony eight years ago represented my first date with Jen. And what a date it was...

I mean, Jesus — she gave up the pussy later that night.

But, mind you, this wasn't just any ol' pussy. This was the pussy that changed my life: the pussy that turned me into a married man and father (and not necessarily in that chronological order, either). This was the pussy that aided and abetted in me falling in love with Jen (although, I could argue that I'd kinda done that when I interviewed with her a month prior).

Shockingly, this'll be the first time we've attended the Spirit Awards since that fateful afternoon. You'd imagine that, based on sentimentality alone, Schwalbach and I would've made Spirit Awards attendance an annual thing. And yet, oddly, neither of us have stepped foot in that tent on the beach in Santa Monica in eight years. So today's being treated as something of an anniversary date (even though, technically, the date of that Spirit Awards/first fuck in '98 was March 21st). M'lady and I are getting gussied up (which, for me, means putting on a jacket instead of a shooter), and we're gonna trip the lights fantastic, waltzing down memory lane, this time hand-in-hand.

And then, post-ceremony, we're gonna bone our brains out — just like we did eight years ago.

Today marks another anniversary in the Askewniverse as well. Peep this...

Date: Mon, 4 Mar 1996 14:46:16 0500

From: Kevin
To: ming
Subject: Let's go!

Ming

Call anytime you'd like.

I'd love to hear what you've thought about thus far. As for me, I've been checking out some other web pages (Film Zone, the Unofficial Kevin Smith home page — which is by some guy who isn't me, but is named Kevin Smith — and of course yours) and I'm starting to get some ideas:

1) I'd like to have sub-sections about each flick we've done so far, with hot-links to other pages already existing.

a) a Clerks section, which we can update periodically with any pertinent info — ie, the animated series, the failed sitcom, reception around the world, blah, blah, blah. I've got a slew of pix that have never seen print we can put up there, as well as updates of what the cast may be doing or where they can be seen.

b) a Mallrats section, with all the same trimmings, including the graphics from the opening of the film (the cool comic book covers). There's a slew of footage that didn't make it into the flick, so we can include them as Quicktime movies if you want (people would love that — it'd be the only place to see the lost footage, as the geniuses at MCA are only issuing a standard letterboxed version of the flick on laser disc, without any cool extras).

c) a Chasing Amy section — the film we're toiling on now. We could talk about the production (pre- and post-) include some cast impressions of the flick as it unfolds, show people how it develops (marketing, trailers before they're in the theatre, etc). We'll have video dailies of the movie while we're cutting it (on the AVID system) so we can put up scenes that people can take a look at months before the flick gets into theatres!

We can list festival info as well.

2) I'd like to have a Team Askew section, that talks about the movers and shakers here at View Askew, what they're doing, which ones are going to be making movies of their own. By being the brains behind this potential website, that makes you a member of the team, as far as I'm concerned, so of course there must be a Ming section.

3) A section where we people can order stuff (signed posters, hats, shirts, etc).

4) A section about the smaller budgeted films we're producing.

5) A section that we can update weekly that's all gossip about the industry — not necessarily about what we're doing, but what the studios are doing. We're tapped into the system, so we find stuff out long before it sees print (for example, we knew about

this George Clooney as Batman thing long before it was reported). I think people would dig that sort of thing. I know I would.

6) And most importantly — once a week, I'd like to do a chat-room thing, where I can get on and answer questions live and stuff like that. We can post chat sessions with people from the casts of the flick, as well as just famous people we know. And we could do it every week. Whether five hundred people show up or only five, I think it'd be neat.

What do you think? I'm sure there's a shit load more we can and will do. I'd love to hear what you're planning as well. Call me and let's go! I'm tres, tres excited — my nipples are hard. Let me know where to send the graphics I have, and if you act now, I'll send you the original, no studio music, 105 minute cut of Clerks that has stuff on it that wasn't even on the laser disc! Also, I love the way the Clerks page starts. Can we start our page with a moving graphic of the clown from our logo, 'Vulgar'? Maybe I can get Walter to draw new art for it — Vulgar at a terminal or something?

Yours,

Kevin

Ladies and gentlemen, in that document, emailed ten years ago today, lay the origins of www.viewaskew.com. A few months later, Ming and I took the site live, and it changed both of our lives forever (and, happily, I would stop using terms like "tres, tres").

Ming Chen is, oftentimes, the unsung hero of the Askewniverse. Had I never been directed to his *Clerks* shrine site a decade back, you probably wouldn't be reading this now. www.viewaskew.com became the stage from which we grew our audience and met so many of the folks who've kept me employed for the last ten years. Without Ming, I wouldn't have been as in touch with the folks that watch our flicks as I am; and keeping in touch with those folks has made all the difference in not just my career, but my life as well. www.viewaskew.com has shaped and defined my life and career in such a way, that Ming has become about as indispensable to me at this point as Scott Mosier or Jason Mewes is; meaning he's not just a guy I work with, but also a great sounding board and friend.

The websites in the Askewniverse family number many at this point (www.viewaskew.com, www.clerks2.com, www.silentbobspeaks.com, www.moviepoopshoot.com, www.moviesaskew.com, www.jayandsilentbob.com, www.newsaskew.com, etc, etc); none of them would've existed at all, were it not for Ming Chen.

Take a bow, Asian Design Major.

Sunday 5 March 2006 @ 4:43 p.m.

Having spent the night at Shutters on the Beach in Santa Monica following the Spirit Awards, Jen and I wake up somewhat early and order a mess of room service. This is the second round of room service in ten hours: the previous night, post-Spirits, we briefly hit the after party downstairs, then retired to the bar, where Jen enjoyed some squid and wine, before hitting our room and ordering up a cart-load of crap to down, while watching *Fun With Dick and Jane* (a comedy that seemed to have forgotten to include actual comedy). As we plow through this morning buffet, we click around the channels on TV and find IFC repeating the uncut Spirit Award broadcast. I'm able to check out my Best Director presentation and finally clarify for the wife whether I said of host Sara Silverman "Finally, there's a host I'd wanna fuck" or "Finally, there's a host you'd wanna fuck" (the not-so-subtle distinction puts to rest a near-fight from the night before). My name cleared, Jen and I get into some rare, post-meal morning sex (she usually doesn't like to fuck 'til after two in the afternoon), then pack up all the swag I got as a Spirit Award presenter (two suitcases literally full of stuff, including a video iPod), load into the car, and head home.

Since we live a mere two blocks up from the Kodak Center (home of the scheduled-for-today Academy Awards ceremony), we take an alternate route back to the house, careful to avoid La Brea and Franklin altogether. We chill with Harley for most of the day. I check email and the board and find some pretty good notices about the Spirit Awards press.

Around three-ish, Harley and I make a pre-Oscars junk food run, stopping at Baja Fresh and Ralph's. Back home, Pinto bean-covered nachos and Snyder's peanut butter pretzel sandwiches in hand, I sack out with the wife and kid and watch yet another disappointing Oscar telecast, that culminates with the best picture of the year (in my opinion, at least) not winning Best Picture of the Year. Both of us tuckered out from our early rise, Jen and I fall asleep to a *News Radio* season three DVD.

I'd rather spend the night in the Four Seasons
Monday 13 March 2006 @ 10:51 a.m.

I love the picture of Paris Hilton accidentally exposing herself. It represents the realization of Warhol's "In the future, everyone will be famous for fifteen minutes" prediction. I mean, even though she comes from wealth, this woman's celebrity is based on stuff like "accidentally" showing off her gash, or having sex on camera.

There's an entire industry full of the distaff who do the exact same thing on a daily basis, and aside from the biggest of them (like a Jenna Jameson), their names aren't nearly as well known as this vapid dork's. And really — what has she done that's any different than what Racquel Darrian or Tori Welles have been doing for years (and done more convincingly)?

This is the new pornography: naked famous people. And this isn't just Sharon Stone airing-out her labia in an interrogation room; it's a movement that's based on watching famous people fuck. People like Colin Farrell. People like Pamela Anderson and Tommy Lee. But at least those cats did something else for a living before their nookie went public; *this* chick never did anything beyond being born into wealth with a surname that used to mean something. Then, she had sex and sucked a little dick (well, a little *big* dick, really) on camera, and suddenly, she became something of a household name.

Warhol was right, man. If you can get world-renowned for doing something anyone can do, the bar has been dropped substantially. Hell, the bar doesn't even *exist* any more.

So based on that, I say let's make any and all of these people famous...

Naked ladies and dudes (at http://pichunter.com)

I mean, really? What's the difference? At least these folks can probably *use* the cash that comes with fame.

Let's give it up for the random chick with the grossly oversized labia; at least her shit's a little different than most. Or the guy with the thick-as-a-coke-can cock; he stands apart. Or the lady (or man) who can stuff two dicks in one hole; they're going where even angels fear to tread. But giving it up for a mannequin who plays peek-a-boo on the red carpet and offers only a lackadaisical fucking on night-vision video? That's like celebrating the person who walks in the NY marathon when everyone else is running: sure, they're *in* the race; but everyone else is doing such a better job than they are.

Championing mediocrity has replaced baseball as the national pastime.

And thank God, I say — otherwise I might not have a career.

The Middle East
Tuesday 14 March 2006 @ 10:08 a.m.

In reading *Time* this week, I've come to the conclusion that I never want to go to the Middle East. I don't think they'd really care for my particular brand of whimsy over there.

The region is so fucking volatile, it seems like the crazy dude on the subway you just don't want to sit near. At all. And yet, said crazy dude needs to be watched by a transit cop — lest he start getting all crazy violent on folks in the other cars. At the end of the day, the crazy dude needs to be policed, to keep him from hurting people. I'm just sorry our troops are the transit cops in question.

Naturally, I haven't factored into the equation how the crazy dude is also a fucking geyser of petro-dollars. Maybe it's a crazy dude on the subway that nobody wants to sit near who needs to be policed… who's holding pockets full of winning rub-off tickets. And not just the free ticket rub-offs either; we're talking $10,000-a-pop winning rub-off tickets. And his pockets are *bulging* with them, too. And the transit cop's boss is like "Watch that nut-bar and make sure he doesn't kill anyone on the train…" but his *real* agenda is to secure all those winning rub-off tickets for himself.

And meanwhile, in the midst of all this, said crazy dude on the subway who's stuffed to the gills with winning rub-off lottery tickets is building a suitcase bomb that'll take out a large section of the train, if not the *whole* fucking thing at once.

This is why I don't teach civics or social studies.

I don't know. It's just wacky over there in the Middle East. And you don't need Nostradamus to figure out the end of the world is gonna have something to do with that region. For years, this country was deeply afraid of the Russians. Now, the Middle East makes Khrushchev beating his shoe on a podium and telling the US "We will bury you!" seem as threatening as Elmer Fudd during wabbit season.

I mean, back during the Cold War, the two "Super Powers" held one another in check with the threat of Mutually Assured Destruction; neither side would rush into battle, because neither side saw the benefit in being dead. But with Middle Eastern extremists, you have an adversary who couldn't give a fuck about M.A.D., so long as the decadence of the west is wiped out (not to mention all western inhabitants).

Even in their most cartoonish, Rambo-like villainy, the "Commies" still seemed human; and that, I believe, had a lot to do with their investment in this world. As a Godless bunch, they didn't look to an afterlife for justice/reward; it was all about right here, right now. Now, the US is at odds with a bunch of religious zealots who couldn't give a fuck about the present, beyond making sure we're not in it for very long. They look to the next life, where shit's gotta be better than it is for them in the here and now. And when you read about what life over there is like, who can blame them? I, too, would be looking to run to Jesus (or Allah) if my world was as full of unrest, poverty, hatred and fear as their world seems to be. Fuck life, at that point — "Let's get busy dying; anything's gotta be better than this horse-shit existence."

I've got no answers, and I'm too terrified to even ask the questions. And even if I was equipped with all the facts, who am I to tell a motherfucker how to run their kitchen? Even if their kitchen threatens to blow up mine? All I know how to do is make movies (and some would say I can barely do that), so I should just shut my mouth and jot down some dopey shit for Jay and Silent Bob to do next.

Whoever said "May you live in interesting times" needs a smack in the mouth. I'd prefer shit to be PBS-boring over the current geo-political climate any day.

Me and my big mouth
Saturday 25 March 2006 @ 7:21 a.m.

At the UPenn gig the other night, I told a fifteen minute story that detailed Jason Mewes's amazing journey from severe heroin abuse to sobriety, giving the man props for coming up on his third anniversary of being completely clean (April 6th) — a stellar accomplishment that should serve as inspiration for anyone looking to kick any monkey off their back. It's an anecdote filled with tons of love and pride for my boy, which culminates with a conversation Mewes and I had two and a half years ago about what he noticed the big differences were between life on drugs and now off.

And in the age of internet gossip, that heroic tale of a guy who was able to beat his demons has been reduced to a brief snippet on thesuperficial.com about Mewes's "romp" with a celebutante from a reality TV show whose name we can't print here, lest we get sued (but dig deep enough online and you'll figure out who I'm talking about).

It's not like I haven't told this story at other college gigs over the last few years, but for some reason, it's now news. I got an email from someone at the NY Daily News regarding not just this bit, but another story that came from a question that night regarding my enmity for Reese Witherspoon (which is pretty well-covered in the book Silent Bob Speaks) that they want to run on Monday. This was my response…

"It's one thing to tell that tale out of school at a college Q&A (in the context of a far larger, longer story about Mewes's hard journey from heroin abuse to three years of total sobriety), and a completely different thing to just pull the stuff about bathroom sex and run it in a gossip column. So unless you're gonna run the whole, unedited transcript of me talking about how amazing it was for Mewes to get clean (a fifteen minute oral story), I'd rather you not include just that bathroom sex snippet, which makes it all seem like unsavory locker-room chit-chat."

Naturally, I'm not expecting they'll keep the context. Sadly, it's not news that Jay — with nearly both feet in the grave at the lowest point in his life — was able to single-handedly pull himself out of the self-made hell of drug addiction and work his way back to the land of the living, clean and sober; what's news is that he had sex in a bathroom stall with a dork from a reality show.

sigh

Slow News Day
Monday 27 March 2006 @ 3:31 p.m.

Much ado about nothing, over some shit I said in the UPenn Q&A...

All stemming from the same poorly-worded story. All insisting I'm still harping on Reese when it was in response to a question. All treating it like it's new info, when the Reese story alone's been around for five years, online, and in print...

Lots of folks in talk-backs teeing off on me as being irrelevant or unfunny, which other cats in the real world, not cyber-snipers, apparently disagree with. The great irony is, the talk-back people on the blog/gossip sites are taking me to task for being a gossip. Kettle, I call thee black.

Also, I'm being called "egocentric". Anyone who's ever seen the *Evening With Kevin Smith* DVD knows how very little ego I have, as I spend far more time blasting myself than other people.

Lots of sound and fury signifying nothing. The sun still rises and sets, I've still got a job, *Clerks II* is still coming out on August 18th, at which point some folks will go see it, some folks won't, some will dig it, and some will hate on it.

Same as it ever was.

Me and My Shadow, Pt. 1
Tuesday 28 March 2006 @ 4:00 p.m.

Since the gossip sites have seen fit to print only the portion of the Jason Mewes story I told at UPenn (that portion being what said sites seem to feel is the only interesting aspect of Mewes's life), I figured why not put the whole tale of Jason's battle with drug addiction into print here, where folks can get a better idea of who Jason truly is and maybe why he fell victim to heroin abuse in the first place. I'm thinking it's gonna be at least a four-parter, and I'm hoping to wrap it up by April 6th, the day Mewes celebrates his "sober birthday", when Jay will mark his third straight year of living completely drug and alcohol free.

At the least, it's a more comprehensive profile of a guy who's accomplished a lot more than celebrity bathroom sex; at the most, it's an ode to a very unlikely hero of mine and a man I love (in a decidedly hetero way).

Enjoy.

On a mid-December early morn, circa 2003, on the balcony of my house in the Hollywood Hills, Jason Mewes, my friend of seventeen years and co-star in five films at that point, dropped a bomb that should've repulsed the shit out of me, or at the very least, made me vomit a little in my mouth.

"Last night, at the Spider Club, ****** ****** dragged me into the bathroom and fucked me."

And yet, instead of retching, I found myself battling another type of growing lump in my throat — the kind induced by watching your child enter the world, or the last ten minutes of *Field of Dreams*. I was suppressing tearful joy, momentarily setting aside the compulsion to smack Jason upside the head, hollering "Don't fuck the vapid, dammit!" due to the fact that I was so insanely proud of how far the boy had come and relieved that we were having this conversation at all.

See, for years, Jason had had what seemed like an unbeatable, untreatable addiction to, alternately, heroin and oxycontin. It was a heartbreaking, trying and puzzling five-year stretch for me, so I can't imagine how bad it was for him (well, that's not entirely true. Mewes would periodically flash self-awareness with statements like "If I'm still like this when I turn thirty, I should probably kill myself.").

Those who've never struggled with drug dependency themselves, or loved anybody who has, will often dismiss the props more empathetic folks extend to the ex-junkie with caustic bon mots along the lines of "So he/she quit drugs? Big deal. Why celebrate someone for finally exhibiting common sense? They didn't have to get hooked in the first place. It's not like someone held a gun to their head and told them to try drugs." Oftentimes, these are the same people who think being gay is a choice, too.

But in the case of drug abusers, not every addict has the luxury of choosing a glamorous existence of despair, lies, theft and self-loathing. Some people are born genetically predisposed to chasing the dragon.

Like Mewes.

Born the son of a heroin abuser, Mewes spent most of his childhood raised by an aunt while his mother fed her jones or spent years in jail. She wasn't above stealing credit cards from neighborhood mailboxes, which resulted in the only Christmas gift of his childhood Jason recalls receiving from his mother: a new bike. The bike came in handy when, during a brief period of her smack-addled fifty years, his mom operated as a drug dealer, using an oblivious nine year old Jason as a bag-man who delivered drugs to locals his mother didn't trust enough to deal with herself.

With no father on the scene (to this day, Jason still doesn't know who his dad is), the story of young Mewes plays out in an almost depraved Dickensian fashion. The nights when his mom wanted to party, she'd drop him and his sister off at the houses of total strangers. The origins of Jay's fear of confined spaces can be traced back to said drop-offs when, shortly after his mother lit off for brownstone pastures, he and his sister would be locked in a closet for safekeeping.

And yet, given the astounding level of parental neglect, Mewes somehow managed to grow up to be a good, if somewhat offbeat, kid — the guy with the million-dollar heart (and, sometimes, a nickel fucking head). It was that combo that made me fall in hetero love with him seventeen years ago, though it was far from love at first sight.

Highlands, the town we're both from, isn't a sprawling metropolis by any stretch of the imagination. Classified as a borough, Highlands is primarily a sea-farming town, with clamming as its largest industry. Roughly one square mile in length, it was rumored that the town had once made the Guinness Book of World Records for having the most bars in the shortest distance. However, the decade-old addition of a ferry into the financial district of across-the-river Manhattan has since sent real estate in Highlands sky-rocketing to dizzying heights: my childhood home — a small, three bedroom ranch-style house in the once inexpensive downtown area, purchased in the late sixties for $14,000 and sold by my parents in 1998 for $90,000 — is again up for sale, this time with an asking price north of $300,000. The waterfront condos that've sprung up around town like coffee bars in the last ten years, start at easily over half a mil.

But back in the day, all men (and women) were not as equal, as the pre-ferry Highlands was distinctly separated into two classes: the more affluent uptown and the lower income downtown. The latter was the home to a young Smith and Mewes, separated by about two blocks. While I hadn't really known Mewes growing up, I'd known of him: locals referred to the boy as "That Mewes kid".

You'd hear stuff like "There's that Mewes kid. He broke the window at Beedles' Pharmacy." Or "There's that Mewes kid. I heard he fucked a dog once." Neither, of course, were true, but that was Mewes in the eighties: a sonic boom with dirt on it, often at the epicenter of any number of suburban legends.

I was formally introduced to Jason by my friends Walter Flanagan and Bryan Johnson, shortly after completing a year-long stint as a latch-key kid after school activity director (ie I oversaw many games of kickball, foosball and billiards from 3 p.m. to 6) at the Bob Wilson Memorial Recreation Center — a building named in memory of the town's greatest celebrity, the former mayor who moonlighted as a prop man in the movie biz while managing to pick up a few bit parts along the way (the cameraman on the soap opera in *Tootsie* who passes out when Dustin Hoffman finally reveals himself, live and on-air, to be a man? That was Bob Wilson). After I'd moved on from the Rec Center, Bry and Walt began regaling me with tales of Jason Mewes, who they'd started hanging out with, after weeks of digging on his Rec-related monkeyshines. On our way to Devils' games or mall trips, Bry and Walt would lavish the highest of praise on the absent Mewes with "Isn't he fucked up?"

It was only a matter of time, I knew, before he'd be incorporated into our group — a group that I'd only recently joined myself. On a Saturday trip to a NY comic book show, Bry and Walt sprung the young Mewes on me, insisting we bring the fellow comics enthusiast (who owned no comics) with us to the city.

"You're serious?" I asked, giving Mewes the once-over. "He's a kid. You want me to transport a minor over state lines in my car? No way."

Mewes, my junior by four years and Walt and Bry's junior by six, was still a high school student at this point — something my compatriots and I hadn't been in years. But that wasn't nearly as threatening to me as the addition of a fourth party into our merry band. I'd been hanging with Walt and Bry for roughly a year, so I was the new funny guy. I knew that bringing on a newer, funnier guy meant relegating my cachet to the backseat.

And the backseat was, indeed, where I'd wound up, as Bry trumped my refusal to let Mewes into my car by opting to drive his Firebird into the city instead, thus accommodating the minor a golden ticket into our clan. Worse still, Mewes had screamed "Shotgun!" thus usurping my hallowed front seat position. For the duration of the hour-long trek into mid-town Manhattan, I was forced to listen to my two friends cackling at Mewes's braying, as he punctuated every outlandish comment with "NEH!" — a post-script that essentially meant "I'm kidding." (Hence, the ass-kicking-inducing declaration "I fucked your mom last night!" was rendered benign, so long as it was quickly followed with the requisite "NEH!")

Beneath the guffaws of Bry and Walt, I could be heard muttering, arms crossed, "He ain't so funny."

Mewes became a constant fourth wheel in our triumvirate. If we went ice-skating, Mewes came along. If we went to the mall, Mewes was in tow. Late night trips to the Marina Diner? Mewes was not only there too, but always in need of a few bucks for fries. And through it all, I always regarded the kid as an interloper. My conversations were invariably directed at Bry and Walt, while Mewes listened in, ever sporting a puzzled look at the topic of conversation until he saw the opportunity to offer up some sort of outlandish what-if scenario that featured him fucking something or someone inappropriate nearby, topping it all off with a resounding "NEH!"

The truly noteworthy aspect of any of these hang sessions was the complete and total absence of booze or drugs. I'd fallen out with my former high school crew over the introduction of mandatory weekend keggers into our social agenda, distressed by the fact that hours of pre-star-69 crank calls had been replaced by obsessive quests to lay our hands on beers. Bry and Walt offered sober-living fun — not by virtue of any desire to lead clean, drug-free lives; simply because none of us were particularly fond of getting loaded. The addition of Mewes didn't change that at all, as a young Jason declared himself "straight-edge", which he defined as "no booze, no drugs, no chicks". We'd tried to explain to him many times that a straight-edge life wasn't defined by the absence of pussy, but a then-girl-shy Mewes opted to include it into his program anyway, to relieve himself of the pressure of trying to score. The vast amount of jerking off he'd engaged in on a daily basis, as related to me, Walt and Bry regularly and in vast detail, whether we wanted to hear about it or not, probably would've precluded any shot he might have had left over to offer potential girlfriends anyway.

But as Bry and Walt became less interested in Mewes and more interested in their respective chicks, the then-single me would often answer the doorbell at my house to find Mewes standing outside.

"What's up?" I'd ask.

"What're we doing today?" he'd anxiously inquire.

"Look, man — we're not friends," I'd tell him. "You're friends with my friends. We don't hang out together, you and I. We hang out as a group with Bry and Walt. Get it?"

"Right, right…" Mewes would respond, seeming to understand, then quickly add "So what're we doing today?"

It was in this fashion that I sort of reluctantly inherited Mewes. And while I had volumes in common with Bry and Walt, on the surface, Mewes and I were about as different as could possibly be. Without Bry and Walt around, I bristled at his what-if scenarios. I'd spend double or triple time in a conversation with the kid, as I'd have to define over fifty percent of the words I used for him. And all the while, I remained resistant to his charms.

Until that day at the Rec Center.

Walt and I had just come back from our weekly new comics run, and were quietly sitting in the Rec library, bagging and boarding our books. The kids hadn't gotten out of school yet, so it was deaf-child silent in the building, save the metal rantings of King Diamond emanating on low volume from a nearby boom-box. Then, suddenly, the stillness was shattered, as a sent-home-from-school-early Mewes kicked the Rec door open, marched into the building Groucho Marx style, and proceeded to fellate everything somewhat phallic in the room.

Walt and I watched with wonder as Mewes grabbed a pool cue and pretended to suck it off. Losing interest, he ran up to the phone on the front desk, grabbed the receiver from the cradle, and pretended to suck that off. He grabbed the flag pole and did the same. He grabbed a whiffle ball bat and did the same. This went on for twenty minutes, with seemingly no regard for our presence whatsoever. He never looked at us as if to say "Are you seeing this shit?" He never looked at us at all. He didn't seem to care that we were even there. This wasn't a show for our benefit. It was as if he'd been walking around Highlands moments earlier, took a gander at his watch, and was like "Wow — it's two o'clock. I'd better get down to the Rec and suck everything off." The kid had an agenda, and he was actively fulfilling it.

It was when he finally reached the Rec's only video game — a standard Asteroids kiosk that time had forgotten — that he finally paused. Studying it momentarily and finding nothing dick-like to pretend to suck off, he seemed stymied. There was no joystick to give him purchase; just a roller ball and a fire button. Walt and I watched with great curiosity, waiting to see how he'd overcome this unforeseen obstacle.

After what felt like five minutes, Mewes shrugged, bent down to the game controls, and started working the roller ball like it was a clit — his tongue darting in and out of his mouth, lapping at the orb as he spun it with his finger.

That's when I finally caved and fell completely in love with Jason Mewes. I thought "This kid's a comic genius. And if nothing else, he knows how to suck a dick. So if I ever get really bored hanging out with him, at least there's always that to fall back on."

From then on, Mewes and I became inseparable. We were a very unlikely pair, but we somehow found common ground. He became my adopted son of sorts, and I wound up being his biggest advocate in our little group, bringing him into our weekend street hockey games (for which I had to buy him roller blades) or taking him with us to the movies (for which I'd have to buy his tickets).

Bry, Walt and I made it our mission in life to get him laid, as Mewes — the most uninhibited, say-anything pottiest of potty mouths — would clam up around girls. At one party, we hooked him up with a chick who dragged him into the bathroom to make out, while we waited outside the door for news that he'd finally busted his cherry. Through the door, we heard stuff like "That's not it" and "Eww, gimme some toilet paper." Later, we'd learn he didn't make it into paradise before going off like a broken hydrant against her hip.

For years, Jason would crack me up with his weird observations and impromptu comedic sketches. Even though the dude never did the high school plays or showed any interest in theater or acting, I'd constantly commend him with "Someone should put you in a movie, man."

One day, I decided that I'd be that someone, when I finally left Highlands for a brief stint at the Vancouver Film School. I was gone for only six months before dropping out and heading back home, where I discovered the once-straight-edge Mewes, in my absence, had become a weekend warrior: booze, weed, and chicks were the order of the day for him, as he racked up bed-post notches that left my own in the dust. He'd changed somewhat, with the addition of blueberry schnapps and dime-bags, but was still very much the same loveable nut-bar regardless: the kind of guy who, after knowing you for five minutes, would say things like "It's warm in here, isn't it?" and then pull his cock out.

It was that Jason Mewes who I'd co-opted for the Jay character in *Clerks*, the script I'd written shortly after dropping out of film school. The role was written to Mewes's strengths, so much so that his complete inexperience in acting wouldn't be a hindrance. The part was peppered with his colloquialisms and catchphrases, written to Jason's intonations and verbal patois. And yet, after reading the script, Mewes first words were "I don't know if I can do this, man."

"Why not? It's just you on a page."

"Yeah, but why would I say something like 'Neh'?"

"I don't know. Why DO you say something like 'Neh'?"

"I do?"

I spent a month teaching Jay how to be Jay, during which time I accepted the fact that I'd never be able to pull off the role of Randal — the part I'd written for myself — and concentrated on finding something else for me to do in the flick, on camera. Since the part didn't require the memorization of any lines, I opted to slip into the role of Jay's quiet muscle, figuring Mewes and I would at least look visually interesting standing beside one another (him wiry and full of energy, me not). And together, dressed in costumes not at all unlike what we normally wore at the time, we became Jay and Silent Bob, the neighborhood drug dealers.

The great irony, of course, is that it'd be drugs that would one day not only threaten the continuation of Jay and Silent Bob, but also Jason's life.

Me and My Shadow, Pt. 2
Wednesday 29 March 2006 @ 3:54 p.m.

The great irony of the *Clerks* theatrical release is that very little attention was given to Jay and Silent Bob in the profile pieces or reviews. Aside from identifying me as the director who also played a small role in the film, the arrival of the two characters — characters I'd not only forever be most closely identified by, but who'd go on to feature prominently in all my subsequent flicks, right up to the who'd've-thunk-it lengths of the pair actually headlining their own movie seven years later — went largely unheralded. To wit, the only notice Jason Mewes received for his performance in *Clerks* while the flick was still in theaters came from a small review in *People* magazine, in which the author wrote "You want to find the rock he crawled out from under and make sure there's no more like him under it."

So when I opted to include the stoner duo in *Mallrats* a year later, it wasn't to capitalize on their insane popularity. For all we knew, there was none. Popping Jay and Silent Bob into *Rats* was simply a matter of sating my desire to put Jason on film again, and solely because he always made me laugh.

As far as the studio was concerned, however, I stood alone. The execs at Universal were dead set against giving Jason the part of Jay, so much so that they insisted we bring alternate Jay choices to the final round of casting sessions. When both Seth Green and Breckin Myer asked me why they were being considered for the part at all when Jason Mewes was so, as they put it, "genius" in *Clerks*, I told them I was as puzzled as they were. Here was a role that wouldn't have ever existed without Jason Mewes, and yet Jason Mewes was far from the frontrunner, inasmuch as the studio folks were concerned.

Still, Mewes worked his ass off throughout the auditioning process, and when I made the final, big push for him, Universal relented and said I could cast him with the following conditions:

1) Unlike the other cast members, he wouldn't be flown out to Minnesota on

the studio's dime.

2) Unlike the other cast members, he wouldn't be put up in his own hotel room during rehearsals. As a result, he would live in my room during his trial period.

3) Unlike the other cast members, he wouldn't be paid for the month-long rehearsal run in Minnesota.

4) If after his first day of shooting dailies were reviewed by the studio and deemed unworthy of the film (a film, mind you, called fucking *Mallrats*), Jason was to be shit-canned and immediately replaced with Seth Green.

Never having made a studio feature before, I assumed this was somewhat normal. Mercifully, so did Mewes.

In one of the few turn-of-events that I can ever truly define as poetic justice, the same suits who were so down on Jason's casting as Jay wound up being so over-the-top up with him after his first full week of dailies, that not only were they sending kudos back from LA, they also began building the marketing plan around his character and the catch-phrase "snootchie bootchies".

How Mewes arrived at "snootchie bootchies", a nonsensical utterance of which he is the sole author, is a fascinating study in linguistics. Whenever Mewes used to say something borderline insulting that might warrant an ass-kicking from the short-fused or the ill-tempered, he would immediately follow it with the exclamation "NEH!" as if to quickly editorialize the objectionable declaration in question and render it null and void. For example "I felched your mom's ass last night after I cocked her in the doody-hole" when punctuated with "NEH!" became less inflammatory to the recipient, because the "NEH!" communicated the caveat "I'm kidding. Don't hit me." But as with all living things, only evolution would insure its survival over time, and "Neh" soon gave way to "Nootch" as in "I felched your Mom's ass last night after I cocked her in the doody-hole. NOOTCH!" "Nootch" hung on as long as it could, until it gave way to "Snootch!" "Snootch" later birthed "Snootch to the nootch" which then begat "Snootchie nootchies", which in turn led to the now-legendary-in-some-circles *Mallrats* exclamatory "SNOOTCHIE BOOTCHIES!" There's nothing quite like watching language grow before your very eyes. An etymologist could have a field day with Mewesian slang.

And Mewes had a field day on *Mallrats*. He very quickly became the most beloved (and most frequently fucked) person on set. About four weeks in on the shoot, *Rolling Stone* magazine finally gave Jason long-overdue *Clerks* props in an article entitled 'Five Minute Oscars', in which the author listed the best performances in movies that year by people with the least amount of screen time.

Mewes's Jay was among the honorees, and in an expression of cast and crew pride, the piece was hung on the back of the office door for all to see.

It was only at the single best theatrical screening *Mallrats* would ever boast — the 1995 San Diego Comic-Con screening — that we learned how deep an impression Jay and Silent Bob had actually made in *Clerks*. A true art-house release, during the film's theatrical life it never played on much more than fifty screens at once, which meant reviews in high-brow, big city papers and some national magazines only. And since, with the exception of the aforementioned *People* blurb, none of those reviews ever singled out Jay and Silent Bob, not to mention the fact that the internet hadn't taken off as it would two years later, we all assumed that nobody gave two tin shits about the stoner duo.

However, our eyes were opened at that July screening in San Diego when, upon their first appearance on screen, the packed-house erupted in excited recognition so enthusiastically you would've thought Yoda had, instead, been standing in front of the pet store in the flick, in CGI form, shredding mother-fuckers with dual lightsabers. *Clerks*, by this point, had found its way to home video, and it was in video stores across America where the film had been finally discovered by its true audience: people not much different than the filmmakers themselves. And if this reaction was any indication, said audience LOVED Jay and Silent Bob.

The studio brass in attendance likened the flick's reception in Diego to the *Animal House* test screening of lore. Dollar signs danced in their eyes, and Mewes was heralded as the Next Big Thing.

However, nobody took into consideration that the flick about a comic book geek playing to an audience full of comic book geeks at the world's largest gathering of comic book geeks was perhaps a weighted exercise in self-selection, and hardly an indicator of how the movie would be embraced in the real world. When *Rats* was released a few months later, it opened to a paltry million and change on 800 screens. By the second weekend, it was out of theaters, damned to the video dustbin (where it, too, would find its eventual audience who'd, thankfully, turn it into a cult classic).

Mewes, meanwhile, had gone off to shoot a flick in Vancouver. Helmed by my friends Malcolm Ingram and Matt Gissing and entitled *Drawing Flies* the flick afforded Jason his first non-Jay role. It also afforded Jason his first taste of heroin courtesy of a girl whose name he doesn't remember, on a jungle gym in a park lit by the Canadian moon.

By this point, Mewes had become something of a partier, keeping a ceiling on his activities that amounted to merely booze and weed. Had I been more educated on the subject of drug addiction and the genetically predisposed, I would've known that these were merely gateway drugs: brief stops on the road to something more harsh. Jason's drug affinity wasn't a worry in those days; hell, it was regarded as kinda cute. While in mid-*Rats* production, a bunch of us got together to record the commentary track for the *Clerks* laser disc (which would eventually become the original *Clerks* DVD), and on it, Mewes can be heard getting progressively more drunk over the ninety minute duration of the film. This wasn't a big concern back then; he was just having a good time, I thought. Just because I'd never been a big fan of getting drunk or stoned didn't mean I had to poo-poo everyone else's parade. What, me worry?

Besides, the safeguard was in place already; the roadblock we all assumed would keep Jason from ever progressing to harder drugs. Mewes's mother, released from jail around early '95, was diagnosed as HIV positive — a lifetime of shared needles the presumed culprit. Seeing his mom drop unhealthy amounts of weight and suffer AIDS-related ailments was, at one point, enough to make Mewes swear off ever even trying heroin.

But alas, there was that park in Canada. And nobody ever caught AIDS because they SNORTED heroin, Mewes rationalized. As long as he never shot-up, he'd be okay.

By the tail-end of the *Rats* post-production, I'd gotten involved with the actress Joey Adams, and soon, I was spending much more time in Los Angeles than New Jersey. This meant much more time away from Mewes, which in turn meant much more time for Mewes to experiment further with drugs. The high was the lure, and the between-films downtime didn't help matters much either. Post-*Rats* and *Flies*, having squandered most of his movie money, Jason was forced to go back to work in non-performance roles. Some days, he was a roofer. Some nights, he delivered pizza. When, mid-delivery, someone would ask him "Weren't you in a movie?" even the level-headed, non-egocentric Mewes would succumb to slight bouts of depression. Movie-making is a rush that's sometimes followed by a hard come-down. On a set, an actor's catered to: dressed, fed, and waited on. When all that goes away, and you suddenly find yourself waiting on others (or at least dropping off their pizza and hoping for a two buck tip), even the least big-headed of actors can succumb to a "Where have all the good times gone?" case of the blues.

So snorting heroin led to snorting coke. And snorting coke led to smoking coke and a one-time dalliance with a crack pipe as well. And I did nothing about it. It was Jason's life, I figured. He was a big boy now, and he could handle himself.

"At least he'd never spike his veins," I'd say. "Because of his mom. Of that much, I'm sure."

The next time we worked together was on *Chasing Amy*. Mewes, at this point, was living with his mother in Keansburg. We'd still hang out when I was in town, and sometimes, he'd come out to LA. But for the two year period I was involved with Joey, our one-on-one time was pretty limited. *Amy* didn't change that, as the Jay and Silent Bob scene in the flick was shot over the course of one night at the Marina Diner in Belford. Mewes was on his game that evening, having memorized all of his dialogue, pulling it off without a hitch. As the night wore on, I'd get sluggish, but Mewes would never tire. Coke'll do that to you.

Amy came out and put View Askew back on the map in a big way, with stellar reviews and awards to boot. The success of the film paved the way for *Dogma*, a flick I'd written prior to *Clerks* but stuck in a drawer for when I had enough cash to pull it off. Thanks to the $12 million theatrical gross of the $250,000 *Amy*, we were given $10 million to make *Dogma*, a film in which Jay and Silent Bob figured more prominently than they ever had in any previous flick.

By this point, my relationship with Joey had ended, and I was back in Jersey full time, moving out of my post-*Clerks* condo and into a lush apartment on Broad Street in Red Bank. I started seeing Jason more and more, and together, we took a trip back out to LA to empty my stuff out of the apartment I shared with Joey, but primarily to convince *The X-Files* star Gillian Anderson to play the lead in *Dogma*. Harvey Weinstein, the chairman of Miramax, was co-sponsoring a charity fashion show to benefit AIDS, and he'd invited Scully to sit at his table. Our mission was to convince her that our angels-run-amuck picture was a worthy counterpart to the *Files*. So, in rented tuxes, Mewes and I spent the night wooing the little redhead, blissfully unaware that she'd later read the script and reportedly hate it.

Harvey gave us a lift back to the east coast on the Miramax jet. Over the course of the five hour and change flight, the three of us smoked (Harvey's jet was dubbed "the flying ash tray") and chit-chatted, with Harvey getting to know Jason better than he'd had time to in the past. When Jason uncharacteristically told Harvey he was really happy with his involvement in the AIDS benefit, due largely to the fact that his mother was HIV positive herself, the conversation got very serious, with Harvey insisting that he'd get Jason's mom to the best doctors in New York City. A promise he'd later make good on multiple times over.

"We're not gonna let your mother die," the chairman of Miramax told Mewes.

It was around this time that I'd taken over a local comic book store on Monmouth Street that was going out of business and turned it into Jay and Silent

Bob's Secret Stash. Mewes, a longtime comics enthusiast (Deadshot and Vigilante being his favorite characters), asked if he could work at the store full time. Charmed by this notion, I gave him the run of the joint.

Months in, when the shop would sometimes open two hours late, or I'd walk in to find a customer hanging out in front of the register, telling me "Jason said he'd be right back. He went to meet someone for a few minutes," it dawned on me that entrusting Mewes with this much responsibility maybe wasn't such a hot idea. More than that, it was a massive red flag that something was truly amiss.

When we recorded the *Chasing Amy* commentary track for the Criterion laser disc (which, later, became the DVD commentary track as well), Mewes was looking pretty bad. He was nodding out during the record so often, I said to Affleck "I think Mewes might be narcoleptic." Affleck, a bit more learned on the subject of drugs and addicts, offered "Bro, that ain't narcolepsy." The cut scene intros on the *Amy* DVD offer a portrait of Mewes that ain't pretty: thin, dirty, and barely conscious.

At this point, I sat Jason down and said "You're doing more than snorting heroin from time to time, aren't you?" After an hour of denial, Mewes finally copped to crossing the boundary he'd so long ago set for himself upon seeing how HIV-ravaged his mother had become: he was shooting up.

Almost immediately, I moved him out of his mother's house in Keansburg and into my Broad Street apartment, where I informed him he was gonna kick the brown, cold turkey. We looked into a methadone clinic in Asbury Park, but Mewes couldn't start until the following Monday, two days away. After one day of withdrawls, Mewes became so violently ill, he begged for cash for a fix of heroin that would hold him over 'til the next day, when he'd begin the meth program in earnest. He promised he'd get and stay clean, but he needed this last hit to keep him from succumbing to the DTs. Sweaty, convulsing, anxious and in tears, the boy pleading his case before me was a far cry from the offbeat soul I'd known for nearly a decade; he'd become a full-fledged junkie. Against all better judgment, I agreed to front him the money for the express purpose of scoring heroin, under the condition that he snort it, not shoot it.

One phone call and twenty minutes later, and I laid eyes, for the first time, on what would become the bane of my existence: heroin. As Mewes readied it for snorting on my living room table, he chuckled.

"What's so funny?" I asked.

"Nothing," he said. "It's just weird. I mean, I know this ain't right, and I'm glad you did this for me this one time, but."

"But what?"

"But it's like you just shook hands with the devil. For me. I think that's kinda cool. Not cool-cool, 'cause I know it ain't right. But, y'know: nice."

It was the only time I'd ever knowingly give Mewes money to buy any kind of drug. Even nine years later, he still refers to it as "That day you shook hands with the devil, Moves."

For the next five months, Jason and I became inseparable again, but this time around, I wasn't as much his friend as his babysitter. Granted, we'd have good times and enjoy one another's company; but not letting Mewes out of my sight became an every-waking-moment priority. The hours were organized around keeping Jay preoccupied and busy. Idle hands being the devil's workshop, constant activity was the order of the day and our days went something like this:

1) Get woken up by Mewes around 6 a.m., as he was fiending for his methadone fix.

2) Drive over to Asbury Park to hit the meth clinic, where Mewes would throw back a shot of methadone that, over the following months, would shrink in dosage, until he was off it completely.

3) Hit Dunkin Donuts for Mewes's favorite sugar fix, the "manager's special" (a glazed donut covered in icing and sprinkles).

4) Head to Toys 'R' Us and wait for the store to open, at which point we'd rush the *Star Wars* section to see if any 12 inch Greedo dolls were on the shelf (they were all the rage at that point; packed one-per-case, they were easy to re-sell at the Stash for a premium).

5) Head back to the apartment and shower.

6) Play video games.

7) Watch laser discs.

8) Head back out into the world to other toy stores to look for more 12 inch Greedo dolls.

9) Head to dinner, hit home and watch movies 'til it was time to go to sleep.

And so it went, for nearly half a year. Sometimes, we'd read the *Dogma* script, readying Mewes for his biggest role yet. Sometimes, we'd hang with Bry, Walt or Ed. When the local Toys 'R' Us started drying up for not just 12 inch Greedo dolls, but also 12 inch Hoth Luke on Tauntaun sets, Mewes, who'd replaced the addiction to heroin with the addiction to finding 12 inch *Star Wars* dolls for the Stash to re-sell, would suggest alternatives.

"Moves, we can try Toys 'R' Us's outside of Monmouth County."

"Like where?" I'd ask.

"I dunno. Ohio?"

We'd take long day trips, scouring the land for 12 inch Greedo dolls, bullshitting, laughing, talking about his attitude toward drugs that day. And slowly, as his meth dose lessened, the heroin-induced haze lifted, and the real Mewes began to emerge again.

The methadone clinic trips revealed quite a growing heroin problem in Monmouth County, as there was always a long line in front of the place when we pulled up every morning. Mewes would jump in line, and I'd sit in the car listening to Howard Stern. Invariably, someone in the line would look at Mewes, then look at me, then look back at Mewes wide-eyed, apparently thinking "Jesus, Jay and Silent Bob have a real problem, man." Stoners are cute; junkies are sad.

And I knew a thing or two about excess myself. By late '97, my weight had ballooned to 270 pounds. During this time, I too took to self-improvement, jumping onto an all-liquid diet program called Optifast, run out of the local hospital. Inspired by Mewes's commitment to wrestling the monkey off his back, I battle my demons as well, dropping down to 230 pounds. We were healthier, happier and one of us was hungrier for pussy.

Mewes accompanied me to a Duquesne college gig in Pittsburgh, where, post-Q&A, we hit a comic book store called Eide's. While I was looking for rarities and toys to bring back to the Stash, Mewes was chatting up a girl behind the counter named Stephanie. We were in the store a total of thirty minutes before Mewes pulled me aside.

"I like this girl, Moves."

"Uh-huh," I half-listened, as I flipped through a long-box full of comics.

"She wants to hang out with me. But I know I can't stay here by myself because of the drugs and shit. So I was thinking about asking her to come home with us."

This caught my attention. "What? You wanna ask that girl to come back to Jersey with us? Us two total strangers? Dude, she'll never say yes."

"She already did."

"You already ASKED her?! You said you were THINKING about asking her!"

"I WAS thinking about asking her. So I ASKED her. She invited me to her place, but I told her I can't stay here because I'm on a program. So she said she'd come home with us. So can she come home with us?"

He had me. He knew I wouldn't leave him alone in Pittsburgh, and he knew I needed a break from spending every waking hour with him as well. Stephanie, he and I both knew, would afford me that break.

So Stephanie punched out of work and took the six-hour trek back to Red Bank with us, staying at the apartment for a little over a week. During that time, I was able to go to the office, get some *Dogma* pre-pro and script revisions done, and concentrate on things that didn't have to do with keeping Mewes clean, all for the low, low price of letting a total stranger sleep in my apartment.

When, a month or so later, we settled on Pittsburgh as the location of the *Dogma* shoot, Mewes was ebullient. He'd taken a shine to Stephanie, so he suddenly couldn't wait to get started making the flick, mostly so he could hang out with the girl in her home town.

But the work had to come first. For months, I'd impressed upon him the importance of learning all of his lines in advance, as this time around, we were gonna have real actors in the flick.

"What, like Ben?" Mewes asked.

"I said REAL actors," I corrected. "Like Alan Rickman."

"Who's that?"

"The guy from *Die Hard.*"

"Bruce Willis?"

"No man, the other guy."

"The 'Yippie-kay-ay motherfucker' guy?"

"That's Alan Rickman."

"What's so special about him??"

"He's British. And Brits invented acting. So he won't put up with any of your 'Snootchie bootchies' bullshit. He'll tear you up if you're not excellent, because he's Alan fucking Rickman. So you've gotta know all your lines. We can't be asking people to leave the set because you're nervous, like we did on *Clerks*. This shit's serious — because Rickman will go ballistic if he smells blood in the water. You've gotta come correct."

So naturally, I was pretty nervous when Jason and I sat down for our first, Pittsburgh-based, one-on-one *Dogma* rehearsal, and the boy was scriptless.

"Where's your fucking script, asshole?" I sighed.

"I don't need it."

"You don't need your script for rehearsals. Right. Take mine and let's get going."

"I'm telling you, I don't need it. Go ahead. Try me."

So I turned to the first Jay and Silent Bob scene and fed him Bethany's lines, and without looking at my script, Mewes delivered Jay's lines in a letter-perfect fashion.

"Alright, so you've got the first scene down," I allowed. "Let's mix it up and try a scene from later in the flick."

So I fed him his lead-in lines from the church exterior scene, and Mewes spits out the Jay responses without hesitation.

"You memorized all your lines already?!" I demanded, shocked.

"Uh-huh."

"All of 'em?!"

"Yeah. Everyone else's, too."

"Yeah, right"

"Try me."

I read him Loki's lines from a Jayless scene, and amazingly, he responded with Bartleby's lines. I was dumbfounded, to say the least.

"You memorized ALL the lines in the script?!?!"

"Even the girl parts."

"What're you, fucking Rain Man?! Why'd you memorize the whole goddamn script?!"

"I don't wanna piss off that Rickman dude."

When Mewes wasn't rehearsing, he was spending every waking moment with Stephanie, either at her apartment or in our shared hotel suite: two rooms adjoining a common living room, so I could keep my eye on the recovering boy. Uberproducer Scott Mosier and I told Jason early on that, for insurance purposes, he'd be subject to random piss tests to scan his urine for traces of dope, as a way to keep him on his toes. Mewes obliged, so we felt we had the situation under control, but we wanted a little extra insurance.

"We've got money in the budget to give you an assistant," Scott informed me, three weeks before principal photography commenced.

"I don't need an assistant."

"That's what I figured. So I was thinking maybe we can hire Stephanie to be Mewes's assistant."

"What is she gonna assist him in, getting his cock in her mouth? That guy REALLY doesn't need an assistant."

"I know, but she might be useful in keeping an eye on him, y'know? Like, she could let us know if he's sniffing around for heroin or anything. Kinda like our spy on the payroll."

This was deemed a good idea, and we brought Stephanie into the office to explain the situation to her: Mewes was a recovering heroin addict, only seven months clean at this point, and we wanted to make sure he stayed clean. So we were opting to pay her three hundred bucks a week to be Jason's assistant as far as he was concerned, but really, she'd be reporting back to production, alerting us to any suspicious activity, letting us know if he was backsliding into the brown.

Stephanie agreed, partly because it meant she could quit her job at Eide's and be with Jason all the time, and partly, she said, because she cared about the boy and could see we cared about him too. The deal was struck, and Mosier and I felt like baby geniuses.

Little did I know that'd be the second time I'd shake hands with the devil, as Stephanie became Jay's Pittsburgh connection for heroin.

Me and My Shadow, Pt. 3
Thursday 30 March 2006 @ 5:57 p.m.

About three weeks into the *Dogma* shoot, we spent a day outside a shuttered Burger King that Ratface, our production designer, had outfitted to pass as Mooby's, a fictional fast food franchise with the unlikely corporate icon of a cow as its pitchman (the faux burger joint would pop up again in *Jay and Silent Bob Strike Back* and ultimately feature prominently in *Clerks II*). The scene saw Linda Fiorentino's Bethany, Jason Mewes's Jay and my Silent Bob quizzing Chris Rock's Rufus, the 13th Apostle who'd fallen from the sky moments before. The day will always be noteworthy to me for two reasons: 1) due to a gripe with production, Linda wasn't speaking to me that morning, making it an interesting challenge to my directorial responsibilities, and 2) because Mewes disrupted shooting in a most unique fashion.

We were shooting Rock's coverage, and since Silent Bob had no lines in the scene, it allowed me to ride the monitor instead of sit in for off-camera. In the midst of a take, Rock was detailing Rufus's outrage in being left out of the *Bible*, when all of a sudden, he started laughing, completely breaking character. I called cut and made my way to the table.

"What's up?"

"Check out Mewes," he chuckled.

I looked over at Jason to see him fast asleep, sitting up, in an almost bovine manner. One nudge or two later, and Mewes startled awake.

"Are we going again?" he asked.

"What're you doing?"

"What?"

"You feel asleep in the middle of the take, dude."

"Yeah, but not for the whole take."

"Dude — you FELL ASLEEP IN THE MIDDLE OF THE TAKE."

"But we ain't shooting me, we're shooting Rock."

"You still have to stay awake, man! Just 'cause the camera's not on you doesn't mean you can take a fucking nap!"

"Alright."

"What the fuck?!"

"What's the big deal?"

"You're supposed to be present in the scene for the other actors! Rock needs to act off of you! AND you've got dialogue to deliver, too! How the fuck can you just fall asleep in the middle of a take?!"

"It's the fourth fucking take, though."

"SO?!?"

"I can't help it. They just keep saying the same shit, over and over."

That sentiment became so instantly revered by the cast and crew that it wound up on the back of the production's wrap-gift t-shirt. With that simple and honest observation, the boy was able to succinctly express the unspoken overview of movie-makers the world over: filming any scene can get a bit repetitive. Whether you're making *Schindler's List* or *Weekend at Bernie's*, "they keep saying the same shit, over and over" is the thought that inevitably and eventually floats through the minds of casts and crews everywhere. The tedium of life on a movie set was completely nailed by Jason Mewes.

Years later, I'd learn that Mewes wasn't really bored; he was simply "catching a nod" — his preferred terminology for the heroin-induced state of euphoria afforded shortly after shooting up.

Had I been educated on the subject of heroin abuse, I'd have realized that Mewes had, indeed, started using again on the set of *Dogma*. After seven months of closely-watched sobriety, my responsibilities in governing the film's day-to-day production and my naïve belief that Mewes had, indeed, cleaned up forever, afforded Jason the ability to quietly shoot-up while keeping it on the down-low. Even though the boy was turning in a performance on that flick that was so beyond-belief great it once prompted Matty Damon to observe "Who'd have thought Jay would steal the entire fucking show out from under us?" he was doing so with the dirty brown coursing through his veins on a daily basis, and passing for sober.

His then-largest salary, combined with the additional influx of the three hundred bucks weekly we were paying Stephanie to keep an eye on him and report any suspicious activity back to us, kept the pair flush with "diesel". The withdrawls that would've alerted me weren't a factor, because the loot he was making and immediately spending kept him doped up and free from the DTs.

By the time we wrapped the flick, I'd fallen in love with the woman I'd eventually marry, Jennifer Schwalbach. Having met her shortly before production began while she was interviewing me for *USA Today*, our relationship was on such a fast track that, when I went back to Jersey, she moved out from LA and in with me. Mewes, too, moved Stephanie to Red Bank, post-wrap, so the four of us lived in that apartment on Broad Street, until a few months later, when Jen's pregnancy prompted the purchase of a house. Jen found a home for us in nearby Oceanport, the most prominent features of which were the indoor pool (rare in the Jersey burbs) and the flat roofs (which we'd later discover were designed by the house's builder, a later-jailed pedophile who had window-peeping on his daughters in mind when he was constructing the dwelling).

Mewes and Stephanie were spending so much time at Mewes's mom's apartment in Keansburg that he didn't ask to move into the Oceanport house. Instead, Bryan Johnson and his then-girlfriend took up residence in one of the five bedrooms.

It was at this point that Mewes asked me to co-sign on a red Ford Explorer for him. Feeling guilty for the lack of time I was spending with the boy (due to my new relationship and the vast amount of hours I spent in the editing room, cutting the flick), I obliged. The deal was that I'd take care of lease payments on the vehicle and he was responsible for the insurance. Beyond that, I'd only see Jay when he needed money — which was so frequent that it warranted me adding him to the View Askew payroll.

A glamorous side-effect of heroin abuse is a weakening of the teeth, apparently. Oblivious to this fact, as Mewes's teeth began falling out at an alarming rate, I assumed he was eating far too much sugar. His diet consisted of Hostess cupcakes and the artificially sweetened red drink sold in gallon form at most grocery stores that we referred to as "bug juice", topped off with a steady mouthful of Lemonheads. The most hardcore smoker I've ever known, Mewes could easily go through four packs a day — half of which wound up burning holes in his clothes when he'd nod out, mid-cigarette, and drop the burning cancer sticks on himself. Many times, he'd later report, he'd be woken up by the scent of burnt cotton, if he wasn't startled awake by a Marlboro burning down to the filter, singeing his fingers.

By Jen's second month of pregnancy, Mewes admitted he was in serious arrears on his truck insurance payments. This happened at the worse time imaginable: when Mewes nodded out at a traffic light and rolled into the car of an off-duty Middletown cop. The guy, who was very cool about the incident, asked only that Mewes pay for the damages to his car: some nine hundred bucks worth. Furious at his negligence (as a co-signer on the lease, I would've been liable had the officer wanted to sue), I told Mewes that I'd take care of the bill, but was confiscating the car for a month as punishment. When he surrendered the keys, I took a look at the odometer to mark the mileage, in case Mewes was hiding a second set and had thoughts of spiriting the car away while I spent my days editing *Dogma*. My eyes bugged when I saw Jason had somehow managed to put 20,000 miles on the car in less than three months.

"How the fuck did you manage that? I've had my Jeep for almost two years and I STILL haven't put that much mileage on it!" I barked. "And I've taken the fucking thing cross-country!"

After hours of interrogation, Mewes copped to slipping back into heroin usage. The many miles he put on the car were from constant trips up to Newark to score — five, sometimes six back-and-forth trips of over a hundred miles a day. He pulled up his sleeves to reveal a connect-the-dots worthy series of track marks, accompanied by bruises and burns. Immediately, we took the Explorer back to the leasing lot and abandoned it for the dealers to find, a note on the windshield that read "Can't pay anymore."

Since Stephanie had brought her car with her from Pittsburgh, the pair still had wheels to get around. But the word was out on Jason and his drug activities in Keansburg, and anytime he'd motor down the main drag in town, the fuzz would inevitably pull him over and search the vehicle. One such pullover came about as a result of the police spotting Mewes, his sister, and Stephanie driving around with a deployed airbag, following a minor traffic accident the week before. The subsequent search resulted in an arrest, when a needle kit was found in the car and a bag of dope was discovered in Jason's boot, under his foot. Frustrated and disgusted, I refused to bail him out of his first overnight stint in county. After Scott Mosier sprung the boy, I asked him how he could be so stupid as to not at least attempt to toss the junk once he saw a cop in his rearview.

"I needed to shoot up to keep from getting sick," he offered. "And plus, I'd spent forty bucks on it."

Action was, again, necessary, so I moved Jason and Stephanie into the Oceanport house. The pair took a room at the back of the second floor, and both were put on heavy-duty monitoring, with Stephanie only allowed to leave daily for her job at a health food joint in Red Bank.

This time around, I was mandating a cold-turkey kick, so the methadone route was not an option. On the second day, Mewes was in such bad shape and pain, he took to crying and screaming at me. When I refused to give him dope money, he bashed his head against a wall, drawing blood. I sent him to his room.

Due to her pregnancy, Jen decided to give up the job she'd taken in New York at MTV. As a sort of going-away gesture, she held a Christmas party at our house, inviting the friends she'd made at her city gig. While we prepped for the shindig the morning of the affair, Mewes slipped out of the house, disappearing for hours. He returned while the party was in full swing, briefly muttering hello to the guests and heading upstairs. I excused myself and followed him.

He wasn't in his room. Instead, he was in the upstairs hallway bathroom. Not hearing any noises emanating from the john, I silently stood outside, waiting for him to emerge. He knew I was there, and for an hour and change, we played a twisted game of chicken: him not coming out of the bathroom, and me waiting, stationed quietly outside, leaning against the wall. When he finally gave in and opened the door, he feigned surprise in seeing me.

"What's up?"

"What were you doing in there?" I demanded.

"I was taking a shit and reading comics."

"You weren't taking a shit for over an hour."

"I was reading comics too."

I studied his face.

"What were you doing in there all that time?"

Dead silence.

"What were you doing in the bathroom all that time?"

"I swear, Moves. I was taking a shit and reading comics."

I glared at him for long, silent minutes. He was clammy and making sporadic eye contact.

"What the fuck were you doing in the bathroom for an hour? Because you weren't taking a shit or reading comics."

"I was."

"You weren't. What the fuck were you doing in there?"

"I wasn't doing dope, I swear to God."

"I don't believe you. What were you doing in there?"

"I swear to God, I wasn't doing dope. I was taking a shit and reading comics."

"You're lying to me."

He didn't respond.

"I need you to tell me the truth."

"I'm telling you the truth."

"I'm gonna ask you one more time, and if you lie to me again, I'm throwing you out of this house. If you're honest with me, you can stay. What the fuck were you doing in the bathroom for an hour."

He stared at me. After a minute, he repeated "I was taking a shit and reading comics."

"I want you out of here. Now. I don't give a fuck where you go, but I want you out of here. Get out."

Bitterly, he grabbed some stuff and took off. By the time I returned to the party, it was over.

I'd later learn that he wasn't shooting up in the bathroom. Instead, he was smoking cocaine. The burned tin foil and straw were hidden under some towels in a drawer.

Stephanie came home an hour later, and when she asked where Jason was, I told her I'd kicked him out because he was doing drugs and lying about it to my face. The assumption was that he'd gone back to his mother's apartment, but rather than have Stephanie join him there and have them both backslide, I told her she was welcome to stay in the house without him, so long as she stayed clean.

Mewes called multiple times every hour for the next week, but still, I was steadfast in his suspension. Stephanie pleaded Jason's case and said he'd copped to smoking coke, but was remorseful about it and swore he wouldn't do any more drugs ever again. He desperately wanted to come back. Ultimately, I relented, issuing even more stringent rules than he'd been living under before his ejection.

Stephanie, meanwhile, was looking deathly thin. Already slight in frame, the once-pretty girl Mewes had met in that comic book store in Pittsburgh was now a pale shadow of her former self. She weighed well under a hundred pounds.

Her parents, farm folk from the western Pennsylvania/Ohio area, had called our house one day looking for her. They told me they hadn't spoken to her in months, and that any time they called Mewes's mom's apartment, nobody would answer. They'd somehow gotten my number and were puzzled as to why they couldn't track down their only daughter. I saw my window.

"I don't know how to break this to you, but Stephanie is a pretty bad drug addict," I confessed. The stunned silence on the other end of the line spoke volumes. "She and Jason just moved in with us here at the new house, and they say they're getting clean, but I don't believe either of them. She's sickly thin. I don't want to sound dramatic or scare you guys even more, but your daughter's gonna die if she doesn't make some drastic changes."

It was clear that Jason and Stephanie were, by now, a lethal combination, supporting and fueling one another's addiction, and the only way they'd ever get better would be to disappear from one another's lives completely. They'd never make this choice on their own, so in that phone call, Stephanie's parents, Jen and I made the decision for them.

An intervention of sorts was organized. Actually, it was more along the lines of a kidnapping. We gave her parents directions to our house, and arranged a time for them to show up, unannounced, on a day that Stephanie wasn't working. I'd taken Mewes into Red Bank and left him at the Secret Stash with Walter for a few hours, insisting he had to help Walt with new comics to make up for his coke-smoking hijinx in the bathroom. He was elated by the prospect of getting out of the house for the first time in days, so he kissed Stephanie goodbye, telling her he'd see her later.

Stephanie's parents arrived shortly after I got back to the house, and we quietly let them in and had them wait downstairs. I went to Jay and Stephanie's room and told her she had visitors. Stephanie's mom started crying at the sight of her, and Jen and I excused ourselves, heading outside to afford the family some alone time.

Stephanie packed and loaded her stuff into her parents' car, passing us on the way out. We apologized for the deception, but she said she understood, and asked us to tell Jason she loved him. Her parents, who'd apparently had their daughter late in life, thanked us and asked that we not allow any contact between Jason and Stephanie, should she try to call. With that, the girl drove out of our lives, in tears.

I picked up Jason from the store a few hours later, and on the ride back to the house, I broke the news to him that Stephanie's parents had come to get her and bring her home. Mewes assumed I was kidding, but when we got back to the house and he saw her stuff missing from the room, he realized it wasn't a joke. We sat in the backyard, smoking, putting it all into perspective.

"I get it," he said. "When I met her, she had her own apartment, her own car, a good job. And she left here with, what? One suitcase, maybe?"

"I think she had two suitcases."

"I ruined her life, huh?"

"I wouldn't go that far. She made her own choices. But you two WERE pretty toxic together," I observed.

"Yeah."

Mewes smoked quietly for a minute, and then chuckled.

"Remember that day back at the apartment, before you guys moved into this house? When you saw me laying on the floor outside of my bedroom, and you asked me what I was doing, and I was like 'Shhhhh'?"

"I do," I smiled. "That was weird."

"I was pretty doped up, and I was sure Stephanie was cheating on me."

"I don't think she ever cheated on you, dude."

"No, I thought she was cheating on me right THEN. I was watching her through the crack in the door because she was laying there with her eyes closed but her lips were moving."

I was a bit lost. "And?"

"And I thought she had some guy under the bed. I thought some guy had climbed through our window when I was in the bathroom, and she heard me coming, and hid him under the bed, and she was whispering to him, and that's why her mouth was moving. I thought she was pretending to be asleep. When you found me, I'd been watching her for two hours, waiting for a guy to come out from under the fucking bed."

"You realize that's insane, right?"

"It's pretty nuts, right?"

"It's beyond nuts. That fucking certifiable."

"I'm an asshole," Mewes laughed. Then, as a sober afterthought, he added "But I just loved her so much."

It was at this point that he started crying. I hugged him.

"You think if we both got clean, me and Steph could be together again? Like normal people?"

"Sure," I lied. Harsh truth wasn't needed at that moment.

"I swear to God I'm gonna clean up."

"You've gotta, man. It's really time."

Jason nodded. Then…

"But this is pretty hard to deal with right now, so I want to get some dope."

"I can't let you do that."

"I won't do it here. I'll do it at my mom's. Stay there tonight, then come back here tomorrow, and go cold turkey."

"I get how you're feeling, but I can't let you do that. If you leave now, I can't let you back in. You understand, right?"

Mewes nodded, smoked, then shrugged, as if to say "It was worth a shot." We went inside, ordered pizza, and watched a movie with my then-six months pregnant girlfriend. Even though Jen and I were sure we'd done the right thing, we still felt pretty guilty. Both of us were extra nice to Jason that night. The whole affair ranked as the most Mewes-induced heartbreaking day I'd ever known.

Until a week later, when I learned how he'd burned a dealer at my house.

Me and My Shadow, Pt. 4
Monday 3 April 2006 @ 11:47 a.m.

Sometimes, it's best to learn the details of a potentially dangerous situation only when it's well after the fact. If you're hanging off a cliff, you don't want the person pulling you up to say "Fuck, look at that drop below you! If you don't make it, you're gonna pancake against those rocks so hard, you might just atomize!" Only after you've gotten your two hands, feet and ass on terra firma do you ever really need to know how bad it was truly looking.

So naturally, when I learned the whole story of how Mewes had burned a dealer at my house months after it went down, I was filled with a mix of rage and relief.

It was a Tuesday, of that much I'm sure. Jen, still early on in her pregnancy, was out shopping, Stephanie had been at work in Red Bank, and Judy was cleaning the house. It was week two of the boy's move back into the Oceanport joint, after he'd been caught smoking coke in the upstairs hallway bathroom. I was spending a lot more time babysitting Mewes, keeping him preoccupied in an effort to distract him from the desire to shoot dope.

We were sitting around watching TV when I got the call from Mosier, who was asking that I come to the office and sign off on our *Dogma* picture lock before it got sent to Skywalker Sound for the pre-mix. Without Jen around to take over Mewes duty, I was between a rock and a hard place: the boy was still feeling like shit from withdrawls and didn't want to take the ten-minute ride to the office with me, knowing he'd then be stuck sitting around for two hours while I went through the flick.

"Besides," he observed. "*Columbo's* on."

Uncharacteristically, Mewes was (and still remains) a massive *Columbo* and *Murder, She Wrote* fan. Had we been a Nielsen family, A&E and USA would've displaced ABC and NBC as the nation's most watched networks, based solely on the amount of hours Mewes spent sacked out on the couch, engrossed in the crime dramas, desperate to solve the mysteries before the protagonists. Given his choice between porn and Cabot Cove, Mewes would forego double-penetrations for double indemnity plots.

With the boy enthralled by the cockeyed flatfoot in the trench coat, I came to the conclusion that it was okay to leave him by himself for a bit. He was flat broke, and I was secure in the knowledge that there was no other loot in the house with which he could make mischief in my absence. So I left him there to lay around and watch TV, pulling Judy aside on my way out to ask that she look in on Jay from time to time to make sure he was staying put. Without a car or cash, I figured there wasn't much trouble he could actually get into.

I was wrong.

No sooner had I pulled out of the driveway before Mewes was on the horn with a dealer in Keansburg, giving him directions to my house along with instructions to bring a bag of dope. The boy then tried to bum forty bucks off Judy, who — as a former alcoholic herself — knew not to give the kid more than enough cash to buy a pack of cigarettes. Three dollars in hand, Mewes put his half-assed Mission: Impossible into action.

The backyard of our Oceanport house was situated at the end of a cul de sac, and it was there that Mewes met his dealer, unlocking the gates in the wooden fence that still afforded an easy view of the flat-roofed house. Maintaining a faux study of the windows, he told the dealer that they had to make the exchange quickly, as "Kevin's watching me from the house." The dealer didn't know I wasn't home, but since the customer was always right, he palmed the bag of dope and extended it out of the driver's side window of the car toward Jason. Instead of doing the same with the money and shaking hands to make the dope swap, Mewes tossed the crumpled three dollar bills across the dealer into the passenger seat, snatching the dope from the man's hand in the process. He then dashed into the backyard, quickly locked the gate, and ran into the house.

It didn't take Columbo to deduce that three crumpled dollar bills was thirty seven crumpled dollar bills shy of the true purchase price, nor did it take a keen, Jessica Fletcher-like power of observation for the dealer to figure out which house Mewes had run inside. Pulling around to the front door, he rang the bell. Mewes told the oblivious Judy to inform whoever was there that he wasn't home. Judy maintained the party line, even when the dealer said "But I saw him run into this house a minute ago. I KNOW he's here." Unwilling to cause a ruckus over thirty seven bucks, the dealer let his longtime customer off the hook with a warning of "Tell him he owes me double now."

Blissfully unaware of all this, I wound up giving Mewes the boot from my house again anyway, shortly after Stephanie's departure. He'd backslid and been caught, at which point I sent him packing back to his mom's, where his drug abuse took on a new facet: Oxycontin dependency.

Mewes's mom, ravaged by HIV, was regularly prescribed the morphine replacement that provided the same numbing pain-relief minus the eventual tolerance build-up. One could become inured to the effect of morphine over time, necessitating larger doses to kill discomfort, but Oxycontin didn't come with these same strings attached. Apparently, the same dosage that relieved pain one week into usage would do the trick one year in, regardless of user-frequency. Mewes's mother started sharing her pills with her son when he was penniless and unable to purchase heroin. Since he wasn't spiking up to get high anymore, I mistakenly viewed this as a step toward recovery for the boy, and invited him to accompany us to Cannes that May for the world première of *Dogma*.

Jason pointed out that he'd never been abroad before, so he was anxious to make the trip. In reality, he was anxious to get his hands on the copious amounts of readily available heroin he assumed was waiting for him in France, after having seen the film *Killing Zoe*. Filled with expectation and worried he might be caught holding and wind up in a foreign jail (*à la Midnight Express*), he opted against bringing Oxys or heroin with him on the plane.

By the time we landed in the South of France, Mewes was going through some pretty heavy withdrawals, throwing up more than once in the forward-cabin bathroom on the plane. When we arrived at the hotel, he immediately took off on a desperate hunt for brownstone. What he discovered rather quickly was that film — particularly movies about bank robbers — doesn't always offer accurate depictions of the real world: the streets of Cannes weren't teeming with the junk *Killing Zoe* promised. Unable to score, he hit a local pharmacy, where he discovered that Codeine — a prescription drug in the US that's derived from morphine — was sold in over-the-counter forms in Europe. He bought a one liter bottle of liquid Codeine and a twenty-four pack of Codeine tablets, taking half of the twenty-four pills and washing them down with the full bottle of the narcotic, hoping for an effect approximate to the high his Oxys and heroin afforded.

What would probably stop the heart of a normal person had zero impact on Jason. His tolerance level was so built up after years of drug abuse, that all the Codeine ingestion gave him was a sour stomach. Returning to the hotel from doing press, Scott and I found a French doctor standing in Mewes's room, demanding payment. Mewes had called the concierge and told them he'd fallen, hoping to be prescribed Oxycontin. The doctor refused both to fill the 'scrip and to leave until he'd been paid for his emergency house call. As I peeled off some francs to pay the man, the English-limited physician tapped his fingers to his forearm, nodded at my friend, curled up on the couch and sweating heavily, and barked "Le junkie! Le junkie!"

Our five-day stay at the fest was successful as far as the film was concerned, but tumultuous thanks to Mewes. Unwilling to do press or attend the actual Palais screening of the flick (the legendary red carpet walk up to the grand, main theater of the film festival), Jason begged and pleaded to be sent back to the States. But since it would've cost an additional grand or more to change his already expensive airline ticket, Scott and I declined.

By the time we did fly home as a group, Mewes was belligerently detoxing, unwilling to speak to anybody, convulsing with "the shakes". As the Cannes-to-London flight was touching down, Mewes did something that would get him shot by a Federal Air Marshal in the post-9/11 climate of today: he got up and started stalking the aisles of the plane, opening up all the overhead bins, searching for a blanket. Mere feet from the wheels hitting the tarmac, the British flight attendants screamed at Jason to sit from their buckled-in positions at the front of the craft.

"SIR! TAKE YOUR SEAT NOW!"

"I'm cold and I need a blanket," Mewes yelled back.

"SIR, IF YOU DON'T TAKE YOUR SEAT IMMEDIATELY, YOU'LL BE PLACED UNDER ARREST AT THE GATE!"

"FUCK YOUSE!" Jason shouted, punching overhead compartments on the way back to his seat, where he hurled himself into his chair, adding, for good measure "ARE YOU HAPPY, YOU LIMEY FUCKS?!"

Keeping the boy away from his mother, his source for Oxycontin tablets, became a priority. Once again, I moved him back into the Oceanport house. Once again, we tried to quit cold turkey. After a month, Mewes was still in pain, but managing to stay clean, so long as he was watched.

In June, I had to fly out to Los Angeles for an appearance on the MTV Movie Awards, where I was to present with Ben Affleck. Not wanting to leave the boy behind, Jen and I took him with us. We stayed at the Sofitel on Beverly, across from the Beverly Center Mall.

The awards show presentation went off without a hitch; the same can't be said for the rest of the LA trip.

Around 1 a.m. four nights into the trip, Mewes rang our room, waking me up.

"Moves — I just took a cab back from some party and I don't have any cash to pay the driver. Do you have twenty bucks?"

"I don't have any cash on me."

"What do I do about the cabbie?"

"Just... come up to my room and I'll give you my ATM card. Take out forty bucks, pay the driver, and keep the other twenty."

When he knocked softly at the hotel room door, I passed the ATM card out to Jason and said "Just slip this under the door when you're done with it. I'm going back to sleep."

"Alright. Thanks, Moves."

The next morning, the ATM card wasn't where I asked him to leave it. I called Mewes's room but got no answer. I called down to the valet parkers to have the rental car brought up, but was told that the car had been taken out already. This is when I started putting two and two together and quickly phoned the twenty-four hour hotline for my bank.

"Yeah, I've lost my ATM card," I offered. "Can you tell me the last time it was used?"

After a minute of tapping keys, the customer service agent said "About twenty minutes ago. A hundred dollars was withdrawn. When was the last time you had the card in your possession, sir?"

"Around 1 a.m. Pacific."

"I'm showing ten withdrawls since then."

"Totaling about how much?"

"Looks like eleven hundred dollars."

After putting a freeze on the account (and lamenting to Jen about how I'd never been able to withdraw more than four hundred bucks a day off my ATM card while Jason was somehow able to siphon over double that in the span of ten hours), I got on the horn with Mosier and filled him in on the situation. The valet parkers called to let us know the car had been returned, and Mos and I went banging on Jason's door. He wouldn't answer, so we called the front desk and told them our friend had locked himself in his room and we feared he might have overdosed. Hotel security opened Jason's door, where we discovered a room in total upheaval: furniture tossed, curtains torn down, burnt sheets and comforters stripped from the askew mattress. Jason was curled up in a ball on the floor, staring at the ceiling. After confirming he was still breathing, we ushered the security guy out. Mewes admitted to the theft and detailed his eventful previous ten hours.

He'd taken the money and the rental car and tried to score junk around town. Unsuccessful, he'd come back to the hotel and phoned the emergency room at Cedars-Sinai, the hospital a block down the street, and told him he'd thrown his back out in a fall off his bed. An ambulance had picked him up and brought him to the hospital where the doctors could find nothing wrong with him. He insisted that he'd aggravated an existing back condition, and the only medication that would help was Oxycontin. The doctors denied his request for the heavy narcotic, instead writing him a prescription for the weaker Vicodin — a drug that, along with Percocet, Mewes had outgrown years prior, building up an enormous tolerance level against them. He'd then taken the rental car anew and hit a bunch of pharmacies that refused to fill his prescription without proper credentials. Defeated, he'd returned to the hotel and trashed his room.

For years, I'd been urging Mewes to check himself into a rehab program I said I'd gladly pay for. For years, Mewes had declined, insisting he didn't think he could handle being in a place he wasn't allowed to leave, kicking amongst strangers. At this point, I finally had him over a barrel, in a position where rehab was no longer a choice.

"You're going to rehab today, or you're going to jail for theft," I told him. "It's that simple. You stole enough for me to prosecute you, and that's what I'm gonna do unless you enter a program by tonight."

He laid there for a beat, staring at the floor, until he finally said "Okay."

Scott and I researched some LA rehabs online and found one called Anna Cappa Steps, a few hours outside of the city. I called them to see if we could admit Jason that day, and they obliged us. We drove Mewes out to the clinic and checked him in, at which point I gave the people in charge my numbers and told them to contact me if there were any problems. Before we left, I sat down with Mewes.

"This is the best thing you can possibly do for yourself."

"Can't I just go home with you and kick at the house in Jersey? I swear, I'll do it for good this time."

"I don't believe you anymore. You go through this program and get clean and I can start believing you again. You've gotta do this now."

He was tearing up. "Alright, Moves," he said. "I understand."

The next day, Scott and I went into an LA studio with Jeff and Brian to record some voiceover for the *Clerks* cartoon we'd sold to ABC. Mid-session, my cell phone rang.

"This is Steps. You're the contact for Jason Mewes?"

"I am. What happened?"

"Jason's having a hard time with the program and wants to sign himself out."

"It's only been A DAY."

"A LONG day, Mr Smith — during which Jason's screamed at his nurses and been a disruptive force in the program. People are trying to change their lives here; they don't need this kind of distraction."

"He's one of those people that needs to change his life too, ma'am," I said. "Once he gets used to the program, he'll be better, I promise. But, please — don't kick him out."

"This is a voluntary program, Mr Smith. We're not kicking him out; he's kicking himself out. And right now, we're inclined to accommodate him."

"Can I speak with Jason, please?"

I was put on hold. The next voice I heard was the boy's saying "I can't take this place, Moves! Lemme go back to Jersey and kick in the house! All these people are assholes and they're treating me..." He pulled the phone away from his mouth and yelled out into the room "THEY'RE TREATING ME LIKE A FUCK-ING BABY!!!"

"You're acting like a fucking baby, Mewes. So show a little spine and quit crying."

"I wanna leave!"

"You can check yourself out if that's what you want. But if you do that, I'm having you arrested for theft."

"FUCK!!!"

"You can do this, man. The first few days are always the hardest, but once you get past that, these people can really help you."

He took a calmer approach. "I'd rather have you help me."

"I've taken you as far as I can. Nothing I do works. Nothing I do has ever worked. You need professional help."

After a long beat of silence... "Alright, Moves."

"You can do this."

"Okay."

I hung up. After half an hour, I called back and asked to speak to the program director who'd called me earlier.

"How's he doing?"

"Much better now. He apologized to the nurses and he's cooperating. He says he's serious about getting off drugs."

Relieved, I went back into the recording studio. Twenty minutes later, my cell phone rang.

"Jason's escaped."

Me and My Shadow, Pt. 5
Tuesday 4 April 2006 @ 4:16 p.m.

I stood in the lobby of the sound studio where we were recording voice tracks for the *Clerks* cartoon, phone to my ear, stunned.

"What?!" I demanded.

"Jason's escaped," repeated the program director of the rehab clinic nearly two hours outside of LA where we'd checked Mewes in only the day before. "He asked if he could step outside for a cigarette, at which point he fled the grounds. He won't get far though, because he doesn't have any shoes. We expect to recapture him soon."

Visions of Mewes running through fields, pursued by rehab workers on horseback, a net scooping him up *à la Planet of the Apes*, raced through my head.

When Jay was brought back to Steps, he was placed in a building across the street from the rehab proper. The decision from the top brass was that he could remain in the program, but he wasn't allowed to mingle with the patients in the main building. Instead, he was placed in lockdown in what was tantamount to a psychiatric ward. For one week, he wasn't allowed to take calls.

I'd stayed in Los Angeles to work on the *Clerks* cartoon for a bit after the MTV Movie Awards, but was planning to head back east soon, as Jen was almost ready to deliver Harley, and I wanted my kid born in Jersey, not California. Three days before we left, I was finally able to speak to Mewes.

I'd called the psych ward's main number, and they gave me the digits for a payphone on the unit's floor.

"Hewhoaw?" said the voice on the other end, sounding vaguely like an old, retarded woman.

"Hello. Yes, can I speak with Jason Mewes please?"

"Who's that?"

"He's a patient there. Long hair. Kinda young."

Apropos of nothing, the voice asked "Do you like my glasses?"

"Excuse me?"

"Hold on," the voice said. Then, I heard the voice call out into the room in an almost sing-songy patois "Dum-Dum..."

There was a momentary scuffle until I heard a familiar voice barking "Gimme that!" Then, Mewes snapped into the phone "Fucking Dum-Dum! Do you hear that, Moves? This guy's calling me Dum-Dum! You've gotta get me out of here!"

"That was a guy?" I asked.

"Do you like my glasses?" the apparently male patient said to Mewes.

"I ALREADY TOLD YOU I LIKED 'em TEN TIMES! NOW FUCK OFF!" He followed it with a sotto "Jesus."

"How's it going in there," I inquired, already pretty sure of the impending response.

"I'm in the fucking nut-house, Moves! You gotta get 'em to take me back across the street!"

"They said they're unwilling to have you back there, Jay. You're to do the rest of the program from where you are."

"In a fucking insane asylum?!"

"You wouldn't be in an insane asylum if you hadn't made a run for it. You wouldn't be in rehab at all if you didn't start doing dope."

"I know, but this is crazy. This fucking PLACE is crazy. That glasses guy? He told me he's my mother. And if he asks me one more time..."

And, as if on cue, the patient piped in again from what sounded like a few feet away "Do you like my glasses?"

"GET AWAY FROM ME!" Mewes yelled.

"You get away from me!" the guy yelled back, then called out in the sing-songy tones "Dum-Dum!"

"Moves, I'm not gonna make it in here. I'll go to another rehab — any other rehab. But I can't stay in here. All these people are insane. I'm not insane. I've got a drug problem, yeah — but I ain't nuts."

The boy had a point. We made arrangements to have him moved to another rehab, this time a place called Cry Help in Los Angeles. Once he was securely in the new program, Jen, Scott and I flew back to Jersey on the Miramax private jet Harvey had sent for us, as Jen — waaaay pregnant and set to pop at any moment — wasn't permitted to fly commercially that close to term.

Harley was born in Red Bank at Riverview, the same hospital where my mother had given birth to me twenty-nine years prior. All of my friends and family came to see the baby that first week; all of my friends and family except the rehab-riding Mewes.

A month and change after Harley was born, Jen, the newborn and I were back on a plane out to Los Angeles to do more work on the *Clerks* cartoon, just in time for Mewes's discharge from Cry Help. I swung by the clinic to pick him up and almost wept after seeing how good he looked and hearing how great he sounded. We got him a hotel room at the Nico, a few doors down from ours, and stuck around LA for two more weeks, recording all Mewes's voiceover for the first four episodes of the cartoon, before collectively heading back to Jersey.

It was a sheer delight to be around Jason at this point. He was crisp and clear in a way he hadn't been since pre-*Dogma*. But with this newfound clarity came candor: as part of his Twelve Steps, he started confessing a litany of prior bad acts and sordid activity that I hadn't been aware of. While it was refreshing to listen to the truth coming out of Jason for a change, one of his mea-culpas proved unnerving.

The dealer Mewes had burned at my backyard gate — the one who had simply left with a warning that day? Had he known his Mewes-related troubles weren't about to stop with being owed thirty seven bucks, he might've instead forced entry into the house and taken the boy out altogether. As part of a plea bargain with the Keansburg police that stemmed from the possession charges resulting from the deployed airbag-induced pull-over, Mewes had to turn in his dealer. After ducking the sting operation as long as he could, Stephanie and Mewes were involved in a set-up and arrest that saw the guy ultimately incarcerated.

All of this was done on the down-low, while Jay and Stephanie were both still residents at my house. In retrospect, Stephanie hadn't put up any fight to stick around when her parents showed up to get her that day. I'd always assumed it was because she saw an opportunity to turn her life around. Suddenly, I realized it might've been a self-preservatory move of a different color altogether — because once the dealer they set up got out of jail, he might be looking for a little payback. And if that was the case, he'd probably go looking for Mewes and Stephanie at their last known address.

My house in Oceanport.

But even though Mewes assured me the guy worked alone and wasn't getting out for at least two years, that was the moment I decided I should probably move my family elsewhere.

But the relocation would have to wait, because the *Dogma* première was fast approaching. The film had its domestic début at the prestigious New York Film Festival, where a thousand protesters showed up, shaking Bible-quoting placards at us. The Catholic League-led campaign against the flick had slow-boiled into a 300,000-strong hate mail endeavor, the three legitimate death threats of which resulted in all View Askew mail and packages being opened by bomb squad professionals for four months.

With all the stress we were under, it was nice to know Mewes — thanks to his newfound sobriety — wasn't responsible for any of it. Living with us back in Oceanport, Jason had become a model citizen, just saying "No". He'd visit his mother regularly, steering clear of her readily available Oxys. His one request in months was that Stephanie be allowed to attend the NY Film Fest unveiling of *Dogma*. He hadn't seen his ex since Steph's hasty departure from our lives, and now that they were both clean, he was anxious to spend time with her. After making him promise that drugs wouldn't factor into the visit, I conceded.

Stephanie took a train and joined us in NYC. The one-time Terror Twins rode in the limo with Jen, Harley and I to the Lincoln Center screening of the flick. At the theater, Jason was in attendance for the intro of the film, along with Salma Hayek, Chris Rock, Ben Affleck, Matt Damon, Alan Rickman, composer Howard Shore, Mos and me. When the intro was over, the boy asked if he could head back to the hotel with Stephanie for a little private time. Not wanting to be a cock-blocker, I allowed it, providing he get back to Lincoln Center by the end of the movie.

While the film screened, Jen told me she couldn't be one hundred percent sure, but she feared she saw a needle kit inside Stephanie's jacket while we were in the limo together. I couldn't leave the theater, shoot over to the hotel to check on the pair and hope to be back in time for the Q&A panel that would follow. Instead, I said I'd confront Jason about it when he returned for the post-screening panel.

Had Jay returned to the theater, he would've been able to bask in the glow of the upscale audience's *Dogma*-driven adoration of Jay. Had he shown up at the after-party, he would've been showered with praise by Harvey Weinstein. Instead, all night I fielded "Where's Jay?" queries.

It wasn't 'til the following morning that I'd learn the details of his absence: Stephanie and he had gone back to the Four Seasons on 57th, where they shot up, getting so loaded they forgot to fuck before she had to get on a train back to Ohio the next morning. Rather than spend the night romantically, they opted to spend it narcotically. And with that, Mewes had fallen off the wagon. He'd managed to stay clean a mere four months.

Excuses were made along the lines of "It was just this one time, and I know it was stupid, because I shot up instead of getting down with her." Still, I booted the boy from the house anew, with Jason insisting he was staying sober from then on in.

The next time I saw him was at Harley's christening, the weekend *Dogma* was released theatrically. He didn't stick around at the party very long, and it was clear that his mind was elsewhere.

Shortly after the holidays, Jen, Scott and I moved out to Los Angeles for three months, to work on the cartoon. When we finally returned to Jersey, we needed to record two more episodes' worth of voiceover with Jay. The difference in his voice was noticeable when he showed up in that Manhattan recording studio, but his appearance was even more telling. He looked like a junkie again.

Still, it wasn't all bad for Jason. He'd been dating a girl named Jamie for some time, and one night, he decided to propose to her. He told me about it the day after he'd gotten engaged.

"I proposed to Jamie last night," he said.

"Get outa here!"

"It's true. I put the ring in my fish tank, and when she came into my room, I told her to check out the new fish I bought. She found the ring, and I got down on one knee and asked her to marry me."

"Classy, dude. I wish I could've seen that."

"You can. I videotaped the whole thing."

"Really?"

"Yeah — I hid a camera so that I could get it all on tape."

"I'd like to see that tape," I said.

After a long beat, he added "I made another tape, too."

I knew where this was going before he elaborated. Mewes gave me both his proposal tape and his celebratory fuck tape to watch and critique. Suffice it to say, the proposal tape was easier to watch, as the fuck tape featured an Oxycontin-numbed Mewes engaged in sadly lackadaisical sex. What should've been a hot viewing turned out to be just another reminder of how far from the land of the living the boy truly was.

The *Clerks* cartoon had a short life on ABC, canceled after only two airings. By that time, I was working on a script for *Clerks II*, but started thinking, instead, of making the all-Jay and Silent Bob flick the fan-base had been requesting for years. The reasons for this change of direction were two-fold: 1) after dealing with the scandal of *Dogma*, I thought it'd be nice to make a movie where death threats wouldn't be a factor; and 2) a Jay and Silent Bob-centric flick was my best chance of getting Jason clean again.

I told the boy about my plan, and he got excited. I told him he'd make more money this time around than he had on all the previous films combined, and he got even more excited. I told him the only way any of this would come to pass would be if he got clean, and the excitement dwindled. Resigned to his fate, he agreed to clean up, and back into my house he moved.

Jason had, at this point, lost a bunch of teeth, thanks to heroin abuse. There were unconfirmed reports that Mewes had gone into the dentist and had repairable teeth removed, solely so he could get an Oxycontin prescription. The end result was a mouth that more closely resembled that of an eighty year old than someone in his mid-twenties. A trip to the oral surgeon was in order.

The doctor said roughly thirty thousand dollars' worth of dental work was needed to fix Jason's mouth and fit him with false teeth. We started the month-long process of root canals and drilling with me pulling aside the dentist and asking what type of pain reliever he'd be prescribing.

"The kid's asking me for Oxycontin," the doctor said. "He's got a pretty bad addiction."

"Yeah, we're working on that now," I confessed.

"Point is, I don't know what I can prescribe for him that would even approach the dosage his body's used to now. He's doing twelve hundred milligrams a day."

"Is that a lot?"

"Let's put it this way: if you took four hundred right now, it'd probably stop your heart cold."

"He's built up quite a bit of tolerance, huh?"

"It's amazing he's not dead."

"He comes from sturdy stock."

That stock he came from had been steadily supplying her son with a diet of Oxys that the boy would have to be weaned from. Worse still, Mewes wasn't taking the pills orally: he'd crack open the time-released coating and chop up the narcotic inside, snorting it to get it into his system as quickly as possible. The doctor suggested a slow reduction, dropping Jay a hundred milligrams a week until he was off the drug completely.

I took charge of the pills and began doling them out every morning. Invariably, a soft knock would come at the door around 6 a.m., with the boy asking "I know it's early, but can I get my medicine now?" After nearly two months, we'd only gotten down to four hundred milligrams a day, and even at that dosage, Jason was complaining that he was getting the shakes.

Our program was interrupted when Mewes got a job on another flick in advance of *Jay and Silent Bob Strike Back*. Entitled *R.S.V.P.*, it was to shoot in Vegas, and Jamie — the boy's fiancée — agreed to accompany him for that shoot, promising to take over the dosage-lowering program in my absence. The pair left Jersey a few weeks after Mewes's final dental visit, at which point he had a mouth full of teeth again.

Jen and I packed up the family (Harley, naturally, as well as Jen's parents Byron and Gail) and headed out to Los Angeles. We set up house in Toluca Lake months in advance of principal photography on *Strike Back*. The rental property came with a back house that was designated as Mewes's once he was done with *R.S.V.P.*

The reports out of Vegas were not inspiring. Jamie said Mewes hadn't diminished his dosage, but instead increased it, hovering somewhere around a thousand milligrams of Oxys a day. I told the boy that, once he got to Los Angeles, we'd be sticking him in a rehab. Jason agreed, so long as it was a week-long program: the kind in which the patient is heavily medicated as they detox from their drug dependency. The notion of kicking drugs with different drugs seemed backwards to me, but if I'd learned anything over the last three years it was that I didn't know shit about drug dependency.

I found a program in Beverly Hills that Jason agreed to enter. Based in Cedars-Sinai Hospital, it was a ten-day detox-only regimen, after which drug counseling was stressed. Mewes wasn't interested in meetings as much as he was looking for a painless way to get narcotics out of his system.

The sad truth, by this point, was that Jason was no longer doing drugs to get high. He'd long-since passed the point of ingesting heroin or Oxys for pleasure. By then, he needed the steady diet of narcotics solely "to feel normal", as he would say. When the body builds up the kind of tolerance level Jason's had, you don't fiend for anything else beyond NOT detoxing. It's no longer about feeling good as much as it's about not feeling bad.

When we admitted Jason into the program upon his arrival in LA, he'd discover what "bad" really meant.

Me and My Shadow, Pt. 6
Wednesday 5 April 2006 @ 9:53 p.m.

Rather than admit himself into a normal rehab program, where the initial withdraw from drug dependency is immediately followed by counseling and a maintenance program on the facility's grounds, Mewes had opted to check into a detox program — a ten-day, one-shot affair in which the patient is weaned off his or her particular poison while being medicated with an alternative painkiller meant to relieve the physical trial of kicking, and then released back into the wild. The detox program Mewes entered was located in Cedars-Sinai Hospital. After four days, we were allowed to visit the boy.

While not quite a psychiatric ward, Mewes found himself sharing space with a crew of offbeat, broken and botched individuals that called to mind the cast of *One Flew Over the Cuckoo's Nest*.

"I am Jesus," moaned the man to Mewes's right, on the sun porch where patients and visitors were permitted to smoke. "I am Buddha. I am Satan and Elijah."

Dressed in a hospital gown and a cowboy hat, the man barely opened his eyes. He was talking to no one; at least, no one we could see.

Jen, Malcolm Ingram, Jamie and I eyeballed the clearly troubled contemporary of Mewes, as Jason himself sat in front of us, heavily medicated and barely awake. The cowboy continued.

"Jesus was not born on December 25th, as most Christians believe, but was instead born on October 31st, also known as All Hollow's Eve."

"He says that all day long," Jason sleepily sputtered.

"At least you're learning something while you're in here," I shrugged.

Mewes cracked a half smile. "Is it check out time already, because I'd like to go home now."

"You've got six more days, bro. Then you're out."

Jason nodded, as if doing so took every ounce of energy he could muster. "This really sucks."

"How're you feeling about Oxys now?"

"To be honest?" Mewes began. "If I had a warehouse full of Oxys somewhere, one that would never go empty? I'd never get off drugs."

It was a troubling sentiment, and one I took with me when we eventually left the boy there, surrounded by those with questionable sanity. Clearly, this program wasn't going to "take". This latest round of sobriety was merely a means to an end: getting clean for *Jay and Silent Bob Strike Back*. I could already tell that, once shooting was over, the boy would either meander or rush back to drugs.

The day Jason was released, Malcolm was hired to babysit him while I attended to the duties of pre-production. His job, like mine for so many years, was to police the boy and keep him preoccupied, his mind off drugs. The first three days saw an ultra-cranky Jason complaining of body aches and demanding a small dosage of Oxycontin that wasn't forthcoming. He became so belligerent, Malcolm ushered Mewes out of the Toluca Lake rental house and up to the Universal Hilton, where they spent three days in their hotel room, eating room service and watching in-room movies, until Jay's demeanor softened.

When Mewes moved back into the Toluca house, his whining never stopped. Rather than focusing on the task at hand — preparing for the flick — everyone spent the days trying to come up with activities that'd keep Jason busy. After a week of this, one month out from our production start date, my patience had worn dangerously thin.

We were driving to the CBS Radford lot, home base for the *Strike Back* production, where I was going to spend the day rehearsing with the boy. The car was loaded with Malcolm, Gail, Jamie, Jen, Mewes and me.

"So what're we gonna do tonight?" Jen enthused, trying to come up with a keep-Jason-busy agenda. "How about bowling?"

"I'd totally bowl," offered Malcolm.

"Sure. Why not?" I said.

The sullen Mewes said nothing.

"Jay? You up for some bowling?"

"I'm up for getting some of my pills, because I'm in pain," came his reply.

"Well that's out," I countered. "So how about bowling?"

"How am I supposed to lift a fucking bowling ball feeling like I do? Fuck that."

"You got something else you'd rather do?"

"My pills."

"Aside from that?"

"I don't wanna do shit."

"That's not the right kinda attitude, man."

"That's the way I feel."

"Y'know, it's all about the mind-set. If you're thinking about the pain and the drugs, it's just gonna bring you down."

"I'm thinking about the drugs BECAUSE of the pain. You don't know what this shit feels like. It fucking sucks. And I don't wanna do any fucking bowling, or go to a movie or any other shit you guys keep talking about. I just want my pills."

We were a mere two blocks from the studio when I finally lost it.

"FUCK YOU, YOU JUNKIE-JERKOFF!"

Yes — I was so fed up with him that I busted an alliterative.

"YOU JUST SIT AROUND AND CRY ABOUT YOUR FUCKING PILLS WHEN EVERYONE'S JUST TRYING TO KEEP YOUR DUMB ASS ALIVE! BE A FUCKING MAN AND GROW UP ALREADY!"

With the car still in motion, Mewes opened the back door.

"Kevin!" yelled Jen.

"Mewes, shut the fucking door!" Malcolm tossed in.

"I WANNA GET OUTA THE FUCKING CAR!"

"FINE!" I yelled, yanking the steering wheel to the right and slamming on the brakes.

Mewes stormed out of the car and headed in the opposite direction. I watched him in the rearview until Malcolm asked "Should I follow him?"

"I don't give a shit at this point. Fuck that asshole."

"Follow him, Malcolm," Jen intervened.

Malcolm went after Mewes and I drove the rest of the way to the lot in silence, thinking. When I got to the *Strike Back* production bungalow, I pulled Scott into my office and closed the door.

"We've gotta pull the plug on the flick."

"What?"

"I don't think it's gonna work out with Mewes. He's impossible to deal with now and all he talks about is getting his hands on Oxys. I'm terrified we're gonna get two weeks into production, and he's gonna fall off the wagon and we're gonna be really fucking stuck. So while we're not that deep into this thing, maybe we should just call it quits."

"We're already almost a million in at this point," Scott pointed out.

"Better to kill it now than get four or five million in and have him flip the fuck out on us. The guy's a hardcore junkie, man. There's no avoiding it any more."

Just then, Malcolm knocked on the door and said "Mewes is here. He wants to talk to you."

Scott and Malcolm left me alone with the tear-stained Mewes.

"You can do all the fucking dope you want now, because we're stopping the movie. I'm not risking millions of dollars of someone else's money on you when you're like this."

"I'm sorry," he swallowed. "It's just hard. It's harder than you think. And you keep saying 'Be a man' and shit, and it's not that easy. I can't stay clean."

"Well I can't make this movie if you're on drugs. I just can't. You're the fucking lead. The title has your name in it. You work every day."

"I was thinking maybe I could just drink instead."

"Jesus…"

"At least if I was drinking, like at night, when we're done shooting, I could make it, I think."

I sized him up for a beat, then repeated "Just drinking."

"Just drinking. I swear."

"You can't drink during the day, when we're shooting."

"I won't."

"And if you're going out and drinking at night, you've still gotta show up every morning, on time, to get your work done."

"I can do that."

"Because if you show up drunk, we're shutting down for that day, and it's gonna cost the production, which will come out of your salary."

"Okay."

I mulled it over for a bit. Drinking was better than drugging, I figured. And it'd mean everyone on the show could keep their jobs.

"Fine," I relented, shaking hands with the devil for the third time in my life. We hugged and put what would forever be known as the "junkie-jerkoff" incident behind us, spending the rest of the day rehearsing.

From then on, Mewes was relatively well-behaved. Every morning, we'd get up early and take a mile and change-long walk together to the nearest Jamba Juice, talking about the flick, going over his feelings about drugs that day, and making fun of Malcolm.

The latter was Mewes's favorite *Strike Back* pastime. Mewes would go out at night with Mitch, who kept track of his every move. The morning after, Jason would detail their adventures from the night before, as well as Malcolm's mundane daily activities, which Mewes was always able to put a humorous spin on.

For example: Malcolm made the mistake of ordering a large kielbasa for lunch one afternoon, and Mewes never let him live the phallic food choice down, insisting it was a sure sign of love of cock. A night or two later, while clubbing, Mewes and a few friends wound up getting into a verbal fight with some west coast actors, that resulted in a near brawl-for-all outside the club. It was Leonardo DiCaprio's crew, which included the recently-cast-as-Spider-Man Tobey Maguire, and in a white-boy equivalent of an east coast/west coast rapper showdown, the two sides postured and posed about kicking ass. The cops came to break it up before it got physical, and the next morning, Mewes gave me the play-by-play.

"Where was Malcolm?" I asked.

"He was there. But all he said afterwards was that Tobey Maguire would've kicked my ass."

"How's he figure?"

"Because the dude got all buff for playing Spider-Man or something. And Malcolm kept saying 'He's huge now. He'd have kicked your ass.' He was obsessed with Maguire being Spider-Man buff."

"Maybe you and Malcolm can start your own Sinister Six," I joked, referencing the comic book villains who banded together to defeat Spider-Man.

Mewes started cracking up. It was that amazing display of a hardcore, physically debilitating laughing jag that Mewes could only manage when his system was clear of junk. In tears, his temple vein pulsing to the point of breaking, Mewes sputtered "Fucking Malcolm could be Doc Oc, but instead…" He tried to compose himself to get his thought across. "…instead of metal arms, he's got…" Unable to continue, Mewes leaned against a tree, cackling.

"He's got what?"

"He's got a bunch of fucking kielbasas strung together, sticking out of his back!!!"

Mewes sank to the ground, rolling from side-to-side. I, too, was in tears; the good kind, for a change.

"And he… he… he can't fucking fight with the sausage arms, because whenever he goes to hit Spider-Man, he takes a bite out of the fucking arms instead!"

At this point, neither of us could breathe.

"And I'm like 'Malcolm, get my back!' But he can't help me because he's too busy sticking his kielbasa claws up his ass!!!"

The portrait was complete when Malcolm, whose longstanding catchphrase had always been "Baw!" was renamed "Doc Baw".

And so it went, all the way up to production. Mewes performed like a champ in the film, knocking it out of the park every day. And as soon as we wrapped, the boy would go out clubbing with Malcolm, as well as Dre and Dave, the caterers on the show. He spent most of his salary on club clothes, adorning himself in furry coats and pimp hats. Every morning, we'd drive to the set or location together, the boy fully ready to work.

His relationship with Jamie didn't fare as well. The pair fought constantly, usually due to Jay's post-shooting inebriated condition. One night, Jamie couldn't take it any more and she sought sanctuary in my and Jen's room. Mewes called up to our balcony, demanding she return to their back house.

"She doesn't want to be around you when you're like this, dude," I called down to him.

"You tell her she's got three choices: One, she comes down here. Two…" He thought for a moment, then said "…we go out driiinkin'…" No third option was ever given. Mewes passed out shortly thereafter, and Jamie headed back to Jersey, their engagement ended.

Toward the end of the show, Jason's mom took a turn for the worse, and some room was made in the shooting schedule for the boy to go back to Jersey and visit her. While there, he had the first dose of Oxys he'd had in months. When he returned to LA, he denied taking the drug, but I knew.

The show wrapped in Leonardo, in front of the Quick Stop that kicked off our careers. After the last Jay and Silent Bob footage was shot, Mewes retired to his trailer. An hour later, the Middletown police officers who'd been keeping the streets closed for our shoot asked if they could take a picture with Jay and I in costume. I went to Jason's trailer to retrieve him, but when he opened the door, it was too late: he'd already snorted two hundred milligrams of crushed Oxys. The difference in his appearance and physical demeanor was startling.

That night, we held a small wrap party in a bar in Red Bank. Mewes popped in to drop off a CD to Taylor, the hair department head, as a thank you. He'd completely reverted to Mr Hyde, as if the previous three months had never happened.

The next morning, I dragged the boy out of his room and took him for a ride.

"You can't do this," I pleaded, in tears — this time, the bad kind. "You've come so far, man. You can't go back to doing drugs again."

"I know. I just slipped yesterday. It was just to celebrate the end of the flick. I'm not gonna do it again. I promise."

I left a day later to head back to Los Angeles. Due to the number of effects shots in the film, Scott had decided that an LA-based post-production made more sense than cutting in Jersey and approving CG via Fed-Ex. By late June, we'd locked picture, with just the sound mix left to do. I'd been in touch with Jason via the phone, but I hadn't seen him in two months, during which time his mother finally succumbed to AIDS. I wrestled with the decision of whether or not to fly back home for the funeral, but couldn't bring myself to do it. His mother had long been a sore subject with me, as she had not only introduced Jason to Oxycontin, but had also supplied him over the years. I sent my condolences and remained in LA, hopeful that, with her passing, Mewes might finally seize the opportunity to get his demons behind him.

In mid-June, I flew back to Jersey to shoot a pair of music videos from songs featured on the *Strike Back* soundtrack. I'd arranged to pick Jason up at his mom's house, where he was still living with his sister. When I pulled up, his sister was sitting on the front steps. She said she'd go inside to get Jason. After a minute or two, an emaciated skeleton of a man with skin pulled tight over bones emerged from the house. He bore a striking resemblance to my friend.

"Goddamn," I said to myself. "Mewes is hanging out with crack-heads that look like him now." When that crack-head climbed into my car, I started crying.

Jason had spent the last two months smoking crack, he informed me. He'd lost thirty pounds. When I lose thirty pounds, people say "You look like you've lost some weight." When Jason loses thirty pounds, photos of concentration camp survivors come to mind. It was the most unhealthy I'd ever seen him appear.

Immediately, I made plans to bring Jay back to LA with me where I'd put him back on the home-kick program. The timing couldn't have been worse, as the junket for *Strike Back* was planned for that week. Dimension put all of us up in the W Hotel in Westwood, where we were to spend two days doing round table and one-on-one interviews in support of the flick. Jason, the star of the film, sat in on a few of the interviews, during which most of the journalists commented on how thin he looked.

On the morning of the second day, I was pulled from an interview and shown into the junket office, where the Dimension publicist Gina, Scott, and Malcolm were waiting for me.

"Mewes had his sister Fed-Ex heroin to the hotel," Scott said. "Malcolm found it."

"Worse," Gina added, "the hotel knows about it, and they're saying if we don't get him off the premises, they're calling the police."

We asked Jon Gordon, our Miramax/Dimension exec, to find a rehab we could deliver Jason to that night. He phoned Chris Moore, who hipped us to Promises, a rehab-to-the-stars in Malibu.

Jason was brought up to the room, and I confronted him, pissed beyond words, about the heroin delivery. Once again, he was given the choice of jail or help. He opted for the latter. I didn't even say goodbye. I was too furious.

I didn't see the boy for almost a month after that, during which time we continued post on *Strike Back*. The first time I'd lay eyes on him would be at the San Diego Comic-Con, where, after a month of good behavior, Promises had given him a day pass out of their facility to attend, providing he be accompanied by a sober-living companion — someone essentially paid to do what I'd done for all those years: babysit the boy. Jason looked great, and even better, he had his wits about him again. After the afternoon panel, we sat around the room with Malcolm, Jen and the sober-living companion, telling Malcolm-related stories and laughing it up. When the day was over, I hugged Jason, told him I loved him, and sent him back to Promises.

The week of the première, Mewes told me a story of coming back to the rehab after another day pass outing and being pulled into the main office.

"I didn't do any drugs, I swear," he'd said. "You can give me a urine, man. I'm clean!"

"This isn't about that," he was told by Jim, the program director who I'd grown to know quite well over the phone, when I'd call in three times weekly to check up on Jason's progress. "There's someone here who you know."

"I don't know anybody who needs rehab except me," Mewes scoffed. "And even if I did, I don't know anybody who could afford this place."

"You know this person, and he's very interested in keeping his stay here private. He doesn't want you to tell anyone he's here."

Mewes says that the door to the room adjoining the office was opened to reveal our friend Ben Affleck sitting there, looking at him. Quoting *Chasing Amy*, Mewes said "Well look at this morose motherfucker right here…"

Ben's stint in rehab made all the tabloids, and in most of the long-lens photos of him in Promises, Mewes could be spied in the background. One article misconstrued Jason's presence as Mewes visiting Ben. For a few weeks, Ben's stay was major news.

Until September 11th.

Strike Back had been out for three weeks when Al Qaeda struck, and suddenly, it was a different world. I was still in Los Angeles at that point, and Mewes was just about to be released from Promises, his on-site program finished. The next step in his recovery was a halfway house on the ocean, where Jen and I visited him. The gorgeous locale prompted Schwalbach to utter "I'M an addict. Check ME in."

By mid-October, I was ready to head back to Jersey with the family. With Jason's help, we loaded out of the Toluca Lake rental. Mewes had decided to stay in Los Angeles, where he was planning to move in with some sober-living friends he'd met while at Promises. His life on track, I felt like I could leave the boy in the City of Angels, secure in the knowledge that he was finally on the straight and narrow. Ben was beating his demons, and now too, so was Mewes.

By Thanksgiving, only Ben would remain sober.

Me and My Shadow Pt. 7
Monday 10 April 2006 @ 10:53 a.m.

In the wake of 9/11, Jen and I opted to drive home to New Jersey from Los Angeles. And as if the post-terrorist attack vibe wasn't foreign enough, we were coming home to a house we'd never lived in.

Before we'd left the motherland eleven months prior to shoot *Strike Back*, we'd purchased a new house in Rumson, a few miles down the road from the old Oceanport, flat-roofed abode. In our absence, a moving company had bagged and tagged all our stuff, shipping the contents of our old home into our fresh, new digs. We were now the proud owners of five acres and two floors in the most desirable part of central Jersey, situated around the block from Bruce Springsteen's estate.

The whole family had gotten back to the east coast in October and spent most of the next month getting ourselves situated in the new house. By late November, we were ready to host our first Thanksgiving in Rumson. Mewes, who'd been out in Los Angeles, living in an apartment with some sober pals, called to say he wanted to come back to Jersey for the festivities as well, so, naturally, I invited him.

"You staying clean?" I asked him.

"Totally," he'd responded.

"How long now?"

"I'm coming up on five months."

"And isn't life better now?"

"It is," he said.

"If you stay clean, I've got a role for you in the next flick. A non-Jay role."

"Awesome. I can't wait."

"I'm really fucking proud of you, man."

"Thanks, Moves."

I hadn't seen Jason in two months when he showed up at my door the day before Thanksgiving with a new girlfriend, Amy. I gave the boy a big hug and then whisked him and his lady into a car with me and Mos, so we could head up to the Gizmo Recording Studio in Manhattan to lay down the *Strike Back* commentary track for the DVD. On the hour-long ride, Mewes chatted a bit, then nodded out a few times.

"You tired, man?" I asked.

"Yeah. I didn't sleep last night," he offered, summoning up that old chestnut of an excuse Mos and I had heard so often back in Jay's drug dependency days. Quietly, I started to panic.

During the commentary track record, Mewes continued to catch a nod every few minutes, before excusing himself to hit the bathroom. Any shred of hope I'd been living in that the boy had stayed clean was now dying in despair.

On the ride home, Mewes asked if we could stop for cigarettes. When he popped into the convenience store, I turned in the driver's seat to face Amy behind me and asked "He's using again, isn't he?"

"He is," Amy confirmed, watching the convenience store to make sure Mewes wasn't on his way back to the car. "He was at a college appearance in Colorado two months ago when someone offered him coke. It's been downhill from there ever since."

"Is it heroin or Oxys?"

"Mostly heroin. He scores it a few blocks from my apartment," she confessed. "You've gotta talk to him about quitting. He'll listen to you."

"What charming, child-like naiveté," I thought to myself, as Mewes returned with his smokes. Nothing else was said on the subject for the remainder of the ride home.

The Thanksgiving meal was prepared by Byron and Gail, and gobbled up by Jen, Harley, my parents, our friend Bob Hawk, Judy, Amy, Jason and me. When the dinner was over, Mewes and Amy retired downstairs to the rec room/basement. My then-two-year-old daughter Harley, who'd long harbored a crush on Mewes, solicited Jason time and again to play with her in her room, but Mewes repeatedly gave the kid the kind-yet-distinct brush-off, insisting that he'd hang out with her later. Harley lurked by the basement door for most of the day, waiting for the play date that would never come. Jen tried to explain to the toddler that Jay was just tired, but the wife really suspected it wasn't exhaustion that was making Mewes inaccessible.

"He's using again, isn't he?" Jen asked.

"His girlfriend said he is. I haven't talked to him about it yet."

"I don't even care any more. I've put up with his shit for years because you care about him, but now he's breaking Harley's heart, and I'm not gonna stand for that. I want him out of here."

I called Mewes upstairs and went outside with him to smoke and talk.

"You're using again," I said to him.

"No, man. I'm just tired."

"And now you're lying again. But worse than lying, you're ignoring the kid — the kid that you love. And you're ignoring her because you're high."

Mewes quietly smoked, saying nothing.

"You brought drugs into my house, didn't you?"

"I'm stopping, I swear. It was stupid, I know. But I'm quitting."

"You can't stay here, man. You lied to me and told me you were coming up on five months clean. You made it, what — like three months, really?"

"Ben said he'd pay for me to go back to Promises."

"That's fine. But until you get clean again, you can't stay here. You're gonna have to go stay with your sister while you're in Jersey. I'll drive you and your girlfriend over now."

Rather than fight the decision, Mewes simply said "Alright."

I dropped him off at his mom's old house in Keansburg. It was the last time I'd see him for two months.

Around December, I had to go to Los Angeles to receive the People for the American Way's Defender of Democracy Award. The ultra-liberal organization (headed by *All in the Family* creator Norman Lear) cited *Dogma* as the film that earned me the prize, which I was to be presented with at the same ceremony in which the *South Park* guys, Kim Pierce (the director of *Boys Don't Cry*), and the Dixie Chicks (who'd taken a world of shit for anti-Bush comments in the wake of 9/11) were also being recognized. Byron, Gail, Harley, the wife and I flew out to California and checked in to the W Hotel in Westwood.

The morning after the PFAW Awards Ceremony, we were enjoying a family breakfast downstairs in the hotel restaurant when a discussion about our time in LA sparked a massive change in all of our lives. We'd spent almost a full year in California while making *Strike Back*, and my rationale was that if you spend a full year anywhere short of prison or Calcutta, it takes on the aspects of home. With the Jersey winter approaching, we embarked on an exploratory conversation about snow-birding it: moving back to LA for six months where I'd spend the time writing *Jersey Girl*, and the rest of the family could escape the impending freezing east coast temperatures. The idea snowballed, and soon, we were calling the owners of the Toluca Lake house we'd rented the year before.

When we got back to Jersey, I'd phoned Ben to see whether or not he'd wound up sponsoring Jason's trip back to Promises. He said he had, but Mewes made it only four days into the program before checking himself out. We commiserated over Jason's condition for a while before I announced that I was moving back to LA for the winter, to finish the *Jersey Girl* script.

"Where you gonna live?" Ben asked.

"We're gonna rent that Toluca Lake house again."

"Why don't you buy my place instead? I just bought Drew Barrymore's property on Coldwater, so I'm moving out of this joint. And you know your ol' lady loooooves my house."

I'd been to the house in question only five months earlier, for a fourth of July party, shortly before Ben checked himself into Promises. Nestled in the Hollywood Hills, Ben's place was easily the most beautiful house I'd ever been in. A tri-level mansion with massive high ceilings and a pool on the top floor, it boasted an amazing view of what I felt was a mountain, but the locals called a hill. Jen had instantly fallen in love with it, and when Ben told us that — due to the joint's proximity to the street which afforded all manner of paparazzi the freedom to shoot the shit out of him whenever he walked out of his front door — he was thinking about selling it, she had turned to me and said "I want this house." We'd spoken with Ben at great lengths about taking the joint off his hands, but after the rehab stint, the topic never really came up again... until that moment.

"I just bought a house in Jersey, so I can't buy your place until I get paid for turning in the *Jersey Girl* script," I told my multi-millionaire friend.

"So then just rent the house instead," he countered. "I'll charge you the same monthly that the Toluca Lake people were gonna hit you up for, but go one better: all the money you pay in rent I'll knock off the purchase price of the house when you're ready to buy it."

It was, to say the least, the biggest steal since the US had purchased the island of Manhattan from the Native Americans for some pelts and beads. Thanks to Ben's largess, Jen's dream of not just moving back to California, but moving back to California and living in that mansion became a reality. We put the Rumson house we'd purchased a year earlier and had only lived in for a total of three months on the market and, in January of 2002, headed west for good.

We'd been in the house for about a day when Jason showed up. He looked a lot worse for wear, but he seemed chipper, taking me through our new house and showing me where he'd slept or banged girls when he'd stayed with Ben a few times, pre- and post-Promises. I inquired about his most recent and brief visit to that same rehab, and he said it was a dumb move on his part, and that Ben was generously offering to send him to a different rehab. He talked about the possibility of moving into the house with us if he cleaned up, and I said with all the space we had, I'd happily give him a room, if he could get his life back on track.

The only thing he did with his life and that proverbial track, however, was tie that shit up like it was Dudley Do-Right's girlfriend Nell and he was Snidely fucking Whiplash waiting for a train. The second rehab Ben paid for was a bust as well, with Jason bolting after only two days. Even worse, the Freehold Court back home in Jersey had issued a bench warrant for his arrest, after Jason missed a mandatory appearance. The tragic irony was that the court date in question was the final sum-up to Mewes's old possession case: he'd successfully completed probation, and all that remained was some final face time before the judge, at which point his honor would've declared Jason free to go, case-closed. Too high to make the plane, Mewes never made it back to Jersey, and the bench warrant was issued.

The role I'd told Jason I'd written for him to play in *Jersey Girl* became a moot point, as the boy couldn't step foot in Jersey without being arrested. When we headed back east to shoot the flick, Mewes asked if he could live at the LA house in our absence, taking care of the dogs. Staring at his crack-pipe burned lips and glancing at the track marks up and down his arms, it wasn't difficult to say no. Sadly, it would be the first film in nearly ten years that I made without the boy.

While I was back east, Jason declined further. By the time we got back to LA, the word was that he was living on the streets. He'd lost a great deal of weight, and had burned a low budget production in the southeast that'd cast him as the lead in an indie flick. When the director contacted me, I commiserated with him about Jason's drug-induced behavior in an effort to make it clear that there was little the guy could've done. It wasn't the lack of budget (which Mewes taxed further by insisting they keep him in his "medicine") or the production's fault, I'd told the director; Mewes was just a destructive force of nature.

I called Jim, Jason's former counselor at Promises, to see if they'd take the boy back into the program. Jim finally set me straight, though, as he tried to explain that the Jason situation was out of my hands.

"Part of the problem is you've never let the kid hit rock bottom," he explained. "You're always there throwing a net out to catch him before he hits. He knows he can count on you to get him out of any jam, because that's been your role for years as an enabler. You've gotta change that approach and practice some tough love instead: don't allow him into your life anymore. He worships and loves you; to Jason, you're like the father he never had. And based on his affection for you, you're the only person who's got a shot at reaching him and getting him to clean up. But the way you've gone about it hasn't worked so far, and that's because you haven't hit him with the worst thing he can imagine: being cut out of your life altogether. You've gotta let him hit rock bottom."

"But what if his rock bottom is the grave?" I asked. "What if he winds up overdosing?"

"Then if that's the case, there's nothing you can do to stop that. If Jason's meant to OD, all you've done is prolong his journey to the inevitable. Every addict has to make the decision to clean up his or herself, and each time you've intervened, it's been you making him get clean, so it's never stuck beyond a few months. He needs to want to get and stay sober for himself, not for you. But where you can really help him is by turning your back on Jason — because I believe he feels that not being in your life is as bad as it could get for him — and then, maybe, he might turn himself around for the best."

So while I was in post-production on *Jersey Girl*, I took Jim's advice and laid down the law with Jason: he wasn't allowed in the house anymore, until he cleaned up. He wasn't allowed to see Harley anymore, until he cleaned up. I wouldn't finance his life until he cleaned up. I wouldn't hang out with him until he cleaned up. The tough love approach had begun.

November 2002 saw the first Thanksgiving we'd spend at our new house in LA. The day before the government-sanctioned food gorge, Jason stopped by the post-production office where I was cutting *Jersey Girl*. His relationship with Amy long-since over, he was there with another girl entirely. She waited in the car while I spoke to the boy in the parking lot.

"Thanksgiving tomorrow," he observed. "Gail cooking again?"

"Yup," I confirmed. "What're you gonna do?"

"Me and this chick are gonna hang out in our apartment, I guess," Mewes explained, pulling a thick-frosted banana cake purchased at 7-11 from his pocket, biting into it. "It kinda sucks because we didn't pay the electric bill so they shut the power off. We've been lighting a lot of candles."

"You guys going to her folks' for Thanksgiving or something?"

"Nah. Not allowed."

The girl in the car, a stick-thin junkie with eyes bulging from a hollowed-out face, climbed out of the vehicle and stormed toward us.

"Half of that's mine," she barked at Mewes, snatching the banana cake from his hand and heading back to the car.

Jason shrugged, as if to say "Life's come down to me and some girl I barely know battling over the last bite of convenience store vended single-serving deserts." I pulled a pair of twenties out of my pocket and handed them to the boy.

"Go to KooKooRoo tomorrow and get yourselves some Thanksgiving turkey with this," I insisted. "Do NOT buy drugs with it."

"Thanks, Moves. I won't."

As he shuffled back to his snack cake harpy, we both knew that forty bucks wouldn't make it to the KooKooRoo cash registers.

The next day, as my family finished the Thanksgiving meal, the doorbell rang. I joined Jason on the front steps outside of my house.

"What're you guys doing?" he asked.

"Just hanging."

Mewes nodded his head, then lifted his nose skyward, saying "I can smell Gail's turkey. Was it good?"

"It was." After a beat of silence, I added "This is the first Thanksgiving in three years you haven't spent with us."

"It sucks."

"It sucks on this end, too. But I can't invite you into the house — you understand that, right? I can't let you in until you clean up."

"We're going to the Betty Ford Clinic tomorrow," Mewes informed me, pointing to the car, where the banana cake girl was sitting. "She knows someone who works there, so I think we're getting in for free."

"That's great. Stay in the program this time. Don't leave 'til you're clean. Then maybe next Thanksgiving you can eat with us again."

"Cool," he muttered, wiping tears from his eyes. I hugged the boy and sent him on his way.

The Betty Ford sojourn lasted about as long as Mewes could make it in rehabs around that point. Two days later, he signed himself out and came back to Hollywood. He'd stop by the editing room from time to time, always to bum a few bucks off me "for smokes", which I knew would go into his veins instead. All the while, I was dealing with *Jersey Girl* and other issues that kept my mind off Mewes.

In February, the family and I found ourselves momentarily homeless due to a mini-disaster of sorts. I'd had a fountain coke machine installed for Jen as part of a Christmas gift only two months before, but what none of us knew was that the crew which had installed it didn't do so properly: they'd tapped into a water pipe under the bar sink and in a prime example of the American work ethic, simply electrical-taped the hole closed. While the entire family was up in Aspen where I was a featured guest at the annual Comedy Festival, the electrical tape finally gave out, and the tapped pipe began gushing all over the top floor of the house. By the time we got home, tens of thousands of gallons of water had flooded the house, soaking the third floor until it collapsed the ceiling of the second floor below it, as well as the first floor below that. The entire dwelling had to be stripped to the beams inside and rebuilt. Luckily, I'd just closed on the house in January, finally purchasing it from Ben after a year of renting, at which time I'd been forced to carry a then-seemingly ungodly amount of insurance, which included a flood policy. My former bitching about carrying a flood policy "on a house on a hill in a desert" was quickly negated, as some $200,000 in repairs were covered thanks to that insurance.

The policy also covered rental expenses for the length of time we needed to be out of the house, so we found a place in the flats of Beverly Hills on Sierra Drive. One day, while I was setting up a DVD player in the bedroom, Jen made a heart-stopping discovery in US Weekly that, startlingly, didn't have anything to do with Angelina Jolie or Jessica fucking Simpson.

"Oh my God..." she uttered from the bed, where she was leafing through the magazine.

"What's the matter?" I queried.

"I think something's happened to Mewes."

She pointed to a small, sidebar feature in the magazine. It was about Mewes, who'd been reported missing for months and presumed dead.

Me and My Shadow, Pt. 8
Thursday 13 April 2006 @ 11:17 a.m.

My heart raced, as I feared the eulogy I'd always been preparing in the back of my mind for Jason's eventual overdose would finally find an audience.

Immediately, I called Jay's cell and received a message about discontinued service. I called every number I'd ever had on the boy, but could not locate him. Then, as if on cue, the phone rang.

"What's up, Moves?"

"You're alive!" I yelled.

"So are you," he responded.

"I just read you were missing and presumed dead, you asshole!"

"Really? Where?"

"In a fucking tabloid. You were supposed to be at Slamdance in January for that R.S.V.P. movie, and when you didn't show and you couldn't be found, the filmmakers reported you missing."

"That's weird."

"Where are you?"

"I'm driving to Jersey. I'm finally gonna settle this bench warrant thing and surrender myself to the cops. HBO's doing a documentary about me and the drugs."

He might as well have said "Moves, guess what? I've always secretly been Jesus Christ himself, and I've decided to head back home to be with my heavenly father, so I'm busting out the rapture a bit early. Start praying you don't get 'Left Behind', sir. Also, I'm gay."

"What?!?"

"There's this guy with HBO, and he's doing a documentary about me getting off dope. So they're taking me to Jersey, where I'm turning myself in and hoping I don't go to jail."

"Wow!"

"Yeah. It's fucked up. But I was calling because they want to interview you when they get back into town. Would you be down for that?"

"How much am I allowed to say?"

"You can say whatever you want, sir."

"Then they're gonna need a lot of film. Are you still using?"

"Yeah, but only 'til I get to Jersey. Then, no matter what happens with the court, I'm quitting dope. I'm tired of living like this, sir. It sucks."

"Good for you, man," was all I could muster. By this point, I'd heard it all before.

"But if I can get clean, do you think I can come live with you guys again?"

"I always said you could live with us, as long as you quit doing drugs, sir."

"Alright. Because I'm gonna do it this time. So start making up my room. Nayng!"

I hung up, relieved my friend was still alive, but not very confident in his latest clean-up effort — particularly if he was doing it on camera.

I called around to see if this HBO documentary was legit, and discovered it wasn't: yes, the filmmaker had gotten some exploratory money from HBO, but there was no deal or commitment in place for any documentary. The next time Mewes called me from on the road, I told him as much.

"Really?" he said, gravely.

"As near as I can tell," I replied.

"That sucks, because the guy made me sign some papers."

"Papers that say what, exactly?"

"That I'm doing the documentary and that he's my new manager."

"Oh, sir…"

"I thought it was kinda weird. I told him I didn't want to sign anything, but he forced me to."

"Were you high at the time?"

"Yeah," he muttered, kind of ashamed.

"Well this may be the first time that being on junk might pan out for you — legally speaking."

"Why?"

"Don't worry about it. Meantime, when's your court date?"

"Tomorrow morning."

"Call me after it's over."

"If I'm going to jail, I don't know if I'll be able to call you."

"Excellent point. I guess if you're calling me, then that'd be a good sign."

"True dat."

"Be humble in that courtroom, sir. And don't shoot up beforehand."

"I won't, Moves. I love you."

"I love you, too. Good luck."

The next morning, I woke up and smoked a pack of cigarettes, waiting for Mewes to call. On one hand, I didn't want him going to jail; the dude was far too pretty to make it out of there an anal virgin. On the other hand, maybe a few months in county would scare him straight, and finally make the boy realize that steering clear of junk for the rest of his life was the best option — at least as far as the well-being of his brown-eye was concerned.

When the phone rang, I breathed an enormous sigh of relief. Though I'd long wanted Mewes to be drug free, rectal torture wasn't the preferred impetus I'd had in mind.

"What happened?" I asked.

"The judge gave me a choice: a year in jail, or six months court-mandated rehab."

"Easy decision there."

"Not really. Six months in lockdown? I don't know if I'll make it."

"Just for the record, you DID choose rehab, didn't you?"

"Well, yeah. Like I wanna get ass-raped and shit…"

"Good boy. Where's the rehab? Can you go back to Promises?"

"Nope. I've gotta do it in a Jersey rehab. Guess where it is?"

Marlboro, New Jersey was about half an hour away from Highlands, the town Mewes and I grew up in. It was infamous for being the home to the area's only mental hospital. As kids, it was invoked by our parents as a correctional tool, as in "If you don't start behaving, we're shipping you off to Marlboro!"

"They're throwing you in the booby-hatch?!"

"I guess the mental hospital closed down. They run a rehab out of one of the buildings there now."

"When do you start?"

"Tomorrow. Tonight's my last night to shoot up."

"You sure you wanna even bother shooting up one last time?"

"Oh, I'm sure. If I'm quitting forever, I wanna boot one last time."

"Was the documentary crew allowed to shoot in the court room?"

"Yeah. But the camera guy told me something weird. He said the director was disappointed when I only got rehab. He said he doesn't have the ending he wanted to the doc. What's that mean?"

"You've gotta even ask that question?"

"I don't trust that guy. He's kinda shady."

"Not your problem right now. For the next six months, all you've gotta think about is getting and staying clean. And you can't bolt from this rehab, sir."

"I know. The judge said if I leave the program early, bam! Two years in jail."

"And I hear you're not allowed to sign yourself out of jail."

"Yeah. Listen, I gotta go, but I'll call you when I get to rehab."

"Cool. Keep your nose clean, boy. And I mean that literally."

When I got off the phone, I called Marty Arbus, the lawyer the doc crew had hired to represent Jason in court. I explained my connection to Jason, and he said Mewes had filled him in on my relevance to his life. I asked Marty to go over the judgment with me, in case Mewes had left anything out. He, too, expressed concerns about the documentary director.

Apparently, the guy was representing himself as being tight with not only me, but Ben Affleck and Matt Damon as well. Marty went through a list of claims the guy had made, ninety-nine percent of which could be easily refuted by someone in the know, and then echoed the sentiments the cinematographer had expressed to Mewes in regards to the director's reaction to Jay getting off with rehab. It was becoming more and more clear that Mewes had fallen in with an opportunist with shades of being a con man.

Said con man called me a day later to discuss doing an interview for his documentary. I told him I didn't think the film was a good idea, particularly if it featured, as I was told, footage of Mewes shooting up. When I said the whole affair seemed tabloid-show exploitative, the guy suggested we pray about it, and ask God for guidance on the subject. That's when I got really nervous. After an hour on the phone with him, I came to the conclusion that the man was shifty, to say the least.

April 6th, 2003, Jason Mewes checked himself into court-mandated rehab. I called the Marlboro facility that afternoon to see how he was doing, but was refused phone access to the boy. They said Jason wasn't allowed phone usage for week one, but I could write him as much as I liked. I penned the first letter I'd ever written to Jason, expressing my pride in him for finally dealing with the bench warrant and encouraging him to stick with the program.

At the start of week two, I was able to speak to Jason on the phone for two minutes, during which time he told me he was forced to cut his hair and scrub a toilet with a tooth brush at the rehab. I reminded him it was better than jail time, and that if he got and stayed clean, he could come live with us again. Before I could say more, the phone was taken away.

A few days after our brief conversation, I received a reply to my letter from Mewes. What follows is, verbatim, Jason's response, via snail mail.

Kevin (Moves),

It was so good to get your letter. It made me really happy. Thank you for not giving up on me. I love you and your family (my family) so much. I can't tell you how good it felt to read, and hear on the phone from you that when I do the right thing I can be in your lives again. I love you and miss you all so so much. I can't wait to see Harley. I hate myself for missing out on her growing up. I don't want to miss out on anymore months or years. And I miss laughing with you our walks. Kevin your like the father I never had. In times financially and always emotionally and mentally. I'm sorry for hurting you. It was never intentionally. And I never wanted to hurt your family. I hope you know that in your heart. As for this place, it is so hard to concentrate on why I'm here and I sincerely want to. I'm tired and broken. I don't want to live like this no more.

This place is filled with people who don't give a shit they have to be here. I got elbowed for being a so called 'Rich Boy' and the counselors keep pointing out 'He's a junkie' which I am, but in 3 meetings they embarrassed me for people asking for autographs. And people say stupid shit like 'He never worked so hard' (we have jobs sweeping and mopping). It sounds petty but it is making things tougher, more uncomfortable, and harder to concentrate on why I'm here. There's more but hard to explain.

Give everyone a kiss for me.

Love,

J

I had to chuckle at the irony of Mewes being tagged a "Rich Boy", but felt for him in regards to the autograph situation. Apparently, whenever someone would ask for his signature, a counselor would dismiss Jason as a junkie, and state that junkies weren't to be looked up to. There was some wisdom to the approach, but it sounded awfully harsh. Still, I had to trust that these professionals knew what they were doing, and assume that they figured harsh was what Jason needed at that point.

Two months into his stay at the Marlboro rehab facility, I had to fly east for a comic book convention in Philadelphia. Since I was going to be on the same coast, I made arrangements to visit Jason at the rehab. I waited in the front office of the clinic, and after a few minutes, I was met by a female counselor. She asked me to take a walk with her, in advance of seeing Jay.

The woman requested that I tell her everything about my situation with Mewes, and for the next half hour, I spilled my guts, telling her pretty much the same story you've been reading here these last few weeks. When I was finished, she said "You don't seem to think the movies have much to do with Jason's problems."

"What — our movies?"

"Yes."

"I guess they've had an effect, inasmuch as it's how he earns, and a lot of that money has wound up in his veins. But the few times he's been able to clean up and stay sober for any period of time has been while we were making the movies, so I tend to think of the flicks as having a positive influence on his life."

"He plays a drug dealer in your movies."

"A weed dealer, yeah."

"And he's drug-dependent in real life. You don't think one has something to do with the other?"

"Not really. I think being born to a heroin-addicted mother and all the things I've been telling you have more to do with how Jason came to be an addict than playing a weed dealer in some comedies. I mean, Anthony Hopkins has played a killer cannibal, but from what I've heard, he's never confused his role with his real life."

"That's a convenient analogy."

"Look, I'm sure he's talked about his mother in counseling sessions with you. You've gotta see the role she's played in his life."

"I'm not Jason's counselor."

Suddenly, I was flush with the notion that Marlboro was, indeed, still a mental hospital, and that I'd just spent the last hour talking to a psychopath.

"You're not Jason's counselor?"

"No, I'm in admissions. I checked him in."

"Two months ago?"

"Yes."

"How long did you deal with him when you checked him in?"

"About an hour."

"You talked to the kid for an hour two months ago, and because of that, you think all of his drug problems stem from playing a weed dealer in the movies?"

"I think there are correlations there, yes."

"No offense, but based on your limited exposure to Jason, I think that's an asinine conclusion to draw."

"You're being very defensive."

"With all due respect, you're being very myopic."

The woman gave me the once over and then directed me back to the main building. "You'll meet Jason in the conference room. You have a half hour to talk to him."

"A half-hour?! I flew all the way here from Los Angeles to see the guy!"

"And you'll see him. For one half-hour. Have a seat, Mr Smith."

Stunned and resentful after spending all that time talking to someone who was almost completely unfamiliar with Jason's case, I paced the room while I waited. Five minutes later, Jason was brought it.

It was the first time, since he was a kid, that I'd seen him with short hair. His long locks completely gone, he looked like a boy band front man. Beyond that, however, he appeared healthy.

During the half-hour, we talked about the rehab, which Mewes hated like poison.

"Of course you hate it," I offered. "You're not allowed to shoot up here."

"It's not that. I can deal with not doing drugs. But the people treat me like shit here."

"It's not Promises, that's for sure. They don't cater to the patients as much, it seems. But I'll say this much: Promises dug a lot deeper than 'he plays a weed dealer in movies so he shoots heroin in real life' for a root cause."

"That ain't even the worst of it. These motherfuckers go out of their way to treat me like shit because I've been in the movies," Jason whispered. "And I don't ask for special treatment or nothing either. But because I get recognized from the movies by the other patients, the people who work here come down on me, telling people I ain't shit and that I'm a scumbag like them, or a bigger scumbag because I've had all these breaks and I still turned to drugs. I'm not even allowed to go outside and smoke as much as other people who're in the program. They let me go outside three times a day for five minutes each time to smoke."

"Can't you smoke inside?"

Fuck no. But everyone else gets six smoke breaks a day and I only get three. It's fucked up. And I told you I got elbowed for being a 'rich boy', right?"

"I thought that was pretty funny."

"I keep telling these people that I ain't rich, but they don't believe me. It sucks, man. This place is almost like jail without the ass-fucking."

"But you're staying put, yes?"

"I gotta, man. Or else I go to the jail WITH the ass-fucking."

Soon, the woman from admissions returned to usher Jason away. I gave him a hug and headed back to Philly for the con.

By odd coincidence, my sister Virginia was also in Philly that weekend. Since she lived in Japan with her husband and two children, my parents were rarely ever able to see all three of their grown children at once any more. Seizing the opportunity to do so, my Mom and Dad flew up from Florida with my brother for a family reunion of sorts. My parents attended my Q&A at the Con that Saturday, and afterwards, we all went out to eat at Morton's Steak House, for what would turn out to be my father's last meal.

It was a great night of good food and fun conversation. My parents got to chill with their three offspring and their respective spouses, the only notable exception being my brother's husband Jerry, who was stuck at work in Florida. When the night ended, I gave my old man a kiss and put him in a cab with my mom.

The next morning, I got a 6 a.m. phone call from my brother Don, telling me to get down to the hospital immediately. After two strokes and a cardio episode six months prior, my father had succumbed to complete heart failure in the wee hours of the morning, following our get-together the night before. As devastating as it was to lose him, considering the man spent his last night on Earth surrounded by loved ones, putting away some delicious food and laughing it up, it wasn't a bad way to go.

Funeral arrangements were made for two days later, back home in Jersey. I called the Marlboro rehab to request Jason be granted a day pass to attend the funeral, since he'd known my Dad pretty well from back in our Highlands days.

"I'm afraid that's not possible," the woman said.

"This is my Dad's funeral," I pushed. "The man was like family to Jason."

"I appreciate that. But Jason's not allowed to leave the premises."

"I think these are extenuating circumstances, don't you? Tell you what — I'll pay for a counselor to escort him, if that's what you're worried about."

"If you think that's our only concern about this proposal, then I'm afraid you're being myopic, Mr Smith."

Burned by my own term thrown back in my face, I talked to Mewes and told him not only that my Dad died, but also that the rehab wasn't going to let him out for the wake. Needless to say, he was disappointed and pissed.

Following the funeral, I headed back to Los Angeles. When I checked my messages, I discovered Marty Arbus, Jason's lawyer, had phoned with what he deemed "an emergency".

"What happened?" I asked, returning his call.

He let out a heavy sigh and said "Jason bolted from the Marlboro rehab this morning."

Me and My Shadow, Pt. 9 — The Conclusion
Tuesday 18 April 2006 @ 5:18 p.m.

As Jason's lawyer Marty Arbus passed on the details about Mewes's latest dash from rehab — the dash I was sure was gonna land him in jail — I recalled a conversation Jen and I had once engaged in on the subject of the nature of Jason Mewes.

"Did you ever read *Flowers for Algernon*?" I'd asked her.

"I went to high school too," she replied.

"Well, did you ever see the flick they made of the book? It was called *Charly*? Cliff Robertson played Charly."

"I think I only ever saw, like, five movies before we met."

"It was pretty good. They didn't deviate that far from the short story: Charly Gordon's this retarded janitor, and these scientists experiment on him and suddenly, he gets smarter, turning into a sort of genius. But his condition starts to deteriorate, at which time the intelligent Charly has to deal with the knowledge that he's going to be retarded again soon. And there's this image from the film that's always really haunted me: at the end of the movie, this woman who's fallen in love with the smart Charly finds him with this childlike, beatific smile on his face, and she realizes the intelligent Charly's completely gone forever. He's lapsed back into the retarded Charly."

"Is this your way of telling me that you're becoming retarded?"

"That shot from the flick always comes to mind when Mewes gets clean. Because, when he turns his life around — either for a couple of weeks or a couple of months — it's like he's the intelligent Charly. And I get used to him and figure that's the way he's gonna be from then on. But, sooner or later, he lapses back into the retarded Mewes — the one who shoots up and stops being himself, y'know?"

"But maybe that's where you've got your analogy wrong. Maybe the junkie Mewes IS the real Mewes, and the few moments of sobriety are the manufactured, unreal Jason. Maybe being a drug addict is his natural state."

It was a sobering notion, to say the least — and one that was still bouncing around in my head when Marty capped the Jason escape story with "But he's here with me now, and…"

"What?!" I barked. "You've got Jason?!"

"Yeah, he's here in my office. Do you want to talk to him?"

"God, yes! Put him on!"

I steeled myself to hear Jason's voice, all drug-addled and dope-dimmed. If he was out of rehab, surely he was back on drugs.

"'Sup, Moves?" he said, sounding… lucid.

"You fucking asshole," I snapped. "Why the fuck would you make a run for it?"

"I couldn't take it anymore, man. People were picking fights with me, and the counselors were all nasty too. I just had to get out of there. I'll go back to rehab, I promise; just not to that one."

"Have you shot up?"

"No."

"Snorted?"

"No."

"Have you used anything at all?"

"Nothing, I swear. I'll even take a piss test."

"You know you're going to jail, right?"

"Marty doesn't think so. He says he's going to plead my case with the judge and see if they'll just move me to another rehab. He says that if I take a piss test and pass, the judge might understand that I didn't leave to get high; I left because I was getting harassed. And then maybe he'll just put me in another rehab. I'll probably have to start the six months over again, but I don't care. It'll be worth it to get out of that place."

And thanks to the genius of Marty Arbus pleading Mewes's case to the judge, that's pretty much what came to pass, with one major exception: Jason didn't even have to restart his sentence. When he entered the replacement rehab in Keyport, NJ, he only had four months left to complete the court-mandated program.

Over the course of the next four months, I grew close with the director of the Keyport rehab, checking in with her on a regular basis for updates on Jason's progress. She was a tough cookie, but fair too — dressing the boy down only when he was wrong, and giving him props when he was on the right track. That's not to say Mewes had become the ideal patient; not by any stretch of the imagination. He'd logged some demerits for house disruption, after vehemently bitching about not being able to smoke as often as he wanted to, and had his privileges revoked for a week after disappearing from a group outing to an Alcoholics Anonymous meeting. When he turned up twenty minutes later, he confessed to taking off with a girl he'd met in the meeting for some parking lot sex in her van (with the dope out of his system, his libido was back to its normal, randy level). But by and large, for the next four months, Mewes got — for lack of a more clinical term — better.

I was allowed frequent phone contact with the boy, and with a month to go before his release, he asked that I come back to Jersey to visit him. When I got to the rehab, I had a long sit-down with the program director, who stressed that, while he was still very much a pain-in-the-ass spoiled child of sorts, Mewes had improved one hundred percent from the attitude he showed up with.

"He's a hard guy to hate," I offered, to which the director nodded, getting up to lead me to the sun porch where I'd meet with Jason — this time, with no half hour restriction.

The first thing I'd noticed was how buff he looked. Not only had he shed some pounds, but he'd also used his time in the program to exercise and build his upper body. The hair was still short, but unlike the butchering he'd received at the Marlboro rehab, his current 'do was more stylized. We sat on the porch for hours, talking about his progress, and what was in store for him once he hit the six-month mark and was free to leave.

"I'll have to talk to Jen and see if she's cool with you staying at the house," I offered. "You're gonna have to walk on eggshells for a while around her — you know that, right?"

"I get it," he responded. "I've got a lot of making up to do to her. But Moves, I was thinking: remember you said that if I cleaned up you'd make another Jay and Silent Bob movie?"

"I remember saying that before one of the many times you fucked up, yeah."

"Well, now I'm clean, and I'm gonna stay that way," he said. "So, I was wondering…"

"No."

"No?"

"No, I'm not making another Jay and Silent Bob movie."

Disappointed, the boy nodded "Oh. Y'know, I understand."

"I'm gonna make another *Clerks* instead, in which Jay and Silent Bob'll have small roles."

Mewes processed this, then smiled. "You were fucking with me just now, weren't you?"

"Kinda."

"I deserve that, I guess."

"That and so much more," I added.

Mewes successfully completed the Keyport rehab program in October 2003. The week he was checked out, we threw a shindig for him at Jay and Silent Bob's Secret Stash, the comic book store in Red Bank. Billed as "Stash Bash 2: Welcome Home Jay", the dual day event saw six hundred fans and well-wishers — hand-picked from thousands of entry essays — come through the store to offer the boy their congratulatory, supportive "ups".

Following the Stash Bash, we were on a plane to Los Angeles, where Jason arrived just in time to stay at the Sierra rental for a few days, before we packed up and headed back to our newly-repaired, post-flood home. There, after much soul-searching by Jen, he inherited the small, first floor guest room. Slowly, Jen warmed up to the boy again, and by his one-year-sober birthday — the day before Jen's actual birthday — she threw a big party at the Spider Club, celebrating both milestones in conjunction.

The Spider Club (located above the Avalon on Vine in Hollywood) became Mewes's new haunt. For the first few post-rehab weeks in Los Angeles, Mewes could be found at the club every night, hanging with his sober-living crew of Jack Osbourne, Mike McGuiness, and Brian Milo. In place of heroin and Oxycontin, their new poison was Red Bull — the energy drink that sells itself professing "It gives you wings" but could move boatloads more product if they sold it as "Red Bull: If you've just given up smack, this is the beverage for you!" One evening, I watched Jason pound ten cans of Red Bull in the span of twenty minutes and felt compelled to remark, amazed "How the fuck didn't that explode your heart?"

"Sir," my sober friend offered, with no small amount of irony. "I used to shoot dope three times a day. If that didn't kill me, what the fuck harm can Red Bull do?"

During the day, Mewes would sporadically attend AA meetings, but every night, he went out with his boys. I'd initially expressed concern, suggesting that being around drinkers and druggers might not be the best environment for him, but Mewes assured me that the scene didn't faze him; in fact, it only strengthened his resolve to stay sober.

"Watching people act like assholes when they're shit-faced doesn't make me want to get high, sir," he'd say. "It makes me never want to get high again. I just like to be around people, dance, act a fool, and mack on chicks. That's what Project Falcon is all about."

"What's Project Falcon?" I asked, puzzled.

"That's what me, Jack, McGins and Milo call ourselves. It's a little gay, I know."

"As long as it keeps a needle out of your arm, you can call your posse 'Project Dick-Eater' for all I care."

Every morning around six or seven, I'd get up to let the dogs out. A light sleeper on his best days, Mewes would join me on the library deck, and we'd talk about his adventures from the previous night. I saw it as an opportunity to take the boy's pulse, to see where his head was from day to day.

"You use any drugs?" I'd ask.

"No, sir," he'd reply.

"Were you tempted?"

"Nope."

"Anyone offer you drugs?"

His answer to the third question would vary from morn to morn. Mostly, he revealed, people respected his sobriety. Once or twice, folks who were looking for the character of Jay would get insulted when Jason would decline to do rails with them. If they tried to force the issue, the club's bouncers — always looking out for the easy-to-love Mewes — would explain things to the offended parties with a degree of force. The only relapse he came close to while hanging at the Spider Club was an unintentional one, when a new bartender mistook Jason's order of a Red Bull as a mixed drink version that contained Red Bull and vodka. One sip in, Mewes spat it out and got the order corrected, forever after requesting an unopened can of Bull from that moment forward.

"You gonna use drugs tonight?" I'd round out my queries with.

"Not tonight," the boy would say. "I don't gotta live like that no more."

It was a slight variation on the old AA theme of "One day at a time", but "I don't gotta live like that no more" had become the Mewes mantra, and has kept him strong for over three years of complete sobriety now. There's a maturity in the boy these days that'd been missing all those years he spent spiking his veins and living fix to fix. And for all my pushing and pulling, my threats, my good intentions and angrily desperate actions, what eventually cleaned him up wasn't any external force or pressure. Like every addict before him and the millions who'll follow, Jason had to make the choice to clean up for himself — not for someone else; not even me. And whether it was because he was tired of living that empty lifestyle of waking every morning and immediately setting about to the task of finding more pills or scoring some dope; or whether it was because, with his thirtieth birthday approaching, he realized he'd either have to fulfill his promise to kill himself if he was still a junkie or beat that monkey off his back and start a somewhat normal life, something about that last rehab sojourn clicked with Mewes. There was no cathartic, cinematic moment in which all was suddenly made clear, the music swelled, and everyone knew a happy ending was in store. Indeed, after all that'd gone down since Jason succumbed to a life of addiction, we were all waiting for the other shoe to drop in that first week out of rehab; and that first month out of rehab; and that first year. Until, finally, it became clear that something had shifted in Jay, ever so slightly, and the landscape had changed permanently.

Many folks have given me a bunch of credit for hanging in there with Mewes through all the bullshit, and even tossed me the hosannas for getting the boy clean, but it was never me. The real hero of Jason's story is Jason himself.

More often than not, a hero's most epic battle is the one you never see; it's the battle that goes on within him or herself. And for whatever reason, the boy triumphed over his darker instincts, quietly laying to rest years of heartbreak and anguish. He entered sobriety in a similar fashion to his entrance into drug abuse: with little fanfare. After what felt like a lifetime of perils and pitfalls experienced side-by-side with — and sometimes at the hands of — Jason, I couldn't have been happier with the lack of drama that marked the end of Mewes's drug abuse era.

That first Christmas he spent with us post-rehab, the boy asked what gift he could get me for the holiday. I told him I didn't want anything beyond his promise that he'd never use dope again — at least 'til he was eighty. That morning, he handed me a tape.

You can watch that tape here:

http://www.clerks2blog.com/movies/jayMBAL.mov

His raw honesty was on full display, but it was his newfound maturity that was so staggering. Many times in the past, the boy had made me countless empty promises about getting off smack that he could and would never keep. In acknowledging his unwillingness to offer up another such pact that was beyond his ability to pledge, Jason had finally revealed the grown-up I'd always been hoping he'd become. And in not being able to give me what I asked for, he wound up giving me something so much better…

He gave me hope.

So on that mid-December early morn, circa 2003, on the balcony of my house in the Hollywood Hills, when Jason Mewes, my friend of seventeen years and co-star in five films at that point, dropped a bomb that should've repulsed the shit out of me, or at the very least, made me vomit a little in my mouth, I didn't retch, or smack him upside the head, hollering "Don't fuck the vapid, dammit!" Instead, I asked a question.

"Who is she?" I was blithely unaware, at that point, of her inane TV show, or her famous father. "You fucked her?"

"She fucked ME, sir. She just pulled me into a bathroom stall and fucked me. It was weird."

"Had you ever even met her before?"

"Once or twice. Through Kim Stewart."

"Rod Stewart's daughter."

"Yeah."

"What's with all the kids of eighties pop icons digging on you?"

"Because they know the Mewes is long, and he's strong, and he's down to get the friction on."

"See? There ARE benefits to staying clean."

"Oh, hell yeah. I was thinking about it yesterday: I been living here a month now, since I got out of rehab. And in one month, I've had sex with twenty-eight different girls."

"GOOD FUCKING GOD!!!"

"That's a lot, right?"

"A better advertisement for the joys of sobriety I can't imagine."

Mewes smiled. "I can. Being here, with my family. That beats fucking any day."

"That's a really sweet sentiment, sir. But let's not go nuts."

"It's true, sir. You know I don't lie now."

"You don't gotta live like that no more?"

Looking out at the quiet morning landscape of the Hollywood Hills, Mewes took a draw on his cigarette and uttered six simple words: "Not today, sir. Probably not tomorrow."

That observation contained more power and magic than any method of forced rehabilitation I'd crammed down his throat over the years. The man had paved his own path to hell, and with those six words, he'd paved his path OUT as well. It was the closest thing to a display of heroism I'd ever personally borne witness to.

And with his journey not quite complete but certainly out of the darkest woods, the hero then asked "Can I borrow twenty bucks? I want to go to breakfast with McGins at the Griddle."

I handed over the green, gave him a hug, and watched him go, satisfied that, for the first time in eons, the bucks were going into his belly instead of his arm. It was the best money I'd ever spent.

Fin.

Super-Pal
Sunday 23 April 2006 @ 8:55 p.m.

We're working on the final sound mix of *Clerks II* (although, you're never done-done until the flick comes out in theaters; and even then, there's the DVD release you can tweak... or the ten-year anniversary DVD release), and it's going swimmingly. The flick sounds phenomenal.

The Skywalker Ranch, contrary to what you might imagine, is no sprawling shrine to the Lucas empire (or *Empire*). You'd be hard-pressed to find so much as an Ewok spear, in the way of props, laying around campus — unless you hit the archives building, where everything from a life-sized *Jedi* speeder-bike to the Ark of the Covenant from *Raiders* go to die.

But what rocks about this place is how quiet and woodsy it is. Nestled in the hills of Marin County, Lucas used his *Empire Strikes Back* bankroll to purchase 5000 acres that would make up the ranch, home to the best sound-mixing facilities on the planet. But if you didn't know what went on inside most of the architecture that dots the landscape, you'd never imagine it was in any way tech-oriented: the buildings resemble large bed-and-breakfast Colonials, vineyard houses, and barns.

Roaming the hills and fields are all manner of livestock, from turkeys to steer. Every once in awhile, a ranch-hand vehicle rolls through, but other than that it's so still, you can hear bees buzzing from ten feet away. It's the kinda place you don't want to fart in, for fear that EVERYONE will know it was you; not even the one-cheek-sneak is safe at Skywalker Ranch.

Seven years ago, during our first mix here on *Dogma*, this pastoral beauty and quiet so moved my then-seven-month-pregnant girlfriend, that it caused the avowed Atheist to remark, "This is God's country."

"That it is," I agreed.

"This is the kinda place it'd be great to get married at."

"Yeah," I offered, oblivious to where this was going.

"We should do it."

"I'm all for it," I said, getting up to pull my shorts off, completely missing her point.

"No — I meant we should get married here."

"Oh. Sure. Yeah, one day we should."

"Why not now?" she countered.

"Now?"

"Yeah. This weekend. We could just go for it — kinda like we eloped or something."

"We could, yeah…"

After too long a pause, she nodded. "You don't wanna get married right now. I get it."

"No — I do. I just hadn't… I mean, we just started talking about it."

"We've been talking about getting married since the second time we had sex."

"I know. I meant we just started talking about getting married up here a few minutes ago, so…"

Life comes down to moments, and in those moments, all the big decisions are made. In that particular moment, I could've either deflected a bit, putting into perspective for her all the practical arguments against trying to pull together a wedding on such short notice, or opt out of unnerving an already emotional, hormonal pregnant chick and simply acquiesce.

But as I gazed at the woman in front of me, belly-chubby with my impending spin-off, my mind raced through the whirlwind romance we'd endured and enjoyed over the previous year and change: the instant, love-at-first-sight connection, the passion, the knock-down/drag-out fights, the growing pains and the uncanny comfort and familiarity. And suddenly, a third choice revealed itself.

And therein lies the story of why, on 25 April 1999, I married Jen.

On the Perils of Strip Clubs
Wednesday 3 May 2006 @ 1:07 p.m.

I know a woman who stripped her way through college. She's now a corporate headhunter, pulling down a six-figure annual salary, she's married, and she's got a kid. Her story, as they say, ends happily ever after.

Sadly, she's the only stripper I've ever "known" (and not in the Biblical sense, either). Sure, I've ENCOUNTERED many an exotic dancer back in the day, but I can't say I've ever really known them any better than, say, the guy who delivers my pizza. And that's not because I believe I'm too good to get friendly with a stripper; quite the contrary. I've just always imagined there are lines an exotic dancer doesn't want crossed; some fat dork from Jersey asking "You wanna grab lunch some time?" might be just the sorta line-crossing I'd imagine they're uncomfortable with.

However, I haven't frequented a strip club since Strutters in Long Branch, circa '89/'90, with Big Bry. Strutters was a juice bar, which meant the performers (oh, who am I kidding? the chicks who get their kit off) would get labia-dangling naked, because there was no booze on the premises. What a wild, wonderful world it was to discover...

For about a month. Then, Bry and I got tired of giving away hard-earned cash just to look at naked ladies. Mind you, these were the days before the internet (when the options one had to look at nude women you weren't involved with were limited) and long before I'd ever marry (at which point, I got to see a naked lady for free regularly AND do stuff with her), but that first glimpse at a Live Nude Girl clutching a brass pole with her thighs to the beat of 'I Remember You' still lingers in my cabeza. Oddly enough, it's not the ladies who made it all so memorable, but rather the dudes jockeying the stage.

Beyond the standard "Don't touch unless you're TOLD to touch" there's no universal etiquette for a strip club. After the condom on the banana demonstration, you're not handed a manual in Health class entitled "How to Conduct Yourself and Not Be Creepy at the Peelers", so behavioral patterns in da club range from guy-to-guy. Bry and I were the "We-like-to-see-brown-and-pink-eyes-up-close-but-don't-need-to-slide-the-back-of-our-palms-across-your-lips-while-you-accept-our-cash" types; we were there to get our freak on in the most civilized way possible. Show us your meat curtains, yes, but regard us with enough intelligence to know that you have zero interest in us beyond the exchange of currency for this privilege. We were happy to hand the dancers our tips, rather than make the bill exchange from lips to cleavage, or worse, from fingers to vag/ass. There was no seduction necessary, because we didn't buy into the fantasy — which is probably why we never became regulars. Both of us knew that, in the real world, none of these foin, foin ladies would take a leak on us if we were on fire at their feet in a public toilet after their water pill just kicked in, so we couldn't pretend that the furtive glances and come-hither eye contact was anything more than role-playing. And if I want to enter a magical world of make-believe, I'll watch old *Mister Rogers' Neighborhood* episodes.

While in Strutters, Bry and I spent as much time looking at our fellow patrons as we did looking at pussy. There were the OPEC Guidos — the Italian dudes whose hair was slicked back with so much oil that, fuck Iraq — Bush should've went to war on these dudes' heads. There were the OPs — the guys who came solo, who I always imagined stepping up to the ticket counter at a movie theater and sighing: "One, please". There were the Thread-Bares — the fellas who accepted so many lap-dances that their pants looked like they belonged to the Michael Palin's prisoner character in the opening credits of *Monty Python's Flying Circus*, as he hangs from chains on a dungeon wall, uttering "It's..."

But the most fascinating category of strip-clubbers we used to obsess over were the True Believers — the guys who bought into the myth, and seemed to seriously believe they had a shot with these women once "Girls, Girls, Girls" ended.

I'm sure that, if they ever noticed me gawking at them, the True Believers would've assumed I was into cock — so intense was my fascinated gaze. But I never had to worry about being caught studying them, as they never... NEVER took their eyes off the prize, man. These dudes were locked onto their targets — whichever girl was on the catwalk at the moment — like a NORAD-programmed ICB. This would reach a height of utter disturbance when the ladies finally worked their way over to the fellas in question. The fucking eye contact was so intense, you'd almost buy that there was a Chuck-Woolery-level love connection in their future. But then you'd look at the parties involved — a tanning-bed frequenting, twenty-something gorgeous Goddess, decked out in fuck-me pumps and clothes that'd do the Emperor proud, and a thirty year-old Indian-American in thick specs, thinning, black-matted hair matching that of his father, who, incidentally, was seated beside him, also macking on the stripper with a grin that'd make Mola Ram in *Temple of Doom* look like Gandhi — and realize that the *Pretty Woman* paradigm only works if the guy with the cash doling out strawberries is Richard Gere.

On the night of our second-to-last visit to Strutters, Bry and I took the opportunity to talk to one of the dancers about their Oscar-worthy performances with some of the least desirable-looking men in Monmouth County. The woman in question sauntered over to us, wearing an addled expression, asking if either of us were interested in a lap dance.

"You seem upset?" I observed.

"That prick over there just stuck his finger in my asshole," she replied.

"Like right IN it?" Bry asked.

"Can you believe it? What an animal."

Proving that chivalry wasn't dead, Bry immediately pushed twenty bucks into the woman's hands, saying: "Here — you deserve this."

"Sit down," she said, getting into lap-dancing position.

"No, that's cool," Bry countered. "I'd rather just talk."

Somewhat surprised, the girl sat beside us at the bar. We chatted for almost a half hour, inquiring about her life and what made he want to dance in the first place. Periodically, Bry would hand our new friend another twenty bucks, guilt-ridden over the fact that one of our own gender would breach the girl's exhaust, uninvited, without so much as a "By your leave".

We learned so much about the dancer's life in that half hour, but more than that, we learned that it was possible for the insanely beautiful to find a pair of trolls interesting. I mean, here was this heavenly creature, engaged in a conversation with us, getting to know us not for what we could give her, but because we showed her a little human compassion in her hour of need. We didn't look at her like she was a pair of tits (even though she was completely naked), and she didn't look at us like we were those Hindi True Believers down the bar — one of whom who'd been very forward with his pointer digit.

Before she had to head back to the stage for her set, we asked if she wanted to grab some late-night chicken salad at the Inkwell — the legendary Long Branch bohemian eatery with the dim lighting and the collegiate clientele that closed at 4 a.m. She said she couldn't tonight, because the boss on duty was a real hard-ass about the girls leaving with patrons. We shook hands, and she was off, heading to the stage. Rather than have her see us as the kind of guys who'd talk to her like human beings for half an hour only to ogle her while she worked the pole later on, Bry and I excused ourselves from Strutters and headed home, all-the-while discussing our newfound friend as well as the utter tragedy of the True Believers who thought for a minute that they were being treated with any degree of sincerity as they forked over their bills.

A week later, Bry and I went back to Strutters. As we paid the cover charge, we saw our new friend onstage, pelvis-thrusting into some dope's face. Rather than make her uncomfortable, we opted to hang out on a side couch 'til her set was over, refusing the legion of lap dances offered to us by the ladies waiting for their sets.

When the girl got off stage, she offered us this very concerned look as she approached us. We wondered if we'd done something wrong by coming back to the club during her act, now that we were all friends and whatnot. But as she joined us on the couch, she immediately dispelled that misconception in and oddly familiar way.

"What's the matter?" Bry asked.

"Some prick over there stuck his finger in my asshole," she offered, shaking her head.

"What — again?" I inquired. "Is that like a frequent on-the-job hazard?"

"What?" she yelled over the blaring music.

"That Hindu guy did the same thing to you last week."

The girl nodded at me, a bit perplexed, and then said "You guys want table dance?"

And then, it became clear that not only did the girl not remember us from the week before, but also that finger-in-the-asshole she'd complained about probably didn't happen either. We'd been played; she'd marked us as the wannabe-sensitive types who thought too much of themselves to gawk at gash and mash our faces into boobs. We were too proud to behave like the standard clientele, and y'know what they say — "Pride goeth before the fall". And as we not only fell but plummeted toward the realization that we'd been had, it dawned on me that somewhere in that bar, someone was looking at Bry and I and labeling us as the kinda guys who actually believed they were better than everyone else in the club, because they were sensitive and viewed the women as more than just business-types hell-bent for loot; they saw the working girls as people who, given the chance, would rather have a conversation with them than thrust their Brazilians within an inch of their maw. And the standard label for guys like that?

The Self-Righteous Retards.

Following that, we never went to Strutters again.

The "Clerks II: Electric Boogaloo" Contest!
Saturday 6 May 2006 @ 11:26 a.m.

On Friday, over at my MySpace page, I ran a contest, the prize of which was a signed, well-worn, aromatically-seasoned pair of my old Vans...

The contest was simple: come up with a subtitle for *Clerks II*.

The jist: create a subtitle for *Clerks II*, along the lines of *South Park: Bigger, Longer, Uncut*, or *Breakin' 2: Electric Boogaloo* (neither of which were eligible). Considering the fast food setting, I was looking for something like *Clerks II: Hold the Pickle* (also not eligible, since I already came up with it). The best double-entendre or most creative subtitle was to win the stinky sneakers, signed and personalized.

The contest ran for twenty-four hours, so by the end of page twenty-one of twenty-seven pages worth of entries, we had all the eligible contestants. There were some great ones, yes; but most surprising is how many people apparently think alike. By the end of the list, however, I was pretty convinced the name of the flick should remain simply *Clerks II*.

But that's not to say there weren't some clever-ass fuckers dropping suggestions. Honorable Mentions went to...

John for his naughty suggestion of: *Clerks II: Slapping the Meat in the Buns*
Gonz for his even naughtier: *Clerks II: We Touch Your Meat*
Milke for his ingenious wordplay of: *Clerks II: Eclectic Burger Crew*
Gav for his sexily suggestive: Clerks II: *Meat in the Mouth, Not in the Hand*

Hunter for taking it old school with: *Clerks 2: All Holes Filled With Hard Clerks*

The Jer for his McDonald's-inspired: *Clerks II: I'm Loathin' It*

Adam for the pretty funny: *Clerks II: Too Thick to Suck*

Mike for the simple fucking brilliance of: *Clerks II: Fuck You!!*

Owen for the alliterative: *Clerks II: Contempt and Condiments*

zombieplatypus for the very cute: *Clerks II: Hapless Meal*

2 Cows Fighting for a personal fave: *Clerks II: Toss the Salad*

Ashley for the Pierce Brosnan call-back (and oddly on-point): *Clerks II: Dante's Peak*

Jennifer for the "Snakes on a Plane" riff of: *Clerks II: Clerks in a Restaurant*

Josh for the literary: *Clerks II: Purgatorio*

Jason for the Matty Damon referenced: *Clerks II: The Bored Supremacy*

Jennifer for taking me back to high school with: *Clerks II: Hot Beef Injection*

CJ for the true double-entendre of: *Clerks II: Eating Out*

ElvX for remembering his film history with both: *Clerks II: The Phantom Lettuce* and *Clerks II: The Frying Game*

One, Two, Three and to the George for the porn title: *Clerks II: Hot Beef, Warm Buns, Special Sauce*

Kelvin for the ever-fun: *Clerks II: Fry Harder*

Rodger for his pimp-daddy suggestion: *Clerks II: You Got Served*

And a pair that were on the same page: Gonz and Ward for the good and slightly improved subtitles of: *Clerks II: Back for Sloppy Seconds* and *Clerks II: Sloppy Seconds* respectively.

But the grand prize winner — the dude who walked with the stinky-ass pair of sneakers, signed and personalized — was Joe for his timely (and pretty film-appropriate) suggestion of:

Clerks II: Counter Terrorism

Honorable Mention winners didn't walk empty-handed either: they're getting a *Clerks II* can cooler in the mail!

Good times, good times.

Sunday 7 May 2006 @ 9:03 p.m.

Yahoo has a button for a sneak peak at *Clerks II* on their front page. When you click on it, it brings you to another page where you can peep a bunch of pics from the flick.

The holy *New York Times* put up their summer movie preview, and a pic of Jay and Silent Bob rides the top of the page. This is cool online, but the pic was even bigger in the actual, old-fashioned newspaper version in the Sunday edition of the *Times* this morning.

In *Entertainment Weekly*, I got a shout out on their Must List (Ten Things We Love This Week). Number six was the blog-site My Boring-Ass Life, of which they wrote "Kevin Smith's no-holds-barred online diary is like his best films: raw, openhearted, and mordantly funny." In the mag, there's a nice picture of me having what I can only describe as a bad hair day.

However, on the back page of *EW*, Stephen King does a weekly column, with the current edition being a piece detailing his summer movie predictions.

Alright, they're not King's predictions; they're the predictions of a guy he calls 'The Longhair'. But being that this is the guy who's also worked under the pseudonym Richard Bachman, I'm not convinced The Longhair isn't, in fact, King himself.

Regardless, The Longhair predicts this summer's hits and misses, and under the heading Flop City (below *The Omen*, An *American Haunting*, the Vince Vaughn/Jennifer Aniston flick *The Break-Up*, and M. Night Shymalan's *Lady in the Water*), he lists *Clerks II*. Of it, he (The Longhair) writes "In *Raiders of the Lost Ark*, Major Toht tells Indy, "That time is past." He might have been speaking of the *Clerks* franchise. Uh... what franchise?"

Some folks on the message board at my home-base, ViewAskew.com, thought I might be pissed at *Entertainment Weekly* for running this. But I got no bones with *EW*. Aside from the two times they've given My Boring-Ass Life a shout-out on their Must List, they also hyped *Clerks II* at number ten in a feature last week entitled The Ten Movies We Can't Wait to See, and gave us a nice write-up in their Summer Preview issue.

I also have no bones with someone named 'The Longhair' opining that *Clerks II* will flop. You mean to tell me there's someone out there who doesn't give a tinwhistle about the flicks I do? I'm shocked...

However, the irony is that *Clerks II* CAN'T flop. Since our entire budget was five million bucks, if the flick makes ten million bucks theatrically, we're successful (and that ten million theatrical doesn't even include the DVD windfall that'll eventually follow; our flicks do extremely well on DVD).

And there's DEFINITELY ten million bucks worth of theatrical box office out there for us — maybe a little more than ten million, actually (*Jay and Silent Bob Strike Back* opened to eleven million the weekend it opened in August 2001, on its way to a theatrical gross of thirty million; and *Strike Back* cost fifteen million more to make than *Clerks II* did).

So when folks like The Longhair poo-poo the theatrical prospects of *Clerks II*, they don't come off as offensive to me; they come off as more misinformed than anything else. The Longhair can chicken-little it all he (or she) wants, but *Clerks II* will never have an apartment in "Flop City".

Clerks II won't see *Superman Returns*, *X-3* or even *Snakes on a Plane*-type box office numbers, granted. But relative to the flick's budget, it'll mint some nice coin, to be sure.

However, box office-shmox office: what really counts is whether a flick stays with the viewer after they've gone home, and for how long. Considering the fact that, twelve years later, there was still enough love for/interest in *Clerks* to warrant a *Clerks II*, I'm hoping the latest installment in Dante and Randal's (complete lack of) adventures earns the same amount of affection, if not more. Keep the theatrical grosses, I say; I'm all about longevity.

Except, y'know... in bed. As my wife will tell you, I'm a five minute-max-kinda-guy there. But they're some of the sweatiest, fear-of-being-crushed-inducing five minutes my woman has ever known.

So I got THAT going for me.

Johnny Rotten vs. Stan Lee!
Tuesday 9 May 2006 @ 4:02 p.m.

On Friday, 29 April, we held a Spoken Word Event at my house to benefit the arts program at my daughter's school. Let it never be said that I'm not a philanthropist, okay (but if anyone calls me a philatelist, they're gonna get punched; I fucking hate stamps)? Because we raised twenty grand for that neediest of causes: kids in private school.

This was the second such event we've hosted at the house, the inaugural outing being last year, back when it was dubbed The Poetry Event. This year, I wanted to move away from calling it a Poetry Event and move toward something edgy and cool, *à la* Spoken Word Event, because Poetry Event just sounds too... gay. And I don't mean gay in that awesome, cock-sucking way. I mean gay in that horrible, boring-ass, lame, straight, breeder kinda fashion. See, I'm a friend of the gay community. I've always maintained that I'm just one cock-in-the-mouth shy of being gay myself. And I understand why gay dudes crave a big, luscious dick: hung like a kindergartner as I am, I, too, have always craved a big, luscious dick myself. Sadly, my thirst will go forever unquenched.

When I was a kid, I'd see movies about Hollywood parties and read articles about Hollywood parties (usually in *Hustler*) that portrayed any Tinsel Town get-together as merely an excuse to have an orgy, replete with pounds of blow and unnatural sex. But last year's Poetry Event was a real eye-opener for me: I thought a few folks would rattle off some "Two roads diverged in a yellow woods"-type shit, and then suddenly, BAM! An explosion of jism, with spunk criss-crossing the room, creating a veritable spider-web of bodily fluids. Naturally, I wouldn't have partaken in the debauchery myself, as I'm a happily married man. But, fuck it — I like seeing shit go into other shit, so I'd have been more than happy to watch all that dirty boots-knocking (preferably from beneath a glass table). Sadly, however, I learned that Poetry Event isn't code for Wife-Swapping. It means exactly that: Poetry Event.

For this year's event, we had so many requests for tickets that we over-sold the show, and roughly 100 people at $200 a pop got to cram into my living room and peep an impressive roster of readers, all of whom did a bang-up job busting with the stanzas and iambic pentameter. I was the emcee, and here's how I introduced the evening's readers:

As police psychiatrist Dr. Emil Skoda on three of the four different *Law & Order* incarnations, he's helped convict tons of felons, and as Vernon Schillinger on HBO's *Oz*, he gets to rape all those felons. He's worked with both the Coen Brothers AND Spider-Man, and since he's also the voice of the Yellow M&M in those M&M commercials, he's the only guy here tonight who can get away with the pickup line: "I'll melt in your mouth, not in your hands." Ladies and gentlemen... J.K. SIMMONS.

Our next reader's the only person here tonight who's been a guest on *The Love Boat*, *Hill Street Blues*, *Murder, She Wrote*, *LA Law* AND *Doogie Howser, M.D.* As Hank Kingsley on *The Larry Sanders Show*, he introduced "Hey, now!" into our lexicon, and he played both George and Oscar Bluth on one of my all-time favorite shows, *Arrested Development*. Give it up for a star of stage and screen, and a funny motherfucker... MR. JEFFREY TAMBOR.

I'm pretty sure our next reader is the only cat in the room tonight who's been on the stage at the World Famous Apollo. He's just finished his first season on *Saturday Night Live* as a full-fledged cast member and he's got a comedy DVD coming soon called *I'm Snap Famous*. Give it up for the man from Hot-Lanta, Starkisha himself... MR. FINESSE MITCHELL.

Our next reader is the first of two living legends in the house tonight. Nobody knows who created the Greek gods of myth, but when it comes to twentieth-century mythology, we can all say we KNOW who created some of the biggest icons of pop culture history: Spider-Man, the Incredible Hulk, the Fantastic Four, Iron Man, the X-Men. And since he also created Daredevil, I will always owe this man for providing me with a bottomless well of 'Ben Affleck in tight red leather' jokes. He's a gentleman, a scholar, a friend, and the hottest eighty-four year-old piece of ass you'll ever see. The star of *Mallrats*, ladies and gentlemen... MR. STAN LEE.

Our next reader is one half of the comic duo *Girls Guitar Club*, so finally we're getting someone up here who doesn't have a dick. Besides me. You've seen her on *Mr. Show*, you've seen her on *The Larry Sanders Show*, you've seen her in *Dude, Where's My Car?* but most folks probably know her as the CTU tech analyst Chloe O'Brian on the show that's not habit-forming at all, *24*. Let's hope her poem is called 'Does Jack Bauer Get Out of the Baggage Hold With the Cassette Tape?' Ladies and gentlemen... MARY LYNN RAJSKUB

Keeping the dickless mojo we've got going on now, our next presenter taught an entire generation of girls that it was cool to carry a laser blaster and wear your hair all fucked-up and stupid. In 1987, she published her first novel, *Postcards from the Edge*, and then followed it up with *Surrender the Pink, Delusions of Grandma* and *The Best Awful There Is*. She's been in tons of movies, written the Academy Awards, and she's a mom. I've always wanted her to tell me she loves me while I was being lowered into a carbonite pit, just so I could offer her a pimp-like nod and say "I know". Give it up for an over-achiever... CARRIE FISHER.

Our next reader brings a screeching halt to the all-dickless reader streak we've been on, but while he's all man, he's also been known to get tarted-up a bit. In the year 2000, he took home two Emmys for his brilliant standup show *Dress to Kill* that played every other hour on HBO. If you haven't seen his prior shows *Definite Article* and *Glorious*, you're a fucking disgrace. He's played both Lenny Bruce on stage and Charlie Chaplin on film, but he's a legend in this house for introducing the phrase: "Cake or death?" into our lexicon. One of the funniest human beings to ever walk the earth, ladles and jelly-spoons, I give you... EDDIE IZZARD.

Next up, we're gonna drop a fucking Academy Award-winner on yer asses who's gonna hobble you dirty-birds with a cockadoodie reading. She taught us how to scream "TOWANDA!" in *Fried Green Tomatoes*, busted-dust in *Primary Colors*, and hot-tubbed with Nicholson in *About Schmidt*. And if that's not impressive enough, she's also directed a shit-load of episodes of *Six Feet Under*. Ladies and gentlemen, give it up for the one and only BoBo... KATHY BATES.

Next up is our second Brit of the evening, which means we're gonna hear more poetry the way it SHOULD sound: fucking gay. He's another stage actor, but from the British stage, which means he's better at it than Kathy Bates, simply by virtue of his nationality. You'll probably know him best as Doctor Nigel Townsend on NBC's *Crossing Jordan*. Party people, let's hear it for… STEVEN VALENTINE.

Our next reader is as important an LA fixture as the Hollywood sign. But unlike the Hollywood sign, she's not nearly as old, and you'll never find empty forties or used condoms lying at her feet. She's a writer and columnist for the *Los Angeles Times*, a host of *The Book Show* on PBS, a regular contributor to *Morning Edition* on NPR, a winner of five Emmys, four Golden Mike awards, and a pair of Pulitzer Prizes. But more impressive than all of that? They named a hot dog after her at Pink's. Give it up for the lady in the hat… PATT MORRISON.

Next up, we've got a lady who once gave a piano concert on a freeway overpass in downtown LA. The author of several books, including the semi-autobiographical *A Year in Van Nuys*, she's another NPR regular whose KCRW show *The Loh Life* was cancelled in 2004 after she said the word fuck on air, proving that America truly is the home of free speech. For her recent one-woman show *Mother On Fire*, the *LA Times* dubbed her "The high priestess of Los Angeles humor". For her appearance here tonight, we dub her simply… SANDRA TSING LOH.

Our next reader was on a show my grandmother used to refer to as 'her stories', the daytime soap *The Young and the Restless*. She once spoke candidly in *Rolling Stone* about her affection for vibrators, and as a result, fans started sending her sex toys in the mail. I'm pretty sure my grandmother sent her the three-speed, gyrating rabbit, batteries included. She's on screens right now in *The Sentinel* so I'm sure she appreciates you all sitting here watching this shit instead of buying tickets for her flick. But she's best known as the wandering wife Gaby Solis on the hit ABC show *Desperate Housewives*. Take your hands out of your laps and put 'em together for… EVA LONGORIA.

We've saved the best for last, folks. Our second living legend of the evening is a man who fronted not one but two insanely influential bands. He does my house more honor than I fear my house can bear. Living history will stand here in a minute, but first, I'd like to read a note he sent to the Rock and Roll Hall of Fame, when he declined, on behalf of his band, to attend their induction: 'Next to the Sex-Pistols, rock and roll and that hall of fame is a piss stain. Your museum. Urine in wine. We're not coming.' So imagine our surprise when he said yes to this fucking thing. Ladies and Gentlemen, and other cunts, never mind the bollocks here's… JOHNNY ROTTEN.

To say the event was a howling success would be an understatement. Every reader held the audience's attention rapt. It was a great crowd, too — all whooping and hollerin' and whatnot (the open bar might've had something to do with it, natch).

Some highlights of the evening...

— Sitting at a table on the deck with Johnny Rotten on my left and Stan Lee on my right, and listening to them have-at one another. Always a gentle joker, Stan was saying, "I can't understand a word this guy's saying," about Johnny, and Johnny was hissing, "Listen, Dad — you don't know who you're dealing with. I'm Rotten."

— Jeffrey Tambor wrapping up his set with a dryly delivered "I'll read one more piece, because I've got two more poetry events to hit before the night's over."

— Finesse Mitchell, doing a pair of impromptu poems entitled 'Mapquest Don't Know Where This House Is' and 'Goddamn, This is a Nice House'. As funny as he was, he wrapped his set up with a really moving poem entitled 'There Was Ugly in the Church Today'. That guy's totally cool in my book.

— Stan Lee, working without a microphone, reciting three not-short poems from memory, and then humorously editorializing at the end of each. He was all prepared to do 'The Raven' from memory as well, but decided to hold onto it 'til next year's event. The man, mind you, is eighty-four fucking years old — and yet, he owned that room. The crowd loved him.

— Kathy Bates, riffing on my intro, saying: "Now I wish I'd brought the other poem I wrote with me: 'Big, Luscious Dicks'."

— Carrie Fisher, sweating the event once she heard the intro and some of the other readers, insisting she only came prepared with one short poem. Then, when it was her turn, she took the mic and said: "Sherlock Holmes used to say that the mind can only house so much information. And when new things are learned, old things get pushed out. But this is something that I've been able to hold onto for a long time." She paused, and then began: "General Kenobi — years ago, you served my father in the Clone Wars..." Yes — she did the entire "Help me, Obi-Wan Kenobi" speech from memory. Brought the cheering house to its fucking feet, she did.

— Mary Lynn Rajskub doing not just a really funny excerpt from her forthcoming, one-woman show, but also an extended hysterical intro about being in 24, famous and not knowing shit about computers.

— Steve Valentine rocking some Shel Silverstein, then following it up with reading some morbidly funny epitaphs he'd found online. And if that wasn't enough, he capped his presentation off with a pretty wicked card trick, reciting patter from a 1930s magician, set to a rap beat. He killed.

— Eva Longoria, post-introduction, saying "You mention liking vibrators in one interview, and it haunts you forever."

— John 'Johnny Rotten' Lydon launching into what seemed like a blistering, anti-abortion screed ("Bodies") at a room full of terrified parents, calling one of the audience members out when she uncomfortably chuckled by saying: "Is this fucking funny to you?! Are you an animal?" blaming all of us for electing George Bush and then dismissing petrol-centric politics with: "This is what you need oil for," while rubbing his asshole over his pants and then patting a balding dude in the front row's head, Benny Hill style, adding "Or this," and then finishing up with an a capella version of 'God Save the Queen' with the audience singing along. Fucking amazing.

In terms of a fundraiser, the whole thing couldn't have been cooler. Big props to my wife Jen for pulling it all together, with massive help from PTA head Russell Milton and Daniella, his classy-ass British wife (and the person who suggested getting Johnny Rotten in the first place). All I did was monkey-it-up as the emcee; THEY did all the hard work. And man, was it worth it; truly a once-in-a-lifetime experience.

Clerks II Movin' On Up!
Friday 12 May 2006 @ 10:56 a.m.

Clerks II is coming out EVEN EARLIER THIS SUMMER!

In a ballsy move that says "Fuck you: we're a five-million-dollar flick and we're coming out in the fucking middle of the summer, bitches!", Weinstein Co. has upped the *Clerks II* release date from 18 August to 21 JULY! The wait is now almost a month shorter, folks!

Why the move? Getting into Cannes changed everything. Since the film will have its world début on 26 May, the Weinstein folks thought it'd make more sense to get the film out there sooner, rather than later. They found a weekend in which there wasn't any flick that directly competed with the movie for an audience, and staked their claim.

Now, we're opening against some pretty big flicks (*Lady in the Water*, *Monster House*), but nothing that's appealing directly to our core audience. So while we'll never open at number one (those two flicks alone are pretty mass-appeal movies), we stand to make a decent chunk of change and wind up somewhere in the top ten.

Good news for me, great news for anyone who's been patiently waiting for *Clerks II* to open.

An Eight-Minute Standing Ovation!
Saturday 27 May 2006 @ 10:42 a.m.

Last night, we debuted *Clerks II* at the Cannes Film Festival.

With all the vitriol surrounding some of the press screenings of flicks there this year, I was pretty terrified *Clerks II*, also, might be greeted by a chorus of French boos (and I ain't talking about champagne).

However, after last night, I say "VIVE LA FRANCE!"

When the flick ended and the credits started rolling, a standing ovation began that lasted a full eight minutes. It was surreal and wonderful, and it just kept going and going. I looked to Harvey (Weinstein, our boss), that old Cannes war-horse, to see if the cast and I should start heading out of the theater: as it was two in the morning and the applause wasn't showing any signs of stopping. But from two aisles back, he responded with a waving "no" finger at me, mouthing the words "Don't move". So we all stayed put.

By the time the credits ended, I figured the audience was done applauding as well.

But they weren't.

They just kept on clapping. And thankfully, not only did Zack and Joey get the whole thing on tape to prove it all happened (watch for it in a new Train Wreck video blog, up this weekend), but Roger Friedman over at Fox411 was there as well, documenting what I have to say was one of the twenty most amazing moments of my life.

The applause finally stopped after eight minutes. Harvey was over the moon about it. "In my thirty years of coming here, I've never seen a standing ovation last that long at a midnight show in Cannes," he said. "Ever."

En route to the theater, I prayed that the notoriously fickle Cannes audience wouldn't boo the flick. During the screening, I prayed that the film would keep playing as gang-busters as it had been playing up 'til that point, and that the audience stayed with us, rather than succumb to mid-flick naps. After the screening, I started praying that I never forget that insanely special moment that I shared with Jeff, Brian, Rosario, Mos and Jen — when time seemed to stand still, and at the world's most famous film festival, we all stared wide-eyed (and wider-smiled) at a room-full of cats staring back at us (with equally wide smiles and palms cooked red from non-stop applause) who really, really "got" what we were trying to communicate with *Clerks II*.

Life comes down to a few major moments. Last night was definitely one of them.

The Kansas City Test Screening of *Clerks II*
Tuesday 6 June 2006 @ 2:01 a.m.

So tonight, after dodging the bullet for months now, we had our first (and only) test screening with a general audience for *Clerks II*.

Let me say a few words about test screenings: I hate them. Fuck, do I hate them. I don't mind the actual screening portion, where you're sitting there with an audience watching the flick and listening to their reactions; that part's totally cool. It's when the screening ends, the lights come up, and the folks in charge start handing out survey cards for the audience to fill out... *that's* when shit usually goes south for me. And even worse, twenty or twenty-five people are kept behind to take part in what's known as a 'focus group', where they're asked pointed questions about the movie ("Did you like it?" and "What didn't you like about it?" and "Would you recommend it to people, and if not, why not?") and the filmmakers are forced to hide in the back of the theater and listen to an audience eviscerate something they've worked so hard on for so long; without being able to get up and defend themselves or the flick. Of all the aspects of filmmaking that go into the gestalt of cinematic storytelling, this is definitely the least appetizing. I don't know any filmmaker who enjoys it.

Now normally, one test screens (or is forced to test screen by the studio) in an effort to look for cuts or make changes in the flick, based on how audiences react to the screening. On *Jersey Girl*, we endured ten of these screenings, in a failed effort to make the movie more palatable to a mainstream audience. With *Clerks II*, the idea wasn't to look for cuts or changes (indeed, the prints are locked at this point); tonight's test screening was purely a marketing screening, set up by the Weinstein Company in an effort to shed some light on how to go about selling the flick.

Based on that, there was no real risk to us: if the audience hated the flick, we weren't going to be forced to make changes. After all, the flick only cost five million to make, so the financial risks facing the Weinstein Company are minimal at best. And with the lion's share of our foreign pre-sales taken care of at Cannes

2005 (a year before we'd screen at the fest to an eight-minute standing ovation, plug, plug) the movie's budget, it's been revealed, was already taken care of; in essence, the movie's in profit before opening day.

Still, any screening in which cards are gonna be filled out and comments about the qualities (or lack thereof) of the flick are gonna be made is nerve-wracking to a filmmaker. So when the lights dimmed in this Kansas City theater (chosen because the Weinstein Company wanted to see how the movie would play in the heartland), I was sweating it. This wasn't a room comprised of hard-core fans. The audience recruit for the test screening didn't list any of our previous flicks on the list of movies potential attendees had to have seen theatrically to be considered for inclusion. The 'Qualifying Films' list (of which the audience must have seen at least three) looked like this: *Bad Santa*, *Malibu's Most Wanted*, *The 40 Year Old Virgin*, *Dodgeball*, *White Chicks*, *Team America: World Police*, *The Ringer*, *Old School*, *Anchorman*, *High Fidelity*, *Napoleon Dynamite*, and *Wedding Crashers*. Not a *Chasing Amy* or *Jay and Silent Bob Strike Back* anywhere in sight.

The Demographics they were looking for were sixty percent male, forty percent female, seventeen to thirty-four (sixty percent under twenty-five). Essentially, a mainstream comedy audience — something, I feel, our flick really isn't.

The good news is that it was, apparently, an easy recruit. They had a line that wrapped the building of people looking to get in. Thirty or forty potential attendees had to be turned away. We had a packed house of close to 400. But when the *Clerks II* title card came up, there was no raucous applause (a normally great indicator that the room is full of friendlies).

However, that was about the only point in the screening when there *weren't* applause.

Man, that screening rocked. The audience was with the flick every step of the way. It played even better, I dare say, than it did in Cannes (which I guess isn't *that* surprising, since the entire audience, unlike the Cannes screening, was comprised of folks whose first language was English). There were only three walk-outs (one of whom was a mid-thirties woman who felt the film was "disgusting"), and they all left in the first twenty minutes (by which time anybody who feels the flick isn't their kinda poison heads for the hills). After that first twenty minutes, nobody left. That's rare for us and our flicks (especially considering how out there our flicks can get; this one in particular).

When the flick ended, there was resounding applause (also pretty fucking rare in a test screening). The audience filled out their cards, and twenty-five folks were kept behind for the focus group.

The focus group didn't seem to match the audience reaction we heard while watching the flick. Folks were a bit more reserved in their praise. But the majority of the focus group rated the flick "excellent", "very good", and "good". Only one person rated it "fair". Nobody chose "poor". Marketing data gleaned from the screening: folks felt (thank Christ) that no subtitle (i.e. *Clerks II: The Second Coming*) was needed; *Clerks II* said it all. And much to the delight of the Weinstein Company, no one in the focus group felt that seeing the first *Clerks* was necessary in order to dig *Clerks II*.

That top two boxes score is key in the test screening process: it's the figure that represents the percentage of people who rated the flick "excellent" and "very good". When the scores are tallied from the survey sheets, there are two figures everyone immediately wants to know: the top two boxes score, and the "definite recommends" (the percentage of those surveyed who say they would definitely recommend the flick to friends). Based on the focus group, Scott and I felt that we were looking at a score of seventy percent in the top two boxes, but neither of us could imagine what the definite recommends figure would be.

When Laurie Eddings brought us the score sheet, she had a smile on her face. Scott and I had told her we thought it was a seventy percent top two box score, and Laurie held up the sheet and said: "It's better than that."

The percentage of that audience who rated the film "excellent" was fifty-six percent. The normal average is twenty-five percent. The combined score of the top two boxes was eighty-four percent; the normal top two boxes average is fifty-five percent. We were twenty-nine percent above the average (the average being the score that everyone breathes easier at). Thirteen percent of the audience rated the film as "good". Two percent rated the film as "fair". Only one percent rated the film as "poor" (likely the "disgusted" woman).

The "definite recommends" score norm is forty-five percent. *Clerks II* got a seventy-four percent — nearly thirty percent above the norm. Seventy-four percent of that audience said they would definitely recommend the film to their friends, with a vast lion's share of the remaining twenty-six percent saying they'd "probably" recommend the movie to their friends.

Considering where we were screening, for this flick to score an eighty-four percent with a seventy-four percent definite recommend is nothing short of astounding. Mainstream movies testing in Kansas City score eighty-four percent; a sequel to a black and white indie flick that's filled with some of the crudest, weirdest shit you've ever seen and heard in a movie theater doesn't score an eighty-four percent. And yet, tonight, it did. In the fucking heartland. In middle-America.

Needless to say, we're all thrilled.

So thank you, Kansas City, Missouri, for an amazing, very memorable night; you've made my life considerably easier. And thanks to Harvey for forcing us to do the test screening; it was definitely worth all the worry leading up to it. And thanks to the cast and crew for all their hard work; without them, there's no movie to score in the first place.

But most of all, thanks to that mid-thirties woman who walked out in disgust. Because, for a second there, I was beginning to think maybe I'd gone soft in my old age. I'm relieved to know that my sense of humor is still not to everyone's taste.

Fuck, this movie's been a sweet-ass ride thus far. God-willing, it'll continue through 'til 21 July (and beyond).

Timing is Everything
Thursday 15 June 2006 @ 2:30 p.m.

They say there are only three basic stories that can ever be told: man (or woman) vs. man (or woman), man (or woman) vs. environment, and man (or woman) vs. himself. Every story ever told falls under one of these three basic categories.

A guy posted on the message board over at my home-site, ViewAskew.com, inviting people to the premiere of his new movie, *Amber Sunrise*. I peeped the YouTube trailer for the flick and one thought ran through my head…

"Wow… There goes *Name*, I guess."

Name was a film that long-time View Askew board folks would remember as the flick that I was talking about making after *Chasing Amy*, circa '97. And since this *Amber* picture shares some big similarities with what *Name* was gonna be, I figured my chances of ever making the flick were suddenly null and void. So I wrote a five paragraph synopsis of what the flick was gonna be to share with the folks at the ViewAskew.com board, and then, before hitting "submit"… I opted to erase it instead. I may not ever make the flick now, but it'd make a great comic book story, if I ever get around to it. So I opted to hold onto it instead, for the time being.

Regardless, this whole discovery is further proof that good ideas should be enacted on immediately — lest someone else come up with the same good idea, somewhere down the road, and actually bring it to fruition. I'm in no way, shape, or form suggesting plagiarism on this dude's behalf, mind you; indeed, you can't plagiarize something that only existed in my head and never saw print. It's just weird how people can have the same idea sometimes, albeit years apart, in this instance.

This is the second time I've had this feeling this year, though. Back in '98, I'd pitched this superhero movie to Miramax (that Harvey loved), which was kind of a *Pulp Fiction* anthology flick about a Justice League-of-sorts that is forced to disband, due to a government decree (*à la Watchmen*). The flick would then follow all the characters in different segments, and then bring them together again in the end to take on a common threat (one of their own, gone rogue). The flick was darkly funny and a pretty straightforward take on the superhero mythos; not a tongue-in-cheek affair at all. The *Untitled Superhero Project* was a mainstay in my overall Miramax deal for years, though I never got around to writing it. In 2000, while in pre-production on *Jay and Silent Bob Strike Back*, I pitched it as a show to HBO, and they "bought" it and told me to write a pilot... and, again, I never got around to writing it. Something else always came up.

Anyway, in the segment/chapter of the flick that followed the Wonder Woman-type character, she found out her husband was cheating on her and decided to use her super-powers to do a brutal, *Extremities* kinda thing on the louse (picture the *Reservoir Dogs* ear-slicing scene at twenty minutes long, with super-powers and a lot more than an ear getting cut).

Opening, ironically, on the same day as *Clerks II* is a flick called *My Super Ex-Girlfriend* — which seems to be a light-hearted treatment of similar material.

The moral of the story (which, if you're keeping track, falls under the heading: man vs. himself) is this: don't wait. When you've got what you feel is a cool, original story to tell... fucking tell it quick. Because if you don't, sooner or later, someone else will.

Where the Fart Have I Been?!
Sunday 25 June 2006 @ 3:27 p.m.

I've been everywhere, man. I've been ev-er-y-where.

Spent all of last week going city-by-city, doing advance *Clerks II* press (radio, print, TV) in Minneapolis/St. Paul, Chicago, Detroit and Boston. This week, I'll be in Philly on Monday, New York on Tuesday, D.C. on Wednesday, Atlanta on Thursday, and Toronto on Friday. If you're in any of those markets, and you're up in the mornings, you might be able to hear me on any number of morning radio shows (though none in NYC on Tuesday morning).

Brian O'Halloran and Jeff Anderson (Dante and Randal) have also been out on the road doing press, visiting San Diego, San Francisco, Portland, Seattle, Denver, Houston and St. Louis. This week, they'll be in Kansas City, Cleveland and Miami.

As we get closer and closer to 21 July, there's a bunch of *Clerks II* stuff happening: The final theatrical poster is in theaters…

As are the teaser posters (including a new Rosario poster)…

An exclusive intro by yours truly and an overview Train Wreck is running at the Apple.com's trailer page.

And in the Sunday edition of the holy *New York Times*, there's a two page article about *Clerks II* and me…

While two *Clerks II* commercials ran during the NBA Finals last Sunday, the majority of the TV spots begin in earnest this week, mostly on networks like Comedy Central and Spike. There's a pretty sweet VH-1 *Clerks II* special that starts running in a couple of weeks as well. At this point, if the movie doesn't do okay at the box office, it won't be for lack of press and coverage.

We're now less than a month away from opening day, folks. Fingers crossed.

Am I mad at Ben Affleck?
Thursday 29 June 2006 @ 6:46 a.m.

Been reading about how mad I'm supposed to be for not being cast in *Gone, Baby, Gone*. Not that I should have to clarify this, but it's patently untrue: I am not mad, hurt, or "fuming" at not getting cast in Ben's flick.

Christ, is it really such a slow news week that what was obviously me joking around has become some kind of column item? I swear…

Lesson learned: if you do press in Boston, and somebody asks you about Ben, just refuse to comment or say anything about the man. Don't joke about him. Don't even say the word "Ben". Because when you do, this kinda shit happens.

You've gotta be willfully retarded to take those comments I made seriously. Jesus — irony really is dead.

Was I "fuming" when I cracked that joke? No. Am I "fuming" now? Yes — and NOT at Ben.

Nose-picking and an anal sex primer
Monday 3 July 2006 @ 1:26 p.m.

I get a ton of shit from the wife for how often my finger's up my nose. Anyone else got one of these spouses/girlfriends/boyfriends?

What's the big fucking deal? I'm a smoker, so I get boogers. Where's the harm in digitally cleaning that shit out? It's not like I'm mining for gold then making a salty deposit in the Oral Bank or something. I pick, and depending on where I am, I flick. If I'm near a tissue, I'll stuff the fruits of my labor in it, sure. But if no tissue's handy? Zooooooom! Across the room it goes, for parts unknown. Wherever it lands ain't my problem; it's not up my nostrils anymore, and that's all that matters.

I get a lot of "Just use a tissue to blow your nose, you fucking skeve." However, blowing your nose doesn't necessarily do the trick, y'know? The hard and crusties sometimes don't always budge during the conventional nose-blow. A finger scrub's the best way to guarantee no danglers. And don't gimme any of this "Well use the tissue to scrape 'em out" shit; tissues break, and then I've got this toxic bullshit up my shnoz as well as the nose crud. Tissues (or toilet paper) is for your ass, I say. THAT'S when you don't want tactile contact with something coming out of your body: when a stench accompanies it. But boogers have no odor. I don't use a Kleenex to wipe away sleepers (or eye crud); why the fuck would I use a tissue to get unscented waste out of some other hole in my body?

Why is seeing a finger up someone's nose considered such bad form? I see someone picking their nose, I'm like "Now THERE'S a motherfucker I can TRUST." Kids are notorious nose-pickers, and who's more trustworthy than a child — unless, of course, that child's Damien? However, I don't recall ever seeing Damien pick his nose in either the original *Omen* or the recent remake, which strengthens my point even further: Satan's spawn DOESN'T pick his nose. Who wants to be like that kid, with the bad bowl-cut and the constant scowl (in the remake, at least), pissing off baboons (in the original) and knocking your mother off a top-floor balcony (in both)? If the Anti-Christ is all about doing the opposite of what's righteous, maybe picking your nose has the air of divinity about it?

We can learn a lot from those *Omen* flicks. The first time the concept of ass-fucking was introduced to me was via *The Final Conflict* — the under-appreciated third entry in the original *Omen* saga, starring Sam Neill as the now-adult Damien. He hooked up with this reporter lady, and at one point, they're getting down. Suddenly, he flips the chick over and buries it, all evil-like, in her dumper. As an eleven year-old without the benefit of an internet connection (or an internet, period), I was confused, to say the least. Sure — I knew about conventional sex (I used to shoplift *Hustler* from the local magazine store), but the horror in this woman's eyes and the physical displeasure she was indicating spoke of some unforgivable act I wasn't schooled in. I was watching the scene and imagining this dude's sporting some kind of forked cock (I mean, he IS the devil), that's got a hydra-like head that's snapping at this poor lady's snapper — hence all the crying. I turn to my brother and ask "What the hell's going on, ya' think?" And my brother explains that Damien's getting all sorts of rectal with this chick.

"He's putting it in her butt," Brother Don tells me. "Why?" I ask. "Because he's the devil. That's what the devil does, I guess."

Now, coming from a Catholic household and six years of Catholic school at this point, you'd imagine that'd be some kind of formative moment for both of us: like, from that moment forward, me and my brother would forever associate (or ASSociate) anal sex with Armageddon, and I'd grow up to be one of these "gays are the devil's pawns" kinda guys. Instead, my brother grew up to be gay (married to a man, and celebrating their thirteenth anniversary today, as a matter of fact), and I became something of an ass-man myself (though with the ladies). The only Armageddon it introduced was my brother and I growing up to be like "Armageddon me some ass!"

What I did take from *Final Conflict*, however, was that anal is something to be approached delicately. For that reason, I'm far less agro than Damien when it comes to the booty; I'm smoove. I'd have sex for the first time approximately two years after seeing that flick (I lost it at age thirteen, with a chick named Norma), but it'd be two more years after that before I got into some of my first digital ass-play with my then-girlfriend, in a parked VW Beetle. Oddly, Damien and his hate-fucking antics never once sprang to mind. There was no spooky music and howls of terror; it was actually all kinds of cool, because the two of us (the then-girlfriend and I) worked ourselves up into a teenage frenzy over the trespassing into heretofore forbidden territory... until a cop knocked on the window with his flashlight and told us to move along. But from that moment forward, the genie was out of the bottle, and the ass was in play: any time I went down on a girl, sooner or later, the pinky would aid and abet my cunnilingus.

I remember having a conversation with Mewes about eating girls out, and being shocked to learn that he only did it with the chicks he really liked or was going to spend time with beyond a one-night stand. Going down on chicks was never an option for me; it was the standard. When you grow up fat, you're never any chick's first choice for fooling around, and any nookie you get is predicated more on your personality than your looks. Since I didn't have the aesthetic advantage working for me, I decided that having the oral edge might improve my chances of getting action beyond the mercy-dry hump or third base fumblings. If a girl was gonna do me the courtesy of giving me a shot at the title, so to speak, I was gonna make an impression. So at age thirteen, I bought a gynecological textbook at a physician's bookshop and read that shit cover-to-cover, absorbing all the knowledge I could about the mysteries of the dickless. By age fourteen, I was — as Sam Kinison used to say — a lick-master from the Orient. You'd be surprised how many women will look past a flabby, swingin' gutt if they know they're gonna get eaten out with nearly surgical precision. And when you add digital-to-anal manipulation to the mix, any thought of you as a fat-ass seems to fly out the window (at least until she cums).

I wouldn't have honest-to-goodness anal sex for another few years after that initial parked car experimentation. Then, like now, I was never the instigator; perhaps because of the impolite example Damien provided all those years prior, I figured that first move wasn't mine to make. If a girl wanted to plumb those depths, she was gonna have to tell me to do so. It's common courtesy, I've always figured: if I was a chick, I'd want to make that choice for myself — not have some oversexed horndog who's already being given the gift of a lifetime get all greedy and go for broke of his own volition.

Contrary to what they tell us in porn, I'm of a firm belief that most chicks aren't very into anal, but only opt for it in the heat of the moment. Sure, there are always exceptions that prove the rule; but if a sexual itinerary were to be established upfront, before things got hot-and-heavy, I think most women would be hard-pressed to utter "And then, you can drill my brown." It's only during the throes of passion, when common sense gives way to pure carnality, that anal suddenly becomes a seemingly good idea. For that reason, I've never rushed in with my dick where angels fear to tread; I'll start with the fingers, and if reason doesn't settle in at that point, I'll eventually do as I'm told — though only in a spooning fashion. I mean, look at me: I'm not the guy you want on top of you during traditional sex, let alone when something as delicate as the sphincter's at the epicenter of it all. If a guy my size loses his balance during man-on-top anal sex, the poor woman's looking at a future of colostomy bags. I don't Damien-it; I'm the tenth-of-an-inch at a time type, leaving plenty of room for reversal of opinion. It also helps that I'm hung like a grape.

I guess what I'm getting at is this: I feel it's totally okay to pick your nose. And anal is something you've gotta let your partner call the shots on and during.

However, picking your nose DURING anal? Probably not a good idea.

A Dick in a Mustache is Still Just a Dick
Tuesday 18 July 2006 @ 4:16 p.m.

So last night, at a press screening of *Clerks II* in New York City, *Good Morning*

America movie critic Joel Siegel decided he'd had enough of my shenanigans, and walked out of the flick at the forty minute mark. You'd imagine this would bother me, and yet, I'm as delighted by this news as I was with the eight-minute standing ovation *Clerks II* received in Cannes.

I mean, it's Joel Siegel, for Christ's sake. As Paul Thomas Anderson once said of the man, getting a bad review from Siegel is like a badge of honor. This is the guy who stole his mustachioed critic shtick from Gene Shalit years ago, and still refuses to give it back. This is a guy who seemingly prides himself on being "punny" — that is, he likes to add his own nyuk-nyuk wordplay into the reviews he writes/gives.

For *Pirates* 2, he made us all titter with "Yo, Ho, Ho and a Bottle of Fun".

For Pixar's lastest, he made us squeal with delight when he wrote "Wheelie Good Time for *Cars*".

Can you believe he somehow not only made us laugh, but also think, when he challenged our perception with "*X-Men* Fails to X-cite"?

I mean, Fozzie fucking Bear laughs at this guy (AT, mind you, not WITH).

So while I feel like my life will be a little bleaker now that I'll never know what pun Joel would've dug deeply into his comedic well to produce for *Clerks II* ("*Clerks II*? More like 'Jerks, Too'!"), I've gotta admit that I'm relieved somebody was finally offended by the flick — enough to head for the exit less than an hour in. I was beginning to think I was losing my touch.

I can't fault Mr. Siegel for feeling "revolted" (his producer's description of Joel's reaction) by our flick; in truth, there is a donkey show in it, and I recognize that brand of whimsy might not be for everybody. Film appreciation is very subjective, and maybe Joel just isn't into ass-to-mouth conversations.

However, I CAN fault him for the manner in which he left the screening.

Apparently, rather than quietly exit, both Joel and his Cum-Catcher (my slang for the fancy kind of mustache he sports) made a big stink about walking out, calling as much attention to himself as possible, and being generally pretty disruptive.

Check this shit out: roughly forty minutes into the flick, when Randal orders up the third act donkey show, Siegel bellowed to his fellow critics "Time to go!" and "This is the first movie I've walked out of in thirty fucking years!"

Now, I don't need Joel Siegel to suck my dick the way he apparently sucks M. Night's, gushing over his flick before he's even seen it; but shit, man — how about a little common fucking courtesy? Never mind the fact that when you're paid to watch movies for a living and the only tasks required of you are to a) sit through said movies and b) write your thoughts about them before your deadline, walking out before a movie's over is pretty unprofessional. Never mind the fact that the scene he was offended by (the ordering of the donkey show), with its (misleading) crude references is only the set-up to a third act pay-off that is a true bait-and-switch from where Joel's imagination went (and if you've already seen the flick, you KNOW what I'm talking about). Never mind that this dude is so straight-laced in his tastes and hyperbolic in his praise that when The Onion took a poke at Joel, I was almost unsure whether it was a joke or not...

You never... NEVER disrupt a movie, simply because you don't like it.

Cardinal rule of movie-going: shut your fucking mouth while the movie's playing. They even ask you to do so in the pre-show run-up to every flick ("Cell phones and pagers off, no talking during the show"). This guy went beyond talking, even; he was making a spectacle of himself as he left. I've now spoken to three folks in attendance last night, and all have said that Siegel WANTED everyone to know how disgusted he was, and that he was leaving. If you want to share your displeasure with everyone, that's fine, dude; just do it AFTER the movie, not during. Some folks were enjoying themselves. I don't come down to your job and slap the taste out of your mouth for coming up with a line like "*Shark Tale Is a Halibut Good Time*"; so don't fuck with my stuff WHILE IT'S STILL SCREENING.

Shit, Joel, I know you like being on camera and all, but was it so difficult to not be the center of attention for forty minutes that you just had to sparkle, Neely, sparkle-it up for your peers instead of showing them a little goddamn courtesy by leaving the theater the way most people do, either during or after the picture: quietly? What are you, a twelve year-old boy, cutting loose with your pals at a Friday night screening of *Scary Movie 4* while your parents are in a theater down the hall watching *The Devil Wears Prada*? Leave the diva-like behavior and drama-queen antics to the movie stars, not the movie reviewer, ya' rude-ass prick.

It makes me laugh to think that, had Joel stayed 'til the end (like any good critic would for any movie they're paid to watch), he would've seen that we weren't going where he seemed to think we were going. But apparently, Joel took a cue from his own *Poseidon* review, in which he wrote: "Audiences today wouldn't stand for an hour of exposition before the flood hit. In fact, they wouldn't stand; they'd walk out." Well, Magnum (y'know — because of the mustache), I guess you're a member of that same audience that can't stand exposition.

Look, I don't hate the guy. Shit, I'm glad he survived his fairly recent bout with cancer. But his behavior in that screening was unconscionable and professionally unethical, not to mention childishly disruptive. And while I might get laughed at for saying this... well, I just expected more from Joel Siegel.

sigh

UPDATE!

The *New York Post* ran a rather large item about this story on page six today, and this morning on the *Opie and Anthony Show*, the guys and I were talking about the whole *Affair du* Siegel. Then, the guys got Mr. Mustache on the phone. It was pretty fucking entertaining radio and a fascinating insight into the hubris that comes with being the "punny" movie critic on *Good Morning America*. (Listen here: http://www.viewaskew.com/kevin/joelsiegel.mp3)

The Aftermath
Sunday 23 July 2006 @ 9:14 p.m.

Friday, on the subject of *Clerks II* the *Hollywood Report* wrote "Bowing in 2,150 theaters, the R-rated film is likely to open in the $10 million range."

The other main industry trade, *Variety*, wrote that we did "$11 million for *Jay and Silent Bob Strike Back* on its first weekend in 2001. *Clerks II* bow will likely be close to that."

Today, at the close of our début weekend, the word is as follows…

Reuters writes "Kevin Smith's *Clerks II* was No. 6 with $9.6 million, broadly in line with expectations."

USA Today writes "Among the other newcomers, *Clerks II* did a respectable $9.6 million for sixth…"

Box Office Guru says "Fans showed support for Kevin Smith whose comedy sequel *Clerks II* debuted in sixth place with an estimated $9.6M from 2,150 theaters. Averaging a good $4,477 per site."

Len Klady at Movie City News writes "Additionally, *Clerks II* ranked sixth with a passable $9.8 million"

And *Variety* writes that we "débuted with a lukewarm $9.6 million"

"In line with expectations." "Respectable." "Good." "Passable." "Lukewarm." Not exactly enthusiastic buzzwords — more like the way any woman who's ever been goodly enough to sleep with me has reviewed my cocksmanship.

I'm not gonna try to spin it for you: we'd have liked to have opened better, naturally.

And yet, I'm happy.

Let's get the business stuff out of the way first…

Once again, in what's been termed by some box office analysts as the *Star Trek-Effect*, we saw good Friday numbers dip on Saturday. Essentially, the hardest of hardcore fans show up in full-force on opening day, inflating the returns slightly, leaving Saturday to drop rather than enjoy the standard jump most flicks enjoy on the same day. So while it would've been nice to have done our best opening weekend ever with *Clerks II* (that 11 million *Strike Back* bar didn't seem all that high to reach on Friday night), alas, it's number six for us.

I can't find anything to complain about; I mean, we nearly doubled our budget in the opening weekend. And while there were marketing costs (prints and advertising) beyond the negative cost ($5 mil production budget), they were pretty modest (indeed, we spent far less opening *Clerks II* than we did to open *Strike Back*). The flick should manage to get to $20–$25 mil theatrically, and eke out a minor theatrical profit, leaving all the DVD loot as total windfall.

In essence, we took the *Strike Back* paradigm, plugged in different, lower numbers, and are seeing pretty much the same results. But since *Strike Back* was a pretty profitable endeavor, when all was said and done, *Clerks II* will be even more so (a twenty-million-dollar budget vs. the five-million-dollar budget). Financially, it'll be a winner for all involved.

But box office is a fleeting, opening weekend concern (which, yes, is easy to say when your box office isn't big-tittied). What has been the non-financial upside of *Clerks II*?

As per Rotten Tomatoes the flick was pretty well reviewed, holding steady at a sixty-six percent "Fresh" rating. For the first time since *Strike Back*, the *New York Times* gave us a positive shout-out.

I was able to close down the Askewniverse more fittingly than I felt we did with *Strike Back*. It started with *Clerks* and now it ends with *Clerks II*.

Not only did the flick get invited to the 2006 Cannes Film Festival, it got an eight-minute standing ovation. (I know I keep harping on this, but it was one of the ten best moments of my professional career, so let me enjoy it; it'll never happen again.)

I was able to work side-by-side with lots of friends and family, and added a few new keepers to the mix (Rosario and Trevor) in the process.

We got to document the entire pre-, production, and post experience in the Train Wreck making-of shorts over at www.clerks2.com.

I got to make the exact flick I wanted to make, resulting in my fave of the bunch.

Was *Clerks II* worth the effort? Fuck yes. We made a flick that a lot of folks love (myself included) and thanks to our low budget approach, before the year is out, it'll earn strong profits. So while we can't boast box office bragging rights this weekend (then again, aside from *Monster House*, what newcomer *can*?), we're not sitting here with shotguns in our mouths either. And in this wacky business, that's about the best one can ever hope for, really.

Thanks, all, who checked the flick out already. Thanks to all who may check it out in the future.

FINAL Weekend Box Office Figures (We did better than initially thought)
Monday 24 July 2006 @ 5:03 p.m.

According to FINAL weekend box office numbers, *Clerks II* did a little better than the Sunday estimate of $9,625,000 for the weekend. The ACTUAL figure, according to the Weinstein Co. this morning, is $10,061,132.

Still doesn't move us up the list any (we're still number six), but we DID hit double digits, and were only a million off from our *Jay and Silent Bob Strike Back* opening weekend of $11 mil. We spent $15 mil less making *Clerks II*, and we spent way less marketing this movie. Add to that the fact that we were in profit before we opened, thanks to foreign sales, and you have the reason why both Harvey and Bob Weinstein called me this weekend to say: "We're happy. Now let's keep moving in the right direction."

In other news, our exit polls have been strong, and our tracking is still good. We'll see what the weekday numbers look like, and hopefully, the drop next weekend won't be too steep.

We officially doubled our budget in the first weekend. That feels good.

Final figures should be up at Box Office Mojo later today.

My New (one day) Job and an invitation to hang out
Tuesday 25 July 2006 @ 2:05 p.m.

Looks like I'll be sitting in for Roger Ebert next week, as a guest critic on *Ebert and Roeper*. Kind of a cool honor, I feel.

We'll be checking out *Miami Vice*, *Ant Bully*, *Talladega Nights*, *Barnyard* and maybe (fingers crossed) *World Trade Center*.

We'll be taping next week, just prior to the Chicago *Wizard* Con. I'll let you know how it goes.

Also: are you an East Coaster? Ever been to Jay and Silent Bob's Secret Stash in Red Bank? Heading to Leonardo for the Rolling Roadshow outdoor screening of the original *Clerks* in front of the Quick Stop?

Then drop in on me...

Finke Makes a Stink
Wednesday 26 July 2006 @ 5:57 p.m.

There's a woman named Nikki Finke who writes for the *LA Weekly*, and she seems to have taken issue with the MySpace credits contest we did for *Clerks II*. "This could very well be the most insulting thing I've ever heard," she writes. "A huge diss, to anyone who's ever legitimately earned a credit on a film."

Yes — she's serious.

Aside from the fact that the Lady Finke's finger seems to be pretty far from the pulse (this blog entry's a bit behind the times, considering the contest launched 30 June — nearly a month ago — and was covered by more alert media back then), she's presupposing an industry outrage and ire that simply doesn't exist. No guild has said a word about the credits contest. Know why?

Because there's nothing to be upset about.

What Finke would realize, if she bothered to do her homework (which would require not even a full viewing of the flick, but merely a pop-in during the end credits), is that the MySpace names don't appear in the credits proper of *Clerks II*. The film's credits end (with all the proper logos and copyright legalese), the screen goes to black, and then after five to ten seconds, a new crawl (although "crawl" is hardly the term I'd use to describe the speed with which the names zip up the screen) begins.

Why is this an issue for Nikki Finke when nary a guild member nor other film artisan seems to care? It's so sad. Weinstein Co. finds a fun way to spice up the marketing a bit, and this woman tries to kill-joy the whole endeavor.

In addition, of an earlier promotion the Weinstein Co. did at YouTube for *Lucky Number Slevin*, she also writes: "Yeah, we saw what that promotion did for those movies' bottom-line: Slevin made a pathetic $22 million, and *Clerks 2* is well on its way to more failure."

For someone who covers the film biz, I found that statement rather oblivious. Our flick's budget was five million bucks. We did twice that in the opening weekend. The film's foreign sales more than covered its negative cost. Our marketing budget was pretty modest — especially for a summer release. Even if, after the box office split the Weinstein Co. will make with the theaters, our theatrical run winds up simply being a wash (meaning all costs are covered), that means everything we made on DVD is pure profit. If *Clerks II* DVD is anything like the DVD on *Jay and Silent Bob Strike Back*, we're looking at forty million bucks, easily. Forty million bucks in profit. Where's the "failure"?

Aside from *Little Miss Sunshine* (which opens this week), *Clerks II* may be the lowest budgeted wide release of the summer. We were modest across the boards, in shooting and opening the flick. We did this because we had a model in the *Jay and Silent Bob Strike Back* release. That film turned out to be very profitable, so we simply plugged in lower numbers when doing the *Clerks II* budget, to ensure high profitability for the Weinstein Co. Spending seventy-five percent less to make the current flick, spending far less to market the current flick and opening to roughly the same numbers ($11 mil for *Strike Back*, $10 mil for *Clerks II*)? In what world is that a "failure"? It may not be sexy huge like the *Pirates* numbers, but when it comes to the business half of the show business equation, being in the plus column is all that matters (on the show side of the equation? Making the film you want to make).

And since when are the credits sacrosanct anyway? If Finke feels the post-credits addition of ten thousand names is some kind of "huge diss, to anyone who's ever legitimately earned a credit on a film", what must she think of my end credits "Thank You" shout-out to God, or to *Jersey Girl* for "taking it so hard in the ass and never once complaining". When a dog is listed in the credits, is this somehow an affront to the performers in a film with speaking roles? I dedicated *Jersey Girl* to my recently deceased father (a dubious honor, I know) who had nothing whatsoever to do with the making of the picture; should the filmmaking community be livid that such an undeserving cad as my dead Old Man wound up with his name in the credits?

Bottom line? Ms. (or Mrs.) Finke can try to tempest-in-a-douchebag the contest all she wants; it doesn't change the fact that it was a fun thing to do that all involved seem to enjoy. And if nobody (but Finke) is upset about it, where's the harm?

Shit — had I known she was gonna react like that, I'd have thrown her name in the credits too, as follows...

Crackpot With Too Much Free Time — Nikki Finke

Editorial Note: When I use the term "Crackpot", I am in no way, shape or form implying that this old Hollywood warhorse is crazy. I would never say Nikki Finke is crazy. Never.

(http://gawker.com/news/los-angeles/correction-nikki-finke-is-not-crazy-184254.php)

The WayBack Machine
Wednesday 2 August 2006 @ 4:57 p.m.

I celebrated my twenty-first birthday unceremoniously by working the two to ten-thirty shift at Quick Stop.

I was single then, having recently severed ties with Kim Loughran, my high school sweetheart. She was home from college for the summer, and I'd spent most of that June trying to get our relationship back on a track I'd felt her tenure at Carnegie Mellon had disrupted. Despite my best efforts to get our on-again/off-again status reassigned to active duty, it had become clear that I'd been reduced in status from love-of-her-life to a mere summertime fling — at which point I'd thrown in the towel.

Who could blame Kim, really, for not seeing a future with me as she once did in eleventh and twelfth grade? She was in her sophomore year in a top-notch college, and I was direction-less and drifting through life back home. It became harder and harder for Kim to see me as husband material after my short-lived college career at the New School for Social Research ended after only a winter semester. And while I'd taken a few for-the-fuck-of-it courses with Bryan Johnson at the local community college, it was clear that I wasn't going to put said studies to good use (i.e. I was never gonna be a criminologist). As unattractive as I normally was, my complete lack of ambition must've made me even less so.

As if a twenty-one year-old with no plan wasn't sad enough, I was still living at home with my parents — something neither of my elder siblings had done since graduating high school and heading to university years prior. Mom and Dad weren't kicking me out of the nest, thank God, but they'd been chiding me to find a better job for some time. I knew that the arrival of legal adulthood would only up the ante on their campaign to get me out of the five-buck-an-hour convenience store service industry and into a gig that paid better and might finally deliver me from the realm of the per-hour rate into the promised elysium fields of a grown-up career.

So with no birthday celebration looming, how did I opt to spend my birthday? Behind the register, slinging smokes. My friends stopped by during my shift, but no post-work plans were made. When the steel shutters were closed at the end of the night, it would also signal the close of my first day as a numerical adult.

Around nine at night, my friend and co-worker Vincent Pereira closed up R.S.T. Video for the evening and joined me at Quick Stop, to stock the milk and mop the floors before heading off. We got to talking about movies, as per usual, and I told him about a review I'd read in the Village Voice for a film called *Slacker* that was playing up at the Angelika Film Center, in New York City. This was a film we'd seen a trailer for about a week or so prior, after Vincent and I had read about an Angelika midnight screening of *The Dark Backward* which Judd Nelson and Bill Paxton would be in attendance for and Pig Newtons (a prop food item that featured prominently in the flick) would be distributed at. The *Slacker* review talked about a scene in which Madonna's pap smear was discussed, and that captured both of our imaginations. Since we two Jersey 'burb boys had successfully gotten into and out of the city for the *Dark Backward* screening with our virtue intact once before, we decided to tempt fate with a second trip into the city that night, to check out this *Slacker* picture. And so, after closing up Quick Stop at 10:30 p.m., Vincent and I drove from Leonardo, NJ to the Angelika Theater on Houston in New York City to see a little movie from Austin, Texas.

This was the moment that changed my life forever.

Richard Linklater's *Slacker*, you see, was the film that made me want to be a filmmaker too. As that flick unspooled before the wide eyes of a freshly minted twenty-one year-old version of me, possibility was first introduced into my sphere of influence. This film was at once remarkable and unremarkable, and I viewed it with a mixture of awe and arrogance.

"I've never seen anything like this," I said to myself, following that thought with, "but if this counts as a movie, then I think I can make a movie too..."

It was during that two-in-the-morning ride home from the Angelika, somewhere between the Holland Tunnel and Exit 14C on the Jersey Turnpike, that I first announced my intentions aloud.

"I think I want to be a filmmaker," I said to Vincent. "I think I want to write and direct."

That was fifteen years ago tonight. Since then, I've gotten married, had a kid, and made seven movies. And I finally moved out of my parents.

So, after a small poker party to celebrate what an old fart I've become, I'll climb into bed with my wife and fool around a bit. And once she's fallen asleep, I'll spend the last two hours of my thirty-sixth birthday in the same way I spent the last few hours of my twenty-first: watching *Slacker*.

The Red Bank Stash Signing: A Day That Will Live in Infamy
Tuesday 8 August 2006 @ 12:13 p.m.

With the Rolling Roadshow screening of *Clerks* being the next day, I figured a hundred, maybe two hundred folks would show up at the Red Bank Jay and Silent Bob's Secret Stash signing we'd scheduled for Monday.

To put this into perspective, when I hit puberty, and my dick grew no bigger than it had been in grade school, I figured one day, I'd enjoy a penile growth spurt that'd put me on a par with the dudes in porn who sported more impressive cocks.

In short, I'm an idiot.

When I showed up at the Stash at 2:45 p.m. yesterday (the hotel where I was staying had temporarily shut the water off around noon, prohibiting me from showering on schedule to make the 2 p.m. signing start in time), I saw a line that stretched far deeper into the heart of Red Bank than I'd anticipated.

By the time I started signing at 3 p.m., the official head count outside was over two thousand.

By the time I signed for the last guy (whose sentiments made my morning), it was 4 a.m. today.

Between those two points, there was a moment that kind of defined the whole day for me: Walter pulls me aside at one point and informs me: "The cops are saying there's a woman outside who showed up around four/five, and she's bitching about the line being cut off. Bitching in a big way. Bitching enough for the cop to suggest we have her escorted off. What do you think?"

It's at this point that I'm thinking: "Has it really come to this?"

"Is she right after the cut-off sign in the line?" I ask. "She's further back," Walt explains. "There're about two hundred people after the cut-off mark. She's in the middle of that group." "What are two hundred people doing standing in a line that's been cut off?" Walt had no answer for that except "What do we do about The Screamer?"

And after a moment's fancy of the *Asbury Park Press* headline that might read "*Clerks*-Guy Has Fan Rolled by Cops", I say to Walt: "Let's move the sign. Put it at the end of the two hundred people." "You're kidding," Walt sputters. "I don't see what else we can do." "We're gonna be here 'til the wee hours." "If we're lucky."

We weren't lucky. It wound up being a thirteen-hour signing. It broke our previous record, set September '04, when we opened the Westwood Stash and had a dual *Clerks X/Jersey Girl* DVD signing that lasted from 5 p.m. to 5 a.m. the next day.

Nobody (not the folks who showed up or even the folks in charge) anticipated a crowd that large. This was the first event that the Red Bank Police made us hire an off-duty uniform to patrol (at $56 an hour). This was the first event at which the View Askew message board folks made up maybe two percent of the folks in line, with the majority of the crowd being MySpacers. It wasn't a cluster-fuck, but it was certainly a quagmire of sorts. And yet, thanks to your patience, we got through it in one piece, staying 'til the last man (and woman) got their shit tagged.

Kudos to the Secret Stash crew — Walt, Ming, Mike Zap and Jeff — who kept it all moving fairly smoothly. Kudos to Jen for spending hours outside, glad-handing and chatting with the waiting crowd. Kudos to all the folks in line who waited upwards of thirteen hours. Kudos to the town of Red Bank for not shut-ting us down once they saw the sheer volume of the crowd.

If you showed up, waited as long as you could, and eventually threw in the towel... man I completely understand. I've read posts on our message board from people who made it through to the bitter end, and from a few folks who were bit-ter about not making it to the end.

I'm a big fan of the people who dig our stuff for the obvious reasons (they keep me employed and they improve my self esteem), but sometimes, an event like this illuminates the not so obvious reasons I love my audience: they are pret-ty fucking devoted.

But not devoted enough, mind you, to get naked for me. In all those two thou-sand plus people, you'd imagine at least one couple would offer to put on a pri-vate fuck show for me. Y'know — like a "I love *Mallrats* so much, that if you lock that front door, the wife will lean me over the BluntMobile and bang me with a strap-on for your amusement." That shit never happens to me. What fucking gives? Where's the Goddamned respect, ya' selfish fucking pricks?

Many thanks, all, for making a fat kid from Jersey feel loved, yet again. It helps to salve the wound left by that complete and utter missing penile growth spurt I'd expected in my youth.

Dirty Words Under the Stars
Wednesday 9 August 2006 @ 10:18 a.m.

Last night, the Alamo Draft House-created/Netflix-sponsored Rolling Roadshow hit Red Bank for an outdoor screening of the original *Clerks*.

We packed the house. 2,500 people were allowed into the fenced-off 'theater' and another 1,000 plus had to be turned away. Brian O'Halloran (Dante) and Marilyn Ghigliotti (Veronica) were in attendance, and limited edition Roadshow-themed posters were sold.

It was a pretty cool crowd. Granted, there were some not-so-great questions at the pre-show Q&A I did, but it was all good and damn fun stuff.

Many thanks to Pat Menna and Mayor McKenna for giving the screening a home in Red Bank after Middletown Township unnecessarily gave us the boot from Leonardo. The show started at 7:15 p.m. and everyone was cleared out of the Marina by 10:30-ish, with no reports of the bad behavior the Middletown authorities were worried about. It's a shame, as it would've been really cool to watch the flick right across the street from Quick Stop itself, however, with the giant screen being backed by the river and a full moon, I can't imagine a prettier setting for such an ugly (aesthetically) movie.

Thanks to Tim League and his Rolling Roadshow crew for making it all happen. Thanks to Ming and Ian, who were the Roadshow's local reps. Thanks to John and Janet Pierson for being instrumental in getting *Clerks* on this year's Roadshow menu. Thanks to Netflix for sponsoring this year's fest. And thanks to all who came.

I can't impart this emphatically enough: if you get a chance to attend ANY of the Rolling Roadshow screenings over the next few weeks, GET YER ASS THERE! It's a pretty incredible experience.

Now let's all start bugging Tim about doing *Mallrats* in the parking lot of the Eden Prairie Mall at next year's Rolling Roadshow tour.

Crawling Out from Under a Rock
Monday 28 August 2006 @ 2:35 p.m.

Hey, all. Sorry for the absence of blogging as of late, but I just got home from traveling abroad with *Clerks II*. We hit Australia for premières in Sydney and Melbourne, as well as the Edinburgh Film Festival in Scotland where our little flick won the Audience Award, beating out fest-circuit faves *Little Miss Sunshine* and *An Inconvenient Truth*.

Speaking of festivals, who's up for attending one?

The Movies Askew Fest!

That's right — the year-long Movies Askew Contest is wrapping up with a one-day screening of all twelve finalists, and if you're in or near Los Angeles, you can be a part of the fun! Come chill with us at Cinespace on 6 September, from 6 p.m. to midnight. Kick back, watch some incredible short films, and get drunk as a skunk as we crown the 2006 Movies Askew Champion. Thousands have entered, but only one of twelve will walk away with the Grand Prize Package, which also includes a position on the next View Askew film!

Thursday 7 September 2006 @ 7:38 a.m.

The Movies Askew Fest went off without a hitch, and a good time was had by all (for anyone wondering, Cinespace is a phenomenal place to throw a party, man).

The panel of judges was made up of Richard *Donnie Darko* Kelly, Jason Mewes, Scott Mosier and me (and the entire audience for the Audience Award). And the winners were as follows...

Audience Award — Elias Matar's "Chingaso the Clown"

Special Recognition Award — Scott Rice's "Perils in Nude Modeling"

And the Grand Prize Winner — Duane Graves' "Up Syndrome"

A compilation of all the finalist's short films is on YouTube, called 'Movies Askew – Finalists Montage'.

Thanks to everyone, auteur and audience alike, who attended.

In MySpace-related news, like a total uncouth fucktard, I shot past my 100,000th "friend" without giving him a shout-out.

Ladies and gentlemen, I give you Josh.

http://www.myspace.com/chickenlegman

A day none of us thought would ever come...
Tuesday 12 September 2006 @ 3:25 p.m.

Uber-Producer Scott Mosier is legally off the market.

On Friday, 1 September Scott Mosier married Alex 'Cookie' Hilebronner in a small, Van Nuys courthouse civil service. The pair met on *Jersey Girl* (proving to the critics, once and for all, that *something* good came out of that much-maligned flick), and tied the knot on the fourth anniversary of their first date (i.e. — the first time they boned).

For anyone who knows Mosier, the news of the nuptials was akin to peace in the Middle East: it's something we thought we'd never see. Scott had long maintained a staunch "I'll never get married" position — so much so that it would've been less shocking had Mosier announced "I'm suddenly turning gay" than "I got married". That Cookie was able to change Mos's mind is nothing short of miraculous, and speaks volumes about her charms (both emotional and, one would suspect, sexual).

Join me in extending a hearty Congrats to the happy couple.

Terror and Pleasure are incredibly subjective
Wednesday 13 September 2006 @ 2:41 p.m.

Since many of us spend so much time on the internet, we tend to forget that life is NOT made up of absolutes. Often, we read about how this movie sucks or this person's career is "over", and because it's in some form of print, defended with such vitriol and bluster as to put the Founding Fathers' passion for liberty to shame, we tend to buy it as truth, or at least as a common consensus. But if *Snakes on a Plane* taught us anything this summer (other than what happens when motherfuckin' snakes take over a motherfuckin' plane), it's the following: what often passes for a majority (at least on the internet) barely constitutes a blip in the real world. The most hyped movie since *The Phantom Menace*, tipped to earn 30 to 40 million in its opening weekend, performed like almost any other "thriller" or horror movie: respectable, but not earth-shattering (and relative to its hype, written off by most Monday Morning Quarterbacks as an "under-performer").

There are no absolutes, folks. Life is a subjective experience, different for all of us. What's rapture (in the euphoric sense) for some is Rapture (in the Biblical sense) for others. Universal truths are few and far between.

Which is why I'm so fascinated by this clip…

http://www.youtube.com/watch?v=xSGJKYuLkNk

Taken from the security camera of a theme park ride, it succinctly exemplifies what I'm talking about: two people share a common experience and react as differently as if they had just, respectively, ran amuck in a hostess sample room and broken out of a window in Hell.

More than that, though? This clip is really, really fucking funny.

Friends — there's only one absolute in the world: the grave waits for us all. But as long as there's stuff like this to watch in the interim… well, then I can't complain.

Anarchy in the UK: *Clerks II* Opens on Friday
Tuesday 19 September 2006 @ 5:09 p.m.

I haven't seen the clip in question (nor do I even know who the man is), but a fella named Ross with a TV show in the UK apparently took a dump on my l'il

Clerks II. It's caused a bit of an uproar over at the home site's message board, but really — what can you do? Not everyone enjoys my brand of whimsy.

Still, with whatever he said, the guy seems to be in the minority over there.

Empire gave us four stars.

Total Film gave us five stars.

Future Movies liked us.

The Sunday Times ran a thoughtful piece when we were released Stateside.

Film Focus had really nice things to say.

Maxim (UK) is into it.

The delightfully named Eat My Cheese, Please gave us five stars in a pretty wonderful review.

MTVUK gave us props.

Scotland on Sunday (*The Scotsman*) did as well.

Sunday Mirror mostly dug it.

Film Stalker was surprised.

TNT Magazine is in the hizzy.

BBC.co.uk (the online home of the offending reviewer's network, I'm told) disagreed with their on-air guy.

News of the World gave us four out of 5 stars (yet still somehow managed to bash me in the process).

Tom Brooks from BBC's *Talking Movies* and *Heat* magazine (from what I understand) gave us a strong review.

Clerks II opens in Blighty on Friday. If you're across the pond, give it a look-see.

Jesus... (Literally!)
Monday 2 October 2006 @ 2:46 p.m.

Dogma, our fourth film, resulted in me getting into all sorts of trouble with a group called the Catholic League. Seven years later, that's all a distant memory: *Dogma* hasn't been the focus of religious ire in close to a decade.

Until now. And this time, it ain't Christians who're up in arms.

Buddy Christ has turned up in Iraq, on posters and pamphlets that mysteriously appeared in Baghdad's Sadr City, following a joint US/Iraqi operation. Local Shiite residents have taken offence.

"If it wasn't so serious it would be funny," said a coalition spokesman, Major Will Willhoite. The guy's got a point.

It's a bummer that the Buddy Christ — meant as a symbol of a non-judgmental, forward-thinking, fictional version of the Catholic Church — is being linked to something like this. God-willing, it doesn't go further than this.

In the midst of something like this, you'd think I wouldn't hawk merchandise. And yet... the *Clerks II* DVD is 22 days from release...

Sucks Less
Tuesday 24 October 2006 @ 3:40 p.m.

For the record, I shouldn't be teaching anybody anything. No right-thinking university would hire me to be the instructor for any subject, unless it was...

a) How to Down a Box of Pre-Sweetened Cereal in a Sitting

Or...

b) How to Avoid Any Physical Exertion Beyond Strolling to the Shitter Hourly Because You've Eaten Far Too Much Pre-Sweetened Cereal (a class that'd have a post-studies course called Sedentary Alternatives to the Hourly Bowl March Including, But Not Limited to, Empty Pre-Sweetened Cereal Boxes You Can Keep By Your Bedside; students would only pass once they handed in their thesis, entitled Toy Surprises: Good Wiping Material or Too Harsh for the Hole?).

That being said, UCLA has brought me on as a visiting professor this semester.

Naturally (or bizarrely, as some of my critics would point out), it's in the School of Cinema and Television — a field I know a thing or two about (as I've watched many movies and TV shows). So, for the last month, I've been spearheading a class called Sucks Less, with Kevin Smith, in which we produce a weekly TV show entitled, ironically, *Sucks Less, with Kevin Smith*. It starts airing this Thursday on MTVU (the college-campus only arm of the Viacom-owned Music Television empire), as well as on MTVU.com and, in an uncharacteristic-for-me nod to what's being called "new media", also on the Amp'd Mobile phone. This means we're producing episodes, webisodes, and mobisodes — which, while sounding ambitious as fuck, simply means we're producing one show that airs on three different platforms. Eat your heart out, Dick Wolf.

How did this all happen, you ask? As far as I can remember, it all came down as follows.

About six to eight months ago, I was talking to someone at MTV about working on the Movie Awards show. They'd asked if I was interested in writing or producing, and I responded that, while very flattered, I was not the right guy for the job: I'm an old man, completely out of touch with the current MTV generation.

If you had a gun pointed at my head, I couldn't name a single VJ beyond Kennedy — who, I'm told, hasn't been a VJ in about a decade.

"My tastes, for better or for worse, fall far outside the mainstream," I argued. "And if I could write/create for the mainstream, I'd be one of those successful filmmakers. So, really — you guys want someone else."

"Yeah, but we like your sensibility."

"But my sensibility isn't in line with the masses."

"What makes you say that?" I was asked.

"I'll bet you're trying to get Vince Vaughn and Owen Wilson as hosts."

"We are," they replied.

"Okay. I'd rather see David Cross be the host. You're voting for the most popular kids in class, I'm voting for the class genius. And there's nothing wrong with your instincts; I just don't share 'em."

"Fine. But there's gotta be something you can do in the MTV family. We're edgy, too. Have you ever seen *Wonder Showzen*?"

(I hadn't, at that point, but since that conversation, *Wonder Showzen* has become one of my all-time favorite programs. That exec wasn't kidding, either: *Wonder Showzen* defined the term 'edgy'.)

"What about MTVU?" they continued.

"What's that?"

"It's the campus-only version of MTV. They actually play music videos, along with some short-form programming. And the college audience is your audience, isn't it?"

They had a point: I like college. Never really attended one all that much... or finished any, for that matter. But still, I like college. I used to like to visit my ex-girlfriend at Carnegie Mellon when she attended, years back. I dug walking around the campus, seeing people preparing for the next stage of development — the one I had such a hard time committing to myself. I liked hitting the library and watching laser discs in the media center while my ex was in class (the CMU library is where I first saw *Citizen Kane*). And most of all, I liked the cafeteria: the place where you could eat sixteen bowls of Apple Jacks, two donuts, a bagel, and six glasses of orange juice for, like, four bucks. There's just something about a college campus, y'know? Particularly when you don't have to be there and aren't sweating writing a paper or making a class on time. It's why I do so many Q&As every year: I just dig being on a college campus. College? I like it. And college kids? I like 'em even more.

So I was introduced to Ross Martin and Brian Decubellis, the guys over at MTVU, and I hit 'em with an idea for a short-form program I could host out of

Jay and Silent Bob's Secret Stash called *For Those Who Can't Get Laid* — a tip show that'd provide a list of upcoming movies/music/comics/events college kids might not know about. They went for it, and then came up with an even better idea: rather than simply produce it in-house at View Askew, we set it up over at UCLA and make an accredited course out of it, with the students actually fulfilling all the various production roles. They get experience, make connections and earn college credits, we get cheap labor; everybody wins.

Once Department Chair Barbara Boyle and UCLA were on board, two more players entered the field: Amp'd Mobile and Rory Kelly. Amp'd offered to underwrite the entire course, in exchange for the rights to air *Sucks Less* on their mobile phones (side by side with other original programming, like their *L'il Bush* cartoon). *Sleep With Me* director Rory Kelly, a long-time UCLA Film instructor, graciously signed on to be the teacher-of-record (while I have a pair of doctorates from two different universities, they're the honorary kind that apparently don't qualify me to be a 'real' teacher), so with complete funding and a legitimate teacher in place, we were off and running.

So me, Rory, MTVU Brian, a pair of UCLA animators (whose spiffy title sequence cartoon kicks off every show), and fifteen grad students with various production concentrations (directing, producing, screenwriting, cinematography) have hunkered down to come up with six episodes of what stopped being called *For Those Who Can't Get Laid* (UCLA wasn't comfortable with that title) and quickly became *Sucks Less* — a bi-weekly, eight minute, student-produced extravaganza that starts airing this Thursday, 26 October, on MTVU, MTVU.com (where most of you will wind up watching it, no doubt), and the Amp'd Mobile phone.

If you dig the show, I can take very little credit: it was, from first to last, the students' production (consequently, if you hate the show, I get to dodge that bullet as well).

As for being a teacher... well, that's something I'll be able to address more thoroughly once we're done with the course (second week of December). But thus far? I'm digging it (though not nearly as much as I'm digging the cafeteria).

Don't forget to check out the episode this Thursday, on MTVU.com.

I mean, Jesus — it's only eight minutes.

I am a *Manchild*
Tuesday 14 November 2006 @ 2:56 p.m.

So it looks like I'm gonna be doing a TV pilot...

But, oddly enough, it's not a show I've created; it's a show I've simply been cast in. And, like anything in life, there's a story behind it.

A few weeks back, Brent Morely — one of the agents at Endeavor — called to say: "There's this Showtime pilot I want to send you to take a look at, because I think you'd dig the sensibility."

Every few months, scripts get sent my way from various studios looking for a rewrite or comedic punch-up, but I haven't done one since *Coyote Ugly* — probably because, after all my work on that script, they hired a director who, naturally, wanted to bring his writer aboard the project, and almost all of my stuff got shit-canned. Generally, the scripts just sit on a pile near my desk for close to a year before they hit the trash — which isn't a statement on the scripts themselves as much as as statement about my lack of interest in rewrite gigs.

When it hit the pile, the *Manchild* script caught my eye because a) the script was very slim, and b) the cover letter said nothing about rewriting. I was directed to read with an eye toward the role of Paul.

An acting gig? Were they kidding? I'm not an actor.

So while Jen was sitting on the bedroom couch reading a book with Harley, I sat on the other end of the couch and started leafing through the *Manchild* script, curious as to why anyone would think of me in conjunction with this show.

Then, I laughed. Out loud (or LOLed in the parlance of this medium).

Jen's head immediately snapped up from the kid's book and she stared at me, agog.

"Really?!" she asked, stupefied. "It was a pretty funny line," I explained.

Her reaction was based on the fact that I rarely laugh at anything on the page. Sure, I can split my sides at something like *Arrested Development* or the latest Carlin album (or *Borat*, I'm promised — I haven't seen it yet); but when it comes to scripts, it's rare that I react aloud at all (even at my own shit).

So I go back to reading, and within a few minutes, I laugh aloud again.

And again.

And again.

It was a truly funny script. And the part they'd earmarked for me to look at was a really funny character in a script full of funny stuff.

So I called Agent Brent back and said: "I'd do this, sir. In a heartbeat."

I met with the show creators, Robb and Mark Cullen (*Lucky* and *Heist*), as well as Darren Starr (show producer) and Stephen Gyllenhaal (show director and father of Jake) a few days later, found them all to be good guys, and suddenly, we were off and running.

We shoot the pilot in December, after I finish this other, two-day acting gig on a feature. If Showtime digs the pilot, we go to series two months or so after that. With twelve eps a season, it means I'm out of the directing game (which should please some folks) for only about four months out of the year.

I don't know how Showtime will position the show (if they pick it up), but it'll be a nice addition to their schedule alongside *Weeds*. It's frank, crude, honest and funny: kinda like the flicks I do, if all the characters had high-paying jobs. While it's based on the BBC show of the same name, from what I understand (never having seen the original), the Cullens kept the premise and title and re-built everything else. The original was compared to *Sex and the City*, so it makes sense that Darren is involved.

The only daunting aspect is that I'm surrounded by real, honest-to-goodness actors (James Purefoy, John Corbett, Paul Hipp). Thankfully, I got my first taste of acting beside real actors (the Silent Bob stuff barely counts) in *Catch & Release* (in theaters this January), so I've already got a bit of experience feeling inferior all the time (shit — I've got a lifetime of experience in that department, to be honest).

It should be an interesting exercise that, if the show works as well as the script, will turn into a sweet side-gig for me. At the very least, I'll learn a thing or two about acting; at the most, I'll have something to do four months out of every year, and be proud as punch to be involved with one really insightful and fucking funny show.

To say I never imagined something like this for myself is a gross understatement; this gig really, really comes out of the blue for me. But when someone hands you something as engaging and hysterical as the pilot for *Manchild* and says, "We'd like you to be a part of it"... Jesus, saying no isn't an option.

Hopefully, y'all will tune-in when (and if) we go on air.

You all wear t-shirts, have dead-end jobs, and live in your parents' basements
Sunday 26 November 2006 @ 2:31 p.m.

That's what *Orlando Sentinel* film critic/blogger Roger Moore thinks, at least.

Yes, on almost the same day that the *L.A. Times* gave me a nice shout-out for doing something original with new media, via the *Sucks Less* mobisodes...

...Mr. Moore, in one of his latest blog entries (on a blog he calls 'Frankly My Dear'; get it? he writes about movies, and that's a line from a movie), described (rather dismissively) the audience that's into my stuff (aka, you folks)...

The blog is at:

http://blogs.orlandosentinel.com/entertainment_movies_blog/2006/11/kevin
_smith_the.html

Have a read...

Nice, right? Aside from the condescension that drips from painting a three-color portrait of who he thinks digs my flicks (t-shirt-wearing basement creatures like A.O. Scott of the *New York Times* or the father of Auteur Theory Andrew Sarris), Rog manages, as you read, to get in a fat joke. Class act, that Roger Moore.

But let's set aside, for a moment, poison prose that aspires to *New Yorker* magazine wit but falls clumsily into Ain't It Cool News Talkback bile: how can this clown make an unsubstantiated, easily-refuted claim like the following and still call himself a journalist?

He wrote that, though Harvey and Bob Weinstein were "probably" happy with what *Clerks II* made at the box office, my last several films have done nothing to "ensure" my ongoing career.

Let's analyze this sentiment: how DOES one ensure a career? Well, two factors loom largest: audience and earnings. Let's assume Roger's not suggesting I don't have an audience, as his piece is predicated on bitch-slapping mine while begrudgingly admitting they exist. Roger, then, must be speaking about the financial track record of my flicks. So if we take his meaning of my last "several" movies to mean, say, the last three (*Jay and Silent Bob Strike Back*, *Jersey Girl*, and *Clerks II*), couldn't the man have done a simple Google search to check whether he was on sure-footing in suggesting I'm hurting for business?

I mean, I was able to find a *Variety* piece (entitled 'DVD Spawns a New Star System') pretty quickly, in which the author writes:

"Kevin Smith. Directors can have big DVD followings, too. *Jay & Silent Bob* sold $36 million on DVD after a moderate $30 million in theaters, which may explain why Smith has become a pitchman for Panasonic's recordable DVD player."

More recently, as regards *Clerks II*, the other industry Bible, *The Hollywood Reporter*, ran two pieces which described it as "a modest box office success" and "a nice piece of coin" for the Weinstein Company.

And even the much-maligned *Jersey Girl*, which is too-often described as a bomb, really only came up about ten million shy of its production budget in its box office run. Between the TV sale, the foreign sales, and especially, the DVD sales, that deficit was righted... and a profit was eked out.

If anything, with the last several films, I've ensured my career pretty well — both with the money people and the audience. I mean, he's writing about *An*

Evening With Kevin Smith 2: Evening Harder; you don't get to a 2 if the first edition was met with ambivalence (indeed, doing a sequel to *Evening With* wasn't even my idea; Columbia Tristar, chuffed with the 300,000-plus units they moved on the inexpensive-to-produce first incarnation, pulled the trigger on *Evening Harder* — just as they had on *Evening With*).

This isn't the first time ol' Roger has spent column space puzzling over why I haven't been banished to movie jail or something. In this August piece talking about the horror movie I'm interested in shooting next year:

(http://blogs.orlandosentinel.com/entertainment_movies_blog/2006/08/kevin_smith_wan.html)

He mentions that I need to have a success in another genre if I am to escape the "ghetto" I am in. He also says that the budget of *Clerks II* was ten million.

First off, the *Clerks II* budget was five million, not ten (also an easily checked — and well-publicized — fact). Secondly, why does he consider my seven-film body of work a "ghetto"? The man implies that I shouldn't be happy with what I've done; that I should be doing more. Why? Should HE be doing more than writing for the *Orlando Sentinel*? Like, say, writing for the *Washington Post* on a regular basis (a paper whose Jen Chaney managed to write about *Evening Harder* without looking down her nose at the audience)? No: he's comfy writing for the *Sentinel* and being catty on his *Sentinel*-hosted blog. Why, then, am I somehow not living up to my potential by working comfortably in MY little corner of cinema?

But the closing line of advice in his fan-slamming blog really blows my mind. He advises me to stop wasting my time with fans who already like me, and will buy my latest DVD anyway.

Setting aside the cynical notion that keeping in touch with the audience is all about a quick buck (or even a slow buck) for me, what the fuck is this dude saying? I should be reaching for a different audience than the one that's supported me and my work for a dozen years now? Why? Doesn't every filmmaker play to their audience? Doesn't Spielberg play to his audience? Granted, his audience pushes his flicks to 300 million while mine push my flicks to a tenth of that (at best); but, shit — I'm happy there's one person watching what I do, let alone a few million. And in terms of the folks who dig what we do at View Askew, I've met many of you, and you're all really cool, really wonderful people. Why should I be courting an entirely different audience, as Roger chides? If I'm happy with my audience, what the fuck's Roger Moore's problem with that?

Ask him yourself at Rmoore@Orlandosentinel.Com

Meantime, if you're one of those t-shirt wearing, dead-end job having, parents'-

basement-dwelling cats that Roger poo-poos, you might wanna join us for the signing at the LA Secret Stash, on Tuesday...

Just remember: the last signing we had (on the east coast) was a fourteen-hour affair.

So if you're not into crowds, you can simply order Roger's favorite DVD online...

(Mention "Roger Moore sent me" and receive a FREE GIFT!)

Roger Moore. The retarded one.
So Roger responded in his blog, now no longer dancing around the topic and instead just flat-out calling folks who're into what I do "losers"...

Read it here:

http://blogs.orlandosentinel.com/entertainment_movies_blog/2006/11/oh_to_be_pellet.html

And for a guy who looks down on "fan-folks", he proves he's about as clever as the biggest AICN Talkback troll by including an image of Comic Book Guy from *The Simpsons* — either to represent me or you. This coming from a guy who carps about movies for a living. Give a few of his negative reviews a read and tell me you can't hear "worst movie ever" in your head.

According to his bio, he studied journalism at Radford University, where he wrote film reviews for the college radio station, just like Pauline Kael had when she started out.

And the Pauline Kael comparisons begin and end there. Kael was a master with words and cinema deconstruction. Roger's a wannabe, cracking wise in a paper with a circulation of about 220,000 (perhaps the paper's recent drop in circulation has less to do with hotel distribution drying up and more to do with an audience that thinks their paper's film critic is fucking hapless). In sheer numbers, that means more people will read this blog than will read any one of Roger's reviews. But, y'know — my "rep" and "hip cachet" are "dwindling", so what do I know?

This non-entity (who's, no doubt, now doing cartwheels over the notion that someone... ANYONE... is writing/thinking about him, thanks to my blog) is just pissed and jealous that he's never been asked to sit in on *Ebert and Roeper* once, let alone three times (I'm heading back to Chicago this week to co-host their annual 'Worst Of' show — consistently the highest-rated episode of the year). You don't get invited back unless the reaction from the audience is favorable (thank you "adoring masses").

As for his claim that he hasn't received that many hate emails, well, that's because they're all over at the MySpace posting of the blog, Rog. Click on that for 500 responses from all these "losers" you love to shit on.

Thirdly, when folks refer to someone else's "hip cachet"... that's a pretty clear indicator that they're not the person who should be passing judgment on said subject. It's like those people who will insist to you: "Me and my friends are crazy, man! We do crazy shit all the time! We're nuts!" If you're telling people you're wild, then you're not wild. If you're telling people that someone else is losing their "hip cachet", you have no clue what "hip" is or isn't. Case in point: last year, *TV* fucking *Guide* also told me I was losing my "hip cachet". And *TV Guide's* about as far from the cutting edge as you can get. So with two lame outlets like *TV Guide* and 'Frankly My Dear' insisting I'm not hip... well, that instantly makes me hip, doesn't it?

And, really? Who gives a shit about hip-ness anymore anyway? Even the notion of "hip" isn't hip anymore. What decade is McFly here writing in, for Christ's sake? Hey, Rog: like Kael, the seventies are gone, sir — stop writing like we're still in the midst of them.

Roger writes that he's found my 'real' work disappointing recently. He's talking about my films. And that's fine; taste is subjective (besides, on the last flick, he was in the minority). Honestly, Roger liking or not liking my films means shit-all to me (our Orlando per screen average for *Clerks II* was unaffected by his ramblings); it's the disdain with which he treats my audience that kills me. It's one thing to dismiss people because they wear t-shirts; as fucking strange (and "square", to work with terms Roger might be more comfortable using) as that may be (I mean, what's this guy think they sell in the fucking Gap? Tux jackets?), it says more about Roger ("I don't wear t-shirts... ever!") than the people he's coming down on. But to insist you all have dead-end jobs and live in your parents' basements just because you're fans of mine? I mean, what a snobby thing to write.

Does Janet Maslin have a dead-end job?

How about the previously mentioned Andrew Sarris (a guy who very generously — and very foolishly — pegged me as "the next Scorsese")?

Those are two of the most influential and respected film critics of the last twenty years or more. They're fans. Are they "losers" as well, Roger?

(And for the record, both Maslin and Sarris have Wikipedia entries; at press time, Roger doesn't — though I'm sure he'll correct that immediately).

This is a dude who'd like people to believe I'm ending (or over).

The *L.A. Times* doesn't seem to think so.

Neither does the *Washington Post* (in its positive review for *Evening Harder*).

But, hey — the guy from the *Orlando Sentinel* wrote it, so it must be true.

Cheer up, Rog — now you know at least one person reads your stupid-ass blog. You can finally silence that nagging little voice that grips you as you post each new entry (hand quivering atop your mouse), saying "Why bother? Nobody's reading. Nobody knows who the fuck I am. I'm working in a vacuum. Pauline Kael I ain't. Shit, I'm not even Earl Dittman. Is there anybody out there for me and my two-bit opinions?"

That'd be me, "hip"-ster. That'd be me.

Apparently, less IS more
Monday 27 November 2006 @ 7:20 p.m.

During the *Clerks II* theatrical release, I was supposed to do one of those iTunes Celebrity Playlists; y'know — the collection of songs choices and (brief) explanations for their inclusion that give us an insight into what, say, Minnie Driver likes to rock out to.

(Yes, rather than the myriad other well-known folks who've done an iTunes Celebrity Playlist, I dropped a Minnie Driver reference on your asses — because A) I remember reading her list, years back, with great interest, and B) because Minnie Driver doesn't get name-dropped nearly enough, as far as I'm concerned. Is there anyone out there who'd disagree with the fact that the chick was genius in *Grosse Pointe Blank*? For that performance alone, she deserves more shout-outs.)

Sadly, at the time, I was in the midst of a press tour, and I didn't feel like I had strong enough intervals in which to do a playlist justice. I mean, while folks like to use the Celebrity Playlist as a promotional device, I can't approach it as lightly. Putting together a playlist is incredibly personal and lays the author naked. It's the modern day equivalent of making a mix tape for someone you're crushing on: you run as much risk of winning her/his heart as you do firmly ensconcing yourself on their 'Avoid At All Costs' manifest. So I declined to submit one at that point, asking to be considered again at some future date, when I wasn't flying from city to city and doing ten hours or more of press a day.

Cut to three weeks ago, when — as another promotional vehicle for the *Clerks II* DVD — I was afforded a second bite at the iTunes apple (pun intended). With a more comfortable alottment of hours to lavish on crafting a playlist and honest explanations for track inclusions beyond "Because this song rocks", I buried myself in my iTunes library, culling through ten thousand plus tracks, searching for the songs that'd represent my 'desert island' choices. A day later, I submitted it to the publicity folks at Genius (the home video label of the Weinstein Company).

Two days later, shit went south.

"This is a great playlist," Darin from Apple wrote. "Too great, actually. We don't have the space for comments that run that long. Will he be OK with us editing them (significantly) or would he prefer to do that himself? Two sentences for each track is a good outline."

Pam's follow-up email, while flattering, was little help: "My contact (at Apple) said he's never had this problem before. He shared that usually he receives playlists that don't include any comments. He said yours is the best they've ever received and he wishes they could make it work."

But the idea of trimming down (significantly, apparently) that Rorschach of the Soul known as the Celebrity Playlist didn't interest me. So with no hard feelings on either behalf, I declined inclusion.

And here we are.

The lesson in all of this: never ask a fat non-celeb with over-compensation issues that stem from having a little cock and too much lard hanging from every appendage (except the aforementioned cock) to do a Celebrity Playlist.

As a firm believer in the "manufacture for use" principle, I now present you with my aborted (non) Celebrity Playlist:

Track: 'Cold Sweat' (Live 1968/Dallas Memorial Auditorium), Artist: James Brown, Album: *Say It Live and Loud: Live in Dallas 08.26.68*

This is James Brown doing his best Eddie-Murphy-Doing-James-Brown impression nearly twenty years in advance of Eddie Murphy actually doing any James Brown impression. It's one of the greatest live recordings of a single in history, and with a running time of twelve minutes and fifty-one seconds, you'd be hard pressed to find a better bargain for ninety-nine cents on iTunes. It's like getting four songs for the price of one! If you act now, we'll throw in a set of steak knives.

Track: 'Unsent', Artist: Alanis Morissette, Album: *Supposed Former Infatuation Junkie*

I love songs about loss and the road not traveled, and I love Alanis Morissette, so this track is right up my alley. This chick sings her guts out, but more than that, she's an awesome, almost cinematic writer: you can practically "see" the story she's singing. And, my God, you can certainly feel it: if you don't identify with her regret in some small way when she belts out the line "What was wroooooong with meeeeeeee?" you're a goddamned robot. This song feels like the woman stole pages out of a diary I forgot to keep, so personally do the lyrics punch me in my fat gut. We've all got a heartbreaking letter like this in us somewhere; mercifully, Ms. Morissette wrote it for us so we don't have to self-examine too closely.

Track: 'Among the Living', Artist: Anthrax, Album: *The Greater of Two Evils*

I used this version of the venerable late eighties metal classic in the very first online trailer we put up for *Clerks II*, and man, did it bring all the Anthrax fans out of the woodwork. Most folks were just happy to hear the track again, but some were miffed that I went with this re-recording instead of the original version from the album of the same name. There's no denying the raw power of the OG 'Among', but this stripped down, starker take on the same material is now my all-time-fave Anthrax song. And even though the cover was recorded recently, listening to it immediately takes me back to Highlands, New Jersey, circa '89, when I first started hanging out with Walt Flanagan. During the ride home from many a game of tennis court street hockey, Walt would extol the virtues of the 'Thrax because, as he said at the time, "They do songs about Judge Dredd and *The Stand*." Later in life, I'd come to identify with Anthrax professionally, as well: in our respective work, we both name-check somewhat geeky stuff that appeals to us, neither of us have ever been embraced by the mainstream, and we've both got small but insanely loyal audiences. But I'll never do anything nearly as cool as this song.

Track: 'Easter', Artist: Bill Hicks, Album: *Rant in E Minor*

A very short, but very funny piece of comedic insight from a very big genius who left us very early. If you've never heard any Bill Hicks material, shame on you: start here, with this excerpt from one of his shows. His accent on the line "That's the story of Jesus..." is worth the price of admission alone.

Track: 'Living in Sin', Artist: Bon Jovi, Album: *New Jersey*

Some folks may feel like I've tossed my street cred by ranking Bill Hicks and Bon Jovi in the same playlist, but fuck 'em. I'm from Jersey; what do you expect? Besides — anyone who denies ever enjoying any Bon Jovi track is lying to you. It was a tough call, picking just one Bon Jovi track instead of twelve; and the temptation was there to go with one of the bigger, stadium-rock anthems like 'Wanted Dead or Alive' (because, I've seen a million faces, and I like to think I rocked 'em all, too). But for repeated plays, I lean toward the more ballad-y Jon Bon, and more than 'Never Say Goodbye' and 'I'll Be There for You' (which will forever represent the prom song genre to me), I dig this track. Fuck you — it's sexy, man. This song makes me want to get into some heavy teenage petting. But, y'know — with my wife, not an actual teenager; sex with an actual teenager would be illegal, and as much as I love the Jov, I ain't doing time for any former hair-band.

Track: 'Rosalita', Artist: Bruce Springsteen, Album: *The Wild, The Innocent, and the E. Street Shuffle*

As picking a best Bruce Springsteen song is impossible, I opted to go with the Bruce-penned tune that boasts my favorite Springsteen lyric, about being stuck in the mud in the swamps of Jersey. A few years back, I was emceeing a post-9/11 concert at the Count Basie Theater in Red Bank, N.J. that was to benefit the families in Monmouth County who'd lost loved ones when the Towers fell. Jon Bon Jovi and Richie Sambora performed, as well as a host of other Jersey-based acts. Naturally, the night culminated with a set from The Boss himself. However, after introducing all the acts, a Comcast exec who donated a substantial amount of cash wound up doing the Bruce intro, bringing him to the stage with "And now, a man who needs no introduction." So Bruce and most of the E. Street Band take to the stage to thunderous applause, and I'm watching from the wings as the man plugs his guitar in. He then says into the microphone "Where's the emcee? If we're gonna do this, let's do it right." He waves my giddy ass back out onstage and I get to intro a living legend to a packed house in my hometown. That night, Bruce Springsteen took a longtime fan and turned him into a Secret Service Agent: from that moment forward, I would take a bullet for The Boss.

Track: 'Diarrhea Moustache', Artist: David Cross, Album: *Shut up, You Fucking Baby*

While the faux title of this track is giggle-inducing enough, it's a bait-and-switch: David Cross likes to mislabel all of his tracks. Instead of diarrhea moustaches, we're treated to a spellbinding and hysterical anecdote about a night when Cross got so plastered, he could barely communicate. With *Shut Up*, Cross has released the best comedy album of the last five years, bar none. If your idea of funny is Dane Cook, this may not be your brand of whimsy; but if you like nasty, frank, and bitchy laughs, get nailed to this Cross.

Track: 'Ain't My Type of Hype', Artist: Full Force, Album: *Still Standing, Pt. 1*

If you've ever seen *House Party*, you've seen Full Force: they play the bullies trying to flatten Kid's high-top fade through most of the flick. And as if they didn't do enough for *House Party*, they also produced this track, heard in the thick of the titular house party in question. This song not only makes me want to dance like Kid 'n Play, it makes me want to be black.

Track: 'Laid', Artist: James, Album: *Laid*

A couple years back, while I was crashing at the Hard Rock Casino in Vegas, working on the *Clerks II* script during the day and playing blackjack at night, my wife took me for a ride to the Little White Chapel, where I was surprised to discover around twenty of our closest friends and relatives (including our daughter, Harley) waiting to watch me and Jen get re-married. Since we'd more or less eloped years before, this was our nearest-and-dearest's chance to watch us tie the same knot they missed us tying the first time. 'Laid' was the track Jen chose to walk down the aisle to (don't ask) and whenever I hear it, I remember how beautiful she looked that day. And because of that, this song always gives me a boner.

Track: 'Fuck and Run', Artist: Liz Phair, Album: *Exile in Guyville*

Is it easier to look at Liz Phair or listen to her sing? Especially when it comes to this song? This song really appeals to fat guys everywhere, because it makes us believe there are girls out there who might, sooner or later, give up on the trim dudes who're distant and treat them like shit. Liz Phair wants a boyfriend? I know a legion of lunchboxes who'd give her what she's asking for: all that stupid old shit — like letters and sodas.

Track: 'The Planet is Fine', Artist: George Carlin, Album: *Jammin' in New York*

Carlin may very well be the smartest person I've ever met. This track illustrates why. Listen to the intensity and focus of this performance — not to mention the masterful use of language: it's like watching the world's best cancer surgeon at work... but way funnier.

Track: 'Straight Outta Compton', Artist: NWA, Album: *Straight Outta Compton*

Jesus, do these guys need a hug...

Track: 'The Morning Papers', Artist: Prince, Album: *The Love Symbol Album*

If you've ever seen *An Evening With Kevin Smith*, you know I've got some history with His Royal Badness. Regardless, it's never interfered with my appreciation for the man's musical genius. I came of age in the Prince era, and his albums have made up a good portion of the soundtrack to my life. This track will always take me back to post-production on the original *Clerks*, when I was editing the flick in the video store featured in the flick, and my long-time girlfriend was graduating from college and dumping my fat ass. Needless to say, I was devastated. But had I known that, in six months, my life was gonna change irrevocably (thanks to the Sundance Film Festival), maybe I wouldn't have burned through two copies of *The Love Symbol Album* listening to this track over and over.

Track: 'Welcome to the Terrordome', Artist: Public Enemy, Album: *20th Century Masters – The Best of P.E.*

What I've always loved about this track is how it has a ticking-clock feel to it.

There's such a sense of urgency to the lyrics and music. You ready to be moved, both emotionally and physically? Then here's your ticket. Hear the drummer get wicked.

Track: 'My Philosophy', Artist: Boogie Down Productions, Album: *By All Means Necessary*

If you get a stiff one for wordplay and language, a KRS One track is like porn. This opening track from the album that immediately followed the untimely death of DJ, Scott La Rock, signaled a new maturity in the work that Boogie Down Productions would, from this record forward, be forever known for: deft (and def) socially-conscious hip-hop that was more poetic than what was being offered up by their contemporaries. This is when rap went from "Throw your hands in the air, and wave 'em like you just don't care" to something more political and, therefore, powerful.

Track: 'Here We Go (Live at the Funhouse)', Artist: Run DMC, Album: *Run DMC*

The greatest rappers of all time, bar none. Far less lyrically complicated than almost any rap act who'd follow in their footsteps, Run DMC still stand as the Kings of Rock because they invented the blueprint and took hip hop to a whole new audience: suburban white kids. But their historical significance aside, Run DMC (and the late Jam Master Jay) knew how to get you on your feet, and this track is no exception in that department. If you're not at least doing a subtle sway by the time Run gets to "If you say you heard my rhyme, we're gonna have to fight — 'cause I just made the motherfucker up last night", then you've got no soul.

Track: 'The Last Day of Our Acquaintance', Artist: Sinead O'Connor, Album: *So Far... The Best of Sinead O'Connor*

One of the saddest songs ever penned by one of the baldest chicks to ever shred a picture of a Pope on national television.

Track: 'Sail On', Artist: The Commodores, Album: *Anthology*

Obviously, I love break-up songs ('The Last Day of Our Acquaintance', 'Unsent', 'Fuck and Run'). This track is a stand-out on that list because there's an undercurrent of hope running through it: yes, the author is saddened by the end of the relationship, but he's also mustered enough pride to get off a few parting shots in the process. Next time someone's dumping you, rock 'em with a little "I gave you my heart, and I tried to make you happy. And you gave me nothing in return." Just don't sing it or you'll confirm that you're a dickhead in serious need of dumping.

Track: 'Ghost Story', Artist: Sting, Album: *Brand New Day*

This is one of my favorite sad songs of all time because I'm a total sucker for songs about regret. And people can blast me all they want, but Sting is one of the best lyricists of all time: whether he was with The Police or solo, it's hard to deny the man knows how to craft a metaphor — which, considering he used to be an English teacher, makes sense.

Track: 'Da' Mystery of Chessboxin", Artist: Wu-Tang Clan, Album: *Legend of the Wu-Tang — Wu-Tang's Greatest Hits*

A good rap track that's elevated to classic status by virtue of ODB's verses alone. Rappinin' is, indeed, what's happenin'.

Track: 'Once in a Lifetime', Artist: Talking Heads, Album: *Stop Making Sense*

Stop Making Sense was the first album I ever bought with my own cash at Jack's Music Shoppe in Red Bank — the primary purchase point for my early career in music consumerism. There was this woman who used to work behind the counter who must've been in her late, late forties/early fifties. What was especially noteworthy about her was how into metal she came across: the woman was forever sporting a Sabbath or Maiden sleeveless t-shirt, long hair, and a pentagram necklace. She was dubbed The Metal Lady. I never got the full story on what her deal was, but I'll always remember her because she reluctantly sold me *Stop Making Sense*, insisting I pick up *Shout at the Devil* instead. Years later, I'd purchase a W.A.S.P. cassette from her, and get zero argument.

Track: 'Pictures of You', Artist: The Cure, Album: *Disintegration*

The mother of all sad songs. It's just stinking with regret. Kyle Broflovski was right: *Disintegration* is the best album ever.

Track: 'Freak Me', Artist: Silk, Album: *Lose Control*

The only thing sad about this song is how much I love it (but an even bigger fan would be Jason Mewes: he once listened to this track, in-flight, on a constant loop en route from New Jersey to Los Angeles). The song screams sex, but when I tried to introduce it into one of our boudoir sessions, my wife broke into a laughing fit so disruptive, we didn't wind up fucking. At least, I think it was the song she was laughing at.

Track: 'Tom Traubert's Blues', Artist: Tom Waites, Album: *Small Change*

Another sad song. What a shock. I've always wanted to hear Alanis Morissette cover this song. I've also always wanted to sport a man-sized cock. Something tells me I've got a better shot at the former than the latter.

So... I showed you mine. Now you can show me yours. Lemme see 'em, folks: put together your Celebrity Playlist and let me know who you really are. Ten songs apiece sounds about right. Have at it.

Ladies? Are you looking for Mr. Right?
Thursday 30 November 2006 @ 1:53 p.m.

Gals, do you live in or near LA? Are you looking for submissive, easily bossed-around boys to be your love slaves, with the small price being that you'll have to put up with 'em screeching "EXCELSIOR!" and "SNIKT!!!" all the time (not to mention that you'll probably have to teach 'em how to eat pussy)?

Then you need to get your man-hunting asses over to UCLA this Saturday night at 7 p.m., for the ultimate Sausage Party. Unsullied cocks will abound at this special, one-time only event!

'Marvel: Then and Now' — a discussion between Stan Lee and Joe Quesada (as mediated by yours truly). Come watch as legions of eligible bachelors line up to hear a living legend and an artist-turned-editor-in-chief talk about wall-crawlers and shell-heads, and ask questions so inside and arcane, you'll think they were speaking another language! It'll be like shooting fish in a barrel for you women-folk! You'll have the pick of the litter: unshaped clay you can mold into your own perfect man!

If you're one of those women who're forever grousing that all the best men are either married or gay, quit yer bitchin' and start your mission! Mr. Rights aren't simply found; they're made! Take matters into your own hands this Saturday night at UCLA, with a roomful of certifiably disease-free and undamaged goods!

Yippee-Ki-Yay, Pt. 1
Friday 22 December 2006 @ 3:01 p.m.

My life over the last thirteen years has been a series of wish-fulfillments so consistently mind-blowing (at least to me) as to presuppose that, at some point in my deep, dark past, I sold my soul to Satan (*Angel Heart* style — complete with the caveat that I not recall the diabolical deal until Bob De Niro drops me in an elevator to Hell). Whether it's been warranted or not (and whether I've deserved it or not), it's nonetheless true. There are some mornings when I swear I'm living someone else's life... until I look down, am unable to see my cock beneath my hanging gut, and realize "No — it's you, alright." Truly, I've been blessed. Hate me if you must (some really do).

But, as if that's not enough for me to be slobberingly grateful for, check this out: lately, I've been having dreams I didn't even REALIZE I had, come true.

For example: for years, I have been in love with Bruce Willis. Not the "drop your nuts in my mouth" kinda love, mind you; the "oh my God — Bruce Willis is the coolest motherfucker on the planet" type of adoration we reserve for the people who set the tone of our early, impressionable years.

Back in the day, I was (and still remain) a massive (in spirit and girth) *Moonlighting* fan. David Addison — like Eric 'Otter' Stratton in *Animal House*, Tripper Harrison in *Meatballs*, John Winger in *Stripes* before him — was a smoothie of the highest order: quick with a quip and always in complete control of any situation; even those beyond his ken. Outside of all that delicious rat-a-tat dialogue that comprised nearly every episode of *Moonlighting*, one of my all-time favorite moments in scripted television history (right up there with Cooper's backwards-talking-midget dream in *Twin Peaks*, Dan, Roseanne and Jackie getting stoned in *Roseanne*, and the Galactica "jumping" into a fast-dropping orbit above New Caprica) is in the Paul Sorvino ep entitled 'The Son Also Rises', at the close of which Addison is dancing with Maddie Hayes at his father's wedding to Anita Baker's 'Sweet Love'. Check out that scene, if you ever get a chance: the man is a goddamned pimp. And since David Addison is, essentially, just Bruce Willis with a different name, Willis is, by extension, a goddamned pimp too.

What wasn't there for me to like about Bruce Willis? He was from New Jersey. He did commercials for Seagram's Golden Wine Coolers (the booze of choice for my burgeoning teenage alcoholic taste buds). He recorded an album that was the soundtrack of my entire junior year (*The Return of Bruno*), when Ernie O'Donnell was the first in our class to get his license, and Ern, Mike Belicose and I spent the semester in his shitty old truck with no heat, hitting the movies at Middletown and trolling from party-to-party on the weekends. I learned to drive in that ol' beater with 'Respect Yourself' blasting from a *Bruno* cassette in a sound system that cost more than the used car itself. Bruce Willis was, for all intents and purposes, the phantom member of the trio: the guy we all wanted to be.

And that was BEFORE *Die Hard*.

My summer of '88 was wiled away watching John McClane make fists with his toes, pull glass out of those same feet, curse like a sailor while he desperately kicked the ass of a thug twice his size, and end up stumbling half-dead out of a building by flick's end — one of the first action movie heroes to actually appear damaged by the adventure he'd just undertaken. What started out as a revenge-date I went on with Shannon Furey (in which I'd hoped to make my ex-girlfriend

Kim Loughran jealous enough to reunite with me), ended with my longtime interest in pussy taking a backseat to my newfound interest in the events of Christmas Eve at Nakatomi Plaza. With that viewing, the term *Die Hard* went from being the brand of a car battery Sears made to shorthand for every action movie of the next ten years that aped its formula: *Die Hard* in a bus, *Die Hard* on a train, etc.

Mortal Thoughts, Billy Bathgate, Pulp Fiction, Nobody's Fool, 12 Monkeys, Armageddon, The Fifth Element, The Sixth Sense, Unbreakable — I'd follow Willis's career anywhere (even to *Hudson Hawk*). Last year, I was beside myself when they released *The New Twilight Zone* on DVD, because it meant I could finally re-watch the Wes Craven-directed segment entitled 'Shatterday' — in which Bruce Willis, as Peter Jay Novins, accidentally dials his home phone number and hears an alternate version of himself answer. This past summer, while in Cannes with *Clerks II*, I watched the daily festival coverage in French just to see the man arrive on the red carpet for the *Over the Hedge* screening.

Fuck you all: I am an unabashed Bruce Willis fag.

So last week, after I wrapped the *Manchild* pilot (which went phenomenally), the very next morning, I reported to work on a flick that'd reveal a heretofore unrealized dream I'd unwittingly harbored since I first watched David Addison limbo in the Moonlighting Detective Agency offices, twenty years prior...

For five days, I acted opposite Bruce Willis in this summer's *Live Free or Die Hard*.

Yippee-Ki-Yay, Part 2

Prior to that December morning in the makeup trailer on the Universal lot, I'd only brushed up against the Pride of Penn's Grove, the mighty Walter Bruce Willis, just one other time.

It's May of 1994. Scott Mosier and I are at the Cannes Film Festival with *Clerks*, and our new boss, Harvey Weinstein, invites us to a *Pulp Fiction* soiree aboard a yacht Miramax has rented in honor of the flick that'll eventually bring home the fest's top honor, the Palm D'Or. Being relative virgins to not just the company, but also the film biz in general, Mos and I aren't rubbing elbows and clacking champagne glasses with the bigwigs and super-famous at the stern; we're huddled with a pack of six lower-level development execs, assistants, and interns at the bow of the über-boat, making fun of our betters.

These are the cats we feel most comfortable with and can relate to better than the Power Lords: the Miramaxkateers who can actually recite dialogue from our newbie effort and truly give a shit when we win the Prix de la Jeunesse and the International Critic's Week grand prize — two smaller fest awards that were bestowed on our flick during our initial Cannes visit. But as much as we play it cool and disaffected and giggle about Lawrence Bender's nervous tic or Uma Thurman's lack of a proper bikini-line wax, we still all share this wide-eyed, hearts-in-our throats amazement and appreciation for the fact that we're in the belly of the beast and under the wing of the Man of the Moment. This is Harvey Weinstein's Miramax at its apex: the company that, for a decade straight, could do no wrong and would redefine cinema — bringing the art film into the multiplexes. Granted, it wasn't akin to being in Dallas when Kennedy was shot, but in some small way, it *was* like living through history.

And as our little group of inside outsiders cackled and cracked wise, safely out of the earshot of anyone who could eject us from a party we didn't really deserve to be at in the first place, one of our number — Patrick McDarrah — suddenly puts us into stealth mode with the quiet utterance of "Here comes Bruce."

I followed his glance to see Mr. Willis rounding the bow, casually doing a saunter-lap around the boat, heading in our direction. As a long-time David Addison acolyte, I was dumbstruck: there he was, live and in the flesh, quietly singing to himself in the Cannes' harbor evening, the master of all he surveyed. He moved with effortless cool, as if an invisible posse of scantily-clad hotties led his way, tossing rose petals in this path. He wasn't just pimp-smooth: he was the *Emperor* of Pimp-Smooth.

And he was now four feet and closing from me.

What would I say? Should I say *anything*? Should I blurt out that I, too, was from Jersey, in hopes it'd spark a conversation during which I could bust out the Seussian "I'm looking for a man with a mole on his nose" back-and-forth from the 'Murder's in the Mail' episode of *Moonlighting*? Should I tell him that the album from said show was my go-to fuck soundtrack and I knew I was doing well if I could make it to his cover of 'Good Lovin'' without nutting? Or should I go Willis-smooth and simply drop a "Yippee-ki-yay, motherfucker" on him — which wouldn't be Willis-smooth at all, on second thought, as I imagined him getting that as much as Robin Williams gets "Nanoo-nanoo" from adoring-yet-annoying, desperate-to-be-clever fans.

In the end, I felt that silence was best. And that's what he got from our entire group as he shimmied by us: awed, hushed silence.

A silence that he chose to break.

"You fellas smoking weed up here?" he offered, signature smirk firmly in place.

Patrick, the quickest of us, was able to respond with "No. Why? You got any?"

"Haven't done that in ten years, Holmes," the Man countered, never slowing his pace, his back now to us as he returned to the stern.

And with that, he was gone, leaving a chorus of "Fuck, he's cool"-type accolades in his wake. We spent the next twenty minutes dissecting his momentary dip into our lives, which kicked off an hour of discussion about his filmography and how awesome he was in *Pulp*.

I figured that was the closest I'd ever come to Bruce Willis again in my lifetime, and the only tale I'd be able to rock my grandkids with when they watched *Die Hard* for the first time: a feeble story from a feeble old man who once stood in the presence of greatness and made no impression whatsoever.

Then, twelve years later, Deb Aquila called.

Somewhere in the midst of 2005, someone decided I could act — maybe not act as much as *appear* in movies that I didn't direct. A handful of gigs starting popping up for me, which was odd because the most well-known on-camera performance I'd given over the last dozen years, naturally, was as Silent Bob.

You'd imagine being the fatter half of the white, not-as-groundbreaking-as-Cheech-and-Chong stoner duo isn't exactly a calling card role that makes casting directors and studio heads all wet and hard to get you into their productions. It's not remotely akin to, say, Ralph Fiennes essaying the part of Amon Goeth in *Schindler's List* — which seemed to prompt the movie biz as a whole to squeal "After that killer, breakthrough performance, we've gotta get that Nazi in our pictures!" Let's call a spade a spade: essentially, all I ever did as Bob was a lot of eye work (bug eyes out, roll eyes, close and open eyes really fast eyes when blinking, etc.).

So then how the fuck did I wind up with roles in *Catch & Release*, *Southland Tales* and *Manchild*? Ty Burr of the *Boston Globe* dismissed the phenomenon thusly: "They bring on Kevin Smith, the *Clerks* director and, increasingly, an indie-cred muppet for studio movies..."

I'd like to believe that, I really would; because a) it would mean I have some sort of credibility I'm unaware of which the studios think they can exploit, and b) fuck Ty Burr — who *wouldn't* wanna be a Muppet (especially Fozzie)? But contrary to Mr. Burr's critic-typical Find-a-Pithy-Way-to-Minimize-the-Fun-Someone's-Having-in-Their-Career-and-Undermine-It-So-as-Not-to-Confront-the-Unfulfilled-Expectations-I-Had-for-My-Own-Life assertion, the answer lies in what turned out to be the single best audition I ever unwittingly gave: a DVD called *An Evening With Kevin Smith*.

Somehow, that four hours of collected quasi-stand-up at colleges across

America became my passport into the world of Other People's Movies. Susannah Grant and the Cullen Brothers (the folks behind *Manchild*) cited *EWKS* as the inspiration behind my casting, insisting there's an affability to the way I tell a story that makes me simultaneously naughty and loveable enough for people to root for (their words, not mine). You wanna be in pictures, kids? Here's the easiest way to do so: stand on stage and talk about how small your dick is.

And in this work-breeds-work business of show, it was *Catch & Release* that got me into *Live Free or Die Hard*, courtesy of one woman: *Catch* casting director Deb Aquila. She called me in July/August of 2006, saying there was a pretty cool and very central one-day role that she thought I'd be perfect for in this flick she was working on, and asked if I wanted to come in and meet/read for the director, Len Wiseman (of the *Underworld* movies fame). I barely heard her, though, as after she casually dropped the title of the picture — *Die Hard 4* — I was already passed out on the floor, overcome by Willis-induced vapors.

I was sent a set of sides — pages from the script with which one auditions — that didn't contain the words "Die Hard" or the name "John McClane". The studio was being so tight with security on the picture that they not only numerically coded scripts, they changed the title and the hero's name, in case the script was leaked. So here I am reading eight pages from *Reset* in which "Grayson" is barking at a character they'd like me to read for: "Warlock" — the Harry Knowles of hackers. I was almost in Heaven.

I say *"almost"* because the dialogue kinda sucked ass.

Granted, it's an action picture — so you can't expect it to crackle with scintillating back-and-forth. But there are action pictures, and there's *Die Hard*: the single best action picture ever made, in which all the elements — cast, plot, performance, action, direction, score, look — were firing on all cylinders in such a way that few, if any, films have ever come close, before or since. John McClane, the cop who's always in the right place at the wrong time, deserved better. So I did what any aspiring actor, hungry to land a part would do.

I rewrote it.

I didn't change plot beats, mind you; just put my dialogue into a patois that'd sound a bit more natural coming out of my mouth, and added some better, more current jokes (emo/goth references, some MySpace nods, etc.). I printed out two copies, studied my lines, and shot over to Deb's office, the location of which I was familiar with because it wasn't my first visit there.

A month or so earlier, Deb had also thought I was right for a small part in *Evan Almighty*, the Steve Carell-centric follow-up to the Jim Carrey starrer *Bruce Almighty*. But either my audition blew or famously Christian Tom

Shadyac didn't want the *Dogma* guy in his faith-based flick, because they went another way. So heading into the *Die Hard* audition, pessimistic me was expecting much the same outcome.

In the waiting room, I ran into Kal Penn (he of *Harold and Kumar* fame) and Brad Renfo (he of *The Client* and drug arrest fame), both there auditioning for the role of Matt Farrell, the young hacker who becomes McClane's sidekick in the picture. Brad and I ran some lines and chit-chatted about his road to recovery before he was called in to read, leaving me alone to mutter stuff like "Why'd you bring a cop into my command center?!" to myself. After twenty minutes, I headed in to meet Len Wiseman.

Len's the kinda guy you wanna hate in a big, bad way: he's a talented, good looking man. I'm a troll, right — but at least I've got the filmmaking thing going for me. Here's a guy who's got the filmmaking thing going for him, *and* he's a pussy magnet (indeed, he attracted, then sorta-married, Kate Beckinsale). While you're talking to Len, you find yourself wondering "Why isn't this dude *in front of* the cameras?" Mercifully, he's as insecure as the rest of us — something I discovered while we discussed how unbelievably harsh the TalkBacks at Ain't It Cool News have been on our respective bodies of work. We concluded that we weren't in an exclusive fraternity, as *everyone* gets trashed in the Ain't It Cool News TalkBacks — so much so that the potential sting has been completely blunted by the stereotypical predictability of the over-the-top bad will and bile.

After about a half hour, I read for Len. It wasn't particularly good, to my recollection, and Len was a bit surprised that I'd brought two sets of re-written sides to work off. But he humored me and let me do it a second time, after which we sat around, inside and outside of the building, bullshitting for nearly two hours about his wife's genius performance in *The Last Days of Disco*, comic book movies, and our mutual affection for *Die Hard*. It was on that subject that Len lit up like Christmas. He was a die-hard *Die Hard* fan, insisting that he wanted to hone as closely as possible to the original in the series and honor it in tone, look, and sense of humor. As the guy who shot a sixteen millimeter, backyard *Die Hard* fan-film in his youth, he didn't wanna be the cat who fucked up *Die Hard*. He was all passion and enthusiasm, his eyes lighting up whenever he talked about doing justice to John McClane. Len was good people, and it was pretty clear he was doing the job for the love, not the money (in truth, he took a pay cut to direct this flick). I don't get the chance to talk to many directors, so even though I felt I'd totally blown the audition and revealed myself as a charlatan thespian, when all was said and done, I was still glad I'd gone.

Two months later, Deb called.

"I wanna give you your *Die Hard* dates," she said.

"What?" I asked. "You mean, when the movie comes out?"

"When you're working on the show."

"Are you fucking *kidding* me?! I *got* that part?!"

"You did. You're the *Warlock*."

I'd completely forgotten about it all, it was so long ago. I'd assumed they were already in production — which they were — and assumed, too, that a better actor (or rather, a *real* actor) had been awarded the role. Deb informed me that, after my meeting with Len, I was always the first choice for Warlock; they were just on such an insane schedule shooting back east that they hadn't even thought about the LA-based stuff yet, much less made their casting calls. My shooting dates, it turns out, were two months away, in December.

Getting cast in any movie leaves you with this unparalleled feeling of acceptance; of being told you're worthy in a way few things can. It's not like when someone says "You're good enough to fuck." It's not like simply getting hired for a job. It's a golden ticket of sorts into a world you knew existed but never thought you'd empirically experience. When I was cast in *Catch & Release*, it was the first time since *Clerks* was bought at Sundance back in 1994 that I felt true professional elation.

And getting cast in a *Die Hard* movie blew that away. I was gonna become part of the *Die Hard* mythology, on par with Argyle the limo driver and Ellis, the coke-snorting White Knight. I was gonna get threatened by John Ma-fucking-Clane. But best of all?

I was finally gonna meet Bruce Willis.

I'd arrived at my appointed call-time of 7:30 on the Universal lot that December morning — perhaps the first occasion in years I'd ever been on time for anything, my wedding included. After I chucked my bag into my trailer, Michael Fottrell, the producer, came by to welcome me to the set, with a warning that "Things don't always run on time around here. Well, they run on *a* time; just not *on* time."

That'd be B.W. Time — and not simply because Willis is one of the biggest stars on the planet: it was truly Bruce's world, since he was the only person in the cast or crew to have worked on/been in all three previous *Die Hard* extravaganzas.

A PA named Todd Havern escorted me to the makeup trailer, where Lori McCoy-Bell immediately gave me the geekiest hair-styling this side of *Revenge of the Nerds*, slicked flat to the point of being Alfalfa without the cowlick. I was, after all, she said, an internet nerd. I didn't have the heart to explain that

I was, in fact, a real, live internet nerd, and (despite my big bald spot) none of us really have hair issues anymore. Rather than make waves, I suffered the 'do with a smile.

Said 'do fascinated Justin Long when he took a seat in the chair beside me. The Man Who Would Be Matt (often identified as the "I'm a Mac" Guy) was an instantly likeable fellow with a quick sense of humor. I was familiar, of course, with his body of work from *Dodgeball*, *Galaxy Quest*, *Accepted*, and — since I've got a kid — *Herbie Reloaded*, but we bonded over a conversation about James Duffy and Will Carlough's *Robin's Big Date* — a short film that'd been in the Movies Askew film fest contest a few months back. In it, Justin played an awkward Robin to Sam Rockwell's alpha-male, date-spoiling Batman, both replete with Halloween-grade costumes and masks.

We were in the midst of meet-cute bullshitting when a larger-than-life presence entered the makeup trailer. And I don't mean larger-than-life in that Rip Taylor or Charles Nelson Reilly kinda way; I mean the larger-than-life that accompanies a man who brings a hush to a room without uttering a single sound.

But, of course, he said *something*...

"'morning, kids," smiled Bruce Willis. "Who's ready to live free or Die Hard?"

You couldn't have scripted a better or intentionally cornier greeting.

Everyone in the trailer offered the group hello, as Bruce came over to shake my hand.

"Mr. Smith. Welcome, welcome. Thanks for doing this."

"Thanks for having me," was all I could sputter.

"Lemme ask you this: why do they call Lindsay Lohan 'fire-bush'?"

"Uh... I don't know," I replied, taken aback by the odd conversation starter.

Why's he asking me, I wondered. Does he think I worked with or even know Lohan? Is he mistaking me for someone else? Who cares: Bruce Willis just asked you a question, Fat-Ass; fucking answer the man.

"Because she's got red hair," I asked in return, clearly indicating I was hazarding a guess. "Does she even have red hair? I've never noticed. If she's a real redhead..."

"I was talking to him," Bruce corrected, staring at my hair, indicating Justin, Lohan's *Herbie* co-star.

While Justin provided the correct answer, I silently died a thousand deaths. What had I *done*? I'd foolishly assumed he had anything more to say to me than welcome pleasantries. And now he thinks I'm a jackass. Fucking great.

His question answered, Bruce said goodbye and headed off to his trailer, presumably to get his makeup done. This gave Justin and I enough time to run lines, so we grabbed some sides and went outside to smoke and pretend we were master hackers.

"Another rewrite," Justin said, regarding his sides. When I expressed distress due to the fact that I'd memorized the old lines, he told me the secret to *Die Hard 4* was to never memorize your lines until minutes before the cameras rolled — as, every morning, there were always changes to the dialogue.

I poured over the new lines — hoping to Christ there wasn't too much techno-jargon that I'd have to suddenly commit to memory — and immediately sensed something familiar about them.

"Oh my God — I *wrote* these."

It was true: all the stuff I'd written for my audition had been included in the script. It was either the highest compliment, or the explanation as to why I was cast.

Justin and I spent an hour going back-and-forth with the new lines, rehearsing and re-rehearsing, until Todd appeared and said "It's time." He loaded us onto a golf cart and we motored over to the stage.

When I pictured Warlock's basement as per the script, it was, at best, the size of the Connor's basement in *Roseanne*. When I laid eyes on the Warlock's basement set on the soundstage, it was, at the least, about half the size of a football field. There's never been a basement this huge in the history of basements. Apparently, Warlock dwelled in the sewers, as there was enough faux exposed concrete, pipes, mold and mildew to support the shooting of six *Phantom of the Opera* sequels. If we'd had a basement in my parents' house and it looked like this, I'd still be living there today.

And the décor! Adorned with a multitude of *Star Wars*-related and various geek-centric statues and props, the set betrayed all the earmarks of the twelve year-old me getting his hands on some plutonium, a flux capacitor and a DeLorean and traveling back to the future just to deck these halls. Complete with an old Asteroids kiosk, all the joint needed was a naked lady to be my dream room, circa 1982.

But there was something in there for future (i.e. present) Kev, too: a shitload of big screen monitors and superdrives, not to mention a gaming chair that made the *Enterprise*'s captain's chair look like a port-a-potty.

And it was that chair that cost us an hour and forty-five minutes of blocking rehearsal.

I was delivered to Len at his director's monitors, where I discovered he'd been doing some time-traveling of his own. But it wasn't his bubbly, eager-to-shoot past self who I'd met months back that'd made the jump; the Len slouched at the monitors in front of me was the John-Connor-at-war-with-Skynet future Len — battle-scarred and world-weary. I didn't have to ask what'd happened: the glee and zeal of landing the gig directing the next *Die Hard* had been replaced by the pressure and frustration of not only making a studio film that already had a release date, but also working with a movie star of galactic proportions. I arrived as Charlie Sheen in *Platoon* — bright-eyed and bushy-tailed; Len was Willem Dafoe — the seen-too-many-horrors vet on his third tour of duty, one necklace-of-human-ears shy of utter madness.

Blocking rehearsals are pretty straightforward. The actors figuratively walk through the dialogue and literally walk through the scene, figuring out where they're going to stand and when they're going to move so that the director and DP can plot where their cameras will go and how best they can capture the action. Considering this was one of the only scenes in *Live Free or Die Hard* in which nobody pulled a gun, threw a punch, or blew anything up, there was no action to capture: it was a ten-page, dialogue-driven scene. And since Len was always rolling, minimum, three cameras, I assumed we'd be out of it by day's end. My contract had me locked in for a week, but there was no way something like this was gonna take longer than twelve hours, total.

"You like the chair?" Len weakly inquired, mustering a hint of that "I can't believe I'm making a *Die Hard* flick" enthusiasm.

"I love the chair, sir."

"I looked long and hard for it. It's the perfect Warlock chair. So you're going to spend the whole scene in it."

"You want me to do everything from the chair?"

"Yeah. Warlock's not the kinda guy who gets up and moves around a lot."

"My kinda guy," I offered.

"Justin and Bruce will enter, Justin joins you here while Bruce cleans up at the sink, then Bruce comes down here too, and you guys finish the scene."

"Right on."

Less than twelve hours, I'm now thinking. I might be out of here by lunch.

Problem was, I hadn't factored in B.W. Time.

Bruce arrives, glad-hands and chit-chats with the crew and Len for a beat, and then suggests we run through the scene. Len lays it out for him just as he'd laid it out for me moments earlier. Bruce tentatively nods then says "Let's take a look."

Rosemary Knower, who plays my mother in the flick, escorts Bruce and Justin down a fake set of stairs. Back to them, from my chair, I bark at her for letting people into my inner sanctum, Justin joins me, we run through the dialogue.

We're maybe three lines in when suddenly, everything comes to a grinding halt.

"Len, hold up, hold up," Bruce says, without uttering his first line to me. "If Kevin's sitting, then I've gotta go all the way over there to address him."

"That's right," Len confirms.

"Why would John McClane go to this guy?"

"Because you wanna know about Thomas Gabriel."

"The whole world's ending, I've just been through a bunch of shit, and two strangers come into this guy's basement and he doesn't even get up? It's like he's expecting us."

"He never leaves his chair. It's his command center."

"But it's not logical, Len. I'm a cop. He's a criminal."

"He's a hacker."

"Isn't hacking illegal? I think we've established in this movie that hacking's illegal. So why would a cop go to a criminal? He'd make the criminal come to him. Or at least get him out of his seat to turn to address him. A guy he barely knows and a total stranger come into his basement and he doesn't even get up to see who it is?"

"When I saw this scene in my head," Len began. "Warlock's always in the chair. My shot list is based around Warlock in the chair. It's why I picked this chair."

Dead, awkward silence, as a hundred people wait to hear how the chair saga's gonna unfold. Then...

"You're the director, Len. It's your movie," Bruce relented. It seemed like we'd be moving on, until he post-scripted with "I'm just saying it's not logical that he doesn't get up when we enter."

It was my first shot, so I figured it was too early to point out that he was arguing for logic in a movie that featured his character jumping off an exploding jet's wing. And thank God I didn't, as it would've prolonged the twenty minute logic discussion that ensued even further. Dude had a point, though: me in the chair the whole scene was gonna result in a pretty un-cinematic ten minutes. But considering the simplicity of my body of work, I wasn't gonna pipe in with my two cents on how to shoot an action movie.

Ultimately, a compromise of sorts was reached: the scene would start with me in the chair until McClane and Matt entered, play for the duration with me on my feet, then end with me back in the chair. Len would get what he needed, Bruce was afforded the logic he was craving, and Justin and I could finally go back to rehearsing the scene.

Two more lines into it, Bruce stopped the rehearsal again.

"I don't get this," he interjected, breaking character. "As far as we know, the world's about to end. Me and Justin've been shot at a million times, I'm bloody, I blew up a helicopter with a car, and we've traveled all this way just so these two can make jokes about MySpace and goth chicks?"

Uh-oh, I thought: homeboy wasn't feelin' my pages. * Gulp *

"We're being too jokey," Bruce continued. "This is the start of act three, and we're putting the brakes on to make jokes. Look at this: these guys have two pages, going back-and-forth about ComiCon and shit. McClane wouldn't stand for that. He's trying to find out who the fuck Thomas Gabriel is — that's the whole reason he's here. Why's he gotta bargain with this asshole? He'd be like 'Tell us what we wanna know or I'll beat ya' to death,' and we'd move on."

"The studio always saw this scene as a comedic pause," Len counters.

"I'm not saying it's a bad scene, Len. I'm saying there's too much going on in the movie to stop and make jokes, at this point. We've gotta keep it *Die Hard*."

It was my first shot, so I figured it was too early to point out that he was arguing against humor in a franchise that kicked off with his character having an entire discussion about Roy Rogers that results in the unofficial tagline for every *Die Hard* flick that followed: "Yippee-ki-yay, motherfucker." Humor, as much as bullets, was always a key ingredient in any McClane epic.

"We should be using this time to let everyone know what a bad motherfucker Thomas Gabriel is," Bruce cautioned. "We've got a lot of information to get across, and this is the only scene it makes sense in."

At this point, Bruce turned to me and said "The problem is, we've been shooting for months now, and every time there's a loophole in logic or something we didn't shoot that needs to be explained, we've been saying

'We'll do it in the Warlock scene.' And now we finally get to the Warlock scene, and none of that information's been included. It's just a scene with two geeks talking to each other while my guy's standing off to the side, waiting to get a word in edge-wise."

I.E. — "Has everyone forgotten this is *my* movie?"

"So what do you wanna do?" Len asks, rubbing his temples as if this isn't the first time he's watched his shot list crumble before his eyes.

What followed was another half hour of logic discussions and story plotting that I kept an ear on while playing Asteroids against Justin as the crew slowly dissipated. Occasionally, the urge to interject would arise, and I'd be screaming in my head "LET'S JUST RUN THROUGH THE ENTIRE SCENE AT LEAST ONCE SO WE CAN GET IT ON ITS FEET TO FIGURE IT OUT INSTEAD OF TALKING ABOUT WHAT IT'S NOT AND WHAT IT SHOULD BE!" It was a maddeningly frustrating position to be in, because seventy-five percent of the issues Bruce had could've been addressed simply by getting through one rehearsal in an effort to discuss what could be lost and what we needed to add. But like I said: it was my first shot on my first day. I wasn't the director here; fuck, I was barely an actor.

So, an hour and forty-five minutes into a blocking rehearsal that normally would've taken twenty minutes max, Len finally broke the set to figure out what he needed to do to tell his story.

As we headed back to the trailers, the McClane in me — the guy who's gotta get things done at any cost — finally came out.

"If you guys gimme twenty minutes and a laptop, I can figure all this shit out and we could be rolling right after lunch," I said to Bruce and Len. Rather than offer me a pat on the head or a punch in the face, both shrugged.

"Skip?" Bruce said to a body-builder, bouncer-looking dude to his right. "Give Kevin your laptop. Take him back to Len's trailer and let's see some new pages." Then, to me, Bruce said "Remember: this scene's all about telling the audience what a bad motherfucker Gabriel is. We don't have that in this movie yet. Nobody knows why we're supposed to be scared of this guy. Make him scary."

Skip led me back to trailer world, during which time, I tried to figure out why Bruce felt like I needed his bodyguard at my side. Turns out Skip wasn't Bruce's bodyguard: Skip was Skip Woods — the writer of *Swordfish* and the writer/director of a 1998 indie flick called *Thursday*. Waiting on his next directorial gig, Skip was one of the hundred guys who makes their living doing punch-up on in-production action movies. He'd worked with Willis on something else previously, so Bruce brought him onto *Live Free or Die Hard* for a week. The dude may've looked like a muscle-head, but he was an incredibly sweet movie-geek who'd been 'round the block on pictures like this too many times to be phased by the lack of forward momentum.

"I don't have to do this, Skip," I said, as I settled in to Len's trailer. "You can do this. I don't wanna get up in your kitchen."

"It's not my kitchen," Skip graciously deferred. "I'm only on for the week. You won't bruise my ego taking a crack at the scene. All I did was take your audition tape and transcribe it for the Warlock stuff anyway, because that's what Len wanted."

"Sounds like all that MySpace humor's going away anyway," I offered. "We've gotta keep it *Die Hard*."

"You'll hear that a lot around here," he smiled.

And with that, I started writing.

Bruce rolled by a half hour later to check on the progress. I let him read what I'd had so far, and he was happy.

"That's what I'm talking about," he smiled, eyes on the computer screen. "But the Gabriel stuff can be even more bad-ass. This is the guy who stood up to the Joint Chiefs of Staff."

"Got it," I said. "Gimme twenty more minutes."

As I wrote, Skip filled me in on all the *Live Free or Die Hard* gossip unfit for print. Nothing mind-bendingly juicy, mind you — just all the normal little fires (and a few big ones) that'd been put out along the way. I read my stuff aloud to him to see what he thought. That's when he dropped the bomb on me.

"You can't say fuck," he told me.

"McClane always says 'fuck'."

"Not in this *Die Hard*," he explained. "They're going for a PG-13."

"Get the fuck out of here!"

""It's true," Len said, joining us in his trailer. "That's the only way Fox would approve the budget: if the flick was PG-13."

"What about Yippee-ki-yay?!" I demanded.

"We get away with one fuck in a PG-13. And that's the one."

Bruce joined us again to check on the progress. He read my pages, smiling ear-to-ear.

"I like this speech," he said in regards to Warlock's Thomas Gabriel monologue. "This is like the speech in *Jaws*."

"If the Indianapolis speech had been written by a retard, yeah," I said, successfully deflecting the undeserved compliment. "It'd be a lot better if I could say fuck throughout it."

"We'll shoot one where you do," Bruce countered. "Len and I have been shooting our secret cut of the movie all along, so that when we do the DVD, it'll sound more like the real *Die Hard*."

"Hey! Hey!" Len joked. "This is a real *Die Hard*."

Bruce put Len in a playful headlock, offering "This man's making the best *Die Hard* since *Die Hard*. Y'know how I know that? Because he got a fucking ulcer doing it." Then, heading for the door again, he added, "You should put rewriting into all your acting deals, Kev."

When he was gone, I turned to Len and asked "Did he *give* you the ulcer?"

"Him and the studio, yeah," Len confirmed. "Peptic ulcer. The doctor said to stay away from stress. You wanna finish the movie for me?"

"You don't wanna *see* my version of a *Die Hard* movie," I offered dryly, tapping at the keys. "All the action would happen off-camera. The only reason you'd know it was there would be because the characters would be talking about it between discussions about their dicks and *Star Wars*."

"In retrospect," Len observed, "that might've been the way to go."

I finished the scene and handed it over to Len and Bruce. Both said they loved it, but had to get it approved by the studio before we could start shooting. The pages were faxed to Fox, and we waited for word back.

Four hours later, we were still waiting.

During that time, I watched my Academy screener of *The Departed* in my trailer, hung with Todd and Justin, bullshitted with Bruce, tried to keep Len's spirits up, met Maggie Q, talked movies with Skip, and generally killed time. Lunch came and went. Bruce'd had Tastycakes shipped from back east, and was handing 'em out to cast and crew alike, making converts of the west coasters who'd never had a Krimpet. We set up chairs outside Len's trailer and had barbecued chicken, prepared by Bruce's chef. It was like a party: a low-key party that was costing thousands of dollars a minute.

As night fell, Len finally got word back from the studio: where'd all the humor in the scene go? Why was it suddenly so serious? The Warlock scene was always meant to be a comedic respite from the non-stop action.

Bruce then called the studio himself. Standing three feet away from me, I heard his side of the conversation.

"Fuck the jokes — this is kicking off the third act. We gotta keep it *Die Hard*... Uh-huh... Uh-huh..."

And then, after a long silence during which the increasingly frustrated Bruce listened to the studio side of the equation, I bore witness to one of the most pimp moves I'd ever seen in my life. It was the true mark of movie star power and yet another reason to add to the long list of reasons I'll forever hetero-love Bruce Willis.

"Lemme ask ya' this," he said into the cell phone. "Who's your second choice to play John McClane?" There was a beat of silence, during which Bruce turned on that twenty million dollar smirk, and then wrapped up with "That's what I thought."

He hung up and said to me "Do one more pass on the scene — don't touch that speech. Throw in a joke or two, and let's get going." As I left to do as instructed, Bruce stopped me. "What's with your hair? I've seen pictures of you, and you don't always wear it like that."

"This is how the hair department saw Warlock," I sighed.

"Fuck that. Wear your hair the way you wanna wear your hair," he tossed off, heading back to his trailer. "That's what I did."

Back in Len's trailer, while banging on the keys of Skip's laptop, a stranger entered, offering me a puzzled look.

"Hi," I said.

"Hi," he replied. "I'm Bill Wisher."

Bill Wisher… as in William Wisher — *the* William Wisher who was an unofficial co-author of many an action screenplay (this one included), and the co-author of record of a low budget flick nobody ever heard of called *Terminator 2: Judgment Day*.

And there I was, with my hands in his soup. I felt like he'd caught me fucking his wife.

But I guess decades of being one of many authors on a single screenplay — and often not getting the official credit — tempers a man's ego, because Bill was about as gracious as you can get in regards to my tampering with his work. He read what I'd done, made suggestions, and complimented me on the pages. After that sign-off, I turned the pages back over to Len and Bruce and hung out in my trailer 'til Todd knocked at my door.

"The Man wants to see you in his trailer," he said. I followed him to Camp Bruce: a trailer bigger than my childhood home.

When I entered, I saw Len, Skip, Bill and Bruce. Suddenly, I felt like I was getting fired. Instead, Bruce welcomed me with a drink in his hand. "You a drinking man, Kev?"

"Not really," I replied.

"Well I am." And he threw back a shot, plopped into a recliner, and announced our plans.

"We're letting the crew go home, and starting fresh in the morning. We're gonna shoot two versions of that speech: the long one you wrote, because that's what we want, and a shorter one we cut from what you wrote, just so the studio gets what they want. Everyone's happy."

"Got it."

"You wanna go see the new *Rocky* with me and Justin? Big premiere at the Chinese in ten minutes."

"No, I'll stick around here for a few and cut the speech up into the smaller speech."

"I wanna thank you for your patience with us today, and for all the work you did on the scene. It's not always like this around here. We just kept putting the Warlock scene on the back-burner 'til it snuck up on us, y'know? But it's all good now, and Len's gonna shoot the shit out of it tomorrow, and you're gonna do that speech, and it's gonna be *Live Free or Die Hard*."

With that, we were ushered out. I'd arrived at 7:30 that morning. It was 9:30 that evening. We hadn't rolled a frame of film.

The next day, I opted against arriving at the appointed 7:30 call time, now knowing full well that we weren't gonna start shooting 'til at least noon, if at all.

We started the blocking rehearsal around eleven, worked through some minor issues, and by 12:30, I finally got on film. Barring any heinous edits somewhere down the line, I was now in *Live Free or Die Hard*.

Once we started rolling, things went smoothly. As mentioned, Len never rocked less than three cameras, two of which, naturally, were always pretty much on The Money — Mr. Moonlighting. One of the best ad-libbers I've ever seen, Justin somehow found a way to improve upon any of his already strong previous takes. And me? I managed not to fuck things up too badly.

From time to time, Bruce would ask for line-change suggestions. One particular variation he wanted was in the nicknames he wanted to throw at me in the scene to describe my ample weight. He'd done "dump-truck", but wanted more choices. Having heard them all over the course of my life, I started feeding him the options, each of which made him giggle: "Ben & Jerry's", "Dairy Queen", "Tubby", "Lunchbox."

"*Lunchbox?*" he queried. "What's *that?*"

I *knew* he hadn't seen any of my flicks.

After running the gamut of insults, his enjoyment escalating to a crescendo with "Jumbo", I felt it was fair to give back a little. During one of my takes, I took a slight deviation as well.

"You wanna know about Thomas Gabriel?" Kevin-as-Warlock asked Bruce-as-McClane. "He's crazy dangerous, man! He's scary. You ever listen to *The Return of Bruno*? 'Respect Yourself?' He's scarier than *that*, man!"

His reaction could've gone one of two ways: north or south. Thankfully, Bruce cracked up.

Had I been directing *Live Free or Die Hard*, the three-person, ten-page scene would've been shot in a day... and had all the visual flair of a fourteen year-old's YouTube video. Thankfully, Len wanted to make his movie look like a *real* movie, so the Warlock scene stretched into a four-day shoot. Over the course of that week, I got to chill with a good bunch of people, and finally geek out with Bruce. I quizzed him on *Moonlighting*, his scene in *Fast Food Nation*, and one of his first, meaty TV roles.

"What comes to mind when I say Peter Jay Novins?" I asked him during a long stretch between set-ups.

"*Twilight Zone* and Wes Craven," he responded, without missing a beat. "My first big gig after I shot the *Miami Vice* episode but before the *Moonlighting* pilot aired."

I even got to serenade him with a Seagram's Golden Wine Cooler jingle he'd done in a series of commercials circa 1985/86, and he quickly joined in, finishing the ditty. If I was a chick, I'd have flooded my panties.

Ultimately, however, I had to divorce Bruce Willis after my final take. The cast and crew gave me a round of applause, and headed off to another, Warlock-less set-up. I headed back to my trailer where, for a few minutes, life seemed somewhat emptier, now knowing that I was no longer gonna be living on B.W. Time.

Months later, I ran into Bruce again at the big-ass, Radio City Music Hall premiere of *Live Free or Die Hard*. We chatted briefly, but it wasn't anything remotely as wonderful as that few days I'd spent on set with The Man. When all was said and done, I shook his hand and resumed my Willis-free existence. He was a movie star and I was a cult filmmaker (at best). We just don't travel in the same circles enough to warrant an ongoing relationship.

The film would go on to become the highest grossing of the entire *Die Hard* franchise and probably the most critically praised, too — though I can't take any credit for that; Len simply made the best *Die Hard* flick since the first one — a film that felt like the only true sequel to that 1988 classic. The whole experience is definitely in the top ten of my career highlights, and will forever mark the only time I'll ever work with a legend and a hero of mine.

Maybe.

On July 5th I was in Las Vegas, playing in the Ante Up for Africa charity poker tournament, hosted by Don Cheadle and Annie Duke, to benefit Darfur massacre survivors. Flanked by movie and poker stars, I donked out around the midway point in the game and did what anyone entrenched in Sin City — where you could throw a rock and hit something to gamble on, imbibe, or fuck — would do...

I went back to my hotel room and played online poker.

In the midst of my anti-socialism, my cell phone rang.

"Kevin?" asked the voice on the other end. "Bruce Willis."

"Hey, sir! How are you?"

"Just celebrating the anniversary of our nation's independence here in Sun Valley. Lighting some fireworks."

"Congrats on the huge opening, man," I offered. "And the great reviews."

"It all worked out, didn't it?"

"It did."

"Listen, Kev, I was thinking," said Bruce Willis. "You're from Jersey, I'm from Jersey. You're a writer, I'm an actor. What say you come up with something we can do together?"

My fat-surrounded, weight-taxed heart nearly exploded out of my chest.

"What — like a *movie*?" I sputtered, obfuscating the fact that I make my living writing somewhat clever things.

"Just like a movie. You think of something and let's do it."

After a few more exchanged pleasantries, I hung up. At least, I *think* I hung up; I doubt I could've reached the phone, so pinned to the ceiling was I at that point… until harsh reality slammed me back down onto the bed.

I don't *make* Bruce Willis pictures. I make movies in which donkey shows figure prominently. I make flicks in which plots turn on stink-palms and snow-balling. My mind raced, but I couldn't think of a single idea which the Mighty Bruce Willis might deem worthy of his time and star power. I was suddenly Tantalus, surrounded by a cool lake from which I couldn't drink; reaching for fruit from branches that would forever lift satiety from my grasp.

A few weeks later, I was doing a Q&A at a Google event in Santa Monica, when someone in the audience asked me what video game would I like to see turned into a movie. After a few seconds thought, I chose Dig-Dug — the early 80's trifle in which a helmeted sprite traveled underground and used a pump to inflate and defeat various mini-monsters. My only problem, I said, would be finding someone to play the lead.

"Bruce Willis!" someone playfully shouted from the audience.

And while the audience and I chuckled over this prospect, I immediately started crafting a poster in my mind. "Bruce Willis is Dig-Dug" was the tagline.

If a fat kid from the Jersey 'burbs could grow up to star opposite one of the biggest movie stars in the world in a summer blockbuster, then anything's possible.

Zack and Miri Make a Porno
Wednesday June 6 2007 @ 11:34 am

That's the title of the comedy we're doing right after *Red State* (the horror flick), as reported by Jay Fernandez in his *L.A. Times* Scriptland column today.

Granted, I'm biased because I wrote it; but I really dig this script. It's funny, bawdy, sexy, dirty, titillating (emphasis on the tit) and dripping with heart. If you were gonna do that movie-description thing, I'd say it's like *Chasing Amy* meets *Clerks II*, with a dash each of *Boogie Nights* and *Bowfinger* tossed in.

Some folks have already said "Sounds like *The Girl Next Door...*" or "Sounds like *The Amateurs...*" A few British cats have drawn comparisons to a flick called *I Want Candy*. I certainly can't deny that *Zack and Miri* has nothing in common with said flicks — namely the subject of porn movies; but I can tell you that that's about where the similarities begin and end, as far as I know.

To be fair, all I know about *I Want Candy* are the reviews I read recently in *Empire* and *Total Film* magazines. And in terms of *The Girl Next Door* (a film that always occurred to me as more of an homage to *Risky Business* than the "Let's-Put-On-A-Show" nature of "dirty movies"), *Zack and Miri* is about as far removed from the world of slick, professional porn (the domain of *Girl Next Door*) as can be.

No — the one flick I was sweating was *The Amateurs* (recently retitled *The Moguls*) — a flick I hadn't heard of until I was in the midst of writing *Zack and Miri*. But as it turns out, Laura Greenlee (our long-time line producer) worked on that flick, and after reading *Zack and Miri*, she was able to dispel any fear I had on the subject by offering, "The only thing they have in common is that non-porn people want to make a porn movie. The circumstances, jokes and characters are completely different."

I breathed a huge sigh of relief, because the last thing in the world a writer wants to be accused of is cryptomnesia; or worse, flat-out plagiarism (well, really, the last thing a writer — or even a non-writer — would want to be accused of is child molestation, I'd imagine; then cryptomnesia or plagiarism). But just because a film shares a similar theme/storyline with another film, does that mean it shouldn't be made at all? I don't think so. And I'm not talking about dueling volcano or asteroid movies here; I mean flicks that immediately invoke other flicks. I'm a firm believer that similar subject matter in different hands still has the potential to be original and fresh. I mean, *Chasing Amy* — the flick we get the most credit for — was pretty much the same-old, same-old boy meets girl, boy loses girl story with a bit of a different spin. Were I really sweating the fact that that story had been done to death before, I wouldn't have bothered with *Amy* — and I'd be all the poorer for it (both figuratively and literally). After centuries of storytelling, there's always bound to be some familiarity/similarity in books/shows/movies; it's how each author handles the material that makes all the difference. Just because we've seen *For Keeps*, *She's Having a Baby*, and *Nine Months* doesn't mean we don't want to see *Knocked Up*.

Regardless, I know I'm in for a few months of "That movie sounds like...", but I'm not sweating it; I've read my script (even wrote it) and while it's preoccupied with dirty movies, I know what it's really about.

And about a year from now, you will too.

Rosario...
Wednesday August 8 2007 @ 4:26 p.m.

A few short weeks ago, in this MTV.com interview, I was asked about Rosario Dawson's involvement in our next flick, *Zack and Miri Make a Porno*.

"I wrote it for Rosario Dawson," I responded. "I'd be kind of flabbergasted if she didn't do it."

Yesterday, MTV.com ran an article, in which she was asked about her involvement in *Zack and Miri Make a Porno*.

"It's going to be a really interesting film. I don't think I'm going to be a part of it. He wrote it for me, but I'm just signing on to do [*Eagle Eye*] and that's going to be shooting from November to March."

It has prompted the following internet articles...

Rosario Dawson ditches Kevin Smith's Zack and Miri Make a Porno for Eagle Eye — slashfilm.com

Rosario Dawson Says She Won't Be Making a Porno with Kevin Smith — Cinematical.com

Rosario Dawson Dumps Kevin Smith — Cinemablend.com

What can I say? It kinda sucks. And not inasmuch as "Jesus — we'll never find another actress for this role!" It kinda sucks because, like I've said, I wrote the part with Rosario in mind/for Rosario to play.

How did this happen, you ask?

Well… it's kinda my fault.

I wrote *Zack and Miri* with two actors in mind for the respective leads: Rosario, natch, as Miri, and this other guy as Zack. The idea was to shoot it sometime after the first of the year, post *Red State*, but the reaction to the *Zack and Miri* script was so enthusiastic across the boards (from producer Scott Mosier, everyone at the Weinstein Co., the agents and managers of both Rosario as well as the unnamed male lead, to *Entertainment Weekly*), that it got fast-tracked into first position (something that wasn't hard to do, considering *Red State* wasn't finished yet). Suddenly, we were looking at an Oct/Nov '07 start for *Zack and Miri*.

Then, our prospective male lead needed some time to get some stuff done, so we moved *Zack and Miri* back to a January start — which would mean a late October/early November pre-production start (precluding any pre-*Zack* start for *Red State*). This would've mean Rosario would be sitting on her hands all fall, waiting to shoot *Zack and Miri*. And with the impending strike, with actors not knowing if they're gonna be working at all post-March, that's a tough request to make of any actor.

Then, along comes *Eagle Eye* — the flick starring man-of-the-moment Shia LeBeouf, to be directed by *Disturbia* helmer D. J. Caruso — based on an original idea by…

Wait for it…

Steven fucking Spielberg.

I mean, who wouldn't take that gig?

Problem is, *Eagle Eye* starts shooting in November and doesn't wrap 'til Feb/March. Well, that's not really a problem for anyone… except me and *Zack and Miri*.

So here I sit, momentarily, without a leading lady.

sigh

However, this is the nature of the movie business. It happens all the time. You start off thinking… knowing who your cast is gonna be, and then it changes on a dime.

I rewrote *Dogma* with Joey Lauren Adams in mind for the lead and Sam Jackson as Rufus. The parts wound up going to Linda Fiorentino and Chris Rock instead.

I wrote the first fifty pages of *Jersey Girl* for Bill Murray and Joey Lauren Adams. The parts wound up going to Ben Affleck and Jennifer Lopez.

I wrote *Clerks II* with my wife Jen in mind to play Becky. Then, we went to Liv Tyler, Bryce Dallas Howard, Ellen Pompeo, and Sarah Silverman, before ultimately casting... Rosario Dawson. And Rosario did such an amazing job in that flick, that I wanted to put her in the next flick — *Zack and Miri Make a Porno* But alas, it's not to be.

I'll miss her, to be sure, but spin control dictates that I've gotta say maybe this is a good thing: certainly for Rosario (why be in the donkey show guy's next picture when you're invited into Camp Spielberg?) and maybe even for me and *Zack and Miri*. I've never worked with our (potential) male lead before, so it might be nice to have a female lead I've also never worked with before.

Anyway, there it is. I apologize that the tale's not more juicy or that it doesn't involve delicious bridge-burning and name-calling, but sometimes, schedules just don't blend — no matter how much you want them to — and you just have to be understanding about a great opportunity for someone you dig. Rather than curse my friend for making the right career decision, I'm elated for her. Go, Ro, Go!

Who is and isn't *Zack*...
Wednesday September 12 2007 @ 1:37 p.m.

Monday

I didn't get to sleep until 5 a.m., so when I'm woken up at 7:45 to take Harley to school, it stands to reason that I'm like "Y'know — I used to walk to school when I was a kid..." But in the age of sexual predators and child killers, I slap on some clothes and groggily stumble out the door to the car, where I somehow manage to get the kid to school without driving into a telephone pole or through a Starbucks front window. I come home and almost immediately go back to sleep.

When I wake up, I watch some season three of *The Closer* that I'd downloaded from iTunes (awesome show) and answer email. Google news sends me a link to this story on SlashFilm.com about Jason Bateman saying he's not in *Zack and Miri Make a Porno*.

A few weeks back, I got an email from Brad Pleyvak, one of the fellas who runs News Askew, that read...

Just wanted you to see this... Any truth or denial here? I assume if it's true it's something you'd want kept quiet and not run at News Askew anyway... So I'll wait to hear back from you. And if it's true, very cool news — Bateman is a fantastic comedic actor in my opinion, and really would be a great fit with your words. See below.

The attachment read...

Hello News Askew Scoops,
Reason: I've Got A Scoop!

I was on the set of a new superhero movie coming out called *Hancock* previously known as *Tonight He Comes* (hmm... wonder why they changed the title).

Any way I overheard a conversation between Will Smith and Jason Bateman about working with Kevin Smith. Bateman stated that he was excited to start working with Kevin. I checked Batemans Imdb page and searched around the net and there was no mention of him working with K. Smith so I'm assuming this is a big scoop.

I'm a huge *Arrested Development* fan — and equally as big a fan of Jason Bateman. I'd only ever met him once: at the Baja Fresh on Sunset and Fairfax (the one next to the Coffee Bean & Tea Leaf). I was in line with Schwalbach when I spotted Bateman outside, sitting alone at a table, eating and reading a newspaper. I nudged the wife and was like "Holy shit — it's Michael fucking Bluth." I'm never... never the guy who wants to talk to famous people, but, Jesus — it's Michael fucking Bluth! Sitting not ten feet away from me! After some initial hesitance, I opted to bug the guy while he was eating and tell him how much I loved the show and his work on it, opening with the standard "I hate to bother you, but..." Thankfully, he didn't seem bothered, saying "Thanks, Kev," as I was heading off. The whole exchange lasted about fifteen seconds, and I was shocked as shit the dude knew my name, as I'd never said "Hi, I'm Kevin Smith." (If this story sounds familiar, it's because I'd talked about it in SModcast 4, around fifteen minutes in.)

But as cool as that brief exchange was, and I much as I love Bateman's stuff, I wrote *Zack and Miri* for another guy I love. So I wrote back to Brad and told him not to run the story on NewsAskew, as there was no truth to it.

That's when the story showed up at Ain't It Cool News...

Who is playing the Zack of Kevin Smith's ZACK AND MIRI MAKE A

PORNO? I think I know!

Ahoy, squirts! Quint here. I think this maybe a bit of scoopage. I haven't seen it reported anywhere else, but I have gotten it on good authority that Kevin Smith has found his titular Zack for his upcoming ZACK AND MIRI MAKE A PORNO.

Rosario Dawson just dropped out, but Smith has been tight-lipped on who is playing the male lead. He's only said it's someone he admires, but hasn't worked with yet.

That someone, according to a source known as "Big J", is none other than Michael Bluth himself: Jason Bateman.

I think that's a great marriage of material and actor, personally. Now we'll just have to see who is the new Miri...

Take the scoop with a tiny pinch of salt. The scooper is definitely in a position to know this information, but is untested.

And even though Quint urged folks to take the info with a pinch of salt, it wound up running all over the 'net, at Cinematical, CinemaBlend, SlashFilm, Ugo, JoBlo ...as well as a slew of others. And I never thought to simply say "It's not true" to anyone but Brad at News Askew. Jason, however, was asked and did have an answer for Peter Sciretta over at SlashFilm. Then, over at MTV's Movies Blog, Shawn Adler threw up a link to the SlashFilm article, but it kind of insinuated that Bateman had passed on *Zack and Miri*. So I called Shawn to clear it up and asked him to adjust it on their site.

However, in case folks are still unclear, I'll second what Bateman said: no, he's not Zack in *Zack and Miri Make a Porno*. We never asked him and he never read it. He was a great idea for Zack, as Bateman's a genius who drops performance clinics in even small roles (*Smokin' Aces*, the upcoming-but-gonna-be-retitled *Quebec*), but like I said: I wrote the role for someone specifically, and that specific someone's the only guy I've ever sent the script to.

The Man Who Would Be Zack
Monday November 19 2007 @ 11:47 am

So, a bunch of folks have seen the announcement of Seth Rogen and Elizabeth Banks, and asked "How the fuck did that happen?!?"

If you've got a minute, I'll tell you.

In late 2005, I had a breakfast meeting with Harvey Weinstein at the

Peninsula Hotel in Beverly Hills. Even though we were a few weeks away from shooting *Clerks II*, he was asking what I wanted to do after that. I told him I'd been thinking about this flick called *Zack and Miri Make a Porno*. I'd gotten no further than the title when he said "Done. I'm making that movie."

"Don't you wanna know what it's about first?" I asked.

He replied "I thought the title said it all."

"Well it doesn't."

"Fine. What's it about?"

"It's a meditation on the Holocaust."

He stared at me blankly for a beat.

"Alright," I relented. "The title says it all."

I never got to see *The 40 Year Old Virgin* in a theater. When it was released in the summer of 2005, we were buried in pre-production for *Clerks II*, so it wasn't 'til the flick's DVD release that I was finally able to kick back and enjoy it. It was a significant watch for me, because that day, I fell in love with the bearded guy who talked about watching a chick fuck a horse and feeling bad for her. But I knew I wanted to work with the guy when I watched him play a video game with Paul Rudd's character and utter "I'm ripping your head off right now. It's off and now I'm throwing it at your body. FUCK you!"

The delivery of that "FUCK you!" had me rolling. I rewound that moment multiple times during that viewing.

A few days later, Scott and I had a meeting with Harvey (at the Peninsula again) to talk about the release plans for *Clerks II*. When those discussions were out of the way, he asked "Where's that porno script?"

"I'm working on it," I lied. "But, hey — did you ever see *40 Year Old Virgin*?"

"Yeah. Funny."

"There's a guy in that movie I wanna cast as Zack."

"Steve Carell?"

"No — the guy who worked in the stock room. His name's Seth Rogen."

"I like that guy. I'm meeting with him next."

"What?!"

"He's coming in to talk about *Fanboys*. You wanna meet him?"

I never wanna meet anybody. This guy, though, I did wanna meet. And meet him I did, on our way out, as he was coming in. Harvey introduced us, and I immediately told him how many times I watched him say "FUCK you!" to Paul Rudd. He said he was a fan, but I didn't take him seriously; in Hollywood, people tell you that all the time, even though they don't mean it.

We talked a little bit about *Clerks II* and I said I'd happily show him the flick if he wanted to see it. The guy gave me his phone number and we said good-bye.

When I got home, I slipped the piece of paper with his phone number under the transparent blotter on my desk, beside pics of my kid, my wife, the original cast of *Clerks*, and sundry other mementos. I never called him about that *Clerks II* screening because I figured it'd be awkward somehow — like he'd feel more obligated to go than anything else, and that's a position I never wanna put anyone in, let alone a guy whose work I like.

A year later, I finally started writing *Zack and Miri Make a Porno*. At this point, it was a month out from the release of *Knocked Up*, and I was seeing posters with Rogen's mug on 'em all over town. "I'm an idiot," I thought. "This dude's gonna be huge. I should've written *Zack and Miri* a year ago."

A week later, I was done with the first unofficial draft — the one I send to Scott for a first look and possible edits. A week after that, on May 14th, I was done with the official first draft. When I submitted the script to Carla, our Weinstein Co. exec, I asked her if she, by chance, had Seth Rogen's email address (since she was also the exec on *Fanboys* — a movie Seth wound up doing some cameos for). So, on May 15th, at 3:31 in the afternoon, I wrote Seth the following email...

Sir,

We met very briefly, about a year and a half ago, as I was leaving a meeting with Harvey Weinstein and you were entering a meeting with Harvey Weinstein. I don't expect you to remember it, but I practically blew you over your "I throw your head at you. Fuck you!" moment in *The 40 Year Old Virgin*.

Anyway, I'm a fan, and that day, I started thinking about writing a script for you. But laze (and *Clerks II* promotional duties) got the best of me, so I never got around to writing it.

Until two weeks ago.

I know you're probably buried in *Knocked Up* and *Superbad* stuff at the moment, but if you've got an hour or two, I'd love you to read it. We're not gonna be shooting 'til Jan/Feb '08, so there's no immediate rush, I guess. I also know (or at least suspect) that you generate your own material, so I realize I'm doing you no favors, as you're probably not hurting for work at the moment. Still, I'd love you to read it and, ultimately, be in it, so maybe we can hook up sooner or later.

As I hit send I thought, "Yeah, you wanna hook up with him, alright. You and every studio in town, at this point. You snooze, you lose, fat-ass. Next time, don't be so fucking lazy. This dude's never gonna respond now."

At 4:42, that dude responded.

Dude,

This may sound like bullshit, but when I first moved to LA, I went out to meet with agencies, and one of them asked me what my goals were. I said, "to be in a Kevin Smith movie." That goal has not changed. I would be honored to read anything you wrote, and am truly flattered and amazed that you sent me this e-mail. I wouldn't be a writer if it wasn't for you and your movies. It's as simple as that. Thank you so much.

Naturally, I about fell out of the chair. My man-crush not only responded (quickly, at that), but he paid me just about the highest compliment he could've, short of "And *Jersey Girl* is a misunderstood masterpiece." (Granted, it's not; but a guy can dream, can't he? And also delude himself?)

I made plans to get him the script before he went off on a press tour, then waited for a reaction.

And waited.

And waited.

Thus began the most tumultuous and agonizing summer of my adult life. *Knocked Up* opened huge and kept earning, turning the stock room worker from *40 Year Old Virgin* into a massive movie star. And movie stars don't do my flicks unless I knew them before they were movie stars. Add to all this the fact that he was the writer of a forthcoming flick that was enjoying huge advance buzz as well — which means this was suddenly a man who could not only get cast in anything, but could write it himself. Like I'd said in the email to him: he could generate his own material. A guy who could do that didn't need me, or my script. Maybe the nice things he wrote in his email evaporated the moment he enjoyed his breakout success. The dude had something akin to a movie biz Bar Mitzvah; but he wasn't just a man now — he was THE man.

Then, word came back from his agent and manager that THE man read the script while abroad. Arrangements were made to meet upon his return to the States.

July 6th, Seth came over to my house. I barbecued him some steaks, and we sat around bullshitting about movies, comics, video games and a bunch of other shit. As much as I'd liked him in *Virgin* I now liked him even more. He was laid back like Mosier. He was geeky like me.

And he loved the script.

The plan had been to shoot in January, but we talked about maybe going in November instead, getting the flick done by Christmas. It was all, ostensibly, a go.

Then, a week later, the brakes were suddenly applied big time. Word came back from his agent and manager that we needed to slow down. Seth had other offers to consider, but more importantly, the dude was exhausted. He'd gone from *Knocked Up* to *Superbad* to *Pineapple Express* to *Knocked Up* whirl-wind press tours both here and internationally, to a new, just announced gig writing and starring in *The Green Hornet*. He was looking for a break.

So on July 18th, I wrote him again…

Hey,

Word is you might wanna/need to wait to do *Zack and Miri* 'til after the first of the year. If that's the case, sir, then don't sweat it. I know you got a bunch of stuff going on at the moment with *Superbad* opening and *Pineapple Express* in post, as well as *Green Hornet* now (congrats on that, by the way). It would've been nice to shoot in the fall, but if you doing the flick means wait-ing 'til January, then I'm willing to wait. I mean, I want you to be in it, obvi-ously; I wrote it for you.

But here's the thing: I don't wanna be the nut-biter that's adding more shit to your to-do list, but if we can at least talk notes in the near future, that'd be nice to get out of the way. I keep hearing you've got thoughts/notes on the script, so naturally, since I've got time on my hands, I'd wanna address said notes sooner rather than later. If it's a case of, "I'm gonna wanna ad-lib and pitch jokes/alts while we shoot," then no worries — I'm all for it. If it's a case of, "There are story changes I wanna make," then that's something I'd rather know now, so I can either get back to work on the script or be like, "You're out of your fucking mind, you Canuck Fuck."

So when you've got time to go over it (either on the phone, over email, or in person), give a bitch a shout and let him know. With the exception of Comic-Con weekend and the first week of August, I'll be here in town. Waiting. Like a school-girl.

Twenty minutes later, he responded…

Dude, thank you so much for understanding. It means a lot. The fact of the matter is that I'm just naturally very lazy and the concept of shooting another movie before the new year gives me cold sweats. When we make your movie, I want to be raring to go. Right now I'm not raring to go anywhere but the couch. The notion of making a movie with one of my heroes when I'm in a headspace where I'm anything less than shitting a brick every second of shooting because of how psyched I am doesn't seem right. I think right now, I'm just too worn out to be in that headspace. But not for long... Honestly, making a movie with you is a dream of mine.

I'll read the script again asap and give you some thoughts. Nothing major. Just an idea for a new take here or there, but again, seriously, its one of the funniest things I've ever read.

At that point, we moved our start back to January and waited. Then, all was quiet for about two months, during which time, I was biting my nails, piss-scared this dude was gonna wake up and be like, "Motherfuck a *Clerks* guy. I'm too huge for his bullshit now."

I distracted myself by eating a lot and gained a shit-ton of weight. I also preoccupied myself writing *Red State* — which was weird because it's about as far from *Zack and Miri* as you can get. I ran into Seth again down at the San Diego Comic-Con, and saw him briefly at the *Superbad* premiere — during which time I never hassled him about *Zack and Miri*. I forced myself to stop sweating the situation: dude said he dug the script and wanted to do it. If it doesn't come to pass, it wasn't meant to be. If something better comes along and he opts to do that flick instead, at least I knew he liked what I wrote and, even for a moment, considered being in it.

Then, shortly after the San Diego Comic-Con, we got word that Rosario Dawson (who I'd been championing as the Miri in *Zack and Miri*) took a gig in the new Spielberg-produced, Shia LaBeouf flick. I was about ready to put a gun in my mouth.

On August 8th, Scott, Carla and I started looking to see what actresses were gonna be available in January. With the strike looming, actors and actresses were booking their fall/winter schedules like crazy. Folks started suggesting we do a list of available actors as well, in case Rogen found something else he wanted to do that was gonna be more high profile/pay him more, but I refused. Even though there was no forward momentum on making an official deal with Seth, I had to take the man at his word: he said he wanted to do our flick. Until he said otherwise, I refused to consider anyone for Zack but the guy for whom I wrote it.

Carla pulled together a list of around a hundred actress names. Alphabetically, Elizabeth Banks was at the top of the UTA list. Having dug her in *Invincible* and *Virgin*, I put her into my top five choices. Carla told me her agent had called because she'd specifically asked about *Zack and Miri*. That made me like her even more.

Then, another potential blow came by way of Ain't It Cool News, when they erroneously reported that Jason Bateman was being considered for Zack. I started to panic: what if Seth saw that and was like, "Fuck Fat Smith for looking elsewhere."

But this never came to pass, because in early September, after a long summer of feeling like Andi waiting for Blaine to ask her to the prom, Seth came over to the house again, at which point we ate pizza and talked about his notes on the script. He had exactly one, and it was a good suggestion. The fear that he was gonna ask me to wait 'til after he did *Green Hornet* was allayed when he said he didn't wanna try to make that flick pre-strike. We went over the potential Miris and he went nuts for Banks, telling me that she was really funny and a quick ad-libber. We both agreed she was the perfect Miri.

After that meeting, on September 19th, four months after I first emailed The Man Who Would Be Zack, Weinstein Co. submitted the official offer to Seth's agent and manager. Negotiations were begun in earnest, during which time, we started auditioning folks for the other roles, with Seth reading opposite them. I met with Elizabeth up at the house and instantly fell in love with her sense of humor (and modest romantic history). She'd read the script and loved it, so Weinstein Co. started her negotiations, too.

On October 31st, while I was trick-or-treating with my kid, I got the phone call that Seth's deal had been officially closed. I was thirty pounds heavier than when I'd started this journey, but all the stress-eating was worth it. I can lose weight; I couldn't lose Rogen.

A few days before November 16th, the Weinstein Co. was able to close Elizabeth's deal as well, so the press release could reveal who both Zack and Miri were gonna be.

On November 25th, I head out to Pittsburgh for good, as we prep for our January 16th start of principal photography on my eighth film, starring Seth Rogen and Elizabeth Banks.

Very seldom does a situation work out exactly the way you'd like it to. Very seldom do all your dreams come true. I've led a pretty charmed life for which

I'm thankful every day. I'm convinced I've been as lucky as I've been, both professionally and personally, because I'm gonna die young. As long as that early demise doesn't happen before we put *Zack and Miri Make a Porno* into the world (and *Red State* after it), I got no beef (and when I say "I got no beef", I don't mean "I don't care if I die young," I mean my dick's small; naturally, I'd be pretty pissed if I don't get to see my kid grow up because I'm dead).

I owe a great deal of thanks to many people, before we roll a frame of film.

Thanks, Jen — for putting up with five months of me laying on the bed, in a near-fetal position, moaning "If Seth Rogen doesn't do this flick, I'm gonna make a real porno."

Thanks, Marsha and Blair — for not insisting that your client aim higher.

Thanks, Mos, Carla, and Phil — for never losing faith and staying on top of this from day one.

Thanks, Harvey and Bob — for stepping up and giving us 25 mil to make this flick.

Thanks, Elizabeth — for being Miri.

Thanks, Seth — for reminding me that sometimes in this business, people say what they mean and mean what they say. You could've done anything you wanted, and you wanted to do this flick; I'll be forever grateful for that.

And lastly, Thank God — we're finally making *Zack and Miri*.

Making Porno, Pt. 1: Foreplay
Thursday January 10 2008 @ 10:36 a.m.

Tuesday was day one of rehearsals, and lemme tell ya: it was pretty awesome, hearing Zack and Miri come to life for the first time. Rogen and Banks are genius together (and apart — which, in the flick, is extremely rare): hilarious and rather sweet and touching when called for. The roles fit them like gloves. Shit, better than gloves: the roles fit them like condoms. Like custom-made condoms, even.

Yesterday was two of rehearsals — a term I use loosely, since it's more of a read-through than anything else. This time, all the leads but two were present. So while I read every other role but Zack and Miri on Tuesday, four more people joined us yesterday, assuming their characters for the first time. And it sounds great; just fucking tremendous. We could've put it on wax — if folks' idea of wax was seven people sitting around a hotel room reading a script aloud. But if we were doing a radio play? It would've been air-worthy. We'd have gotten multiple FCC fines for the content, but performance-wise? Totally air-worthy.

Today, we do camera tests (throw the actors into a bunch of their wardrobe/hair "looks" and shoot 'em under a few different lighting schemes) then a nearly full cast read-through (nearly-full since a new baby is, understandably, keeping one of the leads from making it out for the rehearsal/read-throughs). Tuesday, we'll start doing some location(s) rehearsing, blocking some stuff out in advance of our Wednesday start of principal photography. Back in the day, that'd make me nervous as fuck. One day of on-location rehearsal? I'd be nauseous at the thought. Now? It's a different world.

I used to be a real rehearsal Nazi: insisting on at least three weeks of three to four hour days. Over the last few years, though — either based on time restrictions, more faith in the performers, or simply the experience that comes with doing a job for fifteen years now — I've learned to lighten up and do more on-set tweaking than anything else. Took awhile to reach that conclusion, though.

— On *Clerks*, we rehearsed in Quick Stop, every night for three weeks straight. None of us had ever made a movie before, and we didn't have the cash to blow on multiple takes, so it felt like getting the performances and blocking (such as it was, considering Jeff and Brian were simply parked behind the counter most of the flick) as close to perfection made the most sense. We rehearsed *Clerks* like it was a play, really — so much so that by the last week of rehearsal, we weren't just running scenes — we were doing the whole flick in sequence, minus the cat. The process just seemed to make sense, and because of it, when it came time to shoot, we rarely had to do more than two takes of any given scene. In fact, most of the time, we'd do one take and move on.

— On *Mallrats*, we did at least two weeks of rehearsal, starting in a hotel room and moving it to the actual mall to rehearse the scenes on their feet at their eventual locations. Since I'd only made one movie prior, I decided to stick with the rehearsal process that worked the first time — especially since, like on *Clerks*, we had a lead who'd never acted before; so scene drills and repetition felt necessary. One of the biggest differences was that we didn't rehearse at eleven o'clock at night. Unlike our *Clerks* cast, the *Mallrats* cast didn't have day jobs/weren't doing the flick as a lark; these people were professional actors, paid to be in a movie. And since we were stranded in Eden Prairie, I guess they figured rehearsing beat sitting around their hotel rooms 'til the start of principal photography. We also had the luxury of time on our side, because (with the exception of Doherty) none of the cast was that famous or in-demand. Shannon, who'd just gotten the boot from *90210*, had the time to devote to rehearsals, too. She seemed to like it, even. Everyone did, really. We bonded, laughed, and kinda taught each other our jobs. And out of all that rehearsal time, the Jason Lee style was born.

— On *Chasing Amy*, we rehearsed for at least two weeks, probably closer to three. I'd been dating Joey at the time, so she had constant access to the script. Ben and Lee moved out to Red Bank a month before we started shooting, and we devoted lots of time to rehearsing — mostly in the old Red Bank office on Broad Street. Again, we were in a situation of having little cash with which to make the flick; so getting the performances as close to camera-ready was gonna save us from burning film (and stock and processing costs) and help us make our days. I remember getting uppity with the three leads one day, because we were three weeks out, and they were still on book. "How can we really rehearse if none of you have your fucking lines memorized?!" I'd said, pissed, calling an early close to that rehearsal day. When Ben left the office, he went over to the Dublin House bar on Monmouth for five hours and learned his lines. Joey went back to my condo and did the same. Within two days, Lee was, also, off book. That just seems funny to me now: me being mad at those guys for not having the entire script memorized three fucking weeks away from shooting. On *Catch & Release*, I memorized most of my dialogue on the day, repeatedly going over my sides in my trailer after blocking rehearsal. On the fucking day — like most actors. And here I was, bitching these cats out about not committing all their lines to memory three fucking weeks away from shooting. Oh, how naive I was...

— *Dogma* was the first flick in which I learned that, the more famous your cast, the less likely you're gonna get the luxury of two/three weeks' rehearsals. I think we got about a week and a half of serious rehearsal time. Ben and Matt were blowing up off of *Good Will Hunting*, Salma Hayek had just landed a Revlon contract, Chris Rock was still shooting *Lethal Weapon 4* in L.A. (I actually had to go out to Los Angeles to rehearse with Rock before he could join us in Pittsburgh). Unlike my previous three flicks, people had lives outside of the movie. And since all of the actors were getting paid the same amount of money to do the flick, in a "favored-nations" deal, the last thing I could do was get shitty and decree "I need three weeks rehearsal with all of you or you're out of the fucking picture!" Still, you've got people like Alan Rickman in the cast; how much rehearsal does an actor of Rickman's caliber need, really? Ben I'd worked with before, so he knew what I wanted. Mewes had memorized the whole script (his lines as well as everyone else's) so all I had to do with him was modulate and tweak. Matty Damon was... Matty fucking Damon, i.e. — he's genius at every role. At the end of the day, that week and a half was all we needed.

— On *Jay and Silent Bob Strike Back*, I never rehearsed with anybody but Mewes, really (and maybe one or two days with Shannon Elizabeth). Since the flick was so cameo-driven, it would've been impossible to get any kind of full-cast rehearsal going. (Make people show up and stay all day just to rehearse six or eight lines? Ludicrous.) So the rehearsals on that flick mainly consist-ed of me teaching a heroin/oxy-kicking Mewes how to be Jay again — and even that wasn't tough, considering he'd played the role four times already.

— For *Jersey Girl*, I got a week of rehearsals. We had Lopez for two days, though, since her manager wouldn't let her rehearse until Miramax closed her deal — even though she was with us in Philly, sharing an apartment with our leading man. Said leading man had sold me on doing this flick with him a year and change earlier, at a party in a house that'd one day be mine, when he said, "I wanna do something like *Chasing Amy* again — where it's character-driven, and we rehearse for like a month before we shoot. I miss that." What I didn't know was he was just feeling a bit of the ol' libations-fueled sentimentality in that moment, and that when it came time to actually rehearse, the chances of Affleck finding a month with decks cleared enough to concentrate solely on rehearsing were nil and none. Ultimately, it didn't matter: this was my fifth film with Ben and he knew what I wanted, performance-wise. Carlin came loaded for bear; all we did in rehearsals was find his inflection and accent. Tyler is just always great. And Raquel? She mostly came together in editing (I mean, she was eight when we shot the flick). That week was all we needed, really. As it would turn out, we could've done six months of rehearsals, and still gotten fucked by the critics and at the box office. Sadly, that movie was doomed from the start.

— *Clerks II* was a different story. We rehearsed for around two weeks on the flick, both at my house and at the Mooby's. Most of that rehearsal time was spent with Brian and Jeff, since they carry the lion's share of the flick. Jeff had memorized all his lines prior to our first rehearsal, so he was already pretty much off book. After one day of rehearsals with Rosario, it was clear she did-n't need any work whatsoever, so natural was her delivery. Jen and Trevor I spent the second most amount of time with, trying to find the characters. Trevor's Elias we arrived at almost by accident. He was written as borderline-retarded, but Trevor was just too good looking to play that. So instead, we went with extremely sheltered. When Trevor ad-libbed a "'cause" at the end of one of his lines, and I said, "That's it! That's the guy! Do the whole performance like that!" What really helped our rehearsals on that flick was being able to do them on location. Since most of the picture took place in and around the Mooby's, the moment it was construction-sound enough to get inside of, we all started meeting down there to rehearse — because then, we could also block it (the physical activity/actor placement of a scene). But it's rare when you have a flick that's set in one location, so you're not afforded that kinda of time with the space you'll shoot in/on very often.

Which brings us back to *Zack and Miri Make a Porno*. I've got a guy whose inflections I wrote for/to reading the scenes and sounding like he's not acting at all, as much as being the character. I've got a chick who could read the Bible aloud and make it seem charming. They're naturals. They're excellent. There's no need to sweat inflection or do drills; they innately get what they're reading and say it like I heard it in my head when I wrote it. And while they're not off-book yet, I've learned a thing or two about actors and their lines-memorization abilities since that *Chasing Amy* rehearsal back in '96; I'm not sweating that kinda thing anymore.

It's weird to work one way for so long, and slowly realize it's not necessary anymore; that it was just something you did when you didn't know any better. I hired pros; aside from on-set tweaking and an extra take or two, they don't need to be broken like wild horses or worked like puppets. Those days are behind me now. Now I spend more time thinking about/working on what the flick's gonna look like — which, I guess, should be the primary job of the director.

Ratface has done a great job with the sets, as usual. Sal, too, knocked the costumes out of the park. Purcell (the man behind Mooby) has created another stellar corporate logo for our fake world (as well as a few not-so-corporate logos, and a brilliantly simple chair-back design). Scott and Laura have found a way to get Dave and I everything we asked for. Milos has tamed the production beast into a sensible, manageable schedule. Everyone's ready to pull the trigger (or the pud, considering the subject matter). And I am, too.

We start shooting our eighth film on Wednesday.

Making Porno, Part 2: Climax
Friday March 14 2008 @ 11:50 a.m.

It's been a long time since the last update, I realize; over two months, to be precise. My apologies for that and the total lack of SModcast during that period. I was preoccupied. Rest assured, SModcast will return the moment the recording gear gets back to L.A.

Around two in the morning Wednesday, we wrapped *Zack and Miri Make a Porno*. Poetically, it snowed right before we rolled for the last time... just after we'd laid a bunch of fake white stuff for an exterior shot at Zack's job. It nicely summed up the uncooperative nature of the weather we'd grown accustomed to over the course of the production.

Banks did her last scene the night before, so Tuesday became a countdown of "production wraps" (when you check the gate after an actor's/actress's last shot, and if it's good, you announce their work completion on the show to much applause). First, it was Katie. Then, Mewes. Then Ricky. Then Seth. Then Traci. Then, we moved outside, and Craig and Jeff shot the only dialogue scene we had left to shoot. And with that, the last of our amazing cast was gone, leaving us with merely two establishing shots of a building before we had to say goodbye.

The crew was wonderful. Aside from working with people I've worked beside on almost every show, I got to work with people I hadn't worked with since *Dogma* in '98. There wasn't a weak link in the bunch.

Monroeville/Pittsburgh (and all the surrounding towns we also shot in, like McKeesport, McKee's Rocks, Hazelwood, the Southside, etc.) were so kind and welcoming. Thanks to everyone we may have inconvenienced while in your backyards.

Some folks have asked why I've been so stingy with the details on this flick, as opposed to flicks we've made in the past, during which I was blogging and posting pics galore. There's no conspiracy behind it, really; I just wanna try something different this time. I want folks to discover the flick for themselves, instead of me jamming it down their throats. I'm also gonna try to keep from over-selling it with hyperbole and absolutes. I'll let you guys apply those (good or bad) when the time comes. Just know that we had a problem-free, productive shoot in which everyone was firing on all cylinders and the result was THE FUNNIEST FUCKING MOVIE WE'VE EVER MADE!!!

* ahem *

No more hyperbole starting from this point on, I meant.

I spent all of Wednesday traveling and got to sleep in my own bed last night. When I woke up, I instinctively bolted for the shower, fearing I was gonna be late for call time. When I remembered that not only were we done, but that I was over two thousand miles away from our equipment and locales, I smiled and did the next best thing: took a shit on my own toilet.

Can't wait to share it with you.

The movie, not the shit.

Curious George, the Shadow of the Bat, and Other Stuff
Sunday June 29 2008 @ 12:30 p.m.

It's only been a week, and the world feels much emptier without him.

Here's the piece I wrote about my friend for *Newsweek* on Monday.

They say you should never meet your heroes. I've found this a good rule to live by, but as with any rule, there's always an exception.

My first exposure to George Carlin was in 1982, when HBO aired his *Carlin at Carnegie* stand-up special. When I saw the advert — featuring a clip of Carlin talking about the clichéd criminal warning of "Don't try anything funny," and then adding, "When they're not looking, I like to go ...," followed by a brief explosion of goofy expressions and pantomime — I immediately asked my parents if I could tape it on our new BetaMax video recorder.

That was a hilarious bit. But when I finally watched the special, Carlin blew my doors off. Whether he was spinning a yarn about Tippy, his farting dog, or analyzing the contents of his fridge, Carlin expressed himself not only humorously, but amazingly eloquently as well. I was, as they say, in stitches.

And that was before he got to the Seven Words You Can't Say on Television.

I was twelve years old, watching a man many years my senior curse a blue streak while exposing the hypocrisy of a medium (and a society) that couldn't deal with the public usage of terms they probably employed regularly in their private lives. And while he seemed to revel in being a rebel, here was a man who also clearly loved the English language, warts and al — even the so-called "bad words" (although, as George would say, there are no such things as "bad words"). I wouldn't say George Carlin taught me obscenities, but I would definitely say he taught me that the casual use of obscenities wasn't reserved just for drunken sailors, as the old chestnut goes; even intelligent people were allowed to incorporate them into their everyday conversations (because George was nothing if not intelligent).

From that moment forward, I was an instant Carlin disciple. I bought every album, watched every HBO special, and even sat through *The Prince of Tides* just because he played a small role in the film. I spent years turning friends on to the Cult of Carlin, the World According to George, and even made pilgrimages to see him perform live (the first occasion being a gig at Farleigh Dickinson University in 1988). Carlin influenced my speech and my writing. Carlin replaced Catholicism as my religion.

Sixteen years later, I sat across from the star of *Carlin at Carnegie* in the dining room of the Four Seasons Hotel in Los Angeles. It was a meeting I'd dreamed of and dreaded simultaneously. George Carlin was the type of social observer/critic I most wanted to emulate… but he was a celebrity, too. What if he turned out to be a true prick?

What I quickly discovered was that, in real life, George was, well, George. Far from a self-obsessed jerk, he was mild-mannered enough to be my Dad. He was as interested as he was interesting, well-read and polite to a fault — all while casually dropping F-bombs. But most impressive, he didn't treat me like an audience member, eschewing actual conversation, electing instead to simply perform the whole meeting, more "on" than real. He talked to me like one of my friends would talk to me: familiar, unguarded, authentic.

I made three films with George over the course of the next six years, starting with *Dogma* and his portrayal of Cardinal Glick, the pontiff-publicist responsible for the Catholic Church's recall of the standard crucifix in favor of the more congenial, bubbly "Buddy Christ." A few years later, I wrote him a lead role in *Jersey Girl* — as Bart Trinke (or "Pop"), the father of Ben Affleck's character. It called for a more dramatic performance than George was used to giving, but the man pulled it off happily and beautifully. (Something most folks probably don't know about George: He took acting very seriously. The man was almost a Method actor.) Sadly, I consider that *Jersey Girl* part my one failing on George's behalf, and not for the reasons most would assume (the movie was not reviewed kindly, to say the least). No, I failed because George had asked me to write a different role for him.

In 2001, George did me a solid when he accepted the part of the orally fixated hitchhiker who knew exactly how to get a ride in *Jay and Silent Bob Strike Back*. When he wrapped his scene in that flick, I thanked him for making the time, and he said, "Just do me a favor: Write me my dream role one day." When I inquired what that'd be, he offered, "I wanna play a priest who strangles children."

It was a classic Carlin thing to say: a little naughty and a lot honest. I always figured there'd be time to give George what he asked for. Unfortunately, he left too soon.

He was, and will likely remain, the smartest person I've ever met. But really, he was much more than just a person. Without a hint of hyperbole, I can say he was a god, a god who cussed.

G'bye for now, Boss. I hope you were wrong about the afterlife — if only so that I can shoot the shit with you again one day.

Courtesy of Peter Sciretta over at SlashFilm.com, I caught an early screening of *The Dark Knight* yesterday evening.

Without giving anything away, this is an epic film (and trust me: based on the sheer size and scope of the visuals and storytelling, that's not an overstatement). It's the *Godfather II* of comic book films and three times more earnest than *Batman Begins* (and fuck, was that an earnest film). Easily the most adult comic book film ever made. Heath Ledger didn't so much give a performance as he disappeared completely into the role; I know I'm not the first to suggest this, but he'll likely get at least an Oscar nod (if not the win) for Best Supporting Actor. Fucking flick's nearly three hours long and only leaves you wanting more (in a great way). I can't imagine anyone being disappointed by it. Nolan and crew have created something close to a masterpiece.

Also in the Masterpiece Department... If you haven't already peeped *Wall-E*, get thee to a theater. It's the ballsiest animated film ever made (right up there with *Persepolis*, in terms of untraditional cartoons), yet it'll melt your heart. Seriously — Wall-E's so adorable, he makes E.T. look like Josef Mengele. Alright, maybe not Mengele, but at least Rudolf Hess. Y'know what? Let's drop the Nazi comparisons altogether and just leave it at this: Wall-E (the character) is adorable and *Wall-E* (the film) is a must-see.

In the Far-Less-Than-a-Masterpiece department, *Zack and Miri Make a Porno* continues to move ever closer to its October 31st release date. We tested again in Albuquerque, New Mexico last week (where I did, in fact, make a left turn I knew I shouldn't have made), and scored almost exactly the same as we did in the Kansas City test screening the month before — which is to say really, really well. A poster and a theatrical trailer should be making their way to theaters soon (the online teaser we posted a few weeks back met with an early demise).

I put on a shitload of weight during the *Zack and Miri* shoot and have only just recently started to take it off. Been on a diet for the last four weeks and have already dropped twenty five pounds, with many, many more tons to go. By the *Zack and Miri* premiere in October, I hope to look almost human again.

NC17 No More
Friday August 15 2008 @ 1:01 p.m.

At an appeals screening last week, we were able to overturn the MPAA's NC17 rating for *Zack and Miri Make a Porno* to a more audience-friendly R without making any cuts...

All that really means is that what you see in theaters will be exactly what we were hoping to show you in theaters. None of this waiting around for the unrated DVD shit.

I saw *Watchmen*. It's fucking astounding. The Non-Disclosure Agreement I signed prevents me from saying much, but I can spout the following with complete joygasmic enthusiasm: Snyder and Co. have pulled it off.

Remember that feeling of watching *Sin City* on the big screen and being blown away by what a faithful translation of the source material it was, in terms of both content and visuals? Triple that, and you'll come close to watching *Watchmen*. Even Alan Moore might be surprised at how close the movie is to the book. March can't come soon enough.

Soon, there will be "Porno"
Tuesday October 14 2008 @ 3:53 p.m.

We're inching ever closer to that October 31st release date, folks. I'm doing *The Tonight Show* Friday, then the junket all weekend, and the premiere on Monday the 20th at Grauman's Chinese Theater. After that, I head east for some Devils' games and a NY premiere at CMJ on the 23rd, then a homecoming of sorts in Pittsburgh, where we'll debut the flick we shot there last winter. Then, back home for release week.

Getting excited. I've seen a slew of bus stop ads and billboards... TV spots are starting to run a bunch, too.

Seth and I are on the cover of *Complex* magazine this month... Fuck, I wish I was still as thin as I am on that cover. I've porked the fuck out, man. I'm really, really fat right now. Fattest I've ever been. But as soon as this flick's out, I'm taking my life back; gonna drop out of sight and drop a bunch of pounds. It's the deal I've made with myself. Just gotta make it through the next two and half weeks of press and running around.

Big month around here. Hope ya'll can come out and support the flick. Then, come November 1st, if you see me with any junk food in my hand, you are entitled to kick me in the ass. If I'm sitting, remind me I have to comply; I will stand and allow for one free kick.

Carnegie Thrall
Wednesday May 6 2009 @ 8:07 am

For me, the best part of the Carnegie Hall gig already happened.

It was a quiet moment when I first found out I'd been booked to do my Q&A shtick on that venerable stage, long before the public knew anything about it. That was bliss. I'd never dreamed about playing Carnegie Hall because... well, I've never done anything remotely Carnegie-worthy. Oh, sure — when I was eighteen, I could bend and twist just enough to reach the tip of my cock with my tongue. But while I haven't read every book written on the subject of that legendary performance space, I'm relatively sure self-sucking live on stage wouldn't be considered very Carnegie-worthy either.

(Bullshit, I say. I submit that breaking one off in your own pie-hole may be more Carnegie-worthy than anything else for which anyone's ever taken a bow at 57th and 7th. Think about it: not everyone can do it — and isn't that why we go to the theater/movies/sporting events/opera? To see people do what we, ourselves, cannot? And if you're one of those guys who's worried the homophobic public will cluck their disapproving tongues once people get wind of your viewing habits, you can always insist you're intently peeping another dude hose down his own tonsils solely as research.)

So the best moment of the gig already happened. The next best moment won't happen 'til I'm actually on stage at Carnegie Hall on June 17th (and depending on the crowd that night, it could wind up superseding the aforementioned Best Moment).

But between now and then, I will wake up every morning, praying to Jesus that the show sells out.

Here's the thing: playing Carnegie Hall rocks, yes; it's an honor. In this instance, it's even mind-bending to some degree, as I'm not talented at all. But selling out Carnegie Hall? Now there's a challenge.

I know me: every morning until June 17th, I'll wring my hands over whether or not I'm gonna be able to sell out that beastly barn. Because years from now, when I'm telling a Grandkid that I played Carnegie Hall, I know the next thing out of the mouth of that black-oil-eyed alien hybrid from the future will be "Was it sold out, Earth Grampa?" And before I shiv him with that silver spike, I wanna be able to tell him "Yeah, kid — I sold out Carnegie Hall. Now lemme see the back of your neck..."

I've got a few factors working against me. Back in November, I did a show at the Count Basie in Red Bank, and then another Jersey gig at the Bergen Pac Center four months later (there were Ohio and Connecticut shows in the last few months, too). The chances of rallying those auds for the Carnegie gig are bleak: most Garden Staters don't wanna go into Manhattan for any reason, let alone to see a fat, bearded, sweaty 'tard they just saw mere months back for cheaper.

I can't count on Canada to save my ass this time either. Between the two shows at Toronto's Roy Thomson Hall and three nights of mini-q&a's after the Bloor's Kevin Smith Fest I put nearly 10,000 Canuck "bums" (or Ontari-asses) in seats back in February. It was a point of pride then, but now it just means 10,000 less potential hardcores for the Carnegie gig. And while firmly in line with other Carnegie event prices, the "Evening With" ticket price still offers far costlier seats than anyone in their right mind should have to part with to see me — especially in a weak economy.

So what's this all mean? Well, like everything else in my life (except my true weight), in order for it to be real, I've gotta share it with a bunch of strangers. I've told you about the time I got so heavy that I broke a toilet. I've told you about my anal fissure. I told you when I had unprotected sex during a one-night stand with a total stranger while sporting an open-wound on my dork (don't worry: I married her later). So why wouldn't I share this latest nail-biter?

Lemme break down the numbers for you...

Carnegie Hall Capacity: 2804
Comps/Press/House Seats: -300
Tickets to Sell: 2504

2504. Seems huge, doesn't it? Granted, Roy Thomson seats more — and I sold that out four times (two shows back-to-back). But that's not a fair comparison; for whatever reason (I love hockey, worship Gretzky, and have been on Degrassi), they really like me in Toronto. And while I've got some peeps down here in the tri-state area who may enjoy my bullshit from time to time, they've had ample opportunity to see me stalk (and sweat all over) the stage the last six months.

"Then why schedule the Carnegie Hall gig now," you're probably asking. "Why not wait 'til you've been out of circulation on the east coast q&a circuit for a year, then schedule a Carnegie Hall gig, ya' dim irritant from the mid-90s?" In this instance, it doesn't work like that. Jared and David (the show's producers) were lucky to get me any date (I mean, it's Carnegie fucking Hall, not the Elks Lodge Hall in North Middletown). With The Hall, you take what you can get, and what we got was this looming June date.

So 2504 people will fill the place, but I don't know if I'll be able to sell it out. And every day, the uncertainty will haunt me. But why should I sweat it out alone? From now on, every morning on my Twitter page (@thatkevin-smith), I'll keep you updated with the daily sales numbers I'm fed. That way, I won't be alone in fretting over whether I'm even relevant anymore.

Image is built on perception, and perception can be governed by whoever has the most information. Based on that, common sense would dictate that I NOT share sales info with the general public, as some jackass may try to spin the numbers into something negative. But I've never been known for exhibiting a rat's asshole full of common sense.

Giving out this info is like posting a naked picture of myself: the potential for something positive coming out of such an exercise is pretty slim (ironically). But you can't live like a puss-hole your entire life, y'know? Sometimes it's best to throw your hat over the wall, and commit to finding a way to get it back.

I can year you now: "Nut up already, Fatty! Whip it out! You certainly have no problem letting anyone with an eye or ear know when you've sold out a gig!" We're getting there, but first, some further Disclaimers: I used only Twitter (and my website) to announce the gig/sales info. Aside from an ad in *The Onion*, we haven't advertised at all yet (though a bunch of friendly movie sites — CinemaBlend, Cinematical, slashfilm, JoBlo, etc — helped spread the word).

Tickets went on sale April 16. Sales results after twenty days, as of Wednesday, May 6…

Tickets to Sell: 2504
Tickets Sold: -1260
Tickets Left to Sell: 1244

1260 tickets sold thus far (mostly in the pricey seats, oddly). That's something to be proud of, sure. But the first 1000 was always gonna be the easiest, right? Now the daily sales report reads "11 tickets sold" or "6 tickets sold" or "18 tickets sold." It's a gut-wrenching game of inches now, and moving the next 1000 tickets has gotta be akin to finding my dick under my gut (as well as my gut's gut): trying and humbling.

We're just over halfway from selling out. But it's a strong start – and I've still got plenty of time (a month and change) to fill Carnegie Hall. Can it happen? I guess we're gonna see together.

Fuck, I wish I was still eighteen and limber...

Twitter @thatkevinsmith
10:28 PM Jun 17th
I'm up to 875 "You killed at Carnegie" Tweets. Many thanks for all the kind words. And thank you, especially, for making it A SOLD OUT SHOW!

AFTERWORD

A throwaway gag that never fails to induce a smile can be found nestled in the middle of Cameron Crowe's 70's-set study in celebrity, *Almost Famous*: Jimmy Fallon's slick corporate manager Dennis Hope bursts into the lives of Stillwater — the rockers on the verge of *Rolling Stone* coverdom — to take the reins from the band's longtime buddy-manager, since the band is, as the title suggests, almost famous at this stage in their recording careers. They're about to enter the big time, and Fallon's character's assessment is that big time talent needs big time management. While trying to impress upon the band the importance of having an experienced representative steering the ship, he prognosticates a dark day in pop music: "... If you think Mick Jagger'll still be out there, trying to be a rock star at age fifty, you're sadly, sadly mistaken."

The gag works, of course, because we in the present know that — even as you read this — Mick Jagger is probably on or near a stage somewhere, on the cusp of busting into his patented chicken-strut... and he hasn't been fifty in a *long* time. But that's what hindsight humor can do for a gag: use what we know *now* to make fun of innocence from *then*.

Years have gone by since the end of the original printing of *My Boring-Ass Life*, and years had gone by at that point, since the inception of the blog from which the book was derived — a curious development that saw the good folks at Titan dialing back the clock on our species' greatest strides in new media communication by shaping the blog into its analogue equivalent: a book. We figured it'd sell five thousand copies at best, but look very cool on our respective shelves.

When it became a *NY Times* Bestseller, we were so flabbergasted and ill-prepared, we just about shit blood. I was no J.K. Rowling, so we really never expected the book to chart anywhere, except maybe a Cracked.com "8 Worst Books by Quasi-Celebs Whose Time Has Past" article. So thanks to all who bought a copy, and thanks if you bought *this* edition, too.

Some Dennis Hope moments to look forward to…

Looking back on what was, in retrospect, a year and change spent pooping and watching TiVo'ed *Simpsons* and *Law & Order*, the book closes with a two-parter about my brief acting turn as hacker Warlock in *Live Free or Die Hard*, and a post-shoot phone call from the flick's star, Bruce Willis, asking if I'd wanna work on another flick with him, in a directorial capacity. At the close of the essay was my assessment that I don't make Bruce Willis movies. As I write this, I'm five days away from wrapping a Bruce Willis/Tracy Morgan flick currently shooting under a title that's sure to change (I've been titularly-challenged as of late): *A Couple of Dicks*.

In this updated edition, you'll read pieces from the making of *Zack and Miri Make a Porno*, back when we had hope that it could break us out of our $30 million box office ghetto. Nearly a year after the theatrical release, that childlike naivety still embarrasses me: our theatrical grosses were far from record-breaking. So while I love *Zack and Miri*, I'm not the same guy who wrote those blog pieces; older me is much wiser (and more experienced) than year-ago me.

He's also far more stoned. After watching *Zack* under-perform, I swapped cigarettes for marijuana and checked out of the rat race for a while, blazing like a fourteen year-old metal head. I can't say I really re-embraced weed, because it'd never really been a big part of my life before then. My *work*, sure: I made what most folks dismissed as stoner flicks. Ironically, however, I didn't really smoke that much before or while making them. Now? I don't make stoner flicks anymore (Jay and Silent Bob have left the building), but I do wake-and-bake daily. And while that sounds counter-productive, consider this: while transitioning to a total burnout, I was able to land a gig directing a Bruce Willis flick for Warner Brothers, tend goal for the first time in fifteen years in a street hockey tournament, write a twelve-issue comic book mini-series, and play NY's world renowned Carnegie Hall, selling it out. Not trying to tell people how to live their lives, but Kids? Smoking weed will *totally* improve you. Seriously. Don't believe the hype: weed makes you *blossom* (not to mention goofy, fun and very social).

I don't blog as much as I used to. The addictive, speedy Twitter accomplishes what the blog used to: giving folks a glimpse into my boring-ass life. I used to write volumes; now I fire off multiple missives in easy-to-digest 140-character bursts. Back in the day, I'd write ten thousand-word pieces about an anal fissure; today, I've built a small army of a million-plus followers typing far, far less. But fear not: one day, I'll go back to blogging. Life is cyclical, and if you're around long enough, you get to fall in love *again* with long-since back-burnered people and things that used to mean worlds to you. This year alone, I've immersed myself in all things hockey — an old passion of mine I'd been neglecting since *Clerks* kick-started my career — and got back into writing comics.

Yes, everything's different now… as well as the exact same.

— Still only wanna fuck Jen.
— Still making movies.
— Still watching TiVo.
— Still shitting lots.

But leafing through the book now, it's kinda quaint. The guy who wrote all those words had no idea where life was gonna take him in three short years. Now I'm kinda looking forward to the third revised edition of *My Boring-Ass Life* — if for no other reason than simply to see how (in the words of Mr. Miyagi) different-but-same life gets. So I'm gonna keep harassing Titan about updating and expanding *My Boring-Ass Life* every few years; because, like the flicks I've made, the book's a little snapshot of a moment in a weird-but-wonderful life that I'm still not sure is my own. Plus, it looks cool and respectable on my shelves next to the Batman and Mysterio statues.

But what about the people out there who have zero patience? The kind of folks who flip to the end of a book and read it in advance because they can't wait to see how it ends? If we're really gonna just keep expanding editions of *Boring-Ass*, who knows how long it'll be before they get to the author's *true* end?

In deference to those who can't wait for it, I'm going to include an extra special super bonus here: I'm gonna write my final blog entry in this edition's Afterword. It'll have to be post-dated when it's eventually included in some (God-willing) very distant printing, but watch how it bring closure to what's fast becoming a series of backdoor-books about my (boring-ass) life.

Date/Date/Datey-Date

Today, I died. All this means is my tongue won't be in my wife's ass this afternoon. I think.

Thanks, all, for a great ride. Please don't fuck my wife in my absence, and when I'm buried, please reconsider *Jersey Girl*: it wasn't that bad a flick. Have a week.

And that's how it ends: rather anticlimactically, like the third *Matrix* flick. A fitting conclusion to a life squandered on love, laughter, family, good times with friends, bad food, good weed, and TiVo.

And for those of you wondering when I'm gonna have the decency to wrap it all up, this half-life of mine, I say "Courage": we all know I'm not gonna live very long, so you'll be able to move on to other interests with a satisfactory sense of completion soon enough. Because if you think I'm gonna be blogging about jerking off onto my wife's leg while staring at her asshole when I'm fifty, you're sadly, sadly mistaken.

...'cause I'll be taking that year off, I mean. Rest assured, should I live to fifty-one, I'll be back blogging about dong-flogging to a wrinkly, menopausal Jen Schwalbach brown-eye as expected.

I mean, it's not like I have anything else worthwhile to talk about.

Kevin Smith
4 August 2009

Selected Index

Selected Index

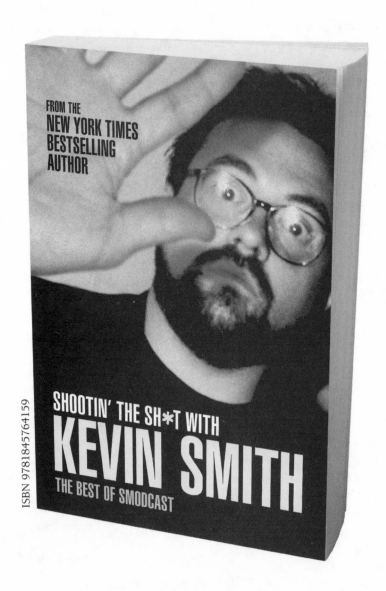